HANDBOOK OF QUALITATIVE RESEARCH METHODS IN ENTREPRENEURSHIP

Handbook of Qualitative Research Methods in Entrepreneurship

Edited by

Helle Neergaard

Associate Professor of Entrepreneurship and Small Business Management, the Aarhus School of Business, Denmark

John Parm Ulhøi

Professor in Organization and Management Theory, the Aarhus School of Business, Denmark

Edward Elgar
Cheltenham, UK • Northampton, MA, USA

Published by
Edward Elgar Publishing Limited
Glensanda House
Montpellier Parade
Cheltenham
Glos GL50 1UA
UK

Edward Elgar Publishing, Inc.
William Pratt House
9 Dewey Court
Northampton
Massachusetts 01060
USA

A catalogue record for this book
is available from the British Library

Library of Congress Cataloguing in Publication Data
Handbook of qualitative research methods in entrepreneurship / edited by
Helle Neergaard, John Parm Ulhøi.
    p. cm.
  Includes bibliographical references and index.
  1. Entrepreneurship. 2. Entrepreneurship–Research. I. Neergaard, Helle,
  1960–   II. Ulhøi, John P.
  HB615.H2659   2006
  338'.04–dc22   2006011747

ISBN 978 1 84376 835 7 (cased)

Printed and bound in Great Britain by MPG Books Ltd, Bodmin, Cornwall

Contents

Contributors

Leona Achtenhagen holds an Associate Professorship at Jönköping International Business School, Sweden. Based on a background in strategy and organization studies, her research interests are mainly related to growth processes of firms, discourse analyses and media industries.

Helene Ahl is a research fellow at the School of Education and Communication at Jönköping University, Sweden, and an affiliated researcher at Jönköping International Business School. Her current research focuses on discourses of lifelong learning. She has published books and articles on the motivation concept, empowerment, pricing practices and inter-organizational learning. Her 2004 book, *The scientific reproduction of gender inequality*, JIBS Dissertation Series, no. 015: JIBS, and Ph.D. dissertation, for which she received an award at the Academy of Management Critical Studies Division, was a feminist analysis of entrepreneurship discourses.

Alistair R. Anderson is Professor of Entrepreneurship and Director of the Centre for Entrepreneurship at Aberdeen Business School, Scotland, UK. After some years of starting and running small businesses, his curiosity about entrepreneurial people drove him to study entrepreneurship at Stirling University. Unfortunately he found that rather than answering his initial questions, he simply found that there were many more interesting questions! He is still trying to answer some of them, especially in the social realms of entrepreneurship. Current themes being explored are social capital, social constructions and associated topic areas.

Henrik Berglund recently received his Ph.D. in Technology Management and Economics from Chalmers University of Technology, Gothenburg, Sweden. He is currently engaged in a number of research projects, including a comparative study of the behaviours and strategies of early-stage venture capital firms in California and Nordic countries. He teaches entrepreneurship and qualitative methodology in various masters and Ph.D. programmes.

Richard Blundel is a senior lecturer at Brunel University, UK and a member of Brunel Research in Enterprise, Innovation, Sustainability and Ethics (BRESE). Current research interests include the role of entrepreneurial networks in technological innovation, business historical perspectives on industrial dynamics, and emerging models of socially and environmentally oriented enterprise. He has published related articles in *Entrepreneurship and Regional Development*, *Industry and Innovation* and the *Journal of Small Business and Enterprise Development*. Richard is also the author of *Effective Organisational Communication: Perspectives, Principles and Practices* (FT Prentice Hall, 2004).

Anne Bøllingtoft is Assistant Professor at the Department of Management, the Aarhus School of Business, Denmark. In 2005, she handed in her thesis titled 'The Bottom-up Business Incubator: A Collaborative Approach to (Entrepreneurial) Organizing?' Her research area covers entrepreneurship with specific focus on business incubators and new organizational structures and forms.

Ethel Brundin is Assistant Professor in the Department of Entrepreneurship, Marketing and Management at Jönköping International Business School, Sweden. Her research interests include micro processes of new business ventures, family businesses and different areas of strategic leadership. She is currently involved in a set of projects in which emotions are in focus. She is project manager for an international research project between Sweden and South Africa on entrepreneurial learning and sustainability. She has published in international journals and edited books on immigrant, ethnic and social entrepreneurship as well as strategic leadership. She was an entrepreneur before entering academia.

Candida Brush is Professor of Entrepreneurship and holder of the President's chair in Entrepreneurship at Babson College, Wellesley, MA, USA. She also serves as Chair of the Entrepreneurship Division and is Director of the Ph.D. programme. She was formerly Associate Professor of Strategy and Policy Director of the Council for Women's Entrepreneurship and Leadership (CWEL), and Research Director for the Entrepreneurial Management Institute at Boston University, USA. She is a founding member of the Diana Project International, a research collaborative of scholars from 20 countries studying finance strategies of women entrepreneurs. Her current research investigates resource acquisition strategies in emerging organizations, the influence of gender in business start-up, and growth strategies of women-led ventures.

William D. Bygrave is the Frederic C. Hamilton Professor for Free Enterprise. He joined The Center for Entrepreneurial Studies at Babson College, Wellesely, MA, USA in 1985 and directed it from 1993 to 1999. He was also the director of the annual Babson College–Kauffman

Foundation Entrepreneurship Research Conference in 1994 and 1995. He teaches and researches entrepreneurship, specifically financing of start-up and growing ventures. He has written more than 50 papers on topics that include venture capital, entrepreneurship, nuclear physics, hospital pharmaceuticals and philosophy of science.

Sara Carter is Professor of Entrepreneurship in the Department of Management and Organization and Director of the Entrepreneurship Centre at the University of Stirling, Scotland, UK. Prior to her Stirling appointment in September 2005, Sara was Professor of Entrepreneurship at the University of Strathclyde, Scotland, UK. Sara has undertaken several research projects in the area of small business and entrepreneurship. Her publications include two textbooks *OEEnterprise and Small Business: Principles, Practice and Policy* (2001, 2006 2nd edition) and *OEWomen as Entrepreneurs* (1992) in addition to several academic and policy papers on entrepreneurship and small business. Sara is editor of *Entrepreneurship Theory and Practice* and a member of the editorial boards of nine peer-reviewed journals.

Torben Damgaard is Associate Professor at the Southern University of Denmark. His research areas include business-to-business marketing, strategy and methodology. He has participated in several research projects in cooperation with both advisers and companies. In these studies interactive research methods are used to develop theories and methods.

Wim During is Emeritus Professor of Innovatory Entrepreneurship at the Dutch Institute of Knowledge Intensive Entrepreneurship at Twente University. He holds a Ph.D. from the University of Enschede and is currently enjoying retirement.

Paula D. Englis is Associate Professor at the Campbell School of Management at Berry College, Mount Berry, GA, USA, and at the Dutch Institute of Knowledge Intensive Entrepreneurship. She holds a Ph.D. from the University of Memphis, TN, USA. Her research has been published in numerous journals, such as the *Academy of Management Review*, *Entrepreneurship Theory and Practice*, *Family Business Review* and *Journal of Small Business Management*. Her research focuses on strategic management with an international emphasis, including application in entrepreneurship, technology and knowledge management, and value chain management.

Bruce A. Johnstone is completing a Ph.D. at Auckland University of Technology, New Zealand. He has a degree in Broadcasting Communications and received his MBA from Henley Management College, UK, and a Post Graduate Certificate in Business Research from Waikato University, New Zealand. He is also a Fellow of the New Zealand Institute of Management. His Ph.D. research uses ethnographic methods to study how advisory and support services associated with New Zealand's Growth and Innovation Framework affect a group of entrepreneurs.

Kim Klyver recently received his Ph.D. from the University of Southern Denmark and is shortly taking up a position as Westpac Post Doctoral Fellow in Entrepreneurship at Swinburne University of Technology, Australia. He works with entrepreneurship, social networks and small business management. In his Ph.D. research he focused on how independent entrepreneurs' social networks develop during the entrepreneurial process. He works with both quantitative and qualitative research methods.

Claire Leitch is a senior lecturer at Queen's University, Belfast, UK. Her research interests include developing an understanding of the learning company and applying it as a company development process; the application of action learning and other client-centred learning approaches, within entrepreneurial and executive education and development; gaining a deeper knowledge of the dynamics of leadership in the process of organizational transformation; entrepreneurial learning and business development; and developing a fuller understanding of the technology transfer process.

Markus M. Mäkelä is Professor of Software Product Development (acting) at the University of Turku, Finland, and works part time as research director at Helsinki University of Technology, from where he obtained a Ph.D. in Strategy and International Business. His domain of research is software business, wherein he studies issues of strategy, technology management, entrepreneurship, internationalization and venture capital finance. Markus has won the Haynes Prize for the Most Promising Scholar of the Academy of International Business and the Eldridge Haynes Memorial Trust. He has previously worked at Stanford University, CA, USA, Helsinki School of Economics and Morgan Stanley Dean Witter.

Brian McKenzie is Assistant Professor of Entrepreneurship at California State University, East Bay, USA. His research and teaching draws heavily on his 30 years as a successful entrepreneur and small business manager. Brian received his BA from the University of British Columbia in 1974, his MBA from the University of Victoria, British Columbia, in 1997 and his Ph.D. from the University of Victoria in 2003. He also holds a certificate of qualification as a master boat-builder. Brian has been awarded the 1999

AOM Entrepreneurship Division Innovations in Pedagogy Award, the 2000 USASBE Model Undergraduate Program Award and the 2004 Entrepreneurship Theory and Practice Best Conceptual Paper Award.

Helle Neergaard currently holds an Associate Professorship in Entrepreneurship at the Department of Management, the Aarhus School of Business, Denmark. Her predominantly qualitative research is published in, for example, *Entrepreneurship Theory and Practice*, *International Small Business Journal*, *Journal of Enterprising Culture* and *International Journal of Entrepreneurial Behaviour and Research*. She has also written several book chapters published in, for example *New Movements of Entrepreneurship*. Her current research interests include strategic and managerial aspects of entrepreneurship, female entrepreneurs and internationalization.

Jesper Piihl is Associate Professor at the University of Southern Denmark. His research interests are focused on organization theory, leadership and entrepreneurship. Jesper Piihl has a special interest in developing theoretical insights from non-modern perspectives such as actor-network theory.

Robert Smith is a doctoral student at the Centre for Entrepreneurship at Aberdeen Business School, Scotland, UK. His research interests include the social construction of entrepreneurship, dyslexia and entrepreneurship, rural entrepreneurship, criminal entrepreneurship and criminology. Robert won the Raymond Family Business Institute Award for the best paper presented on the topic of family business at the 2002 Babson–Kauffman Entrepreneurship Research Conference at Boulder, Colorado, USA.

Romeo V. Turcan is a doctoral researcher at the Hunter Centre for Entrepreneurship at the University of Strathclyde, Glasgow, Scotland, UK. His research interests centre around entrepreneurial international withdrawal and re-birth of small and medium-sized high-technology firms. Before starting his Ph.D. endeavour, he worked as an adviser to the Government of the Republic of Moldova on behalf of the United States Agency for International Development primarily in the electronics, food processing and power sectors. He has been employed in activities related to organizational reengineering; project management; business development; international marketing strategies development; and electric power sector regulatory reforms.

John Parm Ulhøi is Professor in Organization and Management Theory, the Aarhus School of Business, Denmark. His areas of research include technological innovation studies; organization development; entrepreneurship, intrapreneurship; business incubators; and human and social capital theory. His numerous publications appear in journals such as *Journal of Business Venturing*; *European Journal of Operational Research*; *Scandinavian Journal of Management* and *Managerial & Decision Economics*, Dr Ulhøi frequently serves as international research evaluator for different national science councils, the European Science Foundation and the EU Directorate-General.

Ingrid Wakkee is working as a Post Doctoral Researcher at the Vrije Universiteit in Amsterdam. She received her Ph.D. from the Dutch Institute of Knowledge Intensive Entrepreneurship at Twente University in the fall of 2004. Her current research interests include entrepreneurships in networks, international entrepreneurship and global start-up firms.

Friederike Welter is Professor for small and medium-sized enterprises (SMEs) at the University of Siegen, Germany and visiting professor at Jönköping International Business School, Sweden. She also holds the TeliaSonera Professorship at SSE Riga, Latvia. Based on a background in economics and SME management studies, her research interests are mainly related to nascent entrepreneurship, strategy processes in small firms, and discourse analyses.

Caroline Wigren holds a position as research fellow at Jönköping International Business School, Sweden. Her main research interests are entrepreneurship and regional development, and she has a genuine interest in methodological issues, with a focus on qualitative methods and interactive research.

Acknowledgements

The idea of this *Handbook of Qualitative Research Methods in Entrepreneurship* first emerged in a discussion with Francine O'Sullivan from Edward Elgar in the spring of 2003. Edward Elgar had already commissioned a volume on international business and we agreed that the field of entrepreneurship needed a similar effort. However, at the time we did not know where this informal talk would lead. So when Francine wanted to know if we would undertake the responsibility for such a volume, we were more than pleasantly surprised. We accepted the commission and we are very satisfied with the fact that we have succeeded in bringing together such a broad and highly competent group of contributors.

We know many of the contributors from our professional and personal networks, although some also responded to the call for papers, which was distributed at various American and European entrepreneurship conferences and posted on the Aarhus School of Business website. From the suggestions for chapters forwarded to us we selected 17 original contributions for publication in the *Handbook* and one reprint of a seminal article. We thoroughly enjoyed working with the 23 contributors from Scandinavia, Europe, the USA and New Zealand. We were very fortunate to receive abstracts from both junior and more experienced researchers, which has provided an excellent basis for methodological innovation, experimentation as well as refined and well-tested approaches. The contributions cover a wide spectrum and the editorial process has provided us with much opportunity to gain new insight into familiar methodologies and techniques, and to learn about those with which we were less well acquainted. Warm thanks therefore go to all the contributors to this volume. Some have in the process even become personal friends.

During the process we have talked to many people about the book and have consistently encountered encouragement and appreciation of our work with this *Handbook*. According to the comments we have received, the book seems to be much needed and truly fills a gap. We would therefore like to thank all those who have expressed their appreciation of our efforts; it makes all the hard work worth it.

All the chapters have been through a blind review process. Therefore we would like to express our sincere gratitude to our panel of reviewers, who did a marvellous job. All the contributions have benefited tremendously from your helpful comments and careful advice on how to improve the chapters.

We are indebted to Alistair Anderson, Anne Bøllingtoft, Candida Brush, Christian Lystbæk, Colette Henry, Colin Mason, Erik Kloppenborg Madsen, Frances Hill, Grethe Heldbjerg, Hanne Kragh, Isa Kjærgaard Jensen, Jakob Lauring, Jan Karlsson, John Howells, Jon Sundbo, Lars Fuglsang, Maria Anne Skaates, Mary Barrett, Mette Mønsted, Mette Rosenkrans, Mona Madsen, Paula Kyrö, Per Darmer, Pernille Kræmmergaard Jensen, Sara Carter, Susan Ainsworth, Susan Marlow, Thomas Gulløv and Thomas Cooney.

It has been a challenging endeavour for us to produce such an extensive volume, and we have encountered many challenges, some easier to overcome than others. Last, but not least, we would like to thank Francine O'Sullivan for her patience with the process and for her continuous encouragement and support.

Helle Neergaard and John Parm Ulhøi
Aarhus, January 2006

Foreword
Sara Carter

I am delighted to have been asked to write a foreword for this exceptional book. Helle Neergaard and John Parm Ulhøi have compiled a remarkable collection of work that both represents the range of methods and demonstrates the depth of insight that can be achieved through qualitative approaches. This book is not simply a handbook of qualitative research methods, though it well achieves this aim; it is also an important contribution to the field of entrepreneurship research. The development of an academic field occurs in fits and starts, often sparked by the publication of an important article or book. Certain publications emerge, usually unplanned, as being significant points in the development of a discipline that act as 'moments of reflection' within a subject, enabling a periodic stock-taking of the subject's domain, content, approaches and boundaries. This book provides a 'moment of reflection' for entrepreneurship research.

There has been a tendency within entrepreneurship, as with many of the social science and management disciplines, for individual researchers to be associated with either qualitative or quantitative methods, the two approaches erroneously juxtaposed in opposition. One of the founders of entrepreneurship research in Europe, James Curran, viewed research as a craft, and researchers as skilled craftsmen and women capable of using all of the methodological tools at their disposal. No researcher can be expert in all methodologies and personal preferences may favour one approach over another, but every researcher should be aware of the range of available approaches. As the editors state in their introduction, this book represents a 'methodological toolbox' that can be used to refresh the memories of some researchers and introduce new methods and techniques to others.

Three issues emerge from reading this book. First, the book makes plain the sheer range and diversity of qualitative research methods and their potential contributions to our understanding of entrepreneurship. Second, qualitative research emerges as a deeply personal experience, and researchers' passion for their subject shines through each chapter. Third, qualitative approaches, most often associated with the European research tradition, are becoming increasingly valued by North American scholars. Good research is not based on the geographical location of its practitioners, nor on their specific methodological traditions, but on how deeply they engage with their academic and research subjects, their ability to draw together theory and practice, and the truths that emerge from their studies.

This book widens the options for entrepreneurship researchers, allowing them to ask more interesting questions and accommodate greater complexity in their research findings. In so doing, researchers can more accurately reflect the lives of entrepreneurs and their experiences of entrepreneurship.

Introduction: Methodological variety in entrepreneurship research
Helle Neergaard and John Parm Ulhøi

Introduction

Although entrepreneurship in its broadest interpretation is as old as civilization itself, and theory on the individual's role in the organizational genesis can be dated back some centuries, entrepreneurship theory is still considered quite a young academic field (Bygrave 1989; Brazeal and Herbert 1999; Low 2001). Nevertheless, it has become an increasingly popular field of inquiry in the past quarter of a century with a growing research community of scholars from a broad spectrum of disciplines entering the field (Aldrich 1992; Low 2001; Acs and Audretsch 2003; McDonald et al. 2004). The implication is that entrepreneurship can be studied using a variety of methods, including both quantitative and qualitative techniques (Perren and Ram 2004). Despite this richness in methodological approaches, entrepreneurship is still considered a field lacking in methodological diversity and rigour (Wortman 1987; Aldrich 1992; Huse and Landström 1997; Low 2001); a criticism repeatedly directed at both quantitative and qualitative contributions since the late 1980s (Hornaday and Churchill 1987; Bygrave 1989; Low 2001, Hindle 2004). Indeed, it is argued that 'Entrepreneurship is less steeped in the rigors of traditional disciplines' (Low 2001: 20). Whilst this may be so, we would ask whether the pattern is a reflection of entrepreneurship being an applied science rather than a 'pure' science. Further, does not the entrepreneurial phenomenon itself, in all its complexity and dynamics, invite a methodological toolbox of broad variety? Indeed, entrepreneurship is a phenomenon in a state of constant flux, shaped by the behaviour of entrepreneurs whose responses to perceived opportunities may be highly difficult to predict.

In entrepreneurship research, calls for more qualitative approaches are made at regular intervals (e.g. Bygrave 1989; Huse and Landström 1997; Gartner and Birley 2002; Hindle 2004), seemingly without much effect. A less pessimistic angle is that the field is not lacking methodological diversity; rather qualitative entrepreneurship research merely faces a liability of legitimacy from mainstream editors which in part may be due to a varying quality of qualitative contributions. Often researchers who advocate

1

qualitative research blame this on lack of rigour (see e.g. Hindle 2004). Indeed, Hindle (2004: 577) express his opinion in no uncertain terms:

> Unless entrepreneurship ... begin[s] to embrace higher volumes of higher calibre qualitative research, the relevance and potency of the entrepreneurial canon will be severely compromised by a lack of the methodological variety that is so strongly displayed in other social sciences.

Research in entrepreneurship has, in other words, to a large extent been descriptive in nature, and empirical research has predominantly been based on structured surveys (see also Bygrave, Chapter 1 in this volume). When a qualitative research approach was adopted and reached publication, often such studies were based on single or multiple case studies in which the primary sources of information were archival data and/or interview data, the latter being procured by means of a structured or semi-structured survey. More innovative qualitative research in entrepreneurship is more often disseminated via journals explicitly aimed at the qualitative paradigm and anthologies such as the *New Movements of Entrepreneurship* series, also published by Edward Elgar. Keeping in pace with a growing demand for expanding the repertoire of research designs, analytic techniques and more interpretative approaches to understanding the phenomenon of entrepreneurship (Bygrave 1989; Aldrich 1992; Davidsson and Wiklund 2001), it is important to provide an outlet for such approaches. Simultaneously, it is necessary to respond to the call for more stringency in research methods.

This handbook can be perceived as a response to the trend and critique directed at the entrepreneurship field for producing (i) predominantly descriptive research and (ii) qualitative research of doubtful standard. We can only second that qualitative methods are 'demonstrably underrepresented in entrepreneurship research' (Hindle 2004: 577) at least when we are concerned with publications in peer-reviewed mainstream journals. The first reason for this pattern may be that the use of quantitative approaches has traditionally resulted in more publications compared with other methodologies (Huse and Landström 1997). Indeed, Chandler and Lyon (2001) found only 18 per cent of the contributions in their sample of 418 papers to be qualitative. A more recent review of 2234 articles by McDonald et al. (2004) also demonstrates the dominance of positivist approaches and research methods. A second reason for this situation is the pressure for publication for untenured faculty. This is particularly found among American scholars, whereas European academics have until recently been faced with less publication pressure. Therefore they have had the freedom to adopt a greater methodological diversity. Further, Europeans tend to be more tolerant of methodological diversity (Huse and Landström 1997).

Since so few qualitative studies apparently find their way into the mainstream journals, we felt obliged to check whether the pattern found in these journals reflects the direction of the field's research efforts. To this end, we reviewed abstracts from a randomly selected Babson–Kauffman Entrepreneurship Research Conference (2002). This review is by no means exhaustive, but it none the less provides an interesting indication of the pattern of methodological choices of American and European researchers respectively, as illustrated in Box I.1. Simultaneously, it shows that there is a great difference between the kind of research presented at one of the most prestigious entrepreneurship conferences and what is being published in entrepreneurship journals.

As the evidence shows, the number of abstracts purporting to use some form of qualitative research method is considerable, particularly among European researchers. This suggests that qualitative research proliferates,

---

BOX I.1 METHODOLOGICAL CHOICES IN CONFERENCE ABSTRACTS

An assessment of conference abstracts accepted for presentation at the Babson–Kauffman Entrepreneurship Research Conference 2002 revealed that there was a profound difference in the type of research method chosen by American and non-American researchers. Researchers from American universities authored 108 abstracts. Only *six* of these were exclusively case or interview-based, *five* were triangulated using both case method and survey or database, *four* were conceptual, *seven* did not give any method indication and *four* were literature reviews or other method. Further, there was *one* quasi-experiment, *two* experiments and *one* simulation study. The rest were based on surveys (42), existing databases (30), a combination of these (3), desk research and (3) or face-to-face administered structured questionnaires (1).

In contrast, scholars from non-American universities authored 111 abstracts. *Nine* of these were written together with American researchers, of these only *one* was case based. Of the remaining 102 articles there were 47 case or interview-based contributions, i.e. almost 50 per cent in comparison with less than 10 per cent of those written by researchers from American universities. In research teams of mixed origin, quantitative research also dominated.

at least in Europe. It is also a trend that we have encountered in the profile of the contributors to this handbook. Despite our continued efforts, only six of our contributors are from outside Europe. However, although the publication pressure trend has taken considerably longer to hit Europe, European business schools and universities are increasingly hiring and promoting faculty primarily based on research productivity measured by publication in highly ranked international journals (Gartner and Birley 2002). It is therefore time to consider whether and how it is possible to avoid falling into the trap of enforced methodological orthodoxy that such a strategy might well entail. On the other hand, we need to consider the consistent criticism directed at qualitative research for lacking rigour and stringency as a stumbling block to publication of qualitative research. In sum, these observations collectively point to a need for a handbook of qualitative research methods in entrepreneurship research.

As qualitative research in entrepreneurship is often rejected by mainstream journals due to lack of sufficient methodological detail and rigour (Gartner and Birley 2002), a better set of method selection guidelines therefore seems to be needed (Hindle 1994). The aim of this handbook is to introduce a spectrum of the qualitative research methods currently used, to increase the understanding of the versatility, usefulness and systematic rigour of these research methods, and to provide guidance on how they can be appropriately and fruitfully employed. The handbook aspires to assist existing and future researchers to make informed choices of design by providing concrete examples of research experiences, and offering tangible 'how-to' advice. We hope that by clarifying what these methods entail, how they are currently being used, and how they can be evaluated, this handbook may come to be perceived as 'a methodological toolbox'. Ultimately, we hope that it will enable advocates to respond to reasonable criticism, enlighten the critics and cut off unfounded attacks while at the same time demonstrating the width, scope and variety of qualitative methods.

The goal of qualitative research is to develop concepts that enhance the understanding of social phenomena in natural settings, with due emphasis on the meanings, experiences and views of all participants. The general assumption underpinning this handbook is that the phenomenon of entrepreneurship is too dynamic and complex to be captured by a single method. This is not advocating that 'anything goes', but should be seen as an encouragement of methodological pluralism and tolerance. We believe that qualitative research has the ability to explore hitherto uncharted depths in the field of entrepreneurship and to contribute significantly to the advancement of the field.

The audience for this book, therefore, includes all academics who wish to study the entrepreneurship phenomenon, based upon qualitative approaches.

In the process of producing this book we have discussed its potential merits with several national and international colleagues. A question that kept cropping up was 'What is qualitative research?' That is a reasonable question to ask, particularly because several chapters compare qualitative to quantitative research. One definition, provided by Denzin and Lincoln (1994), is considered by many an authoritative contribution on qualitative research methodologies. They define qualitative research as

> multi method in focus, involving an interpretive, naturalistic approach to its subject matter. This means that qualitative researchers study things in their natural settings, attempting to make sense of or interpret phenomena in terms of the meanings people bring to them. Qualitative research involves the studied use and collection of a variety of empirical materials – case study, personal experience, introspective, life story, interview, observational, historical, interactional, and visual texts – that describe routine and problematic moments and meaning in individuals' lives. (Denzin and Lincoln 1994: 2)

Clearly, entrepreneurship is a field that abounds in such empirical material. This handbook will adhere to the definition above.

The next question that springs to mind is 'Why do we undertake qualitative research?' A simple answer is that we use qualitative approaches when we wish to go beyond mere description at a generalizable level in our empirical investigations. Qualitative and quantitative approaches are frequently presented as adversaries in a methodological battle. However, even within qualitative research a similar battle is taking place as we write. Basically, qualitative researchers adopt two opposing approaches. On the one hand, there are those who are totally committed to using qualitative methods and advocate these even to the extent that they may dig new trenches from which they can shoot at quantitative research. On the other, there are those who choose between qualitative and quantitative methods depending on the topic of interest and the related research questions (Brannen 1992).

We perceive 'trench warfare' as unproductive. We embrace the scope and richness of qualitative entrepreneurship research while at the same time acknowledging the qualities of the more established, traditional or well-accepted approaches, both qualitative and quantitative. Various forms of quantitative approaches are indeed useful when there is a need to provide generalizable and representative description as well as statistical analyses. A key issue is therefore to combine respect for the current traditions with an open mind to innovative approaches. However, the adoption of different and sometimes (at least at first sight) contradictory research methods into the same subject, we would hold, may often pave the way for new inspiration and insight. As this is a handbook of qualitative research methods, we do not include contributions that are quantitative in their approach, although some contributions may use certain types of quantification. We further interpret qualitative studies quite broadly and have chosen to include in this volume contributions that represent both well-known and tested as well as some more daring approaches to conducting qualitative research in the field of entrepreneurship. This notwithstanding, we take the stance that qualitative approaches cannot be adequately understood independently of the ontological and epistemological basis and the related research questions. We also hold that concepts, terms and assumptions surrounding qualitative research should be explicitly stated and assessed on their own terms. Finally, we perceive individual approaches as embedded in the research process. In consequence we have organized the book around a procedural perspective.

The structure of the handbook
The handbook aims to provide a reference point for some of the most essential elements and critical choices in qualitative research design, reflecting the steps of the research process. We perceive the various choices in the research process as arising from the research questions; hence we adopt a pragmatic approach to the study of entrepreneurship (Schulz and Hatch 1996). According to Kyrö and Kansikas (2005: 124), 'adopting pragmatism to the research process requires parting from the traditional way of describing it as theoretical and empirical parts and instead views it as a process, in which the previous step creates presumptions and leads to the next step'. Accordingly, we have organized the handbook into four parts, each representing a step in the research process (see Figure I.1).

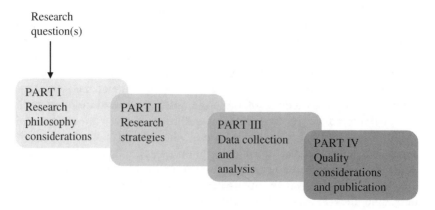

Source: Inspired by Saunders et al. (2003).

Figure I.1   Steps and choices in the research process

Metaphors abound in entrepreneurship research. The most often used is the biological metaphor. Most entrepreneurial processes and acts are likened to the development of human beings and means of sustaining life. However, the research process can be described by means of various metaphors. The vehicle metaphor conveys a number of different associations. For example, according to Collins English dictionary, a vehicle can be interpreted in four ways. Each interpretation may be applied in the production of entrepreneurial knowledge: (i) it may be a medium of expression, communication or achievement of ideas; or (ii) it enables a performer to display his or her talents; or (iii) it constitutes a base in which composite elements are suspended; and last but not least (iv) it may give associations to an automobile. Each of these are valid interpretations with regard to qualitative research methods. Entrepreneurial ideas certainly need to be expressed, communicated and achieved in order to contribute to advancement of society (i). Indeed, entrepreneurs need to display their talents in some way or other (ii). However, most entrepreneurial inventions or innovations are made up of numerous and sometimes complex ingredients without which entrepreneurship could not take place (iii). And finally, entrepreneurship itself and the entrepreneurial process starts with the perception of some idea that is brought to fulfilment, often in a race against time (iv). It is the last interpretation that guides the structure of this book. The research process begins with the choice of vehicle, a paradigm in which the research is anchored. It starts out by delimiting the research challenge and choosing a research strategy. It then gains speed as it proceeds through the turns and straights of planning how to collect data and analyse them. It winds down in considering various approaches to assessing quality and achieving publication.

Part I: Choosing a vehicle
Considerations concerning the ontological and epistemological underpinnings of research or the so-called paradigmatic dimensions of science easily generate controversy and heated debate. It is, however, only through such debate that a field advances. According to Kuhn (1962/70), a paradigm emerges when a group of researchers agree on operating within specifically agreed boundaries, which define what is important, legitimate and reasonable research, an idea that is broadly accepted (McDonald et al. 2004). Over time social consensus is reached on a specific point of reference concerning a definitive set of precepts and methodological procedures (Gummesson 1991). Paradigms in Kuhn's understanding exist primarily in mature fields of science and not, for example, in the social sciences and humanities. Such areas are often described as fragmented in terms of theory and methodology. There are researchers who perceive the field of entrepreneurship as an

example of such a pre-paradigmatic research field, in the Kuhnian sense of the word. However, there are also some who contest this perception. The debate typically hinges on the various definitions of a paradigm that researchers invoke.

However, the concept is often used arbitrarily, thus masking the fundamental meaning (Morgan 1980). Some use the concept about schools of thought, others use the term to describe basic theoretical perspectives or research domains. Not all readers may agree with these definitions. They may instead choose to define entrepreneurship as a discipline, a theoretical field of academic inquiry. Differently put, it is difficult to see how the field of entrepreneurship can be contained within a single or unifying paradigm in the Kuhnian sense; rather it constitutes what Aldrich (1992), for example, would call a pragmatic stance. In methodological terms, according to this stance a researcher should choose the procedure, that is most suitable with respect to the research question(s). It means that for a given research project within entrepreneurship the researcher may choose between a number of research strategies – and even mix them.

The importance of understanding alternative paradigms lies in augmenting the individual's understanding of how certain world-views delimit methodological flexibility and adaptation. This is not to say that 'anything goes', but is rather a question of understanding how important research questions may best be addressed. This sentiment is echoed by, for example, Hofer and Bygrave (1992). We advocate if not an elimination of paradigm boundaries, then a recognition that paradigms are not incompatible, that paradigm boundaries can be penetrated, and that paradigms, even if they cannot be united, may interact instead of being sharply delimited. This approach is proposed by an increasing number of scholars, for example Gioia and Pitre (1990), Hassard (1991), Schulz and Hatch (1996) and Lewis and Kelemen (2002). This invites researchers to look at the world in new ways.

Part I will debate the consequences of a researcher's world-view for the research process. There are fundamentally two ways in which to view the relationship between philosophy and research method: whether the research question(s) (and hence the theory) frame the philosophical stance, or whether the philosophical stance directs the choice of research questions (Creswell 1998; Saunders et al. 2003). In this book we include both approaches. However, the relationship between the philosophical debates and the methods used in the research process is often poorly understood and badly accounted for (Knox 2004), and it is one of the areas that qualitative researchers need to address. The three chapters in this part therefore represent different philosophical arguments and alternatives. However, they should not be seen as exclusive with regard to the approaches that are applied by scholars in the field.

Chapter 1, 'The entrepreneurship paradigm (I) revisited', includes two contributions. The first is a reprint of Bygrave's seminal article, which is next updated with a commentary by Bygrave himself on the developments in the field since 1989. Bygrave invokes the interpretation of the word paradigm as a research domain starting the chapter with 'Entrepreneurship is one of the youngest paradigms in the management sciences' (ibid.: 28). Bygrave's original article probably does not need any introduction. However, in his update he looks back to look ahead, and provides an insight into the background for the original article as well as leaving the distinct impression that the field has not changed significantly in the past 17 years with regard to methodological advancement.

In Chapter 2 Blundel introduces critical realism as one philosophical alternative. 'Critical realism: a suitable vehicle for entrepreneurship research?' provides an outline of the origins and principal features of critical realist social theory and reviews of the methodological implications of this philosophical perspective. The chapter also considers how critical realism might offer a suitable 'vehicle' for qualitative research in the field of entrepreneurship and assesses its explanatory potential.

Berglund in Chapter 3, 'Researching entrepreneurship as lived experience', presents aspects of philosophical phenomenology that are relevant to entrepreneurship and exemplifies how phenomenology can be used to capture and communicate the meanings of different entrepreneurial experiences, allowing for a more detailed understanding of how theoretical concepts and empirical events are understood and translated into action by entrepreneurs.

Part II: Starting out and gearing up
The six chapters in this part deal with focusing and delimiting the research challenge and choosing a relevant research strategy. Some research strategies are deductive (quantitative in nature), others inductive (qualitative in nature). However, research strategies are not necessarily mutually exclusive. To illustrate, Saunders et al. (2003) operate with case studies, grounded theory, ethnography and action research as examples of research strategies. However, a grounded theory study may well be a case study and vice versa. Moreover, in this section we include semiotics and discourse analysis. It is arguable whether these constitute research strategies or are techniques/methods for data collection, because in reality there is no hard-and-fast boundary between the two. A research strategy leads seamlessly into the choice of data collection methods. However, the research strategy is concerned with the overall approach that is adopted, whereas the data collection methods constitute operational, methodological decisions.

The first three chapters in Part II deal with more conventional types of field studies, whereas the last three chapters represent in our view more unorthodox approaches to the study of entrepreneurship, advocating sign and text analysis as a way to produce new knowledge. What distinguishes the latter from the former is predominantly that they do not necessarily include interaction with the field.

In Chapter 4, 'Ethnographic methods in entrepreneurship research', Johnstone invites the reader to consider the potential of an ethnographic research strategy for developing grounded theory in entrepreneurship. Ethnography originates in the anthropological field, and the purpose is to access the interpretation of world of the research subjects. It is a very time-consuming research strategy that requires the researcher to be flexible and responsive to the research subjects. It is definitely a very appropriate strategy for entrepreneurship researchers. Johnstone discusses the cyclical nature of ethnography and considers the strengths and weaknesses of the approach.

Mäkelä and Turcan discuss 'Building grounded theory in entrepreneurship research' in Chapter 5. They describe the history of grounded theory methodology and the location of the methodology within the umbrella of qualitative research methods, reaching out to the field of entrepreneurship. In order to make the discussion more topical, throughout they illustrate the discussion with examples from contemporary grounded theory research.

Chapter 6, 'An action research approach to entrepreneurship' by Leitch, illustrates the relevance of the entrepreneurship discipline to the world of practice through an action research approach. Leitch argues that such an approach not only enhances our understanding of entrepreneurship in action, it also helps entrepreneurs develop their organizations, partly because it creates ownership of the entrepreneurial process.

In Chapter 7 Smith and Anderson propose that semiotics, the doctrine of signs, is a practical tool for exploring the depth and scope of what we mean by entrepreneurship. Consequently the chapter, 'Recognizing meaning: semiotics in entrepreneurial research', argues that an appreciation of entrepreneurial semiotics enables an understanding of the meanings of enterprise; what it is; how it is practised; why it is practised and why it is encouraged. The authors operationalize and explain semiotics so that even the layperson should be able to apply this technique.

Chapters 8 and 9 both present discourse analytical approaches to female entrepreneurship. Achtenhagen and Welter introduce discourse analysis as applied to the representation of female entrepreneurs in the printed media in Chapter 8, 'Media discourse in entrepreneurship research'. Using German newspaper articles as their basis, Achtenhagen and Welter illustrate how discourses continually contribute to shaping the entrepreneurial environment (and vice versa) and provide an understanding of how understanding a particular discourse can generate new insights.

Chapter 9, 'A Foucauldian framework for discourse analysis' by Ahl, develops a discourse analytical approach of research texts on female entrepreneurs building on an interpretation and translation of Foucault's theories of discourse analysis. Ahl provides a detailed description of her interpretation of Foucault and introduces a step-by-step account of her analytical approach. In this unfolding of the research it becomes apparent just how much discursive practices in research influence the general understanding of women's role in and execution of entrepreneurship.

Part III: Gaining speed
The four chapters in this part of the book primarily focus on techniques for collecting information. Apart from the first chapter, which concentrates on the issue of identifying and choosing informants and cases, the chapters are concerned with different ways of working with 'text', making sense of the information and developing the findings for publication. The examples included here are by no means exhaustive of the variety of techniques for collecting and analysing data; indeed the area is so varied that it really warrants a book exclusively on data collection techniques.

Before the researcher can start to collect data and indeed think of analysing it, it is highly appropriate to consider who or what may be the best information source. In Chapter 10, 'Sampling in entrepreneurial settings', Neergaard highlights the need to document sampling procedures and provides guidance on how to select cases and informants purposefully. Neergaard argues that sampling constitutes a crucial element in securing the quality of the outcome of a research project, and that all research projects need to choose cases and informants that are able to provide the best possible information. This can only be achieved through purposeful sampling.

Brundin concentrates on real-time methodologies for collecting empirical material and how these can contribute to enhance our knowledge of entrepreneurial processes in Chapter 11, 'Catching it as it happens'. Real-time methodologies have the advantage that they do not rely on historical recall and therefore the danger of informants recollecting incorrectly or leaving out embarrassing occurrences and the like is reduced. Brundin accounts for a range of real-time methodologies and provides an example from her own research which illustrates a rarely investigated phenomenon, namely the feelings and emotions of entrepreneurs. She shows how using a real-time methodology can lead to an alternative understanding of the entrepreneurial process.

This is followed by McKenzie in Chapter 12, 'Techniques for collecting verbal histories', which focuses on concrete techniques for obtaining the life stories of the entrepreneur. McKenzie's honest and down-to-earth account of the challenges in achieving access to these stories emphasizes the quality dimension of interviews and how to ensure that the reporting is accurate.

E-mails are quite a recent phenomenon research-wise as a means of gathering data, but with the increase in the use of the Internet for business correspondence, they are very likely to become an important source of data in the future. In Chapter 13, 'Using e-mails as a source of qualitative data', Wakkee, Danskin and During seek to explain the value of e-mails, distinguish them from other sources of data, and provide suggestions for analysing the text. They offer a step-by-step account of the procedure from obtaining access to the analysis and presentation of the data.

Chapter 14, 'The scientification of fiction', by Pihl, Klyver and Damgaard, introduces the construction of dialogue and drama as a way to understand entrepreneurial perceptions and processes. They suggest that this alternative way of approaching the empirical field may provide a useful shortcut to theorizing.

Part IV: Winding down and assessing the ride
This part addresses criteria of goodness and quality assessment as well as the challenge of publication. Earlier, we noted that qualitative research was rarely published in mainstream journals. The quality of qualitative research has often been under scrutiny from quantitative researchers – and unfortunately not always unfoundedly. The lack of generally agreed upon rules for what good quality is in qualitative research may indeed be one of the reasons that publication in mainstream journals is notoriously hard to achieve. The two first chapters in this part therefore address the quality control issue from two different points of view. The remaining two chapters focus on the important issue of getting qualitative research published, one from an author's point of view and the other seen from an editor's perspective.

The criteria of representativeness and reliability generally do not belong in the qualitative research tradition. Further, the traditional validity concept is increasingly being substituted by other concepts. The crux of the matter here is that, as researchers, we have an obligation to conduct rigorous, correct and credible research and we must expect to be held accountable in this respect. Therefore we must provide detailed descriptions of how knowledge has been procured and how it is possible to establish that it is valuable knowledge. It has to be transparent how the research has led to certain findings and conclusions. This should not, however, be confused with the existence of any objective truth to which an account should be compared (Maxwell 1996). Validity as a constituent of the research design consists of the strategies used to rule out the threat of alternative explanation. It is, unfortunately, the exception rather than the rule that qualitative research explicitly addresses this issue (Andersen and Skaates 2005). Identifying how to evaluate qualitative research is not a clear cut case, the criteria for evaluation depend on both the paradigm in which the research is embedded and the research strategy chosen, as Wigren shows in Chapter 15, 'Assessing the quality of qualitative research in entrepreneurship'. Wigren starts out by presenting an overview of quality criteria, after which she discusses particular quality criteria that can be applied to ethnographic research.

From a critical realist approach, Bøllingtoft in Chapter 16, 'A critical realist approach to quality in observation studies', focuses on how to incorporate quality criteria into the process of an observation study, and thus overcome some of the potential problems of this technique. Ensuring quality in observation is probably the greatest challenge of all, because observation is inherently subjective and relies excessively on the observer's ability to disengage and be neutral. Bøllingtoft suggests stringent procedures as a solution to minimizing researcher bias.

In Chapter 17 Smith and Anderson present a dialogue on the problems of getting qualitative research published. Smith provides an insightful account into the frustrations of a doctoral student trying to make publication headway. Anderson enters the discussion from a seasoned supervisor point of view providing, probably to some, provocative ideas. 'Daring to be different' is exactly that and, together with Chapter 18, we believe a fitting way to end the book.

In Chapter 18, 'Avoiding a strike-out in the first innings', Brush provides hands-on useful guidelines on how to get published. It answers many of the questions that particularly Ph.D. students and junior researchers may have, not only in entrepreneurship, but across various disciplines.

Finally, in closing we address a few remaining key challenges for those scholars who conduct qualitative research in entrepreneurship.

References

Acs, Z.J. and Audretsch, D.B. (2003) Introduction to the handbook of entrepreneurship research. In Acs, Z.J. and Audretsch, D.B. (eds), *Handbook of Entrepreneurship Research: An interdisciplinary survey and introduction.* Dordrecht: Kluwer Academic Publishers.

Aldrich, H. (1992) Methods in our madness? Trends in entrepreneurship research. In Sexton, D.L. and Kasarda, J.D. *The State of the Art of Entrepreneurship.* Boston, MA: PWS–Kent Publishing Company.

Anderson, P.H. and Skaates, A.-M. (2005) Ensuring validity in qualitative international business research. In Marschan-Piekkari, R. and Welch, C. (2004) *Handbook of Qualitative Research Methods for International Business.* Cheltenham, UK and Northampton, MA, USA: Edward Elgar.

Brannen, J. (1992) *Mixing Methods: qualitative and quantitative research.* Aldershot: Avebury.

Brazeal, D.V. and Herbert, T.T. (1999) The genesis of entrepreneurship. *Entrepreneurship Theory and Practice*, **23**(3): 29–45.

Bygrave, W. (1989) The entrepreneurship paradigm (I): A philosophical look at its research methodologies. *Entrepreneurship Theory and Practice*, **14**(1): 7–26.

Chandler, G.N. and Lyon, D.W. (2001) Issues of research design and construct measurement in entrepreneurship research: the past decade. *Entrepreneurship Theory and Practice*, Summer: 101–13.

Creswell, J.W. (1998) *Qualitative Inquiry and Research Design: Choosing among five traditions.* Thousand Oaks, CA: Sage.

Davidsson, P. and Wiklund, J. (2001) Levels of analysis in entrepreneurship research: Current research practice and suggestions for the future. *Entrepreneurship Theory and Practice*, **25**(4): 81–100.

Denzin, N.K. and Lincoln, Y.S. (1994) *Handbook of Qualitative Research.* Thousand Oaks, CA: Sage, Chapter 1: 1–17.

Gartner, W.B. and Birley, S. (2002) Introduction to the special issue on qualitative methods in entrepreneurship research. *Journal of Business Venturing*, **17**(5): 387–96.

Gioia, D.A. and Pitre, E. (1990) Multiparadigm perspectives on theory building. *Academy of Management Review*, **15**(4): 584–603.

Gummesson, E. (1991) *Qualitative Methods in Management Research.* Newbury Park, CA: Sage.

Hassard, J. (1991) Multiple paradigms and organizational analysis: A case study. *Organization Studies*, **12**(2): 275–99.

Hindle, K. (2004) Choosing qualitative methods for entrepreneurial cognition research: A canonical development approach. *Entrepreneurship Theory and Practice*, **28**(6): 575–607.

Hofer, C.W. and Bygrave, W.D. (1992) Researching entrepreneurship. *Entrepreneurship Theory and Practice*, **16**(3): 91–100.

Hornaday, J.A. and Churchill, N.C. (1987) Current trends in entrepreneurial research. In Churchill, N.C., Hornaday, J.A., Kirchhoff, B.A., Krasner, O.J. and Vesper K.H. (eds), *Frontiers of Entrepreneurship Research*, Babson College, Wellesley, MA.

Huse, M. and Landström, H. (1997) European entrepreneurship and small business research: methodological openness and contextual differences. *International Studies of Management and Organization*, **27**(3): 3–12.

Knox, K. (2004) A researcher's dilemma – philosophical and methodological pluralism. *Electronic Journal of Business Research Methods*, **2**(2), www.ejbrm.com.

Kuhn, T. (1962/70) *The Structure of Scientific Revolutions.* London: University of Chicago Press.

Kyrö, P. and Kansikas, J. (2005) Current state of methodology in entrepreneurship research and some expectations for the future. In Fayolle, A., Ulijn, J. and Kyrö, P. (2004), *Entrepreneurship Research in Europe: Outcomes and perspectives.* Cheltenham, UK and Northampton, MA, USA: Edward Elgar.

Lewis, M.W. and Kelemen, M.L. (2002) Multiparadigm inquiry: Exploring organizational pluralism and paradox. *Human Relations*, **55**(2): 251–74.

Low, M.B. (2001) The adolescence of entrepreneurship research: specification of purpose. *Entrepreneurship Theory and Practice*, **25**(4): 17–25.

Maxwell, J.A. (1996) *Qualitative research design. An interactive approach.* Applied Social Research Methods Series, Volume 41. Thousand Oaks, CA: Sage.

McDonald, S., Gan, B.C. and Anderson, A. (2004) Studying entrepreneurship: A review of methods employed in entrepreneurship research 1985–2004. Paper presented at RENT XVIII, Copenhagen, Denmark, 25–26 November.

Morgan, G. (1980) Paradigms, metaphors, and puzzle solving in organization theory. *Administrative Science Quarterly*, **25**(4): 605–23.

Perren, L. and Ram, M. (2004) Case-study method in small business and entrepreneurial research: Mapping boundaries and perspectives. *International Small Business Journal*, **22**(1): 83–101.

Saunders, M.; Lewis, P. and Thornhill, A. (2003) *Research Methods for Business Students.* Harlow, Essex: Pearson Education.

Schulz, M. and Hatch, M.J. (1996) Living within multiple paradigms: the case of paradigm interplay in organizational culture studies. *Academy of Management Review*, **21**: 529–57.

Wortman, Jr M.S. (1987) Entrepreneurship: An integrating typology and evaluation of the empirical research in the field. *Journal of Management*, **13**(2): 259–80.

PART I

CHOOSING A VEHICLE

1 The entrepreneurship paradigm (I) revisited
William D. Bygrave

Introduction

In 1988, I had one doctorate in physics from Oxford University and was – to say the least – a mature student trying to finish my second doctorate, in business, at Boston University. I was a tenure-track associate professor of entrepreneurship at Babson College. Between my first and second doctorates, I worked in the USA and Europe for a Route 128 venture-capital-backed company – actually the first start-up ever to be backed by formal venture capital; founded a Route 128 venture-capital-backed company; managed a small division of a high-tech company listed on the New York Stock Exchange; and while working on my second doctorate, I took an unpaid leave of absence from academia to co-found a medical database company that we eventually sold to a New York Stock Exchange company. Along the way I had also been a business angel investor. I was born and brought up in a mom-and-pop business in England; many of my relatives in England owned mom-and-pop businesses. One of my enduring hobbies is the history of science, in particular physics.

Entrepreneurship scholarship at the end of the 1980s

In 1988, very few senior scholars were researching exclusively entrepreneurship. Most tenured and tenure-track professors in the field of entrepreneurship had appointments in classic departments such as management, policy, strategy, finance and organizational behaviour. There were no departments of entrepreneurship on a par with the classic business school disciplines. For instance, at Babson College, which by 1989 was regarded as a leader in the emerging field of entrepreneurship, the department of entrepreneurship was part of the management division. To be a scholar solely of entrepreneurship was very risky in 1988 for an untenured faculty member because junior professors who had chosen that lonely career path had rarely received tenure, and as it turned out, a few well-known entrepreneurship scholars were even denied tenure.

There were, however, glimpses that entrepreneurship was gaining legitimacy as an academic pursuit: a few prominent business schools, most notably Harvard and Wharton, were making significant commitments to entrepreneurship. More and more endowed chairs in entrepreneurship were being funded. The annual Babson Entrepreneurship Research Conference with its proceedings, *Frontiers of Entrepreneurship Research*, was established in 1981; and in 1984 the first doctoral consortium was held in conjunction with that conference. In the USA, the *Journal of Business Venturing* was founded in 1985, and in the late 1980s the *American Journal of Small Business* was repositioned and renamed *Entrepreneurship Theory and Practice*; in Europe, the *Small Business Economics* journal was founded in 1987. The Academy of Management reluctantly promoted entrepreneurship from a special interest group to a division in 1986 but did not organize an entrepreneurship doctoral consortium until the early 1990s. Looking back to the 1980s, it is clear that the entrepreneurship paradigm was in the making.

Development as an entrepreneurship scholar
When I enrolled as a part-time student at Boston University's School of Management's doctoral program in 1981, I was the only student – out of more than 80 – who wanted to study entrepreneurship. There was no entrepreneurship department and only one faculty member who specialized in small business. Hence, I had to tailor my own program within the strategy/policy group. By good fortune I knew Jeff Timmons, who was then at Babson College. Jeff invited me to join him and Norman Fast (then vice president of Venture Economics) on a major research project on venture capital. Boston University allowed Jeff Timmons to be my doctoral adviser.

In those days, earning a doctoral degree at Boston University was onerous. Students were required to have an MBA degree, and if they did not, they had to take MBA courses as well as doctoral courses. Between 1981 and 1989, when I finally completed my dissertation, I took at least a dozen courses or waiver exams at Boston University and received transfer credit for another half-dozen courses from my executive MBA degree.

I learned a great deal from some of the courses, but the most valuable learning came through the papers that I wrote in the seminars. Each paper was focused on my venture-capital research with Jeff Timmons and Norman Fast; most of them were presented at the Babson Entrepreneurship Conference and published in *Frontiers of Entrepreneurship Research*, and some were published in the *Journal of Business Venturing*. As soon as I had completed the comprehensive exams at Boston University, I wrote a dissertation based on those papers.

Origins of 'The entrepreneurship paradigm: A philosophical look at its research methodologies'
To be frank, the doctoral program by and large was not an uplifting experience. Too much of it was bogged down in pedantry that drove out

imagination and creativity. In my bleaker moments, earning a business doctorate seemed more like a fraternity hazing than a celebration of intellect. It felt as if I was earning my membership of a guild rather than discovering knowledge that would improve the practice of entrepreneurship. As soon as I had completed my doctorate, I rewarded myself by doing entirely different research for a few months.

I was already a reviewer for the three major entrepreneurship journals. Probably because of my physics background, journal editors had asked me to review papers that tried to introduce the relatively new science of chaos theory into entrepreneurship. Reviewing them actually made me angry because it was obvious that the authors were being opportunistic and simply using 'chaos' as a buzzword. It was doubtful that the authors had even read Gleick's book *Chaos: Making a new science* (1987) that popularized chaos theory, let alone understood even the most elementary mathematics explaining it. My reviews were the harshest that I have ever written because the papers represented entrepreneurship scholarship at its worst. It was the kind of research that invited ridicule from our academic colleagues in established disciplines.

Partly out of remorse at being so harsh and partly out of curiosity, I decided to read some of the scholarly literature on chaos. That led me to develop mathematical models that were metaphors for entrepreneurial chaos. One of the most exhilarating moments in my life as a researcher was when I made an infinitesimal change to one of the model parameters and the beautifully smooth sigmoid curve representing the growth of an industry suddenly and quite unexpectedly broke up into numerous peaks and valleys on the computer screen. It certainly felt like entrepreneurial chaos.

At that point I intended to write a paper on chaos and entrepreneurship, but before embarking on such a task, I decided to look at catastrophe theory, which might be a metaphor for the entrepreneurial event. One thing led to another before I realized that 'physics envy' was getting the better of me. So instead of writing a conceptual article on chaos and entrepreneurship, I combined my thoughts on entrepreneurship methodology that had been presented to the doctoral consortium at Calgary in 1988 with my work on mathematical models that might be relevant to entrepreneurship theory. It resulted in two papers, 'The entrepreneurship paradigm (I): A philosophical look at its research methodologies' (1989), reprinted in this book, and 'The entrepreneurship paradigm (II): Chaos and catastrophes among quantum jumps' (1989), followed by a third paper 'Theorizing about entrepreneurship', co-authored with Charles Hofer (1991). All three papers were published in *Entrepreneurship Theory and Practice*.

By 1989 I was already apprehensive about where the infant entrepreneurship paradigm was heading. My principal concerns were that the field

was being driven more and more by theory often built on flimsy foundations; that the research method was becoming dominated by increasingly
complex statistical analysis, predominantly SPSS; that there was a dearth
of field research; that there were far too few longitudinal studies; that too
many studies were on secondary data sets; that too many of the primary
data sets were produced from self-reported subjective questionnaires; and
that we needed to keep in mind that entrepreneurship is holistic and tends
to decompose when researchers try to break it into its component parts.

Assessment of entrepreneurship research in 2005
Let's see where we have made progress in the last 17 years, and where, in my
opinion, we have either stood still or regressed. But before you read this
section, I ask you to read the following three articles: 'How business schools
lost their way' (Bennis and O'Toole 2005), 'Issues of research design and
construct measurement in entrepreneurship: The past decade' (Chandler
and Lyon 2001); and 'What entrepreneurship research can do for business
and policy practice' (Davidsson 2000).

Demographics of entrepreneurship scholarship
In 2005, there are hundreds of chairs in entrepreneurship at universities
throughout the world. The field has grown so rapidly that the demand for
entrepreneurship academics is still outstripping the supply. Top scholars
are in great demand to fill endowed chairs and as a result salaries have shot
up. The number of entrepreneurship doctoral students increased steadily
throughout the 1990s and continues to rise. This can be exemplified by
looking at the number of students applying to attend the annual Babson
Entrepreneurship Research Conference doctoral consortium. This figure
has increased from approximately 30 per year in 1990 to more than 80 in
2005. Many more scholars are studying entrepreneurship and they are
producing more and more research, as can be seen from the number of
abstracts submitted to the Babson Entrepreneurship Research Conference,
which rose from 39 at the inaugural conference in 1981 to 354 in 2001 to
more than 600 in 2004. What's more, there is now a proliferation of entrepreneurship conferences throughout the world. Likewise, the number of
journals dedicated to entrepreneurship and related fields such as family
business has multiplied. However, the question remains, what has this
growing army of scholars labouring inside and around the perimeter of the
entrepreneurship paradigm produced?

Longitudinal studies
Perhaps the most important advance in the field is the longitudinal studies
that have been undertaken or are now under way. The most prominent one

on the world stage is the Global Entrepreneurship Monitor (GEM), which since 1999 has been making annual surveys of the state of entrepreneurship in 46 countries that comprise more than 90 percent of the GDP and two-thirds of the population of the entire world.[1] More than 120 scholars throughout the world are involved with GEM research. To date more than 620 000 household interviews have been conducted, as have 5000 interviews with key informants. The long-range objective of GEM is to explain the role that entrepreneurship plays in the growth of national economies, a goal that is breathtakingly ambitious – some might even say arrogant. GEM results are already being used by national governments to help set policies to stimulate entrepreneurship at the national level and in some countries such as Germany, the UK and Spain at the regional level.

GEM built on the research method that was used by the Entrepreneurship Research Consortium (ERC) study, which was started in the mid-1990s, and the US Panel Study on Entrepreneurial Dynamics (PSED) study, which is another noteworthy longitudinal study. PSED's method has stimulated similar studies outside the USA.

There is still room for more longitudinal studies because according to Chandler and Lyon (2001) only 7 percent of the 416 empirical entrepreneurship articles published in nine journals between 1989 and 1999 were 'true' longitudinal studies. Further, studies of companies as they develop from conception to adolescence are almost never in real time, which is also a severe shortcoming.

Data sets
Some primary data sets such as the GEM household survey (adult population survey), and GEM key informant interviews, and the PSED are extensive and good but nonetheless have flaws. Too many primary data sets are compiled from subjective replies to multiple-choice questions administered to anonymous respondents via phone, postal mail or email. Chandler and Lyon (2001), for example, found that 195 entrepreneurship articles in their survey used only primary data sets, of which a whopping 142 used paper or phone questionnaires with multiple-item scales. That might be satisfactory when surveying mom-and-pop businesses, but does anyone imagine that busy entrepreneurs with high-potential businesses have time to respond? Or worse yet, does anyone really believe that general partners of leading venture-capital funds respond to such questionnaires? Having said all that, there is one noticeable improvement in primary data sets: nowadays, unlike 20 or more years ago, we almost never see research based on questionnaires administered to students.

Too much research is based on convenient, readily available secondary data sets. There are, for example, far too many papers on venture capital, which funds only one out of 10000 start-ups, and IPOs (initial public offerings), which fund even fewer businesses. On the other hand there is a shortage of research into bank financing. And there is a dearth of research into funding from informal investors – the so-called 4Fs, founders, family, friends and foolhardy strangers – who fund virtually every new business. The amount of research is inversely proportional to the importance of the funding source to entrepreneurs. This situation became so acute that the 2002 Babson Entrepreneurship Research Conference deliberately capped the number of venture capital and IPO papers to 20 percent of all the abstracts accepted.

Statistical analysis
There is far too much complex statistical analysis, almost always with SPSS. For example, approximately 395 of the 416 articles surveyed by Chandler and Lyon used statistical analysis; 78 percent (of the 395) used factor, correlation, regression, discriminant or cluster analysis; 9 percent used analysis of variance; 7 percent used logistical regression; and 10 percent used non-parametric statistics. Only 13 percent simply compared means with T-tests. We are now so addicted to SPSS that my 1990 tongue-in-cheek comment that our leading journals should print on their mast-heads 'Let no one ignorant of SPSS publish here' is in danger of becoming a reality.

But my greatest gripe with statistical analysis in entrepreneurship is that it is a study of central tendency, whereas Schumpeterian entrepreneurship is all about outliers – sometimes extreme outliers such as Wal-Mart, Southwest Airlines, FedEx, Intel, Microsoft, Genentech, Apple, Dell, Amazon.com and eBay that rearrange the economic order. Another related gripe is that when we make a random survey of entrepreneurs or would-be entrepreneurs in the general population, we almost always fail to acknowledge that half the respondents in our data set are part-time entrepreneurs, and half the full-time entrepreneurs have no employees other than themselves. Hence only one-quarter of the respondents have or intend to have employees, and less than 10 percent of those have businesses that have or expect to have at least 25 employees. Thus a data set of 200 responses has only 50 full-time entrepreneurs with employees and only five with 25 or more employees. Put another way, the data set is dominated by part-time and mom-and-pop businesses – hardly the kind of data set from which we should make generalizations to guide our undergraduate and MBA students with entrepreneurial ambitions. No way is this belittling the important role of mom-and-pops in society; it's just that I don't believe that we can learn a lot from mom-and-pops which is relevant to high-potential entrepreneurs.

Theory

No doubt about it, one of the most noticeable differences between articles published in the 1980s and those published today is the increase in the proportion of papers with theoretical front ends. In 2005, except for a few rare instances, it is impossible to get a paper without a theory section accepted for publication in a top entrepreneurship journal. This is an issue where I disagree most profoundly with the journal editors and most members of review boards. It seems to me that more often than not theory developed from sociology, psychology and economics tends to develop esoteric or mundane hypotheses that are of little or no value to the practice of entrepreneurship. Chandler and Lyon (2001) found that 30 percent of all the entrepreneurship articles published in 'A' journals had no empirical data. Hence plenty of theory-only papers are being published, so why are editors and reviewers insisting that empirical papers have conceptual front ends?

Reflecting on the first few years of the *Journal of Business Venturing*, it appears that, in general, authors and reviewers back then had a better sense of what was important to the practice of entrepreneurship. True, authors spent little – if any – effort to root their articles in theory, nor did they use unnecessarily complex statistical machinery, but they had something very important to say to practitioners. What I have in mind is Timmons's work that helped to set up a classification scheme for venture capital; Wetzel's pioneering work on angel investors that led to setting up angel networks (Wetzel 1987); and Sahlman and Stevenson's seminal article on capital market myopia, which is one of only a few journal articles that venture capitalists and investment bankers have ever read (Sahlman and Stevenson 1985). None of those papers would have been accepted by today's generation of reviewers; even worse, they almost certainly would have rejected David Birch's seminal work on job creation, which was published at the end of the 1970s.

Can anyone think of any article published since 2000 in our leading journals that has had as profound an effect on practice as some of the articles published in the 1980s? I should have seen the trend coming in 1988 when one of the reviewers of an article on rates of return of venture capital, of which I was a co-author, commented that it should be presented at a practitioner conference, not the annual conference of the Academy of Management because it lacked theory. Forgive me if this sounds boastful, but the findings in that paper were the most important that I have ever discovered. It changed forever venture capitalists' and their investors' expectations of rates of return.

A more recent example is an anonymous reviewer who rejected an IPO paper submitted to a leading journal because it did not have a strong enough theory section and its empirical method did not pass muster. (I was the other reviewer of the paper.) Unfortunately, the reviewer's critique revealed that he or she did not know what a secondary offering was! For all I know, that reviewer might have an encyclopaedic knowledge of finance theory and might have complete mastery of the armamentarium of statistics for the social sciences, but clearly he or she is ignorant of very basic practical aspects of raising money on public markets. As a result a solid paper on a current topic of substantial interest to practitioners was not published.

My own publications demonstrate that I do believe in theory development. It is simply that I am opposed to making theory a prerequisite for an empirical paper. I repeat what Isaac Newton, the greatest natural philosopher of all time, wrote: 'Hypotheses non fingo.' Newton was not only one of the greatest experimentalists, he was also perhaps *the* greatest theorist who has ever lived. He believed that hypotheses should be induced from experiment and that in sound physics every proposition should be drawn from phenomena and then generalized by induction. I much prefer to heed the findings of a well-designed empirical study with generalizable findings relevant to the practice of entrepreneurship than a paper with hypotheses derived almost entirely from theory.

Recently, I read Eve Curie's touching biography of her mother, Marie Curie, and re-read a compilation of some of the major papers of Luis Alvarez. Curie and Alvarez were two of the greatest experimental physicists of the twentieth century. Both made discoveries that earned Nobel prizes. Nowhere in their articles do you find a theoretical front end from which they derived hypotheses. If we entrepreneurship scholars want to emulate – albeit subconsciously – the hard sciences, then let's not insist that every paper must have a theoretical front end.

Future of the entrepreneurship paradigm

If we continue on our present path I am not optimistic about the future of the entrepreneurship paradigm. Look at the evidence: it's almost impossible to get an empirical-only paper published in an 'A' journal no matter how important its findings; our method is almost exclusively quantitative – 95 percent of the entrepreneurship articles published in nine 'A' journals used statistical analysis; our prime instrument is the questionnaire – 35 percent of the 'A' articles used phone or paper questionnaires with multiple-scale items; only 10 percent were based on interviews, and less than 1 percent on observation; it's extremely difficult to get qualitative research published in 'A' journals; and much of our research is on mom-and-pops instead of high-potentials. Truth be told, our studies derived from theory and driven by methodology produce mostly pedestrian findings that are of little or no interest to practitioners.

Where have we gone wrong?

I think the explanation for the state of the entrepreneurship paradigm today is that we have behaved as if we were researchers in liberal arts departments, especially natural sciences, rather than members of a professional school, such as law or medicine. It seems to me that we suffer from far too much physics envy. In our craving for the respect of our academic colleagues we are squandering the opportunity to build a new paradigm with imaginative research methods that are appropriate to a profession instead of a pure science. We entrepreneurship scholars are not alone in the business school because the same criticism can be made of all management disciplines, and most, albeit not all, of the other business disciplines.

Surely the primary responsibilities of a professional school are to educate and train students and improve practice. With that in mind, read some recent issues of our leading journals and ask yourself what have you learned that is important to your teaching and advising and the practice of entrepreneurship. Per Davidsson (2000) suggested the following possible replies:

- Nothing much, really
- A lot of harm
- Some good
- All the difference in the world.

As I write this piece, I am preparing material for a new textbook on entrepreneurship. I have been reading recent articles in leading entrepreneurship journals, and finding 'nothing much, really'. In one case, I found 'a lot of (potential) harm'. I have not yet found one article that makes 'all the difference in the world', and only a few that have given me even a glimpse of 'some good'. I find that I have to turn to trade articles in magazines such as *Inc.* to get most of the useful insights for the textbook.

To try to stimulate more research with practical implications, the Babson Entrepreneurship Research Conference created a $2500 prize for the paper with the most important findings for practitioners. Alas, even with $2500 at stake, most authors did not write even one sentence linking their findings to entrepreneurship practice, from which it might be inferred that most researchers are indifferent to the practical applications of their work.

Here is a challenge for you, the reader: for the last 25 years, writing a business plan has probably been the most widely used teaching tool in entrepreneurship education and training. It is central in entrepreneurship process frameworks such as the Timmons model. How would you respond to a bright student raring to be an entrepreneur who asks, 'Why are you making me take time out to write a business plan?'

Reach to the academic literature for an answer and you will come up almost empty-handed. One recent paper with a fine theoretical argument and elegant empirical methods reports that if a would-be entrepreneur writes a business plan *before talking to a customer* he or she has a better chance of surviving as a *nascent* entrepreneur. Drill deeper into the paper and you will see that it is based on a panel study that suffers from some of the defects inherent in random household telephone surveys that I have already discussed. The finding may well be robust for the researcher's sample, but it would be wrong-headed to induce a proposition that is generalizable to high-potential entrepreneurship. Anyone who is in day-to-day contact with practitioners knows that many of the most successful entrepreneurs not only talk to customers before they write a business plan but many never write a business plan at all. Here are a few famous examples: Bill Gates and Paul Allen were selling software without a plan; Steve Jobs and Stephan Wozniak were selling Apple computers before they wrote a plan; likewise Michael Dell; and more recently, Google founders Larry Page and Sergey Brin had a working prototype and talked with the major portal companies before they wrote a business plan.

The fact that journal articles do not satisfactorily answer a question as fundamental as whether or not to write a business plan shows that we are not focused on issues that are important for the practice of entrepreneurship, or worse yet, perhaps we don't even know what the important issues are.

Challenges for the future

We are fooling ourselves if we believe we are researching entrepreneurship when we are really studying micro-businesses. It's time to focus on entrepreneurship instead of tiny businesses. It would be a good start if we said that we would study only entrepreneurs who have or expect to have at least 25 employees. Granted, that would capture relatively few Schumpeterian entrepreneurs, but it would eliminate all the micro-entrepreneurs, and it would get us closer to studying the entrepreneurs who are crucial to the health of an economy because they create most of the jobs and many of the new products and services.

Even better from my perspective, it would force us to make in-depth, real-time case studies of actual entrepreneurial businesses from conception to adolescence. Imagine, for example, what we could learn if each of the 600 or so researchers who submitted abstracts to the 2004 Babson conference adopted a high-potential entrepreneur and did a longitudinal study of him or her in action.

Also imagine how the emphasis of our scholarship would change if tenure were granted on the basis of how our research improved the practice of entrepreneurship, just as law and medical schools do. We could still publish in 'A' journals; we could still, if we wanted to, romp in the fields of sociology, psychology and economics to develop theoretical arguments, but it would not be a prerequisite; and above all else, we would keep our eyes on improving the practice of entrepreneurship.

Some of my criticism may seem severe, but it also applies to my own research. I too have tried to conform to what reviewers for the leading journals and competitive conferences want: quantitative empirical research combined with theory. Since 1989, I have produced about 30 qualitative teaching case studies, most of them about high-potential entrepreneurs, but I have lacked the courage to write a qualitative research case because I know that the odds of getting one published in a leading journal are very slim. Let me reiterate that I am not opposed to theory development or complex statistical analysis when appropriate; rather I am challenging journal editors and review board members to be less narrow-minded and to become pluralistic – much more pluralistic. Unless they do, we researchers and reviewers will continue strolling hand in hand down the same primrose path – some of us willingly, and others, like me, kicking and screaming – to irrelevance and maybe oblivion. The losers will be our students and the practice of entrepreneurship.

Note

1.   I confess that my judgment is biased because together with Michael Hay I founded what is now known as GEM in 1997, and I am a member of the GEM Global and US research teams and a director of GERA, the parent organization that governs GEM.

References

Bennis, W. and O'Toole J. (2005) How business schools lost their way. *Harvard Business Review*, May.

Birch, D.L. (1979) The Job Generation Process. Unpublished report prepared by the Massachusetts Institute of Technology Program on Neighborhood and Regional Change for the Economic Development Administration, US Department of Commerce, Washington, DC.

Bygrave, W.D. (1989) The entrepreneurship paradigm (I): A philosophical look at its research methodologies. *Entrepreneurship: Theory and Practice*, **14**(1): 7–26.

Bygrave, W.D. (1989) The entrepreneurship paradigm (II): Chaos and catastrophes among quantum jumps? *Entrepreneurship Theory and Practice*, **14**(2): 7–31.

Bygrave, W.D. and Hofer, C.W. (1991) Theorizing about entrepreneurship. *Entrepreneurship Theory and Practice*, **16**(2): 13–22.

Chandler, G. and Lyon, D. (2001) Issues of research design and construct measurement in entrepreneurship: The past decade. *Entrepreneurship Theory and Practice*. Summer: 101–13.

Davidsson, P. (2000) What entrepreneurship research can do for business and policy practice. *International Journal of Entrepreneurship Education*, **1**(1): 5–24.

Sahlman, W.A. and Stevenson, H.H. (1985) Capital Market Myopia. *Journal of Business Venturing*, **1**(1): 7–30.

Wetzel, W.E. Jr (1987) The informal venture capital market: aspects of scale and efficiency. *Journal of Business Venturing*, **2**: 299–313.

Appendix   The entrepreneurship paradigm (I): A philosophical look at its research methodologies*

William D. Bygrave

Entrepreneurship is one of the youngest paradigms in the management sciences. As with all young paradigms, it has emerged by using the methods and theories of other sciences. But if it is to grow in stature as a separate discipline, it will need to develop its own distinct methods and theories. Consider, for example, three of the most effective paradigms in mankind's glorious pursuit of the origins of the universe: atomic physics, nuclear physics, and elementary particle physics. They have been so successful that some of the leading physicists believe they are close to 'The Theory of Everything' (Davies and Brown 1988). They all had common origins, but as each advanced, it rapidly developed its own instruments and models.

The entrepreneurship paradigm, however, has yet to develop distinctive methods and theories of its own. For the most part, it borrows its methods and theories from other sciences. In so doing, it runs the risk of being driven by them. And that is unfortunate, because borrowed methods and theories may sometimes be unsuitable, mainly for the following two reasons: (1) Entrepreneurship begins with a disjointed, discontinuous, non-linear (and usually unique) event that cannot be studied successfully with methods developed for examining smooth, continuous, linear (and often repeatable) processes.[1] (2) As a science, entrepreneurship is in its infancy. Hence, if we 'force' sophisticated methods from advanced fields such as economics onto entrepreneurship, we may be investigating 'contrived' problems because they can be analyzed with complicated mathematical technology. Instead, we should be studying central questions with appropriate tools, whether they are simple or complex.

Model for the entrepreneurial process

Let us begin with phenomena that most scholars would probably include in a theory of entrepreneurship. We will start with Moore's process model, which has been embellished by me. It is a useful model (or more precisely framework[2]) for the purpose of discussing entrepreneurship concepts because it encompasses the main research themes that entrepreneurship scholars have worked on for the last thirty years or so.

There will be almost unanimous agreement that the phenomena in this model (Figure 1A.1) are an integral part of the entrepreneurship paradigm. However, those who hold the view that entrepreneurship deals only with the starting of new ventures might quarrel with the inclusion of the growth phase.[3]

* This appendix was originally published in the 'Entrepreneurship Theory and Practice' journal, Fall 1989, © 1989 by Baylor University.

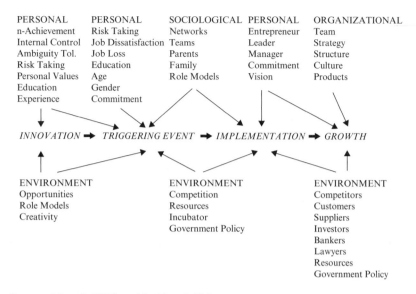

PERSONAL	PERSONAL	SOCIOLOGICAL	PERSONAL	ORGANIZATIONAL
n-Achievement	Risk Taking	Networks	Entrepreneur	Team
Internal Control	Job Dissatisfaction	Teams	Leader	Strategy
Ambiguity Tol.	Job Loss	Parents	Manager	Structure
Risk Taking	Education	Family	Commitment	Culture
Personal Values	Age	Role Models	Vision	Products
Education	Gender			
Experience	Commitment			

INNOVATION ➡ TRIGGERING EVENT ➡ IMPLEMENTATION ➡ GROWTH

ENVIRONMENT	ENVIRONMENT	ENVIRONMENT
Opportunities	Competition	Competitors
Role Models	Resources	Customers
Creativity	Incubator	Suppliers
	Government Policy	Investors
		Bankers
		Lawyers
		Resources
		Government Policy

Source: Moore's (1986) model with embellishments.

Figure 1A.1   A model of the entrepreneurial process

The various ideas contained in the model are rooted primarily in the sciences of business, economics, psychology, sociology, and to a lesser (but increasing) degree, politics. Thus, it mixes theoretical concepts from basic social sciences with practical concepts from applied sciences. The mixing of concepts and methods from widely disparate fields causes difficulties for researchers. We will begin to see how that happens when we position entrepreneurship relative to other sciences in a hierarchy.

Hierarchy of sciences
Auguste Comte (1798–1857) proposed that abstract sciences could be arranged in a hierarchy with mathematics at the top and sociology at the bottom (e.g., Jeans, 1943). Mathematics has the exalted position of 'queen of science' because it is the most fundamental. Since Newton's incredible success with his laws of motion, physicists have increasingly derived laws with mathematics to explain their empirical findings. So physics comes next. Then comes chemistry, which derives its laws from physics. As Dirac pointed out, his equation for quantum mechanics is the basis of 'most of physics and all of chemistry' (Boslough, 1985). Biology, which relies more and more on chemistry and physics for its methods and theories, follows chemistry. Next is psychology, which has links with biology. And finally, there is sociology. When these basic sciences are ranked in descending order

'BASIC'	'APPLIED'
MATHEMATICS	
PHYSICS	ENGINEERING
CHEMISTRY	
BIOLOGY	MEDICINE
PSYCHOLOGY	
SOCIOLOGY	ECONOMICS
	BUSINESS
	ENTREPRENEURSHIP

Figure 1A.2   Hierarchy of sciences

from mathematics to sociology, they are also ordered according to their degree of classical determinism, which for our purpose is their ability to make accurate predictions.[4]

The sciences in the previous paragraph were called basic to distinguish them from applied sciences such as engineering, medicine, economics, business, and entrepreneurship. Figure 1A.2 shows two hierarchies, one for basic sciences and another for applied sciences.[5] The position of an applied science is crudely determined by the position in the basic hierarchy of the fundamental science on which the applied science depends most. When they are placed in that sequence, they are also ranked by their ability to make accurate predictions. Engineering is at the top, and entrepreneurship is at the bottom. Now if we examine where entrepreneurship theories and methods come from, we will see why entrepreneurship research is fraught with difficulties.

Roots of the entrepreneurship paradigm
Sciences contributing most to entrepreneurship theory and methods are shown in Figure 1A.3. Examples of what they contribute are the following: mathematics provides numbers for measuring variables and techniques for analyzing data. Biology produces the population-ecology model. Psychology explains individual behaviour. Sociology interprets the interconnectedness among individuals. Economics studies the allocation of resources to entrepreneurs. And business supplies notions such as strategy. Entrepreneurship research has so many different concepts from such diverse disciplines, it is no wonder that scholars from other fields question whether there is an entrepreneurship paradigm.

One of the biggest dangers in entrepreneurship research is being seduced by the queen of science when we measure, analyze, and theorize. For instance, we often use accounting numbers in our empirical studies. Money

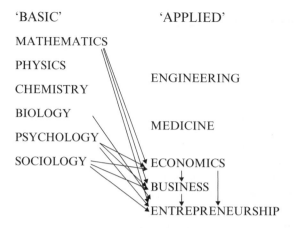

'BASIC'   'APPLIED'

MATHEMATICS

PHYSICS
                        ENGINEERING
CHEMISTRY

BIOLOGY
                        MEDICINE
PSYCHOLOGY

SOCIOLOGY   ECONOMICS

                        BUSINESS

                        ENTREPRENEURSHIP

Figure 1A.3   Linkages to entrepreneurship

is counted with integers. In all of science, there is no more reliable and valid way of measurement than counting integers because, as Eddington (1929) observed, counting is an absolute operation. Bergmann (1947) wrote, 'Counting is, indeed, the only use of numbers that is precise and accurate. The measurement of continuous dimensions, such as time and space, is not precise and accurate in the same sense.' Kronecker is quoted as saying, in arithmetic, 'God created the natural numbers, and all the rest is the work of man' (Devlin, 1988). Every day, we entrepreneurship researchers use natural numbers to count with an accuracy that most experimental physicists never encounter in a lifetime. For example, when we record a number such as $10 000.00, to the penny or $1 million to the dollar, we have an imputed accuracy of 1 in 1 000 000. Indeed, we may have perfect accuracy. We know that when we write a check for $10 000, exactly 10 000 dollars will be transferred out of our account, not 9999.99 or 10 000.01.[6]

What is more, after we have measured our variables with such accuracy (albeit illusory), we look for causal relationships among our variables by using sophisticated statistical tools on powerful computers. The end result frequently is a regression model that appears to have the explanatory power of a law of physics. It is heady stuff. But in our elation, we must not forget that entrepreneurship models have to be rooted in psychology and sociology if they are to have theoretical validity. Those social sciences, in contrast to natural sciences, lack fundamental principles such as the conservation laws of physics from which robust mathematical models can be deduced.

Of course, we know our regression equations are just a way of looking for relationships. They are not really physical models with the predictive power of physics laws such as Einstein's special and general theories of relativity. But when the fallacy of unwarranted accuracy is combined with the illusion of a mathematical model, it is easy to think and behave as if we were physicists rather than social scientists. The entrepreneurship paradigm is simply at too early a stage of development to justify the use of so much mathematics, as we shall see when we compare it with physics, the oldest of the natural sciences.

Comparison of two paradigms

History   Physics can be traced back to the fifth century BC to Democritus, Plato, and Aristotle. Although their theories in general lacked predictive power, there were some spectacular exceptions, notably Archimedes' principle. By the Middle Ages, physics was a central part of the curriculum of the ancient universities. It was taught in conjunction with arithmetic, geometry, and astronomy in the 'core' curriculum.[7] When 'modern' physics was born with Newton's mechanics around the middle of the seventeenth century, Newton used concepts from those four fields to explain planetary motion. As Newton – in an uncharacteristically gracious acknowledgement of the contributions of other scientists – commented in a letter to Hooke (Christianson, 1984), 'If I have seen further it is by standing on the shoulders of giants.' Among the giants of Newtonian mechanics were Copernicus, who proposed that the planets revolved around the sun; Brahe, who charted the orbits of the planets; Kepler, who developed mathematical models for their motion; and Galileo, who studied falling bodies. Newton's accomplishment was a magnificent – perhaps the most magnificent – triumph of human intellect. His Law of Gravitation has been called 'the greatest generalization achieved by the human mind' (Feynman, 1965). It produced an accurate mathematical theory for a dynamic system; and it introduced the notion of force acting at a distance (i.e., between non-contiguous bodies).

Entrepreneurship, unlike physics, has no such august tradition of scholarship. Although there were intellectual rumblings about entrepreneurship in the eighteenth century by economists such as Say and Smith, it was not until 1911 that Schumpeter (1949) gave us the modern version of the entrepreneur as the person who destroys the economic order by introducing new products, new methods of production, new ways of organizing, and new raw materials. Although Schumpeter's classic work was written almost 80 years ago, there was very little systematic empirical research into entrepreneurship until McClelland published his book *The Achieving Society* in 1961. Entrepreneurship education, despite the entrepreneur's central role in moving economies forward, was almost totally ignored by both economics and management departments. Twenty years ago only half a dozen or so management schools offered a course in entrepreneurship. Today there are more than 300 (Vesper and McMullan, 1988). Regrettably,

	PHYSICS	**ENTREPRENEURSHIP**
ORIGINS	5th CENTURY BC *Democritus, Plato*	18th CENTURY AD *Smith, Say*
MODERN	17th CENTURY AD *Newton*	20th CENTURY AD *Schumpeter, Weber*
EMPIRICAL RESEARCH	>2000 YEARS	30 YEARS
THEORY	17th CENTURY AD	-----------
TEACHING	>2000 YEARS	20 YEARS

Figure 1A.4   History of two paradigms

entrepreneurship remains a neglected subject in principles of economics courses (Kent, 1987).

In Figure 1A.4, the histories of the entrepreneurship and physics paradigms are juxtaposed. Unlike physics, which has been central to intellectual thought for more than two millennia, entrepreneurship has barely begun to be noticed.[8] That has important implications for the theory and methods that we use. Sophisticated tools that are suitable for an advanced paradigm may not be proper for an infant one.

Tools for physics and entrepreneurship research   The important tools of a paradigm are its theories and its empirical methods. Included in the theories are concepts, models that are deduced with those concepts, and predictions that are made by those models. And included in the methods are variables, instruments to measure those variables, populations on which those measurements are made, and analytical techniques that are used to interpret those measurements.

A comparison of some of the theoretical tools of entrepreneurship research with those of physics (Figure 1A.5) brings out the lack of definition and precision of an emerging paradigm versus an advanced one. On the abstract level, physics is based on 'six great theories' of Newtonian mechanics: quantum mechanics, relativity, electromagnetic theory, thermodynamics, and statistical mechanics. In general, models produced from those theories explain the behaviour of the physical world with great precision. The parameters in their models are called constants because they have never been found to change with time and place. Some very abstract mathematical models make predictions that take your breath away. For instance, Drac's quantum mechanics equations predicted the existence of the positron before it had ever been observed. Other theoretical physicists have predicted the existence of elementary particles that have never been

'TOOLS'	PHYSICS	ENTREPRENEURSHIP
THEORIES	ABSTRACT *Conservation Principles*	EMPIRICAL *Premises of Social Sciences*
MODELS	ROBUST *Laws, Principles*	FRAGILE *Phenomenological*
PARAMETERS	CONSTANT	CHANGING
PREDICTIONS	ACCURATE	CRUDE

Figure 1A.5   Theoretical 'tools'

observed. Subsequently, experimental physicists have built instruments, sometimes costing hundreds of millions of dollars, and discovered those particles (e.g., Riordan, 1987). It is not surprising that the more robust models of physics are called laws. Of course, physicists do not have models to explain everything they discover. A notable recent example was high-temperature superconductors (Bednorz and Muller, 1986).

In contrast with physics, entrepreneurship has no great theories. At best, we take concepts from other fields and incorporate them into process models such as Moore's. Perhaps entrepreneurship once thought it had a great theory in McClelland's notion that entrepreneurs were different psy-chologically from non-entrepreneurs. His thesis was that entrepreneurs had a higher need for achievement (McClelland, 1961). He thought he had found Schumpeter's heroic entrepreneur, and hence the key to economic growth. He amassed an impressive amount of empirical evidence to support his claim. By studying entrepreneurship longitudinally and in different nations, he implied that his model was universal. So confident was McClelland of his work that he laid claim to being the first investigator of economic development to apply an empirically based, rigorous, scientific methodology. Alas, closer scrutiny of his work (e.g., Kilby, 1971; Schatz, 1971) and subsequent empirical studies (e.g., Brockhaus, 1982) found serious flaws in his theory. McClelland's theory illustrates the frailty of entrepreneurship theory. Unlike physics, where models are robust and para-meters are forever constant, entrepreneurship models are fragile and para-meters are always changing. Today's entrepreneurship models are mainly descriptive. They are empirical or phenomenological rather than theoret-ical models, in much the same way that Kepler's model described planetary orbits before Newton produced the first great physics theory.

If we look at the methods that we use to develop our empirical models for entrepreneurship (Figure 1A.6), we see, in general, a lack of precision starting at the very root of the paradigm, the definition of an entrepreneur.

'TOOLS'	PHYSICS	ENTREPRENEURSHIP
VARIABLES	PRECISE DEFINITIONS *Mass, Length,* *Time*	FUZZY DEFINITIONS *Opportunity* *Resources* *Performance*
INSTRUMENTS	UNIVERSAL ACCURACY *Rulers, Scales,* *Clocks, Meters*	DUBIOUS ACCURACY *Questionnaires* *Likert Scales* *Financials*
POPULATIONS	DISTINCT *Particles, Nuclei,* *Atoms, Gases,* *Liquids, Solids*	NEBULOUS *Individuals* *Firms* *Industries*

Figure 1A.6   Empirical 'tools'

Schumpeter introduced the modern concept of the entrepreneur at about the same time that Rutherford introduced the modern concept of the nucleus. Yet while physicists have essentially solved the puzzle of the structure of the nucleus, we entrepreneurship scholars are still bickering over a working definition of entrepreneurship.[9] Surely, good science has to begin with precise definitions. Entrepreneurs, it seems to me, are our elementary units of analysis, [10] just as particles are the physicist's elementary units of analysis. If we are unable (or maybe unwilling) to agree on a definition of an entrepreneur, it is extremely unlikely that we will have variables with precise definitions, instruments with clear specifications, and populations with exact demarcations.

The fuzziness of the empirical tools of entrepreneurship contrasts starkly with the exactness of the experimental tools of physics. Even what is arguably the most precise tool of entrepreneurship – and of all business science – the certified financial statement, has a purported accuracy that is illusory because of the different accounting methods that may be used to produce it.[11]

Once we start to compare the tools of entrepreneurship with those of physics, we start to realize the futility of an infant paradigm trying to imitate the theoretical and empirical methods of an advanced paradigm. Whey then do we entrepreneurship scholars feel compelled to do it? It is because we are trapped by the basic biases of science.

Science's basic biases
Physics (or natural philosophy as it used to be called) has always played a central role in shaping the way we think about the world. Newton was the first modern scientist. His influence on philosophy was immense. As Dewey

BIAS	EXPLANATION
PROGRESS	• WORLD AND SOCIETY ARE HEADING SOMEWHERE
DETERMINISM	• IDEAS HAVE CAUSES • WORLD AND SOCIETY ARE ORDERED • OUTCOMES ARE PRODUCED BY DEFINITE CAUSES • RANDOMNESS IS SCARY. IT DOES NOT PRODUCE PATTERNS; IT PRODUCES CONFUSION
INCREMENTALISM	• PROGRESS IS SLOW, STEADY, SMALL STEPS
ADAPTIONISM	• WHAT ADAPTS SURVIVES • IT ALL FITS TOGETHER

Figure 1A.7   Our basic biases

(1949) wrote, 'Modern thought, largely under the influence of a Newtonian philosophy of nature, tended to treat all existence as determinate.' Classical determinism is one of our basic biases. It says that a specific set of conditions will produce a specific outcome. If those conditions are present then the outcome is predictable. Models have dominated science since Newton. They are the Laplacian fantasy of a deterministic world (Gleick, 1987).

According to Stephen Jay Gould (1984), scientists have four major biases. Determinism is one. The other three are progress, incrementalism, and adaptionism (Figure 1A.7). Besides determinism, Newton played a major role in two others, progress and incrementalism. The science revolution that began with Newton has been responsible for mankind's rapid progress ever since. And infinitesimal calculus, which Newton invented for analyzing deterministic systems, made incremental reasoning a central tool of science. Our fourth great bias, adaptionism, stems from Darwin's theory of natural selection. What adapts to its environment survives. Unfortunately, adaptionism leads us to believe that everything fits together, it is here for a reason, it all works.

Our biases influence how we view the world. The predominant philosophy in theoretical and empirical research holds that there is inherent, incremental progress in which things happen for a reason, leading to a system in which everything fits (Figure 1A.8). As Gould stated it, 'The world is logical, the world is rational, the world is well-ordered, it's there for a reason.' This view of the world helps us to deal with the major question of natural philosophy: what is the physical nature of the universe? However, when we apply it to the social sciences, especially the business sciences, we are frequently guilty of *physics envy*.[12] Management science suffers from

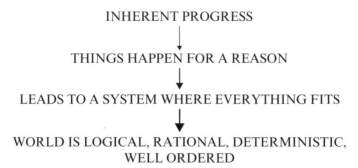

INHERENT PROGRESS

↓

THINGS HAPPEN FOR A REASON

↓

LEADS TO A SYSTEM WHERE EVERYTHING FITS

↓

WORLD IS LOGICAL, RATIONAL, DETERMINISTIC,
WELL ORDERED

Figure 1A.8   Predominant philosophy in theoretical and empirical research

some severe cases of physics envy. That will now be illustrated with the example of business strategy.

Physics envy in business strategy research   I believe that one of the most cherished theories in business science, Chandler's (1962) strategy–structure model and its enhancements, is an example of physics envy. In Chandler's model, a firm scans the environment, determines what strategies it needs to succeed in that environment, puts in place its structure to implement those strategies, and it is on the route to prosperity. Well, Chandler's rational, deterministic model may have worked once upon a time for DuPont, Standard Oil of New Jersey, General Motors, and Sears (Chandler's sample) when they were growing in the relatively benign environment of the first decades of this century, but it bears little resemblance to how businesses start and survive in the hostile environment of the 1980s.

Chandler was not educated as an engineer, but he was very empathetic to engineering. He wrote this about the engineers who built DuPont, Standard Oil, and General Motors: 'The connection between the engineering profession and the rationalization and systemizing of industrial administration in the United States has been close.'

By looking at the education of many of the leading management scholars who have made major contributions to the strategy paradigm, it is possible to paraphrase Chandler's comment as follows: 'The connection between mathematics, physics, and engineering graduates and the rationalization and systemizing of the business strategy paradigm in academia has been close.' One of the strategy pioneers, Ansoff, was once an engineer. No wonder the uninitiated thought his early strategy diagrams looked like electrical control drawings for heating and ventilating the Empire State Building. Hofer was trained in mathematics and Schendel in engineering. They were two of the shapers of the field (Hofer and Schendel, 1978). Hatten, who drove the first vector through strategic groups, was trained as an engineer (Hatten, 1978). Porter, who has done more to influence the competitive strategy field than any other over the last decade, has an undergraduate degree in engineering (Porter, 1980). Cooper (1979), McMillan (1978), and Vesper (1980) have engineering degrees; and there are many more.

Engineers, natural scientists, and mathematicians are steeped in the four basic biases at a very impressionable age. Their education gives them schemata that are rooted in Newtonian mechanics. No wonder their methods and theories have produced a strategy paradigm that is very mechanistic with scant recognition of the whims and vagaries of the human actor. For example, the strategists' bible, *Competitive Strategy* (Porter, 1980), contains only a few pages on how the executive should implement Porter's normative prescriptions for a successful strategy.

There is a warning in all this for entrepreneurship. Physics envy assumes that business progress can be described by smoothly changing, linear, deterministic models than can be analyzed with regression equations. That philosophy is unable to handle entrepreneurship's disjointed events that disrupt stability. It either relegates the acts of the entrepreneur to a dummy variable or, worse yet, leaves them lurking in the ubiquitous error term (Rumelt and Wensley, 1981; Wensley, 1982).

A worrisome trend in recent years is the increasing number of strategy types of papers that are appearing in entrepreneurship. Approximately half the winners of the Academy of Management Entrepreneurship Heizer Award wrote business strategy dissertations. It is an understandable trend because a doctoral dissertation on business strategy is a 'classic' dissertation.

The 'classic' dissertation   An outcome of our four basic biases is a belief that there is a right and wrong way of conducting research. It leads to another bias, the 'classic' dissertation. Many of the dissertations in the business sciences follow an archetype (Figure 1A.9). It assumes that 'good' research follows a fixed sequence. First we select a theory; from that we deduce models from which testable hypotheses can be developed. Then we develop instruments to test those hypotheses on a database with statistical tools – preferably regression analysis (Figure 1A.10). The 'classic' dissertation is seldom the most suitable format for an emerging paradigm such as entrepreneurship because it is too rigid.

The history of science teaches us that in emerging paradigms, successful science rarely follows the sequence of the 'classic' dissertation. Darwin did not have a theory until he 'happened to read for amusement Malthus on *Population*' seven years after he embarked on his field work, and fifteen months after he began his systematic enquiry into the variation of animals and plants (Darwin, 1959). The origins of nuclear physics began with

DEFINITION OF TOPIC

LITERATURE SURVEY

LIMITED FIELD RESEARCH

THEORY DEVELOPMENT

PROPOSITION(S)

HYPOTHESES

QUESTIONNAIRE

DATABASE

STATISTICAL TESTS

CONCLUSIONS

Figure 1A.9   The 'classic' dissertation: a product of our basic biases

IT IS DRIVEN BY

THEORY

MODELS

HYPOTHESES

INSTRUMENTS

STATISTICAL TOOLS

TIME CONSTRAINTS

Figure 1A.10   Classic dissertation is a problem in an infant paradigm

Becquerel's accidental discovery of radioactivity. His discovery was pursued in a spirit of pure empiricism by scientists working with little or no theory to guide them. Madame Curie laboriously separated grams of radioactive radium from tons of pitchblende (an endeavour that eventually caused her death). Rutherford, Soddy, and others carefully investigated the elements that came from radioactivity. It took two decades of experiments before Rutherford produced the 'modern' theory of the nucleus. Similarly, in biophysics, Crick and Watson did not unravel the mystery of the DNA molecule until others, such as Franklin, had made many painstaking experiments with x-ray crystallography. A few years ago, Bednorz and Muller (1986) discovered high-temperature superconductors by experimenting with a variety of materials. They were guided much more by intuition than by theory.

Thus at the beginnings of a paradigm, inspired inductive logic (or more likely enlightened speculations) applied to exploratory, empirical research

may be more useful than deductive reasoning from theory. Natural science
has recognized this for three centuries (e.g., Polanyi, 1964). For some unfortunate pioneers guesswork can be a risky path, as Jones et al. (1989) and
Fleischmann, Pons and Hawkins (1989) found when their putative discovery of cold fusion turned out to be a mirage (Maddox, 1989).

Hypotheses non fingo   It was the inductive method that Newton (1687)
prescribed when he wrote, 'Hypotheses non fingo.' The meaning of this
famous statement has been debated ever since. I think Duhem's (1953)
explanation is as good as any:

> in the General Scholium which crowns his [*Principia*], [Newton] rejected so vig-
> orously as outside Natural Philosophy any hypothesis that induction did not
> extract from experiment; when he asserted that in a sound physics every propos-
> ition should be drawn from phenomena and then generalized by induction.

It is important to note that Newton was not repudiating all hypotheses;
rather he was rejecting those that were not firmly grounded in observations
of natural phenomena. Although Newton firmly held that conviction to his
death, we know he did not always follow its prescription – the best known
instance being his corpuscular theory of light. Nevertheless, it seems to me
that Newton's prescription is a good one for an emerging paradigm.

I believe the emphasis in an emerging paradigm should be on empirical
observations with exploratory or, preferably, grounded research, rather
than on testing hypotheses deduced from flimsy theories. As has been
noted, the 'classic' dissertation emphasizes theory building and the deduction of hypotheses that are tested with an empirical study. And that is a
problem. It is too rigid. Bernard (1865) recognized that when he wrote:

> Men who have excessive faith in their theories or their ideas are not only poorly
> disposed to make discoveries but they also make poor observations. They neces-
> sarily observe with preconceived ideas and, when they have begun to experiment,
> they want to see in its results only confirmation of their theory. Thus they distort
> observation and often neglect very important facts because they do not race to
> their goal.

The 'classic' dissertation stifles imagination. As Bloom (1987) put it in *The
Closing of the American Mind*, 'Cleverness in proposing hypotheses and
finding proofs, inventing experiments is not creativity.'

Suggestions for entrepreneurship research
Some of my suggestions for research methods for our infant paradigm are
listed in Figure 1A.11. It is my wish-list for the paradigm.

LESS PHYSICS ENVY

MORE EMPIRICAL MODELS; FEWER THEORETICAL MODELS

LESS CONCERN WITH SOPHISTICATED STATISTICS

MORE FIELD RESEARCH

MORE LONGITUDINAL STUDIES

DEDICATED RESEARCHERS

ORIGINAL FIELD-DERIVED DATA BANKS

LESS OBSESSION WITH SCIENTIFIC REVOLUTIONS

Figure 1A.11   Needs of an infant paradigm in an applied social science

Less physics envy   It seems to me that we need to suppress our physics envy and cultivate more independence in our research methods. Most of my reasons have been given. But there is another important one: physicists examine nature by remorselessly isolating the parts from the whole. It is a method that is commonly used by social scientists even though it is fraught with difficulty. Does anyone imagine, for instance, that the business strategists who wander around in the PIMS database looking for relationships can really separate strategy from the humans who make the strategic decisions? I doubt it is possible. And I am certain that we cannot separate entrepreneurs from their actions. After all, in a start-up company, the entrepreneur and the company are one and the same. In entrepreneurship research, it is nearly impossible to reduce problems to neat constituents that can be examined in isolation. We should avoid, whenever possible, reductionism in our entrepreneurship research. Instead, we should look at the whole. We can do so with case studies.

Fewer theoretical models; more empirical models   Entrepreneurship, as an emerging paradigm, is in the pre-theory stage. It is rather like biology before Darwin's natural selection theory or nuclear physics before Rutherford's model. At that stage, the emphasis should be on painstaking observations rather than theory building. I must stress that I am not opposed to theories. On the contrary, I fully recognize that theories are central to science. It is just that when I contemplate our present empirical knowledge, it appears to be inadequate for building robust theories of entrepreneurship. At this stage we should rely on frameworks to guide our grounded research. Examples include the Timmons (1985) People–Opportunity–Resources–Uncertainty scheme for analyzing start-ups and the Stevenson framework (Stevenson, Roberts, and Grousbeck, 1989).

What we need at this stage are more empirical models that describe observed phenomena as accurately as possible. But we should be careful not to get caught up in Laplace's dream that all phenomena could be described by formulas. Even in the physical sciences, a model is at best a mathematical metaphor of reality; in the social sciences, it may be nothing more than a caricature. Nevertheless, it can be very useful in helping us understand the world, and, as in the case of Kepler's models of planetary orbits, can sometimes lead to great theories.

Less concern with sophisticated statistical analyses   Poincaré, that prince of mathematicians, said that while physicists had subject-matter, sociologists were engaged almost entirely in considering their methods. As Cohen (1931) commented, 'in this [Poincaré's] remark there is a just rebuke (from one who had the right to deliver it) to those romantic souls who cherish the illusion that by some new trick or method the social sciences can readily be put on par with the physical sciences with regard to definiteness and universal demonstrability.' Poincaré, according to Ekeland (1988), 'will remain in history as the most penetrating critic of quantitative methods, and the great proponent of qualitative ones.' He died in 1912. One shudders at the thought of what he might say if he knew what we were doing today with complex statistical packages. I wonder if he would think that the editors of the *Academy of Management Journal* ought to emblazon its masthead with 'Let nobody ignorant of *SPSS* publish here', in much the same way that Plato is said to have inscribed the lintel at the entrance to his academy in Athens with 'Let nobody ignorant of geometry enter here' (e.g., Dyson, 1988).

As was observed previously, it seems to me that some of us, myself included, imagine regression analysis to be the 'new trick or method' that puts us on a par with physicists. We run our regressions and, eureka, if the R^2 approaches 1, we interpret the equation as if it were a causal law of nature. We forget that the choice of dependent and independent variables is often only a matter of computational convenience (Feigl, 1953). We have refined our methods even more with clever techniques to try to attribute cause and effect. But even in economics, the massive statistical machinery produces indifferent results (Leontief, 1977) – none more so than when economics looks at unique events. Contemplate the stock market crash of 19 October 1987. Economics did not forecast its coming; it was unable to predict what happened on the days following the crash; and subsequently it has failed to explain, unambiguously, the causes of the crash.

Let us never forget that an entrepreneurial venture begins with a unique event. If we believe that understanding the unique event of starting a venture is one of the great aims of entrepreneurship research, we have to concede that no amount of complex statistical machinery can substitute for painstaking field studies of that event.

More field research Entrepreneurship is a process of becoming rather than a state of being. It is not a steady state phenomenon. Nor does it change smoothly. It changes in quantum jumps. No amount of regression analysis will help us understand what triggers the quantum jump or what happens during the quantum jump. At most, a dummy variable in regression analysis will tell us that a change has occurred. But as its name implies a dummy variable is mute. It can only indicate that a change occurred; it cannot tell us the details of why and how the change occurred. One is reminded of what Bridgman (1927) wrote: 'there is behind the equations an enormous descriptive background through which the equations make connection with nature.'

The heart of the entrepreneurship process will be found in the 'descriptive background.' We will not get to the heart of the start-up process unless we observe it happening in the field. Entrepreneurship cries out for more in-depth longitudinal case studies that will help us understand the process of entrepreneurship. The problem with that is (1) many, perhaps most, scientists do not regard case studies as 'proper' research, so it is difficult to get the results published in 'respectable' scholarly journals, and that causes problems with academic careers;[13] (2) complex statistical tools cannot be used for the analysis because the samples are too small by far, which offends R^2 purists who believe there is safety in large numbers (do they know that Einstein's relativity theory was tested on only three celestial cases and no terrestrial ones? or, as Bower (1982) reminded us, that the Hawthorne study involved one small group of women?); (3) longitudinal field research is excruciatingly time consuming, so it does not fit the time constraints imposed on most researchers, especially doctoral students; and (4) most case studies are routine rather than revolutionary research (Kuhn, 1970), and too many young scientists have been inculcated with the belief that only 'startling' findings matter.

More longitudinal studies Entrepreneurship is a process that evolves with time. If we do only cross-sectional studies, we lose much of the richness that comes from longitudinal studies. Let me hark back to what was written earlier: in entrepreneurship, unlike physics, parameters change with time. For example, changes in government policy alter the propensity of entrepreneurs to start companies. Longitudinal field studies are time consuming and costly. But surely we ought to be able to get funding for longitudinal studies of entrepreneurs in view of their importance to the economy, and hence society as a whole.

Dedicated researchers   We need better quality empirical research. It should be exploratory or grounded. We need much more field work. Of course that is laborious; and the output in terms of number of publications may be very small compared to database research. But let us learn from other fields. Where in entrepreneurship among our young scholars are the likes of Charles Darwin, Jane Goodall, and Edmund Halley?

Darwin was fresh out of Cambridge when he embarked on his five-year voyage around the world on the *Beagle*. He meticulously catalogued the species he saw. That was the field work that led twenty years later to his *Origin of Species*. But before he published his masterpiece, he produced four large volumes on the taxonomy and natural history of barnacles.

Jane Goodall was scarcely out of high school when she set up camp in the African jungle. Instead of going to university, she became a disciple of Louis Leakey – one of the great field researchers of all time – and devoted more than fifteen years of her life observing chimpanzees at Gombe.

Edmund Halley did his 'post-graduate' research plotting the stars in the Southern Hemisphere. He spent two years on the island of St Helena – a South Atlantic island so remote that almost 150 years later the British exiled Napoleon to it.

Original field-derived databases   We should gather our own data sets as thoroughly as those great natural scientists gathered theirs. In our field, there have been too many databases that were produced with mailings of self-reported subjective questionnaires or that were generated by others for a purpose other than entrepreneurship research. It is difficult to do valid research on databases that comparative strangers have built because one does not know where the pitfalls lie. It is essential to be able to dig out suspect records and check the reliability of the original raw data. Unless I am mistaken, PIMS disguises the raw data before entering them into its database to prevent researchers from identifying the records of specific companies. That makes it very difficult for outside researchers to be sure that they are looking at reliable and valid records. Entrepreneurship is beginning to develop and tend its own databases. There are a number of longitudinal database studies under way (e.g., Kirchhoff and Philips, 1988; Cooper, Dunkelberg and Woo, 1988). That is a healthy sign. But what I have in mind is observing entrepreneurs from the moment they start to try to exploit their opportunity until they harvest it. To do so will require careful field studies.

Less obsession with revolutionary science   Meticulous empirical research is painstaking, none more so than detailed field work. But all excellent empirical research is very exacting. There are no shortcuts on the road to mastery of a scientific discipline. As Simon (1986) had noted, it takes ten years of tireless endeavor to become world class in any field. We should inculcate our students with the spirit of Louis Agassiz and his training of a biologist (Cooper, 1972). We may do a great disservice to entrepreneurship research if we stress to doctoral students our preference for research that produces 'interesting' findings (e.g., Davis, 1971). The vast majority of research is 'routine' rather than 'revolutionary,' but by having students read Kuhn's book, we may, if we are not careful, glorify extraordinary science and appear to deprecate ordinary science. In judging research, our watchword should be excellence, not routine or revolutionary. If it were not for excellent routine science, Newton would never have stood on 'the shoulders of Giants.'

Concluding comments
A paradigm in the pre-theory stage is like a jig-saw puzzle with a framework but with most of the pieces missing. We must first find the pieces before we see how they are connected together. At this stage we should be carefully finding those pieces with meticulous research. With enough pieces, we will start to see patterns emerge. From those patterns, we can start to build partial theories. And, who knows, maybe one day someone will build a great theory of entrepreneurship from those partial theories. But I doubt that will happen in my lifetime.

We should heed the following quote from Bridgman's (1927) classic, which I believe is the attitude of a physicist that we entrepreneurship scholars *should* strive to emulate. As you read it, substitute *entrepreneurship scholar* for *physicist* and you will have a summary of my position.

> The attitude of a physicist must therefore be one of pure empiricism. He recognizes no *a priori* principles which determine or limit the possibilities of new experience. Experience is determined only by experience. This practically means that we must give up the demand that all nature be embraced in any formula, either simple or complicated. It may perhaps turn out eventually that as a matter of fact nature can be embraced in a formula, but we must organize our thinking as not to demand it as a necessity.

Of course, we should not be amassing undifferentiated empirical data. We must have models to guide us *a priori*. But we should not shun qualitative models because we consider quantitative models to be the only ones that are scientifically valid. Every quantitative statistical model presupposes a qualitative division of reality. It isolates parts of the system that are considered stable and, thus, reproducible (Thom, 1968). But the essence of entrepreneurship is a change of state. And a change of state is a holistic process in which the existing stability disappears. When you try to take it apart, it tends to decompose (Lodge, 1975). With our present knowledge, who is wise enough to tell which parts of the entrepreneurship process are stable enough to be safely isolated from the whole and analyzed with regression models and the like?

Notes

1. The discontinuous nature of entrepreneurship and its implications for research will be examined in a follow-up article entitled 'Entrepreneurship paradigm (II): Chaos and catastrophes among quantum jumps?'
2. In more advanced paradigms, this would not be called a model because it has no predictive power. Rather it would be called a framework or a schematic. For example, Aristotle's theory that everything was made of earth, air, water, and fire was not a model because it made no definite predictions. In contrast, Newton's theory that gravitational attraction between two bodies is proportional to the product of their masses and inversely proportional to the square of the distance between them is a model because it predicts the motions of the sun, moon, and planets to a high degree of accuracy (Hawking, 1988).
3. According to Gartner (1988), 'Entrepreneurship is the creation of new organizations . . . Entrepreneurship ends when the creation stage of the organization ends.'
4. I recognize that the Heisenberg Uncertainty Principle (Heisenberg, 1930) brought an end to determinism in the strictest sense that on an atomic scale we cannot predict what will happen to a specific atom, nucleus, or elementary particle. However, it does not apply at the macro level that we will be dealing with throughout this article.
5. Of course, these are only partial lists. According to Bell (1973), there were more than 900 specializations in the sciences by about 1970.
6. Bertrand Russell put it more colorfully when he said that we are quite certain that Cleopatra had 2 eyes and 1 nose and not, perhaps, 2.000001 eyes and 0.999998 noses.
7. For example, the Oxford University curriculum in the Middle Ages consisted of seven liberal arts: logic, rhetoric, grammar, music, arithmetic, geometry, and astronomy; three philosophies: moral, metaphysical, and natural (physics); and two tongues: Greek and Hebrew (all students knew Latin because it was the universal academic language).
8. Here are two examples: (1) the governing body of the Academy of Management did not bestow division status on the Entrepreneurship Interest Group until 1986; (2) most economics textbooks either do not refer to Schumpeter's theory of entrepreneurship or only mention it briefly.
9. This bickering is illustrated in the Gartner (1988) article, ' "Who is an entrepreneur?" Is the wrong question' and the rejoinder ' "Who is an entrepreneur?" Is a question worth asking' by Carland, Hoy, and Carland (1988).
10. Mitton (1989) put it this way: 'I believe the proper study of entrepreneurship is the entrepreneur.'
11. The great physicist and philosopher Eddington (1929) wrote the following (incidentally, it was before the Great Crash): 'Is [the balance sheet of a public company] true? Certainly; it may be certified by a [CPA]. But is it *really* true? Many questions arise; the real values of items are often very different from those which figure in the balance-sheet. I am not referring to fraudulent companies. There is a blessed phrase "hidden reserves", and generally speaking the more respectable the company the more widely does its balance-sheet deviate from reality. This is called sound finance . . . [The balance-sheet] is not well adapted for exhibiting realities, because the main function of a balance sheet is to balance and everything else has to be subordinated to that.'
12. As an entrepreneurship researcher who was a physicist in a previous academic life, I confess to having more than my share of bouts with physics envy.
13. Case studies are seldom published in scholarly business journals. When they are, the author is more often than not a preeminent scholar (e.g. Mintzberg and Waters, 1982).

References

Bednorz, J.G. and Muller, K.A. (1986). *Zeitschrift für Physik*, B64, 189–93.
Bell, D. (1973). *The Coming of Post-industrial Society: A venture in social forecasting*. New York: Basic Books.
Bergmann, G. (1947). The logic of quanta. *American Journal of Physics*, **15**.
Bernard, C. (1865). *Introduction à la medicine experimentale*. Paris.
Bloom, A. (1987), *The Closing of the American Mind*. New York: Simon and Schuster.
Boslough, J. (1985). *Stephen Hawking's Universe*. New York: Avon Books.
Bower, J.L. (1982). Business policy in the 1980s. *Academy of Management Review*, **7**(4): 630–38.
Bridgman, P.W. (1927). *The Logic of Modern Physics*. New York: Macmillan.
Brockhaus, R.H., Sr (1982). The psychology of entrepreneur. In C.A. Kent, D.L. Sexton, and K.H. Vesper (eds), *Encylopedia of Entrepreneurship*, pp. 39–57, Englewood Cliffs, NJ: Prentice Hall.
Carland, J.W., Hoy, F., and Carland, J.A. (1988). 'Who is an entrepreneur?' is a question worth asking. *American Journal of Small Business*, **12**(4): 33–9.
Chandler, A. (1962). *Strategy and Structure: Chapters in the history of American industrial enterprise*. Cambridge, MA: MIT Press.
Christianson, G.E. (1984). *In the Presence of the Creator*. New York: Free Press.
Cohen, M.R. (1931). *Reason and Nature*. New York: Harcourt, Brace & Company.
Cooper, A.C. (1979). Strategic management: New ventures and small businesses. In D.E. Schendel and C.W. Hofer (eds), *Strategic Management*. Boston: Little, Brown.
Cooper, A.C., Dunkelberg, W.C., and Woo, C.Y. (1988). Survival and failure: A longitudinal study. In B.A. Kirchhoff, W.A. Long, W. Ed. McMullan, K.H. Vesper, and W.E. Wetzel (eds), *Frontiers of Entrepreneurship Research, 1988*. Wellesley, MA: Babson College.
Cooper, L. (1972). *Louis Agassiz as a Teacher*. Ithaca, NY: Cornell University Press.
Darwin, F. (1959). *The Life and Letters of Sir Charles Darwin*. New York: Basic Books.
Davies, P.C.W. and Brown, J. (1988). *Superstrings: A theory of everything*. Cambridge: Cambridge University Press.
Davis, M.S. (1971). That's interesting! *Phil. Soc. Sci.*, **1**: 309–44.
Devlin, K. (1988). *Mathematics: The new golden age*. New York: Viking Penguin.
Dewey, John (1949). *The Quest for Certainty*. New York: J.J. Little and Ives.
Duhem, P. (1953). *Aim and Structure of Physical Theory*. Translated by P.P. Weiner, Princeton, NJ: Princeton University Press.
Dyson, F.J. (1988). *Infinite in All Directions*. New York: Harper & Row.
Eddington, A.S. (1929). *The Nature of the Physical World*. New York: Macmillan.
Ekeland, I. (1988). *Mathematics and the Unexpected*. Chicago, IL: University of Chicago Press.
Feigl, H. (1953). Notes on causality. In H. Feigl and M. Brodbeck (eds), *Readings in the Philosophy of Science*. New York: Appleton-Century-Crofts.
Feynman, R. (1965). *The Character of Physical Law*. Cambridge, MA: MIT Press.
Fleischmann, M., Pons, S., and Hawkins, M. (1989). *Journal of Electroanalytical Chemistry*, **261**: 301–8.
Gartner, W.B. (1988), 'Who is an entrepreneur?' is the wrong question. *American Journal of Small Business*, **12**(4): 11–32.
Gleick, J. (1987). *Chaos: Making a new science*. New York: Viking.
Gould, S.J. (1984). *Stephen Jay Gould: This view of life*. Boston, MA: WGBH Transcripts.
Hatten, K.J. (1978). Quantitative methods in strategic management. In D.E. Schendel and C.W. Hofer (eds), *Strategic Management*. Boston: Little, Brown.
Hawking, S.W. (1988). *A Brief History of Time*. London: Bantam Press.
Heisenberg, W. (1930). *The Physical Principles of Quantum Theory*. Chicago, IL: University of Chicago Press.
Hofer, C.W. and Schendel, D.E. (1978). *Strategy Formulation: Analysis and concepts*. St Paul, MN: West.
Jeans, J. (1943). *Physics and Philosophy*. Cambridge: Cambridge University Press.

Jones, S.E., et al. (1989). *Nature*, **338**: 737–40.

Kent, C.A. (1987). Entrepreneurship suffers textbook case of neglect. *Wall Street Journal*, 4 September.

Kilby, P. (1971). Hunting the heffalump. In P. Kilby (ed.), *Entrepreneurship and Economic Development*, pp. 1–40. New York: The Free Press.

Kirchoff, B.A. and Phillips, B.D. (1988). The effect of firm formation and growth on job creation in the United States. *Journal of Business Venturing*, **3**(4): 261–72.

Kuhn, T.S. (1970). *The Structure of Scientific Revolutions* (2nd edn). Chicago, IL: University of Chicago Press.

Leontief, W. (1977). Cited in Mandelbrot, B. *The Fractal Geometry of Nature*. New York: Freeman.

Lodge, G.C. (1975). *The New American Ideology*. New York: Alfred A. Knopf.

Maddox, J. (1989). End of cold fusion in sight. *Nature*, **340**: 15.

McClelland, D. (1961). *The Achieving Society*. Princeton, NJ: Van Nostrand.

McMillan, I.C. (1978). Commentary on strategy formulation: A social process. In D.E. Schendel and C.W. Hofer (eds), *Strategic Management*. Boston: Little, Brown.

Mintzberg, H. and Waters, J.A. (1982). Tracking strategy in an entrepreneurial firm. *Academy of Management Journal*, **25**(3): 465–99.

Mitton, D.G. (1989). The compleat entrepreneur. *Entrepreneurship Theory and Practice*, **13**(3): 9–19.

Moore, C.F. (1986). Understanding entrepreneurial behavior. In J.A. Pearce, II and R.B. Robinson, Jr (eds), *Academy of Management Best Papers Proceedings*. Forty-sixth Annual Meeting of The Academy of Management, Chicago.

Newton, I.S. (1687). *Philosophiae Naturalis Principia Mathematica*.

Polanyi, M. (1964). *Science, Faith and Society*. Chicago, IL: University of Chicago Press.

Porter, M.E. (1980). *Competitive Strategy*. New York: Free Press.

Riordan, M. (1987). *The Hunting of the Quark*. New York: Simon and Schuster.

Rumelt, R.P. and Wensley, R. (1981). In search of the market share effect. Proceedings of the 41st annual meeting of the Academy of Management.

Schatz, S.P. (1971). N-achievement and economic growth: A critical appraisal. In P. Kilby (ed.), *Entrepreneurship and Economic Development*. New York: Free Press.

Schumpeter, J.A. (1949). *The Theory of Economic Development*. Cambridge, MA: Harvard University Press, 1934; reprinted 1949.

Simon, H.A. (1986). Behaving like a manager. Annual Meeting of the Academy of Management, Chicago, August.

Stevenson, H.H., Roberts, M.J. and Grousbeck, H.I. (1989). *New Business Ventures and the Entrepreneur*. Homewood, IL: Irwin.

Thom, R. (1968). A dynamic theory of morphogenesis. In C.H. Waddington (ed.), *Towards a Theoretical Biology 1*. Edinburgh: Edinburg University Press.

Timmons, J.A. (1985) *New Venture Creation*. Homewood, IL: Irwin.

Vesper, K.H. (1980). *New Venture Strategies*. Englewood Cliffs, NJ: Prentice Hall.

Vesper, K.H. and McMullan, W. Ed. (1988). Entrepreneurship: Today courses, tomorrow degrees? *Entrepreneurship Theory and Practice*, **13**(1): 7–13.

Wensley, R. (1982). PIMS and BCG: New horizons or false dawn? *Strategic Management Journal*, **3**: 147–68.

2 Critical realism: a suitable vehicle for entrepreneurship research?
Richard Blundel

Introduction

Chapter 1 introduced the principal paradigms available to entrepreneurship researchers, and also highlighted some broad ontological and epistemological themes concerning the potential choice of methodological 'vehicle' for a particular study. In the present chapter, I consider how one of the more widely cited social theoretic paradigms, critical realism, might be employed. The opening section comprises a brief account of critical realism ('CR') in the context of social science research, which outlines its principal features, indicates its distinctive ontological and epistemological assumptions, and locates it in relation to its antecedents and to some competing approaches. The central section includes a more focused appraisal of CR as the basis for research methodology, including its relevance to qualitative research in the entrepreneurship field.[1] The discussion is illustrated with examples of recent empirical work that has been informed by a CR perspective. The chapter concludes with a reflection on the methodological issues facing researchers who may be considering the use of CR against rival approaches, and some suggestions for further reading.

Researching in a critical realist perspective
Origins and development

The philosophical perspective now widely known as critical realism has gained in prominence over the last 30 years, during which it has made a transition from the natural sciences into social theory, leading to applications in various fields of social science. The core concepts of CR reflect a long tradition of realist philosophy, but its more recent development can be traced to the work of two philosophers of science, Rom Harré and Roy Bhaskar. Harré's influential (1972) *The Philosophies of Science* and Bhaskar's (1975) *A Realist Philosophy of Science* established what was termed a 'transcendental realist' view of the relationship between the nature of human knowledge and that of objects of investigation in the natural sciences. In his (1979) work, *The Possibility of Naturalism*, Bhaskar extended these principles to the realm of the social sciences. In doing so, he reworked the term 'naturalism', referring to the claim that there can be a unity of method between the natural and social sciences, into 'critical naturalism', which acknowledges real differences in the nature of the objects investigated. The core ideas of CR flow from this combination of transcendental realism and critical naturalism.

The underlying position is that social scientists are engaged in a similar project to their counterparts in the natural sciences, but that researching social phenomena requires a distinctive set of methodological tools. Empirical researchers have attempted to apply, adapt and refine CR's philosophical propositions in various fields, including: economic geography (Sayer and Morgan 1986); economics (Lawson 1997; Fleetwood 1999); and organization studies (Ackroyd and Fleetwood 2000; Fleetwood and Ackroyd 2004), resulting in many different perspectives and emphases (Danermark et al. 2002: 1). Underlying this variety is a common concern with a central question in social science: human agency and its relationship with social structure. This concern can be traced back to the rise of CR, which was associated with the rejection of 'structuralist' grand narratives, and corresponding efforts to recognize the role that knowledge and meaning played among human actors. Interestingly, in relation to qualitative research methods, much of the growing interest in CR appears to have been stimulated by direct experience in the field. For example, like other researchers in urban, regional and industrial studies, Andrew Sayer (2000: 5) found it impossible to reconcile the richness, complexity and sheer variety encountered in concrete social worlds with the tidy abstractions demanded by the 'all-embracing, all-explaining' discourses of this period. CR offered a 'middle way' for social scientific research, avoiding both reductionist forms of modernism, that took little or no account of interpretive understanding, and the problems of relativism and incommensurability that followed from postmodernism's discursive 'turn' (ibid.: 67–80).[2]

Principal features

The aim of this section is to introduce some of the principal features of CR that readers are likely to encounter in the literature, using relatively straightforward language and illustrations. It is clearly impossible to encompass a philosophical position in a few short paragraphs without omitting or compressing many of the complex arguments upon which it is based. Consequently, I have focused attention on the methodological aspects of CR, taking the viewpoint of a researcher who may be considering this paradigm for a particular empirical study. The discussion is divided into four parts. The first two parts deal with CR's world-view, introducing the terms 'structures', 'mechanisms', 'causal powers', 'stratification' and 'emergence'. The remaining parts discuss 'critical naturalism', the focal concept that connects CR to its philosophical roots in the natural sciences,

Critical realist 'world-view'

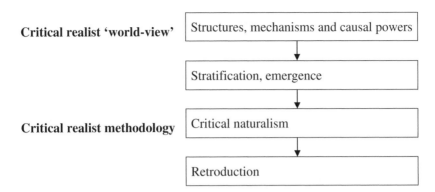

Figure 2.1 Principal features of CR: structure of the argument

and 'retroduction', CR's distinctive mode of scientific inference and explanation. Each part is illustrated with examples from the natural and social worlds; see Figure 2.1.

Structures, mechanisms and causal powers The term 'structure' refers to the way an object is constituted. Hence the structure of a natural object, such as a water molecule, is based on the fusing of one hydrogen atom with two oxygen atoms. Similarly, a social object, such as an entrepreneurial network, is based on interactions between individual human beings. By virtue of its structure, any object has certain 'causal powers'. These are the things that an object is able to do, or more broadly, its 'potentials, capacities, or abilities to act in certain ways and/or to facilitate various activities and developments' (Lawson 1997: 21). Hence water has the capacity to extinguish a fire and an entrepreneurial network can form the basis for a series of different ventures over time (Johannisson 2000). Critical realists also make use of the term 'mechanisms' when referring to the ways that the causal powers of an object are exercised. These mechanisms are sometimes described as 'generative', in the sense that they can give rise to concrete phenomena, such as an event that we might experience. However, activation of causal powers is not automatic, since it depends on the presence of other conditions. Hence, as Sayer (2000: 58) has noted, 'a particular mechanism can produce completely different actions at different times, and inversely, the same event can have completely different causes'. To take a highly simplified example, two individuals might have similar capacities to become successful entrepreneurs, yet due to differing conditions (e.g. prevailing socio-economic conditions in their respective home regions), only one of them might realize her potential. Another implication is that similar events can be the product of an entirely different pattern of causes. Distinguishing

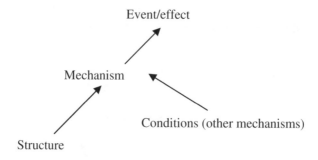

Source: Sayer (2000: 15, Figure 1.2).

Figure 2.2   A critical realist view of causation

these 'contingent' relationships between mechanisms is central to CR's view of causation as depicted in Figure 2.2.[3]

Stratification and emergence   CR asserts that the social world consists of real objects that exist independently of our knowledge and concepts, and whose structures, mechanisms and powers are often far from transparent. This reflects a well-established realist tenet concerning the independence of the world from our thoughts about it (Sayer 2000: 10). As Danermark et al. (2002: 20) have noted, the CR proposition that reality has hidden depths is hardly remarkable. It is not only a prerequisite for scientific activity, but also part of everyday experience, when people conjecture among themselves as to what may be going on 'behind' or 'beneath the surface of' an observed event (e.g. after witnessing extreme weather conditions, or the decline of an industrial district). However, CR does present researchers with a distinctive view of the world, and of their relationship to both natural and social phenomena. In Bhaskar's (1975: 56) terms, reality consists of three domains: the empirical, the actual and the real. The world of human experience and knowledge of events (the 'empirical' domain) is seen as ontologically distinct (i.e. separate and different) from the 'actual' domain in which events occur, irrespective or whether people have observed them. Thus, while different teams of climate scientists may produce competing theories about extreme weather events, the natural phenomena that they study remain the same (*note*: in the case of the social world this relationship with science is rather more complex; social phenomena are themselves products of human knowledge, so do not enjoy the same independent existence as their natural counterparts – see 'critical naturalism', below).[4] The further distinction of a 'real' domain, comprising structures and associated mechanisms, signals CR's decisive break with the so-called 'flat' ontologies, most commonly associated with empirical realist and interpretivist philosophies of science. Realists argue that these paradigms place inappropriate limits on the scope of scientific exploration of the social world, in the first instance ignoring anything that is unobservable by researchers, and in the second, confining research to the direct experiences or accounts of human actors (Sayer 2000: 11). Hence, from a CR perspective, an entrepreneur's account of her experience in starting a new venture only provides a provisional starting-point for explanation (Bhaskar 1979: 80; Whittington 1989: 85–6). One of the primary tasks of science is to probe beneath the 'empirical' and 'actual' domains in pursuit of generative mechanisms that occupy ontologically distinct strata. For human actors, the potential for agency arises from the resulting interactions between different strata:

> Just as for society as a whole, none of these strata provide any unique or dominant determination, but each presents a range of courses according to which actors can direct their activities. At the dinner table, guests are torn between the *physiological* drive of hunger, *psychological* tendencies towards greed and *social* pressures for delicate good manners. (Whittington 1989: 88, emphasis added)

In the case of entrepreneurship research, it has long been recognized that investigations restricted to single strata (e.g. explanations based on efforts to isolate the psychological traits of 'successful' entrepreneurs) are likely to prove unsatisfactory (cf. Low and MacMillan 1988; Aldrich and Zimmer 1986). However, this begs the question of how the properties of different strata are related to one another. CR's response is the proposition that both the natural and social worlds are characterized by the concept of 'emergence'. This suggests that when the properties of different strata combine, they give rise to qualitatively new phenomena, or objects. More precisely, these new objects are emergent in the sense of possessing new properties – structures, causal powers and mechanisms – that depend upon, but cannot be reduced to, those of their constituents (Sayer 2000: 12–13; Danermark et al. 2002: 59–66). Bhaskar (1975: 169) illustrated this point by reconstructing the historical development of chemistry, in which an observable chemical reaction was explained in terms of the properties of objects in successively 'deeper' strata (i.e. electrons, sub-atomic particles). In this example, the structures and associated causal powers (i.e. chemical bonding) of the 'higher' strata are emergent, and therefore fundamentally different in nature, from those of the underlying strata. Social structures, their causal powers and mechanisms are seen as being similarly emergent from human interaction. For example, while recognizing that entrepreneurial networks are a product of interaction between individuals, CR also directs attention to the new and non-reducible properties of the network itself, including its structural form, causal powers and the mechanisms

through which these are exercised. Realists argue that disregard for stratification and emergent powers has undermined social research, contributing
to reductionist explanations, the misidentification of causality and the per-
petuation of territorial disputes between theories and disciplines (Sayer
1992: 120).[5]

Critical naturalism   This concept derives from Bhaskar's efforts to work
through the implications of transcendental realism for the social sciences.
Critical naturalism can be seen, in simple terms, as CR's strategy for accommodating 'messy' and 'ambiguous' social phenomena, without abandoning
the social scientific task. In common with interpretivists, and those who
pursued the postmodern 'turn', critical realists have rejected 'naturalism',
recognizing that the social world cannot be understood in the same way as
its natural counterpart (see also Chapter 4). However, in contrast to these
paradigms, realists have been unwilling to stop their search at the level of
meaning, but prefer to see its interpretation as merely the *starting-point* for
the pursuit of deeper causal explanations.[6] The following short extracts from
the literature indicate some of the more important differences that realists
have attempted to address, as CR philosophy has been translated from the
natural world in order to encompass social phenomena. For researchers, it
has meant taking due account of distinguishing characteristics of the social
world, including: the impact of intentionality on human action (i.e. our purposeful pursuit of perceived goals, such as happiness or profit); the emergent
nature of social structures, such as marriage or organization, which are both
relatively autonomous and inherently meaningful; and the complex relationship between agency and structure that this implies:

> Our pursuit of a separate science in the social sphere, centred upon the inten-
> tionality of human agency and involving a recognition of the reality and rela-
> tive autonomy of action-conditioning social structure, amounts to an
> acknowledgement of the irreducibility of society to nature. (Lawson 1997: 63)

> What does it mean to write of the social world? The natural world is natural
> because it does not require action on behalf of human beings for its existence.
> The social world is social because, by contrast, it does require action on behalf
> of human beings for its existence. (Ackroyd and Fleetwood 2000: 10)

> Critical realism acknowledges that social phenomena are intrinsically meaningful,
> and hence that meaning is not only externally descriptive of them but constitutive
> of them (though of course there are usually material constituents too). Meaning
> has to be understood, it cannot be measured or counted, and hence there is always
> an interpretive or hermeneutic element in social science. (Sayer 2000: 17)

In summary, while the causal powers of natural objects, such as weather
systems, are exercised 'mindlessly', without any (self-conscious) sense of

meaning, interpretation and intent, those of social objects, such as entrepreneurial activities, display these characteristics in abundance. The implication is that social scientists need to engage in a so-called 'double
hermeneutic', generating explanatory knowledge about phenomena that
are themselves 'knowing', in contrast to their natural science counterparts,
whose subject-matter is 'unknowing'. This highlights a central tension
arising from CR's ontology. Given the proposition that science seeks to
explain a world consisting of 'real' objects, which in CR terms represent the
'intransitive' or objective dimension of knowledge, how is it to incorporate
this 'transitive' or subjective dimension? Bhaskar's (1975) concept of *critical* naturalism acts as the conceptual bridge between these competing
demands:

> [C]ritical realism is only partly naturalist, for although social science can use the
> same methods as natural science regarding causal explanation, it must also
> diverge from them in using '*verstehen*' or interpretive understanding. While
> natural scientists necessarily have to enter the hermeneutic circle of their scien-
> tific community, social scientists also have to enter that of those whom they
> study. (Sayer 2000: 17)

It is clear that the concept of critical naturalism represents a far-reaching
methodological challenge to empirical researchers (Danermark et al. 2002:
38–9). Consequently, any conclusions that we reach regarding the empirical *application* of critical naturalism are likely to be central to our assessment of CR as a suitable 'vehicle' for entrepreneurship research.

Retroduction CR has adopted a distinctive form of scientific inference,
termed 'retroduction', which involves the explanation of events in the social
world by seeking to discern the structures and mechanisms that are capable
of producing them (Sayer 1992: 107). This explanatory task involves quite
different methodological operations to those associated with 'induction' and
'deduction'.[7] Consider, for example, a research project investigating the
growth of entrepreneurial firms: *inductive* inference might move from a
series of similar observations to an empirical generalization such as 'rapid
growth is associated with variables X, Y and Z'; *deductive* inference might
move from a set of premises, such as the existence of certain variables, to a
conclusion about their implications for growth in a particular case; while
retroductive inference would move from the description and abstract analysis of the growth process as a concrete phenomenon to a reconstruction of
the basic conditions (i.e. the structures, causal powers and mechanisms) that
make it possible.[8] Retroduction involves a type of scientific generalization
that is concerned with the isolation of fundamental structures whose powers
can be said to act 'transfactually' (i.e. continuing to exist, even though their

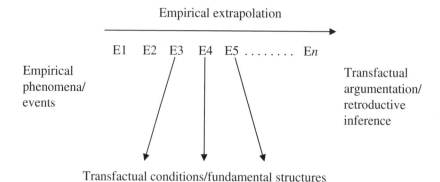

Empirical extrapolation

E1   E2   E3   E4   E5 ....   E*n*

Empirical
phenomena/
events

Transfactual
argumentation/
retroductive
inference

Transfactual conditions/fundamental structures

Source: Danermark et al. (2002: 77, Figure 3).

Figure 2.3   Two types of generalization

operations may not be manifested at the level of events or observations). Its 'analytical' approach to generalization contrasts sharply with the more common type associated with inductive inference, which focuses on the extrapolation of empirical regularities (Danermark et al. 2002: 77) (Figure 2.3). As a consequence, retroduction requires different scientific methods in order to achieve its purposes (Easton 2000: 214).

So what are the implications of retroduction for the working practices of social scientists? Some of the more important issues can be illustrated with reference to an imaginary research study involving case studies of entre-preneurial firms. First, in their effort to reflect the inherent complexity of concrete phenomena, the researchers are likely to draw on multiple sources of data, which may comprise various types of qualitative evidence, derived from ethnography, observation, in-depth interview, historical and archival research, as well as some quantitative evidence, such as industry statistics. Second, in selecting cases, the researchers are guided by the requirements of analytical, rather than empirical, generalization. This means that they select cases in order to explore and to clarify the necessary and contingent relationships between structures (Danermark et al. 2002: 105). To achieve this, their selection might include some extreme or 'pathological' cases, where firms have experienced major transitions or crises (Bhaskar 1979: 48; Collier 1994: 165). In addition, they pay considerable attention to both the spatial and temporal boundaries of case-based research, in an effort to ensure that wider structural conditions are addressed (Whittington 1989: 85). Third, in sifting through their rich idiographic sources, the researchers incorporate the accounts of human actors, not simply in their own terms, but as part of the search for the 'rules' that constitute these accounts

Table 2.1   An explanatory research process involving retroduction

Activity	Nature of activity
1 Description	Prepare a description of the phenomenon, making use of actors' accounts and a variety of other sources.
2 Analytical resolution	Distinguish various components, aspects or dimensions of the phenomenon and establish (tentative) boundaries to the components studied.
3 Theoretical redescription	Interpret and redescribe the different components, applying contrasting theoretical frameworks and interpretations in order to provide new insights (*note*: this activity is sometimes referred to as 'abduction').
4 Retroduction	For each component, seek to identify basic, or 'transfactual' conditions, including structures, causal powers and mechanisms, that make the phenomenon possible.
5 Abstract comparison	Elaborate and estimate the explanatory power of the structures, causal powers and mechanisms that have been identified during activities 3 and 4.
6 Concretization and contextualization	Examine how different structures, causal powers and mechanisms manifest themselves in concrete situations.

Source: Danermark et al. (2002: 109–11, Table 4, modified). Note: the term 'activities' has been substituted for the original 'stages' in order to emphasize the non-linear nature of the process.

(Tsoukas 1989: 555). For example, the researchers treat entrepreneurs' statements about the perceived constraints of the growth of their firms as a starting-point for a retroductive probing of the structural preconditions of these perceptions. Lastly, the study itself proceeds through several iterations, with the researchers moving repeatedly between more concrete and more abstract activities in order to refine their explanation. In Tsoukas's (1989: 558) terms, they are moving concurrently on two tracks, one of which is 'up in the clouds', and concerned with abstraction and theoretical conceptualization, while the other is 'down to earth', engaged in the idiosyncratic details of the case material. The process has been described in a model comprising five distinct but closely related activities (Danermark et al. 2002: 109–11) (Table 2.1). As the authors have emphasized, the model is not prescriptive, nor does it imply a strictly linear process. The emphasis on different activities is also bound to vary, according to the nature of a particular research project, as are the actual research methods employed (ibid.: 109, 73). However, it provides a concise summary of the preceding discussion, illustrating the distinctively retroductive methodological implications that social scientists have derived from the CR paradigm.

The remaining sections of the chapter aim to add some substance to this brief, and necessarily schematic, account of CR methodology. The transition from philosophy to practical fieldwork is made in two stages. The first comprises some general arguments for CR, and their relationship to current empirical and conceptual issues in the entrepreneurship literature. The second includes three examples of recent empirical studies that draw, to varying degrees, on a realist paradigm. This two-stage approach allows us to consider both the 'hypothetical' case for CR in our field and the current state of play as reflected in published research.

Is critical realism relevant to entrepreneurship research?
In this section, I discuss several reasons why the CR paradigm might provide a suitable vehicle for entrepreneurship research, with specific reference to qualitative approaches. As the editors have indicated, the methodological debate in our field is at best at a highly provisional stage. With this in mind, I have presented the material in the form of a rhetorical case for CR-inspired research, intended to stimulate discussion (*note*: critics and alternative approaches are addressed in a later section). The argument builds on five themes: first, that CR can help to revive a longstanding realist tradition in entrepreneurship research; second, that CR can promote the much-needed contexutalization of entrepreneurial phenomena in research studies; third, that CR can facilitate greater theoretical integration between disciplines and across multiple levels of analysis; fourth, that CR can enhance the explanatory potential of existing qualitative research techniques, including the case study approaches; and fifth, that as a consequence, CR has the potential to contribute more 'useful' knowledge than rival paradigms.

Reviving a realist tradition
Realism has long intellectual roots in entrepreneurship research and its contributory disciplines (Ackroyd and Fleetwood 2000: 9; Swedberg 2000: 12–18). For example, it is possible to detect a common thread of ideas in economics, emerging out of its polarization in the *Methodenstreit* (i.e. battle over methods) at the end of the nineteenth century. The pioneering sociologist Max Weber proposed a new approach to overcome the divide between an overly abstract, non-historical version of economics, and an overly historical, non-theoretical one. Weber's *Sozialökonomik*, an attempt to synthesize history with theory, had a great impact on Joseph

Schumpeter's thinking (Swedberg 1991: 83–9), including his approach to entrepreneurship:

> [The] sociology of enterprise reaches much further than is implied in questions concerning the conditions that produce and shape, favour or inhibit entrepreneurial activity. It extends to the structure and the very foundations of capitalist society. (Schumpeter 1951: 224–5)

Schumpeter's ideas influenced Edith Penrose, whose seminal (1959) study, *The Theory of the Growth of the Firm*, reflects a similar realist concern with uncovering structures and mechanisms, and specifically those ignored by mainstream economics in its 'black box' treatment of the firm. Penrose's interest was sparked by involvement in a substantial piece of qualitative research, examining the growth of a former subsidiary of DuPont (Penrose 1960). Her eclectic theory incorporates a subtle treatment of meaning and intentionality in human actors (i.e. the dynamics of entrepreneurial judgement at the level of the managerial team, encapsulated in her concept of 'productive opportunity'), but also acknowledges the relative autonomy of environmental selection mechanisms:[9]

> 'Expectations' and not 'objective facts' are the immediate determinants of a firm's behaviour, although there may be a relationship between expectations and 'facts' – indeed there must be if action is to be successful . . . In the last analysis the 'environment' rejects or confirms the soundness of the judgements about it, but the relevant environment is not an objective fact discoverable before the event. (Penrose 1959: 41)

Penrose's emphasis on the subjective element, whereby firm behaviour is, in the first instance, the product of an 'image' of the environment in the mind of the entrepreneur (Boulding 1956), contrasts with much of the later resource-based literature. However, by elaborating her theory, she helped to perpetuate a strand of research that retains a strong realist flavour (e.g. Lawson and Lorenz 1999; Best 2001). Investigations may start at the level of entrepreneurial perceptions, but their scope should be much broader; researchers are challenged to discover how the phenomenon that Penrose conceptualized as 'productive opportunity' articulates with other structures and mechanisms.

Contextualizing entrepreneurship
Critical realism raises questions about the preconditions for social phenomena. It is therefore well placed to frame an investigation into contextual and process issues. In considering the context in which entrepreneurship occurs, we begin to raise important questions about the boundaries, both temporal and spatial, of our research:

> We need to know not only what the main strategies were of actors, but what it was about the context which enabled them to be successful or otherwise. This is

> consistent with the realist concept of causation and requires us . . . to decide what it was about a certain context which allowed a certain action to be successful. Often the success or failure of agents' strategies may have little or nothing to do with their own reasons and intentions. (Sayer 2000: 26)

Many contributors have called for greater attention to be paid to the context in which entrepreneurial activity takes place (Low and MacMillan 1988; Zafirovski 1999; Ucbasaran et al. 2001). For example, entrepreneurial networks have been identified as important contextual phenomena that display degrees of social embeddedness (Granovetter 1985; Johannisson and Monsted 1997) and latency (Ramachandran and Ramnarayan 1993). Network-based case studies have also been used to deconstruct the (culturally conditioned) myth of entrepreneurs as 'heroic' individuals (Jones and Conway 2000). However, leading figures continue to argue that interaction between entrepreneurial activity and the broader context is a relatively underdeveloped research area (Acs and Audretsch 2003: 329; Davidsson and Wiklund 2001: 81–2). The potential contribution of CR is to facilitate a more nuanced understanding of the context in which entrepreneurs exercise strategic choice; CR's mechanisms-based paradigm is seen as a moderating influence on excessively voluntaristic (and deterministic) accounts of entrepreneurial agency (Whittington 1989: 75). Building on CR's methodological precepts, entrepreneurial research should be capable of better spatial and temporal explanations, tracing the changing 'zones of manoeuvre' of entrepreneurial firms as they interact with the competitive capacities of their contexts (Clark 2000: 303–13).

Integrating different levels of analysis
Entrepreneurship research has blossomed in many academic disciplines, including psychology, anthropology, organization studies, geography, economic history and economics. These activities have generated a rich and diverse harvest of empirical and conceptual material. However, this variety masks the fact that the field is fragmented, with specialists making little use of one another's work (Ucbasaran et al. 2001: 57). Furthermore, in pursuing the methodologies traditionally associated with these disciplines, entrepreneurship researchers have tended to focus their attention on particular levels of analysis. In their comprehensive review of 'past research and future challenges', Low and MacMillan (1988: 151–2) suggested that entrepreneurship researchers may choose among five levels of analysis in pursuit of relevant phenomena: the individual, group, organizational, industrial and societal. They noted a tendency for most previous research to be conducted at a single level of analysis, but argued that a few recent examples of multi-level research (e.g. Aldrich and Auster 1986), demonstrated the

potential for achieving a richer understanding of entrepreneurship processes. This led them to conclude that both entrepreneurship research designs would be enriched if they were able to incorporate multiple levels of analysis:

> The relationships between phenomena that can be observed at different levels of analysis are important not just for academics, but for both practitioners and public policy-makers as well. From the entrepreneur's perspective, the success of the individual enterprise will be affected by factors that can only be observed at different levels of analysis. *To miss any one of these perspectives increases the probability that key factors will be overlooked and that unanticipated events will take the entrepreneur by surprise.* From the public policy-maker's perspective, the insights generated by multi-level studies have the potential to improve targeting of government efforts to encourage successful entrepreneurship. (Low and MacMillan 1988: 152, emphasis added)

However, Davidsson and Wiklund's (2001) review of current research practice, based on a content analysis of articles published in leading US and European entrepreneurship journals, revealed that research was dominated by micro-level analysis, with integrated 'micro/aggregate mix' approaches continuing to represent a small proportion of published work. While our diverse and primarily single-level research programmes have given rise to recurrent debates over the relative importance of, for example, psychological, organizational and socio-cultural dimensions of entrepreneurship, they have achieved little empirical or conceptual integration (Frank and Landström 1997; Davidsson et al. 2001). For example, entrepreneurship researchers employ a variety of strategies to build or refine process theories. Each seeks to understand 'patterns in events', but methodologies differ in the extent to which they probe beyond observed events (i.e. surface-level effects) in order to understand underlying causal sequences or generating mechanisms (Pentland 1999). This is not to deny the many insights into entrepreneurial processes that have already been achieved. For example, population ecologists have made productive use of a single-level methodology, exploring macro-level processes with data that are primarily aggregated and quantitative (i.e. official statistical data sets recording firm entries and exits) (Aldrich and Zimmer 1986; Staber 1997). Similarly, ethnographic researchers, who also tend to apply a single-level methodology, have revealed richly detailed micro-level processes through direct exposure to localized fieldwork sites, making imaginative use of qualitative research methods (i.e. observing entrepreneurs and recording their perceptions and behaviours) (Ram 1999). Rather, as proponents would argue, a CR-inspired methodology is capable of taking entrepreneurship research a step further, supporting new research strategies better geared to achieve integration across its traditional divides (cf. Layder 1993; Danermark et al. 2002).[10]

Enhancing qualitative research

CR is compatible with a range of qualitative research methods. Its potential role in relation to qualitative evidence can be illustrated with reference to one of the leading texts in this field (Miles and Huberman 1994). As the authors suggest, the decision to adopt a realist perspective may have little impact on data collection. However, research strategies will be affected by the imperatives of critical naturalism and retroductive analysis:

> Human relationships and societies have peculiarities that make a realist approach to understanding them more complex – but not impossible. Unlike researchers in physics, we must contend with institutions, structures, practices and conventions that people reproduce and transform . . . Things that are believed become real and can be inquired into. (Miles and Huberman 1994: 4)

Although it has few references to Bhaskar and Harré, this widely adopted sourcebook has added considerable substance to CR's earlier methodological reflections. For example, its approach to 'within case displays' illustrates some of the challenges in causal explanation, contrasting investigations that are limited to a single level of analysis to more complex, multi-level approaches. The authors argue that qualitative research methods are particularly amenable to this type of causal analysis:

> Qualitative analysis, with its close-up look, can identify mechanisms, going beyond sheer association. It is unrelentingly local, and deals well with the complex network of events and processes in a situation. It can sort out the temporal dimension, showing clearly what preceded what, either through direct observation or retrospection. It is well-equipped to cycle back and forth between variables and processes – showing that 'stories' are not capricious, but include underlying variables, and that variables are not disembodied, but have connections over time. (Ibid.: 147)

These techniques are broadly consistent with a CR position, and suggest that researchers should proceed through a combination of what they term a 'variable-oriented' conceptual approach (i.e. looking for patterns, or configurations in the data) and a 'process-oriented' approach (i.e. assembling chronologies, or stories). The overall emphasis is towards retroductive inference:

> [We are] proposing that answering good 'why' and 'how' questions requires us to go beyond sheer association to seeing the actual mechanisms of influence in a bounded local setting, which are always multifold, operating over time. (Ibid.: 170)

The implication, which echoes the previous argument concerning multi-level analysis, is that a CR-inspired methodology can contribute to better outcomes when researchers are employing qualitative research methods.

More specifically, by highlighting the role of unobserved social structures, causal powers and mechanisms, the CR ontology can act as a counterbalance to the 'micro-sociological' tendencies of context-specific qualitative approaches such as ethnography (Porter 2002: 142, 157). Relatedly, CR's fundamental concern with explaining *why* things occur, and with analysis through a process of retroductive inference, can challenge researchers to move beyond the description of social situations to a more critical assessment of the relationship between structural factors and human agency (ibid.: 156–7).

Generating more 'useful' knowledge
In order to intervene successfully in the world, it is useful to obtain a working knowledge of the relevant structures and generative mechanisms. Or, to paraphrase Kant's widely cited aphorism, 'There is nothing so practical as a good theory.' The principal advantage of CR's retroductive methodology, from the perspective of the policy-maker or practitioner, is that its purpose is to develop a theoretical understanding of real mechanisms, and the contingent ways in which they combine to generate effects (e.g. Subramaniyam 2000). While isolated, subjective accounts of entrepreneurial agency may be engaging, they have no referent and therefore lack cumulative explanatory power. With its concern for underlying structure rather than surface-level correlations, its opposition to excessive voluntarism and determinism, and its critique of reductionist explanations, CR seems well placed to deliver a more informed – though, it has to be conceded, not always 'actionable' – understanding of concrete situations. At present, it is difficult to substantiate this argument, given the limited number of published studies that combine a CR methodology with an explicit policy orientation. However, some provisional conclusions may be drawn from three cases presented in the next section, which illustrate contrasting empirical applications of a broadly realist perspective.

Applying critical realism in entrepreneurship research
The empirical challenge
This section provides examples to illustrate the proposition that research drawing on a CR perspective is capable of delivering more informed explanations of entrepreneurial activity. It reflects repeated calls to move beyond *conceptual* integration and attempt to replicate it in concrete, empirical research (Aldrich and Martinez 2001: 51). I will focus on three studies, each reflecting different aspects of the entrepreneurial networks agenda: Best's (2001) analysis of the dynamics of entrepreneurial firms and regional clusters is not explicitly critical realist in approach, yet displays realism's capacity for integration across multiple levels of analysis; Jones's (2001) examination of

divergent strategies of technology- and content-driven entrepreneurs in the early years of the US film industry combines realism with a narrative approach; and Bowey and Easton's (2003) study adopts a CR methodology to explain changes in social capital in relationships between entrepreneurs and other actors. The aim is to connect the methodological debate to concrete research practices, noting both the limitations and potential of the paradigm.[11]

The dynamics of entrepreneurial clusters

Michael Best's recent work addresses 'cluster dynamics', defined as 'interactive processes of capability development and specialization within and amongst firms within a region' (Best 2001: ix). It forms part of a research tradition concerned with processes of entrepreneurship, learning and adaptation both within and beyond the boundaries of the firm (Penrose 1959; Richardson 1972; Lawson and Lorenz 1999). Best's systems integration model extends the spatial and temporal scope of the (neo-Penrosian) 'technology capability and market opportunity' mechanism and suggests how it might articulate with other mechanisms operating at several distinct levels of analysis (Figure 2.4). The resulting analysis of capability development in industrial districts may be interpreted, in CR terms, as highlighting the role of pre-existing structures and their associated latent causal powers, while also isolating the contingent relationships that can lead to these powers being exercised:

This model has been applied empirically to explain the changing fortunes of regional clusters, including the resurgence of high-technology

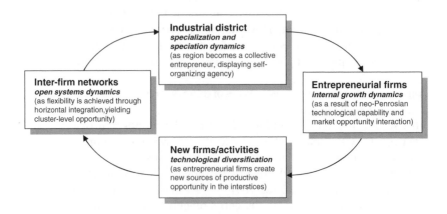

Source: Best (2001: 70, Figure 2.1 – adapted, bracketed annotation added).

Figure 2.4   A cumulative model of cluster dynamics

manufacturing in eastern Massachusetts and emerging cluster dynamics in the Malaysian electronics sector.[12]

> An industrial district, unlike any single firm, offers the potential for new and unplanned technology combinations that tap a variety and range of production-related activities. This protean character of technological capability, particularly evident in the high tech sectors, is a feature of industrial change even in the oldest sectors. . . . Thus, a region's technological capabilities are an outcome of a *cumulative* and *collective* history of technological advances embedded in entrepreneurial firms. (Best 2001: 81, emphasis in original)

Entrepreneurial trajectories in Hollywood

Candace Jones (2001) has conducted a fascinating historical analysis of the interaction between entrepreneurial careers, institutional rules and competitive dynamics in the early American film industry. Jones's methodology combines realist and narrative approaches, while her conceptual framework draws on insights from co-evolutionary, institutional and resource-based theorizing:

> Generative mechanisms are the underlying structures that drive processes (Pentland 1999) and in this study, they are firms' institutional and strategic isolating mechanisms. A narrative approach illuminates how and why change occurs, by examining sequences of events (Van de Ven 1992) to reveal linkages amongst context and action (Pettigrew 1992). (Jones 2001: 913)

The study makes use of a rich variety of qualitative and quantitative evidence, including firm-level archival data, published histories and industry statistics. These are used to probe the contrasting trajectories of 'technology-driven' and 'content-oriented' firms in an analytical scheme that encompasses the firms' entrepreneurial practices, their capability-development and their co-evolutionary relationship and emerging structure of institutional rules (e.g. patent laws and artistic contracts).

Entrepreneurial social capital changes

James Bowey and Geoff Easton (2003) adopt a comparative case study approach, informed by a form of CR explanation, to examine the change of social capital in entrepreneurial network relationships. The two cases in this paper are based on contrasting business relationships involving one entrepreneur, 'Jacques', and two other actors. One of the cases records a process of social capital formation in a blossoming relationship, while the other traces a process of depreciation in a failing relationship. The narratives are framed using a common template that allows the researchers to probe for deeper 'entities' (i.e. structures), mechanisms and relationships. The research reveals similarities and differences that are not evident at the level of 'surface' events:

> Both mechanisms were different because while the entities were the same the necessary and contingent relationships were not only individually different but so was their configuration. As a result they worked in different ways to cause different changes in social capital. (Bowey and Easton 2003: 18)

However, the authors conclude that the most important conclusion coming from their in-depth analysis concerns the difficulty in specifying causal mechanisms. They compare the role played by entities (i.e. social structures) and mechanisms in a realist paradigm with that of variables and correlations found in the 'positivist' research. This prompts the reflection that, though positivism's simple 'linear additive configurations' are unlikely to provide useful representations of reality, 'it is difficult to think in any other way when seeking to ascribe reasonably precise causal explanations' (ibid.: 18–19).

Is it time for a 'test-drive'?

In this chapter, I have assessed the potential of critical realism as a suitable vehicle for exploring the phenomenon of entrepreneurship, with particular reference to qualitative research. I have presented five broad arguments in support of this view. Ultimately, any methodological innovation must be subjected to a simple evaluative question. In short, to what extent can it enhance our understanding of the phenomenon we are studying? The case for qualitative research informed by CR is that it has the potential to produce 'better stories' that could form the basis for more sophisticated causal explanations. Perhaps the most important limitation in narrative-based qualitative research, and one that has long been recognized in the debate between 'models' and 'histories', is that the complexity and idiosyncrasy of narrative data tend to 'crowd out' fundamental mechanisms and relationships. One of the claims of the CR perspective is that it provides a basis for theoretically informed abstraction, reflecting Marx's earlier notion of an *histoire raisonée*. Thus, in the case of narrative-based research, CR demands a more rigorous and analytically sound periodization of episodes than that found in much of the literature (Clark 2000: 115), with more explicit specifications of causality in the processes that it describes (Sayer 2000: 142–3). One thing is certain: the contribution of any methodology cannot be proven in the abstract. As the case examples have illustrated, there is much to gain from further testing and refinement in the field. This would be facilitated by a more creative interaction between the high ground of social theory and more earthly demands of empirical research.

Critics and alternatives

The principal case for CR is that it offers the social scientist a distinctive methodological approach, which rejects both the naive optimism of those expecting to uncover law-like regularities from empirical data and the defeatism of those who deny any possibility of generalizing our under-standing of idiosyncratic phenomena such as entrepreneurship. As we have seen, CR is frequently presented as a kind of 'third way', providing a more sophisticated ontology than either empirical realism or postmodernism in its various forms (Ackroyd and Fleetwood 2000: 4–10; Sayer 1992: 4–7). However, the CR paradigm has also been subjected to sustained criticism, extending from its philosophical roots to the empirical studies it has inspired. The most extensive attacks have been on CR's social theoretic propositions, which have been seen as both internally inconsistent and unoriginal (e.g. Baert 1998: 195–7; Parsons 1999; Roberts 2001). There has also been some questioning of the CR claim to provide a compelling basis for social scientific methodology (Walters and Young 2001). Moreover, the CR community has proved to be an effective (self-)critic, mocking the 'lin-guistic obscurity' of some contributions to the CR literature (Junor 2001: 33), and warning against a common tendency to shift substantive social science issues, 'into the terrain of philosophy' (Potter 2003: 163). As the writer notes, the tendency is problematic because, 'philosophy cannot do social science's job' (ibid.: 163). With this thought in mind, sceptics might find themselves questioning the continuing shortage of substantive pub-lished studies that have adopted an explicitly CR methodology.[13]

In reflecting on these critiques, we should note that critical realists are not the only social theorists who promote a methodology based upon a search for the underlying generative mechanisms that connect different states or events. There is a longstanding debate in sociology, between pro-ponents of variable-centred approaches that make extensive use of statist-ical modelling techniques, and those who argue for mechanism-based theorizing. Advocates of the 'social mechanisms' approach to sociological theorizing would agree with CR on the role played by mechanisms in the routine practice of social scientific research:

> The belief in explanations that provide accounts of what happens as it actually happens has pervaded the sociological literature for decades and has produced an abundance of detailed descriptive narratives but few explanatory mech-anisms of any generality. It is through abstractions and analytical accentuation, however, that general mechanisms are made visible. (Hedström and Swedberg 1998: 15)

However, despite some commonality of purpose, there are important differences between the methodologies adopted by 'social mechanisms' scholars and those associated with CR. In the former case, empirical work tends to have a much stronger quantitative orientation and to be guided by the principles of methodological individualism. The 'middle-range' theori-zing advocated in this tradition is based on the argument that sociological researchers are equipped to pursue only relatively short causal histories (cf. Layder 1993: 19–37). In addition, while sharing with CR the assumption that social mechanisms 'usually are unobserved', they are treated here as analytical constructs that simply assist in the process of theorizing the links between observed events. In other words, these mechanisms, though 'generative', do not enjoy the special ontological status that is granted to them in the work of Harré and Bhaskar (Hedström and Swedberg 1998: 7–17).[14]

'It is in practice . . .'

By way of a closing comment, it seems appropriate to return to the metaphorical image of CR as a potential 'vehicle' for entrepreneurship research. In the course of this chapter, I have reviewed a small proportion of a substantial CR literature that has been generated in a relatively short period, stimulated by the agenda-setting philosophical writings of Harré and Bhaskar that appeared in the 1970s. The review has focused on contributions from entrepreneurship researchers and those in related fields, rather than those of social theorists. Despite this emphasis, one overriding impression is that researchers have invested a disproportionate amount of energy in describing CR's elaborate ontological features, and in debating the merits of its radical epistemological styling. The necessary investment in substantive research – let us call it 'test-driving' CR – has been correspondingly underplayed. As a philosophy of science, transcendental realism was able to reflect on many centuries of empirical practice in the natural sciences. By contrast, CR in the social sciences draws on a much thinner body of substantive work. If CR's critics are to be believed, the tensions inherent in critical naturalism may direct entrepreneurship researchers elsewhere. For example, they may opt for less ambitious studies of particular aspects of entrepreneurship in a 'social mechanisms' framework, or construct much broader geo-historical narratives that are not constrained by social scientific conventions. In any event, the final test will be an empirical one. As the renowned realist, Karl Marx (1818–83), once observed, 'it is in practice that we prove . . . that our thought is true'.

Suggestions for further reading

It is good practice to trace ideas to their original source, but as Junor (2001: 30) has noted, the philosophical texts that underpin CR, such as Harré (1972) and Bhaskar (1975, 1979) are not necessarily the best starting-point for most empirical researchers. The alternative is to turn to other philosophers, such as Collier (1994), who offers a fairly accessible and critical introduction to Bhaskar's ideas, or to scholars from other disciplines, who can mediate between the high plateaux of philosophy and the practical challenges of social science research. Leading contributors in the latter group include: Sayer (1992, 2000), who discusses the methodological implications of CR in various fields, with a particular focus on geo-historical research; Lawson (1997), whose broad methodological critique of 'mainstream' economics methodologies is grounded in a CR perspective; and Archer (1995), who develops a distinctive 'morphogenetic' approach, placing particular emphasis on the time dimension and engaging in a strong critique of structuration theory.[15] Much of this work is summarized by Danermark et al. (2002), who provide a clear and coherent introduction to critical realism in the social sciences, with particular emphasis on methodology and practical application. As noted previously, there are relatively few published accounts of CR as it has been applied in the field of entrepreneurship. However, the volumes edited by Ackroyd and Fleetwood (2000) and Fleetwood and Ackroyd (2004) contain recent conceptual and empirical work in related areas of management and organizational studies (e.g. Porter's (2002) CR ethnography), while the study by Whittington (1989) includes a CR-inspired methodological discussion. In order to develop a balanced view of CR, readers may also wish to pursue some of the leading critics, or to seek comparisons between CR and rival perspectives (e.g. Miri and Watson 2001; Mutch 2002). As noted above, there are many critiques of CR as *social theory*, but these tend to lack the methodological application that is of more immediate interest to empirical researchers. Walters and Young (2001) is an exception, with a challenge to CR's methodological claims that is based on recent applications in the field of economics; the 'debates' section of Fleetwood (1999) contains some counter-arguments.

Acknowledgements
The author would like to thank the organizers of the first Interdisciplinary European Conference on Entrepreneurship Research (IECER), University of Regensburg, Germany (February 2003), conference participants, Stephen Ackroyd, Peter Clark, Michael Rowlinson, the editors of this volume and two anonymous referees for their support, comments and suggestions. The usual caveat applies.

Notes

1. Critical realism has had relatively limited exposure in the entrepreneurship literature, in contrast to its profile in related areas, such as organization studies and economic geography. However, as the editors of this handbook have indicated, there is much to gain from a more critical discussion concerning the often-implicit methodological choices that are made by researchers in this field.
2. This concern to develop 'more open, context-dependent and plural' accounts of the social world was echoed by the rise of postmodernism and post-structuralism, but argues that the development of CR in fields such as urban and regional studies happened 'largely independently' of their emergence (Sayer 2000: 5).

3. 'Necessary relations' (or 'necessity') refer to things that must go together, given the nature of objects in the natural or social world, while 'contingent relations' (or 'contingency') refer to things that might go together. Researchers adopting a CR approach see the pursuit of questions about necessity as fundamental to the practice of theorizing in the social sciences, forcing researchers to sharpen their conceptualizations of their objects of study.

4. Sayer (2000: 33–5) mounts a strong defence of critical realism against the sceptical implication that social phenomena cannot be treated in the same way as their natural-world counterparts (i.e. as 'intransitive' objects of study). However, as one of the reviewers has suggested, while analogies from nature may help to clarify CR's unfamiliar ontological and epistemological claims, they should always be used sparingly and with careful 'translations' to social examples.

5. Bhaskar (1975) presents a *philosophical* case for stratification and emergence, based on the existence of scientific practice. Realists argue that this proposition also corresponds to evidence from the natural and social worlds, giving examples such as the evolution of life on earth (Collier 1994: 46).

6. Sayer (2000) provides an insight into the way this tension between the need for interpretative understanding and that of causal explanation was experienced in the course of his own empirical work:

    The empirical context was the prosaic one of studies of the development of urban and regional systems . . . . In attempting to develop an understanding of these that was both dynamic and spatial, it slowly dawned on me that social systems were necessarily open, and that they evolved rather than equilibrated, not least because people have the capacity to learn and change their behaviour. Consequently, I realized the goal of finding rough regularities, let alone laws, to describe social systems, was a pipe dream. At the same time, realist philosophy was beginning to challenge the regularity or secessionist theory of causation, and to analyse the explanation of change in open systems, so that it became clear that abandoning hopes of finding regularities in no way meant abandoning explanation. (Sayer 2000: 4–5)

7. Retroduction breaks with Popper's hypothetical-deductive form of scientific inference (Sayer 1992: 169–74). Popper's falsificationist criterion of science, according to which a theory must be at least potentially falsifiable by *empirical* observation, was famously illustrated with reference to the appearance of a single black swan. Observation of this event was deemed sufficient to falsify the theory that 'all swans are white'. Some scholars distinguish 'abduction' as a fourth mode of scientific inference, involving the theoretical redescription of underlying structures and relationships (Danermark et al. 2002: 88–95), while others incorporate into accounts of the retroductive process (cf. Lawson 1997).

8. Recent studies pursuing a CR-inspired research agenda in this area (e.g. Blundel 2002; Bowey and Easton 2003), can be contrasted with those adopting the more 'mainstream' approach of inductive inference, based on the analysis of empirical regularities (i.e. the regression of variables derived from a questionnaire-based survey of owner–managers against concurrent firm-level measures of growth) (e.g. Adams and Hall 1993; Barkham et al. 1996).

9. Edith Penrose asserts her realist credentials in a later and more light-hearted comment that seems to anticipate more recent critiques of postmodernist positions:

    Now none but the most philosophically sophisticated businessman will accept the proposition that the opportunities for the expansion of his firm are simply his ideas about what his firm can do; he will insist that the opportunities he sees reflect the 'facts' of the world, facts that may be known with indifferent accuracy to be sure, but facts none the less. (Penrose 1959: 216)

10. This longstanding case for greater integration is reflected in Penrose's (1953) critique of early evolutionary theorizing by economists in relation to the growth of firms. Her argument anticipates CR's rejection of deterministic explanations, on the grounds that they tend to abstract away the essential interplay between human cognition, agency and their environment:

> Once human will and motivation are recognized as important constituents of the situation, there is no *a priori* justification for assuming that firms, in their struggle for profits, will not attempt as much consciously to adapt the environment to their own purposes as to adapt themselves to the environment. (Penrose 1953: 10)

11. Other recent network-related studies adopting elements of the CR paradigm include Neergaard (1999), where the author explores the role of networks in the internationalization of small furniture manufacturers, and Blundel (2002), which addresses the interplay between inter-organizational networks and institutional-level changes in relation to contrasting growth processes in artisanal firms.

12. The realist orientation of this analysis is reflected in its capacity to probe intermediate mechanisms and context-specific interactions. For example, in Best's (2001) account of regional growth dynamics in Northern Ireland, poor performance in innovation and productivity is traced across several levels of analysis to reveal a lack of growth engines. By layering the analysis in a dynamic, open-systems framework, Best is able to make connections between these mechanisms (e.g. the long-run shortage of new entrepreneurial firms can be related to the limited development of technology management capabilities at a regional level).

13. The shortage was evident from my own search for studies to illustrate this chapter, which yielded mostly implicit or quasi-realists. The editors of a leading CR text have reflected on this experience. While acknowledging that three (out of six) of their contributors illustrating contemporary realist practice 'do not make any explicit reference to realism', they argue that in practice the field contains 'much more work that is implicitly realist than that which is implicitly or explicitly postmodernist' Fleetwood and Ackroyd (2000: 19).

14. The authors cite Bhaskar (1975) in support of the argument that mechanism-based explanations usually invoke some sort of 'causal agent' that generates an observed relationship (Hedström and Swedberg 1998: 11). However, the 'social mechanisms' school take a contrary position to CR on the operation of these mechanisms, arguing that social world phenomena must always be explained on the basis of individual actors. This fundamental difference is clarified in the following statement:

> In the natural sciences, causal agents come in a variety of forms such as organic reactions in chemistry and natural selection in biology. In the social sciences, however, the elementary 'causal agents' are always individual actors, and intelligible social science explanations should always include explicit references to the causes and consequences of their actions. This principle of methodological individualism is intimately linked to the core idea of the mechanism approach: Understanding is enhanced by making explicit the underlying generative mechanisms that link one state or event to another, and in the social sciences, actions constitute this link. (Hedström and Swedberg 1998: 11–12)

15. Archer (1995: 102) encapsulates her detailed critique of structuration theory by stating that it involves 'sinking' rather than 'linking' the essential differences between structure and agency (cf. Giddens 1984; Stones 2001). By contrast, Archer's procedure of 'analytical dualism' is based on the CR concept of emergence: social structures and human agency are different strata (hence 'dualism'), whose interactions are only open to social scientific (hence 'analytical') inquiry. Danermark et al. (2002: 178–82) is a helpful summary of Archer's arguments.

References

Acs, Z.J. and Audretsch, D.B. (eds) (2003) *Handbook of Entrepreneurship Research: An interdisciplinary survey and introduction*. Dordrecht: Kluwer.

Ackroyd, S. and Fleetwood, S. (eds) (2000) *Critical Realism in Action in Organization and Management Studies*. London: Routledge.

Adams, G. and Hall, G. (1993) Influences on the growth of SMEs: an international comparison. *Entrepreneurship and Regional Development*, 5: 73–84.

Aldrich, H.E. and Auster, E.R. (1986) Even dwarfs started small: liabilities of age and their strategic implications. *Research in Organizational Behaviour*, 8: 165–98.

Aldrich, H.E. and Martinez, M.A. (2001) Many are called, but few are chosen: an evolutionary perspective for the study of entrepreneurship. *Entrepreneurship Theory and Development*, 25(4): 41–56.

Aldrich, H.E. and Zimmer, C. (1986) Entrepreneurship through social networks. In: D. Sexton and R. Smilor (eds), *The Art and Science of Entrepreneurship*. Cambridge, MA: Ballinger, pp. 2–23.

Archer, M. (1995) *Realist Social Theory: the morphogenetic approach*. Cambridge: Cambridge University Press.

Barkham, R., Gudgin, G., Hart, M. and Hanvey, E. (1996) *The Determinants of Small Firm Growth: An inter-regional study in the United Kingdom 1986–90 (Regional Policy and Development Series 12)*. London: Jessica Kingsley / Regional Studies Association.

Baert, P. (1998) *Social Theory in the Twentieth Century*. Cambridge: Polity.

Best, M.H. (2001) *The New Competitive Advantage: The renewal of American industry*. Oxford: Oxford University Press.

Bhaskar, R. (1975) *A Realist Theory of Science*. Leeds: Leeds Books (2nd edn (1979) Brighton: Harvester).

Bhaskar, R. (1979) *The Possibility of Naturalism*. Brighton: Harvester (2nd edn 1989, Hemel Hempstead: Harvester Wheatsheaf).

Blundel, R.K. (2002) Network evolution and the growth of artisanal firms: a tale of two regional cheesemakers. *Entrepreneurship and Regional Development*, 14(1): 1–30.

Boulding, K.E. (1956) *The Image: Knowledge in life and society*. Michigan, MI: University of Michigan Press.

Bowey, J. and Easton, G. (2003) A critical realist framework for explaining changes in entrepreneurial relationships. In: *Proceedings of the 19th IMP International Conference*, University of Lugarno, Switzerland.

Clark, P.A. (2000) *Organisations in Action: Competition between contexts*. London: Routledge.

Collier, A. (1994) *Critical Realism: An introduction to Roy Bhaskar's philosophy*. London: Verso.

Danermark, B., Ekström, M., Jakobsen, J. and Karlsson, J. (2002) *Explaining Society: Critical realism in the social sciences*. London: Routledge.

Davidsson, P., Low, M.B. and Wright, M. (2001) Editor's introduction: Low and MacMillan ten years on: achievements and future directions for entrepreneurship research. *Entrepreneurship Theory and Development*, 25(4): 5–15.

Davidsson, P. and Wiklund, J. (2001) Levels of analysis in entrepreneurship research: current research practice and suggestions for the future. *Entrepreneurship Theory and Development*, 25(4): 81–99.

Easton, G. (2000) Case research as a method for industrial networks: a realist apologia. In: S. Ackroyd and S. Fleetwood (eds) *Critical Realism in Action in Organization and Management Studies*. London: Routledge, pp. 205–19.

Fleetwood, S. (ed.) (1999) *Critical Realism in Economics: Development and Debate*. London: Routledge.

Fleetwood, S. and Ackroyd, S. (eds) (2004) *Critical Realist Applications in Organisation and Management Studies*. London: Routledge.

Frank, H. and Landström, H. (1997) Entrepreneurship and small business research in Europe – analysis and reflection. In: H. Landström, H. Frank and J.M. Veciana (eds), *Entrepreneurship and Small Business Research in Europe*. Aldershot: Avebury.

Giddens, A. (1984) *The Constitution of Society*. Cambridge: Polity.

Granovetter, M. (1985) Economic action and social structure: the problem of embeddedness. *American Journal of Sociology*, **91**: 481–510.

Harré, R. (1972) *The Philosophies of Science.* Oxford: Oxford University Press.

Hedström, P. and Swedberg, R. (eds) (1998) *Social Mechanisms: An analytical approach to social theory.* Cambridge: Cambridge University Press.

Johannisson, B. (2000) Networking and entrepreneurial growth. In D.L. Sexton and H. Landström (eds), *The Blackwell Handbook of Entrepreneurship.* Oxford: Blackwell.

Johannisson, B. and Monsted, M. (1997) Contextualizing entrepreneurial networking. *International Studies of Management and Organization*, **27**(3): 109–36.

Jones, C. (2001) Co-evolution of entrepreneurial careers, institutional rules and competitive dynamics in American film, 1895–1920. *Organization Studies*, **22**(6): 911–44 (Special Issue on Multi-level Analysis and Co-evolution).

Jones, O. and Conway, S. (2000) The social embeddedness of entrepreneurs: a re-reading of 'Against the Odds'. *Aston Business School Research Papers RP0023.* Birmingham: Aston University.

Junor, A. (2001) Critical realism comes to management. *Journal of Critical Realism*, **4**(1): 30–34.

Lawson, C. and Lorenz, E. (1999) Collective learning, tacit knowledge and regional innovative capacity. *Regional Studies*, **33**(4): 305–17.

Lawson, T. (1997) *Economics and Reality.* London: Routledge.

Layder, D. (1993) *New Strategies in Social Research.* Cambridge: Polity.

Low, M.B. and MacMillan, I.C. (1988) Entrepreneurship: past research and future challenges. *Journal of Management*, **14**(2): 139–61.

Miles, M.B. and Huberman, A.M. (1994) *Qualitative Data Analysis.* London: Sage.

Miri, R. and Watson, A. (2001) Critical realism and constructivism in strategy research: toward a synthesis. *Strategic Management Journal*, **22**: 1169–73.

Mutch, A. (2002) Actors and networks or agents and structures: towards a realist view of information systems. *Organization*, **9**(3): 477–96.

Neergaard, H. (1999) Networks as Vehicles of Internationalization: network relationships and the internationalization process of small furniture makers. Århus: Handelshøjskolen (unpublished Ph.D. thesis).

Parsons, S.D. (1999) Why the 'transcendental' in transcendental realism? In: S. Fleetwood (ed.), *Critical Realism in Economics: Development and debate.* London: Routledge, pp. 151–68.

Penrose, E.T. (1953) Rejoinder to Armen A. Alchian. *The American Economic Review*, **43**: 4.

Penrose, E.T. (1959) *The Theory of the Growth of the Firm.* Oxford: Basil Blackwell (3rd edn 1995, Oxford: Oxford University Press).

Penrose, E.T. (1960) The growth of the firm – a case study: the Hercules Powder Company. *Business History Review*, **34**: 1–23.

Pentland, B.T. (1999) Building process theory with narrative: from description to explanation. *Academy of Management Review*, **24**(4): 711–24.

Pettigrew, A.M. (1992) The character and significance of strategy process research. *Strategic Management Journal*, **13**: 5–16.

Porter, S. (2002) Critical realist ethnography: the case of racism and professionalism in a medical setting. In: S. Ackroyd and S. Fleetwood (eds), *Critical Realism in Action in Organization and Management Studies.* London: Routledge, pp. 141–60.

Potter, G. (2003) Critical realist strengths and weaknesses. *Journal of Critical Realism*, **2**(1): 161–5.

Ram, M. (1999) Trading places: the ethnographic process in small firms' research. *Entrepreneurship and Regional Development*, **11**(2): 95–108.

Ramachandran, K. and Ramnarayan, S. (1993) Entrepreneurial orientation and networking: some Indian evidence. *Journal of Business Venturing*, **8**: 513–24.

Richardson, G.B. (1972) The organisation of industry. *Economic Journal*, **82**: 883–96.

Roberts, J.M. (2001) Critical realism and the dialectic. *British Journal of Sociology*, **52**(4): 667–85.

Sayer, A. (1992) *Method in Social Science: A realist approach* (2nd edn). Routledge: London.

Sayer, A. (2000) *Realism and Social Science.* London: Sage.

Sayer, A. and Morgan, K. (1986) A modern industry in a declining region: links between method, theory and policy. In: D. Massey and R.A. Meegan (eds), *The Politics of Method*. London: Methuen.

Schumpeter, J. (1951) *Essays on Economic Topics.* Port Washington: Kennikat Press.

Staber, U. (1997) An ecological perspective on entrepreneurship in industrial districts. *Entrepreneurship and Regional Development*, 9(1): 45–64.

Stones, R. (2001) Refusing the realism–structuration divide. *European Journal of Social Theory*, 4(2): 177–97.

Subramaniyam, V. (2000) Critical realism and development programmes in Rural South India. *Journal of Critical Realism*, 4(1): 17–23.

Swedberg, R. (1991) *Joseph A. Schumpeter: his life and work*. Cambridge: Polity.

Swedberg, R. (ed.) (2000) *Entrepreneurship: the social science view*. Oxford: Oxford University Press.

Tsoukas, H. (1989) The validity of idiographic research explanations. *Academy of Management Review*, 14(4): 551–61.

Ucbasaran, D., Westhead, P. and Wright, M. (2001) The focus of entrepreneurial research: context and process issues. *Entrepreneurship Theory and Practice*, 25(4): 57–80.

Van de Ven, A.H. (1992) Suggestions for studying strategy process: a research note. *Strategic Managment Journal*, 13: 169–88.

Walters, B. and Young, D. (2001) Critical realism as a basis for economic methodology: a critique. *Review of Political Economy*, 13(4): 483–501.

Whittington, R. (1989) *Corporate Strategies in Recession and Recovery*. London: Unwin.

Zafirovski, M. (1999) Probing the social layers of entrepreneurship: outlines of the sociology of enterprise. *Entrepreneurship and Regional Development*, 11(4): 351–71.

3 Researching entrepreneurship as lived experience
Henrik Berglund

Introduction

> The basis of a *science* of conduct must be fixed principles of action, endur-
> ing and stable motives. It is doubtful, however, whether this is fundamentally
> the character of human life. What men want is not so much to get things that
> they want as it is to have interesting experiences. And the fact seems to be that
> an important condition of our interest in things is an element of the unan-
> ticipated, of novelty, of surprise. We must beware of the temptation to judge
> the nature of our conduct by the way in which we think about it.
>
> (Knight 1921: 53–4)

It is often recognized that entrepreneurship is to a great extent a form of art, a practice-oriented endeavour that requires a sensitive and committed engagement with a range of phenomena in the surrounding world. Still, much of the research and theory development favours large studies and positivist epistemology (Chandler and Lyon 2001), where the liveliness of entrepreneurship tends to be suspended in favour of 'scientific rigour'. There is, however, a growing interest among entrepreneurship researchers to expand the methodological toolbox and widen the scope of inquiry. In introducing a special issue on entrepreneurship theory development, Phan (2004: 619) emphasized the need for diverse and dynamic methods, claim-ing that 'to develop a catechism founded on positivist empiricism may hide the very grail we seek'. Instead Phan and many others (e.g. Busenitz et al. 2003; Steyaert 2003) urge researchers to complement research focused on individual and decontextualized factors with investigations of emergence, interpretation and intersections of various kinds. Sarasvathy (2004) thus invokes Simon (1996) to encourage a focus on the artificial, i.e. the inter-face between inner and outer environments, and proposes the rubric of design as a useful metaphor for entrepreneurship. Similarly Gartner et al. (2003) see enactment (Weick 1979) as a constructive way to comprehend opportunities in the context of entrepreneurial action.

This emphasis on enactive design and interpretation is congenial to philo-sophical phenomenology and phenomenologically inspired methodologies. At the core of phenomenology is an emphasis on 'returning to the things themselves', i.e. to the meaningful ways in which things are experienced, made sense of and enacted in everyday life. A thing in the phenomenological sense does not exist primarily in and of itself, but rather in the meaning that individuals attach to it. Such a conception of phenomena is fundamentally different from 'things' as normally conceived, i.e. in the sense of objective and *a priori* meaningful entities or institutions. This is not to suggest that there is no 'material world' out there, but rather that the world as we experience it is always meaningful to us. In the words of Maurice Merleau-Ponty (2002: xxii) we are 'condemned to meaning'. It is consequently the meanings things have for us, not the things in themselves, that affect our thoughts and behaviours and therefore these become a relevant focus of investigations.

The goal of phenomenological methods is to study the meanings of phenomena and human experiences in specific situations, and to try to capture and communicate these meanings in empathetic and lucid ways. As the entrepreneurship field is still young and grapples with fundamental issues such as the nature and role of entrepreneurial opportunities (Gartner et al. 2003), phenomenology could prove helpful in many ways. Phenomenological methods, as described below, can serve as a powerful tool for exploring and enriching received theoretical constructs such as risks and opportunities, by investigating how entrepreneurs actually interpret and enact them (e.g. Berglund and Hellström 2002). Phenomenology can also be used more directly to explore what meaningful experiences and strategies are associated with different situations such as deciding to start a venture or seeking financial assistance.

The ambition of this chapter is to introduce briefly some relevant aspects of philosophical phenomenology and to exemplify how phenomenological methods can be used to investigate entrepreneurship. To accomplish this, the chapter is structured as follows. First there is a brief review of the phenomenological tradition through the writings of Edmund Husserl and Martin Heidegger. This review is followed by a discussion of how the insights of philosophical phenomenology can be formalized and translated into practical guidelines for entrepreneurship research. Thereafter phenomenological method is illustrated through a worked example of entrepreneurial risk enactment. After that the potential contribution of phenomenological methods to entrepreneurship is elaborated in some detail, especially in relation to cognitive psychological and discursive approaches.

Phenomenological philosophy

Phenomenology deals with a fundamental philosophical question: What is real? In our everyday lives, the realness of the things we encounter is seldom questioned. In modern philosophical discussions, however, the question is often central, and many contemporary social theories such as social constructionism (Berger and Luckmann 1966) and structuration theory (Giddens 1984) draw explicitly on the phenomenological tradition in addressing it.[1]

In the Cartesian tradition the human mind is seen as a passive interpreter of sense data. Phenomenologists object to this description and instead see humans as intentional beings, meaning that each person always actively configures meaning by imposing order on the world (von Eckartsberg 1986). Phenomenologists thus argue that the world and the objects we perceive exist to us through the meanings we give to them, through an act of interpretation. This does not necessarily deny the existence of an external physical world independent of our perceptions, but it does imply that the only way things exist to us is through the way we interpret and give meaning to them. Things such as books, business partners or risks may in this sense exist as more or less independent entities, bombarding us with sense data of different kinds. However, this is not how we know and experience them. Instead, we live in a world filled with books, business partners and risks because we stretch forth into the world and interpret it in terms of those familiar objects. This interpretative way of relating to the world should, according to phenomenology, form the basis for statements about reality (Karlsson 1993).

The contemporary development of phenomenological methodology is rather diverse and has taken place mainly in pedagogy (van Manen 1990), nursing (Benner 1994), and as a general methodology in psychology (von Eckartsberg 1986; Giorgi 1985; Smith 1996). These methods are also influenced by related and more contemporary developments in philosophy and social science such as symbolic interactionism and social phenomenology, and by other phenomenologists and hermeneuticists such as Maurice Merleau-Ponty and Hans-Georg Gadamer. However, phenomenological methods tend to draw mainly on ideas originally developed by Edmund Husserl and Martin Heidegger (Koch 1995; Crotty 1996; Paley 1998). Therefore the following section introduces Husserl's and Heidegger's ideas regarding the nature and basis of human knowledge before discussing phenomenological methods.

Husserl and transcendental phenomenology

Edmund Husserl is commonly recognized as the father of modern phenomenology. He started his career as a mathematician but then turned to philosophy, where he found that the prevailing scientific method was failing to provide true knowledge. Measuring only empirically available properties of reality, unconditional truth was always going to be beyond the reach of scientific inquiry. In Husserl's view the problem was that psychologists and others who tested hypotheses and used specific measurement methods were epistemologically flawed because they focused too much on operational definitions and contingent measures, and too little on actual human experience (Colaizzi 1978).

Husserl, who aspired to establish philosophy and science on 'a basis of unimpeachable reality' (Lauer 1965: 4), was certain that true knowledge could not be reached by observation of empirical manifestations. To Husserl knowledge had to be grounded in individuals' experiences and his alternative was therefore to return to 'the things themselves' (zu den Sachen selbst), i.e. to focus on how individuals truly experience and understand phenomena in their everyday lives. This meant a radical empiricism grounded in an intuitive and unbiased understanding of phenomena as they present themselves to consciousness.[2] In focusing on consciousness and not the empirical world, Husserl wanted appreciation to be holistic and comprise all conceivable aspects of an experienced phenomenon. Therefore he gave no priority to that which was deemed scientific or *a priori* real. The basis for true knowledge of a phenomenon or thing was to be found in the whole range of experiences we have of it as we experience it in everyday life. Phenomena should therefore be analysed for what they are, intuitively and directly, not as what they mean, theoretically and from a particular standpoint.

Husserl wanted to establish a solid and universally valid ground for knowledge about phenomena. To accomplish this, he developed a process consisting of a number of steps aiming to eliminate all preconceptions and reduce experienced phenomena to their essences (Husserl 1982). To Husserl it is because our experiences are grounded on such essences that we are able to find order in our experiences and recognize a meaningful world of things (ibid.: 105). In short, this process entails two steps. First, when meditating on a phenomenon one should bracket or disregard one's natural attitude to things. All the socialized and learned prejudices we have should be suspended so that the phenomenon being contemplated emerges as pure phenomenon. Second, the essential nature of the phenomenon is reached by elaborating it in our minds. By freely and imaginatively varying and thematizing different aspects of the phenomenon, we are able to understand the limits of its identity, which are its transcendental essences and which are its conditional features. Take for example a book: the number of pages and colour of the cover may be seen as conditional features, whereas the existence of pages and a cover may be considered essential.

The goal is thus to focus on the phenomenon as experienced in the everyday life world, then completely bracket its contingent aspects and elaborate the meaning of the pure phenomenon in order to understand its essence. This may seem paradoxical, drawing on a holistic appreciation of life-world experiences and then suspending these in order to reach transcendental essences. It is important, however, to remember that Husserl was strongly influenced by Cartesianism, with its rational ambitions and division of the world into consciousness and matter. From that perspective there could be no other true basis for knowledge than consciousness.

Heidegger and hermeneutic phenomenology

Heidegger was a student of Husserl's but reacted to his teacher's Cartesianism. In fact ever since Plato philosophers had appealed to some form of higher ground to validate worldly experiences. Plato had the ideal world, Dark Age philosophers had God and Descartes had the subject's experience of being. Husserl, while emphasizing the importance of a holistic understanding of experiences, saw no other option but to retreat to transcendental essences when explaining how we can truly know the world.

Heidegger endorsed Husserl's focus on a holistic appreciation of the world and of phenomena, but fundamentally opposed the idea of bracketing as a means of reaching true knowledge (Heidegger 1962; Dreyfus 1991). To Heidegger we always already exist in-the-world and it is therefore in our ever ongoing and situated activities that the source of meaning is ultimately located.[3] As for Husserl, physical objects or sensory data have no meaning in themselves, but as opposed to Husserl, Heidegger did not believe that our experiences rely on transcendental essences to make sense. Meaning instead resides in what Heidegger called a referential totality: the historically learned practices and background understandings we have of the world as a holistic web of interrelated things. Meaning is thus not some stable essence that is *mediated* by interpretations and that can be reached by bracketing or digging through our holistic web of experiences and practices. Meaning resides *in that web*. As an example, consider the following description of coming to a home and being greeted by the smell of freshly baked cookies:

> The pleasant associations we have with the smell of freshly baked cookies are not created by us exclusively, and certainly not at the moment of walking in the door. They are memories of our own previous pleasurable experiences with cookie baking, and they tap into social memories of the meaning of home cooking and a caregiver welcoming us, and deeper human memories of being fed and protected by caregivers. Those memories swirl around us. They are not confined to some dusty file cabinet in the mind, waiting to be called up so we can interpret that lovely smell. They come to light because the fragrance has directed our attention to them. The fragrance is part of a holistic matrix of things and relations that say homely pleasures, care and love. (Steiner 2002)

The meaning of a phenomenon is consequently a result of the historical and holistic ways in which a person has come to make sense of a certain aspect of the world. Similarly, the world becomes better known to us as individuals when we look at more and more aspects of the world and our lives, and try to relate these to each other in an ever more comprehensive structure (Dreyfus 1991: 32). Heidegger's phenomenology thus rests on a truly holistic understanding of the world where understanding any aspect requires knowledge of the greater context of which it is a part.

Phenomenological methods

It is clear that Husserl and Heidegger differ in some of their basic assumptions. These differences are briefly summed up in Table 3.1. Despite these differences, Husserl, Heidegger and other phenomenologists all reject 'natural science' approaches and propose a 'human science' model of understanding human experiences. In doing so they acknowledge that as researchers our privileged access to meaning lies not in measures and numbers but in our capacity to understand and find meaning in other people's stories and experiences (von Eckartsberg 1986). They also share a radical bottom–up approach to understanding reality which emphasizes the role of 'the things themselves' as they present themselves as meaningful to individuals in everyday experiences. In so far as behaviour and thinking are truly influenced by the meanings phenomena and situations have for us, this is a significant point with methodological consequences. It suggests that an important goal of entrepreneurial research should be to capture and communicate the meaning of entrepreneurs' experiences in everyday life.[4]

When moving from philosophy to methodology it is common to distinguish between reflexive and empirical methods, where reflexive researchers use their own experience as data (Colaizzi 1978). It is of course possible to conduct reflexive phenomenological research in entrepreneurship, but this would require the researcher to be in a suitable position to do so, something that is not very common (see, however, Johannisson 2002). There are also differences among empirical methods, some of which lean toward Husserl's

Table 3.1   *Summary of differences between Husserlian and Heideggerian phenomenology*

	Husserl	Heidegger
Metaphysical focus	Epistemological	Ontological
Description of the individual	Person living in a world of objects	Person exists as being in and of the world
Knowledge	Ahistorical	Historical
Enabling the social	Essences are shared	Culture, practices and history are shared
Method for gaining knowledge	Bracketing affords access to true knowledge	Cultural interpretation 'grounds' any knowing

pure descriptions and some of which emphasize the hermeneutic elements of Heidegger's phenomenology (e.g. Karlsson 1993; Colaizzi 1978; Moustakas 1994). As seen above, Husserl sought transcendental knowledge and developed an intricate method for suspending conditional features in order to reach transcendental essences of consciousness. Heidegger on the other hand saw human beings as part and parcel of the world, and therefore saw engaged coping and being immersed in the historically developed web of practices and background knowledge as the fundamental basis for knowing. To illustrate the variety of phenomenological methods available I will briefly present two approaches that can be said to represent polar positions in this respect.

Objectively describing the essential structure of a lived experience
Amadeo Giorgi (1985) represents a Husserlian tradition that seeks to transfer Husserl's philosophical method of reducing lived experiences to their pure essences to a similarly rigorous empirical methodology. The ambition is to collect respondents' lived experiences of a phenomenon, and from those idiosyncratic experiences approach the universal and general aspects of the phenomenon. After a verbatim transcription of the interview protocols, the data analysis consists of four steps:

1. Read and re-read the protocols in order to gain a sense of the whole of the phenomenon as described. This holistic understanding is important for determining how the parts are constituted.
2. Divide the protocol into isolated 'meaning units'. A meaning unit is a purely descriptive term that contains a specific meaning relevant for the study. The division should be based on the researcher's general disciplinary perspective while maintaining a strict focus on the phenomenon being researched. Here it is important not to let one's disciplinary preknowledge dominate the research but allow unexpected meanings to emerge.
3. Translate the protocols from the language of the respondent to the disciplinary language of the researcher. This step corresponds to Husserl's free imaginative variation. The researcher uses his or her 'disciplinary intuition' to translate the subject's everyday language into the researcher's more narrow disciplinary language. Giorgi emphasizes that this step does not entail any interpretation but is purely a matter of describing the essence of the meaning unit in disciplinary language.
4. Synthesize the transformed meaning units to a consistent statement of the structure of the phenomenon. This step is similar to the previous one but here it is the transformed meaning units that are subjected to free imaginative variation. The result is a description of the essential structure of the lived experience from the perspective of the discipline.

By following this procedure, Giorgi claims to develop objective knowledge of the subject's experiences and not necessarily of what actually took place. The result is an objective description of the transcendental structure of the phenomenon as it is experienced.

Poetically re-creating the feeling of a lived experience

Max van Manen's (1990) main interest is not pure phenomenological intuitions. His method instead tries empathetically to capture and transmit the sense and feeling of living through different experiences. Van Manen's approach is explicitly hermeneutic and recognizes the role of the researcher as an interpreter and even inventor of meaning. The goal is to try to describe a lived experience in a way that retains and communicates the essential meaning of that experience. To accomplish this van Manen proposes that researchers first engage themselves thoroughly in the phenomenon to be investigated. The researcher should then reflect on what the essential elements or themes of the interview subjects' experience are. Such themes 'are not objects or generalizations; metaphorically speaking they are more like knots in the webs of our experiences, around which certain lived experiences are spun and thus lived through as meaningful wholes' (van Manen 1990: 90). These themes are then used to craft a composite narrative account which resonates with the original experiences of the participants. This is a fairly extensive process where the researcher engages in a prolonged process of reflective writing and re-writing. Re-writing in this sense does not mean mere editing, but entails new readings of the text that each time reveal novel insights. The end product is a narrative description that is said to capture the essence of an experience if it 'reawakens or shows us the lived quality and significance in a fuller or deeper manner' (ibid.: 10). To capture the essence of a phenomenon is thus to re-create an experience in a way that resonates with the reader, something that requires a poetic or aesthetic quality in the text.

There are benefits and drawbacks with both approaches. Researchers such as Giorgi are criticized for underestimating the interpretative role of the researcher (Karlsson 1993) as well as for writing in an academic prose which loses the liveliness of the phenomenon and in doing so fails to capture the essential experience of the phenomenon (Todres 1998). Similarly, researchers in van Manen's tradition are criticized for drifting too far from the phenomena in themselves and instead focusing on individuals' subjective experiences of phenomena (Crotty 1996). Many phenomenological methods seek a middle ground between outlining the general structure of an experienced phenomenon (what is it?) and re-creating a local experience of encountering a phenomenon (what is it like?) (e.g. Smith 1996; Smith and Osborn 2003). In the following section such a middle-ground approach is illustrated with a worked example of entrepreneurial risk enactment.

A worked example of phenomenological methodology
In a recent project (Berglund and Hellström 2002), a phenomenological method was used to investigate risk among a number of high-tech entrepreneurs in Sweden. This study sought to elucidate the variety of ways in which risk is experienced and enacted by entrepreneurial high-tech innovators as they develop their ventures, and the example illustrates how phenomenological methodology may be used in terms of sampling, data collection, analysis and how the results can be written up and presented.

Sampling
Since statistics are of no concern to phenomenological methods, sampling was purposive, focusing on getting a manageable and relevant group of individuals with whom the investigated phenomenon was relatively salient. The purpose was not to present intrinsically interesting cases nor to represent a general population, but rather to gain a more detailed picture of the phenomenon (Smith et al. 1995). In our case we identified 12 high-tech entrepreneurs distributed across Sweden, who had been active in their technology-based ventures for at least one year, or until such time as the venture had started to stabilize. They had all taken a key role in driving the process of inventing, producing and marketing a technological innovation, whether in the field of information technologies, biotech or advanced services.

Collecting data
When gathering data it is important to be flexible enough to accommodate the richness inherent in the experiences of the participants while staying focused on the research question and the phenomenon explored. To accomplish this we used semi- to non-structured interviews which gave respondents room to speak and allowed us to follow respondents' leads into novel and unexpected areas. The interviews were conducted in the firms and lasted, on average, two hours each. The initial discussions concerned the venture and innovation in general but gradually moved towards the issue of risk, which was discussed very broadly as related to the firm and the innovation, and with regard to the participant, the company and the business environment. The method does not demand detailed content or textual analysis, so taking notes was seen as a viable alternative to taping. In this case we were between two and four interviewers who took turns to interview and document the discussions in detailed notes. The notes were later used to identify specific quotes that were used to distinguish between researcher and interviewee in the results presentation.

Analysis

All interview protocols were read by all the interviewers in order to establish interpretative flexibility and common meaning. In this way the interpretation of the general narratives, as well as of specific quotations, was
agreed upon. The individual protocols were then re-read line by line and
broken down into discrete parts, not according to syntactic rules such as
sentences but with respect to visible changes in meaning, i.e. meaning units
(MUs) (e.g. Karlsson 1993; Giorgi 1985). To illustrate how the interview
texts were divided into MUs, an excerpt from the original (translated) protocol is included in Table 3.2. As shown in the table, each MU was associated with a tentative descriptive concept and broken out of the text together
with its corresponding statements. When the whole text had been broken
down in this way, the resulting list of MUs was re-read and discussed within
the research group. As the researchers worked their way through the list,
MUs with similar meanings were cut out of the original document and
pasted into a new document with a tentative category heading. Each new
MU on the list was similarly either put in an existing category or given its
own new category heading. This process generated a great number of categories, and during the process some categories that were found to be
similar were merged and others split up until all MUs had been clustered
into categories that were agreed to capture specific homogeneous qualities

*Table 3.2   Extraction of meaning units and descriptive concepts from the
interview protocol*

Standard treatment of risk	*NN says he has not thought of risks all that explicitly, but that there is a SWOT analysis in the business plan. These risk analyses are of a fairly general character and you just copy them from a textbook or another business plan.*
External validation	*NN thought the idea was strong. 'I had an idea, a logical trick, concerning how such industrial logical problems could be solved.' He tried to validate the basic idea many times by testing it against colleagues. 'I tried to get my academic colleagues to shoot down the idea on several occasions, but it withstood their attempts. That way I figured the technological risk was accounted for.' In terms of markets NN had seen many problems around in the world, i.e. the Arianne rocket and JAS fighter jets had problems. He therefore judged the potential upside to be big.*
Generic idea	*Another reason the firm was started was that the idea was broad. 'The idea is like a shotgun; it's so versatile that it can be adapted to new applications, if the initially chosen ones for some reason wouldn't work. These additional exits help minimizing the risks.'*

of what was said by the participants. The three MUs above were finally included in the categories 'Risk administration', 'External innovation audits' and 'Technological prowess' respectively (see Table 3.3). The categories and their interrelationships were then focused on in more detail and similar themes were clustered into factors and overarching super-factors, as shown in Table 3.3.

During the analysis procedure, interpretations are continuously made by the researchers as categories and factors are developed. By re-reading the original protocol and questioning the bases of categorizations, the researchers actively sought to minimize the use of pre-existing theoretical categories and be true to the participants' original expressions. If the MUs

Table 3.3   Super-factors, factors and categories of risk and innovation

Super-factors	Factors	Categories
Innovation risk encountered	Human capital	Human capital risk
		Abundance of slack and lack of coordination
	Pace and priority	Missing the time slot
		Lack of time to evaluate decisions
		First-mover risk
	The world moves	*Force majeure*
		Perception of venture capitalists
		Product competition
		Market response
Innovation risk affected	Activating social networks	Managing risks through partnerships
		Matching partnerships to venture pace
		Network activation
	Risk learning	Internalizing routines
		Affecting perceptions of risk
	Risk incrementalism	Risk administration
		Venture incrementalism
		Opportunistic adaptation
	Maintaining venture agility	The venture as a test-case
		Opportunity scanning/market pull
	Creating and sustaining autonomy	External innovation audits
		Technological prowess
		Piggybacking
		Creation of momentum

Source: Berglund and Hellström (2002).

clearly coincide with existing theoretical categories, such categories may however be used (cf. Smith and Osborn 2003).

Results
The results section is a natural extension of the analysis process and contains further interpretative elements. To accomplish a clear distinction between the participants and the researchers, the participants' accounts were presented using direct quotes. The style of such a results presentation is shown with an excerpt from the original article in Box 3.1. This results

---

BOX 3.1   CREATING AND SUSTAINING AUTONOMY

Several of the interviewed innovators found it useful to utilize different kinds of *external innovation audits* in order to ensure innovative integrity of the venture. One way in which an interviewee achieved this is given in the following quote: 'I tried to get my academic colleagues to shoot down the idea on several occasions, but it withstood their attempts. That way I figured the technological risk was accounted for.' Another, more externally oriented version was that 'The most important thing is not to get the product out on the market in a certain space of time, but rather to get an external actor to validate the concept by showing an interest in that particular technology.' *Technological prowess* is a version of the previous category, where the innovator uses the strength of the technology to achieve autonomy. One example of this was: 'The idea is like a shotgun; it's so versatile that it can be adapted to new applications, if the initially chosen ones for some reason wouldn't work. These additional exits help minimizing the risks.' On the administrative/financial side we have found *piggybacking* to be the rule rather than the exception. Piggybacking is clearly a commonplace informal strategy for furthering the autonomy of the venture, e.g.: 'Too little and too dedicated money is another risk. We took money budgeted by S [public utility] for machine purchases and used part of it for developing the innovation . . . . It's easier to obtain forgiveness than permission.' The last category under this general factor relates to the *creation of momentum* for purposes of getting into and staying in the race as an autonomous player. One innovator addressed this phenomenon directly and stated that: 'In a short period of time we have met numerous VC, recruited personnel, made 350 presentations and presented at eight trade-fairs. This has kept the wheels spinning . . . one keeps up the momentum.'

---

section shows how the factor 'Creating and sustaining autonomy' is described using the categories 'External innovation audits', 'Technological prowess', 'Piggybacking' and 'Creation of momentum'.

Summary of methodological procedure
As with much qualitative research, the results are not generalizable in the statistical sense. Instead the hierarchy of risk-related factors and categories, plus their elaboration and discussion, helps produce a relatively comprehensive and varied account of how risk is experienced and enacted by a sample of high-tech entrepreneurs in Sweden. The ambition was to increase understanding of how entrepreneurs perceive and deal with the phenomenon of risk in the course of developing their ventures, but also to explore specific strategies that may be employed by practitioners and used by researchers for further theorizing. In the original paper we used the results to discuss and elaborate on previous research on entrepreneurship and risk (see Berglund and Hellström 2002), but as suggested by Giorgi and van Manen, phenomenological results can be used in many different ways. The next section touches more generally on the potential advantages and drawbacks of a phenomenological approach.

Relevance and potential contributions to entrepreneurship
Phenomenology in a methodological context
The theoretical potential and methodological position of applied phenomenology can be illustrated more clearly by positioning it in relation to cognitive psychology and discursive approaches to entrepreneurship (cf. Smith 1996). In the realm of cognition, research on the use of biases, heuristics and cognitive schemata (Baron 1998; Busenitz and Barney 1997; Mitchell et al. 2002) is rather common. While not all cognitive research on entrepreneurship draws on 'cold cognitions',[5] research tends to focus on cognitive processes (i.e. neglecting specific content or context) where the entrepreneurs' expressions, usually captured using questionnaires and scales, are taken to reflect relatively stable cognitive mechanisms. On the other side there is a growing interest in narrative and discursive approaches to the phenomenon of entrepreneurship. Here researchers (e.g. Hjort and Steyaert 2004) investigate and interpret entrepreneurial expressions and events in relation to emerging and pre-existing discourses. Researchers in the narrative tradition tend to focus on the stories through which entrepreneurial actions and events receive their meaning. They are therefore somewhat reluctant to connect these situated narratives to underlying cognitions.

Cognitive researchers thus seek to isolate entrepreneurs' cognitive processes whereas discursively oriented writers investigate local stories. Phenomenological methods can be seen as occupying a niche in between, by focusing on the way lived experiences are interpreted, what meanings phenomena have for individuals and the strategies by which these phenomena are engaged. A phenomenological analysis may thus enrich findings from areas dominated by quantitative cognition studies by providing 'thicker' elaborations of how things such as entrepreneurial risk-taking are enacted and given meaning by specific entrepreneurs. Such investigations could both develop new theoretical constructs and enhance the potency of existing ones. Phenomenological methods can also contribute to the discursive tradition by providing detailed illustrations of how prevailing discourses are interpreted and made sense of, or by constructing novel narratives based on how individuals think about and deal with specific issues (cf. van Manen 1990).

Limits and criticism of phenomenological methods
Phenomenological methods are often criticized for reasons common to most qualitative methodology. Here I will mention two specific criticisms that are especially relevant to phenomenology, namely its reliance on interpretation and its focus on the individual.

Since findings are grounded in participants' life-world experiences, one main objection is the methods' reliance on interpretation. There is admittedly a fair amount of interpretation in most phenomenological studies. The interpretation is also inevitably double as entrepreneurs first interpret and express their own experiences, after which the researcher interprets these interpretations. One may, however, persuasively argue that most quantitative methods involve at least as much interpretation: in defining the phenomenon to be investigated, in the reduction of variables to be studied, in the choice of indicators to be used, by the respondent who interprets the questions (e.g. in a questionnaire) and by the researcher interpretating the numerical results. The review of philosophical phenomenology also made clear that interpretation is not so much a problem as a basic condition for understanding meaningful experiences. Such understanding is always grounded in individual experiences and framed in a social and cultural context, so while interpretations may seem more or less plausible, the interpretative element is unavoidable in the human sciences (cf. Taylor 1971).

Another criticism is the methodological emphasis on the individual. The method emphasizes individuals' experiences, and the meanings of phenomena are seen primarily in terms of how specific individuals interpret them. Applied phenomenological methods may therefore be accused of reifying the primacy of individuals in entrepreneurship (cf. Ogbor 2000). However, with Heidegger, the basis for intelligibility shifted from the individual consciousness to the historical and social embeddedness of people.

The results of phenomenological studies therefore include the greater context as a vital source of individual interpretations. It is, however, true that the method favours individual accounts.

However, the issue of methods is not primarily one of right or wrong but rather a matter of 'fit', where the phenomenon and the knowledge interest of the researcher should guide the choice of method. As the entrepreneurship field is relatively young and tries to come to terms with fundamental issues regarding what its object is, what questions are relevant, and if it can be studied at all (e.g. Davidsson 2003; Gartner 2001), phenomenology provides a constructive and accessible methodology for deeply exploring and revisiting different topics from the perspective of the entrepreneurs' meaningful lived experiences. More such descriptions and perspectives should help increase awareness and understanding about how entrepreneurs are motivated to act as well as what cognitive and practical strategies they employ. Such investigations do not allow for causal prediction and control of behaviours, but can complement more quantitatively oriented findings and thereby permit more thoughtful actions among entrepreneurs as well as policy-makers, researchers, teachers, venture capitalists and incubator managers. Phenomenological knowledge in this sense does not inform so much as enlighten practice.

Conclusion

As indicated in the introduction, positivist investigations of entrepreneurship run the risk of missing 'the very grail we seek' (Phan 2004). The reason proposed here is that entrepreneurs as well as the commonly conceptualized and measured attributes of entrepreneurship are lifted out of the contexts and life worlds in which they receive their meaning. The view of entrepreneurship as difficult to describe in terms of stable and objectively existing entities is also reflected in recent theories which give local sense-making and emergence priority over stable plans and isolated decisions (e.g. Sarasvathy 2001; Gartner et al. 2003). In this light, phenomenological methods can be seen as a structured way of investigating how popular concepts and common events in entrepreneurship (e.g. opportunity discovery, risk-taking, business planning) as well as less explored aspects (e.g. involvement of self, view of time) are experienced, given meaning and translated into action by entrepreneurs. Phenomenological methods are especially well suited for investigating the gaps between real-life occurrences and theoretical concepts on the one hand and individuals' interpretations of these occurrences or concepts on the other (Smith 1996). As shown in the case of risk, phenomenological investigations can enrich concepts theoretically and give them fuller and broader meaning by exemplifying how they are manifested in entrepreneurs' lived experiences.

In addition to the methodological contribution, the philosophical underpinnings of phenomenology have been used more directly to theorize entrepreneurship. Much entrepreneurship research seeks to understand the relationship between entrepreneurs and their life worlds via entrepreneurial cognitions (e.g. Krueger 2003), Scott Shane's person–opportunity nexus program (2003), and Saras Sarasvathy's (2001) notion of effectuation. These theories all entertain a view of entrepreneurs as contextually embedded human beings trying to make sense of their local and extended life worlds. Some writers have used phenomenology and hermeneutics to explicitly theorize entrepreneurial action. One example is Israel Kirzner's student Don Lavoie (1991), who sees entrepreneurs as cultural interpreters. Lavoie rejects the notion that entrepreneurial discovery is either systematic search or arbitrary alertness: 'profit opportunities are not independent atoms but connected parts of a whole perspective on the world. And the perspective is in turn part of a continuing cultural tradition' (Lavoie 1991: 45–6).

Phenomenological theory and methods thus seem to suit the needs of entrepreneurship researchers since the field is young, struggles with conceptual definitions and faces questions regarding its proper focus and identity, and since entrepreneurship is increasingly becoming theoretically infused with personal meaning and interpretations via terms such as emergence, enactment and effectuation.

Notes

1.   The modern use of the term phenomenology is rooted in Immanuel Kant's distinction between 'that which shows itself' (phaenomenon) and 'the thing in itself' (noumenon).
2.   Phenomenology is therefore not a simple critique of positivism. Husserl rather claimed that: 'If "*Positivism*" is tantamount to an absolutely unprejudiced grounding of all sciences on the "positive", that is to say, on what can be seized upon originaliter, then *we* are the genuine positivists' (Husserl 1982: 39).
3.   Heidegger completely rejects the dualism of mind and world. The meaning of 'in' in the phrase in-the-world should therefore not be seen as describing objects in spatial relation to one and other such as 'I live in Gothenburg', but in its involved and existential meaning such as 'I am in love' or 'he is in business'. Since we as humans have *always already* lived in-the-world, the world has always already had natural meaning for us (Dreyfus 1991: 40–45).
4.   It is of course very difficult, perhaps even impossible, to fully capture and communicate lived experience. It is therefore important to remember that phenomenological research 'is always in conflict with its material, which is beyond language and concept' (Schütz 1982: 70).
5.   Cold cognitions usually refer to reasoned and deliberate cognitions. These are often contrasted with warm or hot cognitions, which rely more on affect and emotions.

Recommended further reading

Benner, P. (ed.) (1994) *Interpretive Phenomenology: Embodiment, caring and ethics in health and illness.* Thousand Oaks, CA: Sage. This edited book discusses the implications of Heideggerian phenomenology with special emphasis on the nursing profession. The first half of the book introduces the philosophical background and the other half describes a number of studies.

Giorgi, A. (1985) *Phenomenology and Psychological Research*. Pittsburgh, PA: Duquesne University Press. Giorgi is an authority in the Husserlian tradition of phenomenological psychology. This book describes his research programme, including a detailed description of his method.

Packer, M. (1985) Hermeneutic inquiry in the study of human conduct. *American Psychologist*, **40**: 1081–93. Oft-cited paper that compares hermeneutics to the empirical and rational traditions in psychology. Emphasis is placed on knowledge claims and explanations of human action.

Smith, J.A. (ed.) (2003) *Qualitative Psychology: A practical guide to research methods*. London: Sage. Practical handbook of qualitative methods that includes detailed guidelines for conducting research using most of the major approaches. Includes chapters on phenomenology by Amadeo Giorgi and Jonathan Smith.

Smith, J., Harré, R. and van Langenhove, L. (1995) Idiography and the case study. In *Rethinking Psychology*, ed. Smith, J., Harré, R. and van Langenhove, L. London: Sage, pp. 59–69. This book provides an exposé of the developments of psychological research from empirical and cognitive towards more discursive approaches. The specific chapter contains an interesting discussion of the tradeoffs inherent in different methodological approaches, viz. view of individual, sample size and time frame.

Spinosa, C., Flores, F. and Dreyfus, H. (2001) *Disclosing New Worlds: Entrepreneurship, democratic action, and the cultivation of solidarity*. Cambridge, MA: MIT Press. This brief volume discusses how concepts and approaches from Heideggerian phenomenology can be used to comprehend entrepreneurship as a practical skill involving a heightened sensitivity to everyday anomalies.

References

Baron, R. (1998) Cognitive mechanisms in entrepreneurship: Why and when entrepreneurs think differently than other people. *Journal of Business Venturing*, **13**(4): 275–94.

Benner, P. (ed.) (1994) *Interpretive Phenomenology: Embodiment, caring and ethics in health and illness*. Thousand Oaks, CA: Sage.

Berger, P. and Luckmann, T. (1966) *The Social Construction of Reality: A treatise in the sociology of knowledge*. New York: Doubleday.

Berglund, H. and Hellström, T. (2002) Enacting risk in independent technological innovation. *International Journal of Risk Assessment and Management*, **3**(2/3/4): 205–21.

Busenitz, L.G., West, G.P., Shepherd, D., Nelson, T., Chandler, G.N. and Zacharakis, A. (2003) Entrepreneurship research in emergence: Past trends and future directions. *Journal of Management*, **29**(3): 285–308.

Busenitz, L.W. and Barney, J.B. (1997) Differences between entrepreneurs and managers in large organizations: Biases and heuristics in strategic decision-making. *Journal of Business Venturing*, **12**(1): 9–30.

Chandler, G. and Lyon, D. (2001) Issues of research design and construct measurement in entrepreneurship research: The past decade. *Entrepreneurship Theory and Practice*, **25**(4): 101–14.

Colaizzi, P. (1978) Psychological research as the phenomenologist views it. In R. Valle and M. King, (eds), *Existential Phenomenological Alternative for Psychology*. New York: Oxford University Press, pp. 48–71.

Crotty, M. (1996) *Phenomenology and Nursing Research*. Melbourne: Churchill Livingstone.

Davidsson, P. (2003) The domain of entrepreneurship research: Some suggestions. In J. Katz and S. Shepherd (eds), *Advances in Entrepreneurship, Firm Emergence and Growth*. Oxford, UK: Elseveir/JAI Press, **6**: 315–72.

Dreyfus, H. (1991) *Being-in-the-World: A commentary on Heidegger's being and time, division I*. Cambridge, MA: MIT Press.

Gartner, W.B. (2001) Is there an elephant in entrepreneurship? Blind assumptions in theory development. *Entrepreneurship Theory and Practice*, **25**(4): 27–39.

Gartner, W.B., Carter, N.M. and Hills, G.E. (2003) The Language of Opportunity. In C. Steyaert and D. Hjort (eds), *New Movements in Entrepreneurship*. Cheltenham, UK and Northampton, MA, USA: Edward Elgar.

Giddens, A. (1984) *The Constitution of Society: Outline of the theory of structuration*. Berkeley, CA: University of California Press.

Giorgi, A. (1985) *Phenomenology and Psychological Research*. Pittsburgh, PA: Duquesne University Press.

Heidegger, M. (1962) *Being and Time*. New York: Harper and Row.

Hjort, D. and Steyaert, C. (eds) (2004) *Narrative and Discursive Approaches in Entrepreneurship*. Cheltenham, UK and Northampton, MA, USA: Edward Elgar.

Husserl, E. (1982) *Ideas Pertaining to a Pure Phenomenology and to a Phenomenological Philosophy*. 1st book: *General Introduction to a Pure Phenomenology*, trans. by F. Kersten. The Hague: Martinus Nijhoff.

Johannisson, B. (2002) *Enacting Entrepreneurship Using Auto-Ethnography to Study Organization Creation*. Conference on Ethnographic Organizational Studies. University of St Gallen, Switzerland.

Karlsson, G. (1993) *Psychological Qualitative Research from a Phenomenological Perspective*. Stockholm: Almquist & Wiksell International.

Knight, F. (1921) *Risk, Uncertainty and Profit*. Boston, MA and New York: Houghton Mifflin.

Koch, T. (1995) Interpretive approaches in nursing research: The influence of Husserl and Heidegger. *Journal of Advanced Nursing*, **21**: 827–36.

Krueger, N.F., Jr (2003) The cognitive psychology of entrepreneurship. In Z. Acs and D.B. Audtresch (eds), *Handbook of Entrepreneurial Research*. London: Kluwer Law International.

Lauer, Q. (1965). Introduction. In E. Husserl (ed.), *Phenomenology and the Crisis of Philosophy*, trans. and ed. Q. Lauer. New York: Harper and Row.

Lavoie, D. (1991) The discovery and interpretation of profit opportunities: Culture and the Kirznerian entrepreneur. In B. Berger (ed.), *The Culture of Entrepreneurship*. San Francisco: ICS Press.

Merleau-Ponty, M. (2002) *Phenomenology of Perception*. London: Routledge.

Mitchell, R.K., Smith, J.B., Morse, E.A., Seawright, K.W., Peredo, A.-M. and McKenzie, B. (2002) Are entrepreneurial cognitions universal? Assessing entrepreneurial cognitions across cultures. *Entrepreneurship Theory and Practice*, **26**(4): 9–32.

Moustakas, C. (1994) *Phenomenological Research Methods*. London: Sage.

Ogbor, J.O. (2000) Mythicizing and reification in entrepreneurial discourse: Ideology-critique of entrepreneurial studies. *Journal of Management Studies*, **37**(5): 605–35.

Paley, J. (1998) Misinterpretive phenomenology: Heidegger, ontology, and nursing research. *Journal of Advanced Nursing*, **27**: 817–24.

Phan, P. (2004) Entrepreneurship theory: Possibilities and future directions. *Journal of Business Venturing*, **19**(5): 617–20.

Sarasvathy, S. (2001) Causation and effectuation: Toward a theoretical shift from economic inevitability to entrepreneurial contingency. *Academy of Management Review*, **26**(2): 243–88.

Sarasvathy, S. (2004) The questions we ask and the questions we care about: Reformulating some problems in entrepreneurship research. *Journal of Business Venturing*, **19**(5): 707–17.

Schütz, A. (1982) *Life Forms and Meaning Structure*. London: Routledge and Kegan Paul.

Shane, S. (2003) *A General Theory of Entrepreneurship: The Individual-Opportunity Nexus*, Cheltenham, UK and Northampton, MA, USA: Edward Elgar.

Simon, H.A. (1996) *Sciences of the Artificial*. Cambridge, MA: MIT Press.

Smith, J. Harré, R. and van Langenhove, L. (1995) Idiography and the case study. In J. Smith, R. Harré and L. van Langenhove (eds) *Rethinking Psychology*, London: Sage, pp. 59–69.

Smith, J. and Osborn, M. (2003) Interpretative phenomenological analysis. In J. Smith (ed.), *Qualitative Psychology: A practical guide to methods*, London: Sage, pp. 55–80.

Smith, J.A. (1996) Beyond the divide between cognition and discourse: Using interpretative phenomenological analysis in health psychology. *Psychology & Health*, **11**: 261–71.

Steiner, C. (2002) The technicity paradigm and scientism in qualitative research. *The Qualitative Report*, **7**(2). [http://www.nova.edu/ssss/QR/QR7-2/steiner.html]

Steyaert, C. (2003) *Entrepreneurship: In Between What? – On the 'Frontier' as a Discourse of Entrepreneurship Research*. Best Paper Proceedings of the Academy of Management.

Taylor, C. (1971) Interpretation and the sciences of man. *Review of Metaphysics*, **25**: 3–51.

Todres, L. (1998) Pearls, pith and provocation: The qualitative description of human experience: The aesthetic dimension. *Qualitative Health Research*, **8**: 121–7.

van Manen, M. (1990) *Researching Lived Experience: human science for an action sensitive pedagogy*. Albany, NY: State University of New York Press.

von Eckartsberg, R. (1986) *Life-world Experience: existential–phenomenological research approaches in psychology*. Washington, DC: Center for Advanced Research in Phenomenology, University Press of America.

Weick, K. (1979) *Social Psychology of Organizing*. Rev. edn. Reading, MA: Addison-Wesley.

PART II

STARTING OUT AND GEARING UP

4 Ethnographic methods in entrepreneurship research
Bruce A. Johnstone

Introduction

> For over three decades, a quiet methodological revolution has been taking place in the social sciences. A blurring of disciplinary boundaries has occurred. The social sciences and humanities have drawn closer together in a mutual focus on an interpretive, qualitative approach to research and theory.
> (Denzin and Lincoln 2003: vii)

This chapter is an invitation to consider the potential an ethnographic research strategy holds to provide fresh insights in the entrepreneurship field. It aims to introduce ethnography and discuss how ethnographic methods may be applied to the study of entrepreneurship as part of a handbook that will guide researchers in this field as they join what Denzin and Lincoln (2003: vii) describe as the 'qualitative revolution' in which fundamental changes in the way researchers attempt to understand the world have been sweeping through the social sciences and related professional fields.

Ethnography as a research strategy usually eschews the widely used linear step-by-step approach to research design in favour of a cyclical approach, and this chapter will begin by discussing the origins and definitions of ethnography. It will continue by describing this cyclical approach and the other aspects of research design that set ethnographic methods apart. Further, it will discuss the strengths and weaknesses of ethnography as a research strategy.

There are many excellent texts on the subject of ethnography and it is therefore not the purpose of this chapter to exhaustively describe and justify the theoretical basis for ethnographic methods but rather to focus on how the methods of ethnography may be applied and justified in the study of entrepreneurship.

This chapter will also deal with practical aspects of data collection and touch on the issues raised by participant observation in emerging ventures, issues of ethics and reflexivity and the need for what Denscombe (1998: 68–9) calls the 'public account of the self that describes the researcher's self'. It will also introduce the analysis and interpretation of ethnographic data and conclude by summarizing how ethnographic methods may contribute to the study of entrepreneurship.

Defining ethnography

In normal usage the word ethnography refers to the research method used in cultural anthropology and also to a written text used to report that research. Indeed, ethnography is often equated with cultural anthropology, and qualitative researchers such as David Silverman (2000) describe it simply as observational research in particular settings, but ethnography entails much more than mere observation, notably a level of participation in daily activities.

Denscombe (1998: 68–9), however, defines ethnography as the description of peoples and cultures and 'understanding things from the point of view of those involved rather than explaining things from the outsider's point of view' and Brewer (2000) offers the following more comprehensive definition:

> Ethnography is the study of people in naturally occurring settings or 'fields' by methods of data collection which capture their social meanings and ordinary activities, involving the researcher participating directly in the setting, if not also in the activities, in order to collect data in a systematic manner but without meaning being imposed on them externally. (Ibid.: 6)

Burgess (1982) provides the further explanation that ethnography involves unstructured fieldwork or field research:

> Field research involves the study of real-life situations. Field researchers therefore observe people in the settings in which they live, and participate in their day to day activities. The methods that can be used in these studies are unstructured, flexible and open-ended. (Ibid.: 15)

Definitions of ethnography provide a general context and describe an approach to data collection and choice of focus or unit of analysis. For example, Hammersley (1990) suggests the following five features as identifying field research as ethnographic.

1. Behaviour is studied in everyday contexts, there are no unnatural or experimental circumstances imposed by the researcher.
2. Observation is the primary means of data collection, although various other techniques are also used.
3. Data collection is flexible and unstructured to avoid pre-fixed arrangements that impose categories on what people say and do.
4. The focus is normally on a single setting or group and is small scale.
5. The data is analysed by attributing meanings to the human actions described and explained. (Ibid.: 1–2)

Hammersley's first point relates to context, his second and third to data collection and his fourth and fifth to the focus or unit of analysis, so these three aspects of the definition are used to outline the remainder of this section.

Context

Ethnographic observation is distinguished from detached scientific observation by the flexible and unstructured approach of ethnographers who seek to understand meaning from the viewpoint of the subjects, and Malinowski (1922) stresses the need for an ethnographic work to 'deal with the totality of all social, cultural and psychological aspects of the community because they are so interwoven that not one can be understood without taking into account all the others' (ibid.: xvi). This suggests that ethnographers need to take a broad view of a community at least initially and should not begin with too narrow a focus on just one aspect or issue.

Further, ethnography is a research method characterized by extensive fieldwork where the researcher is often immersed as an observer, and sometimes as a participant observer. Researchers often remain immersed for an extended period and usually produce a quite detailed account of their exploration of a social environment or culture.

Ethnographers relate to how situations, lives and meanings are lived rather than just observing and reporting what occurs. In understanding their subjects' viewpoints, ethnographers, who may be initially motivated by curiosity towards, or a lack of understanding of, their subjects, often develop empathy towards the people they are studying.[1] However, Malinowski (1944) cautions that 'In dealing with people of a different culture, it is always dangerous to use the short-circuiting of "empathy," which usually amounts to guessing as to what the other person might have thought or felt' (ibid.: 23).

Data collection

Ethnographic research designs adopt cyclical patterns of investigation that accommodate ethnography's flexible approach to data gathering, in contrast to a linear design that follows a predetermined path and requires a much more structured approach to gathering data.

This tendency for ethnographic research to follow a cyclical pattern of investigation rather than the more normal linear design is perhaps a key element in distinguishing ethnography as a research strategy. Spradley (1980) describes an example of a linear research design as following a clearly defined set of steps beginning with the definition of a research problem, the formulation of hypotheses and the making of operational definitions. This linear approach goes on in clear steps to design a research instrument, gather data, analyse the data, draw conclusions and finally report the results. Spradley points out that 'ethnography seldom fits this

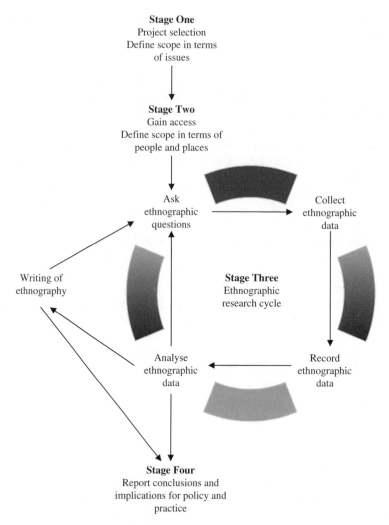

Stage One
Project selection
Define scope in terms
of issues

Stage Two
Gain access
Define scope in terms of
people and places

Ask
ethnographic
questions

Collect
ethnographic
data

Writing of
ethnography

Stage Three
Ethnographic
research cycle

Analyse
ethnographic
data

Record
ethnographic
data

Stage Four
Report conclusions and
implications for policy and
practice

Figure 4.1   A typical cyclical design for an ethnographic study

linear model' (Spradley 1980: 28) and instead follows a cyclical pattern that is repeated over and over. Figure 4.1 shows how a study can be designed using a cyclical ethnographic model.

Spradley further explains that the ethnographic research cycle begins with the selection of an ethnographic project, at which time the scope of the investigation is considered. Ethnographers then begin a cycle of asking ethnographic questions (general research questions that will be a focus for observation or from which a set of more specific interview questions or conversation starters may be derived), collecting ethnographic data, making an ethnographic record and analysing ethnographic data. At this point they return to the asking of more ethnographic questions, although having analysed data they can, and should, divert from the cycle to begin or continue the process of writing an ethnography. The focus of the research is refined as the cycles continue; this process can be viewed as a method of developing grounded theory. Moreover, Spradley notes that 'Ethnographers can only plan ahead of time the course of their investigation in the most general sense' (Spradley 1980: 35) and warns that researchers confront unnecessary problems and will end with a mountain of unanalysed data if they 'confuse ethnography with the more typical linear pattern of research' (ibid.: 35). As the ethnographic research cycle continues, researchers discover both questions and answers within the social situation they are investigating and gain alternative or multiple perspectives that can help them to think and inscribe in more complex and sophisticated ways about the phenomena and provoke insights into situations that are new and useful.

Longitudinal, real-time study of samples of emerging business activity, using the venture itself as the level of analysis, holds the potential to address the very central questions of entrepreneurship, according to Davidsson (2003: 55), who also notes that 'entrepreneurship is about emergence' and that this kind of research is in short supply. Entrepreneurial emergence, like art, is a dynamic process. By its very nature it is a process of innovation and change and it is surely difficult to understand such a disruptive and dynamic process using only cross-sectional techniques that work best when used to document a state of relative equilibrium. It is perhaps like trying to understand a dance by viewing snapshots of the action when you really need to be an observer of the whole process, or better still one of the dancers, to experience and understand the whole performance.

Davidsson (ibid.) suggests that it is the longitudinal information-gathering techniques that follow the emerging venture's progress over time that have the best potential to allow new insights and understanding. Perhaps the depth and detail of ethnography can offer those new insights by enabling researchers to follow the action as it unfolds over time, to see the viewpoints and hear the voices of insiders and to document, interpret and gain a greater understanding of the processes of venture emergence.

Unit of analysis
In discussing the selection of a project and the definition of its scope, Spradley describes how the social situations studied by ethnography are bounded by three elements: actors, activities and places. Although a

particular place is seen as a key element of a social situation, he also acknowledges the possibility of studying clusters and networks of social situations occurring in a number of places. Barth (1969) sees social boundaries as defining groups, although those social boundaries may have 'territorial counterparts' (ibid.: 15). Marcus (1998) takes the place aspect of scope further by describing multi-sited ethnography where sites are linked together in a way that 'defines the argument of the ethnography' (ibid.: 90). To summarize by listing Marcus's headings, multi-sited designs can be constructed by following *the people, the thing, the metaphor, the plot story or allegory, the life or biography* or *the conflict*. This multi-sited approach as depicted in Figure 4.2 seems likely to be useful in entrepreneurship research by allowing the flexibility to pursue answers to questions using research designs that link different actors, activities and places.

Because it can be multi-sited, ethnography is not limited to case studies of individual enterprises and it is possible to use ethnographic methods as more than just a data-gathering technique for case studies of individual entrepreneurs or ventures. As a research strategy, ethnography's cyclical and flexible approach to design and ability to link multiple sites makes it a methodology capable of accommodating complexity, detecting nuances and uncovering explanations within the social world.

Perhaps the disadvantages of choosing ethnography as a research strategy are that researchers begin without the benefit of a clear linear path and the certainty of a conclusion, and must deal with complexity and make design choices as their research progresses.

Origins and evolution

Ethnography began as a way of studying primitive cultures. Anthropologists such as Malinowski (1922) found that to really understand a group of people, they needed to engage in an extended period of observation and would often immerse themselves in a culture for a period of years, learn the language and participate in social events with the people of that culture. This approach was also used in the study of people in Western societies. Schwartzman (1993) notes that ethnography began to be used in the USA to provide valuable insights into organizations some 65 years ago.[2]

Hence there is nothing new or revolutionary about the use of classic ethnographic methods, as this approach dates back to around 1900. While an objective, positivist and rather ethnocentric approach was the norm at the dawn of the twentieth century, ethnography has since then evolved its range of possible approaches across the spectrum of epistemologies and the objective–subjective divide. Ethnographers can now choose from a diverse menu of approaches depending on the political and philosophical stance of the researcher, the issues and questions to be addressed and the

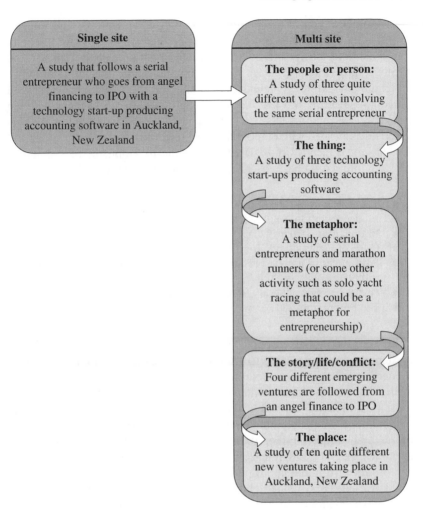

Figure 4.2   Examples of how a single-site study could be extended to become a variety of multi-site studies

people and environment to be studied. It is also possible to mix perspectives and take the role of what Denzin and Lincoln call a 'researcher-as-bricoleur-theorist' who 'works between and within competing and overlapping perspectives and paradigms' (Denzin and Lincoln 2003: 9).

The different paradigms process and value the data gathered by ethnographic methods differently. Denzin and Lincoln (ibid.: 33) define a paradigm as an interpretative framework and 'a net that contains the researcher's epistemological, ontological and methodological premises', and suggest that there are four major interpretative paradigms in qualitative research: 'positivist and postpositivist', 'constructivist–interpretive', 'critical' and 'feminist–poststructural', each with its own 'concrete specific interpretive communities'. Although researchers cannot perhaps move easily between paradigms, Denzin and Lincoln assert that researchers can move between *perspectives* as these are less-well-developed systems. The paradigms and perspectives associated with ethnography have evolved over the last century and Denzin and Lincoln (ibid.: 3) categorize the development of qualitative research into seven phases or 'historical moments' as follows:

- Traditional from 1900 to 1950.
- Modernist or Golden Age from 1950 to 1970.
- Blurred genres from 1970 to 1986.
- Crisis of representation from 1986 to 1990.
- Post-modern – a period of new and experimental ethnographies from 1990 to 1995.
- Post experimental inquiry from 1995 to 2000.
- The Future from 2000 onwards.

Brewer (2000) takes a somewhat different view and suggests four basic epistemological approaches to ethnography: 'positivist', 'humanist', 'postmodern' and 'post post-modern', the last being an approach that has evolved in response to the challenges of postmodernism. He asserts that the 'post post-modern' approach is characterized by being less naïve in its beliefs about what is real and perhaps being concerned with the *relevance* of research outputs rather than claiming validity or reliability. It is an approach that reclaims at least in part the idea that ethnographic research can produce truth and could perhaps be allied to the critical realism view that knowledge may relate to how things really are but accepts that a truth may be partial and may need to be revised as knowledge is developed.

Perhaps the range of epistemological approaches to ethnography has expanded and become more subjective over the last century in order to keep pace with an increasing willingness by researchers to take a critical approach to society and challenge the status quo. In Western societies, where the dominant form of earning a living is to be employed by someone else, many emerging entrepreneurs are motivated by a desire for individual freedom and empowerment, or in other words a desire to escape from forms of domination and subjugation, and there may therefore be a useful role for critical theory to explore these issues in entrepreneurship research. Kincheloe and McLaren (2003: 433) caution that critical theory produces 'undeniably dangerous knowledge, the kind of information and insight that upsets institutions and threatens to overturn sovereign regimes of truth'.

Subjective or objective approach

> Of all the oppositions that artificially divide social science, the most fundamental, and the most ruinous, is the one that is set up between subjectivism and objectivism. (Bourdieu 1990: 25)

Ethnographic researchers can position themselves on either side of the objective–subjective divide, and this choice is perhaps less likely to be ruinous if careful consideration is given to the advantages and disadvantages of each approach. Smith et al. (1989) offer a framework for selecting either a subjective or an objective methodology and suggest the use of a subjective approach when the focus is on strategic intentions rather than behaviour. They point out that, for various reasons, entrepreneurs may not accurately describe their organization's strategies to external researchers and propose a subjective approach to overcome this.

Extending this thinking, the selection of a subjective approach may allow researchers to go further and discover not only the strategic intentions of entrepreneurs but also deeper meanings of those intentions, things that are never talked about and the tacit rules that are taken for granted by a group. Ethnographers often seek to understand the boundaries of what is taken for granted in a social setting and what is open to argument. Bourdieu (1977: 169) explains how dominated classes seek to push back the limits of *doxa* (the undisputed) while those that dominate seek to defend it, or failing that to establish *orthodoxy* in its place to counter the *heterodoxy* or heresy that threatens the established order. The strengths and weaknesses of the objective and subjective approach respectively are listed in Table 4.1.

The choice of an epistemological approach is likely to be influenced by the background, discipline and ontology of the researchers involved, according to Perren and Ram (2004), who discuss the strengths and weaknesses of the objective and subjective approaches in the context of case studies of entrepreneurs. They point out that objective and positivist approaches offer the advantages that complexity may be reduced and causal connections more easily made. Disadvantages, however, are that the conclusions may be too simplistic or ignore nuances or explanations that lie outside of the conceptual framework being employed. The more subjective approaches allow the complexities of the social world to be explored but have the disadvantage that they may result in research that concludes without clear findings or contributions to practice or policy.

Table 4.1   *The strengths and weaknesses of objective and subjective*
             approaches

	Objective approach	Subjective approach
Strengths	• Complexity is reduced • Causal connections are more easily made • Suited to the study of behaviour rather than strategic intentions	• Complexities of the social world can be explored • Deeper meanings may be uncovered • Reluctance of entrepreneurs to report may be overcome • May uncover the deeper meanings of strategic intentions
Weaknesses	• Conclusions may be simplistic • Nuances or explanations outside conceptual framework may be ignored • Not suited to finding the deeper meanings of strategic intentions	• Research may conclude without any clear findings or contribution to practice or policy

Data-gathering techniques

This section discusses the various systematic data-gathering techniques used in ethnography and examines how they can be applied in practice and contribute to the achievement of research objectives, how the information collected may be processed, and the implications of the choice of ethnographic techniques for the ultimate relevance and legitimation of the conclusions. A list of ethnographic data-gathering methods would include the following:

- Observation, including various forms of participant observation.
- Journal keeping by the researcher. This can take the form of text, audio, video or perhaps a web log.
- Interviews. These are likely to be semi-structured or even unstructured or conversational.

Studying the accounts of others such as a journal, diary or testimonio in written, audio or video form, or communications, such as e-mails, videos, audio recordings, news items, reports, memos, letters or speeches.

Participant observation

By choosing participant observation as a research method, researchers become the research instruments and their behaviour becomes a vital

Table 4.2 *Participation and identification by observers*

	Identified	Not identified
Non-participant	Non-participant	Complete observer
Participant	Participant as observer/ or observer as participant	Complete participant

element of the research design. Researchers must balance their role as an outsider with their role as a participant. As a participant they must be able to interact with the subject group, share lives and activities, and understand their language. At the same time they must maintain their position and integrity as researchers and their ability to reflect critically on what they are observing. They must be both involved and detached. Spradley suggests how participant observation can be used as a strategy to focus ethnographic research: 'Participant observation begins with wide-focused descriptive observations, although these continue until the end of the research project . . . the emphasis shifts first to focused observations and later to selective observations' (Spradley 1980: 34).

Brewer (2000) draws a distinction between a participant observer and an observant participant. The former takes up the participant role in order to observe; the latter is already a participant and takes on the role of observer. In both cases the observer can be overt or covert, or observation can take place under the disguise of activities such as questionnaire research. An observant participant has the advantage of already fitting into the group and the role but there may still be issues of access to data; for example observant participants may not be in a position to ask searching questions or access all activities of the group. They may also be too close to the action and be hampered by existing relationships, so the suitability of the participant role must be carefully considered.

Distinguishing further between those participants that are identified and those who are not creates five potential researcher roles, as described in Table 4.2. See also Chapter 17 for an account of the various roles.

Participant or non-participant observation is typically relatively long-term. Kondo (1990: 23) writes that 'The final months of fieldwork are generally the best and most productive: the months of laying groundwork pay off in the increasing intimacy and comfort in your relationships and the depth of the insights you are able to reach.'

Participant or non-participant observation also typically involves the observer being immersed in organizational life and the extensive use of field notes. The writing of ethnographic field notes is discussed at length by Emerson et al. (1995), who stress the value of immersion and note that no researcher can be a neutral, detached fly on the wall. Because the researcher must interact with the subjects, there is bound to be consequential presence and reactive effects where the researcher's participation affects how members of the group talk and behave. They suggest that this should not be seen as contaminating what is learned and observed, but rather that these unavoidable effects should be studied for what they reveal.

> Through participation the field researcher sees first-hand and up close how people grapple with uncertainty and confusion, how meanings emerge through talk and collective action, how understandings and interpretations change over time. In all these ways the field worker's closeness to others' daily lives and activities heightens sensitivity to social life as process. (Emerson et al. 1995: 4)

Clifford notes that 'Insiders studying their own cultures offer new angles of vision and depths of understanding and their accounts are empowered and restricted in unique ways' (Clifford 1986: 9). An insider (complete participant) studying an entrepreneurial venture would have the advantage of beginning with a rich knowledge of the protagonists, the background and history of the venture, its culture and the social situation. Insider participants are also likely to have personal experiences and attributes that will help them gain acceptance and access. However, as involved participants they face the challenge of adopting the more detached viewpoint of an observer and accounting for their own roles as participants.

It is also possible to introduce subtle variations into how roles as participants are adopted and/or existing roles adapted to enable observation. For example, researchers may already be one kind of insider, but change their role for the purposes of observation. If teachers of entrepreneurship overtly or covertly observe the behaviour of entrepreneurial students, they are making use of an existing role but changing from instructor to observer. If bank-lending managers take on the roles of entrepreneurs and apply for loans, they are adopting a different opposing insider role in order to observe behaviour from the other side of the process.

Journal keeping

Practical suggestions for fieldwork provided by Zorn (2001) include keeping a journal of field notes, refinements, expansions and hunches. In preparation for fieldwork, observers are advised to plan how they will lay out their notes, how and when they will take them, and plan the abbreviations and codes they will use. Field notes should map and describe the physical setting and leave space for expansion and comments. He suggests that written field notes should begin by listing the time and place of the observation and describing the setting, then drawing a vertical line down the page and using one side to record descriptions and direct observations of what is said and done. Verbatim comments should be placed in quotation marks so that they can be distinguished later from general descriptions of what was said. The other side of the page should be used for the researcher's inferences, reactions, questions, hunches and thoughts. Keeping descriptions separate from inferences will greatly facilitate interpretation of the data. If events take place more quickly than they can be recorded, space should be left to fill in observations immediately afterwards, when an end time to the observation is noted.

Observers who have identified questions to guide their observations will be able to focus on a subset of the phenomena. Zorn (2001) suggests posing questions such as: What are the issues on which there is conflict or different points of view? How are the differences or conflicts handled? How do individuals influence each other and attempt to make decisions and/or build consensus within the group? He suggests that inferences, reactions and comments made during or after the observation should be clearly tied to direct observations so that they are explained by actions that have been observed and recorded. In this way the analysis and interpretation of data is taking place at the same time as data are being gathered. By reviewing field notes on a regular basis, perhaps by typing them up, researchers can review and reflect, and may discern patterns of data or become aware of issues.

Brewer (2000) makes the point that participant observation is neither quick nor easy. Time is needed to re-socialize the observer into the practices and values of the group and win acceptance for the role, but especially time is needed to experience the full range of the events and activities of the setting. He also points out that participant observation certainly has its limitations as a research method. An observer is bound to be selective and present a partial account, and this may be skewed towards observations of abnormal, exceptional or aberrant behaviour or may be a personal viewpoint that is not representative. Brewer concludes that participant observation should therefore never stand alone as a research method.

Interviewing
Simply put, an interview is a series of questions by an interviewer and a series of responses from a subject. Interviews can range from structured to semi-structured to unstructured; the level of structure is an important design choice. The structured interview is favoured by positivist and quantitative researchers as data can be collected systematically and put into numerical form. A highly structured interview has the advantage of allowing many people to be interviewed quickly over a wide geographical area using a number of interviewers who do not have to be very highly trained.

However, ethnographers searching for thick description, nuance and meaning rather than numerical data generally favour semi-structured or unstructured interviews. These can be more like conversations with perhaps just an initial general focus or direction imposed by the interviewer. Ethnographers also elicit life stories and testimonio, and elicit and compile narratives. In doing so they often gather data through quite unstructured interviews or interactions with subjects.

Ethnographers, or any researchers, who employ the semi-structured interview need to pay attention to their interviewing techniques. Problems with any interviews can be categorized as problems with questions and problems with answers. Looking first at questions, are they understood by the subject and do all subjects understand their meaning in the same way? Second, are the questions being asked reliable indicators of the subject or purpose of the research, and will the answers be useful? Is the subject seeking social approval by providing socially acceptable answers? If there is an imbalance in the relationship between the interviewer and subject in terms of status, class, education, age, ethnicity or gender, this will influence the response, perhaps by making the subject reluctant to admit to an attitude or belief. By standardizing questions and designing a formal or structured interview these problems can be minimized; however, in the ethnographic semi- or unstructured interview there is much more reliance on the ability of the researcher to communicate with and elicit and record the views of the subject.

Zorn (2001) offers nine suggestions for semi-structured interviewing:

1. Plan the interview and write topics and questions in advance and consider different ways of arranging them.
2. In the first interview with a subject, explain your purpose and how you will use the interview data, how you will protect confidentiality and anonymity. Also discuss and obtain permission for tape recording or note taking.
3. In the first interview with a subject, ask general background questions first. These provide necessary information and warm up the subject by allowing them to answer easy questions.
4. Questions on the topic of interest should be broad and open ended, for example 'Tell me the story of . . .'
5. Try not to ask leading questions. If following up on an observed behaviour you might ask 'What did you mean when you said . . .?' but not 'When you said . . . did you mean . . .?'
6. Use probes carefully to get more in-depth answers. For example ask 'Can you give me an example of that?'
7. Simply being silent can encourage the subject to continue.
8. Give thought to how you will end the interview, perhaps by asking 'Is there anything further you would like to tell me?'
9. Check your recording of the interview, complete any gaps in notes and record your impressions. (Zorn 2001)

Table 4.3   Examples of different question types

Question type	Example
Descriptive	When you consult your accountant about a new venture, what would you typically say to each other?
Structural	You used the words 'going it alone' and you also talked about 'a sense of achievement'. Is a sense of achievement something that comes from going it alone?
Contrast – dyadic	What is the difference between borrowing from a family member and from an angel investor?
Contrast – triadic	Thinking about borrowing from family or from an angel investor or from a bank, which two of these three sources of finance seem most similar? (or which seems most different?)
Contrast – rating	Thinking about borrowing from family or from an angel investor or from a bank, which seem the most difficult and which the least difficult?

The semi-structured interview described above should offer topics and questions to subjects and elicit their ideas and opinions. Interviewers should avoid leading subjects towards preconceived choices, but questions can certainly be used tactically to focus and organize information. Questions can be aimed at eliciting descriptive data or to examine how meanings are structured or connected together or how they are contrasted as separate. Contrast questions can be dyadic, triadic or may ask the subject to rate or rack a number of things, and are suggested by Spradley (1980) as techniques to understand differences. Table 4.3 provides examples of how these different types of question might be used to elicit meaning.

Accounts and communications
A variety of data-gathering techniques can be used within the realm of observation and interview, and a number of other data-gathering methods fall outside and are additional tools for ethnographers. For example, researchers can study personal documents, biographies or histories for the tales they can tell. Techniques such as written journals or perhaps audio or video diaries can be used by researchers to record observations; they can also ask insiders to maintain such journals in their own voices and to tell their tales of the inside.

Tales can be categorized as 'realist,' 'confessional,' 'impressionist' or 'critical' (Zorn 2001). The realist tale is a traditional form of ethnography describing a culture or cultural phenomenon that is assumed to be integrated and capable of being objectively reported. There is usually little self-reflection and the author is absent from the account. The problem with a realist tale is that the culture may not be as static and integrated as it is depicted. This is especially likely in a dynamic entrepreneurial environment. A realist account purports to discover a culture whereas perhaps it is rather too shaped by disciplinary conventions, intellectual climate and personal beliefs.

A confessional tale aims to 'demystify fieldwork by showing how it is practised' (Zorn 2001). There is recognition of the researchers' biases and emphasis on researchers' points of view. Research is not assumed to be objective and culture is not assumed to be unified; there is empathy with the group being studied rather than focus on their differences.

An impressionist tale takes a more dramatic approach, often presenting information in fragments and memorable glimpses. The teller of an impressionist tale assumes cultures to be fragmented and, as there is no big picture, offers glimpses of insight.

Finally, critical tales are likely to be rather activist. Groups are selected for study for what they may reveal about political or economic issues. Tellers of critical tales may examine structures of domination and control and aim to free people from these structures. They may also examine institutional constraints that restrict the emergence of new ventures and advocate change.

Reflexivity
When researchers adopt a subjective epistemological approach they need to critically examine how their research has been carried out and understand its limitations. Long-term, involved, immersed and empathetic relationships between ethnographic researchers and the people they are studying will certainly affect the data that are gathered and how those data are interpreted and represented, and examining this relationship is vital to the legitimation of findings or outputs. Brewer (2000) asserts that reflexivity should be bound up with interpretation and be an integral part of the writing process as researchers' selves and identities will affect the meaning they attribute to the data. Researchers taking a positivist or humanistic approach are likely to believe that adopting good research practice will ensure the objectivity of their observation, and their interpretation will not be coloured by their personal values and beliefs. Those taking a postmodern or post postmodern approach will accept that they are themselves very much a part of the social world they are studying, that it is therefore futile to try to eliminate the effects of themselves as researchers, and that reflexivity is the process through which they will seek to understand these

effects. This approach accepts that there are many different competing versions of reality, that any account can only be a partial account and that reflexivity, by providing accounts of researchers' personal backgrounds, biases, preconceptions and research activities, will reveal that partial nature and, importantly, 'improve legitimation of the data' (Brewer 2000: 130). In ethnographic research the most important aspect of conducting good research is perhaps the role of the researcher.

Role of the researcher
The process of being reflexive begins with description of the processes of research. Perhaps beginning with a description of how, when and where fieldwork was carried out and how, when and where notes, journals or records were kept and organized. How was the social environment stratified in terms of age, race, ethnicity, gender, social class, occupation or education, and how did the researcher fit within this social environment? How were the data processed and interpreted – for example, what methods of filing or coding were used and how did these evolve? What was difficult or problematic in the research process? In answering these questions researchers are seeking to account for their own role.

At a deeper analytical level researchers need to engage in reflection. Brewer (2000: 131) suggests they should 'ask themselves questions about the theoretical framework and methodology they are working within, the broader values, commitments and preconceptions they bring to their work, the ontological assumptions they have about the nature of society and social reality'. In describing and analysing oneself as a researcher it may be useful to take another step back and produce what Denscombe (1998: 68–9) calls the 'public account of the self that describes the researcher's self'. This accounting for the self that accounts for the self is perhaps particularly important for researchers who are involved as participants or practitioners. Kondo (1990) provides an excellent example of this accounting for self as she examines in detail the social complexities of her role as a participant observer in Japanese workplaces. These complexities are influenced by her gender, age, status as a student, and her plight as a Japanese American adapting to Japanese society.

Reflexive analysis legitimates research by establishing a vantage point for critically assessing the researchers themselves, their integrity, their decisions on questions of research design, strategy, methods and theoretical framework and the data that result.

Analysis and interpretation
The role of the ethnographer is, according to Geertz (1973: 19), 'To write or *inscribe* social discourse'. By using the word 'inscribe' he is recognizing that

an ethnography need not be a written account and may take the form of photographs, drawings, diagrams, tables, video, audio or a museum display. But he stresses that in writing or inscribing ethnographers must bring clarity.

> The claim to attention of an ethnographic account does not rest on the author's ability to capture primitive facts in faraway places and carry them home like a mask or a carving, but on the degree to which he is able to clarify what goes on in such places, to reduce the puzzlement – what manner of men are these? (Geertz 1973: 16).

He goes on to point out that the value of an ethnographic account lies in its attention to detail and nuance, 'Whether it sorts winks from twitches and real winks from mimicked ones' (ibid.).

The need for ethnographic writing to have a thesis is advanced by Spradley, who suggests that a thesis may emerge from major themes of the research, from the goals of the research or be a set of recipes or tacit rules for behaviour that emerge from the research.

> To communicate with your audience you need to have something to say. All too often, ethnographic descriptions appear to be like meandering conversations without a destination. Although of interest to the ethnographer and a few colleagues, such writing will not hold the attention of many more. A thesis is the central message, the point you want to make. (Spradley 1980: 169)

Spradley also urges researchers to start writing early, noting that the act of writing is best seen as part of the ethnographic research cycle rather than something to be done after fieldwork is complete. New questions will arise from the data during the writing process that need to be asked in the field, and if fieldwork is complete, those questions will be left unanswered and result in gaps.

Zorn (2001) suggests thematic analysis of ethnographic data as a means of interpreting the discourse participants use in conceptualizing their current, ongoing relational episodes. A theme is described as a patterned issue or locus of concern around which interaction centres (Owen 1984); themes are prominent patterns of participants' meanings, actions or responses to situations. Zorn suggests questioning why these themes have emerged, when and under what conditions, looking for sub-themes and super-themes, and observing how the themes have manifested themselves and what is not present that might be expected. Researchers can play back interpretations to participants to affirm, refine and build authority. Researchers should seek to place their interpretations within a theoretical framework and question the social and political influences.

Emerson et al. (1995) suggest that filed notes should be re-read to develop themes and open coding used to ask questions of the notes, for example: What are they doing? What are their goals? How do they do it? How do they describe it? Researchers are advised to write analytic memos, explore rich excerpts, and select core themes based on relevance to theory or the research questions, or based on the frequency they occur or their salience. Field notes and memos should be sorted around themes and focused coding should be carried out – a line-by-line analysis based on major issues, themes, connections and theory. Researchers should then write integrative memos to clarify and link themes and categories.

> Any classification is superior to chaos and even a classification at the level of sensible properties is a step towards rational ordering. It is legitimate, in classifying fruits into relatively heavy and relatively light, to begin by separating the apples from the pears even though the shape, colour and taste are unconnected with weight and volume. This is because the larger apples are easier to distinguish from the smaller if the apples are not still mixed with fruit of different features. (Lévi-Strauss 1966: 15)

There is also a range of software available to assist in classifying the fruit of ethnographic research, including Ethnograph, ATLAS.ti, WinMAX, NUD*IST and NVivo®. Taking NVivo® as an example, this application clearly makes it possible to carry out very complex coding of texts into categories of meanings or nodes and to show, shape, filter, assay, slice and dice the data in various ways. This process can, of course, be done manually, traditionally using highlighter pens of different colours; however, ethnographic researchers can find themselves interpreting literally hundreds of thousands of words, and software allows researchers to process and make sense of the data much more quickly and easily. Search tools in the software also greatly facilitate this process and in NVivo® these are more sophisticated than the search function in a word processor and, for example, make it possible to search for combinations of words in proximity to each other. This is important because these searches are for meanings rather than words, and meanings can be expressed with a variety of words. It can also be valuable to identify words that are used by one group of people but not by another.

NVivo® allows a single comment to be coded in a number of ways – something that is difficult to do with highlighter pens. Researchers can insert comments into the text being analysed in italics which will be ignored by the software. Text elements can be coded by a simple drag-and-drop process, and NVivo® also offers an electronic means of building node trees and expressing relationships between nodes that can be displayed as diagrams and exported as bitmap files. This graphic method of interpreting relationships seems a powerful tool to focus research, uncover a thesis for ethnographic writing and facilitate the development of grounded theory.[3]

Ethical considerations

The use of observation, especially if covert and/or coupled with participation, raises ethical questions that researchers must carefully address and, although a full discussion of those questions is beyond the scope of this chapter, it is perhaps worth noting that it is possible to take two quite different approaches to the ethical questions of ethnographic entrepreneurial research, 'ethical absolutism' and 'ethical relativism' (de Laine 2000). The latter approach is based on an interpretative or critical paradigm and assumes that the world is socially constructed and open to various interpretations. In the case of the critical paradigm, it may also be assumed that there are powerful groups in society that may seek to restrict or distort knowledge for their own ends. De Laine notes that in ethical relativism, actors are granted the liberty to exercise individual conscience in ethical matters. In this she includes the issue of consent. A critical ethical relativist may choose to weigh the right to consent against the need to combat exploitation or the actions of those with power seeking to protect their interests. For example, if a person is acting in an official role, researchers may decide that they must covertly study the behaviour of that person. The justification for this may be that if they were to obtain consent, the very behaviour they wish to study may change and they may further justify covert study on the basis that the performance of a role laid down by public policy makes that role a public one that, in a democracy, should be open to public scrutiny.

It is also possible to justify observing people in public places without their permission or knowledge. Spradley observes that 'anyone has the right to observe what others are doing in public and to make cultural inferences about patterns of behaviour' (Spradley 1980: 23). However, Spradley is in no doubt that researchers have an ethical responsibility towards the people they study and should protect their welfare, dignity and privacy. Therefore a justification for covert research that revealed personal information would need to be one in which the potential harm to the people being covertly studied was obviously, or could be shown to be, either negligible or minor and outweighed by the benefits of the research.

In practice, researchers involved in studying entrepreneurs are likely to obtain informed consent from their main subjects but also may use a justification of lack of harm to allow the covert observation of people who are incidental or peripheral to a subject entrepreneur (see also Brundin, Chapter 11 in this volume for an example).

Conclusions

Researchers in the field of entrepreneurship aim to discover knowledge that will help entrepreneurs be more successful, support the teaching of people to be better entrepreneurs and inform policy and practice for people and institutions that seek to support and facilitate the activities of entrepreneurs within settings such as organizations, communities or regional or national economies.

In this they are no different from other fields where social research using ethnographic methods aims to support practice. Ethnography is a tried and tested tool for generating knowledge in fields such as education and nursing, and undoubtedly results in many advances in the quality of teaching and health care. Further, urban, street or subculture ethnographies are used to inform public policy, lawmaking and social work, work-based or occupational ethnographies inform managers about the workings of social organizations within the workplace and hold the potential to produce knowledge that can be used to make workplaces happier and more productive. It surely follows that ethnographic methods have the potential to contribute to entrepreneurship research and education.

However, examples of the use of ethnographic methods are rarely found in the mainstream journals of entrepreneurship research, which mainly publish studies using quantitative methods. When Paula Kyrö and Juha Kansikas carried out a study of the methodology used in a sample of 337 refereed articles published in a selection of entrepreneurship journals in 1999–2000, only one was classified by the authors as ethnography (Kyrö and Kansikas 2004). They reported that only 38 (or 11 per cent) of the articles used qualitative methods. Discursive methods were used in 26 of them, eight were case studies, two were narratives, one was a history and (as already noted) just one was classified as an ethnography.

Why are ethnographic techniques so little used by researchers in entrepreneurship? It surely cannot be because the dominant quantitative approach is providing all the answers. Jay Barney (Barney 2003) recently pointed out that the field of entrepreneurship research has yet to produce answers to central questions, such as why some firms make more money than others, and that entrepreneurship research has yet to make a contribution back to its parent disciplines. Many quantitative data sets are compiled and complex statistical analysis is carried out, yet it seems the central questions remain largely unanswered and furthermore there is little ability reliably to predict the future. Bygrave (2004) observes that entrepreneurship scholars, despite the fact that many intensively study venture capital, have in recent years been unable to accurately predict either the dotcom bubble or the subsequent dotcom crash.

Ethnographic methods have certainly been adopted by a subgroup of entrepreneurship researchers, although they tend to publish in books or non-entrepreneurship journals. A number of researchers have put ethnographic methods to good use in the study of a range of entrepreneurship issues. For example, Down and Reveley (2004) studied how entrepreneurial identity is shaped by generational encounters and Taylor et al. (2002) examined managerial legitimacy in small firms. Ram's work (Ram and Holliday 1993; Boon and Ram 1998; Ram 1999; Ram 2000a; Ram 2000b; Ram 2001; Ram, Abbas et al. 2000; Ram, Sanghera et al. 2000; Perren and Ram 2004) includes studies of entrepreneurs in family and community settings, and Holliday (Ram and Holliday 1993; Holliday 1995) has studied employment relations in small firms. Kondo's work (Kondo 1990) touches on how entrepreneurs and artisans craft their identities in Japan where white-collar careers with large companies are highly valued. Examples of doctoral research using ethnographic methods to study entrepreneurship include the work of Down (2002) and Fletcher (1997). Perren and Ram (2004) point to the use of ethnographic methods in case study research into small business and entrepreneurs and cite the work of Fletcher (1997) and Holliday (1995) as ethnographic examples that consider methodological issues at length.

Ethnographic studies of entrepreneurs may shed light on wider issues relating to the changing values of a culture or society because of the role entrepreneurs play in initiating bridging transactions that set the relative values assigned to various human activities, ideas, time, money, goods and services. Barth (1966) points out that 'The big potentialities for profit lie where the disparity of evaluation between two or more kinds of goods are the greatest and where this disparity has been maintained because there are no bridging transactions' (ibid.: 18). Barth notes that entrepreneurs make those bridging transactions and also describes 'political entrepreneurs' (ibid.: 19) as 'interpreters and mediators of basic cultural dilemmas' who 'force a showdown through their rival offers of transactions' (ibid.: 20).

Indeed, Kondo's work (Kondo 1990) offers rich insights into the behaviour and values of Japanese people. In describing how her subjects crafted their identities, her tales from the workplace made an important contribution to the understanding by outsiders of Japanese culture and society.

Ethnographic studies of entrepreneurship could reveal understandings about a society and its values that cannot be easily expressed or interpreted in numerical form, and that therefore cannot be pursued with the statistical tools of science and physics but instead require the different and challenging tools of narrative and art. In his book, *The Ethnographic Imagination*, Willis writes that 'Art as an elegant and compressed practice of meaning making is a defining and irreducible quality at the heart of everyday human practices and interactions' (Willis 2000: 3).

If life and work can be viewed as forms of art, then entrepreneurship can also undoubtedly be viewed as an art form. The world is their canvas and entrepreneurs, just like painters or poets, create works of beauty and value by combining resources in new and more attractive forms. In using ethnographic methods to capture the social meanings of entrepreneurs, researchers are observing a dynamic process of meanings in the making, rather than static meaning, and can trace the evolution of new meanings as new ventures emerge.

Ethnography is well accepted as an appropriate approach to qualitative research in the social sciences and therefore should also be seen by researchers in the field of entrepreneurship as a valuable tool with which to study the process of entrepreneurship from the viewpoint of the people involved. In addition to a role in exploratory research and hypothesis development, ethnographic methods can contribute grounded theory and produce rich narratives that hold relevance for practice, teaching and policy.

Ethnographic methods uncover nuances in social settings and offer insights into underlying cultural trends and shifts in meaning. They therefore surely have the potential to uncover greater understanding of entrepreneurial behaviour, new insights into how entrepreneurial ventures emerge and grow, and explain the cultural and institutional factors that surround and either constrain or enable the emergence of a venture.

Finally, because entrepreneurs have a creative role in the bridging transactions that form the values of a society, the study of entrepreneurs using ethnographic methods may offer wider insights into societies and cultures.

Acknowledgements

I would like to thank the editors and anonymous reviewers for their valuable guidance, Chris Batstone and Simon Milne (my supervisors at Auckland University of Technology) for their advice and support, and my wife Janet Johnstone for her constant encouragement.

Notes

1. However, this is not always the case and it is quite possible to use ethnography to study people, such as neo-Nazis for example, for whom researchers may feel no such empathy and may actually despise.
2. In a series of groundbreaking studies undertaken at the Hawthorne Works in Illinois, researchers turned to the observational techniques of anthropologists in an attempt to understand variations in worker productivity. They found that groups of workers formed their own *social organizations* and that these often worked against management's efforts to achieve results through the official and formal organization. Researchers realized that they were shedding new light on the economic and management theories of the day that had previously been based on the expectation of rational behaviour.
3. Further information on NUD*IST and NVivo® can be found at www. qsrinternational.com

Suggestions for further reading

While all the references used in this chapter would be well worth reading, a few stand out as worthy of particular mention.

Denzin and Lincoln's (2003) excellent *Strategies of Qualitative Inquiry* is a general text that contains much useful content on ethnography while the works of Geertz (1973), Barth (1966, 1969), Spradley (1980) and Brewer (2000) have a place on the desk of anyone planning to use ethnographic methods. Of these, Spradley's *Participant Observation* is a very practical and useful guide for a novice ethnographer.

Kondo's (1990) account, *Crafting Selves: Power, Gender, and Discourses of Identity in a Japanese Workplace*, is well worth reading as an example of an ethnographic narrative that shows how thick description can be employed to capture subtle cultural nuances, while the insights of Lévi-Strauss (1966), Malinowski (1922, 1944), Barth (1966, 1969) and Bourdieu (1977) provide a valuable philosophical background.

Finally, the publications of Down (2002), Down and Reveley (2004), Holliday (1995), Ram (1999; 2000; 2001) and Boon and Ram (1998) are excellent examples of ethnographic methods used in the study of entrepreneurship.

References

Barney, J. (2003) Speech to Babson College Doctoral Consortium. B. Johnstone. Boston.

Barth, F. (1966) *Models of Social Organization*. Glasgow: The University Press.

Barth, F. (1969) *Ethnic Groups and Boundaries: The social organization of cultural difference*. Boston, MA: Little, Brown and Company.

Boon, S. and M. Ram (1998) Implementing quality in a small firm: an action research approach. *Personnel Review*, **27**(1): 20.

Bourdieu, P. (1977) *Outline of a Theory of Practice*. Cambridge: Cambridge University Press.

Bourdieu, P. (1990) *The Logic of Practice*. Cambridge: Polity Press.

Brewer, J.D. (2000) *Ethnography*. Buckingham: Open University Press.

Burgess, R.G. (1982) *Field Research: A sourcebook and field manual*. London: Allen and Unwin.

Bygrave, W. (2004) Opening Address AGSE–Babson Entrepreneurship Research Exchange. B. Johnstone. Melbourne.

Clifford, J. (1986) Introduction: Partial truths. *Writing Culture: The poetics and politics of ethnography*. J. Clifford and G.E. Marcus. Los Angeles, University of California Press.

Davidsson, P. (2003) The domain of entrepreneurship research: Some suggestions. *Advances in Entrepreneurship, Firm Emergence and Growth*. J. Katz and D. Shepherd. Greenwich, CT: JAI Press, **6**: 55–9.

de Laine, M. (2000) *Fieldwork Participation and Practice. Ethics and Dilemmas in Qualitative Research*. London: Sage Publications.

Denscombe, M. (1998) *The Good Research Guide for Small Scale Social Research Projects*. Buckingham: Open University Press.

Denzin, N.K. and Y.S. Lincoln (2003) *Strategies of Qualitative Inquiry*. Thousand Oaks, CA: Sage Publications.

Down, S. (2002) *Clichés, generations, space and friendship: the self-identity narratives of two entrepreneurs*. Wollongong, Australia: University of Wollongong.

Down, S. and J. Reveley (2004) Generational encounters and the social formation of entrepreneurial identity: 'young guns' and 'old farts'. *Organization*, **11**(2): 233.

Emerson, R.M., Fretz, Rachel I. and Shaw, Linda L. (1995) *Writing Ethnographic Fieldnotes*. Chicago: The University of Chicago Press.

Fletcher, D. (1997) *Organisational Networking, Strategic Change and the Family Business*. Business School, Nottingham Trent University.

Geertz, C. (1973) *The Interpretation of Cultures*. New York: Basic Books.

Hammersley, M. (1990) *Reading Ethnographic Research*. London: Longman.

Holliday, R. (1995) *Small Firms: Nice Work?* London: Routledge.

Kincheloe, J.L. and P. McLaren (2003) Rethinking critical theory and qualitative research. *The Landscape of Qualitative Research, Theories and Issues*. N.K. Denzin and Y.S. Lincoln. Thousand Oaks, CA: Sage Publications.

Kondo, D.K. (1990) *Crafting Selves: Power, Gender, and Discourses of Identity in a Japanese Workplace*. Chicago: University of Chicago Press.

Kyrö, P. and J. Kansikas (2004) Current state of methodology in entrepreneurship research and some expectations for the future. *Entrepreneurship Research in Europe: Perspectives and Outcomes*. A. Fayolle, P. Kyrö and J. Uljin. Cheltenham, UK and Northampton, MA, USA: Edward Elgar.

Lévi-Strauss, C. (1966) *The Savage Mind*. Chicago: University of Chicago Press.

Malinowski, B. (1922) *Argonauts of the Western Pacific*. London: Routledge.

Malinowski, B. (1944) *A Scientific Theory of Culture and Other Essays*. Chapel Hill, NC: University of North Carolina Press.

Marcus, G.E. (1998) *Ethnography Through Thick and Thin*. Princeton, NJ: Princeton University Press.

Owen, W.F. (1984) Interpretive themes in relational communication. *Quarterly Journal of Speech*, (70): 274–87.

Perren, L. and M. Ram (2004) Case-study method in small business and entrepreneurial research: Mapping boundaries and perspectives. *International Small Business Journal*, 22(1): 83.

Ram, M. (1999) Management by association: Interpreting small firm–associate links in the business services sector. *Employee Relations*, 21(3): 267.

Ram, M. (2000a) Investors in people in small firms: Case study evidence from the business services sector. *Personnel Review*, 29(1): 69.

Ram, M. (2000b) People and growth: The WhitCo experience. *Human Resource Management International Digest*, 8(5): 15.

Ram, M. (2001) Family dynamics in a small consultancy firm: A case study. *Human Relations*, 54(4): 395.

Ram, M., T. Abbas et al. (2000) 'Currying favour with the locals': Balti owners and business enclaves. *International Journal of Entrepreneurial Behaviour & Research*, 6(1): 41.

Ram, M. and R. Holliday (1993) Relative merits: Family culture and kinship in small firms. *Sociology: the Journal of the British Sociological Association*, 27(4): 629.

Ram, M., B. Sanghera et al. (2000) Training and ethnic minority firms: The case of the independent restaurant sector. *Education & Training*, 42(4/5): 334.

Schwartzman, H.B. (1993) *Ethnography in Organizations*. Newbury Park, CA: Sage Publications Inc.

Silverman, D. (2000) *Doing Qualitative Research – A Practical Handbook*. London: Sage Publications.

Smith, K.G., M.J. Gannon and H. Sapienza (1989) Selecting methodologies for entrepreneurial research: trade-offs and guidelines. *Entrepreneurship Theory and Practice*, 14(1): 39.

Spradley, J.P. (1980) *Participant Observation*. New York: Holt, Rinehart and Winston.

Taylor, S., R. Thorpe et al. (2002) Negotiating managerial legitimacy in smaller organizations: Management education, technical skill, and situated competence. *Journal of Management Education*, 26(5): 550.

Willis, P. (2000) *The Ethnographic Imagination*. Cambridge, UK: Polity Press.

Zorn, T.E. (2001) Lecture Notes on Ethnography (unpublished), Hamilton, NZ: B. Johnstone.

5 Building grounded theory in entrepreneurship research

Markus M. Mäkelä and Romeo V. Turcan

Introduction

In this chapter we describe the process of building of theory from data (Glaser and Strauss 1967; Strauss and Corbin 1998). We discuss current grounded theory in relation to research in entrepreneurship and point out directions and potential improvements for further research in this field.

The chapter has two goals. First, we wish to provide an explicit paradigmatic positioning of the grounded theory methodology, discussing the most relevant views of ontology and epistemology that can be used as alternative starting points for conducting grounded theory research. While the chapter introduces our approach to grounded theory, we acknowledge the existence of other approaches and try to locate our approach in relation to them. As an important part of this discussion, we take a stand on how to usefully define 'grounded theory' and 'case study research'. Second, we seek to firmly link our discussion to the potential value of grounded theory research to the field of entrepreneurship and thus the need in this field of further grounded theory.

The procedures of applying grounded theory are basically no different in entrepreneurship than in other fields of research, and while a basic task of our chapter still is to introduce the grounded theory methodology, we bring the entrepreneurship discussion alive by introducing examples of grounded theory research in entrepreneurship. Based on this analysis of ours, we describe current ways of employing grounded theory in entrepreneurship research and suggest improvements, continuing this discussion throughout the sections of this chapter that pertain to the design and management of the grounded theory process.

A number of authors have published their views on how to conduct research that they implicitly or explicitly recognize as grounded theory research (e.g. Glaser and Strauss 1967; Glaser 1978, 1992; Strauss 1987; Eisenhardt 1989; Strauss and Corbin 1994, 1998; Yin 1994; Charmaz 1995; Locke 2001; Dougherty 2002). In this chapter, we describe the conduct of grounded theory research much in the spirit of Strauss and Corbin (1998), with some imports from procedures outlined by Eisenhardt (1989) and Yin (1994).

The remainder of the chapter is structured as follows. The next section provides an overview of the methodology, including its history. The following section discusses the positioning of the methodology within the field of social research in terms of paradigms and perspectives, techniques for collecting and analyzing empirical materials and interpretation and evaluation of quality. The subsequent section introduces an analysis made for this chapter of recent grounded theory research into entrepreneurship. Thereafter, the appropriateness of choosing the grounded theory methodology in various research situations is elaborated. After this, we provide a phase-by-phase description of the research process. Concluding remarks are then presented with considerations of the future of grounded theory inquiry.

An overview of grounded theory research

We define grounded theory as *theory derived from data that has been systematically collected and analyzed using an iterative process of considering and comparing earlier literature, its data and the emerging theory* (see Glaser and Strauss 1967; Strauss and Corbin 1998).

Before introducing the research process, we wish to note that we address grounded theory methods as a part of the family of qualitative research methods. What is qualitative research, then? Definitions abound. Qualitative research has no theory or paradigm that is distinctly its own; several paradigms claim the use of qualitative research methods (e.g. Denzin and Lincoln 1994a).[1] Qualitative research involves interpretive and naturalistic (Lincoln and Guba 1985) approaches to data collection and analysis and is multi-method in focus (Denzin and Lincoln 1994a), with the goal of outlining a set of essential qualities of complex social phenomena (Dougherty 2002). Researchers often study phenomena in their natural settings, attempting to make sense or interpret their research objects in terms of the meanings people bring to them (Glaser and Strauss 1965; Denzin and Lincoln 1994a). They emphasize situational constraints, stressing the 'value-laden nature of inquiry' (Denzin and Lincoln 1994a: 4). Qualitative research chiefly employs qualitative data. In a way, the use of qualitative data could be viewed as a starting point for qualitative research, because research methods that are termed 'qualitative' mainly use qualitative data.

It is worthwhile to note that 'qualitative research' has come to mean many kinds of inquiry, including efforts that may include some statistical analyses: for instance, a grounded theory analysis can employ statistical analyses of cases and it can be based on data collected using a survey. Thus the term 'qualitative research' that refers to the absence of employing quantitative data may be somewhat misleading, if one starts from the common definition provided above.

The grounded theory research process begins with defining the research question and potential early constructs, and then proceeds to sampling. Some reference to existing literature can be used in making these choices. Cases, groups and smaller units of data are sampled for analysis in a theoretical manner, meaning that instead of looking for representativeness, researchers will seek to find variation in key underlying variables (Eisenhardt 1989) and other theoretically interesting characteristics of the units of analysis.

Researchers then prepare vehicles and protocols of data collection and thereafter proceed to fieldwork or to another process of collecting the data on which the resulting theory is to be grounded. Collection of data is often concurrent with analysis to allow the data collection plan to be changed and a better theory discovered (Eisenhardt 1989).

Of further note is that grounded theory researchers may, depending on the circumstances, usefully benefit from triangulation of data collection methods (Jick 1979; Yin 1994), data types (for instance as divided by the quantitative–qualitative dimension) or investigators (Eisenhardt 1989). The convergence of findings enhances confidence in the quality of the study, adding to the empirical grounding of the results, whereas conflicting findings help prevent premature closure of data collection or analysis.

Advocates of grounded theory often note that theory grounded in data is more likely to fit with reality and be relevant than one formed by combining insights from prior literature, experience and common sense (see Eisenhardt 1989; Strauss and Corbin 1998). Analysis – the interaction between researchers and data – can be viewed as both a science and an art, so that the former refers to requirements for rigor, analytic orientation, systematic work and quest for validity that are placed on grounded theory research (of the form that we review in this chapter) and the latter refers to a requirement of researchers to be open to new interpretations and fresh perspectives (see Strauss and Corbin 1998).

Following analysis, propositions that state the relationships of the emergent theoretical framework are formulated and a research report written. Throughout the analysis and proposition formulation stages of the process, intensive rotation between data, the emerging theory and earlier literature has to be sought (Eisenhardt 1989; Yin 1994; Strauss and Corbin 1998).

The history of grounded theory inquiry[2]
Barney G. Glaser and Anselm L. Strauss originally developed the grounded theory methodology in their book *The Discovery of Grounded Theory* (1967). They had published some of their earlier work by using this methodology and, in their book, they referred to a number of earlier publications that had reported similar research. This book, however, was the

first publication to present a thorough account of how to build grounded theory.

In their book, Glaser and Strauss questioned the hegemony of quantitative research in the social sciences, which had marginalized the rich ethnographic tradition of their field, sociology (see Charmaz 2000). Glaser and Strauss spoke for the concern that the gap between theory-generating and empirical studies is too wide. They hoped to help bridge this gap and advocated for qualitative research to move more towards a theory-development goal. They challenged arbitrary distinctions between theory and empirical research; beliefs that qualitative methods generally are unsystematic, impressionistic and lacking rigor; the separation of data collection and analysis; assumptions that qualitative research could produce only description; claims that qualitative research is only 'pre-research' to 'more rigorous' quantitative research; and views that the quest for rigor made qualitative research illegitimate.

Later, Glaser's book *Theoretical Sensitivity* (1978) made grounded theory techniques more explicit, and Strauss's book *Qualitative Analysis for Social Scientists* (1987) improved the accessibility of grounded theory to readers. Glaser and Strauss parted in their views on building grounded theory. In later books, Strauss and Corbin (1990, 1998) presented a detailed viewpoint of theirs into analysis techniques of grounded theory. Glaser (1992), on the other hand, criticized Strauss and Corbin's 1990 book by maintaining that their approach forced data and analysis through a preconceived set of questions, techniques and hypotheses, thus preventing an emergent theory from being formed in a sufficiently objective way.

Glaser (1992), for his part, advocated just abiding by general, systematic comparisons and perceived Strauss and Corbin's approach as invoking contrived comparisons.[3] An objection has been raised that Strauss and Corbin's techniques introduce too large a set of procedures, risking that the attention of researchers may be diverted from the data, an occurrence that could result in loose theory (Charmaz 2000). Despite these criticisms, we will present the key points of Strauss and Corbin's (1998) techniques later in the chapter for the purpose of illuminating grounded theory analysis by presenting one view on doing it.

Glaser and Strauss originally presented a positivistic paradigm of grounded theory (Glaser and Strauss 1967; see also Glaser and Strauss 1965). Later, when Glaser and Strauss had already deviated in their views, Strauss and his key co-author in the 1990s, Juliet Corbin, advocated a somewhat more post-positivistic approach whereas Glaser preserved a more traditional positivistic stance. In the view of Charmaz (2000), Strauss and Corbin (1994, 1998) have since the mid-1990s shifted slightly towards the *constructivist* paradigm but remain predominantly positivistic–post-positivistic. Some others have taken even more constructivist viewpoints to grounded theory. Notably, Charmaz (2000) herself argued for using grounded theory as understood in the constructivist paradigm, thus entailing a relativistic ontology and a subjectivist epistemology. In her work, she criticized Strauss and Corbin (1990, 1998) for giving 'a behaviorist, rather than interpretive cast to their analysis' (2000: 512) and advocated a newer paradigmatic stand towards grounded theory.[4]

While evident disparities abound on what, if any, may be a 'correct' view, it remains necessary for researchers to choose from among different views, none of which can be proved superior to others. Equally important is to be cognizant of the basic tenets of other approaches.

Potential outcomes from grounded theory research

Grounded theory research can have many outcomes. Among other things, it can lead to 'causal theory', wherein relationships of mutually interacting constructs are explained, or 'process theory', wherein the explanation specifically focuses on sequences of temporally evolving action such that changes can be traced to structural and environmental changes (Strauss and Corbin 1998: 163). Other possible outcomes amount to essentially less mature building blocks of theory (see Sutton and Staw 1995), such as individual concepts, typologies and suggestions for enablers of statistical research like measurement items.

While a strong theoretical connection is often a desired characteristic of academically oriented grounded theory research, studies do in reality often lead to 'idiosyncratic theory' (Eisenhardt 1989: 547), with the theorist unable to raise the theory's level of generality. For this chapter, we have conducted a search and analysis of grounded theory papers in entrepreneurship, and indeed, 'idiosyncratic theory' is often the outcome of today's research. However, while raising the level of generality is one goal, any field of research does need *substantive theory* – theory particular to a substantive area such as complementing the entrepreneurial team or selecting venture capital investors. If well elaborated, substantive theories can make building blocks of *formal theory* – theory of a higher level of generality (but one still lower than 'grand theory'), and thus the final contributions of substantive theory do not remain idiosyncratic (Glaser and Strauss 1967).

The grounded theory-based entrepreneurship papers that we analyzed led to causal theory, process theory and less mature theorizing in forms of conceptual classifications and descriptions of structure, and outlines of important issues such as typical problems in a development process or similarities of different types of business organization.

The position of grounded theory in social research

An account of a research methodology benefits from a structured classification of research efforts so that the methodology in question can be put into context. We employ the following four-level classification that Denzin and Lincoln used in organizing their influential *Handbook of Qualitative Research* (Denzin and Lincoln 1994a);[5] we have, however, adapted their classification by labeling items two and three as research methodologies and methods, respectively (see Strauss and Corbin 1998):

1. *Paradigms* (Kuhn 1970; Denzin and Lincoln 1994b; Guba and Lincoln 1994) include, among others, those of positivism, post-positivism, critical theory and constructivism.
2. *Research methodologies* are viewed here as ways of thinking about and studying social reality (Strauss and Corbin 1998: 3), that is, stands towards the question of how researchers can find out what they believe can be known of social reality. Viewpoints that have been considered as research methodologies include for example ethnography, grounded theory, clinical study, biography, historical research and the case study (see Denzin and Lincoln 1994a).
3. *Research methods* are techniques for collecting and analyzing empirical materials (see Strauss and Corbin 1998: 3), such as interviewing, collecting documents, observational techniques, personal experience methods, various visual methods and coding and iteration procedures.
4. *Interpretation and evaluation* includes the interpretation of qualitative research and the evaluation of its quality (see, for instance, Yin 1994; Janesick 1994; Altheide and Johnson 1994; Strauss and Corbin 1998). Quality can be analyzed, among others, via the concepts of validity and reliability (for instance, Yin 1994).

Our stand on the position of grounded theory in this classification is the following: we view grounded theory much in the positivistic–post-positivistic spirit communicated by Strauss and Corbin (1998) and by some procedures and viewpoints presented by Eisenhardt (1989) and Yin (1994), nevertheless acknowledging the existence of other paradigms. Regarding methodologies, we view them as comprising partly overlapping *viewpoints* to the study of social reality. An important implication of this stance to our chapter is that we do not consider 'case study' as a distinct methodology but choose to conceptualize a case as a choice of *object of study*, one common in research following the grounded theory methodology.[6]

Grounded theory can usefully employ all known techniques for collecting empirical material and has a useful set of procedures for analyzing data.

We discuss these elements, as well as the interpretation and evaluation of grounded theory, later in the chapter.

Prior use of grounded theory in entrepreneurship research
For the chapter, we conducted a review for identifying entrepreneurship research that employed the grounded theory methodology. The review resulted in 42 articles that we classify in Table 5.1.

We conducted a search from the Emerald, Infotrac, ProQuest and ScienceDirect databases for articles published between January 1993 and June 2004. Our search criteria first included keywords chosen for identifying relevant research, such as 'entrepreneurship', 'grounded theory' and names of well-known grounded theory methodology authors. Of the articles we found, we excluded those that either did not have a grounded theory methodology or a focus on entrepreneurship. The exclusion was based on comparing the articles with our definitions of grounded theory (presented above) and entrepreneurship (defined as discovering, evaluating and exploiting opportunities to create future goods and services; this definition is derived from the work of Shane and Venkataraman 2000).

The selection of papers was based on a careful but admittedly (and necessarily) subjective comparison with the definitions. According to the definition used for grounded theory, articles needed to demonstrate that analysis involved iterative rotation between three elements – data, emerging theory and existing literature – to produce their results. Authors had to explicitly recognize their work as grounded theory: they needed to be cognizant of their pursuit of a grounded theory approach.

The rationale for the review was to reach a basic understanding of how grounded theory is currently being conducted in the field of entrepreneurship. For each article, we analyzed its research focus, its way of applying grounded theory, key findings and the way of writing up the research. Analysis of applying grounded theory included studying the articles' procedures of sampling, data collection and analysis.

Figure 5.1 graphically presents the distribution of the identified grounded theory entrepreneurship articles by publication year. To illustrate the division of grounded theory entrepreneurship research into publication outlets, Figure 5.2 presents the distribution of the articles by focus domains of journals in which the articles were published.

The search of the four article databases covers several dozens of journals that potentially could publish grounded theory-based entrepreneurship research. As shown in Table 5.1, the procedure for identifying articles that we used does not indicate many pieces of such research having been published each year. Results presented in Figure 5.1 imply that there is no trend towards more of this research (even though some authors, such as Lichtenstein and

Table 5.1 Summary of entrepreneurship articles employing the grounded theory methodology by publication outlet and year

Year	Entrepreneurship					Management & organization, general				Small business		Public administration & research policy		Total
	ETP	IJEBR	JBV	JDE	JPE	AMJ	ASQ	SMJ	Other	ISBJ	JSBM	ARPA	RP	
2004			3						2					5
2003					1				1		1		1	4
2002	1					1		1						2
2001						1		1	2					5
2000							1		3					4
1999				1					2					3
1998			1											1
1997						1	1							2
1996			1					1	2	1		1		6
1995	1	1				1	1		1					4
1994		1	1			1			2					5
1993											1			1
Total	2	1	6	1	1	5	3	3	15	1	2	1	1	42
%	4.8	2.4	14.3	2.4	2.4	11.9	7.1	7.1	35.7	2.4	4.8	2.4	2.4	

Notes:

Abbreviations of journals

AMJ: Academy of Management Journal; ASQ: Administrative Science Quarterly; ARPA: American Review of Public Administration; ETP: Entrepreneurship Theory and Practice; IJEBR: International Journal of Entrepreneurial Behaviour and Research; ISBJ: International Small Business Journal; JBV: Journal of Business Venturing; JDE: Journal of Developmental Entrepreneurship; JPE: Journal of Private Equity; JSBM: Journal of Small Business Management; RP: Research Policy; SMJ: Strategic Management Journal.

Journals in column 'Other'

European Management Journal; Financial Management; Human Relations; International Journal of Organizational Analysis; International Studies of Management and Organization; Journal of Management; Journal of Organizational Change Management; Journal of Purchasing and Supply Management; Management Decision; Qualitative Market Research.

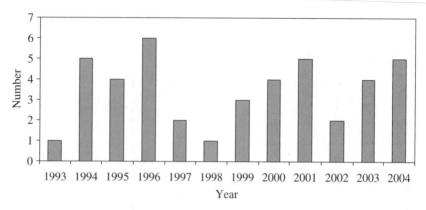

Figure 5.1   Number of grounded theory-based entrepreneurship articles by publication year

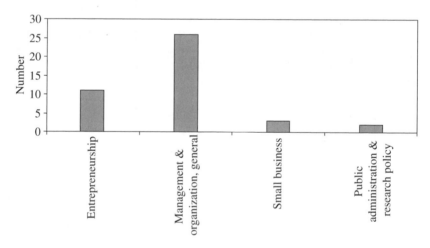

Figure 5.2   Number of grounded theory entrepreneurship articles by focus domains of publication outlets

Brush 2001, have argued that grounded theory building is on the increase in entrepreneurship). The subsections 'Entrepreneurship' and 'Management and organization, general' do not contain clear trends either.

Figure 5.2 implies, first, that much of grounded theory-based entrepreneurship research is published in outlets that are general to the management and organization field. This is not surprising, given that there are many more general management and organization publication outlets than there are entrepreneurship publication outlets. On the other hand, the result may indicate that those publication outlets that go by an entrepreneurship-related name and that are studied in our analysis may lean towards 'traditional' methodologies more than general 'management and organization' journals. Second, the figure illustrates the fact that entrepreneurship research is published not only in 'entrepreneurship' and general 'management and organization' outlets but also elsewhere, including 'small business' journals. But then again, some definitions consider all 'small business' activity as entrepreneurship and entrepreneurship may even be defined by the size of business. Classification used here for journals by their focus areas is indicated in Table 5.1.

In the following, we outline key observations from our review of the articles. As a central outcome, our analysis points to several areas where the grounded theory research practice should be generally improved. Generally, only articles of the most highly regarded outlets were typically 'good' in terms of all or nearly all relevant aspects. In the remainder of the chapter, we outline our suggestions for improvements in more detail than in here.

First, a significant minority of the papers failed to present an appropriate justification for using the grounded theory methodology. Second, despite the claimed use of the grounded theory methodology, many articles were in fact descriptive or exploratory, with no rigorous commitment to an actual theoretical contribution. The meaning of 'theory' (see, e.g., Bacharach 1989; Sutton and Staw 1995) may be unclear to some authors.

Third, potentially related to the first point, while most papers were detailed in describing the sampling and data collection procedures, very few were sufficiently detailed in describing the data analysis. For the purposes of increasing reliability and credibility of the results of a grounded theory effort, wherein a new theoretical framework is proposed from the analysis of data, authors should present a detailed account on how they conducted their analysis. It is known that publication editors put strict limitations on the length of papers, but authors should try to describe all main phases of their analyses. Exemplary works are available (see, e.g., Eisenhardt and Bourgeois 1988; Brown and Eisenhardt 1997; Edmondson et al. 2001).

Very few articles reported to have followed detailed guidelines of coding such as those advocated by Strauss and Corbin (1998). While we think that researchers' thinking and consequently objectivity should not be limited by the strict requirements that coding procedures can be seen to put on them (Glaser 1992), it is our stand that a coding procedure more elaborate than just comparison can serve to ensure a systematic analysis and thus bring about increased credibility to grounded theory research. Acknowledging Glaser's (1992) argument that elaborate coding procedures could invoke contrived comparisons, we urge grounded theory analysts to be careful not to let a procedure become a straitjacket for their theorizing.

Fourth, in a minority of articles, appropriate theoretical sampling is not conducted. Sampling may not be described at all or it may be totally random, echoing the requirements of theory-testing (and not theory-building) research. (See also Neergaard, Chapter 10 in this volume, for a discussion of appropriate sampling procedures in qualitative research.) Fifth, a majority of the articles do not have an explicit assessment of the quality of the study.

Sixth, we observed that many articles reported longitudinal research. This is comforting, because longitudinality may improve the quality of research and is often needed, especially in process research. Seventh, most articles included a literature review, and they explicitly linked their findings to existing literature. This is positive in that it assists the reader in understanding how the authors came to their conclusions and how they have linked their findings to the existing base of knowledge.

Finally, two comments of a more detailed level emerged from our analysis. First, many studies might have benefited from evidence source triangulation, such as obtaining observational data and documentation to complement data obtained through interviews (see Yin 1994). Second, advanced techniques of tabular and graphical displays (see, e.g., Miles and Huberman 1994) should be used more often in the presentation of results. Often in reporting grounded theory research, tables and other displays provide authors with a way to compress information and thereby make the key meanings of their data more easily understood. For instance, rows can be used for cases and, in the columns, authors can present summary information based on which they developed their measurements underlying their model.

Due to the small number of grounded theory entrepreneurship articles found, we cannot say that some substantial area of entrepreneurship research would be 'better covered' by grounded theory efforts than some other area. Most articles that we analyzed were in the areas of innovation, corporate entrepreneurship and entrepreneurial networks. Other areas represented were new venture creation, strategic change in entrepreneurship, international expansion, public-policy-related questions, business exit and team formations. The smallest number of articles was found in the areas of venture capital, family entrepreneurship, risk and entrepreneurial learning. The differences in the number of articles could be due to some areas of entrepreneurship simply being generally under more scrutiny. Finally, we consider the number of articles that we analyzed to be too small to facilitate pointing out distinct directions for grounded theory efforts in entrepreneurship.

Feasibility of the grounded theory methodology
When can or should a researcher use the grounded theory methodology? Newness of the research area is often mentioned as a justification for building grounded theory. Theory-building can often benefit from qualitative

research in which researchers identify important constructs from a novel viewpoint. Thereafter, theory-testing researchers can deduce hypotheses from constructs proposed by theory-builders. Grounded theory fits well with situations where there is little empirical validation of current perspectives or where existing perspectives conflict (Eisenhardt 1989), or where a new perspective is sought (see Hitt et al. 1998). Grounded theory researchers may benefit from unique means to facilitate an understanding of the complexity of social phenomena (Dougherty 2002). The collection and analysis of qualitative data may enable researchers to drill deep into phenomena where obtaining reliable quantitative data would be troublesome.

Our analysis of grounded theory entrepreneurship research showed that entrepreneurship researchers most often justified their use of the grounded theory methodology by the often-used argument of the inadequacy or inexistence of theory on the subject. Complexity of the studied phenomenon was also cited as a motivation to engage in grounded theory research (Garud et al. 2002). Another argument was that boundaries between the phenomenon and its environment were not evident (see, e.g., Amit and Zott 2001). Lichtenstein and Brush (2001) quoted the lack of empirical validation as one justification for employing a grounded-theory-producing case study approach.

We wish to emphasize that substantive theory is often an important ingredient of research into areas where formal theory is already present (Glaser and Strauss 1967). Researchers should not misinterpret our notion about too 'narrow' theory to mean that substantive theory would not be valuable. Grounded theory-building is particularly appropriate in the aforementioned situations because grounded theory research does not rely specifically on existing literature or previous empirical evidence (Eisenhardt 1989). Next, we move on to discuss the grounded theory research process.

The research process
Designing research
Research design can usefully be defined as a 'logical sequence that connects the empirical data to a study's initial research questions and, ultimately, to its conclusions', involving an action plan to getting from the initial research question to conclusions (Yin 1994: 19). We begin our overview of the research process by discussing the definition of the research problem, potential initial constructs and planning for quality.

Research problem and initial constructs   At the start of research, researchers should carefully define the research problem. Often it is useful to present the problem in the form of a research question. Explicit formulation of the research question entails the ability to articulate a justification for using the grounded theory methodology and to define a focus for the study. It also helps in specifying the type of people or organizations that should be approached for data collection and the type of data to be collected.

It is our experience that in addition to specifying the research question, it is often useful to specify some early constructs before beginning data collection. We also feel that researchers should be cognizant of relevant prior literature so that they can effectively focus their efforts on probing new issues and taking useful standpoints and inquiring into all relevant phenomena during their data collection. However, researchers should be aware of the potential biases in findings that may result from certain ways of using prior constructs as indicated in earlier literature. We agree with Glaser and Strauss (1967) and Eisenhardt (1989) in that researchers could end up being guided in their thinking by earlier results *in a manner restrictive to their theorizing*. Researchers should try to avoid this pitfall by regularly analyzing their own research and thinking processes with respect to the potential effect of being knowledgeable about prior literature.

Planning for quality   The focal goal of research design is to maximize research quality (see also Wigren, Chapter 15, and Bøllingtoft, Chapter 16 in this volume for a discussion of the assessment of quality in more detail).

There is no universally accepted standard for developing a high-quality study. Standards for evaluating quantitative research should not be directly applied to grounded theory (see Strauss and Corbin 1998: 266). Following Strauss and Corbin (ibid.: 273), we maintain that criteria for evaluating grounded theory are meant as guidelines and should not be understood as 'hard-and-fast evaluative rules'.

Our review of grounded theory entrepreneurship research points out that a majority of the articles do not have an explicit quality assessment. We suggest that grounded theory researchers take up, to present in their reports, an analysis of (1) *theory–data compatibility*, (2) *consistency of process* and (3) the *generalizability, reproducibility and significance of the theory generated* – that is, aspects of validity, reliability and the value of the results. The theory generated should be logically coherent and, if possible, readily testable. Strauss and Corbin (1998: 265–74) presented an informative overview of the evaluation of grounded theory.[7] Reading this account in advance will help grounded theorists design their research well in the first place. Keys to achieving high quality are in designing research carefully, maintaining a strictly analytical grip during the research process, documentation of the process and rigorous iteration between data, emerging theory and prior literature.

Of note is that because generalizability is an objective in our approach to research, research designs with more than one object of study (multiple-case designs) are preferable. Such design will allow *replication*, obtaining similar results from two or more objects of study (see Yin 1994: 45–50), which will enhance trust in generalizability.

Sampling issues are important in increasing the quality of grounded theory studies. They are covered in detail in this handbook by Neergaard (Chapter 10). *Theoretical sampling* allows the grounded theorist to build variation into theory, thus enhancing its explanatory potential (Strauss and Corbin 1998). Another alternative, random sampling, is possible and may be justified in rare situations, but will often hinder the discovery of variations. It often makes sense for the grounded theorist to select extreme cases in which variation is easily observable (Eisenhardt 1989).

Our review of the literature shows that grounded theorists of entrepreneurship have conducted and explained their sampling in a variety of ways. While many papers – two-thirds of all reviewed – reported and undertook theoretical sampling, a number conducted a random sampling in the spirit of statistical research (e.g. Amit and Zott 2001). Some conducted an intermediate sampling where the paper had a broadly defined scope, and cases fitting the scope were selected apparently without planning on variation (see Lichtenstein and Brush 2001). Sometimes, the use of convenience sampling was acknowledged (Clarysse and Moray 2004). Although sampling should be theoretical, in most cases it was not. Despite the significance of sampling, a significant proportion of articles that used the grounded theory methodology did not sufficiently articulate their grounds for sampling.

Data collection

Data collection in grounded theory research is similar to other qualitative research. Yin (1994) presented a thorough description of potential sources of evidence that is useful to grounded theorists. In the following section, we discuss issues of triangulation and overlap between data collection and analysis that are of special interest to the grounded theorist.

Triangulation   Triangulation is an important issue and tool in qualitative research generally (Huberman and Miles 1994; Altheide and Johnson 1994). Many aspects of triangulation closely pertain to the data collection phase (Eisenhardt 1989; Yin 1994). Triangulation refers to the combination of multiple methods, empirical materials, observers or perspectives in a single study. The use of triangulation is an attempt to obtain a deeper understanding of the studied phenomenon and may add rigor and breadth (Jick 1979; Denzin and Lincoln 1994a). In grounded theory research, triangulation provides an important means to reduce the likelihood of misinterpretation, and thus its use is generally recommended. For instance, it is often useful for the entrepreneurship grounded theorist to make use not only of the interview, but also of documents and observations. Likewise it is often useful to use several people to collect and analyze data. (The downside in this is that the interpretation of data may of course be *different* between interpreters as conducted by different investigators.) What was described was triangulation in terms of sources of evidence and researchers, respectively.

In the research analyzed here, various documents were often used to complement interviews in data collection. The semi-structured interview was the most common way to collect data. We believe that documentary and observational evidence are in reality used in many papers where authors do not explicitly acknowledge this.

Overlap of the collection and analysis of data Generally, an important feature of many qualitative research efforts is that there is significant overlap between the data collection and analysis phases. This enables the study to be properly refocused and the appropriate theoretical sampling to be conducted during the course of research (Glaser and Strauss 1967; Eisenhardt 1989; Strauss and Corbin 1998). Such freedom to adjust the working protocol is an important advantage of grounded theory research, representing 'controlled opportunism in which researchers take advantage of the uniqueness of a specific case and the emergence of new themes to improve resultant theory' (Eisenhardt 1989: 539). Such opportunism is legitimate because researchers are attempting to understand the data in extensive depth (Eisenhardt 1989).

If the part of research after which data collection is refocused is distinct from other parts of research, it can be considered a *pilot study*. A pilot study can be pivotal in helping prevent costly pitfalls by enabling researchers to reformat their research protocol in time. Both the content of data and the procedures of investigation may be revised.

In the research that we analyzed, data collection typically had temporal overlap with data analysis. Only a handful of articles commented on issues of the research process in such detail as to describe, for instance, reorganization of data collection methods or changing the analysis procedure. It is, of course, possible that reorganization is rarely needed. In any case, it is important to describe the data collection and analysis process to the reader in sufficient detail.

Data analysis

Literature illustrates a variety of approaches that can be taken to qualitative data analysis. Analysis is the phase of grounded theory research which can perhaps more than any other phase make use of methods that are distinct just to grounded theory. In this phase, the grounded theorist attempts to conceptualize, reduce, elaborate and relate data and categories to integrate them as novel theory. One way to do this is to conduct coding in three phases as presented by Strauss and Corbin (1998). In the following, we briefly introduce these phases.[8]

The first phase, *open coding*, comprises finding and naming categories and discovering their properties and dimensions. (Categories, or themes, are concepts found from the data that stand for phenomena. Properties are characteristics of a category, and dimensions are about the location of a property along a continuum.) Researchers should try to generate as many categories as possible to make sure that this phase of the analysis is open to whatever is going on in the data. They should engage in open coding each time a new insight emerges, or if there are ambiguities in existing categories. They can do this throughout the analysis process, even though the bulk of open coding is generally conducted in the beginning phase of the analysis.

In the second phase, *axial coding*, researchers relate categories to their sub-categories by coding around the axis of a single category at a time, linking categories at the level of dimensions and properties. In this phase, the extent to which a category fits the data should be checked. In axial coding, cumulative knowledge is produced about the relationship between the focal category and others. Researchers look for answers to questions such as why, when, where and how. This helps them contextualize phenomena.

The third phase, *selective coding*, comprises coding systematically for those core categories that best hold categories together as a coherent framework. In this phase, researchers refine these categories and integrate them into a parsimonious theory. Selective coding is a process of searching for the main problem – the essential 'skeleton' that sums up the substance present in the data and holds it together. The central category needed for this has to be coherent and logical. Once the central category is found, major categories need to be related to it by propositions. The techniques of writing a storyline, reviewing notes, using displays and using software products can help in this integration process. When a theoretical scheme is outlined, researchers should refine the theory by removing excess and filling in poorly developed categories, saturating them via further theoretical sampling if necessary.

At this point, we wish to bring into explicit discussion the aspect of enfolding existing literature. In grounded theory research, it can at times be very challenging to distinguish one's results from those already achieved by others, except possibly when generating substantive theory of a low level of generality: the vast amounts of theory that exist and are published in some field of social inquiry could well explain a part of your data. Grounded theorists in entrepreneurship will benefit from carefully comparing their results with the findings of prior studies. Of essence is that a large enough body of literature is considered and similarities and contradictions sought so that truly novel contributions can be distilled. Contrasting literature can even be helpful in producing new insights into factors such as new dimensions or constructs (Eisenhardt 1989). However, contrasting literature may also just reduce confidence in the validity of the results: such literature may point to the results being incorrect or idiosyncratic to one instance in the data.

It can be valuable to study literature in such substantive areas that are not under study but whose phenomena nevertheless are analogous to those investigated. For instance, various types of strategic alliances may have characteristics that might be useful in the study of venture capital co-investment syndicates. Such literature can point out similarities that are typically not analyzed in connection to each other, and again, new insights can result. Improved levels of conceptual representation and external and internal validity can follow from such comparison.

Propositions[9] generated in the process are validated by comparing them with raw data. More iterative coding is needed if the propositions do not fit the data. Here, it is worthy to note that replication (see section 'Planning for quality' above) can be claimed even when an instance in the data shows different results than a comparison instance if there is a theoretical explanation that credibly accounts for the different results. In other words, replication can be claimed if there is a theoretical reason to believe that different results were reached because of an intervening external factor. Such replication has been labeled 'theoretical replication' as opposed to 'literal replication' (Yin 1994: 46).

Regarding the presentation of propositions, we advocate presenting propositions as explicit sentences, preferably sorted out from the body text by some form of emphasis, and not embedded in the text. Explicit presentation makes it easier for readers to grasp the entirety of the theoretical framework presented and will facilitate discerning the structure of the results and the contributions to knowledge.

An important and often difficult part of the process is to know when the iteration can be stopped. A meticulous research process is resource intensive. Too much iteration will consume time, attention and other resources, and this could negatively impact the quality of research. At some point in time, saturation occurs in the emerging propositions such that further iteration will be unlikely to provide significant incremental learning of new aspects of the framework (Eisenhardt 1989). Experience will enhance the recognition of the correct moment to stop iteration.

For further reading on the grounded theory process, we especially recommend the works of Dougherty (2002) and Strauss and Corbin (1998). Dougherty (2002) has provided one of the most succinct practical descriptions of how to do grounded theory analysis by using the three coding phases outlined above. Her text includes good practical examples of the process, as does that of Strauss and Corbin (1998). We also direct the reader to this chapter's section on suggested further readings.

In our review of grounded theory articles, we rarely encountered authors claiming a careful, detailed analytical process. However, results were typically linked with existing literature at least in the substantive area of the study. While some authors agreed with Glaser (1992) in that strict coding procedures may bring about contrived comparisons, we nevertheless find that a majority of grounded theory efforts would benefit significantly from a more strictly guided research procedure that we feel would enable increased credibility of the results.

Discussion and conclusions

We have attempted to distinguish this chapter from many prior grounded theory methodology reviews primarily by two means. First, we have presented an explicit discussion on how the paradigmatic position of grounded theory can be and has been viewed, and how these views affect the use of grounded theory. We have purposefully presented this discussion to allow for linking our approach better to the entire array of potential approaches to grounded theory. Like other grounded theory authors, we did introduce in detail just one approach to using the methodology: we view grounded theory much in the positivistic–post-positivistic spirit of Strauss and Corbin (1998), with some imports from procedures outlined by Eisenhardt (1989) and Yin (1994).

A main guideline that we sought to follow in our presentation of the grounded theory process was that we wanted to introduce the process to the reader with emphasis on those aspects that are specific to this methodology – the other aspects are covered well elsewhere in this handbook. Especially the phase of designing research and the phase of analyzing data and formulating propositions have aspects discernibly specific to grounded theory.

Second, we particularly discussed grounded theory as a research methodology within the entrepreneurship domain. We facilitated our discussion by looking at an analysis of 42 prior papers that presented grounded theory-based entrepreneurship research. The chapter echoes the results of our analysis throughout the sections that discuss the design and management of the grounded theory process. We have used the analysis to illustrate potent ways of employing the methodology and we have pointed out areas that call for improvement.

The most important areas that call for improvement are (1) presenting a justification for using the grounded theory methodology; (2) carefully planning and conducting appropriate sampling; (3) using a rigorous and systematic analysis process and describing the process to the reader; and (4) explicitly assessing the quality of research in the report. Generally, we urge authors of future entrepreneurship studies using the grounded theory approach to consider what actually constitutes a theoretical contribution (see Whetten 1989) and to aim to produce not only substantive theory (theory specific to a substantive domain) but also formal theory (theory of a higher level of generality). We do not by any means belittle the value of substantive theory, because such theory, if properly built, can be important by itself in some domains and help in building theory of a higher level of generality.

Minor suggestions for improving grounded theory research are that evidence source triangulation should be used more often and that well-prepared graphical representations and tabular displays should be employed to enhance the presentation of the contents of data to the reader.

Building theory is imperative for knowledge creation. It constantly complements testing theory; some form of theory-building is, in fact, a necessary antecedent for testing. Based on our discussion of the feasibility of grounded theory, we encourage entrepreneurship scholars to explore the potential of their research questions to accommodate rigorous grounded theory research and to dare to go on using this methodology with all research problems that could benefit from building theory and that allow for empirical inquiry. In the research agendas of academic institutions, entrepreneurship is a young and immature field, and as such it will benefit from rigorous attempts at theory development. We believe that grounded theory holds important promise for the field and thus should gain a somewhat stronger foothold. We wish to support the further use of the methodology and hope to have contributed to the spreading of knowledge on its employment.

Acknowledgements
We wish to thank Richard Harrison, Leila Hurmerinta-Peltomäki, Markku Maula, Helle Neergaard, Vesa Puhakka, Henrikki Tikkanen, John Parm Ulhøi, and two anonymous reviewers for their helpful comments. We acknowledge the financial support of the Emil Aaltonen Foundation and the Carnegie Trust.

Notes
1. We define the paradigm as a basic set of beliefs that guide action (see, e.g., Guba 1990), considering that paradigms 'deal with first principles, or ultimates', 'are human constructions', and 'can never be established in terms of their ultimate truthfulness' (Denzin and Lincoln 1994a: 99). Paradigms can be viewed to be composed of a set of stances towards three subquestions (Guba and Lincoln 1994): questions of *ontology*, *epistemology* and *methodology*. For discussions on paradigms in qualitative research more broadly, see, for instance, Lincoln and Guba (2000) or Guba and Lincoln (1994).
2. Strauss and Corbin (1994) and Charmaz (2000) presented more detailed accounts of the history of grounded theory.
3. See Charmaz (2000) for an overview of the controversies between Glaser and Strauss in the development of the methodology after its early period.

4.   Charmaz's (2000) work includes a detailed discussion and one of the rare accounts on the paradigm of grounded theory research. The constructivist paradigm may have important insights to offer to the grounded theory research community: the consequences of successful constructivist grounded theory could perhaps eventually result in a more pluralistic and therefore perhaps better understanding of what is studied. While we view grounded theory from a positivistic–post-positivistic standpoint, we refer the reader to Charmaz's (2000) text for an overview of grounded theory from the viewpoint of the constructivistic paradigm and for a comparison of that viewpoint with the positivistic viewpoint. A further view into grounded theory from a constructivist approach can be obtained from an earlier paper of hers (Charmaz 1995; see also Locke 2001). Glaser (2002) repudiated Charmaz's (2000) view that grounded theory could be constructivist. Lincoln and Guba's (1985, 2000) positions, on the other hand, do not regard a positivistic paradigm as necessarily essential to the methodology.

5.   We do not wish to use the division into 'qualitative research' and 'quantitative research' as a classification item. In our view, the label 'qualitative research' describes a set of research methods. We follow the stance of Guba and Lincoln (1994), maintaining that both 'quantitative methods' and 'qualitative methods' can be used appropriately within any paradigm of research, questions of method and methodology being secondary to questions of paradigm.

6.   'Case study research' is a term with several meanings (Ragin 1992 discusses these in detail); the term is commonly used as a euphemism for qualitative research. Stake (1994) was the first author that we know of to define the case study as a choice of the object of study. This definition is relatively seldom used and sometimes argued against (e.g. Yin 1994: 17). Cases are an important object of study in grounded theory research: qualitative data often come to grounded theory research from what can be called cases, and consequently many grounded theory studies will benefit from insights from top authors using the 'case study' label such as Eisenhardt (1989) and Yin (1994). Case study and grounded theory research obviously are not wholly overlapping domains: many case studies are descriptive and some test theory (Johnston et al. 1999 and Hillebrand et al. 2001 discuss theory-testing by case studies in detail) and inductive ones may have methods that could not be regarded as grounded theory methods. Correspondingly, some grounded theory is built based on empirical materials that can be argued not to come from 'cases' (examples are presented by Glaser and Strauss 1967).

7.   In addition, the discussion provided by Yin (1994: 32–8) on construct, internal and external validity, and reliability is suggested as useful reading for grounded theorists.

8.   We acknowledge that Charmaz (2000) and Glaser (1992) presented critique towards Strauss and Corbin's earlier work from 1990, from which Charmaz (2000) considered their 1998 book to be an improved and more accessible version. We view the 1998 book of Strauss and Corbin as a recommendable set of instructions that can ensure a systematic analysis and thus bring about increased credibility to research. The development of the thoughts on coding outlined here was started by Strauss (1987).

9.   'Proposition' is an appropriate term for the formulations of grounded theory end-products, as a proposition is viewed as a statement of a causal tie that connects *constructs* to each other, and 'hypothesis' for its part as a statement of a causal tie that connects *variables* to each other (Bacharach 1989: 498–9). That is, 'hypotheses' are usefully presented at the stage of preparing to enter empirical inquiry, and thus are appropriate for theory-testing research.

Suggested further readings

Dougherty, D. (2002) Grounded theory research methods. In: Baum, J.A.C. (ed.), *The Blackwell Companion to Organizations*. Padstow, UK: Blackwell, pp. 849–66. This book chapter provides a succinct practical description, including real-life examples on how to do grounded theory analysis following the three coding phases outlined by, for instance, Strauss and Corbin (1998) and in this chapter.

Glaser, B.G. (1992) *Basics of Grounded Theory Analysis: Emergence vs. forcing.* Mill Valley, CA: Sociology Press. This book presents Barney G. Glaser's approach to conducting grounded theory research. Glaser preserves a realist stance towards grounded theory research and criticizes the approach of Strauss and Corbin (1990) as invoking contrived comparisons and preventing objective theory formation.

Glaser, B.G. and Strauss, A.L. (1967) *The Discovery of Grounded Theory: Strategies for qualitative research.* Chicago, IL: Aldine. This book is the original, landmark work of Barney G. Glaser and Anselm L. Strauss that introduced the grounded theory methodology. While additional insights and newer views on how to interpret this book have been published later, the reader is advised mainly to consult contemporary texts.

Strauss, A. and Corbin, J. (1998) *Basics of Qualitative Research: Techniques and procedures for developing grounded theory.* Thousand Oaks, CA: Sage. In this book Anselm L. Strauss and Juliet Corbin advocate an approach that is rather more post-positivistic than that of Glaser (1992). The book provides a thorough description of the analysis procedures discussed in our chapter and illustrative examples of actual research situations.

References

Altheide, D. and Johnson, J.M. (1994) Criteria for assessing interpretive validity in qualitative research. In: Denzin, N.K. and Lincoln, Y.S. (eds), *Handbook of Qualitative Research.* Thousand Oaks, CA: Sage, 485–99.

Amit, R. and Zott, C. (2001) Value creation in e-business. *Strategic Management Journal*, **22**: 493–520.

Bacharach, S.B. (1989) Organizational theories: Some criteria for evaluation. *Academy of Management Review*, **14**: 496–515.

Brown, S.L. and Eisenhardt, K.M. (1997) The art of continuous change: Linking complexity theory and time-paced evolution in relentlessly shifting organizations. *Administrative Science Quarterly*, **42**: 1–34.

Charmaz, K. (1995) Grounded theory. In Smith, J.A., Harré, R. and Van Langenhove, L. (eds), *Rethinking Methods in Psychology.* London: Sage, pp. 27–49.

Charmaz, K. (2000) Grounded theory: Objectivist and constructivist methods. In: Denzin, N.K. and Lincoln, Y.S. (eds), *Handbook of Qualitative Research.* Thousand Oaks, CA: Sage, pp. 163–88.

Clarysse, B. and Moray, N. (2004) A process study of entrepreneurial team formation: The case of a research-based spin-off. *Journal of Business Venturing*, **19**: 55–79.

Denzin, N.K. and Lincoln, Y.S. (eds) (1994a) *Handbook of Qualitative Research.* Thousand Oaks, CA: Sage.

Denzin, N.K. and Lincoln, Y.S. (1994b) Introduction: Entering the field of qualitative research. In: Denzin, N.K. and Lincoln, Y.S. (eds), *Handbook of Qualitative Research.* Thousand Oaks, CA: Sage, pp. 1–17.

Dougherty, D. (2002) Grounded theory research methods. In: Baum, J.A.C. (ed), *The Blackwell Companion to Organizations.* Padstow, UK: Blackwell, pp. 849–66.

Edmondson, A.C., Bohmer, R.M. and Pisano, G.P. (2001) Disrupted routines: Team learning and new technology implementation in hospitals. *Administrative Science Quarterly*, **46**: 685–716.

Eisenhardt, K.M. (1989) Building theories from case study research. *Academy of Management Review*, **14**: 532–50.

Eisenhardt, K.M. and Bourgeois, L.J., III (1988) Politics of strategic decision-making in high-velocity environments. *Academy of Management Journal*, **31**: 737–70.

Garud, R., Jain, S. and Kumaraswamy, A. (2002) Institutional entrepreneurship in the sponsorship of common technological standards: The case of Sun Microsystems and Java. *Academy of Management Journal*, **45**: 196–214.

Glaser, B.G. (1978) *Theoretical Sensitivity.* Mill Valley, CA: Sociology Press.

Glaser, B.G. (1992) *Basics of Grounded Theory Analysis: Emergence vs. forcing.* Mill Valley, CA: Sociology Press.

Glaser, B.G. (2002) Constructivist grounded theory? *Forum: Qualitative Social Research* 3(3). Available at http://www.Qualitative-Research.net/Fqs/Fqs-Eng.htm, Accessed on 8 January 2004.

Glaser, B.G. and Strauss, A.L. (1965) *Awareness of Dying.* Chicago, IL: Aldine.

Glaser, B.G. and Strauss, A.L. (1967) *The Discovery of Grounded theory: Strategies for qualitative research*. Chicago, IL: Aldine.

Guba, E.G. (1990) The alternative paradigm dialog. In: E.G. Guba (ed.), *The Paradigm Dialog*. Newbury Park, CA: Sage, pp. 17–30.

Guba, E.G. and Lincoln, Y.S. (1994) Competing paradigms in qualitative research. In: Denzin, N.K. and Lincoln, Y.S. (eds), *Handbook of Qualitative Research*. Thousand Oaks, CA: Sage, pp. 105–17.

Hillebrand, B., Kok, R.A.W. and Biemans, W.G. (2001) Theory-testing using case studies: A comment on Johnston, Leach, and Liu. *Industrial Marketing Management*, **30**: 651–7.

Hitt, M., Harrison, J., Ireland, R.D. and Best, A. (1998) Attributes of successful and unsuccessful acquisitions of US firms. *British Journal of Management*, **9**: 91–114.

Huberman, M. and Miles, M.B. (1994) Data management and analysis methods. In: Denzin, N.K. and Lincoln, Y.S. (eds), *Handbook of Qualitative Research*. Thousand Oaks, CA: Sage, pp. 428–44.

Janesick, V.J. (1994) The dance of qualitative research design: Metaphor, methodolatry, and meaning. In: Denzin, N.K. and Lincoln, Y.S. (eds), *Handbook of Qualitative Research*. Thousand Oaks, CA: Sage, pp. 209–19.

Jick, T.D. (1979) Mixing qualitative and quantitative methods: Triangulation in action. *Administrative Science Quarterly*, **24**: 602–11.

Johnston, W.J., Leach, M.P. and Liu, A.H. (1999) Theory testing using case studies in business-to-business research. *Industrial Marketing Management*, **28**: 201–13.

Kuhn, T.S. (1970) *The Structure of Scientific Revolutions*. Chicago, IL: University of Chicago Press.

Lichtenstein, B.M.B. and Brush, C.G. (2001) How do 'resource bundles' develop and change in new ventures? A dynamic model and longitudinal exploration. *Entrepreneurship Theory and Practice*, **25**: 37–58.

Lincoln, Y.S. and Guba, E.G. (1985) *Naturalistic Inquiry*. Beverly Hills, CA: Sage.

Lincoln, Y.S. and Guba, E.G. (2000) Paradigmatic controversies, contradictions, and emerging confluences. In: Denzin, N.K. and Lincoln, Y.S. (eds), *Handbook of Qualitative Research*. Thousand Oaks, CA: Sage, pp. 163–88.

Locke, K. (2001) *Grounded Theory in Management Research*. Thousand Oaks, CA: Sage.

Miles, M.B. and Huberman, A.M. (1994) *Qualitative Data Analysis: An expanded sourcebook*. Thousand Oaks, CA: Sage.

Ragin, C.C. (1992) Introduction: Cases of 'What is a case?'. In: Ragin, C.C. and Becker, H.S. (eds), *What Is a Case? Exploring the foundations of social inquiry*. Cambridge: Cambridge University Press, pp. 1–18.

Shane, S. and Venkataraman, S. (2000) The promise of entrepreneurship as a field of research. *Academy of Management Review*, **25**: 217–26.

Stake, R.E. (1994) Case studies. In: Denzin, N.K. and Lincoln, Y.S. (eds), *Handbook of Qualitative Research*. Thousand Oaks, CA: Sage, pp. 236–47.

Strauss, A. (1987) *Qualitative Analysis for Social Scientists*. New York: Cambridge University Press.

Strauss, A. and Corbin, J. (1994) Grounded theory methodology: An overview. In Denzin, N.K. and Lincoln, Y.S. (eds), *Handbook of Qualitative Research*. Thousand Oaks, CA: Sage, pp. 273–85.

Strauss, A. and Corbin, J. (1998) *Basics of Qualitative Research: Techniques and procedures for developing grounded theory*. Thousand Oaks, CA: Sage.

Strauss, A.L. and Corbin, J. (1990) *Basics of Qualitative Research: Grounded theory procedures and techniques*. Newbury Park, CA: Sage.

Sutton, R.I. and Staw, B.M. (1995) What theory is not. *Administrative Science Quarterly*, **40**: 371–84.

Whetten, D.A. (1989) What constitutes a theoretical contribution? *Academy of Management Review*, **14**: 490–95.

Yin, R.K. (1994) *Case Study Research: Design and methods*. Thousand Oaks, CA: Sage.

6 An action research approach to entrepreneurship
Claire Leitch

Introduction

More than 30 years ago, Susman and Evered (1978: 585) observed that, 'the findings in our scholarly management journals are only remotely related to the real world of practicing managers'. They suggested that this lack of relevance resulted from the fact that traditional positivist approaches to science, which have dominated much organizational research, were unable to provide managers and employees with the appropriate knowledge to understand and manage the affairs of their businesses. Therefore they proposed that action research, which constitutes a different kind of science with a distinct epistemology leading to the production of another type of knowledge, might be more appropriate: 'As a procedure for generating knowledge, we believe it has a far greater potential than positivist science for understanding and managing the affairs of organizations' (ibid.: 601). This approach, which was specifically developed as 'a way of overcoming a seemingly perennial problem in social science: the relation and relevance of theory to practice' (de Cock 1994: 791), focuses on integrating theory and practice by aiming to contribute both to the practical concerns of individuals within an organization and to the goals of social science. As the knowledge developed in this approach is contingent on a particular situation, it should assist in the development of organizational members' ability to solve their own problems. Even though Susman and Evered's (1978) comments were made with specific reference to organizational science, these remarks could equally be valid in the field of entrepreneurship. Indeed the introduction of an alternative perspective to knowledge production, which combines theoretical content and practical relevance, might help to alleviate some commentators' concerns about the applicability of entrepreneurship research in a practical context. For instance, Aldrich and Baker (1997: 398) have argued that even though entrepreneurship research is improving, it is still of limited topical concern and value to practising managers. This view concurs with that held by Brazeal and Herbert (1999: 31), who are not convinced 'that the field has reached its full potential as a field with substantive managerial applicability'. One potentially useful means by which this might be achieved is through a robust focus on context-of-application-based problems instead of attempting to develop grandiose integrative theories within a single paradigm. By concentrating on the latter there is a danger that the research focus of a discipline becomes little more than a retreat into academic fundamentalism (Burgoyne 1993). Such a perspective does not easily allow research to understand or explicate practice and, thus, if theory is to be made more relevant to the world of practice, new methods must be found by which to formulate, validate and employ knowledge. The challenge, therefore, for researchers, including those in the field of entrepreneurship, is to overcome the concerns of the practitioner community that the findings of much research frequently bear little relation to the complexities of the managerial situation (Tranfield and Starkey 1998). Thus entrepreneurship academics need to, on the one hand, develop the skills to advance knowledge and understanding of their respective field, and, on the other, improve understanding of and potentially provide practically relevant solutions to the issues and problems that an entrepreneur is likely to encounter in the birth and/or development of his/her venture.

By way of providing an exemplar of the benefits of adopting a more applied perspective to research within an entrepreneurial context, a longitudinal study based on an action research approach will be presented and discussed in this chapter. This approach was employed so as to appreciate better the process of collective understanding among a group of managers engaged in a strategy formulation exercise in a small to medium-sized entrepreneurial venture. This chapter is structured as follows. First, the philosophical underpinnings of action research are briefly reviewed and summarized. Second, the study site, including an explanation of the entrepreneurial context in which this research was conducted, is presented. Third, the main challenges that had to be managed within the study, including gaining and maintaining access, initiating the process of critical reflection as well as managing the 'insider'/'outsider' relationship, are discussed. The chapter ends with a concluding section that highlights how the adoption of an action learning and research perspective can contribute to the process of self- and organizational development in an enterprise.

Action research: A brief overview
Given the fact that action research is relatively new and is derived from a range of intellectual origins, it has been described as 'a work in progress [that which has] many unanswered questions and many unresolved debates' associated with it (Brydon-Miller et al. 2003: 11). Indeed, due to the disparate nature of its origins and subsequent complex history, it is impossible to provide a coherent history of action research (Reason and Bradbury 2001). It is not a single academic discipline, but an approach to research that has emerged from a broad range of fields including anthropology, management

and organizational change, education and social theory (Brydon-Miller et al. 2003; Ladkin 2004). Many, however, consider Lewin (1946), who used the term to describe a revolutionary approach within social science in which he attempted to combine theory-building with research on practical problems, to be the pioneer of this research perspective (Ladkin 2004). His approach was premised on the belief that practitioners engaged in uninformed research while researchers developed theory without application. As a result neither practitioners nor researchers produced consistently successful or indeed meaningful results (Dickens and Watkins 1999). Lewin's approach was intended to enable practitioners and social scientists to collaborate to find different means by which to bring about necessary change (Susman and Evered 1978), and thus he worked towards achieving a democratic approach to research sciences. By integrating the user and research communities, as occurs in action research, not only could theory be potentially informed but social change could also occur.

Contemporarily with Lewin's work in the USA, an interdisciplinary group in the UK was developing a similar approach. Even though their work was located in the field of psychoanalysis and social psychiatry rather than in social psychology, the researchers were 'committed to the social engagement of the social sciences, both as a strategy for advancing fundamental knowledge and as a way of enabling the social sciences to contribute solutions to important social problems' (Susman and Evered 1978: 587). In turn, the socio-technical experiments conducted there strongly influenced the links between action research and social democracy developed in Scandinavia, initially in Norway through the work of Thorsrud (Gustavsen 1992; Greenwood and Levin 1998). In the Scandinavian context the political values of increased democracy, political equality and social justice were especially influential in the adoption of action research approaches designed to assist in the creation of workplace democracy and self-management (Elden and Levin 1991). The emphasis on reforming work life resulted, for example, in ground-breaking research which shifted approaches to work design from a Taylorist perspective to more flexible forms of semi-autonomous work organization (Reason 2001).

However, the origins of action research are not just restricted to Western social science but can be observed also in the work conducted by non-Western writers such as Freire (1970) and Gramsci (1971) who developed approaches to research, evaluation and education which focused on creating tools for social change and development (Reason 2001; Reason and Bradbury 2001). The emphasis on democracy and collaboration, implicit within action research, underpins many of the other perspectives that have influenced its development such as humanistic psychology, organization development, feminist thinking, experiential learning and action learning

(Reason 2001). Indeed, as Reason (2001) observes, these approaches, along with participatory research, action science and cooperative inquiry, are all contemporary forms of action-oriented research. Elsewhere, Reason and Bradbury (2001: xxiii) have described 'action research as a "family" of participative experiential and action oriented approaches to research', which are intended to foster change on the group, organizational and even societal levels (Dickens and Watkins 1999).

Since the term 'action research' was first advanced, various writers (see, e.g., Sanford 1970; Argyris and Schon 1991; Cunningham 1993) have elaborated upon and at times even reinterpreted Lewin's definition and approach (Elden and Chisholm 1993). However, despite the disparate nature of the traditions represented by these researchers and the wide range of approaches to action research (Reason 2001), the overriding perspective that contemporary forms of this approach have in common is the belief that research with human beings should be participative, democratic and inclusive, and emphasize the full integration of action and reflection. This is no less true in the field of management where, although action research has been interpreted in a variety of ways by management researchers, three common themes can be identified (Saunders et al. 2000).

First, the purpose of an action research study is to focus on the promotion and management of change within a particular organizational setting (Cunningham 1995; Marsick and Watkins 1997). Indeed, Reason (2001) goes further in suggesting that organizational members should be encouraged and assisted in developing the businesses in which they work into learning organizations in which learning is promoted as the means by which companies can change and develop. Second, emphasis should be placed on collaboration between all those involved in the research project. By encouraging the active inclusion of organizational members in the research process alongside researchers, it is more likely that the findings and conclusions drawn from an action research perspective will be meaningful to the user community as they arise from 'involvement with members of an organization over a matter which is of genuine concern to them' (Eden and Huxham 1996: 75). However, care has to be taken to ensure that the research process engaged in has both research and practical relevance. For example, Alderfer (1993) warns that some researchers use the terms 'action research' and 'organizational development' as if they were synonymous, whereas action research is not solely about creating organizational change. Third, the results of action research should be capable of either informing or being applied in other contexts. For instance, in an academic context Eden and Huxham (1996) recommend that such findings should be explicitly employed to further inform theory development, while they suggest that consultants should be able to transfer knowledge gained from one specific context to another. This emphasis on relating research findings from a practical context back to theory is the element that differentiates action research from participatory action research (Whyte 1991), where the motivation for the research and resultant action derives solely from the need to improve an organization's workings (Park 1999). In this approach the researcher or professional expert, assuming a consultancy role, not only initiates but also implements a particular project within an organizational setting. As such, members in an organization may only have a minor role to play in the research and implementation process.

Adopting an action research approach should not be undertaken lightly, as it is not always easy to deal with both action and theory in the same context. Indeed, according to Gummesson (1991) it can be one of the most demanding and far-reaching methods of doing case study research. However, this should not daunt researchers interested in adopting an action research approach, not least because, as Reason (1999) notes, ways of using participatory inquiry approaches both inside organizations and in the community need to be developed. While there is some evidence of increased interest in the adoption of action research within the sphere of management (see, e.g., Coghlan 2001; Smith 2001), there is no evidence to suggest that this perspective has been applied within an entrepreneurial context.

The entrepreneurial context

The entrepreneurial context in this research is viewed as 'an inherently dynamic phenomenon', the study of which extends beyond a focus on new venture creation (Cope 2005), thus encompassing consideration of the post-start-up phase as well. This is consistent with Naffziger et al.'s (1994) opinion that an expanded view of entrepreneurship, in which the entirety of the entrepreneurial experience, 'that is, the behaviours necessary in the operation of the firm, its performance, and the psychological and non-psychological outcomes resulting from firm ownership' (ibid.: 31), should be adopted. While acknowledging that there is an ongoing debate surrounding the notion that small business owners are only 'entrepreneurial' during the business initiation and creation stage (Chan and Lau 1993; Cope 2005), Cope and Watts (2000) argue that an interdependent development relationship exists between an entrepreneur and his/her new venture beyond the start-up phase that cannot be ignored and which offers a potentially rich arena for examining the ways in which entrepreneurs not only learn to adapt to their changing roles ('innovator, manager, small business owner, division vice president' (Gartner 1988: 26)) but also how they develop new behaviours to cope with the changing demands of their business.

In this study the research site is a local family-owned small-to-medium-sized manufacturing enterprise employing approximately 260 employees in

Northern Ireland. The current chairman, who continues to play an active role, formed the business in 1965. However, strategic responsibility for the running of the business lies with his son, who is the managing director. His daughter is also employed in the company as a sales and marketing manager. The enterprise comprises two divisions, 'Hairco' (which designs and manufactures a branded product range targeted at the haircare and beauty sector) and 'Mouldco' (which designs and manufactures injection-moulded plastic components for a range of industries). Each division operates in very different markets and the company has been structured so as to allow each division to function as an independent strategic business unit. In addition, each division is geographically discrete as they are located on separate sites, a couple of miles apart. However, as the two units have a number of staff in common, in the areas of finance, design and quality, the divisions are only partially independent.

The research was initiated when the managing director of Plastico approached the researcher seeking assistance with making strategy formulation within the company a more inclusive process. At the time strategy was determined by a small group of directors (comprising the chairman, financial director, managing director, marketing director and a non-executive director). While the company was fairly successful and growing in terms of turnover, increased international presence and in staff numbers, the sector in which it operates was facing increasing competition from offshore-based competitors. The managing director felt that including more managers, from senior managers to front-line managers, in the strategic process might provide a better basis for shaping the future development of the company. The request came at an opportune moment for me, as at that time I was engaged in action research projects in other businesses in an attempt to ascertain the extent to which organizations could be construed as learning companies, and wished to extend my expertise in this approach (for further details, see Harrison and Leitch 2000). With reference to the enterprise Plastico, the remainder of this chapter will provide insights into how action research unfolds in practice.

Action research: Some insights into the process
Easterby-Smith et al. (1991) have suggested that there are at least three factors that make research conducted within a business and management context potentially distinctive from other arenas. First, management is a multidisciplinary subject drawing on knowledge developed in other disciplines. Second, as has already been discussed, there is a need for research to have a practical consequence. Third, managers, especially in senior positions, tend to be powerful and busy people who are unlikely to allow a researcher access to an organization unless they can see a personal or commercial

advantage. In this project there were three main challenges that had to be managed. These were gaining and maintaining access, initiating a process of critical reflection through action learning, and the maintenance of the 'insider'/'outsider' relationship.

Gaining and maintaining access

While gaining access to an organization can pose problems for management researchers in general (Saunders et al. 2000), in the case of action research this can be more problematic given the collaborative and participative nature of the research process as well as the fact that the project may be longitudinal in nature (Buchanan et al. 1988; Raimond 1993). Indeed, many writers do not consider gaining access to be an initial or single event but instead view it as a continuing process (Gummesson 1991) which is likely to be iterative in nature, in that access has to be negotiated to different parts of the organization or to different people who might not have been involved in the initial decision to allow the research to be conducted. In this case initial access was relatively easy as the researcher was approached by the managing director and invited into the company. A good working relationship already existed between the researcher and the managing director, as he had been a participant on an experientially based, university-led executive education programme managed by her.[1] The relationship with the company was further strengthened when the financial director of Plastico also became a participant on the same course. It is important to note that the management of this company display a high commitment to education and development and are keen to stress that it is available to everybody at whatever level they might be. The positive attitude towards higher education and academic research evident in this company, which can be unusual among SME owners (Choueke and Armstrong 1998), was undoubtedly beneficial in this study. Indeed, this emphasis on learning and knowledge in the company probably made it easier for the researcher to be accepted by the other managers and employees at the start of the research process, because in general the management team were keen to learn how to manage the business more effectively.

Even though initial access was relatively straightforward, the researcher was careful to establish good working relationships with all of those with managerial responsibility. This involved making presentations, attending meetings and workshops as well as spending time on the shop floor. The result of this was that the researcher not only gained a deeper understanding of the company and its culture, but also gradually became accepted as a non-threatening and legitimate presence. In addition, employees were constantly reassured that anything she was told in the course of the research would be treated in confidence. As Saunders et al. (2000) note, it is important for researchers to demonstrate competence and integrity: they suggest that the role of an external researcher can be beneficial 'as participants are willing to accept you as being objective and without a covert organisational agenda, where they see your questions as being worthwhile and meaningful' (Saunders et al. 2000: 116).

Critical reflection through action learning
All 41 managers in Plastico participated actively with the researcher from the initial design of the study to the final presentation of results and discussion of their action implications. While initially some employees did consider that the researcher was a management consultant, care was taken throughout the action research study to treat organizational members as coresearchers and not as objects or even subjects (Dickens and Watkins 1999). Indeed, the researcher was neither consultant nor professional expert, but instead engaged in a relationship of 'symmetric reciprocity' with employees in the organization (Fals Borda 2001). Such a participative approach was adopted so as to ensure that Plastico's employees were not treated as passive subjects or that the researcher acted as a professional expert who ultimately recommended action to the organization (Park 1999). This meant that the managers were continually asked their views and opinions with regard to every aspect of the process and were encouraged to take ownership of it.

In keeping with an action research approach, care was taken to ensure that the process was as inclusive as possible and engaged those involved in it as much as possible. If employees are not fully committed, outside consultation or intervention may result. This was not what either the researcher or the senior management team wished in the case of Plastico. One means by which the researcher felt that this problem could be overcome was by introducing action learning into the process. The rationale for this was that, while the explicit intention of action research is to bring about change through the research process and learning is implied, the concept of learning either at an individual or organizational level is not expressly emphasized. However, with other action-oriented approaches such as action learning, especially as articulated by Revans (1971), learning is implicit (Marsick and O'Neill 1999).

There has been a burgeoning interest in organizational learning in recent years due to an increasing awareness of the importance of knowledge and learning where organizations are faced with uncertain and changing or ambiguous market conditions (Edmondson and Moingeon 1996). Indeed, more than a decade ago Day (1992) suggested that virtually every aspect of organizational learning has relevance either directly or indirectly for entrepreneurial management, including structures and processes which encourage learning, differences in learning across the levels of the organization, and transfer mechanisms and learning. More recently, Smilor (1997: 344) has argued that

> learning is central to the entrepreneurial process: effective entrepreneurs are exceptional learners. They learn from everything. They learn from customers, suppliers and especially competitors. They learn from other entrepreneurs. They learn from experience. They learn by doing. They learn from what works, and more importantly what doesn't work.

While research has suggested that there is a close link between learning and entrepreneurial achievement, there is less understanding with respect to the process of learning (Rae and Carswell 2001). However, many commentators suggest that learning by experience and discovery is the preferred and predominant method of knowledge creation in an entrepreneurial context (Dalley and Hamilton 2000; Rae and Carswell 2001; Gibb 1987; Deakins and Freel 1998). One means by which this learning can be made more explicit and formalized within an enterprise is by the introduction of action learning.

Action learning is a theory of learning in which a manager or entrepreneur learns by reflecting on actions being taken in solving a real organizational problem with peers of similar position also experiencing challenging situations. This process takes place within an action learning set comprising six to eight managers in comparable situations. As well as providing a forum for managers to meet on a regular basis (often for a fixed period), these learning sets also afford managers the opportunity to use the rest of the group as peer tutors or coaches or for mutual support. Revans (1971), who proposed this approach, based it on the scientific method and thus conceptualized action learning as a model of problem-solving in three stages. He believed that students (in this case, an entrepreneur and his managers) learnt most effectively with and from others in comparable circumstances while attempting to find solutions to actual, real-life problems. In the process of doing so they not only discuss the practical implications of their solutions but also the applications or misapplications of theories and concepts to proposed actions and solutions. To achieve this they engage in a learning cycle that involves a number of stages, including action and reflection, until the problem under consideration has been resolved. This is generally an iterative process involving experimentation as new or different ways of addressing an issue are attempted and the experience subsequently analysed. Experiential learning is especially appropriate in an entrepreneurial context (Rae and Carswell 2001), as such learning can encourage an entrepreneur to alter his/her behaviour (Deakins and Freel 1998). By reflecting on experience, new meaning can be generated, consequently bringing about change in thinking and behaviour that can impact on the recognition of opportunities as well as in the organization and management of the entrepreneurial venture (Rae and Carswell 2001).

Advocates of the action learning model as advanced by Revans (1982) deliberately ensure that learning is highlighted through the cyclical process of action and reflection and is not left to chance, as might be the case in a normal and informal task and learning experience situation (Mumford 1995). Even though action learning is based on 'the straightforward peda-gogical notion that people learn most effectively when working on real-time problems occurring in their own work setting' (Raelin 1999: 117), it has strong parallels with an action research perspective. In fact, Pedler (1998) has described it as an educational process that makes extensive use of action research methods. Marsick and O'Neill (1999: 170) note 'the over-riding factor which differentiates action learning from other action ori-ented methodologies is its pragmatic focus on learning for the sake of more effective problem solving'. In addition, they observe that while action learn-ing approaches are philosophically rooted in theories of learning from experience, they are practised collaboratively through some form of action research. Indeed, Revans (1982) believes that the development of a learn-ing ethos through his action learning model is not only particularly effective but also 'highly appropriate for the development of effective SMEs' (Choueke and Armstrong 1998: 130).

Within Plastico three action learning sets comprising about 14 managers from the top management team to first-line managers were established and members were encouraged to reflect, with the support of the other group members, on various issues that were of importance at a strategic and oper-ational level. Membership of these sets was determined by the geographic location and responsibilities of each manager. As explained above, Plastico comprises two divisions and thus the managers of Mouldco formed one set while the managers of Hairco made up a second. Those managers who had joint responsibility for both sites joined the top management team to create the third group. The researcher acted as a facilitator in this process and avoided the role of consultant by making sure that the learning sets identi-fied solutions to the problems they were facing themselves. Managers had to propose action plans with realistic deadlines that would subsequently be introduced into the working practices of the business. Hence change could be actively initiated, ensuring that simply repeating previous patterns was avoided (Marsick and O'Neill 1999). While in theory this cyclical process appears to be discrete and well defined, it is often quite messy and frustrat-ing. Even though in this case managers were well briefed about the process, they did not really know what to expect and, indeed, did not realize how demanding it can be. Two particular issues to be handled in the sets were pri-oritizing the problems under review and managing managers' expectations that the results of any changes that were implemented would not be instantaneous. This was not the case, as both self- and organizational development is challenging and time-consuming. In order to make the process of strategy formulation more manageable and to structure discussion within the learning sets initially, the researcher suggested to the top management team that the learning company framework and instrument as developed by Pedler et al. (1991) should be adopted. The results subsequently generated by the application of this tool assisted all those with managerial responsibility within Plastico in identifying the problems and issues to be critically reflected upon in each learning group.

The learning company as defined by Pedler et al. (1997: 3) is an organization that 'facilitates the learning of all its members and consciously transforms itself and its context'. Adopting a proactive approach to learning is, they believe, important as it allows organizations to change, develop and potentially alter themselves in response to the needs and aspirations of all their employees and stakeholders. This is especially important in an ever-changing world for, as Schein (1993a, 1993b) observes, for companies to survive and develop they have to adapt faster and faster, otherwise they will be naturally weeded out in the economic evolutionary process. Learning is, thus, the key to survival and development for companies. While the learning company literature is essentially oriented towards large businesses (Wyer et al. 2000), the idea has also been developed within an SME context (Choueke and Armstrong 1998). Indeed, as Gibb (1997: 20) has observed, 'the real criteria for success in SME learning relate to the ability to learn and adapt, in a creative sense, from the key agents with whom it interfaces'. However, even though 'brainpower', 'intellectual capital' and 'learning' are common currency in a knowledge-based economy, few managers know how to manage or exploit a company that favours the importance of learning and knowledge (Nonaka 1996). One of the benefits of employing the survey instrument as developed by Pedler et al. (1991) is that strategic issues, internal and external processes and relations, including inter-company learning opportunities, as well as the learning climate of a business are all assessed. For the managers of Plastico, application of the learning company framework meant that organizational learning opportunities as reflected in the perceptions of employees in the organization were identified.

The concept of the learning company, in the form to which it is referred to here, has been the subject of considerable debate, which is beyond the scope of this chapter (for further information see, e.g., Coopey 1995, 1996; Dovey 1997; Easterby-Smith 1997; Easterby-Smith et al. 1998; Leitch et al. 1999; Harrison and Leitch 2000). However, in this context organizational learning is viewed as a process and the learning company as an outcome of that process, and thus the 'learning company' is considered to be a 'learning technology' that can be applied in a developmental manner to identify organizational self-development and renewal opportunities. The learning company framework serves as both a diagnostic and a developmental tool. On the one hand it is diagnostic in that it provides a mechanism for an enterprise's employees to self-audit the position of their company along a learning continuum. On the other hand it is developmental in that it provides indicators of opportunities for individual, team and company learning and thus can serve as a starting point for an action-based self- and organizational developmental process. This is possible due to the fact that the learning company, as conceived by Pedler et al. (1991), was influenced by theories of experiential learning, including Bateson's (1973) theory of 'deutro-learning' and Argyris and Schon's (1978) idea of organizational learning as well as Revans's (1971) concept of action learning.

To initiate the process of strategy formulation, the learning company instrument, based on the learning company characteristics outlined in Table 6.1, was administered to all managers within the two divisions that comprise Plastico.

The questionnaire employed in the research covers each of the 11 characteristics identified in this model of the learning company (Pedler et al. 1997). It consists of 55 stated elements (five questions per characteristic), each of which is measured on a seven-point Likert scale, ranging from 'a lot like this' to 'not at all like this'. Each statement prompts replies on two dimensions: 'how it is', that is, what in the opinion of the respondent is the current state of the company with regard to that particular element; and 'how I would like it to be', that is, what in the opinion of the respondent is the aspired future state of the company for that particular element. The key measure for each of the 11 characteristics of the learning company is the opportunity index, which is expressed as a standardized ratio of the 'how it is' and 'how I would like it to be' scores for each element. This is calculated as follows:

$$\text{Opportunity index} = 100 \times \left(\frac{\text{how it should be} - \text{how it is}}{\text{how it should be}} \right)$$

In Pedler et al.'s (1991) work the term used to describe this ratio was the 'dissatisfaction index'. Although this is strictly accurate, it was discovered through the course of the research that in an organizational development context this term engendered strongly negative reactions. The alternative terminology, adopted in this study, reflects the comments of one participant in the study, who stated that the index represented an indication of the opportunity for improvement in the company, and thus the index was renamed the 'opportunity index'. This index can range in value from 0 per cent (no perceived opportunity for improvement) to 100 per cent

Table 6.1   The learning company characteristics

Characteristic	Definition
1. Learning approach to strategy	Company policy and strategy formation, together with implementation, evaluation and improvement, are consciously structured as a learning process
2. Participative policy-making	The sharing of involvement in the policy- and strategy-forming processes; that is, all members of the company have a chance to take part, to discuss and contribute to major policy decisions
3. Informating	The state of affairs in which information technology is used to inform and empower people rather than, as so often is the case at present, disempower them
4. Formative accounting and control	Part of informating, this aspect ensures that systems of accounting, budgeting and reporting are structured to assist learning
5. Internal exchange	All internal units and departments see themselves as customers and suppliers, contracting with one another in a partly regulated market economy
6. Reward flexibility	The exploration of new, alternative ways of rewarding people. Money need not be the sole reward, and for many people a whole range of things may be considered 'rewarding'
7. Enabling structures	The creation of opportunities for individual and business development. Roles are loosely structured, in line with the established and contracted needs of internal customers and suppliers, and in such a way as to allow for personal growth and experiment
8. Boundary workers as environmental scanners	The collection of information from outside the company. Scanning is carried out by all members who have contact with external customers, clients, suppliers, neighbours and so on
9. Inter-company learning	Engagement in a number of mutually advantageous learning activities with customers and suppliers, including joint training, sharing in investment, in research and development and job exchanges
10. Learning climate	Managers see their primary task as facilitating members' experimentation and learning from experience. Senior managers give a lead in questioning their own ideas, attitudes and actions

Table 6.1 (continued)

Characteristic	Definition
11. Self-development opportunities for all	Resources and facilities for self-development are made available to all members of the company – employees at all levels and, ideally, external stakeholders too

Source: Adapted from Pedler et al. (1991: 18–23).

(maximum opportunity for improvement): the higher the index, the greater the perceived opportunity for improvement in that element of the company.

Traditional forms of data collection can be used in what have been termed third-person inquiries (Torbert 1991; Marshall and Reason 1998), such as action research 'which aim[s] to create a wider community of inquiry [but not necessarily exclusively so] between people who may not have face-to-face contact, but who share a common interest' (Ladkin 2004: 7). However, such forms of data collection, including questionnaires, interviews and quantitative data, would not be used unilaterally. Instead, those participants involved in an action research project would make sense of the data that had been gathered as well as generating the steps for which the data might be used. In the case of this action research, study feedback generated from the learning company questionnaire was not formally presented to the managers as data with unequivocal epistemic status, but was used to start discussion and critical reflection around particular issues that emerged after analysis of the data.

In this study the researcher had complete access to this business over a three-year period and was thus able to facilitate seven workshop sessions during which time the three learning sets were able to consider a number of issues of concern to them. Throughout this period the learning company instrument was applied annually and thus it was possible to track any changes that had occurred with respect to any action plans that had been initiated. Comparing the opportunity indices generated by subsequent applications of the survey formed the basis for discussion in the action learning sets conducted in years two and three. At the introductory workshop in year one the action research approach, including the use of action learning sets, was discussed in detail. In addition the learning company framework was presented and each element explained with reference to practical exemplars drawn from the researcher's own experience as well as from the work of Pedler et al. (1991, 1997). Before this session, the learning company instrument had been circulated to each manager in Plastico. The questionnaire was self-completed in the absence of the researcher so

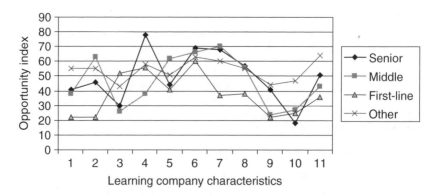

Notes:
$n = 2$ (senior managers), 7 (middle managers), 5 (first-line managers), 5 (other).
Key to learning company characteristics:
  1. Learning approach to strategy
  2. Participative policy-making
  3. Informating
  4. Formative accounting and control
  5. Internal exchange
  6. Reward flexibility
  7. Enabling structures
  8. Boundary workers as environmental scanners
  9. Inter-company learning
  10. Learning climate
  11. Self-development opportunities for all

Figure 6.1   Learning characteristics in Mouldco by management group

that each individual's response would not be influenced in any way. Using a software package developed especially by the Learning Company Project (Pedler et al. 1991), the opportunity index for each managerial level for each division was calculated (Figures 6.1 and 6.2). These figures are based on the aggregate profiles of each respondent at a particular level. Within Plastico six executives have joint responsibility for both divisions and thus the data for this group of respondents have been presented with the indices for the top management team (Figure 6.3). Presenting the data in this way allows for comparison of trends across all levels in the enterprise to be made.

As the focus of this chapter is on the process of action research, the findings from the first application[2] of the learning company instrument only are presented to demonstrate how the data generated were employed to initiate a process of critical reflection within a company (see Figures 6.1, 6.2 and 6.3). The benefit for the managers of presenting the material in this way demonstrated any potential differences in perception that the different groups of managers in each division had with respect to each characteristic

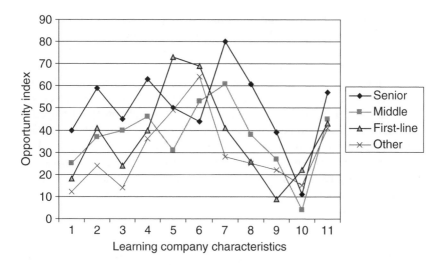

Notes:
n = 2 (senior managers), 6 (middle managers), 2 (first-line managers), 2 (other).
Key to learning company characteristics: see Figure 6.1.

Figure 6.2   *Learning characteristics in Hairco by management group*

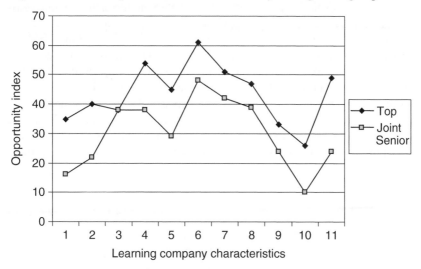

Notes:
n = 6 (top managers), 5 (joint senior managers).
Key to learning company characteristics: see Figure 6.1.

Figure 6.3   *Learning characteristics of the top and joint senior managers*
            in Plastico

in the learning company framework and highlighted issues of similarity as well as difference between the two divisions. For example, Figures 6.1 and 6.2 demonstrate that, on the whole, there is a degree of consistency between the opportunity indices calculated for each managerial group in both divisions. Indeed, during the research, managers expressed surprise that the general pattern between the two divisions was so consistent given the different markets served by the two units and the technology employed in the manufacturing process of each division. The similarity in profiles obtained for these divisions demonstrates that the learning company diagnostic instrument is not necessarily distorted by inter-plant variations with respect to product, technology or market. The value, therefore, of using such a framework is that it considers generic issues that include assessing a company's learning culture instead of focusing solely on operational aspects.

Once the results had been presented to the entire group, the managers separated into the smaller learning sets and started the process of identifying two to three issues that were of particular concern to them (see Figure 6.4). This was a useful process as it meant that the group had to reach consensus as to which problems they felt needed to be addressed in the first instance. Once this element of the process had been completed, the sets then began to generate improvement targets and to establish action achievement steps designed to overcome each problem. Before the workshop ended, a plenary session was held and representatives from each learning set summarized the discussion of each group and presented the action plans that had been proposed. This allowed all managers within Plastico an opportunity to make observations and provide feedback on what they had heard.

One of the benefits of engaging in a process of collective reflection, as occurs in action-oriented perspectives to research (McTaggart 1997), is that it allows for a broad perspective of issues and concerns to be obtained and potentially addressed. As all managers were involved in the strategy

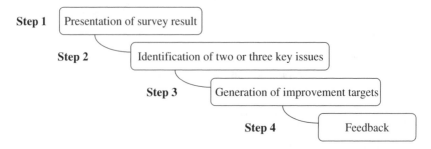

Figure 6.4   The process of collective reflection

formulation process, it was possible to collect the views of a wide cross-section of staff instead of relying solely on the perceptions of one group of individuals alone. This reduced the bias implicit in surveying only one group of managers and also diminished the potential distortion that can arise from power relations in an organization (Coopey 1995). By involving more managers in the reflective process it was hoped that as much learning as possible would occur. As Pedler et al. (1997: 82) have observed, 'all learning proceeds from differences. When we notice what is different from what we expected, there is the learning opportunity.' Indeed, as Weick (1995) has observed, sense-making can be more robust when challenged by different interpretations of phenomena. The managers within Plastico did not always find the process of reflection and understanding easy and at times there were robust discussions: 'becoming aware, debating, learning and deciding are part of this process' (Pedler et al. 1997: 83). However, conditions of heterogeneity and constructive conflict can often lead to the development of significant innovations by teams (West 1994). In this instance, the fact that the managers at Plastico were participating in an action research study focused on strategy formulation and organizational development provided both a context and framework in which issues could be debated in as productive a manner as possible.

While the discussions in the learning sets were useful, some individuals demonstrated a lack of understanding of the importance of learning from past experience and from thinking strategically. One explanation advanced by the general manager of Mouldco was the fact that Plastico had previously adopted a reactive approach to situations, and it was therefore alien for managers to consider a more proactive orientation. In addition, due to a lack of experience in considering strategic issues, the management team found it difficult to address the issue of implementation. In discussions they tended to focus on historical information at the expense of considering the importance of action plans and deadlines for implementation in the future. In order to overcome these areas of weakness in the company and to effect change as well as to ensure that the development process continued, it was suggested by the researcher that ownership of projects should be assigned to individuals or teams, timescales and targets agreed and resources allocated. In doing this it was hoped that the proposed action plans would actually be implemented and that the feelings of frustration of staff who were involved in the design phase of a process which was then not implemented, either at all or not quickly enough, would be addressed.

The insider/outsider relationship
Despite the good working relationship that the researcher had with the managers in Plastico, she was concerned about how she and the managers

would interact with one another throughout the action learning and research process, most especially as each party was approaching it from different perspectives. According to Benington and Hartley (2004: 361), this need not necessarily be problematic, for 'differences in perspective can be productive of high quality collaborative research when recognised and addressed'. Thus, in this action research study the idea of co-learning by all the parties involved in the study (Elden and Levin 1991) was adopted. Such a perspective acknowledges that all the participants can function as equal partners because while the expertise and frames of reference differ, they are equally valuable. One of the aims throughout the course of this research was to consciously 'establish a dialectical process of enquiry by drawing on the complementary, and sometimes conflicting perspectives, interests, skills and knowledge bases of both academics and practitioners' (Benington and Hartley 2004: 362). In this research there were two main groups involved in the process: the 'insiders' comprising the employees of Plastico and the 'outsider', in this case the researcher, though in other cases external experts could fall into this category. In order to obtain as holistic a view as possible of a complex situation (Hughes 1990; Weber 1949), the knowledge and perspectives of insiders is vital. This is especially the case in entrepreneurship, where it is necessary to generate concepts and models that lead to increased or improved understanding of problems and issues (Huse and Landström 1997). Organizations, whatever their size or stage of development, are complex phenomena that require insider knowledge to be understood so as to produce theory and knowledge with high reliability and validity (Easterby-Smith and Malina 1999). Indeed, insiders are experts in the context of the organization in which they work, and know from personal experience how the business operates as well as being aware of the culture, values and attitudes of that particular environment. In addition, the size and complexity of many organizations may mean that a researcher, the outsider, needs assistance in understanding and interpreting particular organizational norms and practices as well as assistance in translating these organizational phenomena to the concepts under study (Benington and Hartley 2004).

As Elden and Levin (1991) have observed, organizational knowledge not only tends to be individual and tacit, but also is generally not reflected upon. For the managers in Plastico, considering issues and establishing goals within their respective action learning sets started a process of reflection. In order to initiate this process in this context, the researcher in the role of a facilitator prompted set members to reflect on why problems might have arisen and to suggest a number of ways in which they might be addressed, as well as anticipating what difficulties, both personal and organizational, might be encountered, why, and how these might be overcome.

Even though the managers began to develop self- and organizational aware-ness, the researcher was part of the organizational context in which the research and potential change process occurs (Zuber-Skerritt 1996), and indeed, the expertise that she was able to bring to the action research study was the ability to engage in systematic inquiry and analysis as well as 'to have a high degree of interpersonal skills and be able to design and manage learning events' (Elden and Levin 1991: 132).

Initiating the process of collective reflection as described in this research represented a powerful means of crystallizing development needs and opportunities that might otherwise have remained unrecognized or unex-plored. While the managers felt that a solid foundation had potentially been established for further strategy formulation sessions, one manager observed that senior management had to demonstrate continued commit-ment to the process, otherwise there was a danger of future workshops being little more than 'talking shops' or indeed not being organized at all. This was a concern given the tendency for managers in the enterprise to focus on operational issues at the expense of strategic considerations. An important outcome of this research, therefore, was to ensure that employ-ees within Plastico did not become overly dependent on the researcher and were provided with tools and techniques that allowed them to adopt an internally managed action learning and research approach which pro-gressed beyond the confines of the research study. Over the course of a suc-cessful action research study, the relationship between the insiders and outsider should alter. At the start of a project the insiders are unlikely to have much experience in the process and therefore tend to be partially involved. As this research progressed and the managers improved upon their expertise within their learning sets, they gradually took on more responsibility for considering operational and strategic issues within the enterprise sets, and at the end of the process the researcher or outsider was no longer necessary for stimulating and facilitating discussion.

Conclusion
In this chapter a longitudinal research study illustrates how an action learn-ing and research approach can be applied successfully within an entrepre-neurial context. In particular, it considers the main challenges faced by those involved in the process and outlines how these were tackled through-out the course of the study. The use of the learning company tool, with its diagnostic and developmental capabilities, represented for managers in Plastico a systematic and novel means of approaching strategy formula-tion. In this research, the learning company framework not only provided a stimulus for significant learning and development for managers within the company, but also offered a means of steering and guiding a change

process. While the data generated within the course of this research provided a snapshot view of managers' perceptions of various elements within the business over a three-year period, they nevertheless encouraged managers within Plastico to collectively reflect and learn from previous experience before engaging in action.

In this research there was evidence of benefits for both the insiders and outsider in engaging in the process. From the insiders' perspective the experience provided a valuable learning opportunity for each manager, leading to an increase in their self-awareness as well as informing strategy planning sessions for the company. Indeed, the outcome of the strategy formulation process was the decision for both divisions of the business to embark upon an aggressive growth strategy, which meant that the company's vision had to be realigned so as to include the exploitation of overseas opportunities. For the outsider or researcher, one of the advantages of the study was that it contributed to knowledge with respect to the development of the learning company concept and in particular confirmed the researcher's belief that the learning company is difficult, if not impossible, to achieve in practice.

Although the adoption of an action research approach can be demanding for both the researcher and the employees of an organization, it is a worthwhile methodology to pursue for it can produce insights that cannot be gleaned from traditional research methods. In particular, it allows researchers to access information about complex situations that at times can be problematic to disentangle. As Gartner and Birley (2002: 389) note, in relation to qualitative research in entrepreneurship, 'there is typically an immersion into the muddled circumstances of an entrepreneurial phenomenon that is cluttered and confusing . . . Yet, it is in this experience of information overload that a certain knowledge and wisdom can occur.'

In this context action research represents a potentially powerful methodology to be adopted within the field of entrepreneurship as it not only allows as holistic a perspective as possible of a complex situation to be gained, but it also goes some way to addressing commentators' concerns that the needs of practising managers are not being met.

Notes

1. Fifty per cent of the participants (approximately 30 individuals) over the duration of this course were entrepreneurs or owner–managers of family-owned enterprises while the remainder were senior executives from either large publicly quoted companies or public sector organizations.
2. The questionnaire was administered to the same managers once a year over the three-year period and the opportunity indices generated were presented at the first workshop session each year. This allowed the managers to compare the indices on a year-by-year basis and make any adjustments to action plans as necessary.

Suggested further readings

Carson, T.R. and Sumara, D.J. (eds) (1997) *Action Research as a Living Practice.* New York: Peter Lange, draws on a wide range of sources to develop an understanding of action research. Particular emphasis is placed on the role of the researcher in the process.

Quigley, B.A. and Kuhne, G.W. (eds) (1997) *Creating Practical Knowledge through Action Research.* San Francisco: Jossey-Bass, is a guide to action research that outlines the process involved. Six case studies, including a hospital and a university, illustrate how the process can lead to organizational development.

Denzin, N.K. and Lincoln, Y.S. (eds) (2000) *Handbook of Qualitative Research* (2nd edn). Thousand Oaks, CA: Sage, is a useful multidisciplinary guide to qualitative research in general, including chapters on action research.

References

Alderfer, C.P. (1993) Emerging developments in action research, *Journal of Applied Behavioural Science (Special Issue)*, **29**(4): 389–492.

Aldrich, H. and Baker, T. (1997) Blinded by the cites? Has there been progress in entrepreneurship research? In D.L. Sexton and R.W. Smilor (eds), *Entrepreneurship: 2000.* Chicago, IL: Upstart.

Argyris, C. and Schon, D. (1991) Participatory action research and action science compared. In W.F. Whyte (ed.), *Participatory Action Research.* Newbury Park, CA: Sage.

Bateson, G. (1973) *Steps to an Ecology of Mind.* London: Paladin.

Benington, J. and Hartley, J. (2004) Co-research: Insider/outsider teams for organisational research. In C. Cassell and G. Symon (eds), *Essential Guide to Qualitative Methods in Organizational Research.* London: Sage.

Brazeal, D.V. and Herbert, T. (1999) The genesis of entrepreneurship, *Entrepreneurship Theory and Practice*, **23**(3): 29–45.

Brydon-Miller, M., Greenwood, D. and Maguire, P. (2003) Why action research? *Action Research*, **1**(1): 9–28.

Buchanan, D., Boddy, D. and McAlman, J. (1988) 'Getting in, getting on, getting out and getting back'. In A. Bryman (ed.), *Doing Research in Organisations.* London: Routledge, pp. 53–67.

Burgoyne, J. (1993) Managing Research, Background paper to inform the British Academy of Management submission to the ESRC Commission on Management Research.

Chan, K.F. and Lau, T. (1993) Are small business owner/managers really entrepreneurial? *Entrepreneurship and Regional Development*, **5**: 359–67.

Choueke, R. and Armstrong, R. (1998) The learning organisation in small and medium-sized enterprises: A destination or a journey? *International Journal of Entrepreneurial Behaviour and Research*, **4**(2): 129–40.

Coghlan, D. (2001) Insider action research projects: Implications for practicing managers, *Management Learning*, **32**(1): 49–63.

Coopey, J. (1995) The learning organisation, power, politics and ideology, *Management Learning*, **26**: 193–213.

Coopey, J. (1996) Crucial gaps in the 'learning organisation'. In K. Starkey (ed.), *How Organisations Learn.* London: Thompson Business Press.

Cope, J. (2005) Towards a dynamic learning perspective of entrepreneurship, *Entrepreneurship Theory and Practice*, **29**(4): 373–98.

Cope, J. and Watts, G. (2000) Learning by doing: An exploration of experience, critical incidents and reflection in entrepreneurial learning, *International Journal of Entrepreneurial Behaviour and Research*, **6**(3): 104–24.

Cunningham, J.B. (1993) *Action Research and Organisational Development.* Westport, CT: Praeger.

Cunningham, J.B. (1995) Strategic considerations in using action research for improving personnel practices, *Public Personnel Management*, **8**: 217–19.

de Cock, C. (1994) Action research: In search of new epistemology, *International Journal of Management*, **11**(3): 791–7.

Dalley, J. and Hamilton, R. (2000) Knowledge, context and learning in the small business, *International Small Business Journal*, **18**(3): 51–9.

Day, D.L. (1992) Research linkages between entrepreneurship and strategic management or general management. In D.L. Sexton and J.D. Kasarda (eds), *The State of the Art of Entrepreneurship*. Boston, MA: PWS–Kent Publishing.

Deakins, D. and Freel, M. (1998) Entrepreneurial learning and the growth process in SMEs, *The Learning Organisation*, **5**(3): 144–55.

Dickens, L. and Watkins, K. (1999) Action research: Rethinking Lewin, *Management Learning*, **30**(2): 127–40.

Dovey, K. (1997) The learning organisation and the organisation of learning: Learning power, transformation and the search for form in learning organisations, *Management Learning*, **28**: 331–49.

Easterby-Smith, M. (1997) Disciplines of organisational learning: Contributions and critiques, *Human Relations*, **50**: 1085–113.

Easterby-Smith, M. and Malina, D. (1999) Cross-cultural collaborative research: Toward reflexity, *Academy of Management Journal*, **42**: 76–86.

Easterby-Smith, M., Araujo, L. and Burgoyne, J. (1998) *Organisational Learning: Developments in theory and practice*. London: Sage Publications.

Easterby-Smith, M., Thorpe, R. and Lowe, A. (1991) *Management Research: An introduction*. London: Sage Publications.

Eden, C. and Huxham, C. (1996) Action Research for management research, *British Journal of Management*, **7**(1): 75–86.

Edmonson, A. and Moingeon, B. (1996) Organizational learning as a source of competitive advantage. In B. Moingeon and A. Edmondson (eds), *Learning and Competitive Advantage*. London: Sage Publications.

Elden, M. and Chisholm, R.E. (1993) Emerging varieties of action research, *Human Relations*, **46**(2): 121–42.

Elden, M. and Levin, M. (1991) Co-generative learning: Bringing participation into Action Research. In W.F. Whyte (ed.), *Participatory Action Research*. Beverly Hills, CA: Sage Publications.

Fals Borda, O. (2001) Participatory (action) research in social theory: Origins and challenges. In P. Reason and H. Bradbury (eds), *Handbook of Action Research: Participative inquiry and practice*. London: Sage Publications.

Freire, P. (1970) *Pedagogy of the Oppressed*. New York: Herder and Herder.

Gartner, W.B. (1988) Who is an entrepreneur? Is the wrong question, *American Journal of Small Business*, **13**(1): 11–32.

Gartner, W.B. and Birley, S. (2002) Introduction to the special issue on qualitative methods in entrepreneurship research, *Journal of Business Venturing*, **17**(5): 387–95.

Gibb, A. (1987) *Enterprise Culture – Its Meaning and Implications for Education and Training*. Bradford: MCB University Press.

Gibb, A. (1997) Building on the small business as a learning organization, *International Small Business Journal*, **15**(3): 13–29.

Gramsci, A. (1971) *Selections from Prison Notebooks*. New York: International Publishers.

Greenwood, D.J. and Levin, M. (1998) *Introduction to Action Research: Social research for social change*. Thousand Oaks, CA: Sage Publications.

Gummesson, E. (1991) *Qualitative Methods in Management Research*. London: Sage Publications.

Gustavsen, B. (1992) *Dialogue and Development*. Assen–Maastricht: Van Gorcum.

Gustavsen, B. (2001) Theory and practice: The mediating discourse. In P. Reason and H. Bradbury (eds), *Handbook of Action Research: Participative inquiry and practice*. London: Sage Publications.

Harrison, R.T. and Leitch, C.M. (2000) Learning and organization in the knowledge-based information economy: Initial findings from a participatory action research case study, *British Journal of Management*, **11**(2): 103–19.

Hughes, J.A. (1990) *The Philosophy of Social Research*. London: Longman.

Huse, M. and Landström, H. (1997) European entrepreneurship and small business research: Methodological openness and contextual differences, *International Studies of Management and Organisation*, **27**(3): 3–12.

Ladkin, D. (2004) Action research in practice: What the books don't tell you. In C. Seale, D. Silverman, J. Gubrium and G. Gobo (eds), *Qualitative Research Practice*. London: Sage Publications.

Leitch, C.M., Harrison, R.T., Burgoyne, J. and Blantern, C. (1999) Learning organisations: The measurement of company performance, *Journal of European Industrial Training*, **20**(1): 31–44.

Lewin, K. (1946) Action research and minority problems, *Journal of Social Issues*, **2**: 34–46.

Marshall, J. and Reason, P. (1998) Collaborative and self-reflective forms of inquiry in management research. In J. Burgoyne and M. Reynolds (eds), *Management Learning*. London: Sage.

Marsick, V.J. and O'Neill, J. (1999) The many faces of action learning, *Management Learning*, **30**(2): 159–76.

Marsick, V.J. and Watkins, K.E. (1997) Case study research methods. In R.A. Swanson and E.F. Holton (eds), *Human Development Research Handbook*. San Francisco, CA: Berrett-Koehler.

McTaggart, R. (1997) Revitalising management as a scientific activity, *Management Learning*, **28**(2): 177–95.

Mumford, A. (1995) Managers developing through action learning, *Industrial and Commercial Training*, **27**(2): 19–27.

Naffziger, D.W., Hornsby, J.S. and Kuratko, D.F. (1994) A proposed research model of entrepreneurial motivation, *Entrepreneurship Theory and Practice*, Spring: 29–42.

Nonaka, I. (1996) The knowledge creating company. In K. Starkey (ed.), *How Organizations Learn*. London: Thompson Business Press.

Park, P. (1999) People, knowledge, and change in participatory research, *Management Learning*, **30**(2): 141–57.

Pedler, M. (ed.) (1998) *Action Learning in Practice* (3rd edn). Aldershot: Gower.

Pedler, M., Burgoyne, J. and Boydell, T. (1991) *The Learning Company: A strategy for sustainable development*. London: McGraw-Hill.

Pedler, M., Burgoyne, J. and Boydell, T. (1997) *The Learning Company: A strategy for sustainable development* (2nd edn). London: McGraw-Hill.

Rae, D. and Carswell, M. (2001) Towards a conceptual understanding of entrepreneurial learning, *Journal of Small Business and Enterprise Development*, **8**(2): 150–58.

Raelin, J. (1999) Preface – special issue: The action dimension in management: Diverse approaches to research, teaching and development, *Management Learning*, **30**(2): 115–26.

Raimond, P. (1993) *Management Projects: Design, research and presentation*. London: Chapman and Hall.

Reason, P. (1999) Participatory research: Letters to Peter Park and his response, *Management Learning*, **30**(2): 231–4.

Reason, P. (2001) Learning and change through action research. In J. Henry (ed.), *Creative Management*. London: Sage Publications.

Reason, P. and Bradbury, H. (2001) Introduction: Inquiry and participation in search of a world worthy of human aspiration. In P. Reason and H. Bradbury (eds), *Handbook of Action Research: Participative inquiry and practice*. London: Sage Publications, pp. 17–26.

Revans, R. (1971) *Developing Effective Managers*. London: Longman.

Revans, R. (1982) *The Origin and Growth of Action Learning*. London: Chartwell Bratt.

Sanford, N. (1970) Whatever happened to action research? *Journal of Social Issues*, **26**: 3–23.

Saunders, M., Lewis, P. and Thornhill, A. (2000) *Research Methods for Business Students* (2nd edn). London: Financial Times/Prentice-Hall.

Schein, E.H. (1993a) On dialogue, culture and organizational learning, *Organizational Dynamics*, **22**: 40–51.

Schein, E.H. (1993b) How can organizations learn faster? The challenge of entering the green room, *Sloan Management Review*, Winter: 85–92.

Smilor, R.W. (1997) Entrepreneurship: Reflections on a subversive activity, *Journal of Business Venturing*, **12**(5): 341–46.

Smith, P.A.C. (2001) Action learning and reflective practice in project environments that are related to leadership development, *Management Learning*, **32**(1): 31–48.

Susman, G.I. and Evered, R.D. (1978) An assessment of the scientific merits of action research, *Administrative Science Quarterly*, **23**(December): 582–603.

Torbert, W.R. (1991) Teaching action inquiry, *Collaborative Inquiry*, **5**.

Tranfield, D. and Starkey, K. (1998) 'The nature, social organisation and promotion of management research: Towards policy', paper presented to the British Academy of Management Directors of Research Network, Coventry, March.

Weber, M. (1949) *The Methodology of the Social Sciences*. New York: Free Press.

Weick, K. (1995) *Sensemaking in Organizations.* Thousand Oaks, CA: Sage.

West, M.A. (1994) *Effective Teamwork*. Leicester: British Psychological Society.

Whyte, W.F. (ed.) (1991) *Participatory Action Research*. Newbury Park, CA: Sage Publications.

Wyer, P., Mason, J. and Theodratopoulous, N. (2000) Small business development and the learning organisation, *International Journal of Entrepreneurial Behaviour*, **6**(4), 239–59.

Yin, R. (1994) *Case Study Research*. California: Sage Publications.

Zuber-Skerritt, O. (1996) Emancipatory action research for organisational change and management development. In O. Zuber-Skerritt, (ed.), *New Directions in Action Research.* London: Falmer.

7 Recognizing meaning: semiotics in entrepreneurial research
Robert Smith and Alistair R. Anderson

Introduction

Entrepreneurship has become fashionable and, as a theme, arises in some extraordinary places: promoted by politicians, patronized by royalty, 'taught' in schools, colleges and universities across the world and very much in vogue in academia. Yet a fundamental problem is the lack of agreement, perhaps even understanding, of exactly what we mean by entrepreneurship. Entrepreneurship is a poorly defined concept and people use parts of its meaning to suit their purposes. For example, politicians talking about entrepreneurship often construe it as some sort of universal panacea for all sorts of economic problems – unemployment, innovation, growth, and new firm formation. All seem to be lumped together under enterprise. Academics are generally more cautious and set out careful definitions. None the less, the width of the application suggests that the meaning of the term really is broad: it means different things to different groups or people. Moreover, how groups employ these different meanings may also be significant. We are not arguing that there should be one universal interpretation of the term. Not only is this unrealistic, but it could also be counterproductive in trying to build understanding about entrepreneurship. However, it is only by exploring the margins of meaning and practices that we can hope to paint a complete picture. For example, how might 'social' or 'criminal' entrepreneurship be understood, if we didn't compare it to more conventional forms? We ask what is similar, what is different and in this way we come to construct a fuller appreciation of meaning, practice and content. But setting aside the semantics of definition, the breadth of the concept is intriguing. It indicates that entrepreneurship, as a concept, is a socially constructed phenomenon with different layers of meaning.

Does this matter, the classic academic question, so what? Even if it is a social construct, what difference does this make? We argue that it makes a big difference to how academics, practitioners and entrepreneurial promoters come to understand enterprise and entrepreneurship. In particular, understanding how entrepreneurship is portrayed enables us to see what meanings lie behind the concept and its applications. This is neither pedantic nor trivial, but aids understanding of the big issues of how and why. By understanding these applications of meaning we can help discern their purpose and power, and perhaps even make some informed predictions based on that understanding. So there are sound academic reasons for trying to understand these different meanings.

In this chapter we argue that semiotics, the doctrine of signs, is a useful tool for exploring the depth and scope of the meaning of entrepreneurship. The entrepreneurship process involves discontinuity and change, where entrepreneurs create disequilibria and exploit change. This fundamental characteristic makes it difficult to pin down, to categorize or to appreciate the meanings that underpin the phenomenon. Yet, although the constituents of enterprise inevitably change through time and space, some continuity can be maintained by framing entrepreneurial explanation within traditional linguistic and semiotic methods such as storytelling. For example, in telling culturally accepted entrepreneurial stories, one recreates the previous state, and meaning, of 'taken-for-granted-ness' of enterprises' externalizing structures (Pile 1993). But power and purpose lie behind these externalizing structures, and understanding meaning may reveal these underpinnings. Consequently, an appreciation of the entrepreneurial semiotic enables a richer understanding of the meanings of enterprise – what it is; how it is practised; why it is practised and why it is encouraged. Many of these meanings lie at the ideological level; they are taken for granted, often implicit, rarely explicit; but analysis of entrepreneurial symbolism gives us some purchase on understanding. By reading and analysis, the decoding of 'texts' (any carrier of signs, books, films, pictures, almost everything that people use becomes an object for analysis) enables us to get beneath the taken-for-granted and iconographic, and begin to understand the nature and purpose of entrepreneurial meaning[1].

Semiotics
According to Leach (1974), meaning lies in the linguistic domain of semantics (the study of meaning), but we argue that semiotics enables us to *recognize* meaning, a first step towards understanding it. The chapter first explores the nature of semiotics. We note that whilst some fairly extravagant claims have been made for the utility of semiotics, a particular problem is the subjectivity of interpretation and the risk of being too self-referential. Moreover, the topic is often clouded by jargon and a bewildering array of approaches. Accordingly the second part of the chapter is an attempt to demonstrate how we have tried to use semiotics to help our understanding of entrepreneurship.

Defining semiotics is problematic because of the diversity that characterizes it. None the less it is useful to explore how semiotics is described; we can then talk about it and think around it. In many ways this talking around the subject mirrors the techniques of semiotics in that we are trying to get beneath the surface to establish what semiotic analysis means. A classic paper on semiotics in business, Barley (1983), describes how many organizational theorists have, in noting how culture is embodied and transmitted by stories, myths and symbols, urged researchers to scrutinize these vehicles closely. Although culture, like entrepreneurship, can be variously defined, there does seem to be some agreement that culture is about a socially constructed system of meaning. If we wish to actually understand what meanings lie behind the narratives that circulate, we need some way of dealing with these signs and symbols. If we don't tackle this issue, we have to relegate 'meanings' to a background assumption. Semiotics makes representations the focus of inquiry and problematizes the process of representations. It offers an approach for analysing signs and the meaning systems of entrepreneurship. For the purpose of this chapter, we argue that entrepreneurship is 'the creation, extraction and communication of value' and that semiotics permits 'the creation, extraction and communication of meaning'. Thus two phenomena, symbols and practices, combine symbiotically, as in dance. To misquote Yeats (1956), we have no need 'to know the dance from the dancer'; dancing can explain the dance.

Eco (1979: 6) describes semiotics as a formal mode of analysis to identify rules, whilst Greimas (1987) notes how patterns of beliefs are grounded in the underlying meanings attached to self and to others. But identifying these patterns (Fiol 1989) also requires a methodology able to detect the meanings assigned to events and situations while specifying the rules that govern meaning in a given context. Semiotics provides such a methodology. Lawes (2002) stresses that semiotics takes an outside-in approach and is concerned with establishing how reality is formed cognitively. For Lawes, semiotics is a visionary methodology that helps understand the past while looking to the future. This view demonstrates the utility for entrepreneurship. Semiotics offers the analysis of communication, operating via the complex system of signs, signals, codes, texts and genres, which form semiotic, sign systems or mental maps. In this way, knowledge, meaning, intention and action are fundamental to semiotics. Chandler (1994) sees it as a conceptual crowbar with which to deconstruct the codes at work in particular texts and practices. He considers its power to lie in the visual availability of seeing a genre in movement and action, which Shanks (1995: 7) refers to as 'a notion of semiotic reality' and not merely expressed via the frozen modality of the printed word. Semiotic analysis allows us to deconstruct cultural myths and separate the ways in which codes operate within particular popular texts or genres, thus revealing how certain values, attitudes and beliefs are supported while others are suppressed. It helps us denaturalize theoretical academic assumptions and raise new theoretical issues (Culler 2001). It provides us with a unifying conceptual framework, a set of methods and terms encompassing the full range of signifying practices, including gesture, posture, dress, writing, speech, photography, film, television and other media. It can uncover hidden meaning beneath the obvious. Chandler (1994) suggests that it enables us to cross academic boundaries, making connections between apparently disparate phenomena.

Constructivist methodologies and semiotics

Semiotics lies within the broad school of social constructivism whose philosophical underpinning is that reality is socially constructed and cannot be understood by resorting to facts. In social reproduction, we draw upon interpretative schemes, resources and norms via existing structures of signification, domination and legitimation (Gregory 1981: 940). Chell (2000) argues that it allows us to understand the ways and mechanisms which individuals use to interpret their social environment, showing how language guides our sense of social reality by framing, filtering and creation to transform the subjective into the plausible.

Ontologically, reality is constructed, and is rooted in viewing 'reality' as a social construction, with mankind being its creator. Thus all 'truth' claims are socially negotiated. It is the researcher's role to try to understand reality intersubjectively. Epistemologically, social constructions are not based on facts but values (Lincoln and Guba 1985), including those of the researcher. The epistemological aim of semiotics is thus to identify the codes and recurring patterns of a particular sign system and to understand how these are used to communicate meaning (Echtner 1999; Fiol 1991). Indeed, its power lies in its utility to analyse the visual and textual carriers of the entrepreneurial story line. We argue that the principal benefit of a semiotic analysis is in revealing the underlying structures, not just of signs, but also of all phenomena under investigation. If we compare semiotics with other techniques for exploring text, for example, content analysis, we can see how these benefits accrue. Content analysis is a quantitative approach measuring the manifestation of content, themes or patterns. In contrast, a semiotic analysis of the pictorial and textual looks holistically: by investigating the meanings behind the sign it develops a deeper, broader, more complete textual picture and challenges the natural and taken-for-granted of appearance.

Social constructionism is claimed to be a liberating methodology placing no particular constraints or demands in terms of preferred visions of the future (Gergen 2001). Yet semiotics possesses an archetypal element, whereby the power of the symbol lies in its ability to attract people and lead them towards that which they are capable of becoming (Singer 1994). Aldrich and Fiol (1994) stress how entrepreneurs develop new meaning through the process of social construction, thus moving social construction away from being a unit of analysis to being the subject of analysis, and present it as a way through which entrepreneurship is achieved. Aggestam and Keenan (2002) view the entrepreneurial act as socially constructed and relationally responsive, emerging in discourse and talk, thus embedded in the linguistic process and grounded in the entrepreneur's experience. Moreover, they also note that the entrepreneurial outcome has no intrinsic meaning separate from the meaning entrepreneurs create through their lived experiences. Casson (2000) regards entrepreneurship as an integrated social science incorporating anthropology, with social constructionism playing a central role. However, social constructions both inform and misinform expectation and we are bounded by social construction and 'reconstructions of reality' (Aldrich and Zimmer, 1986: 11). With justification, Anderson (2003: 11) argues that as a social construct, entrepreneurship is both fact and fiction. Indeed, Gergen (1998) urges us to observe 'a range of variegated and overlapping conversations and practices that draw from various resources and with varying emphases and combinations . . . nothing is fixed – including the meaning of constructionism itself'. However, as Table 7.1 illustrates, there is a bewildering choice of constructivist approaches.

The subtle differences in these categorizations seem to obfuscate rather than clarify, particularly as the terms are often used interchangeably or even erroneously. None the less, the common argument of such stances is that any phenomenon resulting from human agency does not occur naturally, but is shaped by particular social, historical and cultural contexts.

Table 7.1   Constructionist stances

Stance	Emphasis upon
Radical constructivism	The way in which individual minds construct reality
Constructivism	How the mind constructs reality within systematic relationships with the external world
Social constructivism	How the mind constructs reality in its relationship to the world, but informed by social relationships
Social representation	Takes cognizance of broad social conventions
Social constructionism	Uses discourse as a vehicle through which self and the world are articulated and the way in which they function within social relationships
Sociological constructionism	The way understandings of the self and world are influenced by the power that social structures exert over people

Ultimately, what constitutes reality is unknowable except as a mediated phenomenon. There is no one reality, instead there are multiple, socially constructed realities (Yin 1993). As a research methodology in its own right, constructionism has a double hermeneutic: as a unit of analysis and as subject matter under review. Incisively, Nicol (2003: 29) noted that the literature itself forms part of a social construct. Broadly speaking, we can say that social constructionism leans towards the general, whilst semiotics illustrates the specifics.

The origins and development of semiotics

Semiotics has a long, if not entirely respectable, history; signs and meaning were systematically studied during the medieval and renaissance periods (Echtner 1999). Semiotics is rooted in the structural linguistic principles of Saussure (1974), but in semiotics, emphasis is placed on the use of sign systems as a model to identify and make explicit the rules. The key assumption is that meanings are related to diverse signs or expressions because they are grounded in a common set of underlying rules. Semiotics has taken two differing pathways which form distinctive approaches: Saussurian, European and closely related to the Swiss linguist Ferdinand de Saussure's work and termed semiology; and Piercian, American and developed by the pragmatist philosopher Charles Sanders Pierce. This latter form is usually termed semiotics and, as the most common, is the focus of this section.

Saussure typifies structuralist thinking by concentrating his linguistic inquiry on the underlying rules that allow language to operate, so grammar rather than usage, and langue (language) rather than parole (speech) investigated the infrastructure that operates at an unconscious level. This concern with discovering underlying rules, rather than surface phenomena, found an anthropological home in the work of Lévi-Strauss, so semiology came to look beyond language to culture and more general social artefacts. More generally, Roland Barthes took up semiotics for cultural studies: his *Mythologies* (1970) increased awareness of the value of this approach and *Camera Lucidia* (1981) increased awareness of the importance of photography and visual images for social research.

Semiotics has moved away from the original Saussurian interpretation. Not only in terms of the alternatives of Piercian semiotics, but in the last few decades there has been a shift from the classification of sign towards trying to understand the 'work' that signs do. This fits rather neatly with social construction because it allows the recognition that signs are not simply transmitted, but that readers of these texts actively engage in the construction of their meaning. Hence it becomes particularly relevant for the study of entrepreneurship. For example, consider our understanding of the power of the notion of the enterprise culture – issues such as whose power, the legitimation processes associated with entrepreneurship, even enterprise itself; what it is; how it is practised; why it is practised and why it is encouraged. All these become appropriate targets for semiotic analysis. Understanding entrepreneurial symbolism can enable us to appreciate the ideological and taken-for-granted meanings by giving us some purchase on understanding. 'Reading' and analysis enables us to get beneath the taken-for-granted iconographic and fathom the nature of entrepreneurial meaning.

We turn now to consider some of the critiques of and problems with semiotics. Semiotics has so many different elements that it is confusing. We believe that it is certainly not a science, but then too 'entreprenology' has similar problems! In the same way as entrepreneurial scholars have different approaches to studying their phenomenon, varieties of semiotics can offer some insights into meanings. It is probably best to see semiotics as an approach, a way of looking at the issue of meaning. Others might argue that it is a 'world-view', but we feel that this may place just too much emphasis on the 'significance of signs'. Although semiotics has been defined as the 'science of the sign', the idea of it being a science is rather misleading. There is no broad consensus on the theoretical assumptions or empirical methodologies of semiotics. Indeed, many theorists are still trying to establish the scope and even the general principles. Because all signs are open to subjective interpretation: 'you see it this way but I see it another way', there is no bedrock of objectivity. Signs are meaningful but there is a significant risk of becoming self-referential. Another major criticism of constructionist stances and semiotics is that their exponents merely 'talk around' a subject, over-analysing and stating the obvious. Many constructionist tracts do make simplicity complicated. Semiotic analysis has at times been justifiably stigmatized; Chandler (1994) even described it as the last vestige of the academic charlatan.

Semiotics has been criticized as jargon riddled and this is certainly true. Semiotics can be encountered under a perplexing array of pseudonyms, for example semiosis (Sonneson), sémiologie and semiology (Pierce) and even as visual sociology (Baker 1994). (In the last case semiotic attribution is denied, such is the academic stigma it can carry.) The denseness of 'linguistic' terminology can be off-putting. Eugene Gorny (1995) acknowledges that even when explained in print, semiotics can appear to be obscure, abstruse, laden with special terminology, schemes and formulas, sufficiently so to make it unintelligible even to university-educated students. With justification, Gorny (1995) refers to the pretensions of semiotics. For example, the lexicon of semiotics is complex, for example it contains phonemes, morphemes, hyposemy, hypersemy, graphemes and sememes. Thus the definition of semiotics as a science of signs carries little explanatory value. Gorny (1995) expresses surprise that people continually ask him 'what is semiotics?', but considers it a normal reaction to the word. Gorny notes that few people ask what mathematicians and biologists do. Nevertheless, he finds it a difficult concept to articulate succinctly and deliberately evades the direct question. Candidly he admits that he does not know what it is. He describes it as being a cross between philosophy and philology (the science of language). Perceptively, Gorny considers semiotics to be a state of mind despite, or perhaps because of, the basic semiotic concepts being indefinable. None the less, as Baker (1994) argues, research using visual methodologies is particularly useful when researching fields, such as entrepreneurship, that are not clearly defined.

According to Lewis (1982), visual images carry and convey messages, so an interesting subset is semiotic analysis of pictures. For Schere (1990), we picture cultures whilst Harper (1996) argues for 'seeing sociology'. However, the practice of visual semiotics transcends the descriptive. Words describe, while pictures illustrate and illuminate. Visual semiotics or 'Pictorial Semiotics',[2] like all branches of semiotics, is a nomethetic science concerned with generalities and their qualities. Such pictorial significations permeate many qualitative works but are often not chosen for presentation. Baker (1994) argues that visual images present material for descriptive and analytical purposes, but more importantly, photographic images allow us to think visually (Curry and Clarke 1977). Bignell (1997) proposes that photographs function as the proof that the text's message is true, and for Becker (1974) visual images bridge the gap between concepts and behavioural indicators. Baker (1994) notes that certain research problems lend themselves more readily to incorporating visual images because pictures are direct referents. The semiotic analysis of images deals with themes and general meaning, whilst the semiotic analysis of literary text deals with the way in which meaning is produced by the structures of interdependent signs, by codes and conventions. Visual semiotics therefore assists in the production of meaning. Banks (1995) argues that images must be evaluated in tandem for content and context, thus considering image and text. Capturing visual meaning is difficult because there is a lack of structured research approaches to code and categorize such information. Whilst meaning is produced and conveyed in messages that are primarily visual, each viewer constructs their own meanings from visual communication cues. Overcoming the subjectivity inherent in this construction of individual meaning presents great difficulty in semiotic analysis, but some elements of technique can help.

Operationalizing semiotics

Semiotics is a practical science. For entrepreneurship, two schools of semiotics seem important, the structuralist and the social. Chandler (1994) explains that structuralist semioticians focus on the internal structure of the text and language rather than on the processes involved in its construction or interpretation, whilst social semioticians focus on the social processes. Social semiotics, on the other hand, is the study of situated semiotic practices that are revealed using ethnographic and phenomenological methodologies. Interest focuses on the semiotic chain that begins with the basic units of communication, such as phonemes, which are built into words and sentences and formed into texts and stories. Communication and semiotics can metaphorically be likened to a chain because with each level of competence that one adds, the length and strength of the semiotic chain extends. Kress and van Leeuwen (1996) stipulate that semiotic systems have three essential metafunctions:

1. Ideational – to represent aspects of the experiential world;
2. Interpersonal – to project the relations between the producer of a sign and its receiver; and
3. Textual – to form internally and externally understood cohesive texts and signs.

Noth (1995: 89) refers to a 'semiotic triangle', composed of sense, sign vehicle and referent. It is not the object or symbol we are concerned with, but the message, which can be iconic, symbolic or indexical. In reading a text, we check it for coherence – textual, pragmatic and semantic. However, signs can mean anything we agree that they mean, and can mean different things to different people. *Iconic* signs look like what is being represented, whilst *symbolic* signs are determined by convention. They are arbitrary and based upon agreement and learned through experience. *Indexical* signs provide a clue or link. As an example, visual communications often use all three sign types. Within cultural communities, 'communities of visual meaning' and 'meaning clusters' develop. These occur over time through convention, conformity and cultural preferences. Certain items and artefacts become 'visual metaphors' revered by the culture that shares their perceived qualities and values. Thus we can see that the semiotic system includes language, ideology, myth, images, sounds, objects and acts. Importantly, these have no intrinsic meaning and become signs only when we attribute meaning to them.

The plethora of possible elements in semiotics makes it confusing for practitioners. Many constructionist tracts do complicate simplicity. Another criticism is that semioticians do not construct a specific model of how to conduct semiotic analysis but concentrate upon individual abstract linguistic notions and categorical identity generally epitomized as metaphors (Sonesson 1994). Gorny's (1995) explanation of semiotics, Table 7.2, by method and theory is helpful because it illustrates the underlying assumptions. Gorny's (ibid.)

Table 7.2   Explaining semiotics

Canonical definition by subject	Considering semiotics as the science of signs and/or sign systems is problematic – is it a science? Second, who establishes what is/is not a sign? Semiotics permits us to consider anything as signs and sign systems
Definition by method	The application of linguistic methods to objects other than natural language is a way of viewing anything as constructed and functioning similarly to language. Similarity is the essence of the method and everything is capable of being described via language. Specifically, Gorny regards semiotics as a transfer of metaphor from language to object – an extension of the linguistic domain. Semiotics considers anything as a metaphor of language
Theoretical perspectives	Theories that emphasize the significance of language, e.g. hermeneutics (opposed to semiotics), regard language as the universal medium of human experience. Conversely, semiotics considers signs as symbolic apparatus

Source: adapted from Gorny (1995).

explanation of semiotics as a transfer of metaphor from language to object, thus becoming symbolic, broadly explains the process that we want to investigate.

Applying semiotics
Another facet of semiotic application, also akin to metaphor, is that of morphological figures or metamorphs. This operates by addition, subtraction, permutation and substitution. Morphing is the process by which we insert commonly understood images or phrases into others to subtly change their meaning. For Gorny (1995), inter-textuality renders this achievable and works on the conception of culture as a reservoir of meanings interpreted in the sense of information, that is, naturally given knowledge. Thus our ability to find linguistic similarities in quotations, paraphrases, metaphors and the like permits us to understand new worlds. Semiotics reduces culture to the level of migratory 'ready-made knowledge'. Such linguistic and semiotic borrowings from other literal interpretative codes (myth/metaphor) enable us to construct and interpret understandable texts. Semiotics has a social aspect because the same image and text can invoke different meanings in different subjects. Therefore what is regarded as obvious, natural, universal, given, permanent and incontro-

vertible is the result of socially constructed discourses and sign systems. For example, consider the entrepreneurial narrative as a carrier of taken-for-granted values about what is good about entrepreneurship. Words such as entrepreneurial hero permeate such narratives and pictures of these heroes, such as Richard Branson, present an entrepreneurial iconology. A practical way of approaching semiotic analysis is to consider the different domains that contain semiotic significance, the semiotic, the personological, the environmental and the philosophical, as described in Figure 7.1.

Each of the domains impinges upon how meaning is constructed and projected. They may combine to construct a visual imagery, as for example, the visual image of the entrepreneur; or textually in stories about entrepreneurs. Intuitively, they can be ranked by importance, yet to fully describe them in relation to each other would require an extensive tome. Semiotics bypasses this lengthy process by recourse to visual, linguistic, phonetic and culturally specific linkages. We have merely to recognize their significance. Signs provide a raft of socially occurring sense-making inductive linkages; semiotic analysis makes these linkages manifest.

Semiotic analysis is a wide domain. However, all are concerned with identifying the constituent units in a paradigmatic semiotic system and the structural relationships between them: paradox, oppositions, correlations and logical relations. The broad approach is textual analysis, where the objective is to understand the system or rules. This is often followed by a system analysis, where we attempt to access the system of meaning, that is, how and in what ways these symbols belong to a constellation of meaning; how they conform, and how they can be ascribed to a category. It may be helpful to provide a brief worked example of semiotic analysis. One of our recent studies involved criminal entrepreneurs (Smith and Anderson 2003). Since this 'group' is relatively under-researched, we applied some semiotic techniques to try to understand the meanings that lay behind this group. Although semiotics was only one of the research techniques we employed, the range of material available, including books, pictures and magazines, lent itself to semiotic analysis. The categorization of criminal entrepreneurs was ours, but we quickly found strong semiotic evidence to support such a grouping. Dress codes – expensive suits with long jackets which reached beyond the knee, heavy gold jewellery and long dark overcoats and short hair – all symbolized belonging. Yet these artefacts in conjunction with the trappings of success, such as expensive motorcars, set this group apart from other criminals or businessmen. In conforming to the dress code they signalled their belonging to this category and set themselves apart from others. The obvious coding for success, the ability to own these trappings, signalled to us that material wealth was a significant part of the meaning system. Within the criminal group it also indicated some success in evading the

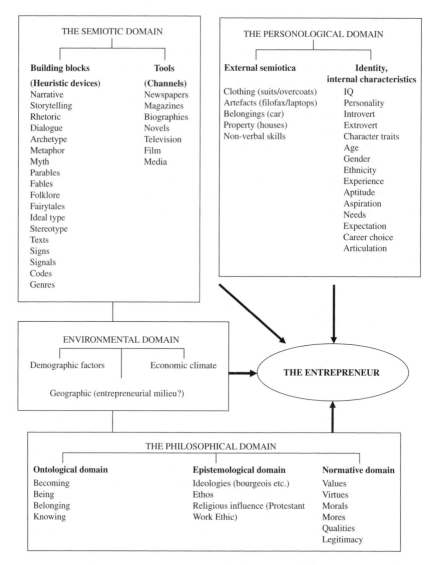

Figure 7.1   The projection of semiotic entrepreneurial identity

clutches of the law! We were able to make this categorization on a visual basis, from our own observations and from pictures. However, this told us very little about rules, yet given the illegal work of this group, we suspected that there had to be powerful rules to control interactions. Obviously legal sanctions could not be applied to extortionists. However, we had access to alternative sources, since this group was involved in making a film about their exploits, and several books had been written about them. We found that there were implicit rules of acceptable behaviour, and group members were expected to conform. For example, drug dealing was taboo, but threatening and acting out serious violence was permitted. Yet this violence was approved only when somebody had themselves infringed a moral code of behaviour. So in fact there was a very powerful system of codes and rules of what was acceptable and what was not acceptable. Moreover, we found that the group identified their interactions by words such as trust and reliability. For us this was another indicator of group coherence and rule-following behaviour, albeit in deviant circumstances.

Another technique, which can be applied to understand meaning, is experimental semiotics. This simply involves showing images and symbols to a particular referential group and recording their responses. A specific text can also be used. Sonesson (1994) criticizes the artificiality of experimental semiotics. Certainly there is a high risk of researcher bias and it can also be very difficult to analyse diverse responses. The classic semiotic methodology follows a favoured 'didactic' method of presentation, the 'Semiotic Reading', where an expert points out significance with a guided tour through a text.

Whilst there is no universal method of conducting semiotic analysis, there are basic generic steps. first, an extensive reading or scanning to appreciate the message and extract levels of abstraction from the data; second, a reflective analysis of the subject matter, essentially asking what is going on here; third, a comparison and asking the important 'who, why, what, where' questions to challenge, refute or support the perceived message; fourth, often an 'imaginative' explanatory (an inductive) 'leap'. Barthes (1988: 127) refers to 'shifting up a semiotic gear'. Normally this involves comparative analysis of the patterns perceived and discerning what these mean. Finally, and often problematically, there is a requirement to present the findings by 'telling a convincing story', in other words, sharing the logic and process of signification with the reader, so that they too can appreciate structure and meaning.

The logical way to begin is by trying it out. Semiotic analysis is a tool, but the interpretation of a text is, and must be, that which the author negotiates with the reader. The best way to learn is by doing semiotics. Baker (1994) provides some instructive pointers, which have been adapted and are presented in Table 7.3.

Semiotic analysis is a comparative, interpretative methodology that permits the subjectivication of the objective. Indeed, it demands that one be subjectively analytical. This often involves much trial and error. We offer the following pragmatic advice as ways of overcoming some of the issues.

Table 7.3   Some pointers for doing semiotic analysis

Generic to all categories	• Beware of judgmental evaluations, of ambiguity and idiosyncratic interpretations • Consider dominant images, characters and objects, background/environmental images and how the various message elements function in terms of semiotic meaning: iconic, symbolic, indexical? • Look for contrasting pairs of images, attempt to identify common themes • Use several people to conduct the analysis (Delphi methodology?) • Consider the personal qualities of the researcher
Pictorial/Visual	• What are the dominant visual images – how are they described and what do they symbolize? • Consider colour imagery, the size of the photograph in relation to the text. Images/pictures are anchored to text by heading/caption. Paradigmatically, photographs involve connotations • Consider the presence of iconical signs, and of indexicality in pictures and the possibility of dividing up the picture into units with independent meaning, and the question of what makes up the specificity of particular picture types. The semiotic character of pictures, and their peculiarities, differentiate pictorial meaning from other kinds of signification • Consider aesthetic appeal of cultural images and whether it is possible to dissolve the picture into layers
Newspapers	• All that appears in print has been selected and is thus socially constructed via learned journalistic behavioural codes. Newspaper articles attach significance to people/events. Headlines act as linguistic syntagms attracting the attention of the reader to new stories/topics • Consider the connotations of the linguistic and visual signs presented • Tabloids use oral-based vocabulary, slang and dramatic, sensational language and short, terse sentences – mixed small and large font sizes. More authoritarian papers use proper grammar/structure with longer sentences/paragraphs – same font size. This connotes authority and formality to the reader • Consider the distancing process of using surnames to vilify and the use of typographic devices to break up the text, e.g. bold text to extend the headline and the use of bold and one-word sub-headings directing the reader to a conclusion • Be aware of editing

Table 7.3 (continued)

Film/televisual	• Action and sound can be iconic, indexical and symbolic. Consider the use of slow motion as a liminal device, sound, motion and interpretation of dynamics and message elements – actions, colours, clothing and sounds • Importantly, films are representations of original data, not recollections
Textual analysis	• Textual analysis treats as meaningful any phenomenon occurring in a culture, e.g. a story, an image, a behaviour as being reducible to a series of repeatable elements and the rules for their combination. Literary texts provide a framework pointing out certain parts as being of relevance • Consider the dialectic between system and text and the relationship between related images

Source: constructed from Baker (1994).

- Do not dismiss semiotic analysis out of hand as it is a useful corroborative methodology.[3]
- Learn by doing and experimenting.
- Do not adhere rigidly to textbook advice (although textbooks are an aid).
- Do not attempt to understand everything at one reading.
- Do not expect your first or second attempts to succeed.
- Persevere and do not consign failed attempts to the bin: initial failure can aid the recognition of meaning.
- A failure to produce meaning may be an important research finding.
- Consider semiotic analysis as a complementary approach.

In reflecting on the earlier section about the critiques of the semiotic method, we believe that it is useful to consider how to avoid some of the problems. These issues and suggestions are set out in Table 7.4. We are particularly obliged to one of our anonymous reviewers for these suggestions.

Doing semiotics
According to Barthes (1988), semiotics is full of blockages of knowledge. This was certainly our experience in doing semiotics. None the less we have been modestly successful, at least in our own terms, in finding and demonstrating the deeper meaning which underpins a number of entrepreneurial artefacts. Table 7.5 provides some examples of where we have managed to employ semiotics to some advantage. The principal benefit of the studies

Table 7.4   Problems associated with doing semiotic analysis

Problem	Discussion and ways of addressing the problem
The issue of when signification ends	There appears to be no simple correspondence between signifier and signified (or referent). Indeed, is any signifier ever free of any other signifier? It could be argued that everything is linked together in a kind of infinite semiosis and that semioticians' merely 'talk around in circles'. This can be resolved by acknowledging the problem and by being sensible and confining arguments to those applicable to the subject matter being studied
Choice of research methodology	It can be argued that choosing a qualitative approach should be justified by the nature of the research question. For semiotics, with its particular strengths and weaknesses, it seems likely that the research question should reflect the need and benefits of applying semiotic analysis
The accusations of theoretical arrogance and mastery	There is no justification for considering semioticians' accounts of the deep structure of texts as being any better, more reliable, more accurate or more scientific than anyone else's view. Indeed, it could be argued that semioticians are guilty of 'theoretical arrogance' and the appearance of manufacturing mastery through the use of exclusionist jargon. One can partly avoid this accusation by avoiding the over-use of semiotic jargon and by providing a reflective account of how the analysis was conducted. In this way a more convincing case can be made. At the very least the reader is permitted to share the logic of the analytical process
The accusation that we are prisoners of language	Semioticians argue that we are prisoners of our language and signifying systems. It is still open to debate as to whether this argument can reasonably be defended. Take for instance the 'Cartesian linguistics' approach, i.e. based on the premise that the brain has a language acquisition device with an understanding of 'universal grammar' built into it at birth, which proposes that the acquisition of language is an instinct. Such a belief has far-reaching consequences. Thinking of language as an instinct reduces language to nothing more than a manifestation of a general intellectual capacity to use symbols. Seeing language not as the essence of human uniqueness, but rather as a biological capacity of adaptation to communicate information, it no longer seems relevant to see language as an insidious shaper of thought
Explicating the limitations of semiotic techniques	It is important to make explicit the limitations of semiotic techniques. It is not a general-purpose tool concerned with, and applicable to, anything and everything. Its employment requires justification, awareness and presentation of the problems

Table 7.4 (continued)

Problem	Discussion and ways of addressing the problem
The issue of the objectification of 'analyses and interpretations'	It is dangerous to present semiotic studies as if they were purely objective 'scientific' accounts rather than subjective interpretations. Thus it is important to provide empirical evidence for particular interpretations. This helps prevent semiotic analysis becoming too impressionistic and highly unsystematic. Such false objectification can generate taxonomies with little evident practical application. To prevent this, semioticians should take care to make their analytical strategy sufficiently explicit, thus enabling others to apply it either to the examples used or to others
Assessing what is good semiotic research	Because semiotics is a loosely defined critical practice rather than a unified, fully fledged analytical method or theory, it is often difficult to assess what constitutes 'good' semiotic analysis. It is helpful to separate good semiotic analysis from that which is little more than a pretentious form of literary criticism applied beyond the bounds of literature and based merely on subjective interpretation and grand assertions. The inclusion of a rigorous methodology section can help prevent this problem but ultimately the effectiveness of any qualitative research lies in its power to be convincing

listed was the exploration of many taken-for-granted issues, but readers may also be interested in the range of material examined. The paper 'Inspirational tales' (Smith 2002) is rather different in that it actually employs and applies semiotics to create meaning. In turning the research method into the production of meaning, a series of semiotic pictures and texts was created which combined to tell a story about entrepreneurship. This story used and capitalized upon a diverse, but established, range of entrepreneurial icons and image to promote entrepreneurship as a worthy practice for children.

Probably the most developed of our semiotic work is Anderson et al. (2004), 'Becoming, being and belonging'. This study looked at the images and texts of successful entrepreneurs who were members of Babson College's Academy of Distinguished Entrepreneurs. A consistent pattern of meaning was presented and promoted: e.g. success equals hard work; entrepreneurs overcome difficulty; poor boy makes good. We argued that these all underpinned the entrepreneurial ethos. We noted how these meaning systems were employed as a form of legitimization. First, Babson as an academic institution legitimized the actions of the selected entrepreneurs. Second, these distinguished entrepreneurs legitimized Babson as a suitable place to learn

Table 7.5   The semiotic/constructivist research stream of the authors

Paper	Category	Purpose/meaning
Smith and Anderson (2001) 'Crossed words: Entrepreneurship as criminality'	Pictorial	To demonstrate the power of semiotic imagery in projecting a criminal identity conflated with entrepreneurial imagery. Entailed the use of slides of London Gangster Dave Courtney contrasted with images of the fictional Del Boy and Arthur Daley
Smith (2002) 'Inspirational Tales: Propagating the entrepreneurial narrative amongst children'	Pictorial and textual	To conduct textual analysis and content analysis to develop common themes in entrepreneur stories. It also entailed the author writing an entrepreneur story specifically for children entitled 'Ernie the entrepreneur'. This was a picture-book story, which was piloted in primary schools using action research
Smith (2003a) 'Entrepreneurial identity and bad-boy iconology'	Pictorial, textual and experimental	The presentation revolved around the pictorial methodology by presenting 20 images associated with entrepreneurship and criminality, discussing their individual significance in building up the overall construct. Audience interaction demonstrated the significance of the universality of the bad-boy image (projected via artefacts) of the entrepreneur across national boundaries. At the same seminar the author also piloted the experimental methodology by distributing a survey/questionnaire accompanied by line drawings of several negative, masculine entrepreneurial types
Smith (2003b) 'Constructing The Heroic/Fabled Entrepreneur: A Biographical Analysis'	Textual	To conduct a semiotic analysis/textual analysis of several biographies and novels of entrepreneurs drawing out common themes and culminating in a diagram depicting typologies of entrepreneur stories and highlighting the anthological nature of the construct
Smith and Anderson (2003) 'Conforming Non Conformists: A semiotic analysis of entrepreneurial identity'	Pictorial and textual	To conduct a semiotic analysis of pictures, images and photographs associated with entrepreneurship. In Britain entrepreneurial iconology is conflated with images of class and criminality. However, we argue that despite this maverick imagery entrepreneurs are nevertheless conforming non-conformists. The power point presentation of the images provoked intense discussion. The paper

Table 7.5 (continued)

Paper	Category	Purpose/meaning
		developed from an appreciation that many entrepreneurs employ semiotics as part of their *modus operandi*, cultivating a visible image/personal trademark or were prone to semiotic exhibitionism and 'clowning' about
Anderson, Smith and Wade (2004) 'Becoming, being and belonging: The Stories about Babson distinguished entrepreneurs'	Textual and pictorial	To conduct an analysis of storyboards at Babson College containing the photographic images and eulogistic text of 80 or so entrepreneurs who make up the Academy of Distinguished Entrepreneurs. Few of the distinguished entrepreneurs fitted the common narrative of the heroic entrepreneur being from humble beginnings. The majority were of the corporate mould and from privileged backgrounds, but paradoxically where the classical entrepreneurial narrative could be bent to fit their individual stories, it was. The distinguished entrepreneurs adopted a serious, conservatively dressed, non-smiling persona and were surrounded by images associated with tradition. Conversely, those who conformed more closely to entrepreneurial ideology presented themselves as casually dressed, smiling personas and were less likely to surround themselves with traditional images

about enterprise. This convergence of legitimacy was made possible only because of the power of the underlying meaning in the texts and pictures. In this way the semiotic analysis showed both meaning and purpose. Given the nature of the data, we feel that this study demonstrates the power of semiotics to look beneath the obvious. Moreover, we cannot envisage any other methodology that would have allowed us to explore the relationship between the entrepreneurs and Babson College in such a purposeful way.

Reflections on semiotic analysis
For us, semiotics required to be learned over time and through experience. En route we developed a model to help us analyse image and text (see Figure 7.2). It is not a complete process model because, as we have argued, semiotic analysis is rarely linear, but it does describe some helpful stages and highlights areas of useful data. Of course it is neither complete nor perfect; moreover it suited our way of doing things, and semiotics is

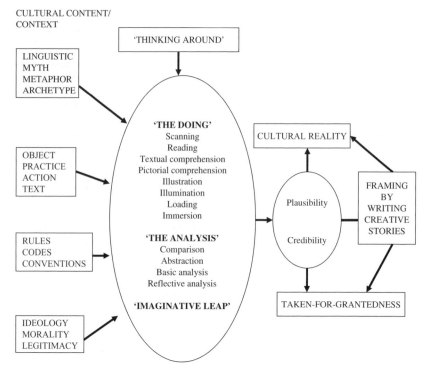

CULTURAL CONTENT/
CONTEXT

'THINKING AROUND'

LINGUISTIC
MYTH
METAPHOR
ARCHETYPE

OBJECT
PRACTICE
ACTION
TEXT

RULES
CODES
CONVENTIONS

IDEOLOGY
MORALITY
LEGITIMACY

'THE DOING'
Scanning
Reading
Textual comprehension
Pictorial comprehension
Illustration
Illumination
Loading
Immersion

'THE ANALYSIS'
Comparison
Abstraction
Basic analysis
Reflective analysis

'IMAGINATIVE LEAP'

CULTURAL REALITY

Plausibility

Credibility

FRAMING
BY
WRITING
CREATIVE
STORIES

TAKEN-FOR-GRANTEDNESS

Figure 7.2   Interpreting semiotic phenomena

subjective. But readers can use it as a guide, employing those bits that work for them, and rejecting the bits that don't. Like most research efforts, our work is never over; all we can offer is to say this is where we have got to thus far.

We now move swiftly from the descriptive to the reflective. Reflection is the final analytic phase in the philosophical construction of meaning. In reflection, we look back on what has been posited and try to understand what has occurred and what it means. In doing so we evaluate the effectiveness of our actions and words. Many research methodologies (particularly quantitative) are sequential, requiring one to conduct analysis in an ordered, chronological manner. Semiotics is not such a methodology, as recognition, interpretation, analysis, synthesis and conclusion can all occur simultaneously. Human cognition enables stages to be short-circuited; hence the speed of perception attributable to semiotic imagery.

The research described above challenges expected notions of entrepreneurial research enabled by qualitative research methodologies. In particular, it emphasized the pictoriality of the entrepreneurial construct. Appreciation of semiotics requires a creative state of mind and thrives upon experimentation. As has been argued in this chapter, if entrepreneurship is the creation, extraction and communication of value, then semiotics permits the creation, extraction and communication of meaning. This is apt because as Barthes (1988: 203) points out that the French word '*sémiotique*' originates from the battlefields of medieval Europe where it described a system of marshalling troops by signalling with flags. From the very same battlefields the word *entrepreneur* originated as descriptor of bold action (a forgotten connection reaffirmed).

Semiotic analysis and associated qualitative methodologies are often misunderstood or avoided completely as being too complex. However, semiotics investigates the continuous dialogue between a culture and its own otherness and, as such, is a potentially rewarding methodology. Yet it is wise to heed the advice of Gorny (1995) that semiotics is a science institutionalized by semioticians themselves by virtue of the language system of conventional semiotic terminology – sign, code, signification, semiosis and so on. It is thus that which is called semiotics, by self-styled semioticians. This has important implications for the articulation of entrepreneurial research because there is a danger that we will fall into the same trap. When the majority of the population instinctively appreciate what we do as a discipline, we will have succeeded in our objective. Simplicity and clarity of explanation should be our aims. Further excellent advice comes from Casson (2000: 22), who argues that the study of discourse has completely supplanted the study of reality, with many academics now merely deconstructing 'each other's texts rather than re-examine reality'. Properly constructed, semiotic analysis allows an understanding of the actual signs and symbols of a given system as they occur naturally, rather than deconstructing the texts of others. Leach (1974) argues that meaning itself is notoriously difficult to define; therefore to try to understand the indefinable (entrepreneurship) by recourse to the indefinable (meaning) requires patience, skill and humility. The virtue of semiotics is that it permits us to recognize meaning.

Notes

1.   Initially in terms of quantity, we found studies concerning the semiotic analysis of visual images to be rare. As is often the case, our search parameters were perhaps not extensive enough. In researching this chapter (ironically after we had conducted the actual research) we found a wealth of useful articles. Academic texts that discuss semiotic analysis, include – Becker (1974), Eco (1979), Curry and Clarke (1977), Lewis (1982), Hockings (1985), Harper (1987), Schere (1990), Merrill (1992), Coote and Shelton (1992), Collier and Collier (1992), Edwards (1992), Bryson et al. (1994), Baker (1994), Chaplin (1994), Chandler (1994), Gorny (1995), Banks (1995), Harper (1996), Bignall (1997), MacDougall (1997), Edwards (1997), Preziosi (1998), Barry (1999), Deely (1990), Barry (1999), Emmison and Smith (2000) and Holliday (2000). Alternatively, one can

research it on the web, although few sites are focused specifically on analysis of visual images. See Chandler and Ryder under 'Websites'. Also, what we had set out to do on our own, enterprising anthropologists and sociologists had done before us.

2. Pictorial semiotics includes the study of still photographs, video footage, films, CDs and anything capable of being portrayed visually. There are critics of visual semiotics; e.g. Emmison and Smith (2000: 20) suggest the adaptation of criticality and of researching the visible social world, not pictures of it. They argue that visual data are simply illustrative and elsewhere argue that visual sociology is an isolated sub-field of marginal interest to other sociological researchers. One of the dangers is that one must be constantly aware of posed material and also of researcher bias.

3. By using a series of complementary qualitative and quantitative methodologies such as constructivism in its many guises – semiotic analysis; content analysis; ethnography; ethno-methodology; surveys; in-depth interviews; the Delphi methodology; and action research – one contributes to a richer understanding of the meaning of entrepreneurship.

References

Aggestam, M. and Keenan, J. (2002) Entrepreneurial Act as Languaging, Languaging as Entrepreneurial Act. Paper presented for consideration of presentation at the ESBRI New Practices of Entrepreneurship Workshop. Stockholm, Sweden 23–26 May.

Aldrich, H. and Zimmer, C. (1986) Entrepreneurship through social networks, In D. Sexton and S. Raymond (eds), *The Art and Science of Entrepreneurship*. New York: Ballinger. pp. 3–23.

Aldrich, H. and Fiol, M. (1994) Fools Rush In? The Institutional Context Of Industry Creation, Academy of Management Review, **19**(4): 645–70.

Anderson, A.R. (2003) Entrepreneurial performances: using a dramaturgical perspective to improve understanding, working paper.

Anderson, A.R., Smith, R. and Wade, G. (2004) Becoming, being and belonging: The stories about Babson Distinguished Entrepreneurs, paper submitted for consideration of presenting at the British Academy of Management Conference, St Andrews, Scotland, August 2004.

Baker, T. (1994) *Doing Social Research* (2nd edn). New York: McGraw-Hill.

Banks, M. (1995) Visual Research Methods, Social Research Update, University of Surrey, http://www.soc.surrey.ac.uk/sru/SRU11/SRU11.html. (Accessed 22.04.2004.)

Barley, S.R. (1983) Semiotics and the study of occupational and organizational cultures, *Administrative Science Quarterly*, **28**: 393–413.

Barry, J. (1999) *Art Culture and The Semiotics Of Meaning: Culture's changing signs of life in poetry, drama, painting and sculpture*. Basingstoke: Palgrave Macmillan.

Barthes, R. (1970) *Mythologies*. Paris: Seuil.

Barthes, R. (1977) *Elements of Semiology*. New York: Hill and Wang.

Barthes, R. (1981) *Camera Lucidia: Reflections on photography*. New York: Hill and Wang.

Barthes, R. (1988) *The Semiotic Challenge*. (Howard, R. trans). London: University of California Press.

Becker, H.S. (1974) Photography and Sociology, *Studies in the Anthropology of Visual Communication*, 1: 3–26.

Bignell, J. (1997) *Media Semiotics: An introduction*. Manchester: Manchester University Press.

Bryson, N. et al. (eds) (1994) *Visual Culture: Images and interpretation*, Middleton, CT: Wesleyan University Press.

Casson, M.C. (2000) *Enterprise and Leadership: Studies on firms, markets and networks*. Cheltenham, UK and Northampton, MA, USA: Edward Elgar.

Chandler, D. (1994) 'Semiotics for Beginners', http://www.aber.ac.uk/media/Documents/S4B/ [29.11.2001].

Chandler, D. (2001) *Semiotics: The Basics*. London: Routledge.

Chaplin, E. (1994) *Sociology and Visual Representation*. London: Routledge.

Chell, E. (2000) Towards researching the 'opportunistic entrepreneur': A social constructionist approach and research agenda, *European Journal of Work and Organizational Psychology*, (91): 63–80.

Collier, J. Jr and Collier, M. (eds) (1992) *Visual Anthropology: photography as a research method*, Albuquerque: University of New Mexico Press.

Coote, J. and Shelton, A. (eds) (1992) *Anthropology, Art and Aesthetics*, Oxford: Clarendon Press.

Culler, J. (2001) *The Persuit of Signs*. London: Routledge.

Curry, T.J. and Clarke, A.C. (1977) *Introducing Visual Sociology*. Dubuque. IA: Kendall/Hunt.

Deely, J. (1990) *Basics of Semiotics*. Bloomington, IN: Indiana University Press.

Echtner, C.M. (1999) The semiotic paradigm; implications for tourist research, *Tourism Management*, **19**: 47–57.

Eco, U. (1979).*Theory of Semiotics*. Bloomington, IN: Indiana University Press.

Edwards, E. (1997) Beyond the boundary: a consideration of the expressive in photography and anthropology. In Banks, M. and Morphy, H. (eds), *Rethinking Visual Anthropology.* London: Newhaven Press.

Edwards, E. (1992) (ed.) *Anthropology and Photography 1860–1920*. New Haven: Yale University Press in association with the Royal Anthropological Institute, London.

Emmison, M. and Smith, P. (2000) *Researching the Visual: Images, objects, contexts and interactions in social and cultural inquiry*. London: Sage Publications.

Fiol, C.M. (1989) A semiotic analysis of corporate language: Boundaries and joint venture, *Administrative Science Quarterly*, **34**: 277–303.

Fiol, C.M. (1991) Seeing the empty spaces; towards a more complex understanding of the meaning of power in organizations, *Organizational Studies*, **12**: 547–66.

Gergen, K.J. (1998) Constructionist dialogues and the vicissitudes of the political. In Velody, I. (ed.), *The Politics of Social Construction*. London: Sage.

Gergen, K.J. (2001) Social Psychology as social construction: the emerging vision, http://www.swarthmore.edu. (01.11.01.)

Gergen, K.J. and Gergen, M.M. (1988) Narrative and self as relationship. In Berkowitz, L. (ed.), *Advances in Experimental Social Psychology*. Vol. 21., New York: Academic Press, pp. 17–56.

Gorny, E. (1995) What is semiotics?, Creator Magazine no. 3, London.

Gregory, D. (1981) Human agency and human geography, *Transactions of the Institute of British Geographers*, n.s. 6: 1–18.

Greimas, A.J. (1987) *On Meaning: Selected writings in semiotic theory.* University of Minneapolis, MN: Minneapolis Press.

Harper, D.A. (1987) *Working Knowledge: skill and community in a small shop*. Chicago, IL: Chicago University Press.

Harper, D. (1996) Seeing Sociology, *American Sociologist*, Fall, **37**(3): 69–78.

Hjorth, D. and Johannisson, B. (2003) Conceptualising the opening phase of regional development as the enactment of collective identity, *Concepts and Transformation*, **8**(1): 69–92.

Hockings, P. (1985) *Principles of Visual Anthropology*, (2nd edn). The Hague: Mouton.

Holliday, R. (2000) We've been framed: visualising methodology, *Sociological Review*, **48**(4), 503–21.

Kress, G. and van Leeuwen, T. (1996), *Reading Images: The grammar of visual design*. London, Routledge, pp. 130–35.

Lawes, R. (2002) Demystifying semiotics: Some key questions answered, *International Journal of Market Research*, **44**, Third Quarter 251–64.

Leach, G. (1974) *Semantics*. Harmondsworth, UK: Penguin Books.

Lewis, G.H. (1982) Image-ing society Visual sociology in focus, paper presented to the Hawaiian Sociological Association.

Lincoln, Y.S. and Guba, E.G. (1985) *Naturalistic Enquiry.* Beverly Hills, CA: Sage.

MacDougall, D. (1997) 'The Visual in Anthropology', in Banks, M. and Morphy, H. (eds), *Rethinking Visual Anthropology.* London: Newhaven Press.

Merrill, F. (1992) *Sign, Textuality, World*. Bloomington, IN: Indiana University Press.

Nicol, R.A.E. (2003) *Social Constructions of Environmental Quality and Opportunities for Enterprise in Rural Scotland*, Ph.D. thesis, School of Sustainable Rural Development UHI Millennium Institute and Open University.

Nicolson, L. (2001) Modelling the Evolution Of Entrepreneurial Mythology, M.Sc. Entrepreneurship, University of Aberdeen, September 2001 (unpublished).

Noth, W. (1995), *Handbook of Semiotics*. Bloomington, IN: Indiana University Press.

Ofverstrom, H. Vahlne, J.E. and Nilsson, A. (2002) *Constructing ideas – a process of communication*. Paper presented at the ESBRI New Practices of Entrepreneurship Workshop. Stockholm, Sweden 23–26 May.

Pile, S. (1993) Human agency and geography revisited: A critique of new models of the self, *Transactions of the Institute of British Geographers*, n.s. **18**: 122–39.

Preziosi, D. (1998) *The Art of History: A critical anthology*, Oxford: Oxford University Press.

Saussure, F. de (1974) *Courses In General Linguistics*. London: Fontana.

Schere, J.C. (1990) (ed.) Picturing cultures, historical photographs in anthropological inquiry, Special issue of *Visual Anthropology*, 3.2D3, Harwood Academic Publishers.

Shanks, G. (1995) Semiotics and qualitative research in education: The third crossroad, *The Qualitative Report*, **2**(3).

Singer, J. (1994) *Boundaries of the Soul: The practice of Jung's psychology*. Sturminster, UK: Prism Press.

Smith, R. and Anderson, A.R. (2004) The devil is in the *e-tale*: form and structure in the entrepreneurial narrative. In Hjorth, D., and Steyaert, C. (eds), *Narrative and Discursive Approaches in Entrepreneurship*. Cheltenham, UK and Northampton, MA, USA: Edward Elgar, pp. 125–43.

Smith, R. and Anderson, A.R. (2001) Crossed words: Entrepreneurship as criminality, paper presented at the Global Entrepreneurship Research Conference in Lyon, April.

Smith, R. (2002) 'Inspirational tales: Propagating the entrepreneurial narrative amongst children', paper presented at the Babson–Kauffman Entrepreneurship Research Conference, Boulder, Colorado, June 2003.

Smith, R. (2003a) Entrepreneurial Identity and Bad Boy Iconology, paper presented at an Entrepreneurship Research Seminar at Strathclyde University, April 2003.

Smith, R (2003b) Constructing The Heroic/Fabled Entrepreneur: A Biographical Analysis, paper presented at the Babson–Kauffman Entrepreneurship Research Conference, Boston, June 2003.

Smith, R. (2003c) Rural rogues: A case story on the smokies' trade, paper presented at the 2nd Rural Entrepreneurship Conference, Dumfries, October 2003.

Smith, R. and Anderson, A.R. (2003) Conforming non conformists: A semiotic analysis of entrepreneurial identity, paper presented at the Babson–Kauffman Entrepreneurship Research Conference, Boston, June 2003.

Smith, R. (forthcoming) Constructions of the entrepreneur: as hero and villain, unpublished PhD thesis, Robert Gordon University, Aberdeen.

Sonesson, G. (1994) The ecological foundations of iconicity. In Rauch, Irmengard and Carr, Gerlard F. (eds), *Semiotics Around the World: Synthesis in diversity. Proceedings of the Fifth International Congress of the IASS, Berkeley, June 12–18, 1994*. Berlin and New York: Mouton de Gruyter, pp. 739–42.

Yeats, W.B. (1956) 'Amongst school children', In the *Collected Poems of W.B. Yeats*, New York: Macmillan.

Yin, R.K. (1993) *Applications of Case Study Research*. CA: Sage Publications.

Websites

Daniel Chandler – http://www.aber.ac.uk/media/Documents/S4B/semiotic.html

Martin Ryder – http://carbon.cudenver.edu/~mryder/itc_data/semiotics. html#resources

8 Media discourse in entrepreneurship research

Leona Achtenhagen and Friederike Welter

Why discourse analysis in entrepreneurship research?

Language, and its use, is increasingly being understood as one of the most important phenomena in social and organizational research (Alvesson and Kärreman 2000a: 1126). Language offers a system of categories for our experiences and how we assign meaning to them. However, as will be shown in this chapter, the use of language in entrepreneurship research has potential far beyond the use of interviews (which are often seen as the most appropriate method of gathering data in qualitative social science research).

Broadly speaking, discourses refer to the practices of writing and speaking (Woodilla 1998). Discourse analysis, as a set of different research methods under a common heading, can be fruitfully employed to analyse spoken and written 'texts' (cf. discussion in van Dijk 1997: 4). According to Phillips and Hardy (2002: 3),

> [S]ocial reality is produced and made real through discourses, and social interactions cannot be fully understood without reference to the discourses that give them meaning. As discourse analysts, then, our task is to explore the relationship between discourse and reality.

Originally used predominantly as a linguistic approach (e.g. Gee 2002), discourse analysis is now being successfully applied in a variety of fields, such as sociology, philosophy and anthropology (Schiffrin 1994: 5). More recently, the potential of discourse analysis has also been recognized by a few scholars in the field of entrepreneurship who apply it to various forms of text, e.g. media, research articles etc. (see e.g. Chapter 9 in this handbook). The analysis of media discourses can help us to better understand contemporary processes of social and cultural change in the entrepreneurship context (cf. Fairclough 1995: 2).

Discourse analysis is highly reflexive and allows researchers to move beyond the taken-for-granted. It can thus play an important role in generating new knowledge in the entrepreneurship field. Consider the following example: by and large, the field of entrepreneurship is connected to (and partly built on) a range of established stereotypes and images. For example, entrepreneurship is viewed as *per se* beneficial for societies, a panacea for reducing unemployment, creating economic wealth, and a facilitator for combining career and family. As language acts as a mediator for constructing reality, discourse analysis can be employed to understand the social construction of these assumptions (Burr 1995: 11). Understanding a discourse and how it is created can then generate new insights into an investigated topic, for example when the discourse around fostering female entrepreneurship focuses on how to enable women to work from home, rather than putting into question the social reality that many women carry that double burden in the first place. The underlying assumption is that discourses play an important role in producing social realities, as they have an impact on, for example, entrepreneurial identities, activities and perceptions (cf. Phillips and Hardy 2002: 1–2). Discourse analysis can assist in reconstructing patterns of these social realities and thus in identifying the structuring of phenomena (Bublitz 2001: 228). Studying and analysing written and spoken texts can, for example, reveal the discursive sources of power, dominance, inequality and bias (van Dijk 1998).

In this chapter, we aim to discuss discourse analysis as a research methodology for entrepreneurship research and assess its advantages and challenges. Current research by discourse analysts points to three different loci of 'producing' discourses: first, institutions and organizations (e.g. organizations supporting entrepreneurial activities, as well as ventures themselves); second, individuals and inter-individual interaction; and third, media (Donati 2001: 154). We will focus on media as a locus of producing discourse, reviewing selected examples of the application of discourse analysis in entrepreneurship research. However, we would like to point out that discourse analysis could be just as fruitfully employed for investigating the other two loci.

Outlining the basics for discourse analysis
The role of social constructivism for discourse analysis
Compared to several other qualitative research methodologies, discourse analysis is more strongly based on a social constructivist paradigm (Phillips and Hardy 2002: 2). According to Berger and Luckmann (1969), knowledge is socially constructed, meaning that it is not developed based on observations alone. Rather, understanding is created in a social context, implying that people construct knowledge and act based on their perceptions and experiences. In this way, social constructivism implicitly draws attention to the cognitive processes connected with entrepreneurial activities featuring prominently in theories of opportunity recognition (e.g. Kirzner 1979; Beattie 1999). Entrepreneurship is then understood as a socially constructed phenomenon, which is reflected in, for example, the

emergence of opportunities, as individuals make sense of information and their actions, thus retrospectively 'discovering' and 'recognizing' business ideas (Gartner et al. 2003). Entrepreneurship hence takes place in an 'enacted' environment (Weick 1995).

In short, social constructivism builds on a number of key assumptions (Burr 1995). First, our reality is produced in social processes. Second, meanings of reality are produced by the interaction of people. We perceive reality through meanings, based on which we construct different versions of reality and accordingly make knowledge claims. Truth and facts are also socially negotiated, implying that the ways in which we usually understand reality and the concepts we use to interpret it are historically and culturally specific. Third, different ways of understanding are specific to particular cultures and periods of time, and depend on the 'particular social and economic arrangements prevailing in that culture at that time' (Burr 1995: 4). Fourth, language offers a system of categories for our experience and for assigning it meaning. Thus language serves as the mediator for constructing reality.

Here lies the potential contribution of discourse analysis as a qualitative methodology in entrepreneurship research: it permits the exploration of the processes of socially constructing entrepreneurship-related phenomena, and their economic/societal implications (Ainsworth 2001). Discourse analysis investigates 'how the socially produced ideas and objects that populate the world were created in the first place and how they are maintained and held in place over time' (Phillips and Hardy 2002: 6).

The role of context in discourse analysis
Texts are a material manifestation of discourse, but discourses exist beyond the individual texts that compose them (cf. Chalaby 1996; Phillips and Hardy 2002). Texts are not necessarily printed texts; they can rather take a variety of forms, such as written texts, spoken words, cartoons and symbols (Grant et al. 1998). However, a discourse cannot be identified based on a single text; rather discourses emerge from the interaction between different social groups, their 'texts', as well as from the context in which the interaction is embedded. Therefore the understanding of the context is crucial in discourse analysis, which has often been criticized for its inadequate attention to context (Cicourel 1981; Fairclough 1992).

Different levels of context exist (cf. Table 8.1). Keller (2004: 96) differentiates between historical–societal, institutional–organizational and situational contexts of a discourse. Schegloff (1992) and Wetherell (2001: 388) distinguish between proximate and distal contexts. Relating this to context as discussed in entrepreneurship research, both proximate and distal context indicate the systemic (economic) and substantive (political and cultural)

Table 8.1   Levels of context in discourse research

Institutional–organizational context	Context in which data have been created: which are the distinctive elements of these fields (e.g. language, topics, power relations)? For which audience have texts been written? How are texts and data distributed?	
Situational context	Who are the authors of texts? What is their position and background?	
Historical–social context:	What are the important characteristics of the context in which the data emerged and texts were written?	
	Proximate context: direct, local environment, in entrepreneurship micro-social and micro-economic environment of entrepreneurs	*Distal context:* social class, institutions where discourse occurs, cultural and regional settings, in entrepreneurship macro-environment of entrepreneurs

Source: based on Keller (2004), Schegloff (1992) in Wetherell (2001) and Johannisson
et al. (2002).

embeddedness of entrepreneurship (Johannisson et al. 2002), which is reflected in the overall institutional settings, norms and values, as well as political and social environments of entrepreneurs. Linking this to notions of context as discussed in discourse analysis, the proximate context and the distal context would reflect the micro- and macro-environments of entrepreneurs respectively.

While discourses cannot be understood without their context, it should also be clear that context does not determine a certain discourse (cf. Potter 2001: 318). Indeed, contexts are not 'fixed' or 'given'; rather they are flexible and changing, and according to van Dijk (1997: 16): 'contexts, just like discourse, are not objective in the sense that they consist of social facts that are understood and considered relevant in the same way by all participants. They are interpreted or constructed, and strategically and continually made relevant by and for participants'.

Referring back to the role social constructivism plays in discourse analysis, the following possible area of 'conflict' in employing discourse analysis in entrepreneurship research needs to be pointed out: an 'objective' context of entrepreneurship also exists, as indicated by numbers of newly founded companies, numbers of women entrepreneurs, or the amount of venture capital distributed to entrepreneurs. But this 'objective' context is not only objective – it is also subjective in that individuals may assign meanings to the numbers, and as a social collective they reproduce and transform it into communicative practices. Thus collectives create a coherent social reality that frames their sense of who they are (cf. Mumby and Clair 1997: 181).

How can we reconcile this with our proposal to use a method based on a social constructivist understanding for entrepreneurship research? First, social constructivism itself pays attention to the fact that different layers of reality exist, as shown by Berger and Luckmann (1969) in their in-depth discussion on society as both an 'objective' and 'subjective' reality. This allows us to consider context as both an 'objective' and 'subjective' phenomenon. Second, a discourse method in entrepreneurship research would not be employed to assess numbers or amounts, but rather concentrate on analysing the 'subjective' reality and context of entrepreneurship, which could be supplemented with 'objective' context data (e.g. cf. Achtenhagen and Welter 2003, 2004, and the next section in this chapter).

For example, discourse analysis applied to entrepreneurship topics could investigate the power implications of venture capital in entrepreneurial processes or the role of venture foundations as a discursive argument for why certain infrastructural means are needed. Another example can be found in the discourse on women's entrepreneurship: here 'traditional' entrepreneurship research could provide 'objective' context data on characteristics and development of women's entrepreneurship and the general policy environment, whilst a discourse analysis of media could concentrate on analysing how a particular social identity of women entrepreneurs is constructed through transporting images and role models (for specific examples see next section).

Different types of discourse analysis
Different 'schools' or 'types' of discourse analyses exist (for extensive reviews and comparisons of these see, e.g., Fairclough 1995; Keller et al. 2001; or Phillips and Hardy 2002). Discourse analysis became most prominent as a linguistic analysis of how language is being used, often focusing on the analysis of communication processes. To exemplify, critical linguistic focuses on grammar in an ideological analysis, as the grammatical form of texts is seen as meaningful in reproducing relations of domination and power. Schiffrin (1994) provides a comprehensive overview of the different linguistics-oriented approaches to discourse analysis and their application.

Another type of discourse analysis has been developed in France since the 1960s. An important contribution here has been made by the political scientists Laclau and Mouffé (1985). In their view, '[d]iscourse theory aims at an understanding of the social as a discursive construction whereby, in principle, all social phenomena can be analysed using discourse analytical tools'

(Phillips and Jørgensen 2002: 24). Phillips and Jørgensen (2002) provide an extensive discussion of this approach and contrast it with other discourse analytical theories. The best-known scholar in this 'school' is Foucault, who wrote, among other things, the seminal book *The Order of Discourse* (*L'ordre du discours*) (1972). Foucault's interest lies, for example, in the formal prerequisites of producing knowledge, the rules of producing and control of discourses, or the relationship between knowledge and power (Keller et al. 2001: 12). Foucault's ideas have been applied to investigate the symbolic and structural dimensions of discourse, the production of discourses and discursive power struggles. Ahl (2002 and Chapter 9 in this volume) applies Foucault's work to deconstruct the image of female entrepreneurs in research texts.

More recently, a number of efforts have been made to reconcile different schools of thought. For example, van Dijk (1997) attempts to integrate them into 'discourse studies'. Van Dijk introduces cognition into discourse analysis to show how societal structures influence discourse structures, and how societal structures are in turn enacted, instituted, legitimated, confirmed or challenged by texts (Fairclough and Wodak 1997: 265–6). Socio-cognitive studies, then, focus for example on the abuse of power and how ideologies reproduce inequalities.

Carrying out discourse analysis in entrepreneurship research
An important issue to keep in mind when conducting a discourse analysis is that it is hardly possible to assess an entire discourse. The aim with employing discourse analysis is to reveal the relation between a discourse and social reality. This analysis is based on a number of individual texts to identify the nature of a discourse: 'We cannot simply focus on an individual text, however; rather, we must refer to bodies of texts, new textual forms, and new systems of distributing texts that constitute a discourse over time' (Phillips and Hardy 2002: 5).

Often, discourse analysis attempts to reconstruct the argumentation structure applied to define a problem or object (Donati 2001: 155). In order to understand the structure of discourses, and to facilitate the analysis of the discourse of interest, researchers might consider the following (cf. Jäger 2001a: 96–7). First, discourses might be specialized discourses, for example the discourse of researchers on topics related to female entrepreneurship, as analysed for example by Ahl (2002). In the overall entrepreneurship discourse, different topics emerge and those discourse processes referring to the same topic can be regarded as 'strands of discourse' (see Figure 8.1). Each strand of discourse in turn consists of a number of 'texts'. Each of the texts normally would refer to different topics, but at least part of the text needs to be related to the strand of discourse. Thus different texts make

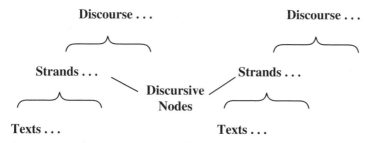

Figure 8.1   The structure of discourses

up the strands of a discourse, and different strands of a discourse make up an overall discourse (Jäger 2001a: 97). The different strands of a discourse might be linked by 'discursive nodes' found in the same text. For example, a text on a successful entrepreneur might refer to the discourse strand on entrepreneurs' characteristics as well as to the discourse strand on the impact of entrepreneurship on employment and social welfare.

Second, different strands of entrepreneurship discourses operate in different discursive fields, such as sciences, politics, education, everyday life, business or administration (Jäger 2001a: 99). Texts are voiced from these 'locations'. The different discursive fields influence each other, refer to each other and make use of each other. For example, to legitimize its existence a typical discourse in entrepreneurship research draws heavily on the need for job creation focused in the social and political discourses. The same is the case with the discourse on entrepreneurship education: this draws on the wish to increase the number of newly founded ventures. The media pick up fragments of these different discourses and influence them, for example regarding the image of entrepreneurs in society. But media in turn are also influenced by discourses from different fields; for example, they make selected use of research results. Here, an interesting question to investigate would be whether and how recent issues in entrepreneurship research are linked to and discussed in the discourse in media.

Third, discourses cannot be directly grasped and understood; rather they have to be distilled methodically from the discourse material. Discourses can be recognized based on patterns and their frequency; they either become obvious from the texts or can be interpreted from the arguments and discourse elements used in the texts (Bublitz 2001: 246). This is a challenge for the entrepreneurship researcher, who has to know about a discourse before analysing it in order to be able to recognize discourse strands in the analysed texts.

Fourth, the discourse analysis can take place on different levels. A discourse analysis on the *meso level* refers to analysing contents as well as language patterns. With regard to entrepreneurship, this allows us to identify and understand the images transported through media, which in turn influence the role of entrepreneurs and their identity, thus determining the extent and nature of entrepreneurship. Examples are our own studies (Achtenhagen and Welter 2003, 2004) and the research by Langowitz and Morgan (2003) on female entrepreneurship, which illustrate that public media discourses reduce female entrepreneurship to being an exception to the male norm, and construct images of successful female entrepreneurship based on a male norm (see the next section for more details on examples and methods employed).

A *grand-scale* discourse analysis allows us not only to determine general patterns of discourse (i.e. what is voiced), but also to identify 'hidden' discourses that take place through *not* discussing a phenomenon, which illustrates both the boundaries of a discourse and its power aspects. Undertaking grand-scale discourse analysis, that is, analysing general patterns of coverage, constitutes a frequent starting point of applying discourse analysis to entrepreneurship topics. One such example is the study by Baker et al. (1997) (cf. the next section for more details).

As an example of how discourse analysis can be conducted, we will refer to a methodology developed by Siegfried Jäger. His approach is also heavily influenced by Foucault. He focuses on grasping sup-topics in different discursive strands and on each discursive level, and groups these to (lead) topics, which build up the discourse. Jäger (2001a: 103–4; see also 2001b) suggests the following procedure for conducting a discourse analysis after the research topic has been specified and linked to a specific discourse strand:

1. *characterization* of the *discursive level*, e.g. newspaper(s) or research text;
2. *gathering of the data*: collecting and filing of the texts in a database;
3. *structural analysis*: analysis of the filed texts in view of the discourse strand under analysis;
4. *fine-grained analysis* of one or more texts typical for the position taken by the media under analysis in respect to the discourse topic;
5. *integrative analysis* of the entire discourse strand and the chosen discursive level; *critical reflection* of the findings and *abstraction to 'condensed findings'*. A lead question for this analysis could for example be: what contribution does this discursive level make to entrepreneurship today, and what further development could be expected?

Keller (2004) adds to this 'check-list' by drawing attention to the fact that the data collection for discourse analysis needs to be focused on a specific

Table 8.2   Steps in the analytical approach applied in our project

Step 1	Step 2	Step 3
Analysing the 'grand-scale' discourse	Analysing the meso-level discourse	Linking discourse analysis with context
• patterns of search term(s) over time	• focus of discourse: main versus side issues	• analysing discourse in relation to 'objective' data, e.g. numbers of women-owned businesses or policy environment
• embeddedness of search term(s) within newspaper: systemic versus substantive	• images transported through language	

discourse right from the beginning, in order to develop criteria for a 'threshold' where data collection is stopped. Moreover, in categorizing the data collected, the researcher needs to decide on which kind of data are needed to understand the context of the discourse or for reconstructing it. Table 8.2 illustrates how we employed this method (more details will be provided in the next section). Note that there is no best way or simple recipe to conduct this type of analysis.

As in any research, quality criteria of discourse analysis can be established. An analysis can be said to be exhaustive when it no longer derives new insights regarding its content. Discourse researchers should keep in mind that, depending on the discourse that is being studied, exhaustiveness may be reached relatively quickly, as often there is only a limited range of arguments and contents within a particular discourse or discourse field at a certain point in time (Jäger 2001a: 101–2). A large amount of texts would then mainly assist in quantifying which arguments are mentioned most often. This quantification can be used to establish which arguments are used as major 'slogans', thus being interesting for historical analyses of patterns of discourses over time. In order to enhance the quality of a study, the analysis of the empirical material can be illustrated with details from the data and presented in a way that allows the readers to reach their own conclusions (cf. Potter 2001: 324).

Examples of discourse analyses in entrepreneurship studies
To exemplify the rather abstract discussion above, the following presents a range of (the few) discourse studies that have been conducted in the field of entrepreneurship using different printed media. So far, some entrepreneurship researchers have analysed fiction or academic research texts. Others have analysed gender discourses on women entrepreneurship in printed media such as newspapers and the popular business press.

Entrepreneurship discourse in fiction

Feldmeier (2001) analyses the functions of different kinds of fiction related to entrepreneurs and entrepreneurship. Her study is grounded in a text-oriented hermeneutic approach as represented by Paul Ricoeur (Feldmeier 2001: 49–57), and the method she employs is new historicism (ibid.: 57–65). This method allows her to interpret texts and discourses across disciplines, simultaneously looking at the novel, its author and the time of origin, thus placing the entrepreneurship discourses in fiction into their respective contexts (ibid.: 227).

Feldmeier selects fiction texts based on five criteria, as no single definition exists of what constitutes a fiction text on entrepreneurs (ibid.: 19ff.). In order to qualify as fiction, a text needs to be (a) a novel (excluding dramas and poems) and (b) written in the twentieth century either in the German-, French- or Anglo-American speaking countries. Further, (c) the entrepreneur needs to be the main actor of at least one major strand, and (d) (s)he should be described in detail. Furthermore, the author differentiates between (i) explanatory, (ii) teaching, (iii) reflection, (iv) critique and (v) entertainment functions (Feldmeier 2001: 67). Each function is reflected in a specific novel genre. The *explanatory* function is linked to genuine business novels, the *teaching* function is linked to novels that enlighten the reader, whilst the *reflection* function and realistic novels go hand in hand. The *critique* function is related to satirical novels, and the *entertainment* function to entertainment novels.

Feldmeier identifies 31 novels that fulfil her criteria, five of which she analyses in depth, using the remaining ones to discuss her results. The work then proceeds to analyse the texts along four main and ten sub-dimensions, which are reflected in a variety of individual and text characteristics (ibid.: 69) as illustrated in Table 8.3.

By drawing on the different functions, the author argues for the practical relevance of her analysis in that entrepreneurs can learn from the discourses created in these different works of fiction through the way fictional entrepreneurs are described in these works. Moreover, the method employed allows her to link the text analysis to the specific historical, political, economic, social and cultural contexts necessary to understand the entrepreneurship discourse in fiction texts.

Entrepreneurship discourse in research texts

Although discourse methods have been used frequently in research texts in, for example, organization theory, few authors have so far employed this methodology to analyse the entrepreneurship discourse in research texts, mainly Ogbor (2000) and Ahl (2002).

Table 8.3 Feldmeier's dimensions

Main dimensions	Sub-dimensions
Entrepreneur	Personal context
	Professional context
	Societal–political context
Work	Formal criteria/stylistic means
	Time and history of origins of work
	Positioning within complete works of an author
Author	Author's own background, and background regarding entrepreneurship and interest in entrepreneurship
Reader	Audience
	Reception

Ogbor (2000) discusses the effects of ideological control in conventional entrepreneurial discourses and praxis. He draws on postmodernist, deconstructionist and critical theory approaches in order to review the 'conventional discourse on entrepreneurship' (ibid.: 610). In practice, this is undertaken by a critical analysis of a variety of important entrepreneurship texts and concepts, although without clearly revealing the underlying logic of text/concept selection. First, the author used Schumpeter's work on entrepreneurship to analyse (a) the predominant biases and (b) knowledge claims of the mainstream entrepreneurship discourse. Going through Schumpeter's main contributions, Ogbor reviewed their reception (or rejection) within academia. This allowed him to detect processes through which research ideas and new theories are legitimated by ideological peer control (ibid.: 611). The latter refers to both elements of political influence as well as to outright hostilities within the academic community towards new and unconventional ideas. Second, the author critically reviewed definitions and concepts of entrepreneurship throughout history. Ogbor's work takes us on a tour from Cantillon's and Knight's risk-taker from the 1920s, Schumpeter's innovator, McClelland's entrepreneurial personality, Collins and Moore's 'special breed' (Collins and Moore 1964: 244, cited in Ogbor 2000: 617) to newer concepts of defining entrepreneurs either ethnocentrically through race, gender and other demographic variables (thus understanding it as a culturally inherent variable), or as a product of the environment (which implicitly refers to the 'nature versus nurture' debate). Third, the author set out to analyse how ethnocentrism and gendering of conventional entrepreneurship ideas assist in legitimizing the dominant entrepreneurship discourse. Summing up his analysis, Ogbor concluded that the entrepreneurship discourse in the texts analysed reproduces societal myths, implicitly referring to the context of the texts as an important element in discovering those myths. Hence, by deconstructing academic ideas expressed about entrepreneurship, the author shows that the concept of entrepreneurship is discriminatory, gender-biased, ethnocentrically determined and ideologically controlled (Ogbor 2000: 605).

Ahl (2002) deconstructed the discourse of female entrepreneurship in 81 academic research articles published in high-quality entrepreneurship journals. More details of the method she employed, which is grounded in Foucault's concept, are to be found in her contribution to this handbook (Chapter 9). She found entrepreneurship to be male gendered, although thought of as neutral. Male and female entrepreneurs are assumed to be essentially different. The articles she analysed, for example, stressed small differences in entrepreneurial behaviour, presented female entrepreneurs as exceptions from 'normal' women, or constructed an alternative, feminine entrepreneurship model.

Entrepreneurship discourse in magazines and newspapers

In a discourse analysis of a Finnish entrepreneurship magazine, Pietiläinen (2001) arrives at similar conclusions as Ahl (2002). She questions the way we tend to decipher gender information with its culturally bound implications. For example, if equal opportunities really existed, why would it still seem natural to ask female entrepreneurs about balancing work and family responsibilities when discussing their entrepreneurial behaviour, which typically does not occur in interviews with male entrepreneurs?

The author used articles published in a so-called pro-SME magazine (*Yrittäjä*) between 1990 and 1997 to show how gender is constructed in media talk. She understands 'talk' as referring both to spoken and written language use (Pietiläinen 2001: 4). The magazine is published by the Federation of Finnish Enterprises, which is the largest SME association in Finland; in 2000 around 23 000 SME owners subscribed to this magazine. Within the period investigated, the author selected all 18 articles explicitly talking about women entrepreneurs or female entrepreneurship. These fell into four categories: eight were interviews with women entrepreneurs, six were interviews with experts on female entrepreneurship, two were reports of research findings, and two were comments from women entrepreneurs on one of the research articles.

In a next step, the author focused her analysis on 'detecting the discursive practices of a dominant discourse' (Pietiläinen 2001: 26) by using textual analysis as a critical reading. In order to look more closely at the way gender is constructed, she divided the texts into statements. Her analysis illustrates that the common way to produce gender in media is to compare businesses owned by women, and female entrepreneurs, to businesses owned by men, and men entrepreneurs. Moreover, all texts showed a strong tendency to discuss female entrepreneurship in the context of gender equality. The author attributes this to the journal being published in a Nordic society, which traditionally has a strong focus on gender equality (ibid.: 11). Grounded in this background knowledge, she grouped the articles' statements into categories of 'sameness' and 'difference' (ibid.: 23), thus identifying the comparison of female and male entrepreneurs as the main discursive practice in the equality discourse.

Langowitz and Morgan (2003) employed a different method to analyse the discourse on women entrepreneurship in the popular business press in the USA. They studied the image and coverage of female entrepreneurs, comparing the discourse created there with results from a survey of female entrepreneurs. Their method focuses on the profile of female entrepreneurs, as these fulfil different tasks. Directly, those portraits could convey a 'human image' of the respective entrepreneur as well as attract potential investors or clients. Indirectly, profiles of female entrepreneurs shape perceptions of society and the business world about the characteristics of a typical female entrepreneur as well as about their business acumen. More specifically, the authors were interested in whether these profiles in the popular business press reinforced the 'glass barrier' for (potential) female entrepreneurs.

The authors set out to identify normative themes across women entrepreneurs' profiles in the business press with the highest coverage in the years 1996–2000. The themes can be considered normative as they describe 'common or even imitable characteristics of the entrepreneur' that significantly contribute to business success (Langowitz and Morgan 2003: 115). The authors then contrasted these norms with the experience of successful entrepreneurs.

Their research design consisted of three steps. In a first step, the authors identified substantial profile articles on women entrepreneurs. These articles contain (a) features of business case studies and (b) personal biographies. The authors started out by doing a search across 24 out of 46 online computer library centres, using the keyword 'women entrepreneurs' for the period beginning of July 1996 through end of June 2000. Out of the 514 entries, 142 are individual or business profiles in the popular business press. A total of seven newspapers with a nation-wide coverage and high circulation (*Black Enterprise, Forbes, Hispanic, Inc., Nation's Business, Success, Working Woman*) were selected, and a total of 43 relevant articles identified. Those articles sub-sampled had to classify as substantial profiles; that is they had at least a 500-word content.

The second step was a content analysis of the identified substantial profile articles, aiming at 'exploring the influence of media upon social

understanding' (Langowitz and Morgan 2003: 105). This included the identification of main themes in the profiles and a basic quantitative analysis of
the 43 articles. Based on entrepreneurship research, the authors identified
six domains of content, which assisted them in understanding and interpreting the business press discourse on women entrepreneurs. The domains
included (i) the origin of the story, (ii) the industry context, (iii) sources of
start-up financing, (iv) characteristics of entrepreneurs, (v) success indicators and (vi) future plans. These domains were then subdivided into dimensions, for example different modes of opportunity recognition and
motivations in the category 'origin of story', sources of financing the business establishment in the category 'start-up financing' or demographic
characteristics, professional experience and family background in the category 'characteristics of the entrepreneur'. Both authors independently conducted the content analysis and coding of the business profiles in order to
cross-check and ensure reliability of the domains.

In the third step, the authors compared the results obtained with survey data on female entrepreneurs. They used a survey undertaken in
Massachusetts on women-led businesses. Sixty-six female entrepreneurs
out of a total 92 participants in the second phase of the survey were
selected for the comparison. The survey included topics such as entrepreneurial experiences, firm and entrepreneur demographics, industries, and
firm development. Although the survey was limited to one state in the
USA, Massachusetts represents one of the leading US state economies:
thus the authors deemed the survey results reasonably representative for the
USA as a whole.

As one important result of their media analysis, the authors stressed that
the media profiles in the business press provide significant messages about
social norms with regard to female entrepreneurs and enterprises. This
refers to the stereotype about women starting businesses in 'women-related'
areas such as professional services, consumer products, or apparel and
accessories. The 'typical woman entrepreneur' emerging from the portraits
in the business media has been in business for less than seven years, she has
no significant plans for business development, she accidentally stumbled
across her business opportunity, and saw opening her own business as a way
of overcoming adverse personal conditions such as illness, death of spouse,
while finances were scraped together 'from personal contacts' (Langowitz
and Morgan 2003: 110).

However, the comparison of the norms to be found in the profile articles
with the reality of women entrepreneurship resulting from the survey data
shows a diverse picture as the normative standards rarely fit the survey data.
While the business press emphasized having a great idea as well as adver-
sities that need to be overcome as starting points for entrepreneurship,

survey data showed that women entrepreneurs generally start their business through a more deliberate process. Moreover, in portraying mainly lower-value companies, the business press reinforced the attitude 'that women entrepreneurs "aren't really serious" ' (Langowitz and Morgan 2003: 114). All this adds to our conclusion (Achtenhagen and Welter 2003), namely that not only newspapers, but also popular business media, often paint a 'restricted' picture of women entrepreneurs, not taking into account academic research results, and thus indicating a gap between discourses on entrepreneurship in popular media and those found in research texts.

In our study, we analysed how entrepreneurship and related notions were reflected in major German newspapers and how these have changed over time (Achtenhagen and Welter 2003, 2004). In Achtenhagen and Welter (2003) we conducted an analysis of the use of a key female entrepreneurship term in two major national newspapers in Germany over the period of 1995 to 2001. We discussed the discourse around female entrepreneurs as presented in *Die Welt*, which is a conservative paper, and the *Süddeutsche Zeitung* as a more leftist paper, employing a longitudinal perspective, as changes in culture and society are usually rather slow. In Achtenhagen and Welter (2004) we concentrated our analysis on the notion 'entrepreneurial spirit' (*Unternehmergeist*), as the lack of entrepreneurial spirit in Germany has been on the political agenda for years, using the *Frankfurter Allgemeine Zeitung* as our main newspaper. We identified gaps between entrepreneurship discourses and public policies, and showed how images of entrepreneurs are being created. Our analysis illustrates how the discourse is strongly embedded not only as an economic topic, but also as a political and/or cultural topic.

In both contributions, we employed the following steps. First, newspapers' online archives were searched for articles covering the key notions to be analysed. In Achtenhagen and Welter (2003) this refers to female entrepreneur (*Unternehmerin*), female business founder (*Gründerin*), woman AND business-owner (*Frau* UND *selbständig/selbstständig*), as well as female AND business-owner (*weiblich* UND *selbständig/selbstständig*) between 1 January 1995 and 31 December 2001, whilst in Achtenhagen and Welter (2004) we searched the newspapers' CD-ROMs for the notion 'entrepreneurial spirit' within the period 1 January 1997 to 31 December 2001, as no earlier archives were available for computer searches. In both our works, we included the period before, during and after the Internet hype, covering a period of major changes in the entrepreneurship policy context.

Because of the large total number of articles found related to women entrepreneurship (2676), in the 2003 article we concentrated the analysis on one key notion, the 'female entrepreneur'. All 539 articles identified were downloaded without any pre-selection along article topics, as we wished to gain a picture of all instances in which female entrepreneurs were considered noteworthy in these newspapers. The same method was applied in the second paper (Achtenhagen and Welter 2004), for which we downloaded a total of 146 articles.

Second, we decided on categories for classifying the information in the newspaper articles. This includes categories with *general information* about the article (e.g. newspaper, key term, date of publication, section/subsection, headline) as well as *content-related categories* such as 'major idea', 'key statements regarding search term', 'images regarding search term', 'country focus' and 'assessment of search term'. (Jäger 2001b provides a helpful 'toolbox' for conducting this kind of discourse analysis.) Relevant text passages were converted into a data file, assisting us in identifying the topics discussed around female entrepreneurship or the entrepreneurial spirit as well as the characteristics attributed to it. This file also allowed us to conduct bivariate statistical operations, analysing changes in categories over time. All entries into the data file were double-checked by both authors for content and consistency of categorizing the text, referring to the original newspaper articles in order to increase the robustness of both studies.

In order to ground the discourse analysis in its wider context ('the distal context'), we additionally analysed the environment for entrepreneurship in Germany, concentrating both on the development of business start-ups and entrepreneurship as well as on relevant trends in entrepreneurship-related policies and support in the study period.

We drew on discourse methodologies to define important key concepts for the articles collected. This refers both to different levels of analysis such as the macro and meso level (Achtenhagen and Welter 2004) and to different levels of embeddedness of the newspaper discourse. With regard to the former, the macro level represents the 'grand discourse' of the chosen topic, where the analysis looks at aggregated patterns of the discourse (Alvesson and Kärreman 2000a: 1145). This is depicted in Figure 8.2, which gives an overview of the development of articles related to women entrepreneurs in the analysed newspapers. With a meso-level analysis we leave this level of abstraction and look more closely at the discourse as texts, rather than the claims it expresses. In line with Alvesson and Kärreman (2000b: 137) we assume a relationship between language and social reality, but we do not posit that language represents reality. Like a discourse, a language is a complex building of different elements and relationships between them. To further stress the importance of language for a discourse and to voice the diversity of discourses in the chosen newspaper, we presented the discourse on entrepreneurial spirit in grammar terms (Achtenhagen and Welter 2004), thus conducting not only a discourse on the grand scale, but including elements of the meso level as well (cf. the previous section).

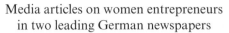

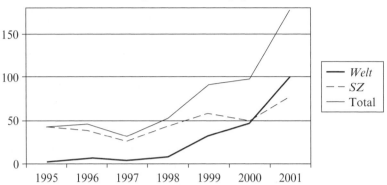

Figure 8.2   Example of a discourse on a grand scale

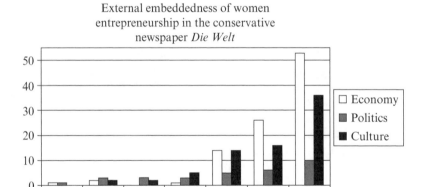

Figure 8.3   External embeddedness of women's entrepreneurship in a German newspaper

With regard to levels of embeddedness, we distinguished between *systemic* (economic) and *substantive* (political and cultural) embeddedness (Johannisson et al. 2002), and between the *internal* and *external* embeddedness of the key term. The first category is related to the macro-level analysis, referring to the newspaper categories where articles on the relevant subjects are to be found (e.g. the reviews stand for cultural, the business news for economic embeddedness). Figure 8.3 shows examples of how this relates to the key term 'woman entrepreneur' in a German newspaper.

The second category is linked to the question whether the respective key term was a main or side focus of the newspaper discourse. A 'main focus' is associated with a higher internal embeddedness, referring to whole series, company or individual portraits as well as to articles on support measures. We employed this category in Achtenhagen and Welter (2003), stating that the discourse on female entrepreneurs shows a 'side focus' or lower internal embeddedness when the notion 'female entrepreneur' simply referred to one of the actors in the article, which often went hand in hand with a completely different article topic. This included expressions such as 'the female entrepreneur from Milan' in an article about her kidnapping or 'the 93-year-old widowed female entrepreneur who was robbed in her apartment'.

Female entrepreneurship has been a popular topic for media analysis, looking at the topic treatment and discourse both in academic texts (see previous section) and business journals as well as in newspapers. Here, Baker et al. (1997) set out to examine 'a paradox', referring to the low coverage of women entrepreneurship in both mass media and scholarly journals in the USA against a background of increasing women business ownership. Their article is an example of undertaking discourse analysis on the grand scale (cf. the previous section). The authors did not analyse the contents and language of the articles in more detail, but instead focused on general patterns of media coverage (Baker et al. 1997: 223).

The authors searched media indexes for their key terms, which include key words related to business ownership and women (for a detailed overview cf. Baker et al. 1997: 237). Their search routine by year included three steps: first, searching for any articles about business ownership, regardless of gender; second, searching for any articles mentioning women, regardless of other content; and third, searching for articles about ownership that mention women. The indexes they used were the Information Access Company's (IAC) index for the popular business press (from 1982 onwards), the Lexis/Nexis electronic database for elite newspapers with full coverage for the *New York Times* and the *Wall Street Journal* from 1980 and 1989 respectively, partial coverage for the *NYT* back to 1969, for the *WSJ* from 1973. The IAC's Academic Index was used to search four main academic journals, namely *Entrepreneurship Theory and Practice*, *Journal of Business Venturing*, *Academy of Management Review* and the *Academic Management Journal*.

Their review shows a distinctive general pattern of the discourse on women entrepreneurship and women business ownership in US media (Baker et al. 1997: 227). Whilst in general business periodicals the number of articles on women business owners increases between 1982 and 1995, this goes hand in hand with a general increase in articles on business ownership, thereby reducing the relative coverage. Both surveyed elite newspapers slightly increased their coverage in the study period, although the overall share of articles reporting on women entrepreneurs remained low, in 1994 amounting to 5 per cent for the *WSJ* and 4 per cent for the *NYT*, respectively. The pattern for the academic journals showed an increase of articles covering women in general between 1982 and 1995, whilst coverage on women entrepreneurs and business owners declined substantially during the same period. The results illustrate a 'quiet revolution' (Baker et al. 1997: 222), as most media keep silent about the growing share of women ownership. In this regard, undertaking discourse analysis on a grand scale allows not only to determine general patterns of discourse (i.e. what is voiced), but also to identify 'hidden' discourses that take place through *not* discussing a phenomenon (i.e. the boundaries of a discourse, illustrating the power aspect of discourses).

Looking to the future: is there a 'best way' of doing discourse analysis in entrepreneurship research?
The examples outlined in the previous section illustrate how discourse analysis of entrepreneurship in different kinds of printed media can add to our understanding of the phenomenon, either by setting the scene on a grand scale and/or by doing discourse at the meso level, analysing language patterns and grammar. They also reflect a broad variety of methods, underlining that there is no best way of doing discourse analysis (Jäger 1999). Thus, there is no one correct and comprehensive definition of a discourse and its content; rather it is produced and reproduced differently by the different social actors. This corresponds to Alvesson and Kärreman's appeal for 'discursive pragmatism' (Alvesson and Kärreman 2000b: 147), which recognizes the various meanings of a discourse stemming from the multitude of social realities. However, it is important that the procedure of conducting a discourse analysis, as well as the own discursive position, are made clear in the analysis.

What are the kinds of questions for which discourse analysis can be fruitfully employed in entrepreneurship research? Rather obvious areas of topics relate to power and control relationships, and how these are produced and reproduced, as well as to discourses of differences, for example in terms of social identities such as gender, cultural background or age (cf. discussion in Phillips and Hardy 2002: 29–33). Discourse analysis can be used for a whole range of different topics, and on different levels in the area 'entrepreneurship' (see also Fairclough 1995: 5), for example:

- *Entrepreneurship as a field:* How is new knowledge introduced into the field? How is it legitimated? How is the development of the field steered? Who is involved in introducing new knowledge and in determining the direction of the discourse? When and how do new discourses related to new trends in entrepreneurship research arise; when and how do they vanish? How are new developments in entrepreneurship theory such as the recent focus on opportunity recognition and sense-making of entrepreneurs reflected in the media discourse? Which actors are involved in transporting research knowledge into media discourses and vice versa?

- *Entrepreneurship as an individual's identity:* How are entrepreneurs depicted in the discourse in media? What metaphors are used to describe individual entrepreneurs? How is the discourse in non-academic media linked to academic research on the person of the entrepreneur? How does media discourse construct identities of entrepreneurs? How does this influence nascent entrepreneurs in creating legitimacy when starting their venture?
- *Entrepreneurial practices:* How do members of a venture produce a sense of social order within the organization through texts? How are meaning and action generated in ventures, for example in different speech acts of an entrepreneur, such as requesting, promising, thanking, appointing or asserting? What role do discourses play in entrepreneurial practices? What relationships are set up between those involved (e.g. entrepreneur–reporter, entrepreneur–politician/policy-maker, entrepreneur–venture capitalist)?
- *Entrepreneurial episodes:* What is the symbolic value of events such as venture capital pitches or entrepreneurship award ceremonies for (potential) entrepreneurs? How does this symbolic value add meaning and structure to social life in ventures? How is the 'world' of entrepreneurship represented? How is this linked to the issue of legitimacy in new ventures?

This list is by no means exhaustive, and different types of discourse analyses can be employed for different kinds of research questions. To facilitate the choice of questions and methods, see the selected readings below.

Acknowledgements
Both authors gratefully acknowledge the financial support of the Media Management and Transformation Centre at Jönköping International Business School, Sweden.

Suggested further readings
Stefan Titscher, Michael Meyer, Ruth Wodak and Eva Vetter (2000) *Methods of Text and Discourse Analysis.* London/Thousand Oaks: Sage. This book provides an excellent overview of different methods of analysing written and spoken texts, such as content analysis, discourse analysis and conversation analysis. The authors discuss the different

underlying theoretical assumptions of each method presented, and compare and contrast these. The book is written by scholars from linguistics and sociology, but much of their discussion can also be applied to entrepreneurship research.

Nelson Phillips and Cynthia Hardy (2002) *Discourse Analysis: Investigating processes of social construction.* Qualitative Research Method Series No. 50, Thousand Oaks: Sage. This short (87pp.) and easy-to-read book is an excellent introduction to conducting discourse analysis in social sciences. The authors point out a number of challenges when conducting discourse analysis and how to overcome them.

Sara Mills (1997) *Discourse.* London: Routledge. This book provides an introduction to the term 'discourse', as well as the development of different discourse theories and discursive structures. The aim of the book is to clarify the term discourse from the perspective of literary theory.

Ruth Wodak and Michael Meyer (2001) (eds.) *Methods of Critical Discourse Analysis.* London/Thousand Oaks: Sage. This book is highly recommended as it not only discusses the historical developments of the different strands of discourse analyses, but also provides 'toolboxes' of how to go about conducting a discourse analysis. Unlike many of its counterparts, this book is easy and interesting to read.

Norman Fairclough (1995) *Media Discourse.* London et al.: Edward Arnold. This book presents different approaches to discourse analysis in the media. It focuses mainly on mass media. The book is primarily interesting for researchers interested in different kinds of linguistic analyses.

References

Achtenhagen, L. and Welter, F. (2003) Female entrepreneurship as reflected in German media in the years 1995–2001. In: *New Perspectives on Women Entrepreneurs*, edited by J. Butler. Greenwich, CT: Information Age Publishing, pp. 71–100.

Achtenhagen, L. and Welter, F. (2004) Linking the entrepreneurship discourse to its context – The development of entrepreneurship in Germany in the years 1997–2001. In: *Advances in Interdisciplinary European Entrepreneurship Research*, edited by M. Dowling, J. Schmude and D. zu Knyphausen-Aufsess. Münster: LitVerlag, pp. 1–25.

Ahl, H.J. (2002) The Making of the Female Entrepreneur: A discourse analysis of research texts on women's entrepreneurship. Jönköping International Business School Dissertation Series No. 15. Jönköping: JIBS.

Ainsworth, S. (2001) Discourse analysis as social construction: Towards greater integration of approaches and methods. Paper presented at the Second International Conference on Critical Management Studies, Manchester, 11–13 July.

Alvesson, M. and Kärreman, D. (2000a) Varieties of discourse: On the study of organizations through discourse analysis. *Human Relations*, **53**(9): 1125–49.

Alvesson, M. and Kärreman, D. (2000b) Taking the linguistic turn in organizational research: Challenges, responses, consequences. *The Journal of Applied Behavioral Science*, **36**(2): 136–58.

Baker, T., Aldrich, H.E. and Liou, N. (1997) Invisible entrepreneurs: The neglect of women business owners by mass media and scholarly journals in the USA. *Entrepreneurship & Regional Development*, **9**: 221–38.

Beattie, R. (1999) The creative entrepreneur: A study of the entrepreneur's creative processes. *Frontiers of Entrepreneurship Research 1999.* www.babson.edu/entrep/fer/papers99/III/III_B.

Berger, P.L. and Luckmann, T. (1969) *Die gesellschaftliche Konstruktion der Wirklichkeit: Eine Theorie der Wissenssoziologie.* Frankfurt: Fischer.

Bublitz, H. (2001) Differenz und Integration: Zur diskursanalytischen Rekonstruktion der Regelstrukturen sozialer Wirklichkeit. In: *Handbuch Sozialwissenschaftliche Diskursanalyse*, Band 1: Theorien und Methoden, edited by R. Keller, A. Hirseland, W. Schneider and W. Viehöver. Opladen: Leske + Budrich, pp. 225–60. [Handbook of Discourse Analysis in the Social Sciences, Volume 1: Theories and Methods]

Burr, V. (1995) *An Introduction to Social Constructionism.* London: Routledge.

Chalaby, J.K. (1996) Beyond the prison-house of language: Discourse as a sociological concept. *British Journal of Sociology*, **47**: 684–98.

Cicourel, A.V. (1981) Three models of discourse analysis: The role of social structure. *Discourse Processes*, (3): 101–31.

Donati, P.R. (2001) Die Rahmenanalyse politischer Diskurse. In: *Handbuch Sozialwissenschaftliche Diskursanalyse, Band 1: Theorien und Methoden*, edited by R. Keller, A. Hirseland, W. Schneider and W. Viehöver. Opladen: Leske + Budrich, pp. 113–44. [Handbook of Discourse Analysis in the Social Sciences, Volume 1: Theories and Methods]

Fairclough, N. (1992) *Discourse and Social Change*. Cambridge: Polity Press.

Fairclough, N. (1995) *Media Discourse*. London et al.: Edward Arnold.

Fairclough, N. and Wodak, R. (1997) Critical discourse analysis. In: *Discourse as Social Interaction*, edited by T.A Van Dijk. London/Thousand Oaks: Sage, pp. 258–84.

Feldmeier, J. (2001) *Der Unternehmer in der Erzählliteratur: Betriebswirtschaftliche Studien zur Darstellung der Romanfigur des Unternehmers und Bedeutung der Romane für Unternehmer anhand ausgewählter Beispiele*. Ph.D. Dissertation, University of St Gallen. [The Entrepreneur in Literature: Business studies depicting the entrepreneur in fiction and the importance of fiction for entrepreneurs reflected in selected examples]

Foucault, M. (1972/1991) *Die Ordnung des Diskurses*. Frankfurt: Fischer. [German translation of *L'ordre du discours*]

Gartner, W., Carter, N. and Hill, G. (2003) The language of opportunity. In: *New Movements in Entrepreneurship*, edited by C. Steyaert and D. Hjorth. Cheltenham, UK and Northampton, MA, USA: Edward Elgar, pp. 103–24.

Gee, J.P. (2002) *An Introduction to Discourse Analysis: Theory and method*. London: Routledge.

Grant, D., Keenoy, T. and Oswick, C. (1998) Organizational discourse: Of diversity, dichotomy and multi-disciplinarity. In: *Discourse and Organization*, edited by D. Grant, T. Keenoy and C. Oswick. London: Sage, pp. 1–14.

Jäger, S. (1999) Einen Königsweg gibt es nicht. Bemerkungen zur Durchführung von Diskursanalysen. In: *Das Wuchern der Diskurse: Perspektiven der Diskursanalyse Foucaults*, edited by H. Bublitz, A.D. Bührmann, C. Hanke and A. Seier. Frankfurt: Campus, pp. 136–47. [The Rampant Growth of Discourses: Perspectives of Foucault's discourse analysis]

Jäger, S. (2001a) Diskurs und Wissen: Theoretische und methodische Aspekte einer Kritischen Diskurs – und Dispositivanalyse. In: *Handbuch Sozialwissenschaftliche Diskursanalyse, Band 1: Theorien und Methoden*, edited by R. Keller, A. Hirseland, W. Schneider and W. Viehöver. Opladen: Leske + Budrich, pp. 81–112. [Handbook of Discourse Analysis in the Social Sciences, Volume 1: Theories and Methods]

Jäger, S. (2001b) Discourse and knowledge: Theoretical and methodological aspects of a critical discourse and dispositive analysis. In: *Methods of Critical Discourse Analysis*, edited by R. Wodak and M. Meyer. London/Thousand Oaks: Sage, pp. 32–62.

Johannisson, B., Ramirez-Pasillas, M. and Karlsson, G. (2002) The embeddedness of inter-firm networks. *Entrepreneurship & Regional Development*, **14**(4): 297–315.

Keller, R. (2004) *Diskursforschung: Eine Einführung für Sozialwissenschaftlerinnen*. Opladen: Leske + Budrich. [Discourse Research: An introduction for social science scientists]

Keller, R., Hirseland, A., Schneider, W. and Viehöver, W. (2001) Zur Aktualität sozialwissenschaftlicher Diskursanalyse: Eine Einführung. In: *Handbuch Sozialwissenschaftliche Diskursanalyse, Band 1: Theorien und Methoden*, edited by R. Keller, A. Hirseland, W. Schneider and W. Viehöver. Opladen: Leske + Budrich, pp. 7–28. [Handbook of Discourse Analysis in the Social Sciences, Volume 1: Theories and Methods]

Kirzner, I. (1979) *Perception, Opportunity and Profit: Studies in the theory of entrepreneurship*. Chicago: University of Chicago Press.

Laclau, E. and Mouffe, C. (1985) *Hegemony and Socialist Strategy. Towards a radical democratic politics*. London: Verso.

Langowitz, N. and Morgan, C. (2003) Women entrepreneurs: Breaking through the glass barrier. In: *New Perspectives on Women Entrepreneurs*, edited by J. Butler. Greenwich, CT: Information Age Publishing, pp. 101–19.

Mills, S. (1997) *Discourse*. London/New York: Routledge.

Mumby, D.K. and Clair, R.P. (1987) Organizational Discourse. In: *Discourse as Social Interaction*, edited by T.A. Van Dijk. London/Thousand Oaks: Sage, pp. 181–205.

Ogbor, J.O. (2000) Mythicizing and reification in entrepreneurial discourse: Ideology-critique of entrepreneurial studies. *Journal of Management Studies*, **37**(5): 605–35.

Phillips, L. and Jørgensen, M.W. (2002) *Discourse Analysis as Theory and Method*. London/Thousand Oaks: Sage.

Phillips, N. and Hardy, C. (2002): *Discourse Analysis: Investigating processes of social construction*, Qualitative Research Method Series No. 50. London/Thousand Oaks: Sage.

Pietiläinen, T. (2001) *Gender and Female Entrepreneurship in a Pro-entrepreneurship Magazine*. Swedish School of Economics and Business Administration Working Paper, 458. Helsinki.

Potter, J. (2001) Diskursive Psychologie und Diskursanalyse. In: *Handbuch Sozialwissenschaftliche Diskursanalyse, Band 1: Theorien und Methoden*, edited by R. Keller, A. Hirseland, W. Schneider and W. Viehöver. Opladen: Leske + Budrich, pp. 313–35. [Handbook of Discourse Analysis in the Social Sciences, Volume 1: Theories and Methods]

Schegloff, E.A. (1992) In Another Context. In: *Rethinking Context: Language as Interactive Phenomenon*, edited by A. Duranti and C. Goodwin. Cambridge: Cambridge University Press.

Schiffrin, D. (1994) *Approaches to Discourse*. Oxford: Blackwell.

Titscher, S., Meyer, M., Wodak, R. and Vetter, E. (2000) *Methods of Text and Discourse Analysis*. London/Thousand Oaks: Sage.

Van Dijk, T.A. (1997) Discourse as interaction in society. In: *Discourse as Social Interaction*, edited by T.A. Van Dijk. London/Thousand Oaks: Sage, pp. 1–37.

Van Dijk, T.A. (1998) *News Analysis: Case studies of international and national news in the press*. Hillsdale, NJ: Lawrence Erlbaum Associates.

Weick, K.E. (1995) *Sensemaking in Organizations*. London/Thousand Oaks: Sage.

Wetherell, M. (2001) Debates in discourse research. In: *Discourse Theory and Practice*, edited by M. Wetherell, S. Taylor and S.J. Yates. London/Thousand Oaks: Sage, pp. 380–99.

Woodilla, J. (1998) Workplace conversations: The text of organizing. In: *Discourse and Organization*, edited by D. Grand, T. Keenoy and C. Oswick. London/Thousand Oaks: Sage, pp. 31–50.

9 A Foucauldian framework for discourse analysis
Helene Ahl

Introduction

The idea for this research arose from of a literature review about women's entrepreneurship (Ahl 1997). This review highlighted some peculiarities about women and entrepreneurship that motivated a number of questions. Why, for example, did many articles start with the assumption that women must be different from men? Why did they compare men and women on gender stereotypical scales? Why was women's entrepreneurship talked about in such an enthusiastic manner as a solution to the childcare problem, but not men's? What effects did such assumptions on the part of researchers have for the positioning of women entrepreneurs? Did they risk doing women entrepreneurs a disfavor rather than help making them visible? Such observations and questions warranted a closer look at how research texts construct the woman entrepreneur.

The study builds on a social constructionist epistemology, according to which research not only describes and explains reality, but is also part of the reality-constructing process. According to this view, there is no reason to give researchers a different ontological status from practitioners. Practitioners and researchers in a given context usually share some assumptions about social reality. These go into the research process in the forms of theories, research questions and methods. They are then repackaged and sent out again in the form of research articles. The consequence of this is that research texts are valid study objects for studying social reality.

Using a Foucauldian framework, I undertook a discourse analysis of 81 research articles on women's entrepreneurship published from 1982 to 2000 in order to identify how they constructed the female entrepreneur (Ahl 2004). I found that she was consistently positioned as inferior to her male counterpart, irrespective of which facet of entrepreneurship was studied – be it growth, profitability, networking, strategy or management practices. Most startling was that such conclusions were drawn even if the studies did not show any significant differences between men and women entrepreneurs. Certain research practices, as for example assumptions about men and women, preferred theories and methods, and ontological and epistemological points of departure caused research to reconstruct women's subordination, even if the authors had no intention to do so.

This chapter reports the methodology used to produce these findings. The method developed builds directly on Foucault's inaugural speech to the Collège de France in 1970. However, Foucault's theories require both translation and adaptation to the research material as well as a measure of ingenuity. This chapter provides a step-by-step description of the analysis, and I explain in detail how I translated Foucault's theories to practical, methodological use.

The chapter starts by situating the work in its theoretical and epistemological context. I briefly discuss social constructionist theory and feminist theory and proceed to a definition of discourse. This is followed by a presentation of the texts to be analyzed, followed by a detailed interpretation of Foucault's theories about discourse analysis and a translation of these theories into an analytical framework. The framework consists of a list of ten research steps, which I use to guide the analysis. At this point, I take the reader through each step of the analysis, describing both the methods and the findings of each step. The chapter finishes with a discussion of the benefits and potential problems of using discourse analysis in entrepreneurship studies and in feminist analyses.

The chapter aims at conveying two points: the usefulness of research texts as a study object, and a practical method for analyzing such texts. While doing this, I also discuss constructions of gender, the role of research practices in such constructions, and the role of research practices in the construction of any research object. The method provided is applicable for research questions other than the one in this particular study, and the findings regarding the construction of the entrepreneur are relevant for everyone involved in entrepreneurship research.

Constructionist and feminist departures on discourse analysis

As Berger and Luckmann (1966) claimed, social reality is constructed in interaction between people in a process of *externalization* (of 'knowledge', 'facts'), *objectification* (where knowledge and facts are made objective), and *internalization* (where one learns from others' objectified knowledge). When knowledge becomes taken for granted it becomes *institutionalized*, that is, people habitually do certain things and they have a normative explanation for doing it. Taken-for-granted knowledge can of course be questioned, renegotiated and reconstructed. Since reality was socially constructed in the first place it is, in principle, always in flux. Renegotiation of social reality is, however, often difficult and may meet resistance. Giddens (1991) writes that taking most things for granted gives people a sense of ontological security. It brackets out threats and anxiety and it maintains social stability. It also provides a stable frame of reference for the creation of one's identity. According to Foucault (1969), there might also be resistance to renegotiation, as knowledge has power implications. It orders people and objects, it determines what is right and true and what one might act upon, as well as the opposite, and it does thereby affect the social order.

Feminist theories are good examples of how different versions of knowledge imply different sorts of social orders. Feminism is defined as the recognition of women's subordination, and the desire to do something about this (Calás and Smircich 1992). But the explanations for why women are subordinated and the consequent advice for changing this state of affairs vary. Following Harding (1987), feminist theories might be classified in three groups. In the first group men and women are seen as essentially similar, in the second they are seen as essentially different, and in the third group similarities and differences are seen as socially constructed. These will be elaborated in the following.

1. In liberal feminist theory men and women are seen as essentially similar. It is inspired by liberal political theory where what makes a human a human is the ability to think rationally. Men and women are seen as equally endowed with this ability, and any subordination of women must depend on structural barriers, as for example unequal access to education. Such barriers can be partly or totally eliminated. A problem with this view is that it has an unstated male norm. It does not question taken-for-granted constructions of bureaucracy, leadership and so on. Women are advised to adapt to the existing order in society (Calás and Smircich 1996).

2. In social feminist theory, psychoanalytical feminist theory or radical feminist theory men and women are seen as essentially different. Feminine traits are seen as benefits rather than drawbacks and as resources to be used constructively (Gilligan 1982; Chodorow 1988). Management research within this tradition has studied organizations where one tried to tear down the corporate ladder altogether, and build flat organizations with shared leadership and consensus-oriented decision making (Iannello 1992). This view also does not question the male norm; it merely provides an alternative, or a complementary, norm. Constructing men and women as different means that one understands 'man' and 'woman' to be essential, unitary (and different) concepts, which gives both sexes a limited repertoire. As studies on gender differences show over and over again, the differences between individuals within each sex are actually much larger than the mean differences between the sexes (Doyle and Paludi 1998).

3. Social constructionist (or post-structuralist) feminist theory is not pre-occupied by what men or women are, but how masculinity and femininity are constructed, and what effects this construction has on the social order, particularly in regard to gender/power relations. Gender is not seen as an essential attribute, but as something that is performed, and that varies over time and place. Any seeming stability depends on the repetitive performance of gender. One is not free to perform gender in any way one chooses, however; one is restrained by each culture's norms for proper gender behavior, and these norms have social effects (Butler 1990). Post-structuralist feminist work investigates and challenges such norms, or such taken-for-granted notions about gender.

This chapter studies constructions of gender in research texts, and their social effects. In line with the theory presented, research texts are not innocent, objective reflections of social reality. Research texts are part of the reality-producing process. The discourses in research texts are particularly important study objects since researchers enjoy an expert status in society. They are seen as those who are supposed to know and are often asked for opinions by the popular media. These texts are also used in teaching; hence they are bearers of reality.

Consequently, this study also co-produces social reality. Is there a place for such a position in a scientific discourse with its traditional notions of objectivity and neutrality? According to the theoretical framework outlined here, the only perspective available is a partial perspective. The ideal of objectivity presupposes that the observer is not part of that which is being observed, which is antithetical to the position taken in this chapter, that the researcher co-constructs social reality. This study, then, takes a feminist position (broadly defined as the recognition of women's subordination and the desire to do something about it) and looks for gender constructions and their effects on gender/power relations. This might be rephrased as saying that I am looking to analyze the discourse on female entrepreneurship.

Defining discourse
Foucault defined discourses as 'practices which form the object of which they speak' (Foucault 1969/1972: 49). Borrowing from Foucault, discourse has been described as 'a group of claims, ideas and terminologies that are historically and socially specific and that create truth effects' (Alvesson and Due Billing 1999: 49), 'a system of statements, which construct an object' (Parker 1992: 5), or 'a set of meanings, metaphors, representations, images, stories, statements and so on that in some way together produce a particular version of events' (Burr 1995: 48). What is common to these definitions

is that discourses have some kind of effect. Hence discourses have power implications in that they form what is held as knowledge or truth.

Discourse analysis builds on the idea of language as constitutive as opposed to the idea of language as representational (Saussure 1970). Language circumscribes (and makes possible) what one can think and feel and imagine doing. It 'typifies our experiences', as Berger and Luckmann (1966) expressed it. Analyzing language as enabling or restricting a discourse thus becomes a focus for discourse analysts. Foucault, however, made it clear that he referred not only to linguistic practices (or statements), but also to the material and other practices that bring about a certain type of statements (Foucault 1972). Based on this discussion, the focus of my analysis is thus the discourse on women's entrepreneurship, which is made up both of linguistic and other social practices. Additionally, I am analyzing the 'power implications' of the discourse, which may be rephrased as the positioning of women in the research texts.

Matching the material with a method

My material consisted of 81 research articles on women's entrepreneurship published between 1982 and 2000. I included all articles on the topic in the four entrepreneurship research journals identified as 'leading' by the entrepreneurship research community (Ratnatunga and Romano 1977). These were *Journal of Business Venturing, Entrepreneurship Theory and Practice, Journal of Small Business Management* and *Entrepreneurship and Regional Development*. Because of frequent citations in these, an additional 13 articles from other journals were included (please refer to Appendix 1 for a list of the articles arranged in order of research topic). Before arriving at this selection I made a search of all the so-called 'A journals' in management and organization theory but found that they published very little on entrepreneurship, and hardly anything on women's entrepreneurship (Busenitz et al. 2003). Even in the specialized entrepreneurship research journals, the number of articles on women's entrepreneurship is relatively limited (Baker et al. 1997). The topic is marginal in the academic community, and is often included in both journals and conferences under the heading 'minority entrepreneurship'.

My empirical material thus consisted of about 2000 pages of text. The next step was to find a suitable discourse analytical method for this material. As the previous chapter demonstrated, there are many different approaches to discourse analysis (Achtenhagen and Welter, Chapter 8 in this volume). Several excellent handbooks are also available (Bergström and Boréus 2000; Kendall and Wickham 1999; Söndergaard 1999; Winther Jörgensen and Phillips 1999). I found the handbooks' advice problematic for my purposes for two reasons, however. First, the different methods under this label sometimes had conflicting epistemological assumptions, and not all of them were compatible with my particular research agenda. Second, the methods that were indeed compatible were often intended for analyses of very short texts. For most of the codified methods, my material was too voluminous. But what about turning directly to Foucault, then? Foucault analyzed large volumes of material. Unfortunately, he never formulated a research method in any technical sense. He even resisted such attempts actively, being afraid that a codified method would also entail a limitation. I found, however, a short text that was helpful for my purposes in his inaugural speech to the Collège de France, *The Discourse on Language* (Foucault 1972), which I have used as the basis for developing an analytical framework and for choosing analysis methods.

The following presents a description of a three-step process. The first step is reading Foucault. The second step is translating his thoughts into an analytical framework suitable for my study. The third step is the actual analysis, where different methods were used for each of the ten points in the analytical framework. The next section describes steps one and two of this process.

Translating Foucault and developing an analytical framework
According to Foucault (1972), the production of discourses in any society is controlled, selected, organized and redistributed by certain procedures. He also describes certain principles to bear in mind when analyzing these procedures. In the following I relate those of Foucault's procedures and principles that are relevant for the present study, and demonstrate how I translated these into an analytical framework. I describe the process in some detail, in order to facilitate a similar process for the reader who wants to use Foucault for another type of study. Below I first discuss some of Foucault's *procedures*, using his own terminology, and how these translate into research questions. This is followed by a discussion about the different methodological *principles*, since they also contributed to the research questions.

Foucault's procedures

1. The prohibition   The prohibition is the most obvious of the exclusion procedures, says Foucault (1972), but he does not refer to legal prohibitions as much as to the assumed understanding that you cannot speak about everything, you cannot say anything at anytime, and not everyone can speak about everything. This is taken for granted; it is not questioned. I translate this to my study to imply that I should look for *ideas, or assumptions, that are taken for granted* about women, society, research, entrepreneurship and so on that are reflected in the reviewed studies.

2. The will to truth   The 'will to truth' is understood as the historically contingent manner in which false is demarcated from true, and what counts as knowledge. This is dependent on institutional support, such as schools and university systems, publishing systems, libraries, laboratories and so on. This implies that what counts as valid entrepreneurship research will be determined by the research community's institutions. I take it to mean to study what bearing *the institutional support for entrepreneurship research* has on the issues studied and the questions asked. Research financing is an issue here, and so are university research centers and their status in the academic community.

3. The commentary   Foucault talks about internal rules, concerned with the principles of classification, ordering and distribution. The first is the commentary. Each culture or discipline has a number of texts that are hailed as important and that are constantly commented upon. Whether the comments celebrate the original texts, try to explain them or criticize them, their role is 'to say *finally*, what has silently been articulated *deep down*', writes Foucault (1972: 221) and in this way the discourse is repeated and reproduced. This means that my study cannot neglect the *founding fathers and the foundational texts* on entrepreneurship. These texts will have bearings on research on women's entrepreneurship. The foremost such text in the field of entrepreneurship research is Schumpeter's (1934/1983) *The Theory of Economic Development*.

4. The author-function   Another screening or sorting procedure concerns the author(s). Authors choose what they write, but not entirely freely, and once they have written one work, the next is expected to show at least some cohesion with the first. 'What he writes and does not write, what he sketches out, even preliminary sketches for the work, and what he drops as simple mundane remarks, all this interplay of differences is prescribed by the author-function' (Foucault 1972: 222). Each epoch provides a certain author-function and the author in turn reshapes it. This 'author-function' may sound somewhat abstract, but it is very relevant for this study, since the procedure of writing scientific articles is highly shaped and controlled through the peer review system. This point means that my study must include the *writing and publishing practices* that shape and delimit the discourse.

5. The disciplinary regulations   The disciplines, here in the sense of academic domains, carry out a restricting function. The discipline regulates what is necessary for formulating new statements, through its 'groups of objects, methods, their corpus of propositions considered to be true, the interplay of rules and definitions, of techniques and tools' (ibid.: 222). What counts and does not count as proper knowledge and

proper entrepreneurship research will be relevant here, as well as what counts as legitimate methods for researching entrepreneurship. These will shape and delimit the discourse on women's entrepreneurship. I thus attend to the disciplinary regulations, particularly the *research methods*, in my study.

6. The screening among the speaking subjects   Foucault discusses a procedure enabling control over the discourses, which he calls 'the screening among the speaking subjects'. 'Here, we are no longer dealing with the mastery of the powers contained within discourse . . . it is more a question of determining the conditions under which it may be employed, of imposing a certain number of rules upon those individuals who employ it, thus denying access to everyone else' (ibid.: 224). Formal qualifications, expert group or other means of excluding people are relevant, but also rituals about who can speak, how and when. The academic system is rich in such rules and rituals, both formal and informal. I thus include the *rules and rituals pertaining to who is allowed to speak* (or write) on the topic of women's entrepreneurship in the research community.

7. Ideas of an ideal truth   Some philosophical themes about an ideal truth as a law of discourse, and an immanent rationality as the principle of their behavior may further strengthen these limitations, continues Foucault. They serve to hide the notion of the discourse being produced through and restricted by the practices discussed earlier. Epistemological assumptions of a neutral and cumulative knowledge development in entrepreneurship research may be such a restriction. *Ontological and epistemological premises* guiding, and limiting, the production of knowledge are therefore relevant for the study.

Foucault's principles   The procedures described above both enable and delimit the discourse. They systematically form the object of which they speak, to quote Foucault's definition of discourse again. Laying bare these restrictions is at the heart of Foucault's project. It is achieved through the following methodological principles, using Foucault's terminology.

1. The principle of reversal   The principle of reversal says not to look for what the discourse conveys, but for what it excludes. What has been cut out in the production of a discourse? Instead of looking for its source and its origin, look for what is not there.

2. The principle of discontinuity   The principle of discontinuity says not to forget that there is no grand narrative. There is no 'silent, continuous and repressed' discourse to be uncovered once the present discourse has

been deconstructed. The discourse does not hide any unknown truth – a series of discourses, sometimes connected, sometimes not, is all there is. This means that a discourse analysis can only result in an alternative story, the value of which is to be judged by ethical, moral or perhaps aesthetic standards. Consequently, it is not possible to analyze the discourse on female entrepreneurship in order to present a truer picture – only to point towards an alternative picture.

3.   The principle of specificity   The principle of specificity is related to the former principle. Since there is no 'silent, continuous and repressed' discourse, this means that a particular discourse cannot be understood by a prior system of meanings. Discourse must be understood as 'practice imposed upon things' as opposed to things being rendered legible through discourse. If discourse shows regularity, it is not because of any inherent regularity, but because of the regularity in this practice. This is another way of saying that there are no social laws and regularities to be uncovered by a study of language as representational of something (which is a common assumption of survey studies); instead the social world is created through discourse. There is no 'depth' beyond any 'surface' (in fact, these two constructs are alien to discourse analysis). Regularities are found because people construct the same thing over and over again.

4.   The principle of exteriority   The principle of exteriority, finally, says to not burrow to any assumed hidden, inner essence or meaning of discourse, but to look for its external conditions of existence. What circumstances make a certain discourse possible? How do these circumstances limit the discourse?

While further explaining Foucault's concept of discourse, the discussion on the principles also expanded my analytical framework. The principle of reversal implies that I should look for the stated, as well as the omitted, *reasons for studying women's entrepreneurship*. It also said to look for what areas are *excluded* from the discussion on women's entrepreneurship. What is not chosen as relevant? What is not, and cannot be, said? Are there any *dissenting voices* indicating points of tension? I translate the principles of discontinuity and specificity to mean that one must study the content and the form, as opposed to any assumed essence. In my research I study *how the research texts position female entrepreneurs*. How are they described? What are they compared and contrasted to?

The analytical framework in summary
Below I summarize the analytical framework. These are the discursive practices derived from the translation of Foucault that are to be analyzed in the

study. The points are reordered so as to reflect the logic in the ensuing analysis.

1. Founding fathers and foundational texts.
2. Ontological and epistemological premises.
3. Research methods.
4. The reasons for studying women's entrepreneurship.
5. How the research texts position female entrepreneurs.
6. Ideas, or assumptions, that are taken for granted.
7. The exclusions, and dissenting voices indicating points of tension.
8. Writing and publishing practices.
9. Rules and rituals pertaining to who is allowed to speak.
10. The institutional support for entrepreneurship research.

Analysis methods and findings
I dealt with each point in my analytical framework as a separate research question, and ended up using several different approaches to cover the ten points on the list. Next I describe the research process and the methods, following the order indicated above. The findings are interwoven in the method discussion, partly for purposes of illustration, but also because the findings of one step often motivated the next step of the analysis.

1. Deconstructing foundational texts
Each field has its foundational texts, which scholars must relate to in order to participate in the scholarly discussion. In the field of entrepreneurship, there are both classical economic texts, and there are contemporary journal articles that are often cited. I chose three different bodies of texts for my analysis. Hébert and Link's (1988) comprehensive overview of economic theory on entrepreneurship covers the classics, beginning with the French Physiocrats in the sixteenth century and ending with twentieth-century US economists. Schumpeter's *The Theory of Economic Development* (Schumpeter 1934/1983). Schumpeter's text can be perceived as seminal due to its influence on scholarly thinking on entrepreneurship. To analyze how entrepreneurship was theorized in the selected journals, I also selected a number of contemporary articles discussing the entrepreneurship concept, published mainly in the same journals as the reviewed articles on women's entrepreneurship (Carland et al. 1988; Gartner 1988; Grégoire et al. 2001; Hornaday 1990; Kirzner 1983; Low and MacMillan 1988; Meeks et al. 2001; Shane and Venkataraman 2000, 2001; Singh 2001; Stevenson 1984). These texts were subsequently analyzed through a feminist deconstruction of the descriptions of the entrepreneur.

A basic idea of deconstruction is that a text says as much by what it does not say as by what it says. The silences in a text can be said to hide, or even make ideological assumptions appear neutral or absent. Analyzing them can make the devalued 'other' visible. A deconstruction is of course always subject to further deconstruction – there is no end point where one has 'revealed it all'. Scholars using deconstruction employ a number of systematic strategies for analyzing the silences and the absences in a text.[1] The technique I have developed in this analysis is inspired by Saussure (1970), who said that one could only make sense of something by picturing what it is not. 'Woman' is 'not man', or 'the opposite of man', and vice versa (Gherardi 1995). I went through the chosen texts and underlined all words used to describe the terms entrepreneur and entrepreneurship. Then I looked for their opposites, using an antonym dictionary. For the concept 'entrepreneur' I chose to compare the lists of words and their opposites to Bem's (1981) widely used femininity/masculinity index in order to pinpoint its gendering. These opposites describing entrepreneurship were words such as 'routine, traditional, habit-like, stable, safe, risk-avoidance, certainty, taking orders, failing, blindness to opportunity, restraining force, stagnation, decay'. I concluded that entrepreneurship is constructed as something positive, associated with innovation, growth and development that one can hardly be against. It seems as if entrepreneurship contributes to the 'betterment of things', fitting nicely into the grand narrative of modernity where development is not only change, but also 'progress', something that is both valued and seemingly inevitable (Foucault 1969/1972; Lyotard 1979/1984).

The entrepreneur was described in words such as bold, rational, calculative, firm, strong willed, achievement oriented, detached and so on. A comparison with Bem's (1981) masculinity and femininity indexes in Table 9.1 reveals that these words are male gendered. The words describing masculinity and entrepreneur are very similar. The femininity words are mostly their direct opposites. Some of the femininity words, such as affectionate, sympathetic, understanding and warm, do not seem to be present in the entrepreneurship discussion at all, neither as words describing the entrepreneur nor as their opposites. Hence entrepreneurship seems to be a male gendered concept.

Getting an overview of the articles

The analysis of the foundational texts covered the first of my ten points. I began the analysis of the remaining points by a thorough reading of all the articles. I used the following reading guide, which was formulated based on the analytical framework. There is, however, no direct and simple relation between the items in the reading guide and the points in the analytical

Table 9.1   Bem's scale of masculinity and femininity

Bem's masculinity scale	Bem's femininity scale
Self-reliant	Affectionate
Defends own beliefs	Loyal
Assertive	Feminine
Strong personality	Sympathetic
Forceful	Sensitive to the needs of others
Has leadership abilities	Understanding
Willing to take risks	Compassionate
Makes decisions easily	Eager to soothe hurt feelings
Self-sufficient	Soft spoken
Dominant	Warm
Masculine	Tender
Willing to take a stand	Gentle
Acts as a leader	Loves children
Individualistic	Does not use harsh language
Competitive	Flatterable
Ambitious	Shy
Independent	Yielding
Athletic	Cheerful
Analytical	Gullible
Aggressive	Childlike

Source: Bem (1981).

framework – drawing a picture of their correspondence would look rather like a spider web. Most of the items in the reading guide were used to provide information for several points in the framework, as further explained below.

- Journal, Author(s), Title, Country
- Research problem and stated reason behind the problem
- Theory base(s), presence of feminist theory (if so, which)
- Method, data sources, measures, analysis
- Sample type and sample size
- Comparison groups used
- Descriptive/explanatory/conceptual
- Independent and dependent variables
- Results
- Ontological/epistemological assumptions (inferred)
- Construction of the female entrepreneur before and after study
- Quotes, comments.

For each article I filled out the relevant information on a separate sheet of paper. The result was a 100-page document that served as the basis for my analysis. The information that could be quantified and compared across the articles was then entered into Excel. I used one line for each article, and columns for the different items. In each column I entered a code for the relevant information, as for example 'B' for British in country of origin, or 'MR' for multiple regression in the analysis column. This made it easy to count and compare across the articles.[2]

2 and 3.   Ontological and epistemological premises and research methods
The overview provided information for a methodological and epistemological discussion. Many of the items above could be presented as descriptive statistics. The articles were for example mainly from the US (64 percent) or from the Anglo-Saxon sphere (83 percent). They were divided about equally between descriptive and explanatory studies. Cross-sectional survey studies comparing men and women through statistical analysis dominated. Half of the studies were not based on any explicit theory, but on empirical results from earlier studies. The remainder departed from psychology, sociology and/or management theory/economics. References to feminist theory were absent from the majority of the papers and only four papers had a point of departure that was explicitly feminist theory.

The studies covered topics such as personal background and firm characteristics, attitudes to entrepreneurship or intentions to start, psychology, start-up processes, management practice and strategy, networking, family, access to capital, and performance. The most common research question was related to differences between male and female entrepreneurs in these areas, but contrary to expectations, few such differences were found. Within-group variation was typically larger than between-groups variation. The results were also contradictory at times. Different explanations were put forth as to the reasons why no differences were found. One said that the research designs were unsatisfactory, with unsophisticated statistical methods, small sample sizes, and convenience samples in combination with insufficient sampling information and/or careless referral practices (Brush 1992; Moore 1990). The idea behind this critique is that the differences are there – if researchers only looked well and closely enough they would find them. Another explanation held that male gendered measuring instruments and pre-formulated questionnaires were used, making it impossible to capture anything 'differentially feminine' since only more or less of what is already imagined is measured (Stevenson 1990). Both these critiques, however, assume that there is something female or male to be measured.

The overview revealed that the studies' ontological and epistemological premises are generally along the lines of the objectivists. The studies assume

that there is something essentially masculine and feminine, with consequences for men's and women's behavior, and that this can be measured with
the appropriate statistical methods. The non-essentialist position taken in
this study questions the existence of stable inner psychological characteristics as well as the causal relationships assumed in much of the reviewed
research (Wicker 1969; Abelson 1972). Hence, essentialist assumptions go
hand in hand with an objectivist epistemology.

Questioning one means questioning the other, and it also means questioning the research methods used (point 3 on the list). If stable inner characteristics do not exist, or at least do not affect behavior, there is not much sense in
using Likert type scales to measure them. Looking for something essentially
female or male is thus to be looking for something in vain. The research,
however unproductive in terms of finding differences, nonetheless produces
something in the making, which of course is the topic of the present analysis.

4.   The reasons for studying women's entrepreneurship

To address the issue of how the research was argued, I performed a detailed
analysis of the introduction sections, in what I would label a genre-specific
argumentation analysis. Scientific journal articles make up their own literary genre with its own distinctive marks. Literary theorist John Swales
(1990) has analyzed articles in international science journals[3] and found
that they use more or less the same rhetorical moves to create interest and
convey their message (see Table 9.2). The introduction section, in particular, almost always follows the same three-step procedure in first establishing a territory by claiming the centrality or the importance of the research
area. Second, a niche is established by indicating a research gap, making a
counter-claim or raising a question. Alternatively, the continuance of a
research tradition is indicated. Third, the established niche is occupied.
This is usually accomplished through the presentation of the work or its
purpose and by announcing the principal findings. The articles in this
analysis were no exceptions. In fact, they followed the pattern to the letter.
I used Table 9.2, adapted from Swales (1990). For each article I filled out
the arguments used, in the appropriate spaces, and then compared across
all articles. The most common step in move 1 was claiming the centrality of
the research area. In move 2 one usually indicated a gap, either by claiming
that women entrepreneurs were under-researched, or that they were not
researched in an adequate manner. Eight percent of the introductions
claimed, however, that women entrepreneurs did not perform to standard,
wherefore this must be further investigated. Concerning move 3, all steps
were present in the introductions.

Research on entrepreneurship is typically argued in terms of its beneficial
effects on employment and economic growth (Birch 1979). The analysis of

Table 9.2   Introduction section structure

Move	Step
1. Establishing a territory	1. Claiming centrality and/or 2. Making topic generalization(s) and/or 3. Reviewing items of previous research
2. Establishing a niche	1a. Counter-claiming or 1b. Indicating a gap or 1c. Question-raising or 1d. Continuing a tradition
3. Occupying the niche	1a. Outlining purposes or 1b. Announcing present research 2. Announcing principal findings 3. Indicating research article structure

Source: Swales (1990).

the introductions showed that the arguments for studying women entrepreneurs in the reviewed articles were largely the same – how can they contribute to employment and economic growth? This was the argument in 88 percent of the reviewed articles. Equality arguments were largely absent. One might conclude that equality arguments are either not interesting or not legitimate as reasons for studying women's entrepreneurship in the selected journals. To single out women's specific contributions they must however be compared to something, which leads me to the next step in the analysis.

5.   The positioning of women entrepreneurs

Following the analysis of the introductions, I analyzed the research problems and the hypotheses to see how they positioned women entrepreneurs. An example would be a hypothesis stating, 'women will be less active networkers than men'. This positions women as inferior to men in terms of networking. I did not use an elaborate scheme as in the analysis of the introductions; instead I categorized the hypotheses and problems as they occurred and looked for patterns. Again, I found some interesting results. The studies followed a certain logic, with one step leading to another, primarily starting with the overall research rationale, namely women's contributions to economic growth. Many studies measure the performance of women's businesses in comparison with that of men. It turned out that they were on average a little smaller, grew a little slower and were somewhat less profitable than male-owned businesses (but controlling for sector, they were comparable).

Given the above rationale, women's smaller average contribution was then constructed as a problem and as a further reason for investigation.

What could be done to make them perform better? The logical next step was therefore to find the reasons for their lesser performance. Some looked for structural reasons, for example discrimination by moneylenders, implicitly following liberal feminist arguments, but obtain mixed results. Women seemed to be discriminated against by banks in several studies, but the explanations appeared to be mainly structural; they own the types of businesses that banks associate with higher risks. If structural barriers did not offer an explanation, maybe there was something about women that did? Indeed, a majority of the studies looked for differences between men and women entrepreneurs (implicitly following the second version of feminist thought, that men and women are essentially different). What sort of differences did they look for? Obviously, characteristics held to be necessary for successful entrepreneurship would be the first thing to study.

This was where the male-gendered entrepreneur from the analysis of the foundational texts enters the picture. 'He' was present both in measuring scales and in hypotheses of the reviewed research. Studies trying to figure out the personality of female entrepreneurs typically envisioned two possible versions. They called one of them masculine and one feminine, and then administered various tests to see how men and women entrepreneurs scored. An example would be a study which modeled two possible ways of management. One model assumed that men and women managed in an identical way. This model was called 'the successful entrepreneur'. The other model assumed that 'women behave differently as entrepreneurs and managers' (Chaganti 1986: 19), and this model was labeled 'the feminine entrepreneur'. Already the labeling indicates that a feminine model is an exception, of less value, and the other one a norm. The model told the story of the successful entrepreneur (who was not feminine), who was detached, rational, calculative, bold, decisive, aggressive and result-oriented. The feminine model was the opposite of that. It was one modest in goals, weak in expertise, irrational (does not use experts or hire trained personnel), unassertive and emotional. The supposedly neutral statistical methods used here actually constructed the research object by using measuring scales that were already gendered.

My analysis of the research problems and hypotheses showed that well beyond half of the articles focused explicitly on some sort of problem or proposed shortcoming associated with women. Women were discussed as having a psychological make-up that is less entrepreneurial, or at least different from a man's (Fagenson 1993; Neider 1987; Sexton and Bowman-Upton 1990). They were thought of as having less motivation for entrepreneurship or for growth of their businesses (Buttner and Moore 1997) be risk-averse (Masters and Meier 1988), to have unique start-up difficulties or training needs (Birley et al. 1987; Nelson 1987; Pellegrino and Reece 1982) or not network optimally (Aldrich et al. 1989; Cromie and Birley 1992; Katz and Williams 1997; Smeltzer and Fann 1989). They were thought to use less than optimal management practices or strategies (Chaganti 1986; Cuba et al. 1983; Olson and Currie 1992; Van Auken et al. 1994), and to behave irrationally (Nelson 1989). The conception of women as being something less than men was thus prevalent in the research.

6 and 7.   *Looking for assumptions, exclusions and dissenting voices*

Addressing points 6 and 7 on my list, I used a different method. So far, the analysis resembles a content analysis in that the presence or absence of the investigated aspects was considered for all articles. When reading the articles I also identified some interesting themes reflecting underlying assumptions that did not lend themselves to this type of analysis. An underlying assumption resides by definition under the text, and can hardly be coded and counted. I therefore left the logic of content analysis, and leaned on the logic of discourse analysis, which says that the presence of a statement, however unusual, indicates that there is a discourse to be drawn upon to produce this statement and to make this statement possible and legitimate. The presence of a statement in these research articles has also passed the discourse community's strict screening devices and is therefore doubly legitimate.

The themes emerged through this exercise. Having formulated the themes, I went back to the articles relevant for each theme and reread the relevant sections. The themes deal with (i) assumptions about the role of entrepreneurship, (ii) assumptions of entrepreneurship as gender-neutral, (iii) assumptions of gender differences, (iv) assumptions about work and family, and (v) assumptions about individual versus collective responsibility. Regarding the last few themes, I found some dissenting voices within the body of articles, indicating the presence of conflicting discourses. The results showed that throughout the reviewed texts, the underlying assumptions positioned women entrepreneurs as secondary to men. Below I formulate five basic assumptions present in the texts, and after this I show the reader how to demonstrate the existence of such assumptions by way of an example.

The first, almost universal assumption, was that entrepreneurship is a good thing, leading to economic growth. Having this as the reason for studying women entrepreneurs excludes alternative reasons, such as those of equality or of correcting the research record in order to include women. It also portrays women as 'less' since their businesses do not, on average, perform as well as men's according to growth-related performance standards.

A second, often tacit, assumption was that entrepreneurship is a gender-neutral concept. This is reflected in the measurements used for both the entrepreneurs and for their businesses. The individual entrepreneur is evaluated on how well she measures up to male stereotypes. The businesses are evaluated on how they perform on narrowly defined growth measures. Controlling for sector and size of business, men and women actually have similar growth and (lack of) growth ambitions (Davidsson 1989), but the reviewed texts portray it as a female problem. Somehow men get to be free riders on their few growth-oriented fellow businessmen, while the women are marked out as the non-growers. Why some men grow their businesses is not explained by how men are, but surprisingly, it seems all right to explain it by how women are not. The construction of the entrepreneur is the stereotypical independent self-made man. This is not an image that fits most women (nor indeed many men) very well, so women are rendered insufficient already by the research design.

The third assumption was that men and women are different and that essential, inner, stable characteristics affecting behavior do indeed exist. This is referred to as essentialist assumptions. The studies frequently looked for essential gender differences, but found many more similarities than differences. This does not, however, lead authors to depart from the idea that men and women are different. I found three ways in which the texts tried to save the idea of the existence of gender differences. The first, which I label *making a mountain out of a mole-hill* entails overemphasizing the few differences that are actually found and ignoring the similarities and the overlaps between the sexes. The *self-selected woman* strategy explains the lack of differences by stressing that women entrepreneurs are different from ordinary women, even if the authors have no research results on 'ordinary women'. The third strategy, which I label *the good mother* strategy, is to cherish the small differences found and from these, combined with general knowledge on women and women's life situations, mold an alternative, female entrepreneur model which is characterized by being relational, ethical and caring. It turns women's proposed differential disadvantages into advantages, but does not challenge the dichotomized and gendered understanding of entrepreneurship. The difference is that the 'feminine' column is still different, but not necessarily 'in lack'. Rather, it is complementary. The 'male way' is still a norm. These three rhetorical strategies serve the purpose of maintaining the idea of the existence of essential gender differences even though the research results indicate the contrary. It is as if the idea of essential gender differences has more power over the mind than have result figures in tables measuring personality. The strategies serve to reproduce traditional notions about masculinity and femininity rather than challenge them.[4]

The fourth assumption concerned the division between work and family, or the division between a public and a private sphere of life. Research on entrepreneurship hardly mentions family. When research focuses on women entrepreneurs, however, it becomes apparent that life consists not only of work, but also of home, family and children, but work and family are seen as separate entities. What sorts under 'family' and 'private' is also seen as an individual and not a collective responsibility, and it is almost universally perceived as the woman's responsibility. Women entrepreneurs are asked if balancing family and work is a problem for them, but male entrepreneurs are not asked the same question. It is taken for granted that his time is for work, only. Giving the woman the responsibility for the private sphere means that she must work double shifts and it means that she cannot compete with male competitors in the same business on equal terms. She is given a secondary, complementary role in business while men's responsibility for children is rendered invisible.

The fifth, and last, assumption was the individualist focus in entrepreneurship research. It is the individual entrepreneur and her business that is in focus, and contextual or historical variables affecting the business such as legislation or family policy are rarely discussed. This precludes collective solutions to problems that are conceived of as individual, as for example public day care as a solution to childcare problems. It severely restricts the study of entrepreneurship, and the effect is that individuals are to be blamed or, even worse, to blame themselves for all the problems in the world, while institutional arrangements remain largely unquestioned. The neglect of social aspects also means that the power perspective is lost. Issues of women's subordination to men are seldom touched upon and there is no talk of collective action to change gender inequalities.

There were some dissenting voices in the texts, most notably from some British contributions (Birley 1989; Chell and Baines 1998; Goffee and Scase 1983; Marlow 1997; Rosa and Hamilton 1994). They opposed mainstream research, questioning and arguing against the individualist assumptions, and the gendered conceptions of entrepreneurship. But the mainstream did not listen. Even if published in the same journals, the dissenting articles were not quoted by the mainstream, and their arguments were not met. The fact that they were published shows that there was room for an alternative discourse in opposition to a dominant one, but that it was so different from the dominant one that they seemed to coexist, but not to mix.

Examples of underlying assumptions   Just as underlying assumptions cannot be coded and counted, one cannot show them neatly and squarely in a table, either. The five assumptions that I formulated above are also products of a certain research perspective, and a result of a certain interpretation. So how does one demonstrate them to the reader? I found that using quotes from the texts was very effective, as the example below shows.

Caputo and Dolinsky (1998) studied the effect of household and family composition on women's choice of self-employment. Like most other studies, they begin by noticing the increase of women's entrepreneurship in the USA as a reason to expand research efforts on this, and they note that the impact of household members' (partners, children and relatives) financial and human capital on women's choice of self-employment is not well researched. Their literature review departs in labor economics, which says that the cost of childcare diminishes the likelihood of females participating in the labor force. Self-employment would be a way to solve this problem:

> One way mothers may begin to overcome child care cost considerations is by pursuing self-employment. As self-employment typically permits a more flexible work schedule, it more readily enables mothers to care for their own children, thus reducing if not eliminating the cost of child care. (Ibid.: 9)

Childcare seems to be mainly the mother's responsibility in the view of these authors. They postulate that the time the father makes available for childcare would have an effect on this equation (increase chances of woman seeking self-employment), by noting that:

> One viable means for a working woman to adapt her work schedule around that of her husband so that he can be available to contribute child care is through self-employment. (Ibid.: 10)

However,

> Regarding the effect of the time a husband makes available for other household chores on a woman's employment choice, no effect is expected a priori. In contrast to a child's need for supervision, which often requires an immediate response, most routine household chores can be completed when time becomes available in the woman's schedule. (Ibid.: 10)

So, necessity might have it that husbands help with children, but other routine household chores seem most definitely to be the wife's responsibility. Having established that self-employment for women is a good thing, since it has the benefits of allowing flexibility so they can care for their own children, the authors go on to investigate factors that increase the likelihood of this. They found that the husband's level of income mattered, but only if he was also himself self-employed. They explain the results as follows:

> these findings may suggest that entrepreneurial husbands, particularly when successful, offer their wives confidence in the pursuit of entrepreneurship. Accordingly, entrepreneurial husbands appear to serve as role models in influencing women's choice to pursue entrepreneurship. (Ibid.: 15)

The authors apparently presume that the men started their businesses before their wives did, and so can serve as role models. They further presume that women are less confident and that their husbands can offer them confidence. It is a patriarchal model where men and men's work is an unquestioned standard, and women, in addition to counting less, are seen as the flexible resource that makes things work. According to the authors, this is quite in order and should be encouraged:

> Quality care, when provided outside the household, can be difficult to find and is often financially draining. In 1993, for example, the Federal government spent nearly $2.5 billion on taxpayers who needed dependent care in order to accept or maintain employment . . . To the extent to which it is a societal objective to minimize such costs and maximize the quality of care, married mothers with children appear to be the most attractive segment to target for programs fostering entrepreneurship, as the flexibility of self-employment makes home-based care most feasible. (Ibid.: 16)

This paints a picture of a society where family and childcare is a fully private responsibility. It also paints a picture of a society where the man is the breadwinner who does things on his terms, and the woman the loyal and flexible adapter who takes responsibility for the children. The problem of combining work and childcare is to be solved by women's self-employment. There is no mention of a collective solution, like public childcare, where men and women can participate in the labor force and provide childcare and perform 'other routine household chores' on equal terms.

The text above demonstrated the underlying assumptions very clearly. The critical reader may of course object, and say that this was just one example. How can I know that the assumptions are shared? To this I have two answers. The purist position says that one example is enough. The fact that the authors above suggest that husbands may be expected to change diapers, but not do the laundry, since the wife can do this when she finds the time, says that there is a discourse around which makes it possible to utter such a statement. The second answer is that I have many more quotes in my study, from many articles, that demonstrate the same underlying assumptions. And I also have quotes from the dissenting voices, which actually make the underlying assumptions even more poignant. An example would be a quote by Chell and Baines, who write that we must:

> recognize the importance of structuring factors in society: extant institutional arrangements – the family, industrial, educational, financial, socio-legal, political and cultural, for example. Such structures, it is argued, shape expectations and create limits and barriers as to what is in fact possible. (Chell and Baines 1998: 118)

Goffee and Scase argue that entrepreneurship may even contribute to the development of a feminist consciousness, which is a far cry from arguing that it is a road to economic growth:

> proprietorship can heighten the awareness of women's subordination and, in this manner, query existing structures to a greater extent than is commonly assumed. (Goffee and Scase 1983: 644)

But the discursive practices go beyond assumptions. Material and other practices also shape the discourse. The last three points shed further light on how the discourse on women's entrepreneurship is formed.

8, 9 and 10.   Writing and publishing practices and institutional support
Information regarding writing and publishing practices and rules and rituals pertaining to who is allowed to speak (points 8 and 9 on the list) came from reading the publishing guidelines of the journals, interviewing the editor of one of them (since many of these practices are not coded), analyzing the composition of the editorial boards and reading Huff's (1999) authoritative guide, *Writing for Scholarly Publication*. I studied entrepreneurship research encyclopedias and interviewed members of several entrepreneurship faculties about institutional support for entrepreneurship, which was the last point on the list.

It turned out that these discursive practices reinforced those discussed earlier. Researchers' careers depend on getting published in mainstream journals. If these encompass the practices outlined above, this means that articles submitted will also conform. They are likely to follow the disciplinary regulations, which favor theories that concentrate on the individual and/or the individual firm. They are likely to adhere to certain methodological preferences, namely surveys and statistical analyses that favor analyses of differences. They will most likely follow an objectivist epistemology, which, combined with the search for essential gender differences and the male norm, renders women secondary. Outliers are less likely to submit, or they might be ruled out or made to conform as a result of the review process. I analyzed the composition of the editorial boards in the four journals included and found that they primarily consist of Americans, many of whom serve on more than one, and most of them go to the same entrepreneurship research conferences. They form a discourse community[5] (Swales 1990), which is likely to attract research that shares its assumptions (Foucault's author-function) and reject studies based on different ones. The training and socialization of researchers may reinforce any of the assumptions and preferences outlined above. Institutional support in terms of research funding and research centers is also part of the discursive practices. Funding is increasingly available for entrepreneurship research, but the interest is either in growth (government funding) or business performance (private funding). None of these focus on gender relations or power issues. The research object is just rendered an inadequate variable in the growth equation.

What lessons can be learned from this research?
The main purpose of this chapter is of course to contribute to the discussion on qualitative methods in entrepreneurship research. Since the research object happens to be research texts on women's entrepreneurship, I believe that there are some implications also regarding entrepreneurship research on gender, as well as regarding the practice of research as such.

Entrepreneurship research on gender
The study showed that the discursive practices of the reviewed research resulted in the recreation of women as 'the Other' (de Beauvoir 1949/1986). To obtain a different result, the discursive practices must be changed. Elsewhere I argue for an expansion of the research area to include factors related not only to the individual, but also structural, historical, cultural, legislative and institutional factors (Ahl 2004; 2006). I also argue for more comparative, international work. More importantly, I suggest a shift in epistemological position, from objectivist to constructionist, from gender as something that *is*, to gender as something that is *done*, from gender as something firmly tied to bodies to gendered anything – concepts, jobs, industries, language, disciplines, businesses and so on. Instead of looking at physical men and women and using their sex as an explanatory variable, one can look at how gender is *accomplished* in different contexts. Study objects would be how individual men and women perform gender in daily interaction and/or the gendering of institutional orders and how they are constructed and reconstructed. Business legislation, family policy, support systems for entrepreneurs, cultural norms, how childcare is arranged, gendered divisions of labor and so on would be objects for study. Such studies would show how gender/power relations are constructed, which, I believe, is more fruitful than looking within individuals for the reasons for gender imbalances.

The practices of research
The discursive practices resulted in the second-sexing of women. I have no reason, however, to believe that this was the intention of the authors. Many of them explicitly say that they want to give women entrepreneurs more attention than they have received in entrepreneurship research. Then why did it turn out this way? The answer is *because* of the discursive practices. The legitimate argument for giving them more attention is the growth and performance argument, which leads to gender comparisons, which leads to . . . and so on. The name of the game produces this particular result.

The way to give women a voice in a field where they are marginalized is to speak *through* the normal discourse – which oppresses women. It is a 'Catch-22' situation. The taken-for-granted research practices delimit what can be researched, and how. The objectivist epistemology, the assumption of essential individual characteristics that affect behavior and the preferred methodology in the reviewed studies have, as shown above, led to a dead end. Still, new papers on gender differences are continuously being published. A shift in epistemological position, the use of other methods and the inclusion of other 'variables' than the individual and his/her firm are, I think, necessary in order to get new and more useful answers.

But even if an individual researcher decides to conduct the research differently, with different research questions, other research objects and different methods as suggested above, at least two problems related to the discursive practices analyzed in this chapter remain. One is to get funding for this kind of research; the other is to get it published in a place that furthers the researcher's career. As of today, critical feminist work is published in one type of journals, and entrepreneurship research in a different type, with no or little exchange between the two. And entrepreneurship scholars are not rewarded for publications in journals focusing on gender issues. This shows the paradox of how the institutionalization of research may be the biggest obstacle of all for untraditional ways of studying the social world.

Using discourse analysis in entrepreneurship research

This chapter provided an interpretation of Foucault for methodological purposes, and a description of a discourse analysis on research texts using this method. I used a feminist perspective to show exactly how the discursive practices of research produce an unintended result – but the discursive practices are likely to have power implications for any research object. This means that the implications go beyond issues of gender inequality. Close at hand are other groups who are marginalized, by for example ethnicity, age, social class or sexuality. There is a growing interest today in the entrepreneurship of immigrants. In Sweden, immigrants are supposed not only to solve their own unemployment problems by starting a business, but they are also thought to revitalize the Swedish small business sector, particularly in the service industries (Nutek 2001). How does this discourse position immigrants, and by what means? Why this focus on small and service businesses? Are large businesses, and manufacturing businesses reserved for another group? Is the discourse on immigrants' entrepreneurship a way to 'cover up' discriminatory employment practices? Does the discourse differ between male and female immigrants' business prospects? If so, how, on what grounds, and with what effects? Questions like these merit an analysis of the discursive practices that constitute this discourse.

Questions may also be asked about how the normal entrepreneurship discourse positions those who are supposed to embody the norm, namely white men. Just as the discourse positions women as the stereotypical Other, it also stereotypes men. The image of the independent, self-made man restricts men's options. Many men may feel uncomfortable with this image and would welcome alternative discourses of masculinity.

Apart from restricting the options for men and women, the entrepreneurship discourse also restricts itself. Using growth and performance as the two main ways of legitimating research on entrepreneurship means that only certain facets of entrepreneurship become visible. There are many imaginable aspects of entrepreneurship worthy of research attention that do not see the light of day, since they are not thought to have a direct bearing on growth or performance. The discourse of entrepreneurship, as carried forth in entrepreneurship research journals, thus severely restrains what notions of entrepreneurship that are legitimate and 'researchable'. The accepted methods serve a similar restricting, as well as shaping, function. This, in turn, limits, and constructs, the phenomena studied by entrepreneurship research. The discursive practices form the object of which they speak, to quote Foucault again. The main point of this chapter is thus the demonstration of how research articles co-produce social reality, along with a useful method for how this can be studied. The method could be applied to other sorts of journals, other research objects and other types of questions. If using it to analyze research texts, the method could probably be taken right off the rack. For other sorts of material, another translation of Foucault might be necessary and different methods applicable. In such case, this chapter serves as an example of how such a translation can be made.

Notes

1. See Joanne Martin (1990) for an accessible introduction to and an application of deconstruction.
2. For complete and detailed information for each item in the overview, see Ahl (2004).
3. Swales cites studies on journals in a wide range of disciplines in the natural and social sciences.
4. Deborah Cameron makes a related point in her research on popular advice for women on speaking. The advice is often about overcoming so-called male–female misunderstandings, but in writing the advice, the authors of this literature actually create these two diametrically opposed categories of ways of speaking. In the ensuing advice on how to overcome the opposition, two things are accomplished. First, the two categories are reproduced, and second, the male category is made the normative one. Women are advised either to adapt to male ways of talking (the career advice), or simply to understand fact that men talk differently from women, as in the relationship advice (Cameron 1995, 1996).
5. Swales holds that a discourse community is a community with a broadly agreed set of common public goals. It has mechanisms for interaction among its members that are used to provide information and feedback. It uses and owns one or more genres in the communicative furtherance of its aims. It has acquired some specific lexis. Finally, it has a

threshold level of members with a suitable degree of relevant content and discourse expertise. All requisites apply. Furthering entrepreneurship research may be the common goal. Scientific articles published in research journals are a mechanism of interaction and also make up a genre. Any one article in these journals will show the specific lexis used and, as the analysis of the composition of the editorial boards showed, the community certainly has a threshold level of members with relevant content and discourse expertise.

Suggested further readings

Burr, V. (1995) *An Introduction to Social Constructionism*. London: Routledge. This is a very well-written and accessible introduction to the epistemological position which lies at the basis of discourse analysis. Burr not only presents social constructionism, but also reports on various criticisms and debates concerning it.

Winther Jörgensen, M. and Phillips, L. (2002) *Discourse Analysis as Theory and Method*. London: Sage. This is a good introduction to three main approaches in discourse analysis, with detailed examples of how one might conduct an analysis within each of the three approaches.

Foucault, M. (1972) *The Discourse on Language* (*L'ordre du discours*). In *The Archaeology of Knowledge and The Discourse on Language* (pp. 215–37). New York: Pantheon Books. The reader who is interested in the kind of analysis carried out in this chapter must read Foucault to obtain more details and a richer understanding of how one might proceed with a different study.

Calás, M. and Smircich, L. (1996) From 'The Woman's' Point of View: Feminist Approaches to Organization Studies. In S. Clegg, C. Hardy and W. Nord (eds), *Handbook of Organization Studies* (pp. 218–57). London: Sage. This is a short and comprehensive overview of feminist theory written for organization scholars.

Weedon, C. (1999) *Feminism, Theory and the Politics of Difference*. Oxford: Blackwell. Weedon provides a readable, current, in-depth overview of feminist theory and of contemporary debates within feminism.

References

Abelson, R.P. (1972) Are attitudes necessary? In B.T. King and E. McGinnies (eds), *Attitudes, Conflict, and Social Change*. New York and London: Academic Press.

Ahl, H. (1997) Entrepreneuship research with a gender perspective: an overview of past research and suggestions for the future. Paper presented at the 14th Nordic Conference on Business Studies, Bodö, Norway.

Ahl, H. (2004) *The Scientific Reproduction of Gender Inequality: A discourse analysis of research texts on women's entrepreneurship*. Malmö: Liber.

Ahl, H. (2006) Why research on women entrepreneurs needs new directions. *Entrepreneurship Theory and Practice*, **30**(5): 595–621.

Aldrich, H., Reese, P.R. and Dubini, P. (1989) Women on the verge of a break-through: Networking among entrepreneurs in the United States and Italy. *Entrepreneurship and Regional Development*, **1**: 339–56.

Alvesson, M. and Due Billing, Y. (1999) *Kön och organisation*. Lund: Studentlitteratur.

Baker, T., Aldrich, H.E. and Liou, N. (1997) Invisible entrepreneurs: The neglect of women business owners by mass media and scholarly journals in the USA. *Entrepreneurship and Regional Development*, **9**(3): 221–38.

Bem, S.L. (1981) *Bem Sex-Role Inventory*. Palo Alto, CA: Mind Garden.

Berger, P. and Luckmann, T. (1966) *The Social Construction of Reality: A treatise in the sociology of knowledge*. London: Penguin Books.

Bergström, G. and Boréus, K. (2000) *Textens Mening och Makt (The Meaning and Power of Text)*. Lund: Studentlitteratur.

Birch, D. (1979) *The Job Generation Process*. Cambridge, MA: MIT Press.

Birley, S. (1989) Female entrepreneurs: Are they really different? *Journal of Small Business Management*, **27**(1): 1–37.

Birley, S., Moss, C. and Saunders, P. (1987) Do women entrepreneurs require different training? *American Journal of Small Business*, **12**(1): 27–35.

Brush, C.G. (1992) Research on women business owners: Past trends, a new perspective and future directions. *Entrepreneurship, Theory and Practice*, **16**(4): 5–30.

Burr, V. (1995) *An Introduction to Social Constructionism*. London: Routledge.

Busenitz, L., West III, G.P., Shepherd, D., Nelson, T., Chandler, G.N. and Zacharakis, A. (2003) Entrepreneurship research in emergence: Past trends and future directions. *Journal of Management*, **29**(3): 285–308.

Butler, J. (1990) *Gender Trouble: Feminism and the Subversion of Identity*. London and New York: Routledge.

Buttner, E.H. and Moore, D.P. (1997) Women's organizational exodus to entrepreneurship: Self-reported motivations and correlates with success. *Journal of Small Business Management*, January; 34–46.

Calás, M. and Smircich, L. (1992) Using the 'F' word: Feminist theories and the social consequences of organizational research. In A. Mills and P. Tancred (eds), *Gendering Organizational Theory*. Newbury Park: Sage.

Calás, M. and Smircich, L. (1996) From 'the woman's' point of view: Feminist approaches to organization studies. In S. Clegg, C. Hardy and W. Nord (eds), *Handbook of Organization Studies*. London: Sage, pp. 218–57.

Cameron, D. (1995) *Verbal Hygiene*. London: Routledge.

Cameron, D. (1996) The language–gender interface: Challenging co-optation. In V.I. Bergall, J.M. Bing and A.F. Freed (eds), *Rethinking Language and Gender Research: Theory and practice*. London: Longman.

Caputo, R.K. and Dolinsky, A. (1998) Women's choice to pursue self-employment: The role of financial and human capital of household members. *Journal of Small Business Management*, **36**(3): 8–17.

Carland, J.W., Hoy, F. and Carland, J.A.C. (1988) 'Who is an entrepreneur?' is a question worth asking. *American Journal of Small Business*, Spring: 33–9.

Carter, N.M. and Allen, K.R. (1997) Size determinants of women-owned businesses: Choice or barriers to resources? *Entrepreneurship and Regional Development*, **9**(3): 211–20.

Chaganti, R. (1986) Management in women-owned enterprises. *Journal of Small Business Management*, **24**(4): 19–29.

Chell, E. and Baines, S. (1998) Does gender affect business 'performance'? A study of microbusinesses in business services in the UK. *Entrepreneurship and Regional Development*, **10**: 117–35.

Chodorow, N. (1988) *Femininum – Maskulinum. Modersfunktion och Könssociologi*. Stockholm: Natur and Kultur.

Cromie, S. and Birley, S. (1992) Networking by female business owners in Northern Ireland. *Journal of Business Venturing*, **7**(3): 237–51.

Cuba, R., Decenzo, D. and Anish, A. (1983) Management practices of successful female business owners. *American Journal of Small Business*, **8**(2): 40–46.

Davidsson, P. (1989) *Continued Entrepreneurship and Small Firm Growth*. Stockholm School of Economics, Stockholm.

de Beauvoir, S. (1949/1986) *Det andra könet* (4th edn), (trans. 'The Second Sex'). Stockholm: Norstedts.

Doyle, J. and Paludi, M. (1998) *Sex and Gender: The human experience* (4th edn). San Francisco: McGraw-Hill.

Fagenson, E. (1993) Personal value systems of men and women: Entrepreneurs versus managers. *Journal of Business Venturing*, **8**(5), 409–30.

Fischer, E.M., Reuber, A.R. and Dyke, L.S. (1993) A theoretical overview and extension of research on sex, gender and entrepreneurship. *Journal of Business Venturing*, **8**(2): 151–68.

Foucault, M. (1969/1972) *The Archeology of Knowledge*. London: Tavistock.

Foucault, M. (1972) The discourse on language (L'ordre du discours), *The Archaeology of Knowledge and The Discourse on Language*. New York: Pantheon Books, pp. 215–37.

Gartner, W. (1988) 'Who is an entrepreneur?' is the wrong question. *American Journal of Small Business*, Spring: 11–32.

Gherardi, S. (1995) *Gender, Symbolism and Organizational Cultures*. London: Sage.

Giddens, A. (1991) *Modernity and Self-identity: Self and society in the late modern age.* Stanford, CA: Stanford University Press.

Gilligan, C. (1982) *In a Different Voice*. Cambridge, MA: Harvard University Press.

Goffee, R. and Scase, R. (1983) Business ownership and women's subordination: A preliminary study of female proprietors. *The Sociological Review*, **31**: 625–48.

Grégoire, D., Déry, R. and Béchard, J.-P. (2001) Evolving conversations: A look at the convergence in entrepreneurship research. Paper presented at the Babson College Kaufmann Foundation Entrepreneurship Research Conference, Jönköping, Sweden.

Haraway, D. (1991) *Simians, Cyborgs, and Women*. London: Free Association Books.

Harding, S. (1987) 'Introduction: Is there a feminist method?' In S. Harding (ed.), *Feminism and Methodology*. Milton Keynes: Open University Press.

Hébert, R.F. and Link, A.N. (1988) *The Entrepreneur: Mainstrean views and radical critiques*. New York: Praeger Publishers.

Hollway, W. (1984) Gender difference and the production of subjectivity. In J. Henriques, W. Hollway, C. Urwin, C. Venn and V. Walkerdine (eds), *Changing the Subject*. London: Methuen, pp. 227–63.

Hornaday, R.W. (1990) Dropping the e-words from small business research: An alternative typology. *Journal of Small Business Management*, October: 22–33.

Huff, A.S. (1999) *Writing for Scholarly Publication*. Thousand Oaks: Sage.

Iannello, K. (1992) *Decisions without Hierarchy. Feminist interventions in organization theory and practice*. New York: Routledge.

Katz, J.A. and Williams, P.M. (1997) Gender, self-employment and weak-tie networking through formal organizations. *Entrepreneurship and Regional Development*, **9**(3): 183–97.

Kendall, G. and Wickham, G. (1999) *Using Foucault's Methods*. London: Sage.

King, B.T. and McGuinnies, E. (1972) Overview: Social contexts and issues for contemporary attitude change research. In B.T. King and McGuinnies (eds), *Attitudes, Conflict, and Social Change*. New York and London: Academic Press.

Kirzner, I. (1983) Entrepreneurs and the entrepreneurial function: A commentary. In J. Ronen (ed.), *Entrepreneurship*. Lexington MA: Lexington Books, pp. 281–90.

Knights, D. and Vurdubakis, T. (1994) Foucault, power, resistance and all that. In J.M. Jermier, D. Knights and W.R. Nord (eds), *Resistance and Power in Organizations*. London: Routledge, pp. 167–98.

Lloyd, M. (1993) The (f)utility of a feminist turn to Foucault. *Economy and Society*, **22**(4): 437–60.

Low, M.B. and MacMillan, I.C. (1988) Entrepreneurship: Past research and future challenges. *Journal of Management*, **14**(2), 139–61.

Lyotard, J.-F. (1979/1984) *The Postmodern Condition: A report on knowledge* (Vol. 10). Manchester: Manchester University Press.

Marlow, S. (1997) Self-employed women – new opportunities, old challenges? *Entrepreneurship and Regional Development*, **9**(3): 199–210.

Martin, J. (1990) Deconstructing organizational taboos: The suppression of gender conflict in organizations. *Organization Science*, **1**(4): 339–60.

Masters, R. and Meier, R. (1988) Sex differences and risk-taking propensity of entrepreneurs. *Journal of Small Business Management*, **26**(1), 31–5.

McCloskey, D. (1994) *Knowledge and Persuasion in Economics*. Cambridge: Cambridge University Press.

McCloskey, D. (1998) *The Rhetoric of Economics* (2nd edn). Madison: The University of Wisconsin Press.

McNay, L. (1992) *Foucault and Feminism: Power, gender and the self*. Cambridge: Polity Press.

Meeks, M.D., Neck, H. and Meyer, G.D. (2001) Converging conversations in entrepreneurship. Paper presented at the Babson Conference 2001 in Jönköping, Sweden.

Moore, D. (1990) An examination of present research on the female entrepreneur – suggested research strategies for the 1990s. *Journal of Business Ethics*, **9**(4–5): 275–81.

Neider, L. (1987) A preliminary investigation of female entrepreneurs in Florida. *Journal of Small Business Management*, **25**(3): 22–9.

Nelson, G.W. (1987) Information needs of female entrepreneurs. *Journal of Small Business Management*, **25**(1): 38–44.
Nelson, G.W. (1989) Factors of friendship: Relevance of significant others to female business owners. *Entrepreneurship Theory and Practice*, **13**(4): 7–18.
Newton, T. (1998) Theorizing subjectivity in organization: The failure of Foucauldian studies? *Organization Studies*, **19**(3): 415–47.
Nutek. (2001) *Marginalisering eller integration: Invandrares företagande i svensk retorik och praktik*. Stockholm: Nutek.
Olson, S.F. and Currie, H.M. (1992) Female entrepreneurs in a male-dominated industry: Personal value systems and business strategies. *Journal of Small Business Management*, **30**(1): 49–57.
Parker, I. (1992) *Discourse Dynamics: Critical analysis for social and individual psychology*. London: Routledge.
Payne, J.W., Bettman, J.R. and Johnson, E.J. (1992) Behavioral decision research: A constructive processing perspective. *Annual Review of Psychology*, **43**: 87–131.
Pellegrino, E.T. and Reece, B.L. (1982) Perceived formative and operational problems encountered by female entrepreneurs in retail and service firms. *Journal of Small Business Management*, **20**(2): 15–24.
Ratnatunga, J. and Romano, C. (1997) A 'citation classics' analysis of articles in contemporary small enterprise research. *Journal of Business Venturing*, **12**: 197–212.
Rosa, P. and Hamilton, D. (1994) Gender and ownership in UK small firms. *Entrepreneurship Theory and Practice*, **18**(3): 11–27.
Saussure, F. d. (1970) *Kurs i allmän lingvistik*. Staffanstorp: Cavefors
Schumpeter, J.A. (1934/1983) *The Theory of Economic Development* (Reprint 1971 edn). New Brunswick, NJ: Transaction Publishers.
Sexton, D.L. and Bowman-Upton, N. (1990) Female and male entrepreneurs: Psychological characteristics and their role in gender-related discrimination. *Journal of Business Venturing*, **5**(1): 29–36.
Shane, S. and Venkataraman, S. (2000) The promise of entrepreneurship as a field of research. *Academy of Management Review*, **25**(1): 217–26.
Shane, S. and Venkataraman, S. (2001) Entrepreneurship as a field of research: A response to Zahre and Dess, Singh, and Erikson. *Academy of Management Review*, **26**(1): 13–16.
Singh, R.P. (2001) A comment on developing the field of entrepreneurship through the study of opportunity recognition and exploitation. *Academy of Management Review*, **26**(1): 10–12.
Smeltzer, L.R. and Fann, G.L. (1989) Gender differences in external networks of small business owner/managers. *Journal of Small Business Management*, **27**(2): 25–32.
Söndergaard, D.M. (1999) *Destabilising Discourse Analysis* (Working Paper No. 7, Kön i den akademiske organisation). Copenhagen: Institut for Statskundskab, Köbenhavns Universitet.
Stevenson, H. (1984) A perspective on entrepreneurship. In H. Stevenson, M. Roberts and H. Grousebeck (eds), *New Business Venture and the Entrepreneur*. Boston, MA: Harvard Business School, pp. 3–14.
Stevenson, L.A. (1986) Against all odds: The entrepreneurship of women. *Journal of Small Business Management*, **24**(4): 30–36.
Stevenson, L. (1990) Some methodological problems associated with researching women entrepreneurs. *Journal of Business Ethics*, **9**(4–5): 439–46.
Swales, J.M. (1990) *Genre Analysis: English in academic and research settings*. Cambridge: Cambridge University Press.
Van Auken, H.E., Rittenburg, T.L., Doran, B.M. and Hsieh, S.-F. (1994) An empirical analysis of advertising by women entrepreneurs. *Journal of Small Business Management*, **32**(3): 11–27.
Weedon, C. (1999) *Feminism, Theory and the Politics of Difference*. Oxford: Blackwell.
Wicker, A.W. (1969) Attitudes v. actions: The relationship of verbal and overt responses to attitude objects. *Journal of Social Issues*, **25**: 41–78.
Winther Jörgensen, M. and Phillips, L. (1999) *Diskursanalyse som teori og metode*. Roskilde: Roskilde Universitetsforlag.
Young, I. (1995) 'Gender as seriality' In L. Nicholson and S. Seidman (eds), *Social Postmodernism*. Cambridge: Cambridge University Press, pp. 187–215.

Appendix   Reviewed studies in order of topic

Table 9A.1

Access to capital

Buttner, E.H. and Rosen, B. (1988) Bank loan officers' perceptions of the characteristics of men, women and successful entrepreneurs. *Journal of Business Venturing*, **3**(3): 249–58.

Buttner, E.H. and Rosen, B. (1989) Funding new business ventures: are decision makers biased against women entrepreneurs? *Journal of Business Venturing*, **4**(4): 249–61.

Buttner, E.H. and Rosen, B. (1992) Rejection in the loan application process: male and female entrepreneurs' perceptions and subsequent intentions. *Journal of Small Business Management*, **30**(1): 59–65.

Carter, S. and Rosa, P. (1998) The financing of male- and female-owned businesses. *Entrepreneurship and Regional Development*, **10**: 225–41.

Coleman, S. (2000) Access to capital and terms of credit: a comparison of men- and women-owned small businesses. *Journal of Small Business Management*, **38**(3): 37–52.

Fabowale, L., Orser, B. and Riding, A. (1995) Gender, structural factors, and credit terms between Canadian small businesses and financial institutions. *Entrepreneurship Theory and Practice*, **19**(4): 41–65.

Fay, M. and Williams, L. (1993) Gender bias and the availability of business loans. *Journal of Business Venturing*, **8**(4).

Greene, P.G., Brush, C.G., Hart, M.M. and Saparito, P. (1999) Exploration of the venture capital industry: is gender an issue? In P.D. Reynolds, W.D. Bygrave, S. Manigart, C.M. Mason, G.D. Meyer, H.J. Sapienza and K.G. Shaver (eds), *Frontiers of Entrepreneurship Research* (pp. 168–81). Babson Park, Wellesley, MA: Babson College.

Riding, A.L. and Swift, C.S. (1990) Women business owners and terms of credit: some empirical findings of the Canadian experience. *Journal of Business Venturing*, **5**(5): 327–40.

Family

Caputo, R.K. and Dolinsky, A. (1998) Women's choice to pursue self-employment: the role of financial and human capital of household members. *Journal of Small Business Management*, **36**(3): 8–17.

Cox, J.A. Moore, K.K. and Van Auken, P.M. (1984) Working couples in small business. *Journal of Small Business Management*, **22**(4): 25–30.

Dumas, C. (1992) Integrating the daughter into family business management. *Entrepreneurship Theory and Practice*, **16**(4): 41–55.

Marshack, K.J. (1994) Copreneurs and dual-career couples: are they different? *Entrepreneurship Theory and Practice*, **19**(1): 49–69.

Nelson, G.W. (1989) Factors of friendship: relevance of significant others to female business owners. *Entrepreneurship Theory and Practice*, **13**(4): 7–18.

Stoner, C.R., Hartman, R.I. and Arora, R. (1990) Work–home role conflict in female owners of small businesses: an exploratory study. *Journal of Small Business Management*, **29**(1): 30–38.

Performance

Anna, A.N., Chandler, G.N., Jansen, E. and Mero, N.P. (2000) Women business owners in traditional and non-traditional industries. *Journal of Business Venturing*, **15**(3): 279–303.

Boden, R.J. and Nucci, A.R. (2000) On the survival prospects of men's and women's new business ventures. *Journal of Business Venturing*, **15**(4): 347–62.

Buttner, E.H. and Moore, D.P. (1997) Women's organizational exodus to entrepreneurship: self-reported motivations and correlates with success. *Journal of Small Business Management*, January: 34–46.

Carter, N.M. and Allen, K.R. (1997) Size determinants of women-owned businesses: choice or barriers to resources? *Entrepreneurship and Regional Development*, **9**(3): 211–20.

Carter, N.M., Williams, M. and Reynolds, P.D. (1997) Discontinuance among new firms in retail: the influence of initial resources, strategy, and gender. *Journal of Business Venturing*, **12**(2): 125–45.

Chaganti, R. and Parasuraman, S. (1996) A study of the impacts of gender on business performance and management patterns in small business. *Entrepreneurship Theory and Practice*, **21**(2): 73–5.

Chell, E. and Baines, S. (1998) Does gender affect business 'performance'? A study of microbusinesses in business services in the UK. *Entrepreneurship and Regional Development*, **10**: 117–35.

Cliff, J.E. (1998) Does one size fit all? Exploring the relationship between attitudes towards growth, gender and business size. *Journal of Business Venturing*, **13**(6): 523–41.

Cuba, R., Decenzo, D. and Anish, A. (1983) Management practices of successful female business owners. *American Journal of Small Business*, **8**(2).

DuRietz, A. and Henrekson, M. (2000) Testing the female underperformance hypothesis. *Small Business Economics*, **14**(1): 1–10.

Fasci, M. A. and Valdez, J. (1998) A performance contrast of male- and female-owned small accounting practices. *Journal of Small Business Management*, **36**(3): 1–7.

Fischer, E.M., Reuber, A.R. and Dyke, L.S. (1993) A theoretical overview and extension of research on sex, gender and entrepreneurship. *Journal of Business Venturing*, **8**(2): 151–68.

Kalleberg, A.L. and Leicht, K.T. (1991) Gender and organizational performance: determinants of small business survival and success. *Academy of Management Journal*, **34**(1): 136–61.

Lerner, M., Brush, C. and Hisrich, R. (1997) Israeli women entrepreneurs: An examination of factors affecting performance. *Journal of Business Venturing*, **12**(4): 315–39.

Miskin, V. and Rose, J. (1990) Women entrepreneurs: factors related to success. In N.C. Churchill, W.D. Bygrave, J.A. Hornaday, D.F. Muzyka, K.H. Vesper and

W.W. Wetzel Jr (eds), *Frontiers of Entrepreneurship Research* (pp. 27–38). Babson Park, MA: Babson College.

Rosa, P., Hamilton, D., Carter, S. and Burns, H. (1994) The impact of gender on small business management: preliminary findings of a British study. *International Small Business Journal*, **12**(3): 25–32.

Attitudes towards entrepreneurship/intentions to start a business

Fagenson, E.A. and Marcus, E.C. (1991) Perceptions of the sex-role stereotypic characteristics of entrepreneurs: women's evaluations. *Entrepreneurship Theory and Practice*, **15**(4): 33–47.

Kourilsky, M.L. and Walstad, W.B. (1998) Entrepreneurship and female youth: knowledge, attitudes, gender differences and educational practices. *Journal of Business Venturing*, **13**(1): 77–88.

Matthews, C.H. and Moser, S.B. (1995) Family background and gender: implications for interest in small firm ownership. *Entrepreneurship and Regional Development*, **7**(4): 365–77.

Matthews, C.H. and Moser, S.B. (1996) A longitudinal investigation of the impact of family background and gender on interest in small business ownership. *Journal of Small Business Management*, **34**(2): 29–43.

Scherer, R.F., Brodzinsky, J.D. and Wiebe, F.A. (1990) Entrepreneur career selection and gender: a socialization approach. *Journal of Small Business Management*, **28**(2): 37–43.

Psychology

Bellu, R.R. (1993) Task role motivation and attributional styles as predictors of entrepreneurial performance: female sample findings. *Entrepreneurship and Regional Development*, **5**(4): 331–44.

Fagenson, E. (1993) Personal value systems of men and women: Entrepreneurs versus managers. *Journal of Business Venturing*, **8**(5): 409–30.

MacNabb, A., McCoy, J., Weinreich, P. and Northover, M. (1993) Using identity structure analysis (ISA) to investigate female entrepreneurship. *Entrepreneurship and Regional Development*, **5**(4): 301–13.

Masters, R. and Meier, R. (1988) Sex differences and risk-taking propensity of entrepreneurs. *Journal of Small Business Management*, **26**(1): 31–5.

Neider, L. (1987) A preliminary investigation of female entrepreneurs in Florida. *Journal of Small Business Management*, **25**(3): 22–9.

Sexton, D.L. and Bowman-Upton, N. (1990) Female and male entrepreneurs: psychological characteristics and their role in gender-related discrimination. *Journal of Business Venturing*, **5**(1): 29–36.

Management practice and strategy

Buttner, E.H. (2001) Examining female entrepreneurs' management style: an application of a relational frame. *Journal of Business Ethics*, **29**(3): 253–69.

Chaganti, R. (1986) Management in women-owned enterprises. *Journal of Small Business Management*, **24**(4): 19–29.

Olson, S.F. and Currie, H.M. (1992) Female entrepreneurs in a male-dominated industry: personal value systems and business strategies. *Journal of Small Business Management*, **30**(1): 49–57.

Van Auken, H.E., Rittenburg, T.L., Doran, B.M. and Hsieh, S.-F. (1994) An empirical analysis of advertising by women entrepreneurs. *Journal of Small Business Management*, **32**(3): 11–27.

Networking

Aldrich, H., Reese, P.R., Dubini, P., Rosen, B. and Woodward, B. (1989) Women on the verge of a breakthrough? Networking among entrepreneurs in the United States and Italy. In H. Brockhaus (ed.), *Frontiers of Entrepreneurship Research* (pp. 560–73), Babson Park, MA: Babson College.

Andre, R. (1992) A national profile of women's participation in networks of small business leaders. *Journal of Small Business Management*, **30**(1): 66–73.

Cromie, S. and Birley, S. (1992) Networking by female business owners in Northern Ireland. *Journal of Business Venturing*, **7**(3): 237–51.

Katz, J.A. and Williams, P.M. (1997) Gender, self-employment and weak-tie networking through formal organizations. *Entrepreneurship and Regional Development*, **9**(3): 183–97.

Smeltzer, L.R. and Fann, G.L. (1989) Gender differences in external networks of small business owner/managers. *Journal of Small Business Management*, **27**(2): 25–32.

Other

Baker, T., Aldrich, H.E. and Liou, N. (1997) Invisible entrepreneurs: the neglect of women business owners by mass media and scholarly journals in the USA. *Entrepreneurship and Regional Development*, **9**(3): 221–38.

Berg, N.G. (1997) Gender, place and entrepreneurship. *Entrepreneurship and Regional Development*, **9**(3): 259–68.

Birley, S. (1989) Female entrepreneurs: are they really different? *Journal of Small Business Management*, **27**(1): 1–37.

Brush, C.G. (1992) Research on Women Business Owners: Past Trends, a New Perspective and Future Directions. *Entrepreneurship, Theory and Practice*, **16**(4): 5–30.

Brush, C.G. (1997) Women-owned businesses: obstacles and opportunities. *Journal of Developmental Entrepreneurship*, **2**(1): 1–24.

Moore, D. (1990) An examination of present research on the female entrepreneur – suggested research strategies for the 1990s. *Journal of Business Ethics*, **9**(4–5): 275–81.

Nilsson, P. (1997) Business counselling services directed towards female entrepreneurs – some legitimacy dilemmas. *Entrepreneurship and Regional Development*, **9**(3): 239–58.

Stevenson, L. (1990) Some methodological problems associated with researching women entrepreneurs. *Journal of Business Ethics*, **9**(4–5): 439–46.

Stevenson, L.A. (1986) Against all odds: the entrepreneurship of women. *Journal of Small Business Management*, **24**(4): 30–36.

Walker, D. and Joyner, B. (1999) Female entrepreneurship and the market process: gender-based public policy considerations. *Journal of Developmental Entrepreneurship*, **4**(2): 95–116.

Personal background and firm characteristics

Birley, S., Moss, C. and Saunders, P. (1987) Do women entrepreneurs require different training? *American Journal of Small Business*, **12**(1).

Carter, R.B., Van Auken, H.E. and Harms, M.B. (1992) Home-based businesses in the rural United States economy, differences in gender and financing. *Entrepreneurship and Regional Development*, **4**(3): 245–57.

Dant, R.P., Brush, C.G. and Iniesta, F.P. (1996) Participation patterns of women in franchising. *Journal of Small Business Management*, **34**(2): 14–28.

Dolinsky, A. (1993) The effects of education on business ownership: a longitudinal study of women. *Entrepreneurship Theory and Practice*, **18**(1): 43–53.

Hisrish, R.D. and Brush, C. (1984) The woman entrepreneur: management skills and business problems. *Journal of Small Business Management*, **22**(1): 30–37.

Holmquist, C. and Sundin E. (1990) What's special about highly educated women entrepreneurs? *Entrepreneurship and Regional Development*, **2**, 181–93.

Maysami, R.C. and Goby, V.P. (1999) Female business owners in Singapore and elsewhere: a review of studies. *Journal of Small Business Management*, **37**(2): 96–105.

Rosa, P. and Hamilton, D. (1994) Gender and ownership in UK small firms. *Entrepreneurship theory and practice*, **18**(3): 11–27.

Scott, C.E. (1986) Why more women are becoming entrepreneurs. *Journal of Small Business Management*, **24**(4): 37–44.

Shabbir, A. and Di Gregorio, S. (1996) An examination of the relationship between women's personal goals and structural factors influencing their decision to start a business: the case of Pakistan. *Journal of Business Venturing*, **11**(6): 507–29.

Shim, S. and Eastlick, M.A. (1998) Characteristics of Hispanic female business owners: an exploratory study. *Journal of Small Business Management*, **36**(3): 18–34.

Spilling, O.R. and Berg, N.G. (2000) Gender and small business management: the case of Norway in the 1990s. *International Small Business Journal*, **18**(2): 38–59.

Zapalska, A. (1997) A profile of woman entrepreneurs and enterprises in Poland. *Journal of Small Business Management*, **35**(4): 76–82.

Start-up process

Alsos, G.A. and Ljunggren, E. (1998) Does the business start-up process differ by gender? A longitudinal study of nascent entrepreneurs. In P. Reynolds, W.D. Bygrave, N.M. Carter, S. Manigart, C.M. Mason, G. Dale Meyer and K.G. Shaver (eds), *Frontiers of Entrepreneurship Research* (pp. 137–51). Babson Park, MA: Babson College.

Goffee, R. and Scase, R. (1983) Business ownership and women's subordination: a preliminary study of female proprietors. *The Sociological Review*, **31**: 625–48.

Kolvereid, L., Shane, S. and Westhead, P. (1993) Is it equally difficult for female entrepreneurs to start businesses in all countries? *Journal of Small Business Management*, **31**(4): 43–51.

Marlow, S. (1997) Self-employed women – new opportunities, old challenges? *Entrepreneurship and Regional Development*, **9**(3): 199–210.

Nelson, G.W. (1987) Information needs of female entrepreneurs. *Journal of Small Business Management*, **25**(1): 38–44.

Pellegrino, E.T. and Reece, B.L. (1982) Perceived formative and operational problems encountered by female entrepreneurs in retail and service firms. *Journal of Small Business Management*, **20**(2): 15–24.

Shane, S., Kolvereid, L. and Westhead, P. (1991) An exploratory examination of the reasons leading to new firm foundation across country and gender. *Journal of Business Venturing*, **6**(6): 431–46.

PART III

GAINING SPEED

10 Sampling in entrepreneurial settings
Helle Neergaard

Why is sampling important?

Fifteen years ago VanderWerf and Brush (1989) berated what they called 'the inconsistencies in research methods' in entrepreneurship research, particularly in the sampling of units of analysis (ibid.: 49). Their survey of sampling procedures used in entrepreneurship found that the three most used criteria for selecting units of analysis were that (i) units were new, (ii) in a particular industry or (iii) of small size. In samples of individuals the first three criteria used were (a) the founder, (b) the owner or (c) the manager of the business. Further, they found that 'convenience of data collection or focus on a particular aspect of entrepreneurship' (ibid.: 50) was decisive for sampling units of analysis. Lacking a general directive for achieving sample comparability, they suggested that, at the very least, the reasons for sampling specific units should be made explicit since 'explicit sample characteristics can unravel apparent contradictions in empirical results' (ibid.: 52). Indeed, the sample selection process has a profound effect on the ultimate assessment of quality of the research findings.

A further argument for paying particular attention to sampling issues is the need to publish. Since reviewers are not generally sensitive to qualitative methods and approaches, and often reject papers on lack of sufficient detail and rigour concerning the methodology used (Gartner and Birley 2002), it is essential to be careful, systematic and explicit about procedures. In their introduction to the *Journal of Business Venturing* 2002 special issue on qualitative methods in entrepreneurship research Gartner and Birley state, 'We believe that quantitative research has tended to drive out what for us would often seem to be common sense . . .' (ibid.: 388), continuing, 'The rules and procedures for engaging in quantitative research are . . . institutionalized and accepted as the standard for how academic scholars will agree that finding is a fact, rather than opinion.' This suggests that in order to argue the qualities of qualitative research it is necessary to agree on some common rules and procedures.

However, sampling procedures in qualitative research are neither as rigidly nor as systematically prescribed as in quantitative studies, and the lack of clear guidelines on the principles of sampling can cause confusion (Coyne 1997). Nevertheless, it is an important issue to address since the lack of a sufficient description of the sampling strategy used in a study makes interpretation of findings difficult and affects the opportunity for replication of the study in other settings (Kitson et al. 1982). This chapter seeks to remedy that shortcoming with particular attention to entrepreneurship research. The chapter will begin by highlighting the difficulties in sampling entrepreneurs and their ventures. This will then be related to entrepreneurship research in an overview of the sampling strategies used in a sample of 47 abstracts from the Babson–Kauffman Entrepreneurship Research Conference (BKERC) 2002. It will continue with an analysis of journal articles published in four peer-reviewed entrepreneurship journals. This will be succeeded by an overview of the sampling strategies available and accounting for their merits and drawbacks. In conclusion, the chapter discusses the challenges in determining how a sample should be constructed.

Difficulties in sampling entrepreneurs and their ventures

Although the choice of research strategy (qualitative or quantitative) should in theory always be guided by the purpose of the inquiry, there are three major difficulties concerning sampling that are particularly pertinent to entrepreneurship research and which may influence the choice of a qualitative over a quantitative strategy:

- Populations are not easily identified
- Populations tend to be very small
- Obtaining access to proprietary databases.

Identification of populations

According to Kuzel (1999), true random sampling assumes knowledge sufficient to define a larger population from which the sample can be drawn. Aldrich (1991: 208) criticizes entrepreneurship researchers for being 'remarkably careless in identifying a population from which to draw a sample'. However, this may often be a nearly impossible task; for example Mankelow and Merrilees (2001) report that researching rural small businesses was difficult because there were no published statistics on the characteristics of these businesses and they were not included in existing studies. Further, there may be legal restrictions on combining data from various databases; for example in Denmark, the National Bureau of Statistics registers all the newly founded businesses but not the identity of who owns them. Although these data can be found in the enterprise register, these two databases cannot be combined due to legislative protection of privacy. Thus a researcher seeking to identify all the newly registered businesses has to go through all the firms in the enterprise register one by one. A very time-consuming activity! A similar obstacle is encountered when trying to identify all the newly founded ventures in, for example, information and communications technology. Although data exist on how many new ventures are established in a given industry in a given year, the specifics of these businesses cannot be divulged. Another example involves the identification of business angels. Such individuals want to protect their anonymity, as they would otherwise be inundated with requests for support (Carter et al. 2003). A research inquiry may therefore have to resort to newspaper articles, word of mouth or other secondary sources in order to identify ventures to investigate. Such a process may be both time-consuming and costly, and fail to identify all business angels, and therefore invites qualitative investigation, which might utilize snowball or chain sampling for circumventing the problem since in these forms of sampling it is not necessary to know the exact population size up front in order to construct a sample.

Size of population
In many countries the previous problem is augmented by the fact that the population of entrepreneurs is not sufficiently large to provide a basis for quantitative analysis and comparison, particularly if the research aims to study a particular subgroup of entrepreneurs, such as a specific industry or, for example, female or academic entrepreneurs, or the research is restricted to studying the entrepreneurial process in newly founded firms, say within a time frame of three to five years. Further, many countries are divided into states or regions that are also often used to delimit the research but provide similar size restrictions. In such instances, choosing a qualitative approach may be preferable, since attempting to undertake statistical analysis on very small samples will provide neither valid nor reliable nor generalizable results. Kemery (1988) found that much research in entrepreneurship downplays or ignores the importance of methodological detail, such as sample size. However, in the case of the women-owned businesses, for example, Carter and Rosa (1998) point out that a random stratified sample would probably not yield enough women for satisfactory statistical analysis. Additionally, in the pharmaceutical industry, the population of ventures founded each year on a European level is so small that a sample of say 100 enterprises in a single country over a period of five years would constitute the whole population (EFPIA 2000). Indeed, Gibb (1992) argues that finding a representative sample is rarely possible in small firm research given the small total populations.

Access to proprietary databases
The last challenge that may lead to a qualitative rather than a quantitative research design concerns gaining access to relevant databases collected by

governments and private or public organizations. Many of these are proprietary and the researcher will therefore have to pay – often prohibitive amounts – for accessing the information required. As research funding is often difficult to obtain, this constitutes a significant obstacle.

Qualitative research as the preferred choice

Most entrepreneurship research is either variables-oriented and quantitative or case-oriented and qualitative. Whilst quantitative research strategies pursue generality, qualitative approaches and designs help elucidate and explain complexity. It is therefore a misconception that qualitative research is a fallback option or only appropriate for the exploratory phase of a research project in a pilot study. Because of the above problems in sampling, however, choosing a qualitative approach may for some be a 'second choice'. For those who believe that qualitative research provides insight that cannot be achieved through quantitative means, qualitative research methods and techniques are preferred above other alternatives. Nevertheless, qualitative studies in entrepreneurship have a tendency to select cases in ways that mirror the random sampling found in quantitative research.

An analysis of 210 abstracts accepted for presentation at BKERC 2002 revealed that of all abstracts purporting a qualitative method, an account of formal sampling rules was frequently lacking in the abstracts (see the introduction to this book for a further description). Notably, abstracts were very short (limited to one page), but when explication was given, it revealed a choice of cases and informants based on 'convenience' sampling rather than purposive sampling. Of the 47 abstracts reporting the use of either in-depth interviews or cases, only 16 (one-third) stated that they had sampled their cases purposefully. Twenty-two abstracts reported that they had used random sampling[1] and nine did not provide any reason at all. This raises the question whether the pattern found in the BKERC abstracts is symptomatic of articles that are sent to mainstream journals. If this is the case, a high rejection rate is likely as the lack of rigour in sampling design, quantitative or qualitative, is tantamount to rejection (cf. Bygrave, Chapter 1 and Brush, Chapter 18 in this volume). Therefore, an investigation of the actual pattern of qualitative publication in mainstream peer-reviewed journals was undertaken.

Journal publications

A search on the EBSCO database including the words 'entrepreneurship' and 'qualitative' limited to scholarly (peer-reviewed) journals from 1995 to 2003 gave 34 hits distributed on 22 different journals. Based on the highest number of hits, the following four journals were chosen for further analysis: *Entrepreneurship Theory and Practice* (*ETP*), *Journal of Business Venturing* (*JBV*), *Entrepreneurship and Regional Development* (*ERD*), and finally *Journal of Developmental Entrepreneurship* (*JDE*). Although *Qualitative Market Research* and *Qualitative Sociology* revealed a high number of hits too, these were excluded for two reasons: first, they do not qualify as 'mainstream entrepreneurship journals'. Second, due to their title they were judged as biased towards qualitative research. However, their appearance in the search suggests that qualitative research within entrepreneurship is being published elsewhere, so maybe the outlook is not so depressing after all. All remaining journals (16) only featured with one hit.

The next step was a search of each journal using combinations of the words entrepreneur, entrepreneurship, qualitative, case, case study, case studies, and interview. I chose to use more search terms for this search in order to capture all articles that used some variety of qualitative methods. The search revealed that *JBV*[2] published 16 articles, *ERD* 15 articles and *JDE*[3] 14 articles using some form of qualitative method in the period. *ETP* published 11 qualitative articles in the nine-year period.

Following the search, all articles were downloaded in full text format. A reading of the articles revealed a number of problems with the search criteria, however. For example, the words 'case', 'case study' and 'case studies' yielded a number of hits that were teaching cases, which are generally exemplars of certain traits such as *Zandiger!* (Tompson 2003) and *Roustam Tariko: Russian Entrepreneur* (Sandberg 2003). However, they constitute a special type of case: what Patton (1990) would denote 'a typical case'. The purpose of a typical case is to describe and illustrate a situation or situations that are typical for an audience who need to recognize such situations in practice. Nine such teaching cases were found in the sample, distributed fairly equally across the four journals. Further, a 'case study' may also use fully structured questionnaires, and three such articles were identified. Even though they are case studies, they do not qualify as qualitative studies. Further, the word 'interview' yielded three articles in which interviews were used synonymously with fully structured interviews distributed face to face. Moreover, six articles were purely *conceptual*. Additionally, some studies *combined* qualitative research designs with questionnaires. Eight such articles were identified. Three articles in the sample were *reviews* of existing research in the field, hence only referring to qualitative studies. Finally, one article was based on *archival* research, and one was the introduction to a special issue. Only a total of 30 purely qualitative articles were identified in the nine-year period. These were defined as studies using, for example, grounded theory, in-depth interviews or ethnographic methods. The final results are shown in Figure 10.1. It should be noted that the review might suffer from what McDonald et al. (2004) call

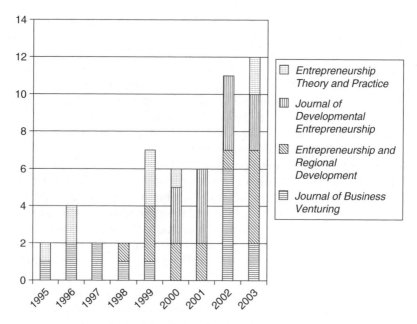

Figure 10.1   Publication of qualitative research in four journals 1995–2003

stochastic variation.[4] Even with these reservations, the acceptance of articles using qualitative research methods either on their own or in combination seems to be on the increase. See also Tables 10A.1–10A.4 in appendix for a full list and categorization of the articles reviewed.

A closer investigation of the contents of the methodology described reveals that a common feature of most of these articles is a very thorough description of and argumentation for selection of cases or informants to interview, even if these were sampled randomly. However, the older the articles, the more limited was the justification for the methodological procedure.

The next section offers an overview of the various ways in which cases may be sampled, since the most urgent problem seems to be that there are no universally agreed-upon standards for how to sample cases and informants (Coyne 1997).

An overview of sampling strategies
Although many authors have provided various overviews of sampling strategies used in qualitative research, for example Goetz and Lecompte (1984), Lincoln and Guba (1985) Strauss and Corbin (1990), Morse (1991) and Sandelowski (1995), Patton (1990) was probably the first to provide a

thorough description of a large number of options for sampling cases or informants purposefully. Patton argued that 'nothing better captures the difference between quantitative and qualitative methods than the logics that undergird sampling approaches' (1990: 169). However, the literature on sampling uses the terms purposeful, selective, and theoretical sampling interchangeably. So the first point of debate is to elucidate this apparent discrepancy.

According to Gilchrist and Williams (1999), there are basically two approaches to identifying which sampling strategy is relevant for any particular study. The first approach is theory driven, the second is data driven. The choice hinges on the paradigm in which the research is grounded. Theory-driven research results from 'the use of prior theoretical knowledge in constructing a framework' (Johnson 1990: 24) in which the decision on sampling is made prior to the beginning of the study according to a preconceived, but reasonable, set of criteria, also termed selective sampling (Sandelowski et al. 1992). Data-driven research, on the other hand, generally does not have an explicit theoretical framework up front; instead new units are sampled as the need occurs, leading to the discovery of new theoretical categories, hence the term theoretical sampling as described in, for example, grounded theory (Glaser and Strauss 1967). Purposeful sampling, a term coined by Patton (1990), goes to the link between sampling strategy and the purpose of a research project. Therefore purposeful sampling can be perceived as an umbrella term covering both theoretical and selective sampling (Coyne 1997). The difference is the timing in the selection of the cases: whether they are selected *a priori* or as the research unfolds.

Sample size

The second point of debate is the number of cases deemed necessary. According to Sandelowski (1995), the adequacy of sample size is relative in qualitative research, unlike quantitative research in which a minimum of 100 respondents is often cited as necessary for valid statistical analysis. In qualitative research it is a matter of judging the optimum size for the intended purpose of the study. In many cases the sample sizes are too small to support claims of having achieved redundancy (Lincoln and Guba 1985) or saturation (Eisenhardt 1989), because in practice it can be difficult to determine whether the point of redundancy or saturation has been reached and inexperience, lack of time, resources or difficulty in negotiating access may lead the researcher to stop sampling prematurely. Further, knowing when to stop sampling is a faculty that is acquired through experience. Indeed, the researcher may often obtain all the data needed through the very first case or informant, but does not know this until more are collected (Sandelowski 1995). On the other hand, some researchers refer to the 'myth of saturation', arguing that when saturation is reached it is not uncommon to look for confirmation of findings from other cases, only to find that the experience reported by these adds a new perspective to those originally reported. In reality, 'there are a myriad of experiences that may or may not be pertinent or significant, and only the researcher is in a position to decide whether new information is significant' (Morse 1991: 141). This problem may be addressed by applying various 'tests of goodness' of the sampling method, for example tests for appropriateness and adequacy (Morse 1991). According to Morse, an appropriate sample is guided by whether informant/case sampling facilitates understanding of the research problem. However, Kuzel (1999: 37) argues that 'issues of appropriateness begin with a consideration of whether the researcher is using an appropriate paradigm'. Adequacy refers to the sufficiency and quality of the data obtained. The researcher thus has to assess the relevance, completeness and amount of information obtained. There should be no thin areas (Kuzel 1999) (see also Chapters 15 and 16 in this volume for information on how to assess the quality of qualitative research).

Levels of sampling
The third issue of debate concerns levels of sampling. In many studies the researcher has to contemplate sampling on more than one level. A case may be defined as an individual, a small group (e.g. an organization or a sub-group within an organization), a larger group (e.g. an organization or an industry) or even an event (e.g. venture foundation or dissolution) or a process of events (Yin 1989). An informant, on the other hand, is defined as 'the individual who provides information' (Gilchrist and Williams 1999).

For example, at the industry level, the researcher has to decide whether the sample should be found within one industry or across two or more industries, for example ICT and life sciences. What is to be gained from a cross-sectional sample? If a matched sample needs to be obtained, for example comparing mature and new businesses, selecting cases across industries would be like comparing apples and pears. Although they may have generic commonalities (both are fruits, both grow on trees), the species are different. At the company level such variables as number of employees, turnover, organization structure and ownership may be used to create either homogeneity or heterogeneity in the sample. At the individual level, demographic variables such as gender, ethnic origin, age, education, experience, position (founder/owner/manager/expert) may be used as selection criteria. Moreover, specific subgroups may be chosen for analysis. The important issue here is that argumentation for sampling specific units has to be deliberated at all levels and not just one! In qualitative research these become analytic rather than theoretical variables (Sandelowski 1995) because they are selected by virtue of a specific characteristic that enables them to provide certain kinds of information pertinent to the study; for example, in studies of gender differences in entrepreneurial behaviour, a sample needs to be obtained that includes both men and women. However, according to Sandelowski (1995: 181), these variables should only be used when they are deemed 'analytically important and where the failure to sample for such variation would impede understanding or invalidate the subsequent findings'. In order to provide some order to this confusion, the following subsection outlines some guidelines for purposeful sampling.

Sampling strategies
Table 10.1 provides a systematic overview of 20 different sampling strategies and the logic and purpose underlying each sampling strategy. Each approach serves a somewhat different purpose. Most of these have been gleaned from a number of different sources and subsequently categorized, with Patton (1990) as the dominant source. Others have been named following the logic of a sampling procedure that I have come across in my research (e.g. matched and linked cases). The various strategies have then been categorized into seven major categories. Each of the sub-categories will be briefly explained in the following, but the explanations serve as inspiration only. For in-depth discussions readers should consult the original works.

Hofer and Bygrave's article (1992: 94) serves to illustrate the link between research design and sampling strategy; for example a study of 'representative exemplars' would seek out 'typical cases'; a study of 'best exemplars' would attempt to identify 'extreme or deviant cases' and 'event sampling' would be used in a study undertaking 'longitudinal comparisons to identify causal linkages'. The following provides a more detailed description of each sampling strategy while also attempting to illustrate with examples from the entrepreneurship literature where these can be found.

Unique or typical case characteristics

- Extreme and deviant cases are often used to drive home a point in a dramatic manner. They may be defined as particularly problematic or successful examples of a phenomenon, for example how to manage organizational change in a fast-growing technology-based venture. The logic is that lessons may be learned that are transferable to improving more typical organizations. In other words, extreme or deviant cases are often seen as 'best practice' cases (Patton 1990; Yin 1989).
- Typical cases are the exact opposite. The aim of such cases is to describe and illustrate what is typical. As mentioned previously,

Table 10.1   Sampling strategies and their characteristics

Categories	Sampling strategy	Logic and purpose
Unique or typical characteristics	Extreme/deviant	Unusual manifestations of the phenomenon to be studied
	Typical	Highlight what is normal or average
	Revelatory	Illustrates common problems
	Intensity	Manifests the phenomenon intensely but not extremely
	Critical	Challenge to existing theory
	Politically important	Attract attention/avoid unwanted attention
Small or great variation	Maximum variation	Document variation and identify patterns of commonality
	Stratification	Illustrate subgroups
	Matched	Comparison of cases that are alike
	Homogeneous	Focus/reduce variation. Facilitates group interviewing
Reference based	Expert/key informant	Define the research field
Specific theoretical	Criterion	Identify regularity; exemplify processes
basis	Theory based	Build upon/exemplify/test a theoretical construct/concept
Event	Critical incident	Describe development processes
Sequential	Snowball or chain	Identify unknown, information-rich sources
	Confirming/ disconfirming	Seek exceptions, variation from the outset
	Opportunistic	Follow unexpected new leads
	Linked	Historical/process interest
Random choice	Convenience	Lack of knowledge/resources
	Random purposeful	Large number of cases to choose from

Source: Based on sampling strategies suggested by Flanagan (1954), Patton (1990), Strauss and Corbin (1990), Miles and Huberman (1994), Sandelowski (1995).

teaching cases are predominantly typical cases so that students can draw inferences to theory about, for example, how founding teams are constructed and can discuss the advantages or disadvantages of various choices (Patton 1990). A number of such cases can be found in the appendix to this chapter.

- Revelatory cases may be seen as a subspecies of typical cases. They are described by Yin (1989) as opportunities to observe and analyse a phenomenon previously inaccessible to scientific investigation even though the problems encountered in these cases are common to a larger group. Such a case could be concerned with, for example, angel financing.

- Intensity sampling involves the same logic as extreme sampling, but with less focus on the extreme (Patton 1990). Whereas extreme cases may distort the manifestation of a particular phenomenon, intensity sampling seeks examples that are remarkable in some way. The choice of an intensity case often requires considerable knowledge of the case up front in order to determine whether it does manifest the phenomenon intensely; for example, in a current research project, a nanotechnology venture showed the remarkable ability to spawn new ideas which were then spun out into new, independent businesses. An in-depth study of this case may therefore constitute central inspiration to other new ventures.
- A critical case is identified by asking the question: 'if it happens here, it can happen anywhere' or oppositely 'if it does not happen here, it is not going to happen anywhere' (Patton 1990). A critical case is often used to challenge preconceived ideas or existing theory (Yin 1989). In entrepreneurship, a critical case could be used to test the applicability of, for example, personality trait theory.
- A variation of the critical case strategy involves the choice of politically sensitive or important cases (Patton 1990). The choice of a political case can be directed by the wish to attract political attention to a certain aspect of entrepreneurship, for example micro/peer lending programmes as described in Kibria et al. (2003). In this study the authors conduct in-depth interviews with 17 members of the nonprofit organization Working Capital. Although the case appears as a politically sensitive case, the informants were chosen according to the maximum variation strategy described below. However, it should be stressed that politically sensitive cases will always be subject to ethical considerations, as the researcher has an obligation to be 'true' to the case even if it is not in line with the political agenda.

Small or great variation across cases

- According to Patton (1990), the advantage of using a maximum variation strategy is that 'any common patterns that emerge from great variation are of particular interest and value in capturing the core experiences and central, shared aspects' (ibid.: 172). A further advantage of the maximum variation strategy is that the data collection and analysis should yield both high-quality detailed descriptions of each case, which are useful for documenting uniqueness, as well as important shared patterns that derive their significance from having emerged out of heterogeneity (Patton 1990). Additionally, the maximum variation strategy increases the robustness of the findings (Herriott and Firestone 1983). This is possibly why maximum variation is by far the most popular strategy with entrepreneurship researchers. Exemplars of the use of maximum variation strategy can be found in, for example, Anderson (2000), Jack and Anderson (2002), Fadahunsi and Rosa (2002), Lechner and Dowling (2003) and Neergaard (2005).

- Stratification is a 'subspecies' of maximum variation sampling and is often used in conjunction with typical case sampling (Patton 1990). Stratified sampling aims at identifying cases that are, for example, above average, average and below average. Contrary to maximum variation, stratified sampling aims at catching major differences rather than commonalities, which means that the focus is on detecting the contingent premises. Each stratum constitutes a relatively homogeneous section of cases.

- Matched cases mean that a researcher compares pairs of cases, i.e. two and two, three and three etc. A matched pair would, for example, be found within the same industry and then differentiated on various analytical variables. However, it is not possible to construct a matched pair by choosing, for example, two large ventures from the biotech industry and two small ventures from the ICT industry. Comparing successful with unsuccessful firms or starters with non-starters within the same industry would on the other hand constitute a matched sample. This is a strategy which is often used in entrepreneurship (see e.g. Kodithuwakku and Rosa 2002). The advantage of such a sample is that it may be possible to detect which factors lead to success or failure respectively.

- Homogeneous cases constitute the direct opposite to maximum variation (Patton 1990). This strategy is predominantly used to describe some particular subgroup and/or topic in depth, for example how media influences women's inclination to start a business (topic: media influence on subgroup: aspiring female entrepreneurs) (Neergaard and Smith 2004). The selection of informants for focus group interviews is typically based on the principle of homogeneity.

Reference-based selection

- It may be difficult to distinguish expert from key informant selection, because basically key informants may also be experts. However, as a rule of thumb experts are generally used in the beginning of a project to help define the boundaries of an investigation or provide ideas about what cases may be chosen (starting off the snowball or chain selection) or at the end of the project to provide insight and information, and supplement the results obtained (e.g. to help interpret focus groups results).

- Key informants, on the other hand, are 'ideal' informants in a study. Most researchers have at some point in their career come across an informant who was very reticent and reserved. According to Tremblay (1957), key informants may be chosen according to criteria such as willingness and ability to communicate or cooperate, and impartiality; in other words they are good interview subjects. Key informants may be selected on reference from, for example, the owner–manager of a firm who can identify employees within the organization with the specialized knowledge that the researcher needs.

Specific theoretical basis

- The logic of criterion sampling is to study cases based on a predefined criterion of importance (Patton 1990). Their ability to elucidate major systems or programme weaknesses based on which these may be improved; for example an understanding of why initiatives to help increase the number of ethnic minority businesses are ineffective may provide opportunity for programme or system improvement. Further, critical events, discussed below, may also constitute a criterion. This is often used in process studies.
- Theory-based (selective) sampling is a more formal version of criterion sampling. The researcher identifies specific theoretical constructs and selects cases or informants, even time periods, on the basis of their potential to manifest or elucidate the chosen constructs. Such sampling is typical of theory-driven research (Johnson 1990; Sandelowski et al. 1992).

Event-based selection

- Using critical incidents or events can both be a sampling strategy and an interviewing technique (Flanagan 1954). When used as a sampling strategy it is important to theoretically define *a priori* what constitutes an event; for example a critical event in a study on how growth is influenced by the provision of external capital could be constituted by the number of capital injections received. When used as a technique either (a) the informants are asked to define what they perceive as critical incidents, or (b) the researcher identifies critical events *ex post*. Critical incident or event sampling is often used in studies of development processes or in inter-organizational network studies to explore the underlying mechanisms that influence the networking processes (Huggins 2000) but the technique has also been applied in a study, for example by Sundbo et al. (2001) to investigate role changes in international franchising.

Sequential cases

- Snowball or chain sampling aims at identifying cases that are rich in information about a particular subject. This strategy is often combined with reference-based selection in which the first informants are experts in the particular topic under investigation, and who therefore have the knowledge to point the researcher in the direction of which case/s or informant/s may constitute exemplars of the subject of interest (Patton 1990). The process begins by asking the experts identified 'who knows a lot about X?' All informants are asked 'who else can I speak to about this?' and the snowball grows. The chain of informants will typically be very varied in the beginning but then start to converge and at the end concentrate on a very few cases/informants. Snowballing is typically used when it is difficult to identify the population from which to select informants.
- Confirming/disconfirming case selection is a strategy often used in iterative theory-building, theory-testing designs or data-driven research. Confirming cases are examples which fit into the already emerging pattern; they enrich the study, give it greater depth, and increase the trustworthiness of the study. Disconfirming cases are examples that do not fit the emerging pattern. Hence they constitute a source of rival explanations of the patterns, whence they delimit the explanatory power of the emerging theory (Patton 1990).
- Contrary to most of the other types of sampling discussed here that depend on some prior knowledge of the setting to be investigated, 'opportunistic sampling takes advantage of whatever unfolds as it unfolds' (Patton 1990). Field research often involves making on-the-spot decisions about sampling either new cases or new informants, and one of the primary advantages of qualitative research over quantitative research is the opportunity to follow unexpected new leads. Opportunistic sampling is often used in grounded theory studies.
- Linked cases may involve, for example, three generations of business owners, in which the process from establishment to current date needs to be investigated. For example succession constitutes a major problem in family firms and survival may be linked to how networks

are handed down from one generation to the next (Tidaasen 2000). The argument for calling them linked is that each often has distinguishing characteristics but the actions and events taking place in the latter cases are dependent on the former – in other words there is a path-dependence. Linked cases are chosen for their ability to elucidate a given development process in a historical perspective.

Random choice

- Convenience sampling entails that the researcher chooses cases in the proximity of the university or cases that it is easy to obtain access to because an organization member is related or other such reasons. This strategy, however, is neither purposeful nor strategic, and leads to bias! The only exceptions when convenience sampling is acceptable are (a) if the population is very homogeneous or (b) if informal, social networks constitute the only means for identifying and selecting cases or informants, for example, 15 informants selected were former students. For the same reason it is also sometimes referred to as 'network sampling' (Kimball and Partridge 1979), but basically, both convenience and random sampling should be avoided in qualitative studies, if at all possible.
- Patton (1990) does not actually reject random purpose sampling, arguing that for many audiences such sampling substantially increases the credibility of the results. However, as the results will neither be representative nor generalizable, it totally defeats the objective and the argument seems to fall apart. Indeed, according to Hofer and Bygrave (1992: 95), 'purposive sampling . . . should be among the more frequently used sampling techniques in the field, whereas *random sampling* should be among the least used techniques' (emphasis added).

Single-case versus multi-case study strategy

Different kinds of sampling require different minimum sample sizes. The choice depends on the purpose of the study. A single, isolated case study often uses the critical case sampling strategy to test, challenge or extend existing theory.

However, the single case study may also be constituted by an extreme or unique case which reveal a rare phenomenon. The danger of an isolated case study strategy is that the case may turn out not to be quite as critical, extreme or unique as first assumed. Further, even a single case may also be 'linked'. Table 10.2 provides an overview of the sampling strategies and the number of cases involved in a typical investigation.

Table 10.2   Relationship between sampling strategy and type of inquiry

Single case	Single- or multi-case	Multi case
Intensity	Typical	Maximum variation
Critical	Politically important	Stratification
Extreme/deviant/unique	Expert/key informant	Matched
	Criterion	Homogeneous
	Critical incident	Theory based
	Opportunistic	Snowball/chain
	Convenience	Confirming/ disconfirming
	Random purposeful	Linked

Whilst isolated cases help investigate a specific problem in depth, a multiple case design helps strengthen confidence in the precision, validity and stability of the result because repetition of the same procedure across a number of cases helps eliminate accidental similarities between theory and case. It should be noted that Yin (1989) exclusively associates the multiple case design with a replication logic rather than a sampling logic. This approach is typically used in a purely theory-building (e.g. grounded theory) or iterative theory-building/theory-testing designs in a critical realist perspective. A multiple case study often highlights complementary aspects of a phenomenon. It is a bit like a jigsaw puzzle: by putting individual pieces together, a more holistic picture is obtained. A common question in this situation is 'how many cases do I need?' Maximum variation tends to require the largest minimum sample size because variation in itself makes it difficult to achieve saturation. However, it is not decisive how many cases are involved, but rather that they are explicitly chosen in a systematic and stringent fashion. Although by far the majority of sampling strategies are associated with multiple case studies, a number of strategies may be used with either single or multiple case studies, such as reference-based and event-based sampling.

Both single cases and multi-case studies may be *embedded* (Yin 1989) or *nested* (Miles and Huberman 1994). This type of case study is a bit like a babushka nesting doll. It contains several 'units' of analysis within the same case and requires several steps of selection. First the main case is selected. This is followed by a selection of the various units to be studied within the case, for example various management levels. Finally, the informants at each level need to be chosen, for example a manager and an employee representative, depending on the purpose of the study. Obviously, if the problem to be studied only involves managers, employee representatives are irrelevant – unless of course the interviews with management reveal that employees are in some way influential. In that case, the researcher will be following unexpected new leads and undertaking opportunistic sampling. That is in fact the strength of qualitative research: the ability to react to new information revealed by the field and include it to build an even stronger argument. However, in this type of study it is crucial to remember that the 'doll' needs to be put back together at the end, so that the analysis does not become an analysis of the parts but of the whole.

It is quite common not to use a single case sampling strategy in isolation. Often several strategies are combined in the same study in order to reach the best choice of cases; for example criterion sampling may be combined with maximum variation sampling in order to increase the robustness of the findings. Reference-based sampling is probably the strategy which may be used in conjunction with most other strategies. Further, when selecting cases and informants at two or more levels, a different strategy is usually applied for each level.

Negotiating access
When a sampling strategy has been decided upon, the researcher encounters the more practical problem of negotiating access to particular cases. Purposeful sampling means just that: the researcher chooses precisely those cases that will yield the most useful information for that particular inquiry given the research question(s). One advantage of dealing with entrepreneurs rather than long-term business owners or managers is that they are often very pleased with their achievements and therefore more than willing to narrate their stories. However, overcoming the suspicion of some entrepreneurs may present a severe problem (see Chapter 12 in this volume for an example). If an entrepreneur fears that his/her venture is easily identifiable as a case in a publication, this may prevent participation in the research project despite all promises of anonymity. Further, entrepreneurship in information communications technology, life sciences and nanotechnology has recently become a very 'hot' research topic, and since these populations are very small, new ventures have been overwhelmed with interest. Hence they may reject participation in inquiries for 'lack of time'. Time is a sensitive issue with entrepreneurs since they often work incredibly long hours, so asking them to give you an hour or more of their time requires very careful negotiation and understanding. Ultimately, the sum of the objections may lead to selecting an 'inferior' case in terms of the potential information to be gained about the particular topic to be investigated. Even if that is the situation, the researcher should still account fully for the sampling process in the research report.

Choosing the 'right' strategy
It is, however, not always easy to determine which sampling strategy to use. Some researchers suggest that certain types of sampling and sample sizes

are favoured in certain types of qualitative research (Morse 1994; Cresswell 1998), others that the purpose of the inquiry directs the choice of sampling strategy (Patton 1990; Maxwell 1996). This tends to be a very personal choice. Further, even the experts whom I have drawn upon here for the above categorization disagree on the terminology; for example Strauss and Corbin (1990) operate with four types of sampling in grounded theory: open, relational, variational and discriminate sampling.

Open sampling takes place in the early stages of an inquiry and is defined as 'sampling open to those persons, places and situations that will provide the greatest opportunity to gather the most relevant data about the phenomenon' (ibid.: 181). In essence this is what Patton (1990) would call opportunistic sampling because the researcher is supposed to follow unexpected new leads in order to lead to theory generation. Strauss and Corbin (1990) continue to suggest that individuals chosen for interviewing could indeed be 'whoever walks through a door or agrees to participate' (ibid.: 184) which, according to Patton (1990), is opportunistic or convenience sampling. As mentioned previously, the latter is a strategy that should be avoided at all costs, because it does not necessarily lead to the best information; in other words it fails to fulfil the quality criteria of appropriateness. Finally, open sampling involves 'going from one person or place to another on a list' (Strauss and Corbin 1990: 184), which constitutes random purposeful sampling in Patton's terminology. According to Kuzel (1999), the basic assumption behind qualitative research makes random sampling inappropriate and the worst choice. It indicates a wish to generalize from sample to population, which all the sources agree is neither possible nor desirable in qualitative research. Qualitative research does not aim to ensure representativeness, but rather the field under study yields substantive information that will contribute to elucidate the problem issue, and on this basis facilitate ideographic, holographic, naturalistic or analytical generalization (Sandelowski 1995). Hence, in the trade-off between generality and complexity, complexity wins.

Relational and variational sampling take place in the process of looking for evidence of variation or differences within and across the data and test how well the emerging theory holds up in new settings (Strauss and Corbin 1990: 185ff.). These purposes can be fulfilled through the selection of, for example, confirming or disconfirming cases, using matched or maximum variation sampling. This qualitative 'testing' of the emerging theory's robustness continues in the final phase of an inquiry through discriminate sampling, which is used to 'maximize opportunities for verifying the story line, relationships between categories, and for filling in poorly developed categories'. Such an approach is often used in critical realist research.

Generalizability

The above discussion leads to the last issue to be addressed in this chapter, namely generalizability. Whether few or many cases are included in a sample, this is an issue that cannot be avoided since qualitative studies are often rejected by reviewers as they disbelieve in the value of small purposeful samples simply because these cannot be generalized to 'a larger universe' (see example in Brush, Chapter 18 in this volume). It is an inherent feature of qualitative studies that they are context dependent and not representative of a larger universe, neither do they allow generalization across time and space. According to Cronbach (1975, in Patton 1990: 487), 'social phenomena are too variable and context-bound to permit very significant empirical generalizations.' In most books on qualitative research, the choice of cases is also closely linked to a discussion about generalization (see e.g. Silverman 2000: 106–10; Miles and Huberman 1994: 29–31; and Patton 1990: 486–90). Typically, such volumes refer to analytical or theoretical generalization. I want to propose a different distinction since those two terms are used interchangeably and have with time come to equate with each other. Hence I operate with analogous versus analytical/theoretical.

Analogous generalization is concerned with *extrapolation* of an insight from the situation researched to recognizing this insight in new and foreign contexts, or with identifying analogous situations. It means that the researcher thinks about the likely application of the findings to other situations under similar, but not identical, conditions (Patton 1990). Extrapolation is not exclusively made by the researcher, but may also be undertaken by the reader who recognizes the situations in question. This is the type of generalization that underlies most case study teaching. Generalization based on analogy does not need an explicit theory, as opposed to *analytical/theoretical generalization*, which finds its application when the researcher operates within a theoretical framework to which findings can be generalized (as e.g. proposed in Yin 1989). This type of argumentation may also be described as abductive reasoning (Danermark et al. 2003), which aims at hypothesis or theory generation.

Conclusion

As the above highlights, there is more to qualitative sampling than meets the eye. It is an elaborate process of making the 'right' choices. Careful sampling pays attention to what can be controlled in terms of characteristics of events, cases and informants as well as to what cannot be controlled. Purposeful sampling may not solve the problems of selection bias but it reveals the selection criteria which reduces the vulnerability to criticism for not being sufficiently rigorous. I have found that in a publication perspective, it is extremely important to argue each and every step in the selection process convincingly and in detail. The usefulness of qualitative research is often judged on the basis of the logic and the purposes that are associated with probability sampling. Therefore, as the review of mainstream, peer-reviewed journals showed, it is decisive that the methodology is sufficiently succinct, well argued and accounted for.

Looking at the long tradition in quantitative research for common rules and procedures and at the more or less standard format of accounting for sampling choices and analytical procedures, researchers using qualitative methods should not be surprised that in a publication perspective qualitative research is lagging behind. Qualitative scholars should provide a thorough account of their sampling strategy and analytical procedure, demonstrating that qualitative research can be as methodologically rigorous as its quantitative counterpart. If they do this, experience shows that it will result in successful publication, even in journals that are known to be inclined towards quantitative research.

Notes

1. It is sometimes difficult to identify truly qualitative research without reading the whole paper because quantitative researchers will also use the word 'interview' when distributing a questionnaire face to face.
2. *ERD* and *JBV* appear in Katz and Boal's Entrepreneurship Journal Rankings as level 1 journals, with *JDE* and *ETP* as level 2 journals.
3. *JDE* only features in the EBSCO database from 1999 and only with full text from 2000, which means that the first four years of the journal's existence are not included.
4. It should be noted, however, that the number of articles included in 2002 in *JBV* is inflated due to a special issue on qualitative research edited by Sue Birley and William Gartner that was published this year. Without this issue *JBV* would have published no qualitative contributions in that year.

Recommended further reading

Patton, M.P. (1990) *Qualitative Evaluation and Research Methods* (2nd edn), Newbury Park, CA: Sage has been my 'bible' on sampling since doing my Ph.D. It provides a comprehensive presentation of sampling strategies. The book is especially aimed at evaluation of programmes but it offers a number of useful suggestions along the way about research strategies, selecting cases, interviewing techniques and methodological triangulation as well as analysis that can be used as a guideline in any qualitative study. The book also contains some 'spice' in the form of a number of insightful observations by 'Halcolm'. I am particularly fond of Halcolm's last evaluation law with which Patton begins the book: 'Qualitative inquiry cultivates the most useful of all human capacities – the capacity to learn from others.'

References

Aldrich, H. (1991) Methods in our madness? Trends in entrepreneurship research. In Sexton, D.L. and Kasarda, J.D. (eds), *The State of the Art of Entrepreneurship*. Boston, MA: PWS–Kent Publishing Company.

Anderson, A. (2000) Paradox in the periphery: an entrepreneurial reconstruction? *Entrepreneurship and Regional Development*, **12**(2): 91–110.

Carter, S. and Rosa, P. (1998) The Financing of Male- and Female-owned Businesses, *Entrepreneurship and Regional Development*, **10**(3): 225–41.

Carter, N., Brush, C.G., Greene, P.G., Gatewood, E. and Hart, M.M. (2003) Women entrepreneurs who break through to equity financing: the influence of human, social and financial capital. *Venture Capital*, **5**(1): 1–28.

Coyne, I.T. (1997) Sampling in qualitative research: purposeful and theoretical sampling; merging or clear boundaries? *Journal of Advanced Nursing*, **26**(3): 623–30.

Cresswell, J.W. (1998) *Qualitative inquiry & research design: choosing among five traditions.* Thousand Oaks: Sage.

Danermark, B., Ekström, M., Jakobsen, L., Karlsson, J. ch. (2002) *Explaining Society: An Introduction to Critical Realism in the Social Sciences.* London and New York: Routledge.

Eisenhardt, K. (1989) Building Theories from Case Study Research. *Academy of Management Review*, **14**(4): 532–55.

EFPIA (2000) *The Pharmaceutical Industry in figures – 2000 Edition.* Report from The European Federation of Pharmaceutical Industries and Associations.

Fadahunsi, A. and Rosa, P. (2002) Entrepreneurship and Illegality: Insights from the Nigerian cross-border trade. *Journal of Business Venturing*, **17**(5): 397–430.

Flanagan, J.C. (1954) The critical incident technique. *Psychological Bulletin*, **54**(4): 327–56.

Gartner, W. and Birley, S. (2002) Introduction to the Special Issue on Qualitative Methods in Entrepreneurship Research. *Journal of Business Venturing*, **17**: 387–95.

Gibb, A.A. (1992) Can academe achieve quality in small firms policy research? *Entrepreneurship and Regional Development*, **4**(2): 127–44.

Gilchrist, V.J. and Williams, R.L. (1999) Key informant interviews. In B.F. Crabtree and W.L. Miller (eds), *Doing Qualitative Research*, (2nd edn), Newbury Park, CA: Sage.

Glaser, B. (1992) *Basics of Grounded Theory Analysis.* Mill Valley, CA: Sociology Press.

Glaser, B. and Strauss, A. (1967) *The Discovery of Grounded Theory.* Chicago: Aldine.

Goetz, J.P. and Lecompte, M.D. (1984) *Ethnography and Qualitative Design in Educational Research.* New York: Academic Press.

Goulding, C. (2002) *Grounded Theory: A Practical Guide for Management, Business and Market Researchers.* London: Sage.

Herriott, R.E. and Firestone, W.A. (1983) Multisite qualitative policy research: optimizing description and generalizability. *Educational Research*, **12**(3): 14–19.

Hofer, C.W. and Bygrave, W.D. (1992) Researching entrepreneurship. *Entrepreneurship Theory & Practice*, **16**(3): 91–100.

Huggins, R. (2000) The success and failure of policy-implanted inter-firm network initiatives: motivations, processes and structures. *Entrepreneurship and Regional Development*, **12**(2): 111–36.

Jack, S. and Anderson, A. (2002) The effects of embeddedness on the entrepreneurial process. *Journal of Business Venturing*, **17**(5): 467–88.

Johnson, J.C. (1990) *Selecting Ethnographic Informants.* Qualitative Research Methods Series, 22. Newbury Park, CA: Sage.

Kemery, E.R. (1988) *Some Psychometric Concerns with Small Business Research.* Presented at the USASBE meeting, Monterey, CA.

Kibria, N., Lee, S. and Olvera, R. (2003) Peer lending groups and success: a case study of Working Capital. *Journal of Developmental Entrepreneurship*, **8**(1): 41–59.

Kimball, S.T. and Partridge, W. (1979) *The Craft of Community Study: Fieldwork Dialogue.* Gainsville: University Press of Florida.

Kitson, G.C., Sussman, B., Willians, G.K., Zeehandelaar, R.B., Shickmanter, B.K. and Steinberger, J.L. (1982) Sampling issues in family research. *Journal of Marriage and the Family*, 44: 965–81.

Kodithuwakku, S.S. and Rosa, P. (2002) The entrepreneurial process and economic success in a constrained environment. *Journal of Business Venturing*, **17**(5): 431–66.

Kuzel, A.J. (1999) Sampling in qualitative inquiry. In B.F. Crabtree and W.L. Miller (eds), *Doing Qualitative Research*, (2nd edn), Newbury Park, CA: Sage.

Lechner, C. and Dowling, M. (2003) Firm networks: external relationships as sources for the growth and competitiveness of entrepreneurial firms. *Entrepreneurship and Regional Development*, **15**(1): 1–26.

Lincoln, Y.S. and Guba, E. G. (1985) *Naturalistic Inquiry.* Beverly Hills, CA: Sage.

McDonald, S., Gan, B.C. and Anderson, A. (2004) Studying entrepreneurship: A review of methods employed in entrepreneurship research 1985–2004. Paper presented at RENT XVIII, Copenhagen, Denmark, 25–26 November.

Mankelow, G. and Merrilees, B. (2001) Towards a model of entrepreneurial marketing for rural women: a case study approach. *Journal of Developmental Entrepreneurship*, **6**(3): 221–36.

Maxwell, J.A. (1996) *Qualitative Research Design*. Thousand Oaks, CA: Sage.

Miles, M.B. and Huberman, A.M. (1994) *Qualitative Data Analysis: An Expanded Sourcebook*, (2nd edn), Thousand Oaks, CA: Sage.

Morse, J.M. (1991) *Strategies for Sampling in Qualitative Research: A Contemporary Dialogue*. Newbury Park, CA: Sage.

Neergaard, H. (2005) Networking activities in technology-based entrepreneurial teams. *International Small Business Journal*, **23**(3): 1–20.

Neergaard, H. and Smith, R. (2004) Images of women's entrepreneurship: Do pictures speak louder than words? Paper presented at RENTXVII 24–26 November Copenhagen.

Patton, M.Q. (1990) *Qualitative Evaluation and Research Methods*, (2nd edn), Newbury Park, CA: Sage.

Sandberg, W.R. (2003) Case study: Roustam Tariko: Russian entrepreneur. *Entrepreneurship Theory and Practice*, **27**(3): 315–19.

Sandelowski, M. (1995) Focus on qualitative methods: sample size in qualitative research. *Research in Nursing and Health*, **18**: 179–83.

Sandelowski, M., Holditch-Davis, D. and Harris, B.G. (1992) Using qualitative and quantitative methods: the transition to parenthood of infertile couples. In J.F. Gilgun, K. Daly and G. Handel (eds), *Qualitative Methods in Family Research*. Newbury Park, CA: Sage.

Silverman, D. (2000) *Doing Qualitative Research: A Qualitative Handbook*. London: Sage.

Strauss, A. and Corbin, J. (1990) *Basics of Qualitative Research: Grounded Theory Procedures and Techniques*. London: Sage.

Sundbo, J., Johnston, R., Mattsson, J. and Millett, B (2001) Innovation in service internationalization: the crucial role of the frantrepreneur. *Entrepreneurship and Regional Development*, **13**(3): 247–68.

Tidaasen, C. (2000) Succession in family firms: the transformation of networks. Paper presented at 11th Nordic Conference on Small Business Research, Aarhus, Denmark, 18–20 June.

Tompson, G.H. (2003) Zandinger! *Entrepreneurship Theory and Practice*, **28**(2): 193–201.

Tremblay, M-A. (1957) The Key informant technique: a non-ethnographical application. *American Anthropologist*, **59**: 688–701.

VanderWerf, P.A. and Brush, C.G. (1989) Achieving empirical progress in an undefined field. *Entrepreneurship Theory and Practice*, **14**(2): 45–58.

Yin, R.K. (1989) *Case Study Research: Design and Methods*. Thousand Oaks, CA: Sage.

Appendix
Key to abbreviations used in tables:

Q	Qualitative
Q_1	Quantitative
TC	Teaching case
C	Conceptual
A	Archival
R	Review
I	Introduction to Special Issue

Table 10A.1

Entrepreneurship Theory and Practice

2003	Zandinger! By: Tompson, George H. Vol. 28 Issue 2, p. 193, 12 p. Methodological Note to Accompany Zandinger! p. 205, 3 p.	TC
	Case study: Roustam Tariko: Russian entrepreneur. By: Sandberg, William R. Vol. 27, Issue 3, p. 315, 4 p.	TC
2000	Human resource management practices in small and medium-sized enterprises: Unanswered questions and future research perspectives. By: Heneman, Robert L. Vol. 25, Issue 1, p. 11, 16 p.	C
1999	Loosely coupled systems for corporate entrepreneurship: Imagining and managing the innovation project/host organization interface. By: Holler, Trudy. Vol. 24, Issue 2, p. 25, 7 p.	Q
	The determinants and consequences of subsidiary initiative in multinational corporations. By: Birkinshaw, Julian. Vol. 24, Issue 1, p. 9, 28 p.	Q_1
	A historical perspective on small firm development. By: Vinnell, Reuben; Hamilton, R.T. Vol. 23, Issue 4, p. 5, 14 p.	A
	Corporate entrepreneurship and cross-functional fertilization: Activation, process and disintegration of a new product design team. By: Hitt, Michael A. Vol. 23, Issue 3, p. 145, 23 p.	Q
1996	Cooperative strategies in non-high-tech new ventures: An exploratory study. By: Brush, Candida G.; Chaganti, Radha. Vol. 21, Issue 2, p. 37, 18 p.	C
	A synthesis of six exploratory, European case studies of successfully exited, venture capital-financed, new technology-based firms. By: Murray, Gordon. Vol. 20, Issue 4, p. 41, 20 p.	Q
1995	Firm-level entrepreneurship and field research: The studies in their methodological context. By: Savage, Grant T.; Black, Janice A. Vol. 19, Issue 3, p. 25, 10 p.	R
	Entrepreneurial opportunities in an entrepreneurial firm: A structural approach. By: Krackhardt, David. Vol. 19, Issue 3, p. 53, 17 p.	–

Table 10A.2

	Entrepreneurship and Regional Development	
2003	Entrepreneurship in biodiversity conservation and regional development. By: Seidl, Irmi; Schelske, Oliver; Joshi, Jasmin; Jenny, Markus. Vol. 15, Issue 4, p. 333, 18 p.	C
	Acquisition, assessment and use of business information by small- and medium-sized businesses: a demand perspective. By: Fuellhart, Kurtis G.; Glasmeier, Amy K. Vol. 15, Issue 3, p. 229, 24 p.	C
	A longitudinal study of habitual entrepreneurs: starters and acquirers. By: Ucbasaran, Deniz; Wright, Mike; Westhead, Paul. Vol. 15, Issue 3, p. 207, 22 p.	Q
	Policies to support ethnic minority enterprise: the English experience. By: Ram, Monder; Smallbone, David. 2003, Vol. 15, Issue 2, p. 151, 16 p.	C
	Firm networks: external relationships as sources for the growth and competitiveness of entrepreneurial firms. By: Lechner, Christian; Dowling, Michael. Vol. 15, Issue 1, p. 1, 26 p.	Q
2002	New models of inter-firm networks within industrial districts. By: Carbonara, Nunzia. Vol. 14, Issue 3, p. 229, 18 p.	Q
	The dynamics of limited breaking out: the case of the Arab manufacturing businesses in Israel. By: Drori, Israel; Lerner, Miri. Vol. 14, Issue 2, p. 135, 20 p.	Q
2001	Innovation in service internationalization: the crucial role of the frantrepreneur. By: Sundbo, Jon; Johnston, Robert; Mattsson, Jan; Millett, Bruce. Vol. 13, Issue 3, p. 247, 21 p.	Q
	Managing the locals: employee relations in South Asian restaurants. By: Ram, Monder; Marlow, Sue; Patton, Dean. Vol. 13, Issue 3, p. 229, 17 p.	Q
2000	Paradox in the periphery: an entrepreneurial reconstruction? By: Anderson, Alistair R. Vol. 12, Issue 2, p. 91, 19 p.	Q
	The success and failure of policy-implanted inter-firm network initiatives: motivations . . . By: Huggins, Robert. Vol. 12, Issue 2, p. 111, 25 p.	Q
1999	The virtual web as a new entrepreneurial approach to network organizations. By: Franke, Ulrich J. Vol. 11, Issue 3, p. 203, 27 p.	Q
	Trading places: the ethnographic process in small firms' research. By: Ram, Monder. Vol. 11, Issue 2, p. 95, 14 p.	Q
	The small firm as a temporary coalition. By: Taylor, Michael. Vol. 11, Issue 1, p. 1, 19 p.	Q
1998	Case analysis of Canadian self-employment assistance programming. By: Orser, Barbara; Hogarth-Scott, Sandy. Vol. 10, Issue 1, p. 51, 19 p.	R

Table 10A.3

Journal of Business Venturing	
2003	An institutional view of China's venture capital industry: Q Explaining the differences between China and the West. By: Bruton, Garry D.; Ahlstrom, David. Vol. 18, Issue 2, p. 233, 27 p. Network-based research in entrepreneurship: A critical review. R By: Hoang, Ha; Antoncic, Bostjan. Vol. 18, Issue 2, p. 165, 23 p.
2002	Metaphors and meaning: A grounded cultural model of US Q entrepreneurship. By: Dodd, Sarah Drakopoulou. Vol. 17, Issue 5, p. 519, 17 p. The entrepreneur's character, life issues, and strategy making: Q A field study. By: Kisfalvi, Veronika. Vol. 17, Issue 5, p. 489, 30 p. The effects of embeddedness on the entrepreneurial process. By: Jack, Q Sarah L.; Anderson, Alistair R. Vol. 17, Issue 5, p. 467, 21 p. The entrepreneurial process and economic success in a constrained C environment. By: Kodithuwakku, Sarath S.; Rosa, Peter. Vol. 17, Issue 5, p. 431, 35 p. Entrepreneurship and illegality: Insights from the Nigerian Q cross-border trade. By: Fadahunsi, Akin; Rosa, Peter. Vol. 17, Issue 5, p. 397, 33 p. Introduction to the special issue on qualitative methods in I entrepreneurship research. By: Gartner, William B.; Birley, Sue. Vol. 17, Issue 5, p. 387, 9 p.
1999	Colas, Burgers, Shakes, and Shirkers: Towards a Sociological R Model of Franchising in the Market. By: Stanworth, John; Curran, James. Vol. 14, Issue 4, p. 323, 22 p.
1998	Small business growth through geographic expansion: A Q comparative case study. By: Barringer, Bruce R.; Greening, Daniel W. 1998, Vol. 13, Issue 6, p. 467, 26 p.
1997	The birth and growth of Toshiba's laptop and notebook computers: TC A case study in Japanese . . . By: Abetti, Pier A. 1997, Vol. 12, Issue 6, p. 507, 23 p.
1996	An examination of the relationship between women's personal Q goals and structural factors . . . By: Shabbir, Amama; Di Gregorio, Silvana. 1996, Vol. 11, Issue 6, p. 507, 23 p. A qualitative study of managerial challenges facing small Q business geographic expansion. By: Greening, Daniel W.; Barringer, Bruce R. 1996, Vol. 11, Issue 4, p. 233, 24 p.
1995	Case study: The rise and fall of the Merlin–Gerin foundry business. TC By: Badguerahanian, Leon; Abetti, Pier A. 1995, Vol. 10, Issue 6, p. 477, 17 p.

Table 10A.4

Journal of Developmental Entrepreneurship

2003	Customer communication and the small ethnic firm. By: Dyer, Linda M.; Ross, Christopher A. Vol. 8, Issue 1, p. 19, 22 p.	C
	An examination of indigenous Australian entrepreneurs. By: Foley, Dennis. Vol. 8, Issue 2, p. 133, 19 p.	Q
	Peer lending groups and success: A case study of working capital. By: Kibria, Nazli; Lee, Susan; Olvera, Ramona. Vol. 8, Issue 1, p. 41, 18 p.	Q
2002	Individual perception of business contexts: The case of small-scale entrepreneurs in Tanzania. By: Kristiansen, Stein. Vol. 7, Issue 3, p. 283, 22 p.	Q
	Building social capital for rural enterprise development: Three case studies in the United States. By: Lyons, Thomas S. Vol. 7, Issue 2, p. 193, 24 p.	TC
	Entrepreneurship and aboriginal Canadians: A case study in economic development. By: Aderson, Robert B. Vol. 7, Issue 1, p. 45, 21 p.	Q
	The internationalization process of the craft microenterprise. By: Fillis, Ian. Vol. 7, Issue 1, p. 25, 19 p.	C
2001	A case study of microenterprise training: Beta test findings and suggestions for improvement. By: Cook, Ronald G.; Belliveau, Paul; VonSeggern, Kristen L. Vol. 6, Issue 3, p. 255, 13 p.	TC
	Towards a model of entrepreneurial marketing for rural women: A case study approach. By: Mankelow, Gary; Merrilees, Bill. Vol. 6, Issue 3, p. 221, 15 p.	Q
	An examination of entrepreneurial motives and their influence on the way rural women small business owners manage their employees. By: Robinson, Sherry. Vol. 6, Issue 2, p. 151, 17 p.	Q
	Evaluating the outcomes of microenterprise training for low income women: A case study. By: Dumas, Colette. Vol. 6, Issue 2, p. 97, 32 p.	Q
2000	Challenges to launching grassroots microlending programs: A case study. By: Freedman, Michael P. Vol. 5, Issue 3, p. 235, 13 p.	TC
	From unemployed to entrepreneur: A case study in intervention. By: Osborne, Stephen W. Vol. 5, Issue 2, p. 115, 22 p.	TC
	Financing the microcredit programs of non-governmental organizations (NGOs): A case study. By: Alamgir, Dewan A.H. Vol. 5, Issue 2, p. 157, 12 p.	TC

11 Catching it as it happens
Ethel Brundin

Introduction

The field of entrepreneurship is witnessing the introduction of new methodological approaches such as experiments, simulation and longitudinal studies (Wiklund 1998; Baron and Brush 1999; Sarasvathy 1999; Fiet and Migliore 2001; Davidsson and Honig 2003; Gustavsson 2004). As valuable as such approaches may be, they mostly approach the phenomenon at arm's length. However, close-up insights are needed if we want to access what actually happens and matters within the entrepreneurial firm. To do so the study of *processes over time* is important. Davidsson (2003) proposes that overall the development within the field is a movement towards a more processual approach (cf. Gartner 1988). According to Davidsson (2003), the emerging interest in processes is closely linked to methodological challenges, which include new levels of analysis and the heterogeneity of the field. The use of real-time process studies represents one way to capture entrepreneurial activities as they happen and be able to uncover the more intangible, yet very important, issues in the daily life of the entrepreneur.

The purpose of this chapter is to illustrate real-time methodologies for collecting empirical material and show that such methodologies have the potential to contribute to our knowledge about entrepreneurial processes. In doing so, the focus will be on micro-processes and real-time methodologies, and the case of emotions will be used as a basis. The phenomenon of emotion is however just one example of many phenomena where there is a need to come close to the process itself in order to understand what is taking place. Other examples include an understanding of how a start-up process proceeds and its endeavours; the rationale behind important decisions and actions; the consequences of certain behaviour; why some entrepreneurial activities succeed while others fail; and the thinking and feeling of the entrepreneur in relation to a range of issues. Addressing emotions can thus be of value for subjects or phenomena within entrepreneurship research when we want to come to grips with the 'sustainable advantage [that] must lie in micro assets that are hard to discern and awkward to trade' (Johnson et al. 2003: 4). The integrative methodologies used in the example here will thus have a bearing for other studies within the field of entrepreneurship with a processual, longitudinal and real-time approach.

The chapter is organized in four sections. Initially, it will be argued that there is a need to move towards new approaches in entrepreneurship research and that much potential lies within micro-processes. The next section initially frames the concept of 'real-time methodologies' and thereafter describes in detail how different and integrative real-time methodologies helped to fulfil the purpose of investigating entrepreneurial micro-processes over time. Section three addresses how to go from micro to macro in order to build theory. In section four, some methodological concerns and ethical dilemmas are addressed that were faced in the process of collecting empirical material and providing a public account for it. This final section also serves to indicate some future challenges for a research agenda including novel methodologies.

From a macro- towards a micro-perspective

Huse and Landström (1997) established that publications in European as well as American journals tend to concentrate on the macro- or meso-levels,[1] albeit with slightly different foci. Macro-level theories may provide ample insight into a range of all-embracing and coherent macro-level phenomena and how they work in a general sense. They result in 'grand' theories such as agency/stewardship theories; resource-based theories; institutional theories and theories about national and organizational growth. However, within all businesses, we also face a myriad of fragmented activities that are not taken into account by a macro-perspective and we might learn less valuable lessons at the individual level with a macro-level approach (Rousseau and House 1994). Since the results of these macro-level perspectives most often derive from methodologies that do not offer close insights into processes and/or individual thinking and acting, they are logically less capable of presenting explanations and understandings for different phenomena on a more detailed level.

Indeed, a number of researchers within the field today call for longitudinal and/or qualitative studies focusing on processes (Aldrich 2001; Bergendahl and Landström 2003; Davidsson 2003; Huse and Landström 1997; Steyaert 1997) – as well as real-time studies (Davidsson 2003) – where more in-depth knowledge is supposed to be found. The emerging trend for micro-processes, where the interest lies in looking for 'know how', 'know when' and 'know where' rather than 'know what' (Balogun et al. 2003), means that there is a renewed interest in an activity-based approach. This would lead researchers into the day-to-day activities within organizations taken by different actors, and it would also meet more practice-oriented demands (Johnson et al. 2003). Entrepreneurial processes are formed in social practices and the focus on realized actions leads to micro-processes. Where individuals are involved, such a focus will have to take social interaction into account. This has a number of important implications, where, among other things, the individual constitutes the central focus of entrepreneurial processes. Hence, understanding the entrepreneurial process means understanding the individual as essentially interactive. Furthermore, these interactions depend on a mutually reinforcing relationship with a variety of forces, which are highly important for the progress of the firm. Johnson et al. (2003) argue that micro-activities are a possible way of studying phenomena that, despite their invisibility, may have a bearing on the business. Parallel to this, Steyaert (1997) claims that entrepreneurship constitutes 'never-ending practises of becoming' and advocates a processual language, such as 'entrepreneuring'; cf. strategizing and organizing (Melin et al. 1999; Johnson et al. 2003).

The strongly emerging interest in entrepreneurial processes and the focus on ongoing human activities hence makes practice the unit of analysis rather than the level of analysis. All levels, from micro to macro, can be included, and they rely on each other in the processes. It is a matter of activities where the outcome and the effect are all to be viewed as entrepreneurship, albeit in multiple forms. However, the lack of studies made in real time with a micro-processual approach probably means that we miss out on how day-to-day activities relate to entrepreneurial outcome, particularly if we assume that individual differences and the context play a role (Rousseau and House 1994). If we are able to understand parts of the complex and non-linear relationship of entrepreneurial processes and gain knowledge from it, there are implications not only for practitioners but also for the scholarly domain within entrepreneurship. Qualitative studies, relying on traditional interviews only, do not meet the challenge of capturing a process as it unfolds over time. Furthermore, retrospective studies are less suitable for process research where rationalization might play a trick on the researcher as well as on the entrepreneur. In fact, methodological difficulties may be one explanation for the lack of theorizing within the field. As a consequence, we need to reconsider methodological issues and in this chapter real-time methodologies are advocated to facilitate learning from entrepreneurial processes.

Real-time methodologies

What, then, are real-time methodologies – and how can they contribute? In Britannica Online (http://www.britannica.com/dictionary) the term is defined as 'the actual time during which something takes place; the computer may partly analyze the data in *real-time* (as it comes in)'. Within research and in a figurative sense, the term is used to illustrate that the collection of data and/or empirical material is instantaneous, that is, takes place at the same time as such data are unfolding and where events depend on each other in a sequential order. Real-time methodologies can in practice be applied in different ways. In this chapter real-time methodologies stand for: (1) the researcher being on site *and* (2) the researcher collecting material when it happens *or* (3) the entrepreneur reporting about and in connection with the events taking place. Real-time methodologies in this chapter hence refer to 'catching it as it happens'.

To be on site does not necessarily mean that the empirical material that is collected emerges at the same time. For instance, a researcher can be on site while interviewing entrepreneurs or asking them to fill in questionnaires and the like about retrospect incidents and events. On the other hand, the researcher can be present while interviewing about incidents and events that are taking place there and then. The former is not defined as a real-time methodology. The novelty of the real-time methodology that will be presented here is that in addition to (1), (2) and (3) above, a set of real-time methodologies is in use.

Even if real-time methodologies are an emerging phenomenon within entrepreneurship research, more common examples exist, such as observations, verbal protocols and experiments. Less common examples include conjoint analysis, *in situ* studies (where the researcher more or less 'lives' with the respondents), personal self-reports and active participation of the entrepreneurs in the interpretations. Gathering material where the researcher makes direct observations has a long tradition within management research and has occasionally been used in entrepreneurship research. Verbal protocols constitute a methodology where the research subjects 'think aloud', preferably in a real-time experiment, primarily regarding entrepreneurial decision-making processes or problem-solving situations (Sandberg et al. 1988; Hall and Hofer 1993; Harrison et al. 1997; Dibben et al. 2003; Gustavsson 2004). An emerging methodology where experiments and verbal protocols constitute the basis is that of conjoint analysis. According to Shepherd (1999) and Shepherd and Zacharakis (1999), this is an excellent real-time tool to capture venture capitalists' decision-making criteria at the time decisions are actually made. Mason and Stark (2004) provide a practical example where they use verbal protocols analysis in order to capture how investors evaluate business plans. The special point here is that the researcher (or respondent) can computerize the result, that is, make an instant analysis as well (cf. the definition above).

The main argument among researchers for applying a real-time methodology is that it prevents rationalization as opposed to *post hoc* material collection methodologies (Hall and Hofer 1993; Shepherd 1999; Shepherd and Zacharakis 1999; Brundin 2002). By collecting material from entrepreneurs in real time they will have a 'fresh memory' and be more likely to answer in a spontaneous manner.

Despite its many advantages, real-time methodology also has some drawbacks. The disadvantages of verbal protocols, experiments and con-joint analyses are that they may be a-contextual, relying on artificial basic data to some extent, and they are carried through in experimental settings. The situations that face the entrepreneur in those cases are most often con-structed by the researcher and may therefore not fully mirror the entrepreneur's actual situation; in addition, the knowledge of being part of an experiment can make the entrepreneur more 'scientific' in his/her approach. *In situ* studies are to date very rare and their drawbacks are that they are time-consuming and result in excessive material that needs to be inter-preted. Self-reports demand openness and genuineness from the entrepreneurs in order to be sufficiently valuable, issues that were discussed by Bergendahl and Landström (2003) in their work, where entrepreneurs provided e-mailed self-reports. However, weighing the pros and cons, the former are considered by far to outweigh the latter when it comes to achieving accounts of more intuitive and subtler micro-processes. As will be illustrated later on, everyday emotions and their implications are considered to need real-time attention.

Real-time methodologies are not necessarily the same as qualitative studies, as Table 11.1 illustrates. Neither are retrospect methodologies nec-essarily the same as quantitative studies. The purpose of Table 11.1 is to bring some clarification with regard to how different ways for collecting empirical material can relate to real-time vs retrospect research method-ologies and how they traditionally relate to qualitative vs quantitative research strategies.

Table 11.1 shows the most common ways to collect empirical mater-ial/data. Ticks indicate whether real-time or retrospect methodologies are usually applied and the traditional method used in relation to these ways of collecting empirical material. Ethnography is in this table both a way to collect empirical material – such as being present in an organization for a longer period of time and experiencing a process together with the organization members – and a study design (see Wigren 2003). The case study design is also added as a comparison, as is action research and a set of novel research designs. As illustrated in the table, the researcher can choose from a range of collection methods depending on his/her ontological and epis-temological stance. For instance, in the study on entrepreneurial emotions presented in this chapter, the natural choice was to collect material in real-time micro-processes in order to produce a micro-level theory. For a research design the case study was chosen. Furthermore, within the case study, design techniques were used that were all related to real time, such as interviews, conversations, successive observations, joint interpretations and self-reports. The chosen method is therefore qualitative due to the way I

Table 11.1   Various data collection strategies

Ways of collecting empirical material	Real-time methodology	Retrospect methodology	Qualitative method	Quantitative method
Interviews	✓	✓	✓	
Conversations	✓	✓	✓	
Observation (participant/non-participant/successive)	✓		✓	
Questionnaires		✓	✓	✓
Documentary studies		✓	✓	✓
Critical incident technique		✓	✓	
Experiments	✓			✓
Conjoint analysis	✓			✓
Self-reports: verbal protocols	✓			✓
Self-reports: e-mails	✓	✓	✓	✓
Self-reports: diaries	✓	✓	✓	
Ethnography	✓		✓	
Direct involvement of practitioners/ entrepreneurs	✓	✓	✓	
Study design				
Case study	✓	✓	✓	
Ethnographic study	✓		✓	
Action research, collaborative research, enactive research, interactive research, follow-up research	✓		✓	

collected empirical material and the interpretive approach. However, as indicated, the key to making progress is probably wider than the choice of novel methodologies and stretches into the researcher's own worldview underlying the research issues.

Time to come out of the closet?

Sutton (1997) comes out of the closet when he admits that he has hidden the fact that he has used qualitative material in his research in order to be published. He argues that it is sometimes better to leave out such material if it 'destroys' the good story that is to be told (cf. Pike 1994; Golden-Biddle and Locke 1997). His reasoning very clearly illustrates where qualitative research stands: in rhetoric it is fully accepted but in practice not. Within the field of entrepreneurship research, this is even truer. Even so, Huse and

Landström (1997) claim that European researchers are better trained in a variety of methods, with a wider openness to 'experiment'. Thus there is hope that the field is not completely methodologically institutionalized. The main challenge for qualitative studies may lie within core beliefs and assumptions about how knowledge is created. Or as Morgan and Smircich phrase it:

> Quantitative techniques may have an important but only partial role to play in the analysis and understanding of the process of social change, and in defining the informational properties of a cybernetic field; however, their utility is much more restricted in the more subjectivist positions identified on our continuum [objective to subjective approaches]. The requirement for effective research in these situations is clear: scientists can no longer remain as external observers, measuring what they see; they must move to investigate from within the subject of study and employ research techniques appropriate to the task. (Morgan and Smircich 1980: 498)

I will refrain here from a dead-end discussion of qualitative vs quantitative methods. It will suffice to draw the conclusion that the current state of the art within the field of entrepreneurship seems to be mainly represented by studies with a preference for quantitative methods. These studies offer a multitude of useful concepts, taxonomies and categorizations, but in order to move forward, researchers in the field have started to consider how to approach more complex and multi-faceted phenomena. This volume on qualitative research is clear evidence of this trend.

In the next section, I will take up Huse and Landström's (1997: 11) call 'to employ venturesome and entrepreneurial methods' by giving an account of my own study of real-time entrepreneurial processes.

Real-time methodologies for the collection of empirical material
This study focuses on two entrepreneurial processes in two different firms. The main interest was in the two entrepreneurs. The one entrepreneurial process was the development and implementation of equipment for quality assurance for the third generation of mobile phones. The other entrepreneurial process was to develop and market a totally new product within a mature market. The project was studied *in situ*, that is, I followed two real-time processes over a period of 20 months, including two intensive four-month periods at both firms. A set of real-time methodologies was applied involving all parties within the process. In order to make the study more comprehensible, I will first frame the micro-process phenomenon in focus here – emotions. This is followed by an account of the real-time methodologies, including some illustrations from the study. I will conclude this section with a discussion of how to account to readers when presenting a process approach.

An example of a micro-process phenomenon: emotions

Emotions and how they matter in entrepreneurial contexts are conspicuously absent in the literature. Even so, there are many reasons to believe that emotions play a major role within entrepreneurial processes where the urge to succeed with the business and make it grow is important. The very essence of entrepreneurship and its many connections to devotion and motivation would be sufficient reason (see e.g. McClelland et al. (1971) on the need for achievement). The underlying research questions in this example were: (1) what emotions are communicated by the entrepreneur during the process of developing the business; (2) when and where do different emotions emerge during such a process and (3) how do emotions influence the process?

According to Sturdy (2003), the choice of theoretical approach is important when studying emotions. However, even if the field is characterized by multidisciplinary approaches, integrative perspectives are perhaps more essential. (For a thorough literature review, see Brundin 2002.) Emotions are part of human interaction in entrepreneurial processes, and in the conceptualization of emotions, I therefore argue for the social constructionist perspective represented by, among others, Averill (1980, 1984), Denzin (1984, 1990), Harré (1986), Cornelius (1996), Parkinson (1995) and Fineman (1996, 2000). Furthermore, and in line with the social constructionist approach, a performative view on emotions was applied (cf. Latour 1986, 1998, and his concept of power). This means that an emotion is not something that a person 'has', but it is interpreted and translated by other people and the emotion is dependent on their – conscious or unconscious – interpretations and decisions about how to understand the emotion. For example, it is not until an outburst is interpreted as anger that it will constitute the emotion of anger. A natural consequence is to look for emotions in linguistic practices included in communication and interaction, and with an emphasis on micro-processes. Dialogues are the starting point in forming emotions and they evolve, transform and take on new directions in 'the space between' formed by institutional and organizational contexts. As such, they are expressed with different degrees of intensity and can be expressed or not. They are either explicitly articulated or fictive in 'tacit dialogues', which could very well arise in solitude. In sum, I here rely on a 'common-sense' definition of emotions as evaluative, affective, intentional and short-term states (Parkinson 1995). Emotion refers to happiness, anger, fear, frustration, hope, joy, surprise, disgust, hate, excitement, anxiety, sadness, depression, contempt, guilt, anguish, envy, jealousy, compassion, pity, embarrassment, shame, indignation, pride, and the like (cf. Averill 1975; Hochschild 1983; Hein 2000[2]), but also more long-term emotions such as loyalty, friendship, team spirit and sympathy.

Examples of real-time methodologies

A consequence of studying a phenomenon that is regarded as socially constructed is to rely on an interpretive approach, for example *à la* Burrell and Morgan (1979). Its purpose is to create a dialogue in which mutual understanding can be reached in order to offer new perspectives and/or expand existing ones. This is a creative process and therefore there was a need to approach a micro-process in a real-time setting in multiple ways. The methodologies applied included interviews; 'intimate' conversations; successive observations; active involvement of entrepreneurs; and self-reports made by the entrepreneurs in diaries and e-mails, as illustrated in Figure 11.1.

During an initial phase, I started out with interviews with the entrepreneurs and the persons closest to them in the professional and private realm. Documentary studies were also part of the initial phase. From there I primarily went from conversations and successive observations to intimate conversations and involvement with the entrepreneurs and to self-reports. However, most of the methodologies were used throughout the whole period and/or on an iterative basis. The special focus on emotions became more and more evident along the process. In the following section, I will discuss each of the real-time methodologies in more detail. First a few words about the case design which formed the basis of the study.

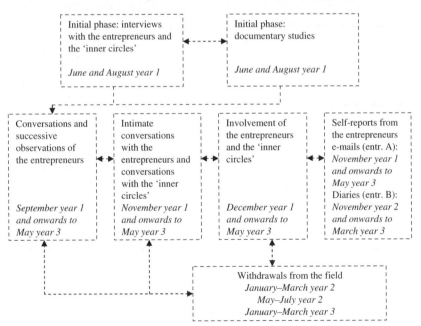

Figure 11.1   The step-by-step application of real-time methodologies

A case study design   The case study design was deemed suitable since it is capable of supplying holism within one or several cases simultaneously with providing local theory (Gummesson 1991; Stake 1995). It involved presence, participation and intervention, and provided experiential understanding and glimpses of multiple 'realities' (Stake 1995). Davidsson (2003) argues that the very heterogeneity aspect might make such a design even more interesting for entrepreneurship research. With an in-depth design, two cases were considered enough. Even if I did not have the implicit ambition to compare the two case companies, I tried to get two cases that initially seemed to be as different as possible in industry and entrepreneurial process. Accessibility was another issue to deal with, but was not a real problem here. Access was achieved in a stepwise manner; that is, I asked for new access from one time to the next. Not until 'real' trust was established was it time to be more close and active in the research process. I did not experience any hesitation towards my presence in either company, not even when it became rather work-intensive for the entrepreneurs. On the contrary, one of them was openly disappointed when I left the company.

Interviews and 'intimate' conversations   Initially, a range of interviews was undertaken with the two entrepreneurs in order to build trust. I spent time with the entrepreneurs and their 'inner circles' in order to gain their respect and confidence, and in order to become acquainted with their situations. Over time, the initial interviews turned into conversations that were more and more personal and I could move on to intimate conversations. I prefer to use the term conversation here since this term implies that two persons are in charge of what is taking place. Gadamer (1994: 383) argues that when 'we fall into conversation, or even when we become involved in it . . . no one knows what will "come out" in a conversation'. Further, he writes, 'all this shows that a conversation has a spirit of its own, and that the language used in it bears its own truth within it, i.e., that it reveals something which henceforth exists' (1994: 383). This fits very well with the interpretative tradition and the understanding, that is sought in the process here. Interviews, on the other hand, connote asking questions that have to be answered, implying that the researcher is in charge and that it is a one-way relation. The word 'intimate' refers to the character of the conversations since they dealt with delicate and very personal thoughts and feelings such as being strained, lonely, or made tense by a specific issue.

Successive observations   Observation as a methodology is widely accepted. Observations can vary on a continuum from complete participation to non-participative observations (see also Chapters 4 and 16 in this handbook). We mainly find observations within *in situ* studies, such as ethnographic studies, where the researcher often stays and lives with those s/he is going to study. Within the field of entrepreneurship, these are rare. Wigren's (2003) ethnographic study of the municipality of Gnosjö and the so-called Gnosjö Spirit provides a recent example of a lived-in type of observation.

The advantage of observations was obvious in my case. I was invited to take part in the process as it unfolded and was able to make interpretations from the spoken word and the action. Intonations in the language could be noted as well as the body language and what was not said. If there were no meetings, I made observations and tried to keep pace with the entrepreneurs. Observations were made successively; that is, when I spent time with the entrepreneurs and 'their' processes I made observations all along; in meetings, in the daily 'rounds', at lunches, at coffee breaks, during informal conversations with people around the entrepreneur, on business trips and so on. What I conducted could be termed 'shadowing'. I always brought my tape recorder along and switched it on when the entrepreneurs got involved in a discussion with someone or when they wanted to express their thoughts more directly in a particular situation. Successive observations do not, however, allow for observations of inner thinking and feeling. Therefore an involvement with the entrepreneurs and their 'inner circles' was deemed necessary.

Involvement with the entrepreneurs   An issue that is not brought up very often is the amount of material that is frequently the result of qualitative approaches: the researcher has to interpret quite a heavy load of notes, tapes, e-mail correspondence, brochures, minutes of meetings, CD material, advertisements, and the like. I claim that it is beneficial not only to get rid of some of this burden but also that the interpretations will increase in value and quality if the respondents in the process themselves are involved. The entrepreneur as well as the researcher will benefit from embarking on such a joint venture; it will yield them joint knowledge (Johnson et al. 2003) where they learn from each other and from the process itself. It is also a way for practitioners to experience that they get something in return for providing access (Balogun et al. 2003).

Not only the entrepreneurial process as such was in focus here; the process also included a relational orientation (Bradbury and Bergmann Lichtenstein 2000), exploring the interaction between individuals. This means that both parties (the researched and the researcher) were involved and that the process co-evolved between them. By tradition, research has been the work of one individual and it has been taken for granted that the researcher is the expert who can conduct the entire research process single-handedly – and even be the interpretative link (Balogun et al. 2003). However, when it comes to more personal phenomena, such as the complex phenomenon of emotion or other intra-personal phenomena in a process, no one is better able to tell us what is happening than the researched subject him- or herself. Of course, the researcher has a huge responsibility to make sure, as far as possible, that trust is developed in order for such openness to take place.

For the reasons above, it was necessary to involve the entrepreneurs closely in the process. Along the way, the increasing intimacy of the dialogues seemed to rest naturally with the entrepreneurs. I usually spent two to three consecutive days at each company, arriving without any prior notice other than making sure that the entrepreneurs were 'at home'. Each visit was built up in pretty much the same way: a conversation took place, where we talked about what had happened since last time we met, including what issues brought them joy or disappointment. If any meetings were planned during my stay, the entrepreneurs were asked for their expectations, fears and doubts before the meeting and in relation to what issue. Moreover, dialogues took place with each of the participating members of the meeting regarding his or her expectations, fears and doubts. During the meeting, I observed the communication, including intonations, body language and the like. Directly after the meeting, reflecting conversations were held with the entrepreneurs in order to reach a joint interpretation of what emotions were expressed, felt or withheld during the meeting – and in relation to what issue. Conversations were also held with the other members of the meeting with a view to understanding their emotions in relation to the entrepreneurs and how their behaviour was interpreted by other members of the company. In short, I first tried to establish a close relationship, where the entrepreneurs would feel free to reveal as much as possible, hence creating a situation where they could be honest with me.

As the study progressed, the entrepreneurs and their immediate working and family environment were engaged more and more actively. The empirical material is therefore represented by a series of detailed micro-processes from a range of formal and informal arenas, where the entrepreneurs and others helped out in interpreting and analysing the process, such as meetings, lunch and coffee breaks, trips, social events and at family gatherings. This study is thus mainly built on an interpretative approach, from the perspective of the researcher as well as from the entrepreneurs themselves and their environment. In order to get even closer to the more 'tacit', I invited the entrepreneurs to take part in the research process by providing self-reports in direct connection to the process.

Self-reports (diaries and e-mails)   Self-reporting is a method that has been used in other disciplines, such as medicine, psychology and psychotherapy, but is very limited within the field of entrepreneurship. Bergendahl and Landström (2003) constitute an exception to the rule, applying a structured electronic diary routine at a venture lab. Self-reports have, however, appeared occasionally within management research (see e.g. Mintzberg 1974; Balogun and Johnson 1998; Buchanan and Boddy 1992; Weiss et al. 1999). Balogun et al. (2003) argue that these are an apt form of gathering empirical material in real-time research. With diary notes it is possible to come very close to an entrepreneurial process and obtain access to thoughts, feelings and reflections. Furthermore, the time lapse between when events are happening in the process to the moment they are reflected upon can be made very short and hence the rationalization effects are reduced. From their listing of different forms of diary techniques, Balogun et al. (2003) suggest logs, memoirs or life-history data in a falling scale from being more depersonalized to more personal (structured to unstructured). However, all three can be either real-time or retrospective in character. Allport (1942; in Burgess, 1993) makes a similar distinction between logs, memoirs and intimate journals. The intimate version, revealing thoughts and emotions as they occur spontaneously, seems to be apt for a processual approach in line with what has been the purpose here; in Denzin's wording diary entries may offer 'uncensored outpourings' (Denzin 1989). In a listing of the advantages of such a method, Balogun et al. (2003) mention that it is less time consuming for the researcher; it is a method at the convenience of the 'researched' regarding frequency and actual time to do them – and how to do them (tape, e-mail, notes); there is less risk of post-rationalization; and notes can be asked for in relation to certain events or at specific times. Inevitably, there are drawbacks as well: depth and detail may be lacking; the informants may feel uncomfortable with the situation; non-relevant material may be excessive; and personal reflections may interfere with future actions (Balogun et al. 2003).

The two entrepreneurs provided their own diary notes. They decided themselves how they wanted to do this. I wanted them to feel comfortable with the arrangement and free to choose the way that suited them best. One of the entrepreneurs made notes on an intermittent basis over the entire period of the study, providing at least one diary note per month via e-mail of one to two pages per occasion. They were mostly recorded and sent to me during trips, when the entrepreneur was waiting for a flight connection or the like. The other entrepreneur chose to use a dictaphone for recording the diary notes on a more concentrated and regular basis. These notes stretched over a period of five months, where the notes for the first two months were kept on an almost daily basis and thereafter at least on a weekly basis. They were mainly dictated on the 75-minute car ride (one-way) to or from work and made up three to five pages in printed form per occasion.

In practice, the advantages of using diaries far outweigh the disadvantages or problems. The study in question did not explicitly ask the entrepreneurs to reflect on their emotions, rather to give an account of what was happening right now and how they related to that. Therefore these diary notes are invaluable, since they have left it to the entrepreneurs themselves to bring up issues of interest and – as will be seen in the empirical part – these notes are loaded with emotions.

'Withdrawal tactics'   At three points I withdrew from the field. I felt a distinct 'data saturation' from being so tightly involved in the entrepreneurial processes and needed 'time out' to absorb the material I had collected and to 're-live' the process. During these time-outs I also attended to other, completely different academic duties, to obtain a distance from the research. Often this is advantageous in a research process in order to approach the data with 'new eyes'.

How to wrap up entrepreneurial processes: narrated chronologies   Inevitably, there comes a time when the empirical material needs to be wrapped up. Pentland (1999) argues for narratives – good stories – as a means to build better theory (cf. Sutton 1997; Golden-Biddle and Locke 1997). In order to create a fuller description of the course of events, I relied on a narrative approach in connection with the chronological, and I have chosen to label the accounts 'narrated chronologies'. This means that the entrepreneurial process is made in a continuous report in the form of a chronology, starting with the first visit in June year 1 and ending with the last intimate conversation in May year 3 (cf. White's 1987 discussion on annals, chronicles and history proper and the discussion on stories vs narratives made by White 1987; Sarbin 1989; Weick 1995; Gergen 1999; Pentland 1999; Clandinin and Connelly 2000 and Stacey 2000).

The main purpose of the narrated chronologies was thus to create and optimize understanding and to give the reader the means to learn from the story-telling. Through the narrated chronologies it was possible to provide the foundation for a mutual understanding, even if neither the form nor the content can in themselves guarantee the creation of this understanding. Rather these are an invitation to the reader to make his or her own understanding and interpretation. Characters, events, discussions, thoughts, atmosphere and so on represent a social reality with a purpose of contextualizing and focusing on emotions in the entrepreneurial process. To quote White, 'the events are chronologically recorded as they appear on the horizon of the story' (White 1987: 3).

Illustrations of a micro-process phenomenon in real-time
Tables 11B.1–11B.4 in Appendix B provide an idea of the empirical material involved. The first illustration is from a meeting in November of the

second year in the high-tech company and is in three parts: Table 11B.1 provides the entrepreneur's expectations before the meeting; Table 11B.2 results from the meeting itself and Table 11B.3 shows the outcome of a short follow-up after the meeting.[3] Table 11B.4 is diary notes from the other entrepreneurial process. From these illustrations, the reader can follow the process and gain his or her own understanding of it.

From micro to macro
Parallel to the vocabulary of entrepreneuring, I argue that theorizing is a process as well. The interpretation that takes place applying real-time methodologies is a starting point for the theorizing process. Ample advice has been provided by scholars on how to build theory from qualitative case study research (Glaser and Strauss 1967; Mintzberg 1979; Yin 1984, Gersick 1988; Van Maanen 1988; Eisenhardt 1989; Miles and Huberman 1994). In line with Huse and Landström's (1997) notion that European researchers tend to build theory from case studies, the narrated chronologies and the dialogues are true micro-processes that build the basis for new knowledge (Lyotard 1993; Steyaert 1997). In this process, generalizations are not the name of the game, since they a-contextualize the material (Geertz 1983; Steyaert 1997). Steyaert (1997) even claims that generalization from interpretative research hinders theorizing.

Naturally, this study cannot be generalized in the traditional sense of the word. However, it is useful for a local theory on the micro-level that can help build theory on the macro-level and hence constitutes a piece of puzzle in order 'to begin to piece [the puzzle] together' (MacMillan and Katz 1992) and relate it to an outcome (cf. the earlier posted research questions of the exemplified study). Some people would perhaps argue that the study is primarily an explorative one, considering the novelty of the subject and the real-time methodology. I claim that it is mainly about understanding – understanding why the process unfolds the way it does and the result within the time frame in question. Research is about trying to 'know how', 'know when and where' (Johnson et al. 2003), and to this I therefore add 'know why'.

The study on the first entrepreneurial process resulted in 41 different emotions that occurred 201 times. The second entrepreneurial process resulted in 68 different emotions that occurred 178 times. In order to interpret how emotions relate to the entrepreneurial process, I classified the emotion words in a two-step process. First, the emotion words were labelled by the different parties involved, including the researcher. The total of 379 emotion words occurred with varying frequency and intensity. This called for further abstraction to allow for an analysis of the occurrence of certain emotions in relation to specific entrepreneurial issues. The next step consisted of a choice of a classification system that would merge similar emotion words into the same classes. Here the extensive work of Shaver et al. (1987) formed the basis. After some modification, mainly in relation to the context of a strategic entrepreneurial change process, this resulted in a final classification of nine groups of emotions: Abandonment, Anger, Bewilderment, Concern, Confidence, Frustration, Resignation, Satisfaction and Strain (see Appendix A). With the classification as a point of departure, the entrepreneurial process was then divided into critical issues. From there it was possible to start building theory about how emotions matter in entrepreneurial processes. The main results point out that emotions help make sense of the process and that emotions work as driving and/or restraining forces related to the intended goal. There are no positive or negative emotions since frustration and anger might work as driving forces, and confidence as a restraining force. Furthermore, emotions play a role as mood setters and for building up emotion sediments that have an impact on behaviour – and thereby on the outcome of the process. A detailed analysis of the result of the study is, however, not within the scope of this chapter (see Brundin 2002).

Methodological concerns
Involving the entrepreneurs in the process adds a new dimension to the empirical material. Balogun et al. (2003) argue that collaboration with managers – and other organizational members – is a way to ensure that researchers bring up interesting and relevant research issues. The entrepreneurs in this study appreciated the joint collaboration with the researcher since it gave them more insight and contributed to personal and eventually organizational development. Furthermore, this way of involving informants in the research agenda helps create more depth, breadth, as well as diversity in process research, from which many can benefit. Inevitably, there are some perceived disadvantages as well.

First, it is a delicate task in an ongoing process to ask people to stop and reflect on what is going on. The methodology applied here demands a great deal from the researcher, and a continuous balancing act results from trying to be sensitive to what is appropriate for each specific moment or situation. The two entrepreneurs have been exposed to a high degree and they have willingly 'opened up'. Even if the two entrepreneurs knew that the purpose was to gain a close insight into their daily work as the process evolved, critical voices would perhaps argue that the entrepreneurs should have been told up front about the specific phenomenon that was to be studied. On the one hand, having told them in the beginning might have yielded a more accurate discussion of how the entrepreneurs felt and possibly more honest accounts. On the other hand the entrepreneurs might have adopted a reserved attitude and hindered the attempt to capture the process (and the emotions) in a more natural and instant way. Not until trust was established did I reveal the explicit focus of the research: emotions. By then, the entrepreneurs and I had established a confidence that easily included being explicit about feelings and emotions. With topics that still seemed too unusual to deal with, bringing them out in the open right from the beginning might exclude the researcher from access. There was, however, an ethical dilemma since the entrepreneurs reacted to the uncommon theme in the account. Confidentiality was guaranteed, but in both cases a local and immediate environment could easily identify the specific cases. As I see it, this fact has been more critical to the entrepreneurs than 'going public'. Given the material one might get access to with a topic like this, it is understandable, and it has put me in an awkward position: what can I reveal in the name of research, and what should I disguise in the name of privacy and to maintain a good relationship with the two entrepreneurs? The conclusion was that there is no perfect compromise, and I have admittedly taken a risk, making the decision to include everything. Entrepreneurs, leading their companies, are always the subject of discussion, and it is hoped that studies of this kind can contribute to such a discussion in a constructive way, trusting that 'local' readers will handle such information with due diligence and in turn deal with it to make further progress. A matter of utmost importance is that the entrepreneurs are involved as co-interpreters and are given the opportunity to read and make comments on the empirical material. To extend this further, it is perhaps also time to invite the practitioners to take an active part in the theorizing process.

Second, applying the real-time methodologies gives rise to considerations about how much the researcher influences the process. Bradbury and Bergmann Lichtenstein (2000) argue that a theorist needs to be conscious of the process and what affects what and whom. In addition, they argue that being involved in research about 'the space between' means that the researcher 'enters an organisation as if it were an extended set of relationships. S/he thereby pays more attention to the 'space between': the space between subject and object, subject and research, researcher and subject, and the reflexivity of the research process itself' (2000: 551).

This argumentation indicates that the judgements and the consciousness of the researcher in a project like this are of the utmost importance. Being 'in charge' of a research project is always a matter of subjectivity. With this follows control over how the research process is carried out and finalized. Following this line of thought I am creating and constructing the research as it goes along. The question of validity and reliability, used in its original sense, becomes almost rhetorical. Validity would here stand for a question that is a door- and window-opener, and reliability for logical reasoning and an understandable report (Helenius 1990). Furthermore, even in a socially constructed world, there is the possibility of local, personal and community forms of truth, and in our daily life we make reliable observations and generalizations, and try to use valid arguments (Kvale 1996). What the researcher can do is to be consistent and truthful (not the same as reporting the truth), and thereby be trustworthy, reliable and give credibility to his/her work. This is good ground for contributing to generative theory, that is, 'accounts of our world that challenge the taken-for-granted-conventions of understanding, and simultaneously invite us into new worlds of meaning and action' (Gergen 1999: 116).

Third, to concentrate on a micro-level is not without pitfalls. To focus on day-to-day activities of an entrepreneur and his/her immediate environment might be to 'overestimate local effects and underestimate cross-level ones' (Rousseau and House 1994). It is essential to include the entrepreneurial context in a wider sense, such as the organizational and probably also the regional/national level and industry level, since human beings – and businesses – are by no means a-contextual. In order to face this dilemma, Rousseau and House (1994) suggest an integration of two or more levels at the same time. Interpreting meso-level research in such a manner opens up the way for integrated research of unthought-of possibilities. In the study presented here, levels other than the individual level were included by the individual entrepreneur who set the limits of the case study.

Finally, a question that can be addressed here is whether this study is a typical or an atypical example. The setting here is the Swedish context. Swedish entrepreneurs – and Swedes in general – are often regarded as more open to research and they are known for their willingness to collaborate. Having said this, it does not necessarily mean that they are open to commit themselves to such a degree that they intervene with the work that has traditionally been that of the researcher. The challenge to the research community must be to make entrepreneurs – and others – aware of the benefits that lie in this kind of approach. To carry out a study such as the one described here has by no means been a one-man show but a collective co-production.

Notes

1. Macro-level in this sense means aggregate or systems-level, such as the industry, the region, or the economy at large. From this it follows that the meso-level equates to the organizational level. By micro-level is meant here the individual, intra-individual or inter-individual level.
2. Averill (1975) labels over 500 emotion words in his semantic atlas on emotions. In an appendix Hochschild (1983) gives names to 19 emotions. Hein (2002) has created a list of over 1600 emotions words.
3. All conversations and diary notes have been translated from Swedish into English by the author/researcher.

Recommended readings

Balogun, J., Huff, A.S. and Johnson, P. (2003) Three responses to the methodological challenges of studying strategizing. *Journal of Management Studies*, **40**(1), January. Special issue: Micro Strategy and Strategizing: Towards an Activity-Based View. This article brings up a set of complementary methods (interactive discussion groups, self-reports and practitioner-led research) for studying micro-processes in strategy formation (strategizing).

Davidsson, P. (2003) The domain of entrepreneurship research: Some suggestions. In Katz, J. and Shepherd, D. (eds), *Cognitive Approaches to Entrepreneurship Research*; *Advances in Entrepreneurship, Firm Emergence and Growth*. Amsterdam: Elsevier, Vol. 6; pp. 315–72. This chapter provides an overview of the development within the entrepreneurship field, including different research agendas.

References

Aldrich, H. (2001) Who wants to be an evolutionary theorist? *Journal of Management Inquiry*, **10**(2): 115–27.

Allport, G.W. (1942) *The Use of Personal Documents in Psychological Science*, Bulletin No. 49. New York: Social Science Research Council.

Averill, J.R. (1975) Semantic atlas of emotional concepts. *JSAS Catalog of Selected Documents in Psychology*, **5**(330). No. 1103. Amherst, MA: University of Massachusetts.

Averill, J.R. (1980) A constructivist view of emotion. In Plutchik, R. and Kellerman, H. (eds), *Emotion*. New York: Academic Press.

Averill, J.R. (1984) The acquisition of emotions during adulthood. In Zander Malatesta, C. and Izard, C. *Emotion in Adult Development*. Beverly Hills, CA: Sage.

Balogun, J. and Johnson, G. (1998) Bridging the gap between intended and unintended change: the role of managerial sensemaking. In Hitt, M.A., Ricart I Costa, J.E. and Nixon, R.D. (eds), *New Managerial Mindsets*, New York: John Wiley.

Balogun, J., Huff, A.S. and Johnson, P. (2003) Three responses to the methodological challenges of studying strategizing. *Journal of Management Studies*, **40**(1), January. Special issue: Micro Strategy and Strategizing: Towards an Activity-Based View.

Baron, R.A. and Brush, C.G. (1999) The role of social skills in entrepreneurs' success: evidence from videotapes of entrepreneurs' presentations. In Reynolds, P.D. Bygrave, W.D. Carter, N.M. Manigart, S. Mason, C.M. Meyer G.D. and Shaver K.G. (eds), *Frontiers of Entrepreneurship*. Wellesley, MA: Babson College.

Bergendahl, J. and Landström, H. (2003) Understanding the entrepreneurial process – some methodological considerations. Paper to the 17th Nordic Conference on Business Studies, Reykjavik, Iceland, 14–16 August.

Bradbury, H. and Bergmann Lichtenstein, B.M. (2000) Relationality in organizational research: exploring the space between. *Organization Science*, **11**(5): 551–64.

Brundin, E. (2002) *Emotions in Motion. The Strategic Leader in a Radical Change Process*. JIBS Dissertation Series No. 012. Jönköping: Jönköping International Business School.

Buchanan, D. and Boddy, D. (1992) *The Expertise of the Change Agent: Public Performance and Backstage Activity*. Hemel Hempstead: Prentice-Hall.

Burgess, R.G. (1993) *In the Field: An Introduction to Field Research* (4th impression, 1990). London: Routledge.

Burrell, G. and G. Morgan (1979) *Sociological Paradigms and Organisational Analysis*. Aldershot, UK: Gower.

Clandinin, D.J. and Connelly, F.M. (2000) *Narrative Inquiry: Experience and story in qualitative research*. San Francisco, CA: Jossey-Bass.

Cornelius, R.R. (1996) *The Science of Emotion. Research and Tradition in the Psychology of Emotion*. Englewood Cliffs, NJ: Prentice-Hall.

Davidsson, P. (2003) The domain of entrepreneurship research: some suggestions. In Katz, J. and Shepherd, D. (eds), *Cognitive Approaches to Entrepreneurship Research: Advances in Entrepreneurship, Firm Emergence and Growth*, Amsterdam: Elsevier, Vol. 6, pp. 315–72.

Davidsson, P. and Honig, B. (2003) The role of social and human capital among nascent entrepreneurs. *Journal of Business Venturing*, **18**(3): 301–31.

Denzin, N.K. (1984) *On Understanding Emotion.* San Francisco, London, Washington: Jossey-Bass.

Denzin, N.K. (1989) *The Research Act. A Theoretical Introduction to Sociological Methods.* Englewood Cliffs, NJ: Prentice Hall.

Denzin N.K. (1990) On understanding emotion: the interpretive–cultural agenda. In Kemper, T. (ed.), *Research Agendas in the Sociology of Emotions.* Albany: State University of New York Press.

Dibben, M., Harris, S. and Wheeler, C. (2003) Export Market development: Planning and relationship processes of entrepreneurs in different countries. *Journal of International Entrepreneurship*, 1: 383–403.

Eisenhardt, K.M. (1989) Building theories from case study research. *The Academy of Management Review*, **14**(4): 532–50.

Fiet, J. and Migliore, P.J. (2001) The testing of a model of entrepreneurial discovery by aspiring entrepreneurs. In Bygrave, W.D. Autio, E. Brush, C.G. Davidsson, P. Green, P.G. Reynolds, P.D., and Sapienza H.J. (eds), *Frontiers of Entrepreneurship Research*, Wellesley, MA: Babson College, pp. 1–12.

Fineman, S. (1996) Emotion and organizing. In Clegg, S., Hardy, C. and Nord, W. (eds), *Handbook of Organization Studies.* Thousand Oaks, CA, London, New Delhi: Sage Publications.

Fineman S. (ed.) (2000) *Emotion in Organizations* (2nd edn) London, Thousand Oaks, CA, New Delhi: Sage Publications.

Gadamer, H.G. (1994) *Truth and Method.* Translated by Joel Weinsheimer and Donald Marshall. New York: Continuum.

Gartner, W.B. (1988) 'Who is an Entrepreneur?' is the wrong question. *American Small Business Journal* (Spring): 11–31.

Geertz, C. (1983) *Local Knowledge.* New York: Basic Books.

Gergen, K.J. (1999) *An Invitation to Social Constructionism.* Thousand Oaks, CA: Sage Publications.

Gersick, C. (1988) Time and transition in work teams: Toward a new model of group development. *Academy of Management Journal*, **31**: 9–41.

Glaser, B. and Strauss, A. (1967) *The Discovery of Grounded Theory. Strategies for qualitative research.* New York: Aldine Publishing Company.

Golden-Biddle, K. and Locke, K.D. (1997) *Composing Qualitative Research.* Thousand Oaks, CA: Sage.

Gummesson, E. (1991) *Qualitative Methods in Management Research.* London: Sage Publications.

Gustavsson, V. (2004) *When it pays (not) to be rational.* JIBS Dissertation Series No. 21, Jönköping: Jönköping International Business School.

Hall, J. and Hofer, C.W. (1993) 'Venture capitalists' decision criteria in new venture evaluation. *Journal of Business Venturing* **8**: 25–42.

Harré R. (ed.) (1986) *The Social Construction of Emotions.* Oxford, UK: Basil Blackwell.

Harrison, R.T., Dibben, M.R. and Mason, C.M. (1997) The role of trust in the informal investor's investment decision: An exploratory analysis. *Entrepreneurship Theory and Practice*, **20**: 63–81.

Hein, S. (2000) *Feeling words. Long list: 'How do you feel?'* Available at: http:www.eqi.org/fw/htm (6 June 2001).

Helenius, R (1990) *Förstå och bättre veta.* Stockholm: Carlsson Förlag.

Hochschild, A.R. (1983) *The Managed Heart. Commercialization of human feeling.* Berkely: University of California Press.

Huse, M. and Landström, H. (1997). Preface: European entrepreneurship and small business research: methodological openness and contextual differences. *International Studies of Management and Organization,* **27**(3); ABI/INFORM Global.

Johnson, G., L. Melin and R. Whittington (2003) Micro strategy and strategising: towards an activity-based view. *Journal of Management Studies*, **40**(1), Special issue: 3–22.

Kvale, S. (1996). *InterViews. An introduction to qualitative research interviewing.* Thousand Oaks, CA: Sage Publications.

Latour, B. (1998) *Artefaktens återkomst. Ett möte mellan organisationsteori och tingens sociologi.* Stockholm: Nerenius och Santérus Förlag.

Latour, B. (1986) The powers of association. In Law J. (ed.), *Power, Action and Belief.* London. Routledge and Kegan Paul.

Lyotard, J.F. (1993) *The Postmodern Condition: a report of knowledge.* Minneapolis: University of Minnesota Press.

MacMillan, I.C. and Katz, J.A. (1992) Idiosyncratic milieus of entrepreneurial research: The need for comprehensive theories. *Journal of Business Venturing*, 7: 1–8.

McClelland, D.C. and Winter, D.G. with Winter, S.K. (1971) *Motivating economic development*, New York: Free Press.

Mason, C., and Stark, M. (2004) What do investors look for in a business plan? *International Small Business Journal*, 22(3): 227–48.

Melin, L., Ericson, T. and Müllern, T. (1999) 'Organizing is Strategizing. Innovative forms of organizing means continuous strategizing'. Paper presented as part of the INNFORM Symposium on Organizing/Strategizing, Academy of Management Annual Conference, Chicago, 9–11 August. Jönköping International Business School, Jönköping University, Sweden.

Miles, M. and Huberman, A.M. (1994) *Qualitative Data Analysis.* Newbury Park, CA: Sage Publications.

Mintzberg, H. (1974) *The Nature of Managerial Work.* New York: Harper and Row.

Mintzberg, H. (1979) An emerging strategy of 'direct research', *Administrative Science Quarterly*, 24: 582–9.

Morgan, G. and Smircich, L. (1980) The case for qualitative research. *The Academy of Management Review*, 5(4): 491–500.

Parkinson, B. (1995) *Ideas and Realities of Emotion.* London and New York: Routledge.

Pentland, B.T. (1999) Building process theory with narrative: from description to explanation. *Academy of Management Review*, 24(4): 711–24.

Pike, L.J. (1994) Writing as a Storyteller's Art, Presented at the 1994 National Academy of Management Meetings, Dallas, TX.

Roussseau, D.M. and House, R.J. (1994) Meso organizational behavior: avoiding three fundamental biases. In Cooper, C.L. and Rousseau, D.M. (eds), *Trends in Organizational Behavior*, Vol. 1. Chichester: John Wiley and Sons.

Sandberg, W.R., Schweiger, D.M. and Hofer, C.W. (1998) The use of verbal protocols in determining venture capitalists' decision processes. *Entrepreneurship Theory and Practice*, 13(2).

Sarasvathy, S. (1999) *Decision making in the absence of markets: An empirically grounded model of entrepreneurial expertise.* School of Business: University of Washington.

Sarbin, T.R. (1989) Emotions as narrative emplotments. In Packer M.J. and Addison, R.B. (eds), *Entering the Circle. Hermeneutic investigation in psychology.* Albany: State University of New York Press.

Shaver, P., Schwartz, J., Kirson, D. and O'Connor, C. (1987) Emotion knowledge. Further exploration of a prototype approach. *Journal of Personality and Social Psychology*, 52: 1061–86.

Shepherd, D.A. (1999) Venture capitalists' introspection: A comparison of 'In use' and 'espoused' decision policies. *Journal of Small Business Venturing*, 37(2): 76–87.

Shepherd, D.A. and Zacharakis, A. (1999) Conjoint analysis: a new methodological approach for researching the decision policies of venture capitalists. *Venture Capital*, 1(3): 197–217.

Stacey, R.D. (2000) *Strategic Management and Organizational Dynamics*, 3rd edn. London Financial Times/Prentice Hall.

Stake, R.E. (1995) *The Art of Case Study Research.* London: Sage Publications.

Steyaert, C. (1997) A qualitative methodology for process studies of entrepreneurship. Creating local knowledge through stories. *International Studies of Management and Organization*, 27(3): 13–33.

Sturdy, A. (2003) Knowing the unknowable? A discussion of methodological and theoretical issues in emotion research and organizational studies, *Organization*, 10(1): 81–105.

Sutton, R.I. (1997). The virtues of closet qualitative research, *Organization Science*, **8**(1): 97–106.

Van Maanen, J. (1988) *Tales of the Field: On writing ethnography*. Chicago: University of Chicago Press.

Weick, K. (1995). *Sensemaking in Organizations*. Thousand Oaks, CA: Sage.

Weiss, H.M., Nicholas, J.P. and Daus, C.S. (1999) An examination of the joint effects of affective experiences and job beliefs on job satisfaction and variations in affective experiences over time. *Organizational Behavior and Human Decision Processes*, **78**(1): 1–24.

White, H. (1987) *The Content of the Form. Narrative Discourse and Historical Representation*. London: The Johns Hopkins University Press.

Wigren, C. (2003) *The Spirit of Gnosjö. The Grand Narrative and Beyond*. JIBS Dissertation Series No. 017. Jönköping: Jönköping International Business School.

Wiklund, J. (1998) *Small Firm Growth and Performance. Entrepreneurship and beyond*. Dissertation. Jönköping: Jönköping International Business School.

Yin, R. (1984). *Case Study Research*. Newbury Park, CA: Sage Publications.

Appendix A

Table 11A.1

ABANDONMENT$^{IV*(5)}$	ANGER$^{*(2)}$	BEWILDERMENT$^{V*(5)}$
Betrayal$^{V(1)}$	Aggressiveness$^{V*(1)}$	Distrust$^{V(2)}$
Dependence$^{V(2)}$	Indignation$^{IV*(8)}$	Doubt$^{IV*(5)}$
Emptiness$^{V(1)}$	Rage$^{I*(3)}$	Hesitation$^{V(2)}$
Helplessness$^{V*(4)}$		Reluctance$^{V(7)}$
Loneliness$^{III*(1)}$		Surprise$^{III*(1)}$
Sense of Unfair Treatment$^{V(1)}$		Suspicion$^{V*(1)}$
		Uncertainty$^{V(5)}$
(TOTAL 15)	(TOTAL 14)	(TOTAL 28)

CONCERN$^{V*(36)}$	CONFIDENCE$^{V*(10)}$	FRUSTRATION$^{II*(15)}$
Disappointment$^{II*(17)}$	Calmness$^{IV*(3)}$	Annoyance$^{II*(2)}$
Easy strain$^{V(1)}$	Cautious optimism$^{III(3)}$	Defensiveness$^{V(4)}$
Empathy/sympathy$^{II*(8)}$	Commitment$^{V(1)}$	Disharmony$^{V(1)}$
Regret$^{II*(3)}$	Conviction$^{V(1)}$	Dissatisfaction$^{V*(7)}$
Uneasiness$^{II*(3)}$	Expectation$^{V*(10)}$	Impatience$^{IV*(14)}$
Worry$^{II*(7)}$	Hope$^{III*(9)}$	Irritation$^{II*(18)}$
	Loyalty$^{V(1)}$	Persistence$^{V(1)}$
	Optimism$^{III*(2)}$	Restlessness$^{V(1)}$
	Reassurance$^{V*(2)}$	Feeling shut in$^{V(1)}$
	Security$^{V*(1)}$	
	Self-assurance$^{V(6)}$	
	Trust$^{V*(1)}$	
(TOTAL 85)	(TOTAL 49)	(TOTAL 64)

RESIGNATION$^{V*(7)}$	SATISFACTION$^{I*(23)}$	STRAIN$^{V(6)}$
Sense of cowardliness$^{V(1)}$	Amusement$^{I*(2)}$	Fatigue$^{V*(1)}$
Hopelessness$^{II*(1)}$	Challenge$^{V(1)}$	Grief$^{II*(1)}$
Lack of motivation$^{V(1)}$	Cockiness$^{V(1)}$	Guilt$^{II*(1)}$
Listlessness$^{V*(1)}$	Excitement$^{I*(5)}$	Hardship$^{V(2)}$
Pessimism$^{V*(1)}$	Happiness$^{I*(3)}$	Inability to express feelings$^{V(1)}$
Sense of giving up$^{V(1)}$	Joy$^{I*(20)}$	Inadequacy$^{V(4)}$
Tiredness$^{V(4)}$	Pride$^{I*(9)}$	Pain$^{V*(1)}$
	Relief$^{I*(10)}$	Pressure$^{V(4)}$
	Self-fulfilment$^{V(3)}$	Shock$^{II*(4)}$
		Stress$^{V(1)}$
		Tension$^{II*(1)}$

Table 11A.1   (continued)

		Threat[V]*[(2)] Vulnerability[V(1)]
(TOTAL 17)	(TOTAL 77)	(TOTAL 30)

Notes:
[I] Categorized by Shaver et al. within the same category.
[II] Categorized by Shaver et al. within a split category.
[III] Categorized by Shaver et al. within a new category.
[IV] Listed by Shaver et al. but not categorized.
[V] Not listed by Shaver et al.
[*] Listed by Averill.

Appendix B

Table 11B.1   Entrepreneur's expectations

Researcher	Answers	Emotions
What is your role today?	To push things forward. Development is too slow. The important thing is to bring out the right products at the right time. Costs are not that important. . . . The Marketing Department has a sales target of 262 million Swedish crowns and is supposed to bring forward the conditions to reach that target in a dialogue with the R and D Department. This is the way it is done this year. We do not ask the market – what the hell do you need this year?	Impatience Frustration Determination
What result do you expect from the meeting?	We will have a quarterly priority meeting next week about the development of new products. I expect this meeting to go a little bit ahead of that one. I think it is irritating to go over things again and again – it's about time something happened. We can make plans and forecasts and projects but we must concentrate in order *to get things done.*	Irritation Frustration Determination
Does the Marketing and Logistics manager agree with this?	Yes, I think so. Actually, I have made it very easy for him – he can raise the standards.	

*Table 11B.2   Meeting between the entrepreneur (E) and the Marketing
and Logistics manager (M) concerning a forecast*

	Statement	Emotions
E	I think you are *incredibly* optimistic at the Marketing Department . . . that the old products will sell. I had been expecting – I think myself that if we are not able to fully develop a standard application of the third generation quality assurance equipment, only half of the figures will be reached. I am *much* more pessimistic.	Irritation Disappointment
M	(increasing the volume of his voice): But this depends on what our agents say that they can sell. They do not know all products in the pipeline.	Annoyance
E	No, I am aware of that.	
M	(in a raised voice): *We* are supposed to make the intelligent decisions, we can't expect the agents to do that. . . . We can't write down 500 and keep our fingers crossed. I mean, we have been talking about the product for over one and a half years. What would be the basis for such an assumption? . . . All those figures are based on what the agents have answered to the question 'how much will you be able to sell?' Of course their answer is in accordance with what we *have available*.	Irritation Anger
E	(somewhat urging): So what you are saying is that you have not revised the figures?	Doubtfulness
M	We are not supposed to reveal the third-generation product yet. We are not able to present future products. So you are implying that we have not revised the figures?	Annoyance
E	Yes.	
M	No, we have not. But we can't do that. We can't change what the agents tell us. Or should we have done that?	Defensiveness Hesitation
E	Yes, I think so.	Resignation
M	(angrily): I mean, if we are to have some dynamics in this, we could have given a damn about asking the agents, and made everything up ourselves. That is another possibility. (In a calmer voice): What we can do now is to discuss the figures . . .	Irritation
E	I agree. We must take another round. This is too insignificant . . .	Disappointment
E	I can't believe this. I think it is – no, (turning to the manager of Marketing and Logistics), I do not think this is good. It's far from good. This is just a summary of what a bunch of agents have told you without your own standpoint.	Irritation Disappointment Worry

Table 11B.2   (continued)

	Statement	Emotions
M	(in a low voice): Of course we have our own standpoint.	Resignation
E	There are only two adjustments. (Silence) No, I really have to stress that – I would have asked for the opinion of the Marketing and Logistics Department – not that of the agents.	Disappointment Concern Frustration
M	(in a low voice): Is that so?	Resignation
E	Really, if it is the truth that is presented here, then the consequence is not that we should increase our R and D Department, but rather the other way around. We should keep it intact.	Irritation
M	(angrily): We are for *God's sake* not presenting any truths today – are we?!	Anger

Table 11B.3   Reflections on the meeting

Researcher	Entrepreneur	Emotions
Can you give me a comment on the meeting?	Yes that was a waste of time!	Dissatisfaction Frustration
Why?	Because there was nothing of the *dynamics* as it should have been.	Anger
Of the meeting or of the forecast?	Of the forecast. It was a sheer summary of the figures that the agents had handed in, with the addition of the Swedish market – but that was all.	Anger Frustration
Isn't that realistic?	No. It does not give the direction for the future. It does not give the stress on the discussion on what products we should develop and prioritize. Maybe the result is good next year – it is possible that we can surf on previous products – but that is all. But it is not enough. It is the same damn products as last year. Not a damn thing has happened.	Anger Worry
Why aren't the new products ready?	A damn good question. I think it's a question of concentration – more than I originally thought . . . There should have been another approach from the Marketing and Logistics Department.	Irritation
The R and D Department did not seem to react either?	No, not at all. That's one reason for this whole thing going to hell. They are all technocrats. They make calculations and file up. Therefore it was a sheer, *a sheer fiasco.* As I see it, anyone can make a forecast like this. The risk is that the dynamics are low.	Irritation Anger Disappointment

Table 11B.4   Diary notes from the other entrepreneurial process

Diary notes	Emotions
Thursday, 11 November 1999 *When I am trying to tell you what I have been doing this week, it is with horror that I realize that I cannot point out that I have been doing this or that, but I have made a hell of a lot of a hell of a lot. It is hard to pinpoint anything in special. And that makes me feel disharmonious, and it makes me afraid that I have not finalized things that should have been finalized. I would like to devote more of my time to customer relationships in the short and long run. And be able to devote my time to strategic issues. However, I am forced to attend to current, operational matters. Do I take part too much in the operational matters? Am I to blame myself? This is certainly not my intention, but sometimes it feels like it. And if so, something has gone wrong.*	Disharmony Inadequacy Frustration Concern
Thursday, 27 January 2000 *We are working full capacity to make the test toys for the exhibition. The toys look very nice. However, whether or not they will sell, we have no idea. We have the same problems as we had before – the sales price does not cover the costs. The risk is that we sell to a certain price just in order to get ready with the toys for the exhibition, and then we are not able to raise them later on. This work takes our full capacity of product development, product design and calculation. I am preparing for a school fair in Germany and an ironware fair, in Germany as well. It is hectic and trying right now. The pressure comes from the profitability being so low, and it is affecting everyone, of course . . . So right now, without being negative, and without having lost the spirit in any way, I feel that I am not up to it right now. I wish I was more competent and had more solutions to all our problems – it feels heavy right now.*	Cautious Optimism Pessimism Pressure Strain
Saturday, 11 March 2000 *The stand is ready, everything is on display, and it looks good, and now we are here with three other companies – we are all satisfied and look forward to the fair and we are all positive. We are going to have an interesting meeting with the wholesaler from the States. If that meeting is successful, if it goes as planned, then it will be pretty good for us. I will get back to you and tell you about it all, later on this week.*	Satisfaction Optimism Expectation

12 Techniques for collecting verbal histories
Brian McKenzie

Introduction

In 1998, the first year of my doctoral studies, I became the associate editor of the Academy of Management's Entrepreneurship Division newsletter. This position put me on a first-name basis with the most active researchers in the field of entrepreneurship, a vantage point from which I was able to watch them at their work. In Clifford Geertz's words, 'if you want to understand what a science is, you should look in at the first instance not at its theories or its findings, and certainly not at what its apologists say about it; you should look at what the practitioners of it do' (Geertz 1973: 5). What I could see entrepreneurship researchers doing, by and large, was collecting survey information using questionnaires. This observation was confirmed by a number of 'State of the art of entrepreneurship research' articles written between 1982 and 1997 (Paulin et al. 1982; Churchill and Lewis 1986; Wortman 1986; Aldrich 1992) as well as by a similar study done in 2001 (Chandler and Lyon 2001). These studies classified research presented at the Babson–Kauffman Entrepreneurship Research Conference (BKERC) and articles published in the top entrepreneurship journals by their subject matter and research methodologies. Brief comments on the prevailing methodology found in each of these 'State of the art of entrepreneurship research' studies are summarized in Table 12.1.

Every one of these studies pointed to the administration of questionnaires as the dominant method of data collection among entrepreneurship researchers. My years as a working entrepreneur had taught me first-hand the inaccuracy resulting from asking entrepreneurs to fill out questionnaires. All the entrepreneurs I had known were busy men and women who disliked paperwork. In addition, research based upon questionnaire surveys faces the difficulty of concise measurement. Entrepreneurship, as it has been described in the literature, is about contingency (Sarasvathy 2001: 17), creation (Meyer, Gartner et al. 2000), market pioneering (Covin, Slevin et al. 2000: 177), newness (Gartner and Brush 1999: 7), and organization initiation (Aldrich and Martinez 2001: 42). These constructs do not lend themselves well to the linear measurement of surveys and questionnaires (Bygrave 1989: 28).

On the other hand, both the literature (Hopkins and Feldman 1989: 29; Jack and Anderson 1999: 111) as well as my own experience with working

Table 12.1 *Comments on the prevailing methodology of entrepreneurship research by 'state of the art of entrepreneurship research' articles 1982–2001*

Article title	Reports studied	Findings
'Entrepreneurship research: methods and directions'	81	'Sample survey was by far the most common entrepreneurship research strategy, employed in 64% of the sampled studies.' (Paulin, Coffee et al. 1982: 357)
'A unified framework, research typologies and research prospectuses for the interface between entrepreneurship and small business'	51	'Throughout these studies, the use of mail questionnaires and interviews with structured or non-structured schedules is the overwhelming type of research methods used by most researchers.' (Wortman 1986: 277)
'Entrepreneurship research: directions and methods'	298	'An examination of the methodologies utilized in the research studies shows a preponderance (77%) of observational and contemplative theory building and surveys and few (less than 4%) field studies.' (Churchill and Lewis 1986: 345)
'Methods in our madness? Trends in entrepreneurship research'	322	'Investigators still relied heavily upon nonsystematic methods of data collection, and when they ventured out to collect data, they depended heavily upon surveys.' (Aldrich 1992: 199)
'Blinded by the cites? Has there been progress in entrepreneurship research?'	528	'Research design and sources of data have not changed very much over the past 15 years, other than a decisive break with journalistic and armchair methods by the journals after 1985.' (Aldrich and Baker 1997: 383)
'Issues of research design and construct measurement in entrepreneurship research: the past decade'	416	'Seventy five percent of the empirical papers used primary data. Of the studies using primary data, 66% used paper surveys, 25%

Table 12.1   (continued)

Article title	Reports studied	Findings
		used interview methodologies, 3% used phone interviews, 4% used experiments. Only four studies (2%) used participant observation.' (Chandler and Lyon 2001: 104)

entrepreneurs suggested that entrepreneurs were generally keen to share their experiences and loved to tell stories about them. The disparity between what I saw to be standard practice in entrepreneurship research and what I had seen to be effective practice led me to investigate the potential of using the verbal histories of entrepreneurs as a source of data for research.

The purpose of this chapter is to outline techniques for verbal history collection in entrepreneurship research. The chapter describes the personal experiences of the author in verbal history collection and includes a description of current state-of-the-art techniques for the collection of verbal histories of entrepreneurs. Issues surrounding data quality are also discussed. A set of protocols for the documentation, transcription and editing of verbal histories using readily available hardware and software is clearly laid out in order to assist other researchers. These techniques and protocols are summarized in table form, for easy reference in the field.

Verbal history collection
Verbal history collection is a particular form of ethnography or participant observation. The collection of verbal histories is a very old phenomenon as well as a relatively recent one. The origin of verbal history collection has been attributed to Homer's 800 BC account of the fall of Troy (Henige 1982: 7). However, it was the invention of portable tape recorders in the years following the Second World War that led to the development of modern verbal history collection. The Columbia University 'Great Man' recording project begun by Allan Nevins in 1948 popularized verbal history collection as a valuable method of collecting important historical data (Evans 1987: 34).

Verbal histories are the life stories told by a *memoirist* in the form of narrative discourse. Narrative has been defined as prosaic discourse which uses complete sentences linked into a coherent and integrated statement (Polkinghorne 1995: 6). Generally, only one person is speaking in a narrative, although the presence of others is implied (White 1981: 3). The term *narrative* emerged during the first century BC as a particular technique of rhetoric (Swearingen 1990: 174). Today, narrative is used synonymously with *storytelling* to describe a report of a sequence of events that a group of characters have engaged in (McGuire 1990). Narrative can be presented in written or verbal form. It can be classified as historical, literary or invented, depending upon the material the author presents (ibid.: 226). Verbal histories are spoken life stories, a particular form of historical narrative.

Verbal history evidence is maintained in the form of an *actuality* (Ridington 2001: 1), the name given to the audio recording of the discourse between a memoirist and an interviewer. It is important for those new to verbal history collection to recognize that the recording is considered to be the primary document in this field of research. Transcriptions of the audio recording are seen as interpretations of the actuality, since the process of transcription from an audio format to a textual one involves judgement on the part of the transcriber. As a scholarly tool, the actuality or verbal history recording is regarded as an accurate collection of the subjective evidence given by the memoirist in dialogue with the interviewer (Moss and Mazikana 1986: 25). The actuality documents the lived-in experience of the data collection and requires little, if any, added detail to transmit the accuracy of the participant observation experience.

In my research, the determination of whether or not verbal histories are factual is not an important concern. My research centers on trying to understand the nature of the phenomenon of entrepreneurship. What is important for my studies is the 'thick description' (Geertz 1973: 6) of the memoirist's understanding of their entrepreneurial experience. Thus, the delayed time and modified perceptions of the facts, which entrepreneurs tell in their life stories, heighten rather than diminish the quality of the data provided. The delayed time involved in verbal histories indicates that these life stories represent the memoirist's attempt to make sense of their relationship to the past. Gummesson (2000) has described historical analysis as being derived from sense-making which bridges our interpretation of the past to our interpretation of the present. Sense-making often takes the form of a series of anecdotes centered on past events (Allen and Montell 1981: 28–9). The modified perceptions involved in verbal histories result from the life histories not being self-initiated, but rather involving a discourse between the interviewer and the memoirist (Thompson 1988: 199). An important role for the interviewer is acting as a sounding board for the memoirist (Evans 1987: 26–7).

There are many advantages to verbal history collection as a research technique. Jerome Bruner has noted that we define ourselves and tell others about ourselves in life narratives (Bruner and Kalmar 1998: 318–22). He claims that narrative can be seen as a legitimate form of reasoned knowledge, providing a distinctive way of ordering reality (Bruner 1986: 11). Polkinghorne points out that the knowledge carried in stories is different from scientific knowledge and complementary to it (Polkinghorne 1995: 9); thus verbal history collection holds the potential to provide research evidence that would be hidden from other forms of qualitative and quantitative exploration. Gardner claims one of the advantages of studying life stories is that they allow the study of development, both of individuals and of their comprehension (Gardner and Laskin 1995: 63–4). More importantly, researchers have access to learning about how an individual understands his or her own development and the development of his or her venture (Atkinson 1998: 8). Finally, verbal history collection minimizes the impact of researcher bias, which is often coupled to the questions being asked (Ferber and Wales 1952: 126–7). Researchers, who are adept at collecting verbal histories, find that they do not have to ask many questions, but rather invite the memoirist to tell their story and then sit back and listen.

There are, however, disadvantages to verbal history collection. The data collected are unstructured, which can provide the researcher with a challenge when doing interpretation. Roemer points out that the data presented in verbal histories are always in the past: 'a story not only *is* past but *has* one' (Roemer 1995:14, italics in original). This past conceptualization is part of what makes storytelling a 'delicate art' (Cavarero 2000: 3). Cavarero claims the delicate art includes the ability to reveal meaning without defining it. However, a significant disadvantage embedded in this delicate art is the reification of the individual's identity. The memoirist both describes himself or herself and situates his or her life in a relationship of self with the world (ibid.: 25–36). Finally, verbal history does not afford the researcher the option of subject anonymity. The institutional review process required by most North American universities requires that verbal history collection be considered to be research involving potential harm to human subjects. Since verbal histories are not anonymous, the researcher is responsible for protecting the memoirist from harm caused by his or her own words. This can be a challenge if the memoirist has disclosed illegal or inappropriate behavior during the interview.

Verbal history interview techniques
This section outlines the techniques used in the collection of a series of recordings of entrepreneurs' verbal histories. The purpose of this section is to provide researchers with information on procedures that have proven useful in fieldwork. The section divides verbal history interviewing into three dimensions: the interview dimension, the technical dimension and the legal/ethical dimension. The section concludes with a table, which summarizes these three dimensions.

The challenge of finding informants

The selection of informants by field researchers is generally an area shrouded in mystery. When an ethnographer works in a foreign setting, the process of selecting informants often involves paying local assistants (Marcus 1998: 121) or associating with individuals who seek status from association with the fieldworker (Thomas 1987: 50). However, when field researchers work in domestic settings, they require a unique solution to the problem of gathering informants. Dorothy and David Counts are field anthropologists who studied North American seniors living in recreational vehicles (RVs). They describe their method of finding informants as 'lurking in the laundromat' (Counts and Counts 2001: 24). The Counts found that the social affinity associated with sharing the chore of doing laundry afforded the intimacy required for full disclosure of the many details of life in RVs.

I began my research by interviewing my cousin Sean Fillion, primarily because I had some depth of knowledge of his life story but also because Fillion and his partner Scott Hendrickson had been recognized as two of Canada's leading young entrepreneurs in the 2000 Business Development Bank of Canada Young Entrepreneur Awards (Arab and Ilchena 2000). Sean Fillion and I met to record his life story in September of 2001. I was surprised to discover the richness of detail included in Sean's narrative. I had known that Sean had started his business at the time when his mother's business had failed. However, I had never before known the impact of those difficulties on Sean. He described the stress he experienced at the start of his retail clothing business this way:

> If it didn't make it, Mom and I and Nick and Erica were looking at going on the street because we were all so screwed. Out of all of us, Erica wasn't working, I had the shop and Mom went bankrupt. Nick was the only one working. And that month that we started doing better, they were going to foreclose the house. So, you know it was just will, pure will. Because I could easily have went and worked for somebody else, and whatever else but I didn't see it that way. I didn't see it that way. (Fillion and McKenzie 2002, 21:20–21:49)

The experience of interviewing Sean Fillion convinced me that important new information about entrepreneurship could be extracted from the verbal histories of entrepreneurs. However, the experience also led me to believe that I would have to build personal relationships with each of the entrepreneurs strong enough to warrant their trust as a confidant.

My challenge in selecting memoirists for entrepreneurship research was to develop a strategy that would ensure a flow of one to two interviews per day over a period of several months. My starting point was my own social network. I solicited interviews of entrepreneurs that I had worked with and asked them to suggest other entrepreneurs who might be interested in participating in my study. This sampling strategy is commonly referred to as *reference-based* (see also Chapter 10 in this handbook).

At the same time, I expanded my search for memoirists by seeking introductions through networking agencies in the field of entrepreneurship. These agencies provided two paths to the recruitment of memoirists. First, I was able to introduce my research project at networking meetings and found that each of these introductions would lead to two or three volunteers. Second, the agencies provided me with lists of entrepreneurs who they thought would make suitable candidates. More importantly, these agencies allowed me the use of their name as a reference when I approached the entrepreneurs. This technique led to a constant flow of leads for new interviews.

Another technique I used to develop leads took a cue from anthropologists Dorothy and David Counts: utilizing social affinity. My data collection area included the coastal waters of British Columbia in Canada and Washington State in the USA. Cruising in the summer months proved to be an excellent source of new memoirists. Some interviews resulted from the social affinity associated with the ownership of the particular type of sailboat I owned (a Valiant 40). Other interviews resulted from a common interest in the marine industry, and some interviews just came naturally from tying up next to an entrepreneur. Only one of the many entrepreneurs I made contact with did not wish to be interviewed. The success of my approach to the development of trust as a confidant is shown in the interview of Stacy Kuiack. He began his verbal history with the story of his childhood in an entrepreneurial family:

> That's where the entrepreneurial history came from. So the good side was I was exposed to a whole bunch of different business issues at a really early age from a whole bunch of different angles. Mostly it was trial by fire. We made a lot of really, really, really bad mistakes. Had three mortgages on the house. I remember being ten years old in 1981 and knowing what mortgage rates were because it was a topic of discussion because there was three of them on the house when it was going when we were in a big recession here in B.C. (Kuiack and McKenzie 2002, 04:14–04:39)

More than once, throughout the process of data collection, I reflected on how open entrepreneurs were to my invitation to be interviewed. I wondered if this openness to participate was a characteristic of entrepreneurs in general or a reflection of my method of recruitment. Counts and Counts reported openness and a feeling of community among senior citizens living in recreational vehicles (Counts and Counts 2001: 185–218). On the other hand, Evans describes the difficulty he initially had in establishing rapport with Suffolk farmers (Evans 1987: 26).

Interview styles

Each researcher will have his or her individualized style of interviewing. I have found that a simple statement such as: 'This research collects the verbal histories of working entrepreneurs. Perhaps we could begin with you describing where you were born' works effectively as an opening. This direct approach has caused reactions such as: ' "Oh you want my real life story . . ." ' (Farmer and McKenzie 2002, 00.33–00.35) and ' "Well . . . yah . . . well let me give you . . . I'll kind of give you a few quick examples. One is I am a twin . . . ahhh supposedly identical . . . we're not sure . . . the doctor just came out of the army . . . and had a drinking problem so we're not sure . . ." ' (Morgan and McKenzie 2002, 00:40–00:56). My asking the memoirist to describe his or her birthplace seems to frame the interview in the context of life history and provide a comfortable starting point. I have also found that I can later locate the memoirist's history in time through their description of their childhood and schooling. This technique avoids the awkward question: 'How old are you?'

Once the interview has begun, I try to stay out of the conversation as much as possible. This can be a balancing act between the need for clarity and the desire to have the memoirist tell their own story in their own way. When I ask questions for clarity, I try to make them as open-ended as possible, adhering to the advice of Thompson: 'A careful or indirect question, previously worked out and confidently put is much better' (Thompson 1988: 201). Otherwise, I tend to rely on the advice of Evans: 'Hang back and in the silence that follows the speaker will grasp that he is intended to fill it. He will then usually get into his stride, and you will be able to interrupt without necessarily breaking his rhythm' (Evans 1987: 27).

I have found that it is good practice to not fiddle with the recorder during the recording. Constant monitoring of the recorder distracts the memoirist's attention from their conversation. I try to set the recorder on my knee or in my lap and glance at the recording level and time remaining indicators infrequently.

I make a habit of thanking each memoirist at the end of each recording. Since the memoirist will be receiving a complimentary copy of the recording, this recorded thank-you forms a polite ending to the actuality.

Technical dimension

The development of the magneto-optical disc led to a revolution in mobile recording. Magneto-optical discs and ATRAC compression offer two significant benefits over traditional cassette recording technology. First, the technology allow the size of a recorder to be significantly reduced while at the same time increasing the quality of the sound. This means that the informant may feel less intimidated by a recorder being present. Second, the quality of the recording is not adversely affected by vibration or shock, making this technology very suitable for field use (Yoshida 1994). The rugged nature of mini-disc technology has made it a favorite for researchers, who need to carry high-quality, reliable miniature recording devices into the field (Ritchie 1995: 58).

It is important to choose a microphone that matches both the frequency range of the mini-disc recorder and your personal style. There are a large number of microphones commonly available for use with the mini-disc recorder. Better-quality microphones have a battery-powered built-in pre-amplifier. The only disadvantage I have found with these microphones is that the researcher has to remember to turn the microphone off at the end of recording or the battery will discharge. However, this is more than made up for by the excellent audio quality captured by the microphone and its convenient size.

It took me a couple of trial recordings to master the use of the mini-disc recorder. I discovered three important things to remember at the beginning of each recording. First, I learned to always have plenty of discs on hand. Each disc is capable of recording up to 74 minutes of data. However, it has surprised me how long it can sometimes take to record an entrepreneur's life story. Second, I learned to always double check to ensure that I have the microphone plug inserted into the correct jack. Unfortunately, the micro-phone jack is the same size as the headphone jack, so it is easy to confuse the two. My double check is to closely monitor the microphone level indi-cator on the mini-disc recorder through the first few minutes of the inter-view. Third, I have learned to place the microphone well away from the mini-disc recorder. The recorder gives off an almost imperceptible noise as it records, but the microphone can pick up this noise if it is placed close to the recorder and this noise is irritating to the listener.

I have found that it is important to consider the sound environment of the recording (Ritchie 1995: 65). The sound environment, what Truax has termed the 'soundscape' of the recording (Truax 1984: 9), can provide a rich texture to the interview or it can provide a distraction. An example of a pos-itive texture provided by soundscape occurred in an interview that I recorded with Melchior (Melchior and McKenzie 2002). Luke is a dynamic young entrepreneur whose ambition is not hampered by his severe physical disabilities. The soundscape for our interview included the mechanical sound of Luke's electric wheelchair and the purr of the orange cat that sat in his lap throughout the interview. On the other hand, a distracting sound-scape occurred when I recorded an interview in a noisy coffee bar in Seattle. The clatter of dishes and the background chatter of the customers seated nearby make this fascinating verbal history very difficult to follow. I have learned to arrange interviews in as quiet a location as possible to minimize the effect of soundscape in the recordings. It is good practice to activate the play-only tab on each disc immediately after each recording session in order to minimize the chance of lost data.

Legal/ethical dimension

There is a tradition in verbal history collection of indicating the authorship of interviews using the convention: interview of '(memoirist name) by (interviewer name)'. It is extremely important to set out clearly the intended designation of authorship and copyright in the participant consent document and to review this document before the interview begins. In verbal history documents, the memoirist is considered the author of his or her actual words, while the interviewer is considered the primary author of the interview (Thompson 1988: 224).

Memoirists who participate in verbal history collection should reasonably expect minimal risk of harm resulting from their participation. Minimum risk of harm is defined as: 'the probability and magnitude of possible harms implied by participation in the research project will be no greater than those encountered by the subject in those aspects of his or her everyday life that relate to the research' (Medical Research Council, Natural Sciences and Engineering Research Council et al. 1998: 1.5).

Nevertheless, the spoken word is open to interpretation (Borland 1996), which can lead to harm of the participants. This harm can come about in one of two ways. First, the memoirist may say something slanderous or defamatory in the interview, not realizing that he or she is creating a public document. Second, the researcher may incorrectly interpret statements made by the memoirist and thus cause harm.

The situation of recording harmful material can be avoided by carefully reviewing the conditions of consent for the interview with the memoirist before the recording. Consent should be formalized in the signing of a participant consent document. This document can be reviewed and approved for use by the Institutional Review Board Committee on Human Subjects Research Ethics at the researcher's sponsoring institution. Each participant should be informed that he or she may withdraw from the research project at any time without any consequences or any explanation. Further, it should be explained to each participant that he or she will receive a complimentary compact disc copy of the actuality for review. The researcher should state in advance that, should the memoirist find any offending material in the recording, it can be edited from the master original before use in the research project. The researcher should be prepared to deal with questions from participants about the research project in an open and honest fashion.

The situation of causing harm through wrongful interpretation can be avoided by careful transcription and thoughtful reporting of results. Each researcher will have to make these decisions based upon his or her best knowledge of the circumstances. For example, this transcribed passage might not be appropriate to publish if the memoirist's father were still alive:

> My dad was a small merchant in New York in the textile business in Lower Manhattan. Unfortunately my mother passed away three days after I was born. So I was raised without a mother. I had two older sisters and lived in Brooklyn in New York until I was about nine or 10 years old. And then we moved to the Bronx till the time I was about 13 or 14. I kind of lived by myself. My dad was a workaholic and while it was a small business, it was him and one or two other guys occasionally. It was a hand-to-mouth kind of business and by the time I was 13 or 14 my sisters had gone off and gone to college and moved out. And so I lived with my dad, but I kind of lived alone because he would work from 8 in the morning and come home at 10 or 11 at night. (Rothman and McKenzie 2002, 01:06–01:57)

However, the passage provides an important insight into the character and upbringing of the entrepreneur, and its publication is appropriate in light of the father having been dead for a considerable time.

Summary of verbal history interview techniques
Each researcher will find that his or her project and fieldwork setting has its own unique set of characteristics. Table 12.2 summarizes the techniques I have found to be effective along three dimensions: the interview dimension, the technical dimension and the legal/ethical dimension. It is hoped that this summary of the techniques will be useful to researchers as a field guide.

Data quality
Researchers who are new to verbal history collection must consider data quality within the framework of their own particular research. Positivist research usually considers data quality in terms of validity and reliability. Interpretive research such as ethnography, in general, and verbal history collection, in particular, considers data quality in relativist terms based upon the memoirist's definition of his or her situation (Goldenberg 1992: 186) (see also Chapter 15 in this volume for an account of quality criteria). Verbal histories contain both recollections of the events of the past and the memoirist's interpretation of these events. Thus, in verbal history collection, the construct of validity is generalized to truthfulness of investigation (Kvale 1995: 25). Since interpretive research deals with unique situations, reliability cannot be defined as a measurement of the likelihood of similar conditions giving rise to similar observations (Aunger 1995: 99), as it would be within the framework of positivist research. Thus, in verbal history research, the construct of reliability is generalized to craftsmanship on the part of the researcher (Mays and Pope 1995: 110).

Table 12.2   Techniques in collecting verbal histories

Interview dimension	Technical dimension	Legal/ethical dimension
Develop trust as a confidant with memoirists through introductions from social networks or the use of social affinity as a keystone.	Monitor interview location for 'soundscape' which does not distract from the verbal history.	Clearly set out the intended designation of authorship and copyright in the participant consent document and review this document before the interview begins.
Begin recording by stating the date, the location and the full name of the memoirist.	Remember to take to the interview lots of discs and spare batteries.	Carefully review the conditions of consent for the interview with the memoirist before the recording.
Open the dialogue with a statement such as 'This research collects the verbal histories of working entrepreneurs. Perhaps we could begin with you describing where you were born.'	Place the mini-disc recorder away from the microphone to avoid noise.	After the interview, send a complimentary compact disc copy of the actuality to the memoirist for review.
Once the interview has begun, try to stay out of the conversation as much as possible and try not to fiddle with the recorder.	Double check to ensure that the microphone plug is inserted into the correct jack.	Avoid wrongful interpretation through careful transcription and thoughtful reporting of results.
Thank the memoirist at the end of the recording session and then turn off the mini-disc recorder.	Activate the play-only tab on each disc immediately after each recording session.	Share any royalties received from the exercise of the copyright equally between the interviewer and the memoirist of that recording.

My research has been exploratory in nature. Exploratory research is inherently inductive in its reasoning: grounding theory development in a small number of cases through a process of theoretical sampling. Research that attempts to use verbal histories in a deductive reasoning process will incur a number of complex issues surrounding the process of random sampling. Such research might best be balanced with the use of questionnaires and the asking of cross-related questions to increase the reliability of the data collected. The following paragraphs discuss the concept of reliability as it relates to verbal history collection in general and to my use of verbal history collection in particular.

In verbal history, there are two types of reliability that must be considered: evidentiary reliability and interpretive reliability. Evidentiary reliability refers to the credibility of the narrative that the memoirist presents. Interpretive reliability refers to the care with which the evidence is collected and presented in the research work.

Evidentiary reliability can be evaluated by checking the internal consistency of the memoirist's narrative (Lummis 1987: 83). Each actuality can be tested for reliability by checking that the narrative has coherence, consistency and is free of contradictions (Fisher 1985: 364). The researcher must, however, remember that it is the sense-making of the memoirist's relationship to past that is being recorded. The following transcription provides an example of how this sense-making can take precedence over factual matters:

> We formed this company. Anyways, I went back to Britain and I got my entry permit. As an entrepreneur, I was allowed into Canada, within . . . well I think that was . . . I'm just trying to think now. That was March. I think it was June I got the OK I could come to Canada. I flew out again on my own in July and bought a house in Prince George. And we arrived in September on the Labour Day weekend. My wife, one daughter was 15 months old and one was three months old. And with all our worldly possessions in 10 suitcases. So from March of '80 until September of '80 we were done, sold off everything in Britain and were here. (Newman and McKenzie 2002, 14:39–15:20)

While the memoirist is unclear of the exact dates involved, he makes sense of this blurred sequence of events by remembering that his emigration from Britain happened quickly and that he and his family arrived in Canada with all their possessions in ten suitcases. Interpretive reliability can be much more difficult to establish. A recording of an encounter is inherently more reliable and accurate than a written record of that encounter (Thompson 1988: 108). Still, care must be taken in the documentation and the referencing of the actuality to ensure that a reliable interpretation of the encounter is developed. Researchers have an obligation to clearly document the process they use in interpretation to ensure interpretive reliability.

Protocols used in verbal history collection
Protocols are intended to ensure the authenticity of data collection and replication. This section looks at documentation, transcription and editing. It also sets out a recommended methodology for accurately copying and archiving actualities that have been collected in the field. Underlying this

methodology is recognition of the verbal history recording or actuality as the primary document of reference.

Documentation
The goal of good documentation is to provide adequate and timely access to information without creating a burden of paperwork. Verbal history documentation requires mastery of the creation and storing of both audio and written documents. The audio documents include the actuality, a master original recording of this actuality and a number of copies made from the master original. The written documents include the participant consent document, an outline of each recording and a catalog of all recordings made.

Audio documentation begins with the actuality or the mini-disc used in the recording session with the memoirist. The actuality should begin with a verbal note of the date, location and name of the memoirist. The actuality should be labeled before the recording session, or if the session extends beyond the length of a single disc, the additional discs should be labeled as soon after the session as feasible.

As soon after the interview as possible, the interview should be copied from the actuality to a recording master. This process uses the mini-disc recorder to reverse the ATRAC compression resulting in an analogue output. The analogue signal is transferred to the microphone input connection of a personal computer audio card. The analogue signal is re-converted to digital using any of a number of readily available digital audio editor software packages. The resulting 16-bit stereo mode audio file will be stored in WAVE format. The WAVE format, identified by the file extension: '.wav', was created by Microsoft and has become a standard PC audio file format for everything from game sounds to compact disc (CD)-quality audio. WAVE files can be recorded on standard recordable compact discs (CDR), which can then be replayed on any CD player. The new disc is referred to as the *master original* and should be labeled with the name of the memoirist and the date of the recording along with the words 'Master Original'. This disc should be recorded on an HHB brand compact disc recordable (CDR) compact disc. HHB brand compact discs have the highest estimated archival stability rating of any compact discs produced (estimated to be in excess of 100 years). Generic compact discs have an estimated archival stability rating of 30–50 years.

It is good practice to develop a strategy for archiving the verbal history recordings early in the research project. One way that security of data can be ensured is through distributed storage. The concept of distributed storage relies on the unlikelihood that disaster will strike more than one place at a given time. Thus the researcher stores data in multiple media

Table 12.3   Summary of storage and access to recordings

Description	Medium	Storage	Access
Original recording	Sony MDW74D recordable magneto-optical disc	Safety deposit box	Principal researcher only to create master original
Master original	HHB brand CDR 74 gold or silver recordable compact disc	Locked fire-proof box in different location from original recording	Principal researcher only to create working copies
Working copy (number)	Generic CDR 74 recordable compact disc	Locked filing cabinet at principal researcher's work station	Principal researcher and others with specific permission
Complimentary copy	Generic CDR 74 recordable compact disc	Delivered to memoirist	Memoirist
MP3 copy	Generic CDR 74 recordable compact disc	Locked filing cabinet at principal researcher's work station and computer hard-drive	General

formats in multiple locations. The master originals are only used for the creation of working copies of the recording. The medium, storage and access restrictions of each copy of the verbal histories that I have collected are summarized in Table 12.3.

Working copies of verbal histories are copied as needed from the master original using any available brand of CDR disc. Each of these should be labeled with the name of the memoirist, the interviewer, the date of the recording and the words: 'Working Copy' or in the case of a copy which is being given to the memoirist, with the words: 'Complimentary Copy'. I have found it convenient to create another version of each interview in MP3 format. MP3 is an acronym for Motion Pictures Experts Group Audio Layer-3 (Jones 2000: 1), an audio coding algorithm developed at the Fraunhofer Institut in Germany. The MP3 format shrinks the size of WAVE files by a factor of 10 to 12 without a perceptual loss of sound quality. MP3 format allows the easy exchange of audio files over networks, allowing data to be stored on the hard-drives of multiple computers to further distribute the data.

The archival stability of all compact discs can be affected by the quality of the label used on it. Researchers should use high-quality labels and take care in the installation of these labels to ensure the archival stability of the compact disc.

Written documentation begins with the creation of an outline of each recording. I have found that the easiest way to create this document is to monitor and summarize the interview in a table in which a summary of the memoirist's conversation is noted against a timescale of two-minute intervals (McCracken, Bronstein et al. 1974: 11; Hitch and Norris 1988: 26). I usually do this as the master original is being created. The outline serves as a quick reference tool for retrieving information from recordings as well as a written record of each recording. Table 12.4 gives an example of the first ten minutes of an interview I recorded with Tony Melli.

I have found it useful to develop a folder for each recording. This folder includes a printed copy of the outline, a working copy of the recorded interview, copies of any correspondence with the memoirist, a copy of the participant consent document and any other information gathered about the memoirist.

More general information about each recording, including the memoirist's contact information, should be stored in a recording catalog. The recording catalog can be created using any convenient database software. This catalog can be used for follow-up mailings to memoirists and serves as a convenient source of demographic information. Again care should be taken to keep several copies of the recording outlines and the recording catalog utilizing a distributed storage security strategy.

Transcription

Transcription was a necessary archival tool in the era of magnetic tape recording due to the poor archival stability of the medium (Ritchie 1995: 41). However, with modern compact discs offering archival stability in excess of 100 years, the tedious task of transcription is no longer required for archival purposes. In contemporary verbal history collection, the actuality recorded with the memoirist is considered the document of reference and so no attempt needs to be made to transcribe interviews in their entirety.

Transcription is a difficult literary form requiring interpretation of the grammar and phrasing of a verbal document (Thompson 1988: 229–32). It also alters the nature of the verbal history, removing both the soundscape and the intonation of the memoirist. Consider this piece of transcription:

> I came back for a couple of months and I just hated it. So I just . . . I can't believe I did it . . . but I . . . one day I came and I took all my staff out for lunch and

Table 12.4   Example of a recording outline

Understanding Entrepreneurship
Verbal History Project
Interview Data Sheet

Memoirist:	Tony Melli
Interviewer:	Brian McKenzie
Recording Date:	April 16, 2002
Tape ID:	013

Recording Outline

Time (minutes)	Outline
Start	Tony begins his story by talking about his family moving from Italy to Canada. His father was a mechanic who ran his own business in the downtown core. Tony was born in Canada in the Cabbagetown area of Toronto.
2	Early education at a Catholic High School. Tony works at his father's garage 'taking carburetors apart and things like that'. He describes himself as a spatial thinker. He describes his brother showing him an early mainframe computer at the University of Toronto.
4	Tony ends his education in the midst of a recession. He describes himself as 'not doing great in any course except those he was interested in'. I ask him about business courses he took in his Computer Science degree.
6	Tony begins his career working for his brother in a small software company developing sophisticated systems on the PC platform. 'It seems my whole life I've been trying to prove that you can do things on smaller equipment than most people think you can.'
8	Lessons learned in developing product: a different way of viewing database retrieval with a windowing feature.
10	Tony states his theory that ideas exist out there . . . a version of the collective conscious.

bought them everything I'd told them we couldn't afford. I went out and bought it all and faxed my resignation to the head office and walked out the door. (laughs) (Vickers and McKenzie 2002, 34:57–36:10)

What the reader cannot determine from this transcription is the gender of the memoirist. The audio recording clearly shows the feminine voice of the memoirist – Shirley Vickers – and thus enhances the power of the statement that the memoirist is making.

Transcription of sections of interviews is necessary for the inclusion of quotations in research reports. I have found Express Scribe Transcription Playback Software (ExpressScribe 2002) produced by NCH Swift Sound to be a valuable aid to accurate transcription. This software allows the transcriber to slow down the playback of recordings to a speed appropriate for his or her level of typing ability. The software uses the function keys of a standard computer keyboard to control the playback of a recording. This makes it easy for the transcriber to stop, rewind and manipulate the speed of the recording without having to remove his or her fingers from the keyboard.

Editing

As a general principle, the actuality created in a verbal history recording session should not be edited (Ritchie 1995: 45–6). However, there will be situations where the memoirist will review his or her complimentary copy of the recording and find material that he or she wishes to have deleted or added. Decisions to edit an interview should be made only after discussion with the memoirist or when the memoirist has specifically asked that certain comments made during an interview be kept off the record. Edits to a WAVE file can be made using commonly available digital audio editing software such as GoldWave Digital Audio Editor (Goldwave 2003). When an edit is made, the master original recording should be used as the basis for the edited recording. The new recording should be labeled 'Edited Master Original' and the original master recording should be destroyed. The current best practice for destroying a compact disc is to place the disc on a non-metallic stand in a microwave oven and subject it to 15 seconds of high-temperature radiation (Ardant 2000).

Major strengths and weaknesses of verbal history collection

This chapter has outlined the value of verbal history collection in entrepreneurship research. Verbal history is a form of ethnography particularly suited to the study of entrepreneurship. As a scholarly tool, verbal history is an accurate collection of subjective evidence (Moss 1974: 11) created by the 'memoirist' (Moss and Mazikana 1986: 25) in dialogue with the interviewer. Verbal history documents contain the self-created life stories of the memoirists. The life stories that entrepreneurs tell represent their attempts to make sense of the events of their past.

However, it should be pointed out that there are limitations to the use of verbal history collection as a research tool. The evidence collected in verbal histories is limited to the individual's sense-making of past events and may not be factually accurate. Since each memoirist describes the events of their life in a unique way, the researcher may have difficulty reconciling different memoirists' interpretation of similar events. Verbal history data collection

Table 12.5   Summary of the strengths and weaknesses of verbal history collection

Strength	Weakness
1 Provides an accurate collection of subjective evidence.	1 Evidence is limited to the individual's sense-making of past events and may not be factually accurate.
2 Actualities provide 'thick description'.	2 Researcher must develop a position of trust as a confidant.
3 Entrepreneurs appear to be very open to recounting their life stories.	3 Researcher may have difficulty reconciling different memoirists' interpretation of similar events.
4 Simple field-proven techniques for data collection.	4 Data collection is time-consuming, limiting the number of cases a researcher may collect.
5 Current technology facilitates accurate distribution of verbal data.	

can be time-consuming, thus limiting the number of cases a researcher may collect. The strengths and weaknesses of verbal history collection are summarized in Table 12.5.

Collection and analysis of verbal histories has provided me with many new insights into the way that entrepreneurs think and act. The weaknesses of verbal history collection are frequently pointed out to me by researchers who adhere to a positivist approach to inquiry. In responding to these colleagues, I have become ever more convinced of the importance of verbal history collection and analysis as an appropriate tool for entrepreneurship research.

Evidence collected in verbal histories may not be factually accurate. However, the individual memoirist's sense-making of past events provides the researcher with a more comprehensive view of past events than the facts would suggest. Action researchers have begun to challenge the assumptions of order, rational choice and intentional capacity that have long been held as presuppositions of factual accuracy (Kutz and Snowden 2003: 462–6). Weick has argued that sense-making combines authoring, interpretation and the creation or discovery of past events (Weick 1995: 8). Thus, what may appear to some researchers as the weakness of verbal histories factual accuracy may appear to other researchers as conceptual richness and thick description.

Researchers who collect verbal histories must develop a position of trust as a confidant. This takes time and effort, which are often precious commodities in the world of academic research. However, my experience in collecting verbal histories has shown that the richness of the material collected and the pleasure of the personal contacts developed has made this time well spent. It must be remembered that verbal histories are co-authored aural documents. Since the researcher is an integral part of the discourse that the memoirist develops in recording his or her verbal history, it is essential that the researcher make the memoirist aware that it is the memoirist's story that is important, not the researcher's special interests or biases (Wetherell, Taylor et al. 2001: 17). Thus, while it does take time and effort to develop a position of trust as a confidant, the researcher is rewarded with rich and reliable data.

Researchers may have difficulty reconciling different memoirists' interpretation of similar events. Information collected in verbal histories can be identical in context, complementary in context, contradictory in context or so different as to have no common features at all (Henige 1982: 71). At best, the variation in differing memoirists' interpretations of similar events can lead to confirmation of a general sense of the event. At worst, the variation in interpretation can lead to the need to further explore the circumstances surrounding the event. This additional research may provide clues to missing links in a chain of events which is extremely complex or may provide the researcher with new insight into the area being studied.

The collection of verbal histories is time-consuming, limiting the number of cases a researcher can collect. However, researchers can mitigate this weakness with two strategies. First, the data collected in verbal histories are very rich and thus lend themselves to use in multiple studies. Second, researchers can easily share data collected by colleagues or students. The development of new recording technologies and the ability to transmit recordings over the Internet are creating new and efficient ways to collect and disseminate verbal history data.

I hope that this chapter will be the first step in the development of a common set of protocols which will assist researchers in developing networks of verbal history data.

Recommended further readings

Chamberlain, M. and P.R. Thompson (1998) *Narrative and Genre*. New York: Routledge. *Narrative and Genre* draws on a wide range of disciplines in the social sciences and humanities to examine how far the expectations and forms of genre shape different kinds of autobiography and influence what messages they can convey.

Dunaway, D.K. and W.K. Baum (1996) *Oral History: An interdisciplinary anthology*. Walnut Creek, CA: Altamira Press. This is a collection of classic articles by some of the best-known proponents of verbal history, demonstrating the basics of verbal history while also acting as a guidebook for how to use it in research.

Ritchie, D.A. (2003) *Doing Oral History*. New York: Oxford University Press. A comprehensive handbook on the theory, methods and practice of verbal history, based on work by the Oral History Association to revise its professional standards and principles.

Thompson, P.R. (1988) *The Voice of the Past: Oral History*. Oxford, UK: Oxford University Press. In this fully revised edition of his pioneering work, Paul Thompson traces verbal history through its own past and weighs up the recent achievements of a movement which has now become international.

Yow, V.R. (1994). *Recording Oral History: A practical guide for social scientists.* Thousand Oaks, CA: Sage Publications. With extensive examples from both historical and social science literature, this book is a practical guide to methods of recording verbal history.

References

Aldrich, H.E. (1992) Methods or madness? Trends in entrepreneurship research. *The State of the Art of Entrepreneurship*. D.L. Sexton and J.D. Kasarda. Boston, MA: PWS–Kent Publishing Company: 191–213.

Aldrich, H.E. and T. Baker (1997) Blinded by the cites? Has there been progress in entrepreneurship research? *Entrepreneurship 2000*. D.L. Sexton and R.W. Smilor. Chicago, IL: Upstart Publishing Company: 377–400.

Aldrich, H.E. and M.A. Martinez (2001) Many are called, but few are chosen: An evolutionary perspective for the study of entrepreneurship. *Entrepreneurship Theory and Practice*, **25**(4): 41–56.

Allen, B. and W.L. Montell (1981) *From Memory to History: Using oral sources in local historical research*. Nashville, TN: American Association for State and Local History.

Arab, D. and K. Ilchena (2000) Clothes make the men: Sean Fillion and Scott Hendrickson win BDC Young Entrepreneur Award for Alberta. Calgary, AB, Business Development Bank of Canada: 2.

Ardant, D. (2000) *The Toasties Nuke Guide*, Asthenosphere. Available at http://toast.ardant.net/guide.shtml.

Atkinson, R. (1998) *The Life Story Interview*. Thousand Oaks, CA: Sage Publications.

Aunger, R. (1995) On ethnography: storytelling or science? *Current Anthropology*, **36**(1): 97–130.

Borland, K. (1996) 'That's not what I said': interpretive conflict in oral narrative research. *Oral History: An interdisciplinary anthology*. D.K. Dunaway and W.K. Baum. Walnut Creek, CA: AltaMira Press: 320–32.

Bruner, J. and D.A. Kalmar (1998) Narrative and metanarrative in the construction of self. *Self-awareness: Its nature and development*. M. Ferrari and R.J. Sternberg. New York: The Guilford Press: 308–31.

Bruner, J.S. (1986) *Actual Minds, Possible Worlds*. Cambridge, MA: Harvard University Press.

Bygrave, W.D. (1989) The entrepreneurship paradigm (II): Chaos and catastrophes among quantum jumps? *Entrepreneurship Theory and Practice*, **14**(2): 7–30.

Cavarero, A. (2000) *Relating Narratives: Storytelling and Selfhood*. New York: Routledge.

Chandler, G.N. and D.W. Lyon (2001) Issues of research design and construct measurement in entrepreneurship research: the past decade. *Entrepreneurship Theory and Practice*, **25**(4): 101–13.

Churchill, N.C. and V.L. Lewis (1986) Entrepreneurship research: directions and methods. *The Art and Science of Entrepreneurship*. D. Sexton and R. Smilor. Cambridge, MA: Ballinger: 333–66.

Counts, D.A. and D.R. Counts (2001) *Over the Next Hill: An ethnography of RVing seniors in North America*. Peterborough, ON: Broadview Press.

Covin, J.G., D.P. Slevin et al. (2000) Pioneers and followers: competitive tactics, environment, and firm growth. *Journal of Business Venturing*, **15**(2): 175–210.

Evans, G.E. (1987) *Spoken History*. London, UK: Faber.

ExpressScribe (2002) *Express Scribe Transcription Playback Software*. Canberra, ACT, NCH Swift Sound.

Farmer, T. and B. McKenzie (2002) *Terry Farmer Oral History*. Sidney, BC.

Ferber, R. and H.G. Wales (1952) Detection and correction of interviewer bias. *The Public Opinion Quarterly*, **16**(1): 107–27.

Fillion, S. and B. McKenzie (2002) *Sean Fillion Oral History*. Sidney, BC.

Fisher, W.R. (1985) The narrative paradigm: an elaboration. *Communication Monographs*, **52**: 347–67.

Gardner, H. and E. Laskin (1995) *Leading Minds: An anatomy of leadership*. New York: Basic Books.

Gartner, W.B. and C.B. Brush (1999) *Entrepreneurship as Organizing: Emergence, newness and transformation.* Lloyd Grief Centre for Entrepreneurial Studies. Los Angeles, CA: University of Southern California: 25.

Geertz, C. (1973) *The Interpretation of Cultures: Selected essays.* New York: Basic Books.

Goldenberg, S. (1992) *Thinking Methodologically.* New York: HarperCollins.

Goldwave (2003) GoldWave Digital Audio Editor. St John's, NFLD, GoldWave Inc.

Government, US (2002) *Copyright Law of the United States of America.* Washington, DC: US Copyright Office.

Gummesson, E. (2000) *Qualitative Methods in Management Research.* Newbury Park, CA: Sage Publications.

Henige, D.P. (1982) *Oral Historiography.* New York: Longman.

Hitch, C. and J. Norris (1988) *Conducting an Oral History Interview.* Willowdale, ON: Ontario Historical Society.

Hopkins, T. and H. Feldman (1989) Changing entrepreneurship education: finding the right entrepreneur for the job. *Journal of Organizational Change Management*, **2**(3): 28–40.

Jack, S.L. and A.R. Anderson (1999) Entrepreneurship education within the enterprise culture: producing reflective practitioners. *International Journal of Entrepreneurial Behaviour & Research*, **5**(3): 110–25.

Jones, C. (2000) *MP3 Overview*, Webmonkey. Available at: http://www.webmonkey.com/webmonkey/00/31/index3a.html?tw=multimedia.

Kuiack, S. and B. McKenzie (2002) *Stacy Kuiack Oral History.* Sidney, BC.

Kutz, C.F. and D.J. Snowden (2003) The new dynamics of strategy: Sense-making in a complex and complicated world. *IBM Systems Journal*, **42**(3): 462–83.

Kvale, S. (1995) The social construction of validity. *Qualitative Inquiry*, **1**(1): 19–41.

Linstead, C. (2001) Preserving digital sound recordings. Victoria, BC. 31 July (unpublished).

Lummis, T. (1987) *Listening to History: The authenticity of oral evidence.* London: Hutchinson Education.

Marcus, G.E. (1998) *Ethnography through Thick and Thin.* Princeton, NJ: Princeton University Press.

Mays, N. and C. Pope (1995) Rigour and qualitative research. *British Medical Journal*, **311**(6997): 109–13.

McCracken, J.W., E. Bronstein et al. (1974) *Oral History: Basic techniques.* Winnipeg, MAN: Manitoba Museum of Man and Nature.

McGuire, M. (1990) The rhetoric of narrative: A hermeneutic, critical theory. *Narrative Thought and Narrative Language.* B.K. Britton and A.D. Pellegrini. Hillsdale, NJ: Lawrence Erlbaum Associates: 219–36.

Medical Research Council, Natural Sciences and Engineering Research Council et al. (1998) *Tri-Council Policy Statement: Ethical Conduct for Research Involving Humans.*

Melchior, L. and B. McKenzie (2002) *Luke Melchior Oral History.* Sidney, BC.

Meyer, D., B. Gartner et al. (2000) The research domain of entrepreneurship. *Entrepreneurship Division Newsletter.* Worcester, MA: Entrepreneurship Division of the Academy of Management, **15**: 6.

Morgan, R. and B. McKenzie (2002) *Ron Morgan Oral History.* Sidney, BC.

Moss, W.W. (1974) *Oral History Program Manual.* New York: Praeger.

Moss, W.W. and P.C. Mazikana (1986) *Archives, Oral History, and Oral Tradition: A RAMP study.* Paris, France: General Information Programme and UNISIST United Nations Educational Scientific and Cultural Organization.

Newman, P. and B. McKenzie (2002) *Peter Newman Oral History.* Sidney, BC.

Paulin, W.L., R.E. Coffee et al. (1982) Entrepreneurship research: methods and directions. *Encyclopedia of Entrepreneurship.* D.L. Sexton and K.H. Vesper. Englewood Cliffs, NJ: Prentice-Hall: 352–73.

Polkinghorne, D.E. (1995) Narrative configuration in qualitative analysis. *Life History and Narrative.* J.A. Hatch and R. Wisniewski. Washington, DC: The Falmer Press: 65–23.

Ridington, R. (2001) *Oral History Practice (an Overview).* Department of Anthropology. Vancouver, BC: University of British Columbia: 2.

Ritchie, D.A. (1995) *Doing Oral History.* New York: Twayne Publishers.

Roemer, M. (1995) *Telling Stories: Postmodernism and the invalidation of traditional narrative.* Lanham, MD: Rowman & Littlefield.

Rothman, N. and B. McKenzie (2002) *Nathan Rothman Oral History.* Sidney, BC.

Sarasvathy, S.D. (2001) *Entrepreneurship as Economics with Imagination.* School of Business, Seattle, WA: University of Washington.

Swearingen, C.J. (1990) The narration of dialogue and narration within dialogue: the transition from story to logic. *Narrative Thought and Narrative Language.* B.K. Britton and A.D. Pellegrini. Hillsdale, NJ: Lawrence Erlbaum Associates: 173–97.

Thomas, S.D. (1987) *The Last Navigator.* Toronto, ON: Random House of Canada Limited.

Thompson, P.R. (1988) *The Voice of the Past: Oral History.* Oxford, UK: Oxford University Press.

Truax, B. (1984) *Accoustic Communication.* Norwood, NJ: Ablex Pub. Corp.

Vickers, S. and B. McKenzie (2002) *Shirley Vickers Oral History.* Sidney, BC.

Weick, K.E. (1995) *Sensemaking in Organizations.* Thousand Oaks, CA: Sage Publications.

Wetherell, M., S. Taylor et al. (2001) *Discourse as Data: A guide for analysis.* London: Sage Publications.

White, H. (1981) The value of narrativity in the representation of reality. *On Narrative.* W.J.T. Mitchell. Chicago, IL: University of Chicago Press: 1–23.

Wortman, M.S. (1986) A unified framework, research typologies and research prospectuses for the interface between entrepreneurship and small business. *The Art and Science of Entrepreneurship.* D. Sexton and R. Smilor. Cambridge, MA: Ballinger: 273–333.

Yoshida, T. (1994) The Rewritable MiniDisc System. *Proceedings of the Institute of Electrical and Electronics Engineers, USA* **82**(10): 1492–500.

13 Using e-mails as a source of qualitative data
Ingrid Wakkee, Paula D. Englis and Wim During

Introduction
Using e-mail in qualitative research methodologies is a fairly recent phenomenon. This is not surprising considering that the World Wide Web with
Internet and e-mail access was only opened to public use in 1991. With relatively low penetration during the first few years, the adoption of the
Internet had sky-rocketed to over 600 million users around the world by
2002. As shown in Table 13.1, business Internet penetration in selected
developed countries reached levels of more than 70 percent by 2001
(OECD 2002). Clearly this offers considerable opportunities for collecting
data not previously available.

So far, e-mail has mainly been used in quantitative research as a means
to distribute surveys, often in combination with online questionnaires.

Table 13.1   Businesses with Internet access, 2000–2001 (%)

Country	2000	2001
Denmark	87.0	93.0
Japan	n/a	91.5
Finland	84.0	90.8
Sweden	n/a	89.9
Australia	77.0	86.0
New Zealand	n/a	84.0
Austria	n/a	83.7
Norway	74.0	82.0
Netherlands	n/a	79.0
Italy	n/a	72.0
Portugal	n/a	72.0
Canada	63.4	70.8
Spain	n/a	67.0
United Kingdom	n/a	63.4
Luxembourg	n/a	54.6
Greece	n/a	54.2

Source: OECD, ICT database and Eurostat, E-Commerce Pilot Survey 2001, August 2002.

There is also some qualitative literature which examines the use of e-mail correspondence between researcher and informant as a means to gather data (Harris 2002; Kralik et al. 2000; Selwin and Robson 1998). This technique of 'e-mail interviewing' creates e-mails for research purposes. Further, some studies have examined the nature and content of e-mail and how it affects intra- or interfirm communication (Kollman 2000; Pantelli 2003). In these studies, e-mail has been the *subject and topic* of the study. However, the aim has not been to describe and explain business processes in general. Also, even though the studies have described what codes or measures were used, they have not offered guidelines on how to deal with the specific characteristics of e-mail messages, nor on the specific complexities of preparing and analysing these messages. Indeed, a void was identified regarding the use of *e-mail as a source of data* in qualitative research on entrepreneurship topics.

The scarcity of references to the use of e-mails as a source of data in entrepreneurship research may not, on the one hand, be surprising considering the relatively short existence of (public access to) the Web. Yet, on the other hand, it is remarkable because using e-mail offers interesting opportunities that do not exist when (only) using other sources of data. For example, using e-mails as a source of data provides researchers with very rich information that may enable them to develop an understanding of phenomena in a way that is similar to observation but without actually being present at the site (Wakkee 2003). In addition to offering such opportunities, e-mail data also present challenges. Company e-mails have several characteristics related to form, structure and technical properties that make this data source different from other sources. This chapter addresses three research questions:

1. What is the value of using company e-mails in qualitative research on entrepreneurship?
2. How are e-mails different as a source of data from other sources of qualitative data?
3. What research method can be used to deal with the complexities of using e-mail and benefit most from their richness?

The value of e-mails as a source of data will be determined on the basis of the richness of the information contained in them, and practical issues related to the method of eliciting and analysing it. The chapter is organized around these issues. The first section contains a short discussion on how the use of e-mails as a source of data fits within the qualitative paradigm. In the second section, e-mails are compared with other sources of data. This comparison is based on insights from communication richness theory (e.g. Daft and Lengel 1984) and previous research experiences (Wakkee 2003, 2004). Third, a step-by-step method is proposed for the use of e-mail as a source of qualitative data. This method was developed during a case study investigation into the global start-up process of a Dutch high-tech enterprise (Wakkee 2004). To illustrate both the benefits and drawbacks of the proposed method, we include specific examples from this case study and reflect upon the findings. The chapter concludes with a discussion of the implications for further research.

E-mail research in the qualitative paradigm

Qualitative research can be positivist, interpretive or critical. The choice of a specific research strategy (such as the case study method) may be independent of the underlying philosophical position adopted. For example, both case study and action research can be positivist (Yin 1994; Clark 1972), interpretive (Walsham 1993; Elden and Chisholm 1993), or critical (Carr and Kemmis 1986).

The use of e-mail as a source of data is not limited to certain ontological or epistemological views on reality or the truth. Data contained in e-mails are created independently of the research, and interpretation of these data is done by the researcher, independent of whether this researcher adopts a positivist, interpretive or critical paradigm. Yet, because of the personal and often informal nature of e-mails, they do offer the researcher the opportunity to come as close to the 'reality' as perceived by the person sending the e-mail message. At the same time we realize that the interpretation of the researcher could affect the outcome of the study. By using multiple investigators and reporting back to the authors of the e-mail for confirmation, the interpretations can be made more objective and less personal.

E-mails and other data sources

When reviewing the literature on qualitative research methods, including classic and contemporary case studies, a large number of potentially valuable data sources can be identified such as observation and participant observation (fieldwork), interviews and questionnaires, documents and texts (e.g. diaries, archival records, reports), (telephone) transcripts, websites (Bell and Loane 2002), and the researcher's impressions and reactions.

In the following paragraphs, we discuss how e-mails differ from other data sources in terms of both content and structure. We examine how this affects the value of e-mails as a source of data, and how research methods used with other data sources have to be adapted to suit e-mail research.

The first clue regarding the value of using company e-mails can be found in media richness theory. Daft and Lengel (1984) present a media richness hierarchy, arranged from high to low degrees of richness. They identify four criteria: (a) the availability of instant feedback; (b) the capacity of the medium to transmit multiple clues such as body language, voice tone and inflection; (c) the use of natural language; and (d) the personal focus of the medium. Face-to-face communication is the richest communication medium in the hierarchy, followed by telephone, electronic mail, letter, note, memo, special report and, finally, flyer and bulletin. As shown in Table 13.2, e-mail can be considered a warm and personal medium (e.g. Walther 1996; Pantelli 2003), carrying equivalent levels of information richness to face-to-face interaction, including characteristics of both written and spoken language. Recent developments in e-mail communication, such as the use of emoticons (e.g. smiley faces) or the use of capitals to express anger or exclamation, have only increased the personal and informal nature[1] of e-mails in the last few years. The presence of signs of emotions can create rich pictures of organizational culture and development. Because richness is one of the important determinants of the value of a specific data source

Table 13.2   Characteristics of different qualitative data sources

	Instant feedback	Transmission of multiple clues	Use of natural language	Personal focus of the medium
Face to face (interview)	Very good	Very good	Very good	Very good
Observation	(Very) good	Very good	Good/ mediocre	Good/ mediocre
Telephone (interview)	Very good	Good	Very good	Very good
Instant messaging	Very good	Good/ mediocre	Good/ mediocre	Good/ mediocre
E-mail	Good	Good/ mediocre	Good	Very good– mediocre[1]
Fax	Mediocre	Poor	Good	Mediocre
Letter	Poor	Poor	Good	Mediocre
Archival records	Poor	Mediocre/ poor	Mediocre/ poor	Poor
Websites	Mediocre/ Poor	Mediocre	Mediocre	Poor
Reports	Poor	Mediocre/ poor	Mediocre/ poor	Poor

Note: [1] The personal focus of e-mails can vary considerably, depending on whether an e-mail is personal and being sent to only one or a small group of individuals or impersonal and sent to a large number of e-mail addresses (e.g. spam).

and case study descriptions (Miles and Huberman 1994), media richness theory suggests that company e-mails are indeed a valuable source of data.

The richness of company e-mails is not a sufficient reason for using them as a source of data. After all, face-to-face communication is still richer than e-mail communication. There are other relevant reasons for including e-mails as a data source.

Using e-mails may, at first sight, seem similar to using paper correspondence as a source of data (i.e. Thomas and Znaniecki 1918 in their classical case study on the Polish peasant in Europe and America). Yet the difference in speed of exchange affects the type of information exchanged by e-mail and letter. Early research by Sproull and Kiesler (1986) also suggests that because of its informal nature, e-mail accelerates the exchange of information to a great extent. In addition, the use of e-mail may lead to the exchange of new information. New information is information the respondents reported they would not have received or sent if there were no electronic mail (Pantelli 2003). New information was obtained both from people the receiver knew and from unknown people. This suggests that the information contained in company e-mails may not be available from any other source.

Although the use of e-mail was reserved for less formal topics of communication initially, it is increasingly being used in business transactions and contracts. For example, whereas a few years ago it would be unthinkable to send an application letter by e-mail, this is now becoming more accepted – and even required by some companies. Especially in communication with external contacts, entrepreneurs or other individuals must be very careful in their formulation of some electronic messages. Also, files such as contracts, computer programs, statistical data, pictures or even audio and video files may be attached to the e-mails. Such information might previously only have been available from archives. The main benefit of obtaining such documents via e-mail is that often the e-mail will also include some additional explanatory information about the documents, while this is not likely to be included in the archive. The additional information helps the researcher make sense of the data and, as such, it will be an important element of the case study database. Hence, e-mail messages are not only an additional source that may confirm data from other sources, but are also an essential source containing information not found in other sources. Further, the exchange of information with both existing and new contacts suggests that analysing e-mails may be a sensible way to map network development. Additionally, unlike archival records, company reports and websites, company e-mails are not produced for the purpose of the investigation. As a result, researchers do not have to take extra measures to deal with issues of socially desirable answers, such as might be obtained through interviews (Nancarrow and Brace 2000). From all this it can be concluded that including e-mails as a source of data becomes increasingly important when studying entrepreneurial processes to obtain a rich, complete and credible picture of these processes.

Research method

The following section describes a method of using company e-mails as a source of data. This method will be described along the four basic steps of any qualitative study: (1) case selection; (2) data collection; (3) data preparation; and (4) data analysis. The basics of the method are not very different from existing methods used for other data sources. Yet, due to the specific nature of e-mails, additional steps and adaptations are necessary that may not be required for other data sources.

Step 1: case selection

Case selection is very important. Basically, researchers have to consider three issues in relation to case selection. First, as in any other research method, formulating selection criteria based on the research question and sampling strategy is critical (e.g. Glaser and Strauss 1967).

Second, researchers have to make sure e-mail is a common means of communication in the case study object. Because e-mail messages are often very short,[2] a large number of e-mails is necessary to be able to understand the processes under investigation. Third, researchers must gain access to interesting cases and ensure the willingness of relevant informants to participate. Gaining access to an organization for research purposes is generally difficult (see also Chapter 10 in this volume for access problems in entrepreneurship). Organizational decision-makers might fear that (1) being involved in a research project is too time-consuming or (2) that sensitive information is being misused or becomes available to the wrong people (Erlandson et al. 1993). Because e-mail collection is less time-consuming and the researcher does not have to be present in the company during the collection, the first issue may present a minor objection when using e-mails as a source of data compared to interviews, direct observation, or even the investigation of archival records. Indeed, collecting e-mails is not time-consuming. E-mails can simply be forwarded from the company's to the researcher's computer. The hesitance to share sensitive information may present a more difficult obstacle. Establishing a fairly high level of trust between the decision-maker and the researcher will be necessary in most cases before researchers will be granted access to the e-mails. Yet, as Leenders et al. (2001: 44) note, 'nowhere in the world have these kinds of excuses proved insurmountable'. Typically, this stumbling block can be overcome by tapping into your network. Researchers should be aware that doing so might lead to selection biases. However, as long as the case-firm is only atypical in that it allows access and not in the business process under investigation, we expect that this selection bias will not affect the outcomes of the study as data (the content of the e-mails) are created independently from the data collection and analysis.

In terms of ethics and confidentiality, it has to be noted that e-mail messages can include information that is highly sensitive and personal. Although individuals employed at the target company will most likely be aware that e-mails are being used in research, external contacts will not know that their writings are being scrutinised. Moreover, disclaimers and privacy statements are increasingly included in e-mails. Researchers need to consider carefully how to deal with such issues. For instance, they may seek permission from all the external informants separately. But this may be a time-consuming process. Therefore, it seems better to use aliases to disguise the real identities of the external contacts and/or not to display literal quotations of these individuals that may lead to their identification in the case study report.

Step 2: data collection
Once a case has been selected and access is gained, data can be collected. Three issues should be taken into consideration when planning and collecting data: (1) real-time versus post-date collection of data; (2) the number and variety of mailboxes from which e-mails are collected; and (3) the timeframe and period of data collection.

The first issue concerns the choice of whether (a) to collect all the e-mails in one go, some time after they have been sent or received (post date) or (b) to collect them instantaneously when they are sent or received (in real time). Both approaches have several benefits and drawbacks.

The major benefit of the post-date approach is that at the time of writing the e-mails no one (not even the decision-maker giving consent to the use of e-mails) is aware that they will be used in research at a later stage, whereas in a real-time approach, at least the decision-maker may be affected by this knowledge and may be more careful when writing e-mails. Thus post-date collection may reduce individuals' tendency to engage in socially desirable behaviour and improve the validity of the data. But a major drawback of the post-date approach is that most likely a pre-selection has already been made. When receiving e-mails, people delete those messages that do not seem important to them. Also, the decision-maker may decide to remove all the e-mails from the 'e-mail archive' that he does not want the researcher to see.

In a real-time approach no such pre-selections have been made as the messages are sent instantaneously to the researcher. Another benefit of the real-time approach is that the researchers can stay up to date on company developments without actually being present on the site. Also, it allows the researchers to start analysing data as soon as received rather than waiting until an enormous amount of data is collected. When adopting this real-time approach, researchers should remain aware of the fact that individuals may decide to use other (personal) e-mail addresses not included in the study or other channels of communication such as telephone or face-to-face meetings when they know e-mail data will be used in investigations.

The second issue with respect to data collection involves which e-mail addresses and mailboxes are being used in the research. Using only the 'sent items' mailbox from a single individual in the company (e.g. the founder) provides a totally different set of data (both quantitatively and qualitatively) than when all mailboxes of all company officials (founders and employees) are included. Again the research question as well as the size and structure of the firm and the type of knowledge sought will determine how many and which mailboxes to include in the study.

The third issue in relation to data collection is the timeframe set. The e-mail data should cover the entire period under investigation. However, it should be taken into consideration that only so much data can be processed. Given that a single person may send dozens of e-mails during a day, one has to be careful not to drown in data.

The volume of data handled depends on the timeframe of the research, the number of researchers involved in the investigation, as well as the level of detail needed to answer the research question sufficiently. For instance, an exploratory research question may be answered sufficiently on the basis of a review and analysis of a very large number of e-mails, whereas an explanatory research question may require more in-depth analysis and allow for a smaller number of e-mails. If feasible, however, the data-collection period should be based on the time-boundaries of the actual process under investigation. Clearly, this issue is strongly related to the issue of post-date and real-time data collection. In some cases researchers will enter the field only once the process under investigation has begun. Combining post-date and real-time data collection may then be necessary.

Step 3: preparation
The actual preparation process will most probably consist of the following steps. In order to prepare for analysis, all files should be loaded into the case study database. Such a database allows researchers to register and structure all data included in the study, to list and describe the relevant concepts and theoretical perspectives used in the study, to make theoretical and methodological notes, and to report about (the progress of) the analysis (Hutjes and Van Buuren 1992). The case study database facilitates cooperation

between researchers while working on a project. Also, it enables others to replicate the study when desired, thereby increasing the reliability of the findings.

Before starting the analysis, researchers should decide whether or not to use computer-assisted qualitative data analysis systems (CAQDAS) in their investigation (Fielding 1994; Weitzman and Miles 1994). This decision is usually based on the personal preferences of the researcher as well as the nature of the research question. When more detailed analysis is required, more benefits can be derived from CAQDAS (Barry 1998; Seidel 1991; Seidel and Kelle 1995; Coffey et al. 1996). From our perspective the most obvious advantages of CAQDAS is that it is faster and facilitates a more complex coding of data, which saves time and improves the quality of the data analysis. Some special features of e-mail communication just increase these benefits, but at the same time these special features may also lead to the inclusion of several additional and time-consuming steps. E-mails often belong to chains of messages and answers or comments to previous messages. Because earlier messages are often included at the bottom of a response, many messages may be included several times in the database since they were included in several documents. The software can allow the researcher to keep track of these chains of e-mails fairly easily by grouping them into sets that can be undertaken manually.

Because most software packages can only read .txt and .rtf files, loading the data into the database is a time-consuming process. Every message and its attachments (which many include Word documents, PowerPoint presentations, Internet links, .pdf files, pictures and even a videotape) will have to be opened, saved as a .txt file, and then uploaded into the database. Because of the time-consuming nature of this process, it may be advisable to review all the e-mails first, while they are still in the researcher's inbox, and remove all non-relevant e-mails such as spam, personal e-mails and messages that include disclaimers before loading them into the database. After this, some 'housekeeping' may be in order. Housekeeping activities may include removal of typing errors to allow for automatic coding, translation of unfamiliar words or concepts (when languages foreign to the researcher are being used in the e-mails, as was the case in our research), and separation of different messages (e.g. responses to earlier messages) in single e-mails. As with other types of data, it is highly recommended that housekeeping activities are tracked in a diary or journal.

The final preparatory step involves grouping the emails into sets and subsets. As the grouping is based on an initial content review, this step could already be considered part of the actual analysis of the data. Sets and subsets refer to groups of messages from the same sender or receivers, or messages about the same topic. Each e-mail can belong to several different sets or subsets (e.g. based on the topic, the period, the location etc.). Although part of this grouping will have to be undertaken manually, basic groups can be identified in the e-mail program where the e-mails were originally stored. Programs such as the recently introduced Gmail from Google automatically create such e-mail chains and store e-mails sent between two e-mail addresses with the same subject line as one file; therefore, this program could be a valuable tool in linking and analysing e-mails.

Step 4: analysis

Next, the actual analysis can begin. Analysing the content of e-mails is not very different from analysing other types of written data. Researchers can adopt an inductive or a deductive approach. In the former, researchers start reading through the data and develop categories and codes as they move forward. This approach allows the data to 'speak for themselves' without the imposition of existing theoretical frameworks (Denzin and Lincoln 2000). Often researchers using this analytical approach to different sources of data adopt a grounded theory approach. However, Kelle (1997: 20) suggests that many researchers have jumped on the 'grounded theory bandwagon' because it is 'an established brand name' and are in fact applying a 'coding paradigm' that is neither inductive nor deductive, but a mixture of both (Kelle 1997).

In order to create a starting point for conducting inductive research, different software packages (e.g. 'WordCruncher') could be used to break down the texts and calculate how often certain words or concepts can be found across all documents, thereby finding recurring themes (e.g. Harveston et al. 2004). This approach is, however, very tricky when using e-mails as a source of data, since many messages will be contained repetitively as chains of questions and responses develop. As a consequence, the words and concepts in these chains will be included several times and therefore the themes identified by the software may not accurately represent reality. One solution could be to create an additional database listing all messages rather than all e-mails and then removing all double messages before conducting this investigation, which will be a time-consuming process.

The deductive approach is more theory driven and builds on previously developed categories and codes derived from earlier studies. This approach was followed in our own research, as we believed that sufficient information on the relevant 'constructs' and 'measures' could be found in the literature on which the case study was based.

Coding process   When following a deductive approach several steps have to be taken. First, researchers have to determine what they want to know from the individual e-mails and/or all relevant sets of e-mails (e.g. all e-mails, only those sent to a specific external contact or a specific topic). These 'questions' are called attributes. An attribute is a named generic property (e.g. Age, Marital Status) that the researcher can give to documents. Each document (e-mail) was given a specific value for the attribute (e.g. 49, Single).

The attributes can be more general, such as the language used in the document, or the number of messages included in a single e-mail. Attributes can also be more theory driven, such as the nature of the relationship between the sender and the receiver or the stage of company development at the time of sending the e-mail (e.g. opportunity recognition phase, growth, etc.).

Thus, the first step is to create an attribute table on the basis of a previously defined theoretical framework including all the relevant attributes and their (expected) values. Second, to be able to find the relevant information in the e-mails, a large number of potential *codes* must be identified or devised. These may be the words (combinations and synonyms) that are frequently mentioned in the literature in relation to the attributes.

Once the coding tables have been developed, all documents can be automatically searched for these codes. When conducting an automatic code search, reports can be generated listing all occurrences. By combining codes belonging to a certain attribute or value of this attribute, sets and subsets can be created. On the basis of these sets and subsets, the attribute tables can be filled in fairly quickly.

Relying only on automatic coding could be dangerous and result in less valid outcomes for several reasons. First, the lists of predefined codes will most probably not prove sufficient for extracting all relevant information from the e-mails. For example, in many cases, organizational names may be used in the e-mails (e.g. Fiat or University of Istanbul). Researchers will be able to classify such organizations (respectively an Italian automotive multinational and a Turkish university) based on their previous knowledge and experience, but such specific names will not be included in a coding table up front, because it is unlikely that the researcher knows all relevant contacts before the start of the analysis, let alone the nicknames or aliases sometimes used in informal e-mails (e.g. company officials used the nicknames 'Mosquito's', de 'Muskietenboys' and 'muskieten' when referring to one of their customers). Also, as suggested by Brown et al. (1990: 136), the existence of synonyms would lead to incomplete retrieval of information. So although it is possible to search for particular terms, variations and derivatives of those terms, the way in which respondents express similar ideas in completely different ways makes it difficult to recover all responses. Alternatively, researchers may overlook or be confronted with the existence of homographs among their codes. Homographs are words that have the same 'names' but different meanings. An example would be the word 'order': (1) in order to; (2) in the following order; (3) sales order.

Finally, when investigating companies that are active in multiple countries, the e-mail database may include e-mails in multiple languages. Even if researchers are able to understand each of those languages, it seems unlikely that they will be able to include a complete codebook in each.

For these reasons, it is recommended to complement the automatic coding process with manual coding before completing the attribute tables. During the manual coding, the generated sets of documents can be reviewed to determine whether the automatic coding actually referred to the required information (e.g. when searching for [sales] 'order' the automatic search tool may also come up with hits for in 'order' to). Further, during the manual coding process, the blanks left by previously unidentified synonyms, personal names and even 'tacit knowledge' can be completed.

In order to improve the reliability of the manual coding process, it is advisable to use multiple coders in the project team. This will allow for comparison of the coding results and attribute tables and to determine the inter-rater reliability.

Parallel to the manual coding on the basis of the previously defined codes related to the attributes, e-mails should also be coded liberally with 'free nodes',[3] as suggested by Richards and Richards (1995). These free nodes can be used to store any other information, such as contact name, origin of the e-mail (internal/external), signs of company culture (e.g. hierarchical structures or openness of communication between employers and employee), or anything else that may prove valuable to the research or to understanding the context in which the investigated process or project takes place.

Location of information   With respect to the 'location' of the information, most of the information used to assign the attributes can be found in the body of the messages. However, information may also be found in the subject header. The nature of the contact with whom the message is exchanged may be found in the (e-mail) address listed in the From/To fields. For instance, some names (such as Fiat) may be well known, or the extension provides a clue about the nature of the organization (.gov or .edu) or its location (i.e. .nl or .uk). Some country-domains (e.g. .tk) are, however, open to non-residents; therefore, it is necessary to search carefully for additional clues regarding the location of the contact. Also, attachments may provide relevant information for answering the research questions.

Finally, combining the findings using both the results from the automatic and manual coding processes, the *attribute table* can be filled in for each document and/or for relevant sets of documents. Not every e-mail or set of e-mails is likely to provide information on each of the attributes included in the table. The e-mails can then be left out of further analysis on these specific topics.

The attribute tables can then be used as data matrices that form the basis of the analysis. They are also useful as a starting point in the reconstruction of the consecutive events and developments in the process under investigation or the relationship between the different actors involved in it. The further analysis process is similar to that for information obtained from other sources of data and is beyond the purpose of this chapter.

Starting global: evidence from company e-mails

In a recent study on global start-ups we examined the role of networking in the global start-up process of high-tech ventures (Wakkee 2004). The following presents an account of the research process.

Step 1: case selection

The case firm was selected on the basis of three criteria:

- it would have to be active around the world;
- it would need to have been founded two or three years before the start of the investigation to ensure that business activities such as sales were already initiated but that the firm would still be involved in its start-up process;
- e-mail would have to be a common tool for communication both internally and externally.

The firm was identified through our network at the University of Twente, and we gained access by using the names of two shared network contacts and explaining the purpose of the study. In our study we did not have to ask specifically to gain access to company e-mails. Instead we suggested a more common type of data collection method combining interviews with observation and archival records. The entrepreneurs, however, suggested that we might want to access their company e-mails instead (in combination with fewer interviews and no observation but access to archival records). As a result, we did not have to deal with some of the complexities described in step 1 above.

Step 2: data collection

In our study, we collected about 800 e-mails in real time during a period of six months between December 2001 and May 2002. In addition, we gained access to 176 e-mails that were stored in the company archives. These 176 e-mails covered a period between 1995 and 2001 but only included those e-mails the entrepreneurs had considered worth saving. It is unclear what percentage this comprised of all e-mails sent and received during the period they were collected. Thus we combined post-date and real-time data collection. The main benefit was that the complete time-period was included, although a limited number of e-mails was included for the post-date period. The main drawback was that potentially interesting data had been removed.

At the time of the investigation, the venture employed five people, including the founders, all of whom were working part time for the company. All company mailboxes were included in the study, and therefore we could gain a fairly complete picture of developments. However, as some company employees were sometimes using personal (university student) e-mail addresses, the coverage was not 100 percent. The percentage of missing e-mails seemed to be relatively small as copies of many of the 'missing' messages were found at the bottom of response e-mails. About 54 percent of all messages included in our dataset were either sent by, or received by, or forwarded to the founder of the firm. Therefore it seems that, in this case, using only his inbox and 'sent items' box might also have generated a relatively complete picture of the global start-up process in this firm. The e-mails were sent to and by 128 external contacts from over 112 organizations, none of which was asked for permission to use their data. So far, we have dealt with this issue by obscuring their identity. Further, we asked the consent from the company's decision-maker before publishing anything about our study.

Step 3: preparation
In our investigation, we adopted QSR Nvivo to store, prepare and analyse the data (Welsh 2002). Nvivo allows for creating and editing primary or secondary data to facilitate their exploration, organization and linking, as well as the searching, modelling and theorizing of an emerging analysis (Barry 1998; Jemmott 2002).

After collecting all e-mails in our mailbox, we loaded each of them and the accompanying attachments individually into the case study database. In order to prepare the e-mails for analysis, we first conducted several house-keeping tasks. To distinguish between multiple messages in a single e-mail, we colour-coded the messages, using black for the 'original' messages and all messages sent by the sender of the original message, green for responses, and blue for comments by forwarded messages.

Step 4: analysis
Next, an attribute table and the codebook were composed (see Tables 13.3 and 13.4 for a small selection of the attributes and codes used in this study). The choice of attributes and codes depends on the research question that is being investigated. In our particular research on the global start-up process, we were interested mainly in the nature and development of the international activities and the development of the venture's network.

Table 13.3   *Selection of attributes and values used in global start-up*
                research

Attribute	Value
Nature of international activities	Innovation, R&D, building a resource base, building an organization, production, setting up distribution channels, sales, service, 'networking'
Timing of international activity	Date of first reference of specific country–activity combination
Network composition and development	
Type of contact	Individual, company, research institute, governmental/agency, sector organization, financial organization (bank, VC), accountancy, consultancy, lawyer; unknown, not applicable
Country of origin	List of countries of the world
Type of relationship	Customer, supplier, investor, banker, employee, trainee, distributor, prof. adviser partner in R&D, partner in production, external researcher, competitor; unknown, not applicable
Origin of contact/ antecedents	Internet/Yellow Pages; introduced by third party, conference or trade fair, previous employment, school, childhood, network event or social gathering; unknown, not applicable

To determine the nature of the contacts, 'the type of organization', 'the location of the organization' and 'the nature of the relationship between the contact and the firm' was established. For instance, when searching the e-mails for customers of our global start-ups, code words such as sales, (sales) order, customer, client, buyer and their Dutch equivalents were used.

First, we searched the e-mails[4] automatically for these codes. Then a manual search was conducted. During the manual inspection, we found many cases where the search terms used did not refer to the actual concept under investigation. For instance, regarding international sales activities, we conducted a search for the word 'order'. This search yielded results for both 'sales *orders*' but also for 'in *order* to . . .'.

After coding the e-mails, we created groups based on sender/receiver, subject header (e.g. creating chains of messages), topic (e.g. sales, human resources, R&D), and because the research focused on internationalization, the different countries to or from which e-mails were sent. For instance, we created a set of e-mails from or to contacts in four different organizations in Italy and seven different contacts in Germany. This information allowed

Table 13.4   Code table for contact type

	English	Dutch
University/ research institute	University, research institute, lab(oratory), researcher, scientist, science, .edu, .ac	Universiteit, Onderzoeks Instituut, Lab(Oratorium), Onderzoeker, Wetenschapper, Wetenschap
Company	Start-up, multinational, firm, venture company, commercial, .com	Starter, Multinational, Firma, Bedrijf, Commercieel
Governmental agency	(Local, regional, provincial) government, ministry, chamber of commerce, innovation relay centre, tax office, customs, .eu	(Locale, regionale, provinciale) Overheid, Ministerie, Uitvoeringsinstantie, Kamer Van Koophandel, Belastingdienst, Douane
Individual	Friend, acquaintance, family (brother, sister, uncle, aunt, father, mother, niece, nephew, cousin), neighbour	Vriend, Kennis, Familielid (Broer, Zus, Oom, Tante, Vader, Moeder, Neef, Nicht) Buurman/Vrouw
Financial institution	Bank, investor, venture capital, angel, loan	Bank, Investeerder, Risico Kapitaal, Lening
Sector organization	Sector organization	Branch Vereniging, Sector Organisatie

us to fill in the attributes tables. Figure 13.1 provides an example of how e-mail data were used to fill in the attribute table.

After completing the attribute tables, we reviewed the remaining set of e-mails in a search for additional information to confirm, complement or reject the information previously compiled. Next, we established a timeline linking different activities to obtain a model of the global start-up process. On the basis of the information obtained from the different external contacts, network models were created to link the different factors to each other as well as to the process, as shown in Figure 13.2.

Reflection and limitations

In the following discussion we will specifically address a number of issues in relation to coding and content of the e-mails. In addition, we will discuss various quality considerations and ethical dilemmas.

Coding and content

With respect to our methodology, several issues must be discussed. Using software in the data analysis process added rigour to the qualitative research (Richards and Richards 1995). In our view, the search facility in Nvivo

From: AK	To: G@fiat[1].it[2]
Sent: tue 05-02-2002, 5:09 PM	subject: Visit

Hello Mr[3]. G

Self evidently we are interested in visiting your establishment in Turin.[4, 5] Since we are a small starting company with only limited financial means, we have to be prudent in travelling expense. If you would consider our visit to be of serious help to you in understanding our Technology[6, 7], self evidently we will come rightaway.

If it would be good enough to have some e-mails back and forth to start with, we would also accept that. Maybe we both would have more of a meeting once you have been working with the goods and a larger amount of questions and ideas have been generated. Most likely, we will visit Italy[8] anyway later this year (August?) trying to combine visits to various prospects.[9]
Let us know what you consider optimal.

Kind Regards
AK

#	Topic	Value
1	Type of organization	Fiat = multinational firm (automotive)
2, 4, 6	Location	1: Extension = .it = Italy; 2: Location: Turin = Italy 3: Italy
3	Level of formality	Use of Mr. suggests they are not close friends but they are either just business acquaintances or they recently met
5, 6	Origin of the contact (timing)	Sentences suggests previous contact, so the relationship started prior to this e-mail being sent
7	Type of relationship	Use of Sound Inc's products / lack of understanding -> suggests: Customer (medium certainty)
8	Topic of communication	Visit? Or (After sales??) service: -> Suggestions for further means of communication
9	Internationalization process	Visit suggests that more sales or representation activities are being undertaken in Italy

Figure 13.1   Linking data to attributes

particularly facilitated data interrogation. In our research, the search function was used to find evidence about how relationships were established between our case company and its external contacts (trade fairs, introduced by third party, direct mail etc.). Clearly, carrying out such a search electronically will yield more reliable results than doing it manually because human error is eliminated. Also, a larger number of codes could be included in the analysis than possible manually. However, while conducting the automatic coding process and comparing the results with the manual coding, problems arose. It became clear that many internal issues (e.g. incompleteness of our coding table/synonym lists, the use of personal names and the existence of homographs) limited the validity of the outcomes of the automatic coding process. Manual coding is essential if researchers want to benefit from the richness of the data. This problem exists when analysing data from many different types of sources. However, the informal nature of e-mails compounded this problem. In our case study, we found that in internal communications between company officials, nicknames and variations of nicknames were sometimes being used for external contacts. For example, one contact was sometimes referred to by his personal name, but he and his firm were also referred to as the Mosquitos, de Muskietenboys, and de Muskieten. This makes it very difficult to rely on automatic coding to get all relevant information about this contact.

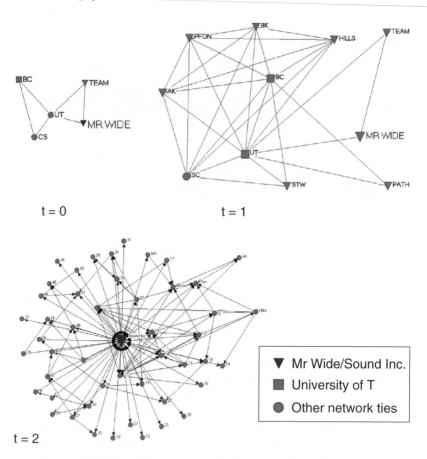

Figure 13.2   Network composition of the firm based on analysis of the e-mails

Another issue in the coding process is the use of multiple languages in the e-mails. In our case study, we originally included Dutch and English translations of the concepts in Table 13.3 as we had expected these languages to be used in the e-mails. However, during the inspection of the e-mails we soon learned that some were written in German. Considering the small number of German e-mails, we decided to use manual coding rather than automatic coding for them. From our experience, we would recommend researchers to use automatic coding processes for the e-mails written in the most common languages and conduct manual coding for those in the remaining (less common) languages. It is unlikely that researchers will be able to produce complete code lists in each of the languages.

Our experience showed that most e-mails had to be reviewed and coded several times before the data contained in the information started to make sense or before the value of the different attributes could be determined. For instance, we were only able to link the nickname 'Mosquitos' to the appropriate real name after reviewing the e-mails several times. Also, sometimes it was not clear where a particular contact was located by reading only one e-mail to or from this contact since address details were only included in one or two of all these e-mails (for instance only when a sales order was placed). This problem is particularly relevant when an e-mail is relatively short. Some consist of only five or six words followed by a salutation and a (first) name.

Because of the informal language used in the e-mails (e.g. use of nicknames) and the wide variety of topics discussed through e-mail, the data in the e-mails proved very rich. E-mails provided a good insight into both the contexts and culture in which the process or project under investigation takes place. If researchers rely only on automatic coding, this richness cannot be appreciated and utilized. From our analysis it became apparent that the casual nature of some e-mail exchanges made tacit knowledge more explicit. Groen and Nooteboom (1998) called this 'intellectual midwifery'. Reading the company e-mails was like listening in on telephone conversations or witnessing face-to-face conversations. Consequently, analysing company e-mails proved to have characteristics similar to direct observation. Subtle meanings became clearer as the analysis of the e-mails moved forward, thereby increasing the researcher's insight into the phenomenon under investigation. It should be noted, however, that in our case study investigation we relied on only one coder; as a result, the findings may have been the result of interpretations of a single individual (Wakkee 2003). We tried to minimize this effect by sending drafts of our reports to the principal decision-makers at various times during the investigation.

One of the drawbacks of qualitative analysis based on company e-mails is the time consumed. Perhaps the most time-intensive portion was the preparation of e-mails. Each had to be prepared separately. Every e-mail was analysed at least twice as information contained in other e-mails improved the understanding of the information contained in the e-mails first investigated. Yet we feel that the actual content analysis did not take more time than would have been the case for other textual sources of information. Also, the richness of the information contained in the e-mails after the preparatory work was done confirmed that the e-mails were very rich in content.

Quality considerations
A number of quality considerations in relation to the use of e-mails as a source of data have to be taken into account. When conducting the analysis

of the data, we relied on existing literature to identify the concepts, attributes and values, and to generate ideas. New concepts, attributes, values and ideas emerged during the data collection and analysis (Wakkee 2004). We contemplated the data and tried to consider them from different perspectives to generate ideas and frameworks. Also, we sent work-in-progress reports to the principal decision-makers to determine to what extent our interpretation of the data corresponded with theirs. Supporting evidence gave strength to the ideas and interpretations, while contradictory evidence led to questions about my original interpretations and ideas. To evaluate the outcomes of the e-mail study we used a number of criteria related to internal validity, credibility and authenticity of the results formulated by Miles and Huberman (1994). Table 13.5 lists these considerations and a reflection of how we incorporated these into our study.

As can be seen, most of these criteria can indeed be used to judge the quality of the e-mail method we propose. However, some other criteria do not depend on whether or not e-mails are being used but more on the design of the study and the quality of its performance. Besides the quality considerations proposed by Miles and Huberman (1994), when conducting a study based on qualitative analysis of company e-mails, researchers should take into account issues related to reliability, construct validity and credibility, in the same way that they would deal with these issues in any other type of qualitative study (Yin 1994).

Origin of the data   Because e-mail messages are not intended to be used in research and therefore non-reactive, the data are not presented in a form that conveys impression management, as might be the case in interviews or official documentation. When investigating archival records, researchers have to keep in mind that a selection has been made in the past about which records were considered important enough for archiving. This means that archives will never contain all data that have been produced about company development in the past. Also, in an interview, respondents will only provide what they remember or consider important. When collecting e-mails in real time, such a pre-selection of data has not yet been made and the researcher can determine which data are relevant for answering the research question. For these reasons it is claimed that e-mails are a non-biased source of data. In this respect, reading company e-mails is similar to being present at the organization and witnessing face-to-face meetings or listening in on telephone conversations.

Selection bias   In the section on case study selection, we argued that a selection bias is unlikely to result in a bias in the outcomes of the study, as the nature of the information contained in the e-mails is independent of the

Table 13.5   Quality considerations in relation to using e-mails as a source of data

Consideration	E-mail studies
How context rich and meaningful (thick) are the descriptions?	E-mail data prove to be very rich and revealing. Reading e-mails feels like being present at meetings or listening in on telephone conversations. Due to the high frequency of e-mail interaction, e-mail chains resemble what Groen and Nooteboom (1998) called 'intellectual midwifery'.
Does the account ring true, make sense, seem convincing or plausible, enable a vicarious presence for the reader?	Because e-mails are not created for the purpose of the research, the story unfolding over the e-mails reflects what happened, but also often how the key actors perceived what happened. To stay close to the actual reality we suggest including as many quotes from the original data as possible.
Is the account rendered a comprehensive one, respecting the config-uration and temporal arrangement of elements in the local context?	This will depend on the individual studies. By describing how the internal and external environment developed we indeed believe that by using e-mails one can provide a comprehensive account.
Did triangulation among complementary methods and data sources produce converging conclusions? If not, is there a coherent explanation?	E-mail can be used as a source of data on its own. Yet, as with any data source, we suggest that e-mail should be used in combination with other sources of data, such as archival records and interviews. Indeed, Wakkee (2004) found that the various data sources may lead to converging conclusions.
Are the presented data well linked to the emerging theory?	This can be established by trying to link the data closely to the measures by using a coding table and using the code (or attribute and values) labels in the report.
Are the findings internally coherent; are concepts systematically related?	Evidence sent by internal and external individuals and at different points in time indicates the same or a similar meaning of the concepts and measures.
Were rules used for the configuration of propositions and hypotheses made explicit?	This will depend on the nature of the study (e.g. whether studies are exploratory or used for testing).
Are areas of uncertainty defined? (Should there be some?)	Due to the richness of the information, few areas of uncertainty are expected. Yet this depends on the research questions and the amount of data. Triangulation with other data sources can further minimize uncertainties.

Table 13.5   (continued)

Consideration	E-mail studies
Was negative evidence sought? Found? What happened then?	This will depend on the nature of the study. E-mail can be used both for success and for failure stories.
Have rival explanations been actively considered?	This will again depend on the study undertaken. The richness of the e-mails will, however, allow for doing so.
Have the findings been replicated in other parts of the database?	Either e-mails from two different time periods can be compared or the findings from the e-mail investigation can be compared with findings obtained from other sources.
Were the conclusions considered accurate by the original informants? If not, is there a coherent explanation for this?	This depends on the design of the study and the quality and carefulness of the interpretation. In Wakkee (2004) the entrepreneurs felt that the report provided a very detailed account. Except for a few remarks, no serious comments were received from the entrepreneurs about the content.
Were any predictions made in the study, and how accurate were they?	This will depend on the individual investigation.

Source: adapted from Miles and Huberman (1994).

research. However, because it can be expected that only a small number of companies or entrepreneurs will be willing to participate in a study based on or including e-mails, establishing external validity may be difficult. Therefore, the use of company e-mails as a source of data may seem to apply best to studies seeking to obtain theoretical generalization rather than generalization based on replication of studies in multiple cases.

Triangulation   In this chapter we have presented our method as if e-mails were the only source of data used in a study. We recognize the value of using multiple sources of data and of benefiting from triangulation as much as possible (Yin 1994). Triangulation between e-mail, interviews, Internet pages, archival records, and other sources of qualitative and or quantitative data will only improve the validity of the findings, as information obtained from one source can complement, confirm or disprove information obtained from another. In fact, based on our own experiences, it seems to be much easier to retrieve and make sense of the information contained in the e-mails if the researcher already has some basic knowledge about the company. However, after conducting our investigation, we agree with

Sproull and Kiesler (1986), who suggest that much of the information obtained from the e-mails would not have been found in other sources. The communication between company officials and external contacts proved to be very rich and formed a highly detailed picture that would not have come to light through other sources of information. Therefore, e-mail messages are not just a means to confirm other sources of data (for which the analysis of documentation is often used); rather, they are a new source of information for researchers. Nevertheless, it is clear that company e-mails only provide part of the picture and need to be investigated in relation with other types of data. Once information is obtained through the e-mails, further probing through interviews may add even better insights. We expect that after analysis of e-mails such follow-up interviews with the company officials can be better targeted and need only focus on confirming findings and filling in some details. In this way researchers need not intrude significantly on entrepreneurs' valuable time.

Ethics   A final issue that needs some attention involves ethics. We wonder to what extent using e-mails sent by third parties is ethical and can be justified, as these third parties do not know that their writings are being read by someone other than the person they initially sent it to and did not give permission to use their data. In our case study several messages included disclaimers at the bottom of the text and we decided to remove them from our database. An example of such a disclaimer found in the collected e-mails is shown in Box 13.1.

BOX 13.1   DISCLAIMER EXAMPLE

The information contained in this e-mail communication is solely intended for the person/legal person to whom it is/has been sent, and as it may contain information of a personal or confidential nature, it may not be made public by virtue of law, regulations or agreement. If someone other than the intended recipient should receive or come into possession of this e-mail communication, he/she will not be entitled to read, disseminate, disclose or duplicate it. If you are not the intended recipient, you are requested to inform XX of this by telephone (phone number: xxxxxxx) immediately, and to destroy the original e-mail communication. XX shall not be liable for the correct and complete transmission of the contents of a transmitted e-mail, or for any delay in its receipt. This e-mail message does not create any contractual obligations for XX.

In our research only a few such messages were found and it seems unlikely that their removal influenced the outcomes of our study. Yet it seems likely that in the future such disclaimers will only be used more frequently, especially once legislation becomes more clear and strict in Europe. In the USA, researchers will generally be required to pass their research through the Human Subjects Committee. This committee reviews content and use of data and ensures that human subjects are treated with respect and that the data are used in such a way as to protect confidentiality. As researchers we have to think about what this would mean for doing research with this new data source. One suggestion could be to ask the case-company to attach a warning at the bottom of their e-mails stating something like: 'E-mails being sent by or to this company will be used in a study of . . .'. Another solution could be to ask each of the third parties for explicit permission to use their e-mails in the investigation.

On the basis of our experiences a table of guidelines including a checklist was developed, which is shown in Table 13.6.

Conclusions and need for further research
This chapter presented a discussion of the value of company e-mails in qualitative research on entrepreneurship on the basis of a proposed methodology and our experiences in using this methodology. Like most qualitative researches, the use of company e-mails results in huge quantities of data to gather, prepare and analyse. Despite this, the most important conclusion of this chapter is that company e-mails are an interesting source of qualitative data. With the amount of e-mail communication continuing to increase, this value will also increase as a more complete picture of company developments will develop with enhanced discussion through this medium. We do, however, stress that company e-mails are best used in combination with other qualitative and or quantitative data sources to develop a more complete picture.

Above we argued that at least in Western Europe and North America, e-mails are often highly informal and similar to speech. In our research, we indeed witnessed this informal nature and as a result a very rich picture emerged of the company developments under investigation. We expect that even when e-mails are used in a more formal manner they will also be revealing and thus worthwhile including in scientific research, just as paper correspondence has proven to be revealing (as was shown by the classical case study of Thomas and Znaniecki 1918 on the Polish peasant in Europe and America). However, it may very well be that more formal e-mails will make it more difficult to develop a picture of the company culture and the persons involved in the venture. Therefore, it will depend largely on the

Table 13.6   Guidelines for using e-mails as a source of data

Step	Action/Considerations
Case selection	Formulation of criteria: • dependent on research question • e-mails should be used regularly Gaining access: • stress that data collection is not time-consuming • existing connection/trust may be necessary (selection bias) Trust – confidentiality • dealing with third parties • legislation and ethics • a contract may be necessary
Data collection	Real-time – post-date • post-date reduces impression management from side of decision-maker • real-time reduces chance of pre-selection and enables 'gradual' analysis Number and variety of mailboxes • depends on nature of the inquiry/research question • discuss with company officials what is best Timeframe • considerable numbers of e-mails may be necessary • longer timeframes allow for reconstruction of processes • best project driven
Preparation	Using software • evaluate pros and cons • selecting package Creating database: • removing spam, non-relevant e-mails • loading individual e-mails in database • linking attachments Housekeeping (especially when using automatic coding) • removing typing errors • resolving language problems, 'difficult words' • highlighting different messages in one e-mail Creating sets and subsets
Analysis	Inductive – deductive If inductive: identify themes using software tools • consider the inclusion of multiple repeated messages • create codes and attributes while coding manually

Table 13.6   (continued)

Step	Action/Considerations
	If deductive: design attributes and coding from theoretical framework
	• create attribute tables from theoretical framework
	• create coding tables including synonyms and translations
	Coding
	• automatic and manual coding of e-mails and sets
	• filling in attribute tables
	• use multiple coders to enhance reliability
	• progress with analysis by reconstructing processes etc.

nature of the research question and the type of knowledge sought whether more formal e-mails are adequate sources of data.

Our findings are based on only one case study focusing on a specific set of research questions. In order to develop a better understanding of the nature of the research questions and the contexts that can benefit from using company e-mails in qualitative research, more extensive investigation is in order. Experience will enable improvement of the method.

Notes

1. These developments have been observed in North America and Western Europe; in other regions of the world such as Eastern Europe, e-mail is still treated more formally in appearance and content.
2. On average the messages contained in our database were only 5.3 sentences long and contained 42.3 words.
3. Free nodes are those sections of coded information which are not (yet) linked to other codes or organized into a tree of related codes.
4. As described in Wakkee (2003), it was decided to conduct a pilot study including only a small subset ($n = 100$) of all e-mail with the sole purpose of determining whether the e-mails would indeed yield sufficient insight into the phenomenon under investigation before engaging in the time-consuming task of preparing and analysing each of the e-mails individually. The reason for this was that we could not find examples of studies using e-mails and thus had no frame of reference. After undertaking this pilot we continued the coding process of the complete dataset. We strongly recommend researchers to include the complete set of e-mails when conducting case studies, as only that will yield a complete picture.

Suggested recommended readings

Like e-mail and websites, an electronic message board provides a wealth of information. The following paper has been particularly inspiring in recognizing the value of electronic data sources.
Bell J., and Loane, S., Entrepreneurship research in Europe: innovative methods in the exploration of internationalisation issues at INPG-ESISAR, Valence, 19–20 September, 2002, see www.epi-entrepreneurship.com

Storing, preparing and analysing large numbers of e-mails and enormous quantities of information in a systematic way would in our view not be possible without the use of software. We recommend in particular the following publications to develop understanding of how NVivo can be used in the research process.

Jemmott (2002) Using NVivo in Qualitative Data Analysis in Dialog, (2) http://www.bath.ac. uk/education/dialogue/dialogue2.7.pdf

Welsh, E. (2002) Dealing with data: using NVivo in the qualitative data analysis process, *Forum Qualitative Social Research*, **3**(2).

References

Barry, C.A. (1998) Choosing qualitative data analysis software: Altas/ti and Nudist compared, *Sociological Research Online*, **3**(3), available at http://www.socresonline.org.uk/ socresonline/3/3/4.html, accessed May 12th, 2001.

Bell J., and Loane, S. (2002) 'Entrepreneurship research in Europe: Innovative methods in the exploration of internationalisation issues, given at INPG–ESISAR, Valence, 19–20 September: see www.epi-entrepreneurship.com

Brown, D., Taylor, C., Baldy, G., Edwards, G. and Oppenheimer, E. (1990) Computers and QDA – can they help it? A report on a qualitative data analysis programme. *Sociological Review*, **38**(1): 134–50.

Burgess, R. (1995) *Computing and Qualitative Research.* Greenwich, CT: JAI Press.

Casti, J.L. (1994) *Complexification: explaining a paradoxical world through the science of surprise.* New York: Harper Collins.

Carr, W. and Kemmis, S. (1986) *Becoming Critical: Education, knowledge and action research.* London: Falmer Press.

Clark, P.A. (1972) *Action Research and Organizational Change.* London: Harper and Row.

Coffey, A., Holbrook, B. and Atkinson, P. (1996) Qualitative data analysis: technologies and representations. *Sociological Research On-line*, **1**(1).

Daft, R.L. and Lengel, R.L. (1984) Information richness: A new approach to managerial behavior and organization design. In L.L. Cummings and B.M. Staw (eds), *Research in Organizational Behavior*, Vol. 6, Greenwich: JAI Press, pp. 191–233.

Denzin, N.K. and Lincoln, Y.S. (eds) (2000) *Handbook of Qualitative Research.* London: Sage Publications.

Elden, M. and Chisholm, R.F. (1993) Emerging varieties of action research: Introduction to the special issue, *Human Relations*, **46**(2): 121–42.

Erlandson, D.A., Harris, E.L., Skipper, B.L. and Allen, S.D. (1993) *Doing Naturalistic Inquiry, a Guide to Methods*, Newbury Park, CA: Sage Publications.

Fielding, N. (1994) Getting into computer-aided qualitative data analysis, *Data Archive Bulletin*, September; http://caqdas.soc.surrey.ac.uk/getting.htm

Glaser, B. and Strauss, A. (1967) *The Discovery of Grounded Theory: Strategies for qualitative research.* New York: Aldine de Gruyter.

Groen, A. and Nooteboom, B. (1998) Environmental innovation: knowledge and networks, unpublished paper.

Harveston, P.D., Osborne, J.D. and Kedia, B. (2004) Examining the mental models of entrepreneurs from born-global and gradual globalizing firms. In Ray Oakley, Wim During and Saleema Kauser (eds), *New Technology-based Firms in the New Millennium*, Vol. III, Amsterdam, The Netherlands: Pergamon.

Harris, J. (2002) The correspondence method as a data-gathering technique in qualitative enquiry. *International Journal of Qualitative Methods*, **1**(4): http://www.ualberta. ca/~ijqm/

Hutjes, J.M. and Van Buuren, J.A. (1992) *De gevalsstudie Strategie van kwalitatief onderzoek*, Open Universiteit, Heerlen, The Netherlands.

Jemmott (2002) Using NVivo in Qualitative Data Analysis in *Dialog* (2); http://www.bath. ac.uk/education/dialogue/dialogue2.7.pdf

Kelle, U. and Laurie, H. (1995) Computer Use in Qualitative Research and Issues of Validity. In U. Kelle (ed.), *Computer-Aided Qualitative Data Analysis: Theory, methods and practice.* London: Sage.

Kelle, U. (1997) Theory building in qualitative research and computer programmes for the management of textual data, *Sociological Research Online*, **2**(2), http://www.socresonline.org.uk/socresonline/2/2/1.html.

Kollman, K. (2000) Changes in electronic communications: What the user figures for the new communications technologies aren't telling us, *Forum: Qualitative Social Research*, [On-line Journal], **1**(1). Available at http://www.qualitative-research.net/fqs-texte/1-00/1-00 kollman-e.html [Date of access: June 2nd, 2002].

Kralik, D., Koch, T. and Brady, B.M. (2000). Pen pals: correspondence as a method for data generation in qualitative research. *Journal of Advanced Nursing*, **31**: 909–17.

Leenders, M., Mauffette-Leenders, L.A. and Erskine, J.A. (2001) *Writing Cases*. London, Canada: Richard Ivey School of Business.

Miles, B.M. and Huberman, A.M. (1994) *Qualitative Data Analysis: An expanded sourcebook* (2nd edn). Thousand Oaks, CA: Sage.

Nancarrow, C. and Brace, I. (2000) Saying the 'right thing': Coping with social desirability bias in marketing research, *Bristol Business School Teaching and Research Review*, Issue 3, Summer.

OECD (2002) ICT database and Eurostat, E-Commerce Pilot Survey 2001, August.

Pantelli, N. (2003) Richness, power cues and e-mail text, *Information & Management*, **40**(2): 75–86.

Richards, T. and Richards, L. (1995) Using computers in qualitative research. In N. Denzin and Y. Lincoln (eds), *Handbook of Qualitative Research*. Thousand Oaks, CA: Sage.

Seidel, J. (1991) Method and madness in the application of computer technology to qualitative data analysis. In R. Lee and N. Fielding (eds), *Using Computers in Qualitative Research*. London: Sage.

Seidel, J. and Kelle, U. (1995) Different functions of coding in the analysis of textual data. In U. Kelle (ed.), *Computer-Aided Qualitative Data Analysis: Theory, methods and practice*. London: Sage.

Selwin, N. and Robson, K. (1998) Using e-mail as a research tool, in Social Research Update, University of Surrey, http://www.soc.surrey.ac.uk/sru/SRU21.html

Sproull, L. and Kiesler, S. (1986) Reducing social context cues: electronic mail in organizational communication. *Management Science*, **32**: 1492–512.

Thomas, W. and Znaniecki, F. (1918) *The Polish Peasant in Europe and America: monograph of an immigrant group*, Vol. I, Chicago, IL: University of Chicago Press.

Wakkee, I.A.M. (2003) Global Startups: Evidence from Company E-mails? Paper presented at the 6th McGill conference on International Entrepreneurship: Crossing Boundaries and Researching New Frontiers, June 10th.

Wakkee, I.A.M. (2004) *Starting Global: an Entrepreneurship-in-networks approach*, Doctoral dissertation, University of Twente, Enschede, The Netherlands.

Wakkee, I.A.M. and Harveston, P.D. (2003) In search of a multidimensional identification method of born global firms. Paper presented at the 11th High Tech Small Firm Conference, Manchester, UK, June.

Walsham, G. (1993) *Interpreting Information Systems in Organizations*. Chichester: Wiley.

Walther, J.B. (1996) Computer-mediated communication: Impersonal, interpersonal, and hyperpersonal interaction. *Communication Research*, **23**: 3–43.

Weitzman, E.A. and Miles, M.B. (1994) *Computer Programs for Qualitative Analysis*. Thousand Oaks, CA: Sage.

Welsh, E. (2002) Dealing with data: using NVivo in the qualitative data analysis process. *Forum Qualitative Social Research*, **3**(2).

Yin, R. (1994) *Case Study Research: Design and methods*, 2nd edn, Beverly Hills, CA: Sage.

Web sources

http://www2.fmg.uva.nl/sociosite/websoc/demografie.html#mensen
http://www.casro.org/faq/faq1099.htm
http://www.iusmentis.com/maatschappij/pcactive0211/
http://www.oecd.org/document/62/0,2340,en_2825_495656_2766782_1_1_1_1,00.html

14 The scientification of fiction
Jesper Piihl, Kim Klyver and Torben Damgaard

Leaving the harbour – with visions of strange lands

The piece of dialogue in Box 14.1 grew out of the work on a paper on the different roles performed by consultants, researchers and entrepreneurs involved in change processes in SMEs (Damgaard et al. 2004; Klyver et al. 2004a, 2004b). The dialogue has never actually been observed in the field, as it was initially improvised by three researchers performing it as a role play. The dialogue has been amended several times before reaching its final form. Actually, it is in a state of continual flux – it keeps developing according to the various settings into which it is translated. In truth, the dialogue is fiction. However, it is not pure fiction – rather a kind of 'scientificated fiction'. Scientificated fiction has played a crucial role in our work on theoretical and conceptual developments and is believed to show promise as an alternative qualitative research method for the future.

The primary argument for developing this distinct approach is a perceived need for a method that may have the potential to turn our more or less unsystematic experiences with a subject into an asset in theory development. All three authors have participated in several projects over extended periods of time with both entrepreneurs and advisers as they perform their roles. In some of our research projects we have been engaged in traditional data collection through structured and semi-structured personal interviews, as well as conducted surveys and meticulously researched secondary material. However, we still felt that conventional qualitative and quantitative methods left insufficient opportunities for merging valuable knowledge from informal experiences with theorizing processes.

The question was: how to transform such intangible and tacit 'knowledge' with a view to contributing to theory development? In the particular project that fuelled the development of the method elaborated here, the question was: how should such experiences be put together in order to build an image of the different individuals' reasoning in certain situations? Ethnographers encounter a similar problem and point to impressionist tales as a way to proceed. Impressionist tales are stories based on experiences gained from fieldwork. However, they are not directly observed or authenticated stories. They are the researchers' own stories derived from their experiences in the field:

BOX 14.1   A PIECE OF DIALOGUE

[The researcher, Robert, has just accused the consultant Claus of delivering the standard consulting buzzwords in response to a question about what he could do to 'help' the entrepreneur Ernest rather than relating his expertise to the daily activities of Ernest's entrepreneurial SME]

Claus: What I'm saying really does mean something in relation to their everyday life. Every morning, Ernest gets up to earn money and, what I would like to say is, I can help him earn more money and – maybe in the long run – grow the business. (It's an absolute certainty that he will now say that he doesn't want to earn more money and that in any case he doesn't want the business to grow . . .)

Ernest: Grow? Growing really depends on what it means to grow. I don't want to see growth as an objective in itself. However, growth may also indicate that my ideas and initiatives make a difference to people – customers and employees, at least. I really enjoy working hard at turning my ideas into reality. If the money comes rolling in, then it is a nice by-product of my efforts, but earning money is not the driving force.

Robert: There is something else that I'm thinking about . . . I have noticed that the importers of cars have begun to reduce and rationalize their network of retailers, because they think they can cover the market with fewer retailers . . . is it going in that direction within agricultural machinery too?

[. . .] the well-told tale will always go behind the bare bones and embellish, elaborate, and fill in little details as the mood and moment strike. Certainly in my written telling of this story I've hedged here and there, added an extraneous point or two, polished up some descriptions, and left others out from previous tellings. Storytelling of the impressionist sort seems to rest on the recall of forgotten details and the editing of remembered ones. (Van Maanen 1988: 117)

With this idea of impressionist tales somewhere in the back of our minds, our solution turned out to be the development of a method of 'scientificating' role playing. Our solution in this particular case was to develop a method starting from the performance of an 'improvised' role play. This we developed into what we have chosen to call a 'scientificated' role play. That is, we developed a method for making fiction scientific. Therefore the aim of this chapter is to describe and discuss the use of scientificated fiction as a method for turning implicit and tacit knowledge gained from fieldwork into theoretical and conceptual development.

In the project giving birth to the approach explored here, our topic was managerial processes in the intersection between small business management and entrepreneurship (Damgaard et al. 2004; Klyver et al. 2004a, 2004b). Our backgrounds for theorizing on this subject were the documented, remembered and forgotten details recalled as the work took shape.

The next section heads towards the strange land of scientificated role plays, commencing with sketching the rough contours of the method. Next, we take a look at the sea which we are sailing, through discussing the paradigmatic foundations underpinning the method. Then we take a closer look at specific elements of the method, as through the lens of a telescope. The chapter concludes with reflections on taking the lessons learned from this journey to other destinations.

Scientificating role play – the landscape of a strange land

The approach presented here was inspired by theatre and acting. When engaged in interaction processes for longer periods, field researchers become familiar with the roles 'performed' by the participants. Ideal types slowly emerge and their roles become familiar to the researcher, facilitating an identification with the characters, in much the same way as actors immerse themselves in a character to be played out on the stage. This willingness or open-mindedness to familiarize oneself with the roles performed by 'real-life players' is necessary when engaging in the usage of role plays for the development of concepts and theories, and we argue that it takes empirical as well as theoretical insight to do so. To draw the contours of the method we have found it helpful to break down the scientification of role play into three phases, as illustrated in Figure 14.1.

Phase one
The first phase involves three steps towards the scientification of tacit knowledge through developing and scientificating an improvised role play. The subsequent phases draw on this scientificated role play as a catalyst for theory development and ultimately for writing specific papers.

Step 1   In the first phase, the initial step is to decide on a theoretical *theme* reflecting the research interest as well as experience of the participants.

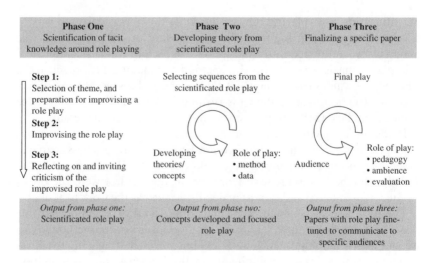

Phase One	Phase Two	Phase Three
Scientification of tacit knowledge around role playing	Developing theory from scientificated role play	Finalizing a specific paper

Step 1:
Selection of theme, and preparation for improvising a role play

Selecting sequences from the scientificated role play

Final play

Step 2:
Improvising the role play

Step 3:
Reflecting on and inviting criticism of the improvised role play

Developing theories/ concepts

Role of play:
• method
• data

Audience

Role of play:
• pedagogy
• ambience
• evaluation

Output from phase one:
Scientificated role play

Output from phase two:
Concepts developed and focused role play

Output from phase three:
Papers with role play fine-tuned to communicate to specific audiences

Figure 14.1   The landscapes of the scientificated role play

In deciding on a theme, it is crucial that the involved researchers all have considerable experience from more traditional research projects regarding the theme – as it is the tacit knowledge developed through these experiences that acts as the impetus for role play improvising. Furthermore, this first step involves detailed preparation for improvising the role play. This preparation may involve initial discussions focused on bringing tacit knowledge to the surface and may also require additional theoretical reading – or re-reading – related to the subject.

In our specific project, which we illustrate in more detail later in the chapter, the preparation first included a decision regarding the roles to be improvised in the second step. Second, the preparation incorporated an initial translation of our individual experiences from the field into archetypical 'lines' characterizing the different roles encountered in the field. These preparations are important first steps in the scientification of tacit knowledge. In the preparation, initial discussions concerning the characters to be played out should be allowed to emerge naturally among the participants.

Step 2   The second step is the performance of the role play as improvisation. Our initial role play was created through improvising a dialogue between three imaginary characters – each of the researchers participating performed the role of one character relevant to the theme. This second step was inspired by the lines and discussions from the first step. Our improvised role play resulted in two hours of tape-recorded dialogue that was later transcribed into a 'raw material' format.

Step 3   To 'scientificate' this improvised raw material even further, it is necessary to go through steps of *reflection and critique*. In our case, the third step, hence, involved reflection on a critical reading of the raw material by ourselves and, more importantly, by colleagues and others who had also been involved in the empirical field that the role play aimed to bring into life. This step resulted in several comments, which we applied in two ways. First, they were treated as an indication of the degree to which our dialogue could be recognized by other experts. Second, the comments received were themselves treated as data and incorporated into the dialogue. After revision of the role play – based on the comments received – the final *scientificated role play* was created.

Phase two
After constructing the scientificated role play in the first phase, the second phase focuses on developing theory or concepts using the scientificated role play as method and data (Phillips 1995). In Figure 14.1, there is a circular arrow between selecting sequences from the role play, developing theories/ concepts and finally using the role play as method and/or data. It is important to note that it may be relevant to make several iterations between these three elements. First, the scientificated role play may elaborate on several themes, where only a few are relevant for a specific conceptual development at hand, leading to a first selection of sequences.

As the theoretical/conceptual work advances, the role play may serve as data like any other kind of qualitative data. Furthermore, the basis in a scientificated role play provides the researcher with an additional opportunity. As the data are in the first place a kind of fiction, they open up the possibility of slightly amending the dialogue based on the researcher's tacit experience to fuel the theoretical and conceptual developments even further. Of course, if these amendments are too far reaching, it may be necessary to return to the third step of phase one, and make them objects of further scrutiny. However, the crucial point is that the role play is also, in this phase, an active part of a method which may be allowed to keep evolving as new elements of hitherto tacit knowledge are activated. Thus the selection of sequences and the decision on how to use the role play in theoretical and conceptual development is a dialectical process, in which the selected sequences and their use are developed as a process of iterative refinement.

Phase three
In the third phase the focus is on writing papers that communicate the theoretical and conceptual developments carried out in the second phase. In this phase, the role play may serve the two related functions of aiding pedagogy and communicating a certain ambience (Phillips 1995). First, the

role play may serve as a pedagogical instrument in communicating otherwise abstract ideas to certain audiences. For example, researchers, consultants and entrepreneurs will view a paper from different angles and therefore, by being exposed to a varied audience the role play, may be fine-tuned for optimal communication. Second, the role play may be a shortcut for creating or communicating certain ambiences experienced in the fieldwork in a way that can bring these soft aspects into research texts. Furthermore, there is an increased opportunity to fine-tune the role play to serve specific purposes which are not available in traditionally collected empirical 'evidence'. This iterative process is illustrated in Figure 14.1 by the circular arrow.

A third function the final role play may serve in this phase is as a device for evaluating the theoretical or conceptual developments. To the extent that they can be brought into life through the role play, it adds a little trustworthiness to the conceptual developments (Phillips 1995).

Considering the function of the role play, it changes throughout the process. In the first phase, it was used to give voice to otherwise tacit knowledge gained from traditional research by creating and scientificating the improvised dialogue. In the second phase, the role play functioned as both method and data. Finally, in the third phase, the main function of the role play became more concerned with the target audience as a source of evaluation of the concepts developed.

The changing role of distance and empathy through the three phases

Traditional qualitative research is conducted through interplay between periods of empathy and periods of distance/reflection (Damgaard et al. 2000: 155). This is also the case using the method described here. However, it is not empathy directly with practitioners under study – rather, such prior activities are necessary for building up the tacit knowledge which this method brings into use. Instead, empathy – in this case – points towards the need for the researcher to take on the role of practitioner.

In the first phase the researchers need to be able to get into the characters to be performed in order to, later on, take on a role in the play themselves. Empathy and the ability to get into the role set the boundaries for the possibility of choosing a theme, which is used as a catalyst to build an improvised role play. Furthermore, on the basis of the researchers' theoretical readings in the first phase, reflection and distance are also parts of the activities to delimit the theme and to prepare for improvising the role play. Improvising the role play is highly dependent on the ability to get into the roles to be brought into life. Further, the improvised role play is scientificated through the empathy of impartial practitioners and researchers as they make comments on the role play. Here, the researchers who perform the improvisation need the ability to distance themselves from the specific ways they perform the roles and work hard to critically evaluate the performances. This phase of distance is highly aided by the comments received.

In the second phase, the researchers need to become immersed in their characterizations, essentially for the purpose of selecting sequences and for making minor modifications of the play sequences according to the theoretical or conceptual development. Distance and reflection are needed in the second phase to make use of the dialogue in this development. Hence empathy as well as knowledge of existing theory is needed to understand whether or not the new concepts and theories contribute in describing and explaining the phenomena under study and also to help determine whether the sequences of the play seem trustworthy. Reflection and distance are needed to evaluate the theoretical concepts developed, as general concepts, compared to the specific sequences of the play.

The third phase requires empathy towards the audience reading the paper in order to be able to fine-tune the role play as a pedagogical tool for communication and for creating the right ambience in the text. Further distance is required to facilitate a final assessment of the practical value of the theoretical and conceptual elements developed in the hands of the potential reader.

Now, as we have left the safe harbour and sketched out the contours of a strange land, it is time to take a closer look at the waters that we, as researchers, are sailing through.

Paradigmatic foundations – outline of the sea we are sailing
This section outlines some of the meta-theoretical considerations that inspired the development of this distinct method. Traditional qualitative methods are used as a basis for comparison as the method, primarily, is thought of as being an alternative to traditional qualitative approaches. The outline is structured around two philosophical approaches for conducting research – modernism and postmodernism – with a special emphasis on how to evaluate a theory. This is undertaken in order to position the method developed in a context and not to discuss modernism–postmodernism in its own right (see for example Chia 1995, 1996).

Following the argument of Astley and Zammutto (1992), research conducted within a modernist framework is committed to a correspondence theory of truth. A theory is true if it corresponds or 'mirrors' (to use Rorty's expression) an independent reality to be found 'out there'. Therefore, modernist evaluation criteria – e.g. construct validity, internal validity, external validity and reliability (Yin 1994: 33) – are designed to evaluate the degree to which theories and concepts developed correspond to existing real-life phenomena.

Gergen (1992) argues that modernistic research is built on four key beliefs. First, modernism has a belief in the power of reason and observation. Second, there is a belief in and search for fundamentals or essentials; for objective and universal truths. Third, modernism has a faith in progress and universal design – as truths are aggregated, they can be used in developing continuously better design of, for example, organizations or societies. And fourth, modernism absorbs the machine metaphor in stressing systematic (typically causal) relationships between or among basic elements.

These key elements of modernism are fiercely attacked by diverse branches of reflexive and critical theorizing which here can be grouped under the conveniently broad heading of postmodernism. However, giving up these solid pillars, at first sight, seems to turn the temple of science into mere rubble. Therefore pressure to give up this set of assumptions has led some critics to argue that if the postmodern critiques of the modernists are true, then why bother writing more research texts (Parker 1995)? If the researchers' theories are just stories in line with the huge amount of stories already existing in and around the area of study and do not even have a stable foundation, then why bother writing more stories? Gergen (1992) poetically formulates the frustration in the following way:

> if we do not base theories on conceptions of rationality, motivation, emotion and the like, where do we turn? [. . .] If we cannot offer truth, objective accounts removed from our own valuational biases, then on what grounds can any new formulations be justified? If there are no foundations for theoretical formulations, and these are only linguistic constructions, then why play the fool – whose serious words turn to mere posturing in the hands of the deconstructionist critic? (Ibid.: 217)

Different researchers find different solutions to this problem of 'why write' when there is no stable independent and universal phenomena that can be described in the written word. Steyaert (1997), as a prominent example within entrepreneurship, argues for the creation of local knowledge through stories that are highly contextually dependent and sensitive to local complexities. The argument is that traditional modernist generalizations can be seen as a kind of reductionism – reducing local complexities and fragmented realities into minimalist principles. As an answer to the modernist urge for progress, Steyaert asks the field of entrepreneurship to be patient and to start creating an identity of its own 'instead of pursuing a nervous search for progress' (ibid.: 16).

Gergen (1992) turns towards another solution to the problem of 'why write' under postmodern assumptions in assessing that the importance of a theory is determined not from correspondence to phenomena mirrored, but from the activities it enables:

we are moved to silence only if persuaded by the modernist presumption that objective truth is the only game in town. If the function of theories is *not* derived from their truth value, but from their pragmatic implications, then the theoretical voice is restored to significance. And the potential of theoretical work is far greater than that assigned to it under modernist conditions. (Ibid.: 217, emphasis in original)

Following this argument, the problem of 'why write' emerges as the traditional modernist criteria for good research are maintained when discussing the implications of postmodern challenges. Instead it is suggested that emphasis should be placed on what the theories may put the beholder in a position to accomplish.

The implications of this radical shift towards the pragmatic implications of theorizing as basis for legitimacy can be seen by comparing it with the philosophical basis for grounded theory. The grounded theory researchers Strauss and Corbin (1994) argue that grounded theory – just as Gergen – closely follows the American pragmatist position (p. 279) in arguing that truths are enacted. However, they still have a commitment to the importance of correspondence. This commitment is not on the form of correspondence to an independent truth somewhere out there, as radical modernists may claim, but correspondence to *data enacted in the field*:

> as noted in *Discovery*, a grounded theory 'must *correspond* closely to the data if it is to be applied in daily situations' (Glaser and Strauss, 1967) And this *faithfulness* to the *substantive data*, this *'fit'* to a *substantive* area, is a powerful condition for usefulness in the practical life of the theory. (Strauss and Corbin 1994: 281, emphasis added)

Thus they strongly emphasize that 'correspondence' and 'fit' with a 'substantive area' are important in constructing theories that are useful. In this way they stay with the modernist idea that research gains its relevance through being a well-polished mirror that reflects the underlying mechanisms of reality. Compared to this, Gergen's (1992) emphasis on pragmatic value is far more radical than that of the 'grounded theorists'. This difference can be illustrated by Figure 14.2.

The difference becomes apparent when distinguishing between context of theory development and contexts of application. The 'grounded theorists' emphasize correspondence to data and fit to a substantive area as a powerful condition of usefulness. Therefore they place a strong emphasis on evaluating theories within the context of development, considering the move to contexts of application to be smooth – at least when proper scientific work has been carried out within the context of theory development.

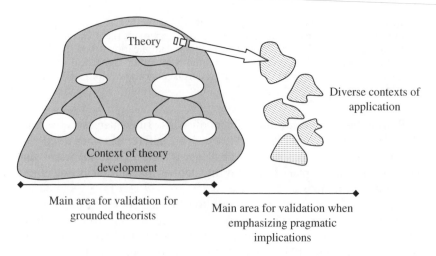

Figure 14.2   Two approaches to evaluation of theories

Gergen (ibid.) does not have these considerations about fit to some external substances. The reason is that the perspective he advances, according to the postmodern assumptions, denies the *a priori* existence of such substances. Instead, there is a much stronger focus on the context of application in evaluating theorizing: thus it can be seen in Figure 14.2 that the arrow from the context of theory development, which points towards contexts of application, becomes crucial.[1]

However, it should be noted that *contexts* of application have to be understood broadly and can consist of many heterogeneous contexts potentially ranging from practical contexts to playing a role in further research. Furthermore, *application* has to be understood in a broader sense than is normally implied when one speaks about taking ideas to the marketplace (Gibbons et al. 1994). Therefore the meaning of the term application ranges from direct practical steps to follow, at one extreme, to new ways of understanding phenomena which make it possible to imagine alternative avenues of action at the other.

Returning to the method of the scientification of tacit knowledge, and placing it within the debates outlined here, the method follows Gergen (1992) and Steyaert (1997) into the realm of postmodernism. Moreover, it follows Gergen's (1992) emphasis on evaluating theories according to the thoughts and activities they enable, rather than the degree to which they mirror some independent reality with some objective essences.

However, it is important to stress that this is not an argument for 'anything goes' (Feyerabend 1975). Anything does *absolutely not* go. First, the ideas presented here ask researchers to drop the heavy tools (Weick 1996) associated with strict and formal methodological procedures, thus letting the researcher's creative potential flourish. However, a heavy burden is placed on the shoulders of the researchers who now need to persuade an audience that their theories are useful. Furthermore, it cannot be sufficient to argue that they are inherently useful *because* they are thoroughly grounded in data and substances. Therefore the demands for showing pragmatic implications are greater. Phillips (1995) suggests that fiction can play two different roles in helping the researcher to remove this burden as fiction can assist in evaluating theories:

> Attempting to dramatize a particular theoretical position injects a measure of realism into an extremely abstract situation. If we can write a convincing dramatization that sensibly operationalizes a theory, then this provides one more bit of confirmatory evidence. On the other hand, if a sensible dramatization is not possible, then either the theory, or the domain in which it is applied, lacks validity. (Ibid.: 641)

We have now left the safe harbour, seen the contours of a strange land, and discussed the characteristics of the sea we are sailing upon. In the following section we will take a closer look at the activities performed in the strange land. However, due to the limits of one chapter, there is no opportunity to go ashore. Therefore, we present the land through the lens of a telescope. This will give a sufficiently accurate impression of the activities going on there to enable some lessons from this journey to be taken on other journeys.

Details of the strange land – through the lens of a telescope
Seeing the destination through the lens of a telescope gives detailed pictures of small parts of the destination. Combined with the outline of the contours of the destination in the previous section, it should give a clear indication of the coast we are heading towards. It is left to the creativity of the reader to fill in the blank spots. For the purpose of illustrating how and what tools might be used in the different phases, we use the former research project – known as the LoS project[2] – as an illustrative example. In this project, consultants, researchers and entrepreneurs heading small ventures joined under a common interest of developing management concepts that could help entrepreneurs lead their ventures into identifying and pursuing new opportunities.

Case: three roles in entrepreneurial change processes
In the LoS project, one of the focal elements was the process of action learning through cooperation among entrepreneurs, consultants and researchers. It involved a wide portfolio of different activities, ranging from traditional consulting activities, workshop forums aimed at training the

entrepreneurs for developing their ventures, diverse research projects directly related to these consulting activities as both kinds of action research and traditional observations. Further, research was conducted focusing more broadly on the managerial and organizational issues related to entrepreneurial management in these ventures. Participating in all these more formal activities – and the resultant tacit knowledge developed – gave rise to a project calling for the approach described here.

As the project evolved, the cooperation among the three groups gave rise to important learning. One issue that became painfully clear was that the different actors had different interests and perspectives, which influenced their views on entrepreneurial change processes. At different moments and in different situations widely different understandings of the situations and the actions appeared. These different understandings are of course related to the different roles played by entrepreneurs, consultants and researchers. Different opinions about the possibility for, and the content of, entrepreneurial change management were pronounced and much disagreement was voiced on how entrepreneurial change management might help develop the ventures in the cooperation among the participating entrepreneurs, consultants and researchers. Therefore this study came to focus on how different people in the process have different perspectives and how this influences how they recognize goals, means and problems.

In the following sections the telescope is directed towards examples of how methodological concepts, tools and working methods were used in the different phases of this project for constructing and developing theories from scientificated role play.

Phase 1. Scientification of tacit knowledge around role playing   The first phase concerned the thematic crystallization and production of an improvised role play as steps in the effort to scientificate tacit experiences developed through fieldwork. As researchers, our pre-understanding was used to guide the development of a theme. In undertaking an improvised role play, the importance of experiences from entrepreneurial practice as well as academic research should be emphasized.

To delimit the theme and sub-themes we reviewed literature that reflected a broad range of perspectives including, for example, strategy, management, organizational theory and entrepreneurial theories (e.g. Johansson 1997, 1999; Sturdy 1997; Chrisman and Katrishen 1995; Frank 1993; Clark and Salaman 1998; Clark and Fincham 2002). This process led to the categorization of themes across the literature reviewed. This part of the work can be seen as theory driven. Together with our experiences from the field, the existing literature inspired the role play. Hence thorough preparation, it could be argued, is a prerequisite of creativity.

Table 14.1   *The use of themes and roles that inspired the improvised role play*

Overall theme: different roles in entrepreneurial change processes

Sub-themes Roles	Role and function	Change processes and change management	Solutions, models and tools	Ontology
Entrepreneur		* 1 *		
Consultant	* 2 *			
Researcher			* 3 *	

At this time the theme was delimited to different roles in entrepreneurial change processes. We wrote an abstract that functioned as a mutual frame of understanding for us. When a theme was delimited, the next step was to identify the roles relevant for improvising the play. The three of us had participated in a project with the aim of developing a model for consultation concerning the guidance of entrepreneurs in change processes. Therefore we readily identified three characters we held to be important for the drama: the entrepreneurial manager, the consultant and the researcher.

A diagram, illustrated in Table 14.1, was used to broaden and deepen the dialogue in the improvised role play. The heading indicates the overall theme of the project. The rows show the three different roles to be performed, while the columns list four sub-themes. These themes arose from our work in the field, which, combined with theoretical insight, indicated what might be interesting variations among the roles. The next preparatory step was to fill archetypical conversation lines into the schema created in combination between the roles and the sub-themes.

To prepare for improvising the role play we tried to find 'lines' of entrepreneurs, consultants and researchers that we could recall from our experiences in the field. We separated the lines in different sub-themes which were mainly drawn from our theoretical review. We discussed different angles and perspectives under each theme and tried to fill in different lines in every box. Table 14.2 provides examples of how the cells of Table 14.1 were filled in. The illustrative line was originally uttered by a surprised and confused consultant just returning to the office from a meeting with an entrepreneur.

Then each of us took on a role and we improvised the role play based on our private experiences, inspired by work with themes, roles and theoretical knowledge from the literature. Improvising the role play revealed subconscious elements and tacit knowledge. It is easier to recognize other

Table 14.2   Application of structure (Table 14.1) to inspire the pinpointing
of actors' typical lines

Returning from a meeting with an entrepreneur, a surprised and confused
consultant uttered the following line:

'Hey . . . he didn't want to grow?'

This line led to the following three lines that were prepared as the background for
improvising the dialogue:

* 1 *	'I don't want my venture to grow if it just means more work and no more money, but if it means more money and the same or less work to me I'm interested . . . of course.'	Place in Table 14.1: the entrepreneur on change processes.
* 2 *	'It's an absolute certainty that he will now say that he doesn't want to earn more money than he does, and that in any case he doesn't want his venture to grow.'	Place in Table 14.1: the consultant's role expectations towards entrepreneurs.
* 3 *	'If this is the case, then the strategic options might be grow or blow!'	Place in Table 14.1: the researcher on the strategic consequences of environmental changes.

people's ideas, different angles and mistakes, and the experiences come out
through performing the role (Gordon and Langmaid 1988). When improvising the role play it is important to step into the roles and stick to them,
and leave theoretical discussions to subsequent phases. After the audio-
recorded improvised role play was finished, it was transcribed.

Next, a crucial step in the 'scientification' of the improvised role
play took place, when the improvisation was subjected to close scrutiny
by practitioners and others with experience in the field. Practitioners read
and commented on the dialogue to strengthen its plausibility or believability. At the same time, their comments enhanced the value of the play in its
later role in theory development. This phase is complex, can take many
forms and have very different content. One of the comments we received
from one of our colleagues was that the researcher acted very much as a
know-all – even in areas outside his field of expertise. This led to several
amendments of the improvised role play. As an example, the line is shown
in Table 14.3.

The lines change from being a statement to being a question, therefore
opening up the dialogue rather than closing it. The changes emerging from
this comment did not have any theoretical implications. However, it was

Table 14.3   Example of amendment caused by comments received

Robert:	'As far as I know, the market for agricultural machinery is under heavy pressure. Isn't it right that there are three times as many combine harvesters as needed in Denmark, and that the distributors are going to reduce the network of retailers – down to one out of every five? If this is the case, then the strategic options might be "grow or blow"!'
Was changed to:	
Robert:	'There is something else that I'm thinking about . . . I have noticed that the importers of cars have begun to reduce and rationalize their network of retailers, because they think they can cover the market with fewer retailers . . . is it going in that direction within agricultural machinery too?'

important as it reduced the level of irrelevant 'noise' in the dialogue experienced by the reader, making it easier to focus more on the theoretical insights developed from the role play.

Furthermore, and of conceptual importance, consultants reading our improvised role play provided us with suggestions on lines for the consultant, which we worked into the scientificated role play. This was both about improbable answers given in response to questions from the entrepreneur (i.e. answers that consultants would be unlikely to give) and suggestions about alternative contributions to the ongoing dialogue in the improvised role play. An example of a comment with potential theoretical implication is that a consultant pointed out that the consultant in the improvised role play talked about his 'clients'. Instead the commentator suggested that they should be termed customers. 'They are not ill', the commentator explained. The possible theoretical implication from this amendment is a critique of an early tendency in consultancy literature to consider the buyers of the services as 'needy clients' (Johansson 1999).

Even these changes, however, do not make the scientificated role play mirror a particular reality. Instead, they make the role play appear more relevant and trustworthy. The intention was not to produce a role play of real lines and observed roles, but to formulate recognizable characterizations and statements. If the people, their lines and their argumentation are all believable, then we have created the basis of a better understanding of the focal study topic. Also, comments on the improvised role play took on the form of new data in their own right which, reinterpreted, can give important insights to the field.

Phase 2. Developing theoretical concepts from scientificated role plays   In the second phase, sequences of the scientificated role play were selected to form part of a specific conceptual development, the selection criteria being the purpose of the paper and its target audience. Experience and field notes from the work with developing the scientificated role play were also considered in the second phase.

An important element of phase 2 is that of conceptualization via the role play. Here, the role play can function as both data and method. When the role play functions as a method, the play is a focal element in the way of working, and when the role play functions as data, the play works as all other kind of data – provoking theory for the purpose of its further development.

The theoretical insights gained from readings made it possible to read the role play from a certain distance. In this phase, reflection on the scientificated role play and notes taken through the development of the role play acted as data in developing new concepts and theories. The working process included a thorough and structured element of reflection. Every line was interpreted according to specific theoretical themes. All researchers did this and the interpretations were compared and discussed. Some of the themes occurred often and in a detailed manner, while others were more superficial. The outcome of this work was an overview of themes with direct links to the play. Examples of themes included evaluation of consultancy, strategic thinking and strategic processes in small ventures, differences in consulting small ventures compared to established companies, the character of the services delivered by the consultant and so on.

Even though we used well-structured techniques in the reflection process, it is important to emphasize that it does not correspond with the conventional research process, where evidence is found in the field through close examination. In the work with the material, in comparing the role play with theoretical elements, moments of crystallization occurred. New models, new structures, new concepts and so on grew out of the process. It is difficult to say exactly why, how and when, but sometimes this leads to 'magic moments of creativity'.

In the example we present here, the work crystallized into a new structure with four perspectives on entrepreneurial change processes, as sketched out in Table 14.4.

When we went through the role play it became apparent that the actors often misinterpreted each others' words. Often they spoke about the same issue but from different angles. The angles presented in the role play came from our experiences from working in the field as well as those drawn from our literature review. However, it was in the work with the role play that it became evident to us that the theoretically extreme positions had a modified 'counterpart' in everyday life. Table 14.5 gives an example of a piece

Table 14.4   Four perspectives and three roles in change management

	Interactive perspective	Modified interactive perspective	Modified linear perspective	Linear perspective
Entrepreneur				
Consultant				* A *
Researcher				

Table 14.5   Piece of dialogue with conceptual notes

Claus:	'I would like to say that I can help him earn more money – and maybe in the long run – to grow the business.' (Line from a piece of the role play.)
Conceptual notes	Here, the consultant suggests that he can identify variables/ factors that can be translated into managerial solutions. The form taken is what we call here a linear managerial change perspective.
* A *	The theoretical and practical examples are many. The dialogue argues for a modified version as practitioners often mix different perspectives in their argumentation. Furthermore, the identification of one position opens the way for reflection on opposing strands of argumentation – in this case the interactive perspective. The arguments for this perspective are found primarily in theoretical sources.

of the role play and conceptual notes associated to a particular line. Such reflections on the lines in the role play lead to the new perspectives.

The work where the role play is translated into concepts and the grouping/juxtaposition of the concepts leads to moments of creativity. For example, the four perspectives and the three roles helped to explain why representatives of particular roles can misunderstand those from other roles, as well as helping to show why people occupying a particular role can misunderstand others with the same role but different perspectives. The activities taken and the tools used can vary in the second phase, depending on the purpose of the conceptual developments. Moments of creativity are results of systematic work with the scientificated role play, and might go on for long or short periods of time. The output of this phase was twofold. First, there is the development of theories and concepts; and second, selections of sequences from the scientificated role play were turned into a focused role play.

Phase 3. Dissemination to various audiences   The third phase concerns the presentation(s) of the constructions. First of all, the researchers have to ask themselves whether the new concepts and theories contribute towards the description and explanation of situations taken from the scientificated role play. Further, can the elements of the scientificated role play contribute to communicating the concepts developed to specific audiences? In this respect, the role play may serve the function of pedagogical instrument or a technique for communicating a certain ambience. When the role play functions as a pedagogical instrument or for ambience creation, the play is fine-tuned to a communication function attuned to the target audience.

The final paper has to be written according to the theme, the theoretical and practical perspective, and also to the audience it addresses. This may again lead to amendments and reselection of the focused role play to fine-tune it according to the theoretical points developed and the audience addressed.

As a pedagogical and more imaginative technique, the role play can be helpful in communicating with audiences not familiar with theoretical concepts by providing illustrations from 'real life'. Hence the paper, and especially the role play, can illustrate entrepreneurial topics for entrepreneurs. The role play can illustrate entrepreneurial change processes and, in the context of the role play, the set of concepts necessary for understanding the change processes can be presented.

For consultants, the paper and the role play might be of similar help. Consultants get illustrations for use in developing tools and plans. Furthermore, these may also be relevant to them in the consultation processes they engage in with entrepreneurs. Hence we argue for the value in the use of scientificated role play due to its pedagogical advantages.

After having constructed the new concepts or theories in phases 1 and 2, a validating step is to return to the role play once again to confront the new concepts or theories with the entire (revised) role play. In comparing the concepts or theories with the role play, the following questions may be asked: Are the concepts or theories developed interesting? Are they coherent? And, when brought together, do the role play, the concepts and theories seem plausible? In line with Phillips (1995), we therefore argue for the use of role play to evaluate theories developed in line with his argument that:

> Attempting to dramatize a particular theoretical position injects a measure of realism into an extremely abstract situation. If we can write a convincing dramatization that sensibly operationalizes a theory, then this provides one more bit of confirmatory evidence. On the other hand, if a sensible dramatization is not possible, then either the theory, or the domain in which it is applied, lacks validity. (Phillips 1995: 641)

This evaluation has to take place within the research society itself. Thus the role play functions in the evaluation of the concepts developed and as a way to present new concepts and meanings in their context.

Taking the lessons to other destinations
The ambition of this chapter was to leave the safe harbour of well-established methodological procedures, in order to explore a way to use fiction as a process to transform unspoken and 'wordless' knowledge into an asset in theory development.

The ethnographer uses the concepts of plausibility and believability in similar qualitative approaches. They construct stories as a way of making presentations about cultures. 'The audience cannot be concerned with the story's correctness, since they were not there and cannot know if it is correct' (Van Maanen 1988: 105).

In relation to scientificated role play and the accompanying theoretical and conceptual developments, the demand for plausibility and believability is a little more extreme, as there has never been a place where the audience could have been. Therefore we lean to the term 'convincing' from Phillips (1995) or a pragmatic interpretation of trustworthiness – meaning *does it 'add value to me' to trust it?*

To succeed with this method it is necessary to have various kinds of experiences with the subject matter researched – both theoretical and empirical. If these experiences are present, we suggest that the use of scientificated fiction – which in this chapter is put into practice as a scientificated role play – can be considered as a new tool in our methodological toolbox. However, a new tool does not provide a solution to any problem on its own. It is necessary to know when to use a particular tool, and whether or not it should be used in combination with other tools, in order to achieve the best results.

The faith of theories stemming from the use of the method presented in this chapter is not determined by its correspondence to a truth. Instead, the theories can be seen as proposals for new perspectives, where faith lies in the hands of the users of the theories (Latour 1987). And of course, the same goes for the method itself. That is, the value of this chapter does not rest on its truth value, but on the way the lessons learned are taken towards other destinations.

In regard to scientificated role play, our imagination leads us towards the belief that the method can be interesting in several instances. In our case, a scientificated role play served as the primary method for developing four different perspectives on the relationship between researchers, consultants and entrepreneurs. In other cases, scientificated fiction may serve as supplementary methodology to breathe life into research using quantitative data. Scientificated role plays may also serve as a 'crowbar' for opening new research themes within areas already exposed to more traditional research methodologies. In this case, the interest is in awareness of where the imagination stops, as this may indicate a frontier of knowledge that might benefit from additional research.

Notes

1.   As a radical example, Gergen and Gergen (1991) suggest that hypothetical data rotation can be used as a short-cut to develop theories within psychology. The argument is that as theories are, nevertheless, developed through observations that do *not fit expectations*, why not try to imagine such observations and let them provoke theorizing, instead of patiently waiting for them to emerge in the field?
2.   LoS is an abbreviation of leadership and management in small and medium-sized ventures (in Danish: Ledelse og Styring i små- og mellemstore virksomheder).

Recommended further readings

Brownlie, D. (1997) Beyond ethnography: Towards writerly accounts of organizing in marketing, *European Journal of Marketing*, **31**(3/4): 264–84. This text is written by a disillusioned ethnographer, reflecting on the difficulties of ethnographic methodologies. Two central arguments should be mentioned here. First, the author recognized that the persons studied used different tactics to make the researcher describe their ways of working in certain ways. Second, the conventions of writing within an academic discipline play crucial roles for our ways of thinking and theorizing within the field.

Gergen, K.J. (1992) Organization theory in the postmodern era, in M. Reed and M. Hughes (eds), *Rethinking Organization: New Directions in Organization Theory and Analysis*, London: Sage Publications, pp. 207–26.

Gergen, K.J. (2003) Beyond knowing in organizational inquiry, *Organization*, **10**(3): 453–5. The first of these texts is not so interesting for its postmodern critique of mainstream organizational research as for its suggestions concerning reasons to go on researching anyway, by pointing towards the pragmatic implications of research. This suggestion is put forward again in the second more recent text in arguing: 'It is my strong belief that the domain of organizational inquiry would be enormously benefited by replacing the search for Knowledge with the development of broadly actionable discourses, that is, forms of language that can be put to use more directly within the sphere of work' (ibid.: 455).

Phillips, N. (1995) Telling organizational tales: On the role of narrative fiction in the study of organizations, *Organization Studies*, **16**(4): 625–50. In this text, Phillips argues for the benefits of encouraging the use of fiction as a legitimate approach to the study of management and organization. He suggests the use of novels, short stories, plays, songs, poems and films. This is done by showing how the boundaries between traditional forms of analysis and narrative fiction are blurred and by pointing towards several roles that fiction can play in theory development.

References

Astley, W.G. and R.F. Zammuto (1992) Organization science, managers, and language games, *Organization Science*, **3**(4): 443–60.

Chia, R. (1995) From modern to postmodern organizational analysis, *Organization Studies*, **16**(4): 580–605.

Chia, R. (1996) The problem of reflexivity in organizational research: Towards a postmodern science of organization, *Organization*, **3**(1): 31–59.

Chrisman, J.J. and F. Katrishen (1995) The small business development programme in the US: A statistical analysis of its impact on economic development, *Entrepreneurship and Regional Development*, **7**: 143–55.

Clark, T. and R. Fincham (eds) (2002) *Critical Consulting*. Oxford: Blackwell Publishers.

Clark, T. and G. Salaman (1998) Creating the 'right' impression: Towards a dramaturgy of management consultancy, *The Services Industries Journal*, **18**(1): 18–38.

Damgaard, T., Freytag, P.V. and P. Darmer (2000) Qualitative methods in business studies, in A.G. Woodside (ed.), *Getting Better at Sensemaking*. Greenwich, CT: JAI Press, Vol. 9, pp. 143–86.

Damgaard, T., Piihl, J. and K. Klyver (2004) The drama of consulting and counselling the entrepreneur, in D. Hjort and C. Steyaert (eds), *Narrative and Discursive Approaches in Entrepreneurship*, Cheltenham, UK and Northampton, MA, USA: Edward Elgar, pp. 160–76.

Feyerabend, P. (1975) *Against Method*. Atlantic Highlands, NJ: Humanities Press.

Frank, H. (1993) Small business owners and consultants: An empirical analysis of their relationship, *Journal of Small Business and Entrepreneurship*, **10**(4): 32–43.

Gergen, K.J. (1992) Organization theory in the postmodern era, in M. Reed and M. Hughes (eds), *Rethinking Organization: New directions in organization theory and analysis*, London: Sage Publications, pp. 207–26.

Gergen, K.J. and M.M. Gergen (1991) Towards reflexive methodologies, in F. Steier (ed.), *Research and Reflexivity*. London: Sage Publications, pp. 76–95.

Gibbons, M., Limoges, C., Nowotny, H., Schwartzman, S., Scott, P. and M. Trow (1994) Introduction, *The New Production of Knowledge*, London: Sage Publications, pp. 1–16.

Gordon, W. and R. Langmaid (1988) *Qualitative Market Research: A practitioner's and buyer's guide*. Aldershot: Gower.

Johansson, A.W. (1997) *At förstå rådgivning till småföretagere*. Bjärred: Academia Adacta AB.

Johansson, A.W. (1999) How can consultants advise SMEs?, in B. Johannisson and H. Landström (eds), *Images of Entrepreneurship and Small Business: Emergent Swedish contributions to academic research*. Lund: Studentlitteratur, pp. 141–64.

Klyver, K., Damgaard, T. and J. Piihl (2004a) Et bryllup i Nørre Snede . . . En dialog om forandringsledelse i mindre ejerledede virksomheder, in P.R. Christensen, T. Damgaard and T. Jørgensen (eds), *Iøjnefaldende anderledes – studier af forandringsprocesser i mindre virksomheder*. København: DJØFs Forlag, pp. 259–74.

Klyver, K., Damgaard, T. and J. Piihl (2004b) Forandringsledelse i ejerledede virksomheder – fire perspektiver, in P.R. Christensen, T. Damgaard and T. Jørgensen (eds), *Iøjnefaldende anderledes – studier af forandringsprocesser i mindre virksomheder*. København: DJØFs Forlag, pp. 275–302.

Latour, B. (1987) *Science in Action*. Cambridge, MA: Harvard University Press.

Parker, M. (1995) Critique in the name of what? Postmodernism and critical approaches to organization, *Organization Studies*, **16**(4): 553–88.

Phillips, N. (1995) Telling organizational tales: on the role of narrative fiction in the study of organizations, *Organization Studies*, **16**(4): 625–50.

Steyaert, C. (1997) A qualitative methodology for process studies of entrepreneurship: Creating local knowledge through stories, *International Studies of Management and Organization*, **27**(2): 13–33.

Strauss, A. and J. Corbin (1994) Grounded theory methodology: an overview, in N.K. Denzin and Y.S. Lincoln (eds), *Handbook of Qualitative Research*. Thousand Oaks, CA: Sage Publications, pp. 273–85.

Sturdy, A. (1997) The consultancy process – an insecure business?, *Journal of Management Studies*, **34**: 389–413.

Van Maanen, J. (1988) *Tales of the Field: On writing ethnography*. Chicago and London: University of Chicago Press.

Weick, K.E. (1996) Drop your tools: an allegory for organizational studies, *Administrative Science Quarterly*, **41**: 301–13.

Yin, R.K. (1994) *Case Study Research*. London: Sage Publications.

PART IV

WINDING DOWN AND ASSESSING THE RIDE

15 Assessing the quality of qualitative research in entrepreneurship
Caroline Wigren

Qualitative studies in entrepreneurship research

A qualitative study is here defined as a study that focuses on understanding the naturalistic setting, or everyday life, of a certain phenomenon or person. They are studies that include the context in which the studied phenomenon is embedded. However, qualitative studies do not represent a uniform perspective. Rather, depending on assumptions about ontology and epistemology, different qualitative techniques and approaches are applicable. Common to qualitative studies is that the researchers do not 'remain as external observers, measuring what they see; they must move to investigate from within the subject of study' (Morgan and Smircich 1980: 498). The main difference between the different qualitative approaches is the degree to which the researcher accepts subjectivity (ibid.: 492). Many researchers who have an objectivist approach to social science operate within the functionalist paradigm of inquiry, while those who accept subjectivity operate within the interpretive paradigm of inquiry (Gioia and Pitre 1990). Denzin and Lincoln (1994: 2) as representative of the interpretative paradigm define qualitative research as follows:

> Qualitative research is multimethod in focus, involving an interpretive, naturalistic approach to its subject matter. This means that qualitative researchers study things in their natural settings, attempting to make sense of, or interpret, phenomena in terms of the meaning people bring to them.

To get to know which meaning people bring to certain phenomena the researcher focuses on different types of texts, oral and/or written (Cassell and Symon 1994). Doing qualitative studies is about coming close to the field and learning from it. Studies in the interpretative paradigm have, however, encountered problems in obtaining legitimacy, even if they contribute with an added understanding to studies in the functionalist paradigm.

A literature review of two well-known journals within the field of entrepreneurship research, *Entrepreneurship Theory and Practice* (*ETP*) and *Journal of Business Venturing* (*JBV*), reveals that little qualitative research is published in these journals[1] (see also Chapter 10), a well-known fact in the field (cf. Aldrich 2000; Gartner and Birley 2002). Moreover, much of the research published has been undertaken in the functionalist paradigm and the authors use the terminology of this paradigm (e.g. post-positivist, validity, causality, accuracy of the interview data, member checks, triangulation and reliability) (cf. Hite 2005; Reuber and Fischer 2005; Howorth et al. 2004; Barringer and Greening 1998). These authors also stress that their studies are generating knowledge that can be tested by a quantitative approach. One reason could be that it is difficult to keep an interpretative qualitative study within the number of pages that are generally acceptable for a journal article (Parker and Gartner 2004). According to Parker and Gartner (ibid.: 414) authors versed in qualitative methods have more experience in using monographs and books for reporting their results. Hence the challenge for interpretative qualitative scholars is to learn to turn novels into short stories (ibid.). Moreover, qualitative scholars need to learn how to ensure and articulate the trustworthiness of their research in a condensed form. In the articles published in *ETP* and *JBV* it is obvious that most authors decide to leave out such a discussion, opting to refer to some well-known qualitative researchers, who then come to represent and answer for the method applied. A frequent reference was for example Eisenhardt's article on case studies (1989).

This may reflect that there are no commonly agreed quality standards in qualitative research. Hence, for qualitative studies to obtain increased legitimacy there is a need to agree upon what good quality means, which is the focus of this chapter.

The chapter begins with a discussion on traditional scientific research criteria, social construction and constructivist criteria, and postmodern criteria. The first type of research criteria mentioned are closely related to those used by quantitative scholars and are suitable for researchers who work within the functionalist paradigm of inquiry, that is, the positivism or post-positivism paradigm of inquiry (Lincoln and Guba 2000). However, for researchers within the interpretative paradigm of inquiry believing that '[t]he qualitative researcher is not an objective, authoritative, politically neutral observer standing outside and above the text' (Lincoln and Denzin 2000: 1049), there is need for supplementary ways of discussing quality in qualitative research. Those researchers are either working with constructivist criteria or with postmodern criteria.

The chapter is structured into three sections. First follows a discussion on different types of research criteria (presented above). Focus thereafter is on quality criteria in ethnographic studies, the discussion is structured according to the criteria that a good ethnographic study is authentic, plausible, and critical (Golden-Biddle and Lock 1993). Finally, the chapter addresses the question who is the judge: the inner academic world, practitioners, or both?

Quality criteria in qualitative research

A question qualitative researchers are frequently asked is: What makes your study a piece of academic research? Isn't it just good storytelling? Fetterman (1998b) argues that a good ethnographer should be both a good storyteller and a good scientist. If the ethnographer manages to come close to the natives and to the studied phenomenon, and manages to convey these experiences to the reader, the better the story and the science becomes. But when is the story good enough, and when is it 'good science'? In qualitative studies, different researchers argue for different criteria. This section discusses different quality criteria in relation to alternative inquiry paradigms.

Depending on the ontological and epistemological standpoints of the researcher, s/he relies on different criteria for judging quality. Table 15.1 presents four different types of quality criteria: traditional scientific research criteria, critical realism criteria, social constructivist criteria, and postmodern criteria. Researchers applying the traditional scientific research criteria and the critical realism criteria are working in the functionalist paradigm of inquiry, while the researchers operating in the interpretative paradigm apply research criteria from the third or fourth column. The four columns illustrate four distinct groups of quality criteria. There are, however, no clear-cut boundaries between these and each researcher makes his or her own choice as to how to handle quality issues. The criteria applied depend, among other things, on the purpose of the study, the method used, and the philosophical orientation of the researcher (Patton 2002). Columns one, three and four are further elaborated below. The criteria presented in column two are elaborated in greater detail in Chapter 16.

Traditional scientific research criteria are applied by researchers adopting the positivist or post-positivist perspective. Such criteria are most common among quantitative researchers but there are also researchers who work with qualitative data who apply these criteria (cf. the articles published in *ETP* and *JBV*). In 1985 Lincoln and Guba posed the following criteria for qualitative research: *credibility, transferability, dependability* and *confirmability*. The four criteria correspond to the traditional scientific research criteria. The four quality criteria are presented in Table 15.2.

Regarding *credibility*, Patton (2002) distinguishes between three inquiry elements, which are distinct but related. These are: *rigorous methods, credibility of researcher* and *philosophical belief in the value of qualitative inquiry*. Regarding rigorous methods, studies should be based on high-quality data, which are systematically analysed. Moreover, presenting complexities and dilemmas adds credibility, which can be achieved by including negative or disconfirming cases, that is, cases that do not necessarily fit into

Table 15.1   A variation of quality criteria in qualitative studies

Traditional scientific research criteria (cf. Glaser 2000; Lincoln and Guba 1985; Miles and Huberman 1994; Ragin 1987, 2000; Yin 1994)	Critical realism criteria (cf. Healy and Perry 2000)	Social construction and constructivist criteria (cf. Guba and Lincoln 1989, 1990; Denzin 1997, 2001; Potter 1996)	Postmodernism and postmodern criteria (cf. Goodall 2000; Richardson 2000; Barone 2000)
Objectivity of inquiry (attempt to minimize bias)	There is a 'real' imperfectly apprehensible world to discover	Subjectivity acknowledged (discusses and takes into account biases)	Opens the world to us in some way
Value-free	Value-aware	Value-laden	Value-laden
Systematic rigour of fieldwork procedures	Methodological trustworthiness	Trustworthiness	Creativity
Triangulation (consistency of findings across methods and data sources)	Triangulation (consistency of findings across methods and informants)	Triangulation (capturing and respecting multiple perspectives)	Aesthetic quality
Reliability of codings and pattern analysis	Contingent validity (generative mechanisms, contexts make them contingent)	Authenticity	Interpretive vitality
Correspondence of findings to reality	Improving interpretation by 'fining' the more appropriate one	Reflexivity	Flows from self; embedded in lived experience
Generalizability (external validity)	Construct validity	Praxis	Stimulating
Strength of evidence supporting causal hypotheses	A family of answers	Particularity (doing justice to the integrity of unique cases)	Provocative
Statistical generalization	Analytic generalization (theory-building)	Enhanced and deepened under-standing (*Verstehen*)	Connects with and moves the audience
Proving assumptions about reality	Critical descriptions and theory-building	Contributions to dialogue	Voice distinct, expressive

Source: Inspired by 'Alternative sets of criteria for judging the quality and credibility of qualitative inquiry' in Patton (2002: 544), exhibit (9.1) and Healy and Perry (2000).

Table 15.2   Criteria for qualitative research

Traditional scientific research criteria	Lincoln and Guba's (1985) criteria for qualitative research
Internal validity: a study is logically sound and free from confounding variables.	*Credibility*, referring to the issue that the inquirer ensures that the respondents' views fit with the inquirer's reconstruction and representation.
External validity: it is possible to generalize from the study to a larger population.	*Transferability*, referring to the issue that the inquirer should provide the reader with sufficient case information so s/he could make generalizations, in terms of case-to-case transfer.
Reliability: the results of an assessment are dependable and consistently measured, and indicate the consistency of scores over time, between scores, or across different tasks or items measuring the same thing.	*Dependability*, referring to the issue that the inquirer should ensure that the research process is logical, traceable and documented.
Objectivity: accurate representation of reality.	*Confirmability*, referring to the issue that data and interpretations are not figments of the inquirer's imagination.

Source: Lincoln and Guba (1985).

the pattern (see also Chapter 10). Another way to increase credibility is to work with different types of triangulation (Patton 2002: 556):

(i)   *Methods triangulation*: consistency of findings generated by different data collection methods.

(ii) *Triangulation of sources*: consistency of different data sources within the same method. That could for example mean to compare:
   ● Observations with interviews
   ● Interviews with written material
   ● What people say in public and in private
   ● If people are consistent and say the same thing over time

(iii) *Analyst triangulation*: Using multiple analysts to review findings.

(iv) *Theory/perspective triangulation*: Using multiple perspectives or theories to interpret data.

The main reason for working with triangulation is to ensure that the findings are not 'simply an artifact of a single method, a single source, or a single investigator's blinders' (Patton 2002: 563).

The credibility of researchers is enhanced by providing professional information about them. Who the researcher is in terms of academic position and track record might influence how s/he was received in the field. Being a credible researcher comes with training and experiences. Finally, regarding intellectual rigour, Patton (2002) asks the researcher to describe, discuss and reflect upon the concepts that are used, for example objective, subjective, trustworthy and authentic. However, since this might result in a lengthy discussion it would not be suitable for a journal article, whereas it would not constitute a problem in a chapter for a book or in a monograph.

Social construction and constructivist criteria. In 1989 Guba and Lincoln re-evaluated their criteria from 1985 and concluded that they were analogous to conventional criteria. Hence they added a second set of five criteria called authenticity criteria, which they perceived as more in line with the constructivist epistemology. These criteria are presented in Table 15.3.

Other researchers have also contributed to the dialogue, such as Stewart (1998), who argues for the criteria veracity, objectivity and perspicacity, and emphasizes the following questions (ibid.: 15–16):

Table 15.3   Criteria for judging qualitative research

Type of authenticity criteria	Definition of the criteria
Fairness	A quality of balance, meaning that respondents' different constructions should be presented in a balanced and even-handed way to prevent marginalization.
Ontological authenticity	Refers to the fact that if the respondents have participated in the inquiry, then their constructions should be enhanced. The author should help the reader to enhance understanding about the social context of the study.
Educative authenticity	Refers to the issue that participants in an inquiry learn from participating and are able to develop a deeper understanding and new perspectives of seeing things.
Catalytic authenticity	Is a reference to what extent action is stimulated and facilitated by the process; has the research acted as an impetus to participants to change things?
Tactical authenticity	Refers to whether or not the participants in the inquiry are, or have been, empowered to act.

Source: Guba and Lincoln (1989).

- How well, with what verisimilitude, does this study succeed in its depiction?
- How well does this study transcend the perspectives of the researchers?
- How well does this study transcend the perspectives of informants?
- Is this study revelatory?
- Does this generate insights that are also applicable to other times, other places, in the human experience?
- How fundamentally does this study explain?

Postmodern criteria are applicable in qualitative studies that have a subjectivist approach to social science, such as ethnographic studies. In the most general sense ethnography refers to the study of culture(s) that a given group of people share to a greater or lesser extent (Van Maanen 1995), or as Wolcott expresses it; 'to make sense of human social behavior in terms of cultural patterning' (1995: 83). The ethnographer focuses on understanding the social context of a certain phenomenon or person and the context is included in the study. While a journalist would write about the unusual, the ethnographer studies and documents the routine, everyday lives of people (Fetterman 1998b). There are many forms of ethnographic research, and as in all research the approach chosen depends on ontological and epistemological standpoints, which further influence the choice of quality criteria. Postmodern ethnographic studies are those studies that have a subjectivist approach to social science.

The postmodern approach to ethnography challenges Stewart's (1998) argument, countering that it is not possible to view the world through the eyes of somebody else. Unfortunately, the scientific debate between postmodernism and naturalism in ethnography sometimes lacks a sense of nuance, and postmodern ethnography is equated with the idea that anything goes. Therefore, more than many other studies, postmodern ethnographic studies need to convince their readers that they are trustworthy.

The ethnographic method has only been used marginally in the field of entrepreneurship research so far, which according to Aldrich (1992) and Gregoire et al. (2002) is an unfortunate loss to the field, since such an approach makes it possible to gain additional knowledge and understanding about entrepreneurs and entrepreneurship. In the few studies that have applied ethnographic methods, the naturalism approach is dominant (cf. Bøllingtoft and Ulhøi 2005; Fadahunsi and Rosa 2002; Jack and Anderson 2002). Yet since there are few ethnographic studies about entrepreneurs and entrepreneurship, there is a limited number of studies that can serve as models. The rest of this chapter deals with quality criteria in ethnographic studies, with a focus on criteria that are suitable for researchers who have a subjectivist approach to social science.

Quality criteria in ethnographic studies

In line with Golden-Biddle and Locke (1993), who rely on an interpretative perspective inspired by Berger and Luckmann (1966) and Burrell and Morgan (1979), I argue that an ethnographic study is good when it is trustworthy, and it is trustworthy when it is authentic, plausible and critical. If the ethnographer manages to fulfil these criteria, then s/he can also convince the reader. Golden-Biddle and Locke (1993) are inspired by literature and literary criticism (Booth 1961, 1967; Iser 1989), 'which rhetorically analyzes written work as "texts" to be constructed and interpreted' (p. 596). Lately, they stress, other fields have also taken up the challenge to 'explore the rhetorical dimension of convincing in the written texts of their respective fields' and they refer to philosophy (Rorty 1982), anthropology (Clifford 1983; Geertz 1973, 1988; Marcus and Fischer 1986), psychology (Bruner 1990), and organization studies (Van Maanen 1988a, 1988b). They point to the relationship that is established between the text, produced by the researcher, and the reader of the text. Focus is on how the researcher 'convince[s] the reader that the findings are credible' and furthermore, 'how do readers convince themselves' (ibid.: 597).

Based on Hunt (1990), Stewart writes: 'truth is what is right to believe, provisionally and critically, based upon our best means of understanding the reality of the subject at hand' (Stewart 1998: 14). This way of reasoning is in line with ethnographic naturalism, where an attempt is made to capture the true, real nature of the phenomena (Schwandt 1997). Believing that no ethnographer can manage to do a completely true study implies an exception to ethnographic naturalism. One reason is, as Burk (1935: 70) once wrote, that 'A way of seeing is always a way of not seeing.' The presence of the ethnographer in the field is the essence of the ethnographic method, and there are always meetings, incidents and discussions that the ethnographer will miss, simply because s/he cannot be everywhere at once. Another reason, in line with the social constructionist perspective, is 'that what exists is what we perceive to exist' (Burr 1995: 2), that is, there is no true reality to discover since reality is constructed by those who, through social interaction, ascribe meaning to it. Rosen (1991: 6) writes:

> The aim of social constructionist research is then to understand how members of a social group, through their participation in social process, enact their particular realities and endow them with meaning . . . – meaning is the focus of investigation . . . The task of the researcher is to describe and analyze the world from the perspective of those involved with its performance.

After having conducted the fieldwork the researcher should reorganize the material and make it presentable. This part of the process is about formulating the results from the time in the field in a convincing way. Conducting an ethnographic study implies that the researcher takes the responsibility to participate in the continuing dialogue to define and redefine it both as a process and as a product (Wolcott 1995). The following subsections deal with the three criteria: authenticity, plausibility and criticality (Golden-Biddle and Locke 1993). The three concepts are discussed in depth and related to the field of entrepreneurship research.

Authenticity
A text[2] is authentic when the readers can see that the researcher has been in the field and is genuine about what s/he has experienced there by having observed and participated in everyday life. Making participant observations means that the researcher takes the role of an observer as well as a participant in daily life activities, in order to create understanding about how people live their lives. It takes time to gain access to everyday life since mutual trust must be established between the researcher and the natives. Alvesson (1999) discusses, metaphorically, qualitative research in geographical terms, showing how the researcher 'is coming closer and closer to the lived realities of other people' (ibid.: 2).

A text is convincing when it offers 'thick descriptions' (Geertz 1973). Thick descriptions are those accounts that in a reliable way make the culture come alive for the readers of the text, through stories that provide meaning to the context studied (ibid.). The researcher should record circumstances, meanings, intentions, strategies and so on that characterize particular episodes that s/he experiences and interpret these (ibid.). It is the interpretations of the episodes that make the descriptions thick, not only the richness of details. In Schwandt's (1994: 123) interpretation the researcher studies the stories that are told, what is said, and takes thereafter the role of constructing a 'reading of the meaning-making process of the people he or she studies'.

Golden-Biddle and Locke (1993: 598) define a text as convincing when the researcher has managed to create a balance of 'novelty and familiarity'. The reader should feel at home while at the same time experiencing new understandings. This implies that it is necessary to go beyond taken-for-granted assumptions about the field and truly try to understand how those living and working in the field actually experience it, and to see and experience daily life through their eyes and thereby 'identify' what Van Maanen (1979) calls their first-order concepts.

First-order concepts, or experience-near concepts, are 'the "facts" of an ethnographic investigation' (Van Maanen 1979: 540), or the descriptive properties in the field. But they are also 'situationally, historically, and biographically mediated interpretations used by members of the organization to account for a given descriptive property' (ibid.). It is those concepts that the people in the field spontaneously use in their daily language. Discussing first-order concepts, Van Maanen (1979) distinguishes between (i) presentational data and (ii) operational data. Presentational data, or stories, are what the people in the field espouse. These data are often 'ideological, normative, and abstract, dealing far more with a manufactured image of idealized doing than with the routinized practical activities actually engaged in by members of the studied organization' (ibid.: 542). Such data are, according to Martin (2002), espoused values, or those that natives ascribe to their organization or community and these values are often chosen 'to make an impression on an audience' (ibid.: 88). The values are often abstract, represent the rationalized talk of an organization, and stand for the formal practices of the organization, although they may not necessarily say anything about informal practices (Martin 2002). Operational data, on the other hand, are those that 'document[s] the running stream of spontaneous conversations and activities engaged in and observed by the ethnographer while in the field' (Van Maanen 1979: 542). Martin (2002) calls these data inferred values, which 'reflect a deeper level of interpretation' (ibid.: 88).

Unfortunately, many researchers focus on espoused values, which Martin (2002) questions since they say very little about the behaviour of people. Values are attitudinal and attitudes do not necessarily have anything to do with oral manifestations written down for internal as well as external marketing purposes. Martin (2002) argues that there are often contradictions and inconsistencies between how people in an organization talk and act. This is what Brunsson (1989) discusses as organizational hypocrisy. According to Holmquist (2003), it seems that the field of entrepreneurship has fallen into the same trap. Holmquist (2003) argues that the Western myth of the entrepreneur is so strong that it hinders a deeper understanding of the phenomenon of entrepreneurship. A similar point is made by Ahl (2004) in her discourse analysis of research texts about women entrepreneurs (see also Chapter 9 in this handbook). By relying and focusing on espoused, male-gendered values about entrepreneurship, as well as espoused (and different) values about femininity, we have fallen into the trap of reproducing the female entrepreneur as being weaker. The research texts end up reproducing gender stereotypes instead of providing a deeper understanding of entrepreneurship. Boje et al. (1999) use the term 'grand narrative' for those stories that are taken for granted and explain these as a sort of hegemony. They quote Clegg's definition (1989: 160), which says that hegemony 'involves the successful mobilization and reproduction of the active consent of dominated groups'. They stress that the hegemony force, or grand narrative, 'of one social class, gender or culture over another, can be an invisible prison of intersecting gazes to those who have little power to negotiate or even voice alternate stories defining and shaping their existence' (Boje et al. 1999: 341). The grand narrative easily becomes the narrative of the studied case (Boje et al. 1999). It could either be one social class, a gender, or a culture that constructs this narrative. People with less power stay silent. The grand story cannot camouflage the meanings of all microstories (ibid.). Both Boje et al. (1999) and Martin (2002) ask for studies that do not merely focus on the values that are articulated by organizations.

Researchers shoulder the responsibility of uncovering the taken-for-granted assumptions that are created by the society of today. In a time when information and knowledge are widely communicated, it is important to remember that a number of professions participate in the construction of grand narratives, for example politicians, journalists, authors of popular-science books, as well as researchers. These opinion-formers have the power to influence how people perceive different things, and they participate in the construction of these taken-for-granted assumptions, which are adopted by the average person on the street. Assumptions are not more or less true, but there is a risk that they might be too one-dimensional and superficial when they are adopted as representing the only true picture. Assumptions should preferably be understood in relation to the context they have been created in, and, moreover, related to the contexts that they are created about. There is a need to give voice to many groups of people, meaning that multivocality should be taken into account in research (Risberg 1999). As discussed in the introduction to this chapter, much of the qualitative research in entrepreneurship has been undertaken within the functionalist paradigm using the terminology of this paradigm. This means that multivocality is not taken into account. Rather, grand narratives are created.

It is easier to focus on the presentational data, since these are the data that the natives express as written or oral stories (Van Maanen 1979). However, according to Whyte (1961: 57), 'the most important things to know about a group of people are the things they themselves take for granted. Yet it is precisely those things that the people find most difficult to discuss.'

Relying on presentational data means that we do not manage to grasp those things an entrepreneur or a group of people take for granted. Moreover, it implies that nor are the readers offered a thick description of the studied phenomenon or phenomena; that is, the text is not convincing. Managing to enter the world beyond presentational data demands that the researcher is present in the studied field. The aim of ethnography is to understand the world from the natives' point of view, to have 'been there' as Alvesson (1999: 5) expresses it. To do so, the researcher should gain access to everyday life. Ethnography implies that a phenomenon is not only studied in depth but also to a certain breadth. Day-to-day activities are to be studied in their context, in real time, and the researcher gets to know the culture from those who construct it, that is, the participants.

To prevent a study being based mainly on presentational data, it is important to reflect upon the methods, or techniques, used to obtain access to the data. It does not matter how good the ethnographer is at analyzing the empirical material, or constructing new theories, if the different techniques used in the field are faulty (Salamone 1979). In an authentic study the researcher has managed to move beyond the espoused values, the presentational data, and has also grasped the inferred values and the operational data. In the case of entrepreneurship this means, for example, that the researcher has managed to move beyond the polished stories told by and about entrepreneurs, and managed to understand the daily life of an entrepreneur, an organization, or an entrepreneurial milieu. To manage to do this, researchers must be critical of the methods used for collecting data and stories. To avoid the domination of espoused values and presentational data, they must also participate and collect data in non-artificial situations, and in everyday life. This demands inquiry from the inside and, furthermore, a move from a focus on 'what' and 'how' questions to a focus on 'why' questions. By following and interacting with entrepreneurs it is possible to learn why they do what they do, which will add to our understanding about entrepreneurs and entrepreneurship.

Plausibility

The second concept, plausibility, is about bridging the empirical and theoretical worlds. This implies, in Van Maanen's words (1979), 'going from first-order concepts to second-order concepts'. Second-order concepts explain the patterning of the first-order concepts and are used by the researcher to organize, explain, and forward what those in the field do and refer to (ibid.). The analysis and the interpretations of the stories lead the researcher to the process of theorizing and to the construction of second-order concepts, or experience-distance concepts. Even if qualitative research, including ethnographic-inspired studies, is contextually bounded, it is possible to learn from them on a general level if the descriptions are thick enough and if the researcher has developed second-order concepts. The concepts of first- and second-order concepts are common in ethnographic studies, but applicable to other qualitative methods too. Going from first- to second-order concepts is a critical part of qualitative research, since the quality of the final research piece depends on how well the researcher manages to bridge the gap between the empirical and theoretical world.

'Stories are theories', according to Draft (1983: 541). He points out that it is not the stories as such that contribute to knowledge but the answers to the question why that are evident in the stories. Draft (ibid.: 543) quotes Oppenheimer (1956: 129): 'Science is the adaptation of common sense.' In essence the researcher comes from common sense and it also that common sense s/he gives back, adding to an ongoing dialogue. Van Maanen (1979: 549) quotes Sherlock Holmes, who says: 'The world is full of obvious things which nobody by any chance will ever see.' The role of the researcher is to see the obvious, create understanding about it, and communicate it.

Van Maanen (1988b) emphasizes three different styles of writing ethnography: (i) the realist tales, (ii) the confessional tales, and (iii) the impressionist tales.

(i)   In the realist tale, the researcher attempts to give a picture that is as accurate as possible, reporting what happens in the field and referring to what natives say and do, but s/he is not present in the text. There is a distance between her/him and the text and s/he avoids the use of the first-person singular 'I'. Indeed, 'The actions and words of singular persons are minimized . . . in favor of what typical natives typically do, say, and think' (Van Maanen 1988b: 49). This implies that there is a way to do, say and think that can be classified as typical. This means that there is one true interpretation, one true understanding, or a 'typical' way of doing, saying or thinking. Such a study is not based on the assumption that reality is enacted and research is constructed, which is rather the base for social constructionist research (see the discussion above on ethnographic naturalism).

(ii)   However, in the confessional tale, the researcher is a participant and infiltrates the text. The text is about the researcher's personal experiences and reactions. This helps the reader to understand how the researcher has learned about the culture in question. Barriers faced in the field are presented and the researcher tells how access was gained to the culture. This is in line with the idea that the researcher merges into the field and both become a whole. During the writing process, the researcher draws on the memories gathered from the field as the stories are constructed in interaction with the people there. It is possible to say that the researcher is present in all stories since 'most storytelling is done in conversation and involves the listeners in various ways' (Boje 1991: 107). In line with this reasoning, the listeners are 'co-producers with the teller of the story performance' (ibid.).

(iii) Finally, the impressionist tale is a text written to startle the reader, focusing on unusual and extraordinary events. The researcher becomes the teller of the tales and takes an active role in the text. By applying the confessional style of writing, the researcher unmasks the fieldwork process (Van Maanen 1988b). This is a relatively new approach to writing a text. The researcher admits things like blind spots, missing information and so on. Doing fieldwork is demasked and demystified at the same time, with an increase in the level of subjectivity in the text and the process of doing fieldwork. Subjectivity is no longer placed on a hidden agenda. The information filters through the researcher. The confessional style is considered here to be an honest way of writing. Its adoption is to avoid ascribing interpretations to people, constructed in the interaction process by those researching and those being researched.

The ethnographic studies published in *JBV* are written in line with the realist tale (cf. Bøllingtoft and Ulhøi 2005; Fadahunsi and Rosa 2002). Regarding quality criteria of the data, Bøllingtoft and Ulhøi (2005) refer to 'the potential lack of reliability', and conclude that the design of their study 'has obvious limits for generalization' (ibid.: 277). Moreover, they conclude that their study is a base for generating hypotheses. Fadahunsi and Rosa (2002) include a discussion about validity criteria in quantitative studies and conclude that qualitative studies need their own criteria. However, although they mention the risk of ethnocentrism, they do not develop this discussion further. Jack and Anderson's (2002) study provides 'insights, rich details, and thick descriptions' (ibid.: 473) and they consider their study as a base for generating hypotheses for further testing. It is interesting to note that none of the studies argues for alternative criteria for judging quality even if Aldrich had already argued that 'a totally pragmatic anti-positivist view' (1992: 208) was present in entrepreneurship. More than ten years later, scholars hang on to a positivistic terminology. However, there are scholars who do the opposite (cf. Steyaert 1997; Wigren 2003). Nevertheless, so far, few studies within the field of entrepreneurship have relied on stories (cf. Steyaert 1997), but qualitative researchers within the field of entrepreneurship should not be too afraid of using stories, as long as these are trustworthy, that is, they originate from ambitious field studies, as it is possible to develop significant new knowledge from solid, qualitative field studies.

Criticality
Criticality means that the text offers its readers the possibility to take a step back and challenge taken-for-granted assumptions. Golden-Biddle and Locke (1993: 614) state that 'the most provocative task and potential of ethnography is the use of the data to reflect not only on the members' world but more importantly on the world of the researcher'. This is a

challenge. However, it is important to challenge not only the research community but also the studied world. Assumptions are put to test in the written text since this is the research phase in which the researcher decides what to tell and how to tell it. This is the time when ideas become clearer and more structured, experiences from the field become part of a bigger context, and thoughts are clarified. It is the time when the researcher realizes which 'pieces' from the field have not been fully investigated and if any information is missing. What makes a text more or less ethnographic is the thickness of field descriptions, in other words, how well the researcher has managed to communicate the culture from the natives' point of view.

The major part of the process of doing field studies is often tacit, and to create trustworthiness it is good to be as open as possible towards the readers of the text, telling about successes as well as setbacks in the field. The researcher should account for the following issues: (1) how the ethnographer entered the field; (2) how s/he developed relationships and interacted with the informants, successfully or not; (3) which arenas s/he visited; (4) if s/he was excluded from any arenas; and (5) how s/he checked the information with others to know which standpoints should be considered general or individual (Wigren 2003).

Even though researchers spend months in the field, there are still many events, conversations and issues that might be missed. The researcher might be in the wrong place; might focus on something else; or might be tired and just not sufficiently observant. The more open the fieldworker is about such issues, the better it is; or in Van Maanen's (1979: 548) words,

> the ethnographer must continually assess the believability of the talk-based information harvested over the course of a study, an evaluation dependent upon the fieldworker's interest, skill, and good fortune in uncovering lies, areas of ignorance, and the various taken-for-granted features of the studied organization. These tasks represent the essence of sound fieldwork and lie at the heart of any faithful description of a studied organization.

Dyer and Wilkins (1991: 618) add to this argument that it is important to 'ask for more personal disclosure of the authors' biases and involvement with a particular setting'. They also call for more information about the contexts from which case studies originate. However, there might be issues that are difficult to write about in the final text, such as the mood of the researcher, as well as the mood of the people in the field. Emotions in the field do influence the process. The researcher will get along with some people better than with others. Writing about such issues in the final text might be difficult; however, it is helpful just to be aware of this problem. The more open and the more honest the researcher can be, the better will be the quality of the final text, or as Fine (1994: 289) claims, 'By knowing oneself, one can improve a bit, but more significantly, one can recognize that the limits of the art are part of the data.'

The researcher plays a significant role when it comes to collecting and constructing texts in qualitative research since s/he is, in many ways, the 'focal research instrument' (Stewart 1998: 6), and s/he influences the process. Van Maanen (1979) writes, 'the ethnographer's own taken-for-granted understandings of the social world under scrutiny are also tied closely to the nature of quality of the data produced'. Therefore it is relevant to argue that the background and history of the researcher should be prominent in the final academic text. Depending on the researcher, the result of a study might differ. The researcher should be open and include a brief description about his or her background in the final text, in order to make the readers aware of how this might influence how the stories are presented and read (see Box 15.1).

BOX 15.1   EXCERPT FROM *THE SPIRIT OF GNOSJÖ: THE GRAND NARRATIVE AND BEYOND* (WIGREN 2003)[3]

I arrived to the field at the age of 27 to carry out a one-year ethnographic study. I chose an industrial district in Sweden situated only about 80 kilometres southwest of my hometown. One could argue that this would be an environment in which I would not be considered an outsider, and I had not really considered myself to be an outsider before arriving to the field. However, I was, since the industrial structure of the region is oriented towards production and the CEOs who run the companies are men. Being a female academic, with a southern accent, made me an outsider. Lacking training in the field of engineering, I had little knowledge about technology and machinery. I was often addressed as a 'secretary' because I constantly took notes, mainly during interviews and meetings. A fifty year-old male professor would probably have had a different experience. Being young and a woman however offered me the opportunity to ask more naïve questions. It was important to share this background when I presented my findings since it gives the reader of the book an understanding about the process in the field. Knowing this makes it easier for the reader to form his or her own opinion about the process, which might influence how s/he interprets the text.

To conclude: being open towards the subjectivity that exists in qualitative studies increases the trustworthiness of the study. The background of the researcher might influence the research process; therefore, it is preferable if the researcher is open about his or her background.

Who is to judge?

An important question for researchers to take into account is: Who is actually judging what good quality is? I would argue that there are at least three 'target groups'. The first group is the research community, the second group is the people that the researcher has studied, and the third group is other practitioners, for example politicians and policy-makers. The different groups have different expectations. Silverman (2001: 267) presents the table reproduced here as Table 15.4.

All groups, principally, make their judgments based on the text, which is the final product of the research process. The art of writing is a question of balancing what the researcher meets in the field with what the natives tell him or her (Van Maanen 1979). As highlighted above, the researcher is part of constructing the stories that are presented in the text. It is important to remember that writing up qualitative data is about interpretations. A researcher makes interpretations while talking with people and is the spectator when reading a text. Each researcher puts down his or her own interpretations as field notes, which are to be read later on. This implies that even those times when the realistic style is applied, the text is a construction. Richardson (1995: 218) addresses the question of how we should write in the following way:

Table 15.4   The audience of research and their expectations

Audience	Expectation
Academic colleagues	Theoretical, factual or methodological insight
Policy-makers	Practical information relevant to current policy issues
Practitioners	A theoretical framework for understanding clients better; factual information; practical suggestions for better procedures; reform of existing practices
The general public	New facts; ideas for reform of current practices or policies; guidelines for how to manage better or get better service from practitioners or institutions; assurances that others share their experience of particular problems in life

Source: Silverman (2001: 267). Table adopted from Strauss and Corbin (1990: 242–3).

> If we wish to understand the deepest and most universal of human experiences, if we wish our work to be faithful to the lived experiences of people, if we wish for a union between poetics and science, or if we wish to use our privileges and skills to empower the people we study, then we should value the narrative.

Narratives should be valued, mainly because 'people by nature lead storied lives and tell stories of those lives' (Clandinin and Connelly 1994: 416). Part of research is to allow the readers of a text to 'relive' the researchers' experiences from the field (cf. Richardson 1994: 521). However, as stressed above, it is important to be aware of the researcher's role in the construction of the narratives, especially when relying on participant observations and conversations that are not taped. It is impossible to remember word for word what people said, no matter how good we might be at stenography. This is not a problem as long as the researcher is aware that this is the case. Ultimately, good quality is a question of openness and honesty on the part of the researcher (Stewart 1998).

The field of entrepreneurship needs new perspectives, new methods, and a new terminology if we want to understand entrepreneurs and entrepreneurship (Hjort et al. 2003; Huse and Landström 1997). If we just apply our already existing management terminology we are not studying entrepreneurs and entrepreneurship in their own right (Hjort et al. 2003). This means that we need significant new knowledge, derived through experiences from interacting with entrepreneurs. We can learn from stories which terminology might be appropriate to use; we can learn to see new things.

Ethnographic studies are time-consuming because it is of great importance that trust is established between the researcher and the native people. When trust is established, the interaction and dialogue between the ethnographer and the natives takes on more sensitive and deeper aspects. In this manner, different meanings can be emphasized and the ethnographer goes from being an outsider to becoming, almost, an insider. An emic understanding (Fetterman 1998a) about the cultures is created, and different meanings are emphasized. Emic terms are those that are specific to a language or a culture, and they refer to first-order concepts, that is, concepts or expressions used by members in a particular group, organization, or community. In contrast, etic terms refer to second-order concepts, that is, concepts used by scientists. These concepts were originally used by cognitive anthropologists, but are today used more broadly. In 1983 Geertz refined the emic–etic distinction and introduced the concepts experience-near and experience-distant and argued that experience-near concepts are those that the natives use and understand while experience-distant are those concepts used by different specialists. A good ethnographic study is based on thick descriptions and on good theorizing, that is, carefully performed analysis and interpretations of first-order concepts, which, through the process of theorizing, are developed into second-order concepts (Van Maanen 1979). As explained earlier in the chapter, many qualitative studies are contextually bounded, but that is not to say that we cannot learn from them, and that generalizations cannot be drawn from them. Actually, we do learn from them and we make generalizations when we work with first- and second-order concepts. Working with second-order concepts implies that our language is developed further. New concepts are taken into account, and perhaps constructed as well. There is a need to trust thick descriptions and first- and second-order concepts.

To returning to the question: Who is the judge? Traditionally, the validity of research has been judged by the academic world, or the inner circle, based on whether the research is published in top-ranked journals and, moreover, how many subsequent citations result. Consequently, researchers tend to deliver what the academic community wants and basically the inner circle becomes the one and only target group. Looking at the language used, it is obvious that academic texts are usually written for those who are in the field and already invited. Others are excluded.

Regarding policy-makers, they quite often show an interest in the research since they, in many cases, are the buyers of the research; the research is commissioned research. An important issue regarding this type of research is that researcher keeps a critical perspective.

Finally, practitioners and the general public, those we study, the outer scientific world, play an insignificant role when we evaluate good research. They do play a role when it comes to member validation, but the question is, how many researchers take the time to work with member validation? Any researcher who is doing ethnographic research shoulders the responsibility of defining his or her work, both the process of doing it and the final product, in a continuing dialogue (Wolcott 1995). It is easy to leave out this part of the ethnographic research and instead focus on writing articles for publishing based on the empirical material.

The field of entrepreneurship research is closely related to practice, and although it is important that research contributes to scientific dialogues, researchers should also try to contribute to dialogues with practitioners. From such dialogue it is possible to gain additional knowledge about entrepreneurs and entrepreneurship, which can influence future studies within the field. Bridging the gap between researchers and practitioners, in this case entrepreneurs, enriches the scientific world as well as the entrepreneurs' worlds. If we want to make a contribution to the field of entrepreneurship research with significant new knowledge (Draft 1983), we have to use those methods that, so far, have been used only marginally, and that bring the two worlds closer to each other, such as ethnography.

Notes

1. The purpose of the review was to see how qualitative scholars publishing in *ETP* and *JBV* deal with methodological issues. The review was conducted as follows: (1) the review was confined to include articles that included the words 'case study' or 'ethnographic'; (2) each article was analysed according to the method applied, techniques applied, and how the authors ensured the quality of the data and the process. In *ETP* it was 11 matches in 11 issues (Volumes 27 to 29(1), 2002–2005) with the concept 'case study' and three with the concept 'ethnographic'; none of those three had used the ethnographic method. In *JBV* it was 25 matches in 20 volumes (Volumes 1 to 20, 1985–2005) with the concept 'case study' and three matches with the concept 'ethnographic'; all had applied the ethnographic method. Among the articles including the word 'case study' a number were cases written for teaching purposes. *JBV* has a special issue on qualitative methods in entrepreneurship research (Volume 17(5), 2002); this issue includes additionally three articles that were not included in the above search. One of these applies an ethnographic approach, one is a case study, and one is a discourse analysis.
2. Using the word 'text' in qualitative work is problematic since the word has different meanings. When writing about the text in this chapter I refer to the final written text, that is, the product of the ethnographic study.
3. The Gnosjö region is situated about 80 km south-west of the city of Jönköping.

References

Ahl, H. (2004) *The Scientific Reproduction of Gender Inequality: A discourse analysis of research texts on women's entrepreneurship*. Copenhagen: Copenhagen Business School Press.

Aldrich, H.E. (1992) Methods in our madness? Trends in entrepreneurship research. In *The State of the Art of Entrepreneurship*, edited by D.L. Sexton and J.D. Kasarda. Boston, MA: PWS–Kent Publishing, pp. 191–213.

Aldrich, H.A. (2000) Learning together: National differences in entrepreneurship research. In D.L. Sexton and H. Landström (eds), *The Blackwell Handbook of Entrepreneurship*. Oxford: Blackwell Publishers, pp. 5–25.

Alvesson, M. (1999) *Methodology for close up studies – struggling with closeness and closure*. Institute of Economic Research Working Paper Series, 4. Lund: University of Lund.

Barone, T. (2000) *Aesthetics, Politics, and Educational Inquiry: Essays and examples*. New York: Peter Lang.

Barringer, B.R. and Greening, D.W. (1998) Small business growth through geographic expansion: A comparative case study. *Journal of Business Venturing*, **13**(6): 467–92.

Berger, P, and Luckmann, T. (1966) *The Social Construction of Reality: A treatise in the sociology of knowledge*. London: Penguin Books.

Boje, D. (1991) The storytelling organization: A study of story performance in an office-supply firm. *Administrative Science Quarterly*, **36**(1): 106–26.

Boje, D., Luhman, J. and Baack, D. (1999) Hegemonic stories and encounters between storytelling organizations. *Journal of Management Inquiry*, **8**(4): 340–60.

Bøllingtoft, A. and Ulhøi, J.P. (2005) The networked business incubator – leveraging entrepreneurial agency? *Journal of Business Venturing*, **20**(2): 265–90.

Booth, W.C. (1961) *The Rhetoric of Fiction*. Chicago, IL: University of Chicago Press.

Booth, W.C. (1967) The revivial of rhetorics. In Martin Steinmann, Jr (ed.), *New Rhetorics*. New York: Charles Scribner's Sons, pp. 1–15.

Bruner, J. (1990) *Acts of Meaning*, Cambridge, MA: Harvard University Press.

Brunsson, N. (1989) *The Organization of Hypocrisy: Talk, decisions and actions in organizations*. New York: John Wiley.

Burk, K. (1935) *Permanence and Change*. New York: New Republic.

Burr, V. (1995) *An Introduction to Social Constructionism*. London: Routledge.

Burrell, G. and Morgan, G. (1979) *Sociological Paradigms and Organizational Analysis*. London: Heinemann.

Cassell, C. and Symon, G. (1994) Qualitative research in work contexts. In *Qualitative Methods in Organizational Research*, edited by C. Cassell and G. Symon. London: Sage Publications, pp. 1–13.

Clandinin, J. and Connelly, M. (1994) Personal experience methods. In *Handbook of Qualitative Research*, edited by Norman K. Denzin and Yvonna S. Lincoln. Thousand Oaks, CA: Sage Publications, pp. 413–27.

Clegg, S.R. (1989) *Frameworks of Power*. London: Sage Publications.

Clifford, J. (1983) On ethnographic authority. *Representations*, 1(2): 118–46.

Denzin, N.K. (1997) Coffee with Anselm. *Qualitative Family Research*, 11(1, 2): 16–18.

Denzin, N.K. (2001) *Interpretive Interactionism*, 2nd edn. Thousand Oaks, CA: Sage.

Denzin, N. and Lincoln, Y. (1994) Introduction: entering the field of qualitative research. In *Handbook of Qualitative Research*, edited by Norman K. Denzin and Yvonna S. Lincoln. Thousand Oaks, CA: Sage Publications, pp. 1–17.

Draft, R.L. (1983) Learning the craft of organizational research. *Academy of Management Review*, 8(4): 539–46.

Dyer, G.W. and Wilkins, A.L. (1991) Better stories, not better constructs, to generate better theory: A rejoinder to Eisenhardt. *The Academy of Management Review*, 16(3): 613–19.

Eisenhardt, K.M. (1989) Building theories from case study research. *Academy of Management Review*, 14(4): 532–50.

Fadahunsi, A. and Rosa, P. (2002) Entrepreneurship and illegality: Insights from the Nigerian cross-border trade. *Journal of Business Venturing*, 17(5): 397–429.

Fetterman, D. (1998a) *Ethnography: Step by step*, 2nd edn. Thousand Oaks, CA: Sage Publications.

Fetterman, D. (1998b) Ethnography. In *Handbook of Applied Social Research Methods*, edited by L. Brickman and D. Rog. Thousand Oaks, CA: Sage Publications, pp. 473–504.

Fine, G.A. (1994) Ten lies of ethnography: Moral dilemmas of field research. *Journal of Contemporary Ethnography*, 22(3): 267–94.

Gartner, W.B. and Birley, S. (2002) Introduction to the special issue on qualitative methods in entrepreneurship research. *Journal of Business Venturing*, 17: 387–95.

Geertz, C. (1973) *The Interpretation of Cultures*. New York: Basic Books.

Geertz, C. (1983) *Local Knowledge: Further essays in interpretive anthropology*. New York: Basic Books.

Geertz, C. (1988) *Works and Lives: The anthropologist as author*, Stanford, CA: Stanford University Press.

Gioia, D.A. and Pitre, E. (1990) Multiparadigm perspectives on theory building. *The Academy of Management Review*, 15(4): 584–602.

Glaser, B. (2000) The future of grounded theory. *Grounded Theory Review*, 1: 1–8.

Goodall, H.L., Jr (2000) *Writing the New Ethnography*. Walnut Creek, CA: AltaMira.

Golden-Biddle, K. and Locke, K. (1993) Appealing works: An investigation of how ethnographic texts convince. *Organization Science*, 4(4): 595–616.

Gregoire, D., Meyer, D.D. and De Castro, J.O. (2002) The crystallization of entrepreneurship research DVs and methods in mainstream management journals. In *Frontiers of Entrepreneurship Research*, pp. 663–74.

Guba, E.G. and Lincoln, Y.S. (1989) *Fourth Generation Evaluation*. Newbury Park, CA: Sage.

Guba, E.G. and Lincoln, Y.S. (1990) Can there be a human science? *Person-Centered Review*, 5(2): 130–54.

Healy, M. and Perry, C. (2000) Comprehensive criteria to judge validity and reliability of qualitative research within the realism paradigm. *Qualitative Market Research: An International Journal*, 3(3): 118–26.

Hite, J.M. (2005) Evolutionary processes and paths of relationally embedded network ties in emerging entrepreneurial firms. *Entrepreneurship Theory and Practice*, 29(1): 113–44.

Hjort, D., Johannisson, B. and Steyaert, C. (2003) Entrepreneurship as discourse and life style. In: *The Northern Lights – Organization theory in Scandinavia*, edited by B. Czarniawska and G. Sevón. Liber, Astrakt, Copenhagen Business School Press, pp. 91–110.

Holmquist, C. (2003) Is the medium really the message? Moving perspective from the entrepreneurial actor to the entrepreneurial action. In *New Movements in entrepreneurship*, edited by C. Steyaert and D. Hjort. Cheltenham, UK and Northampton, MA, USA: Edward Elgar, pp. 73–85.

Howorth, C., Westhead, P. and Wright, M. (2004) Buyouts, information asymmetry and the family management dyad. *Journal of Business Venturing*, **19**(4): 509–34.

Hunt, S.D. (1990) Truth in marketing theory and research. *Journal of Marketing*, **54**(3): 1–15.

Huse, M. and Landström, H. (1997) European entrepreneurship and small business research: methodological openness and contextual differences. *International Studies of Management and Organization*, **27**(3): 3–12.

Iser, W. (1989) *Prospecting: From reader response to literary anthropology*. Baltimore, MD: Johns Hopkins University Press.

Jack, S.L. and Anderson, A.R. (2002) The effects of embeddedness on the entrepreneurial process. *Journal of Business Venturing*, **17**(5): 467–87.

Lincoln, Y. and Denzin, N. (2000) The seventh moment: Out of the past. In *Handbook of Qualitative Research*, 2nd edn, edited by Norman K. Denzin and Yvonna S. Lincoln. Thousand Oaks, CA: Sage Publications, pp. 1047–65.

Lincoln, Y.S. and Guba, E.G (1985) *Naturalistic Inquiry*. Beverly Hills, CA: Sage Publications.

Lincoln, Y.S. and Guba, E.G. (2000) Paradigmatic controversies, contradiction, and emerging confluences. In *Handbook of Qualitative Research*, 2nd edn, edited by Norman K. Denzin and Yvonna S. Lincoln. Thousand Oaks, CA: Sage Publications, pp. 163–88.

Marcus, G.E. and Fischer, M.M.J. (1986) *Anthropology as Cultural Critique*. Chicago, IL: The University of Chicago Press.

Martin, J. (2002) *Organizational Culture: Mapping the Terrain*. Thousand Oaks, CA: Sage Publications.

Meyerson, D. and Martin, J. (1987) Cultural change: An integration of three different views. *Journal of Management Studies*, **24**(6): 623–47.

Miles, M.B. and Huberman, A.M. (1994) *Qualitative Data Analysis*. London: Sage Publications.

Morgan, G. and Smircich, L. (1980) The case of qualitative research. *Academy of Management Review*, **5**(4): 491–500.

Oppenheimer, R. (1956) Analogy in science. *The American Psychologist*, **11**: 127–35.

Parker, S.C. and Gartner, W.B. (2004) Introduction. *Entrepreneurship Theory and Practice*, **28**(5): 413–17.

Patton, M.Q. (2002) *Qualitative Research and Evaluation Methods*, 3rd edn. Thousand Oaks: Sage Publications.

Potter, J. (1996) *Representing Reality: Discourse, rhetoric and social construction*. London: Sage.

Ragin, C. (1987) *The Comparative Method: Moving beyond qualitative and quantitative strategies*. Berkeley: University of California Press.

Ragin, C. (2000) *Fuzzy-Set Social Science*. Chicago, IL: University of Chicago Press.

Reuber, A.R. and Fischer, E. (2005) The company you keep: How young firms in different competitive contexts signal reputation through their customers. *Entrepreneurship Theory and Practice*, **29**(1): 57–78.

Richardson, L. (1994) Writing a method of inquiry. In *Handbook of Qualitative Research*, edited by Norman K. Denzin and Yvonna S. Lincoln. Thousand Oaks, CA: Sage Publications, pp. 516–29.

Richardson, L. (1995) Narrative and sociology. In J. Van Maanen (ed.), *Representations in Ethnography*. Thousand Oaks, CA: Sage Publications, pp. 198–221.

Richardson, L. (2000) Writing: A method of inquiry. In *Handbook of Qualitative Research*, 2nd edn, edited by Norman K. Denzin and Yvonna S. Lincoln. Thousand Oaks, CA: Sage Publications, pp. 923–48.

Risberg, A. (1999) *Ambiguities Thereafter: An interpretative approach to acquisitions*. Doctoral Thesis No. 46, Lund Studies in Economics and Management, The Institute of Economic Research, Lund University.

Rorty, R. (1982) *The Consequences of Pragmatism*. Minneapolis, MN: University of Minnesota Press.

Rosen, M. (1991) Coming to terms with the field: Understanding and doing organizational ethnography. *Journal of Management Studies*, **28**(1): 1–24.

Salamone, F.A. (1979) Epistemological implications of fieldwork and their consequences. *American Anthropologist,* **81**: 46–60.

Schwandt, T.A. (1994) Constructivist, interpretivist approaches to human inquiry. In *Handbook of Qualitative Research,* edited by Norman K. Denzin and Yvonna S. Lincoln. Thousand Oaks, CA: Sage, pp. 118–37.

Schwandt, T.A. (1997) *Qualitative Inquiry: A dictionary of terms.* Thousand Oaks, CA: Sage Publications.

Silverman, D. (2001) *Interpreting Qualitative Data: Methods for analyzing talk, text and interaction,* 2nd edn. London: Sage Publications.

Stewart, A. (1998) The ethnographer's method, *Qualitative Research Methods,* Vol. 46, Thousand Oaks: Sage Publications.

Steyaert, C. (1997) A qualitative methodology for process studies of entrepreneurship. *International Studies of Management and Organizations,* **27**(3): 13–33.

Strauss, A. and Corbin, J. (1990) *Basics of Qualitative Research.* Thousand Oaks: Sage Publications.

Van Maanen, J. (1979) The fact of fiction in organizational ethnography. *Administrative Science Quarterly,* **24**(4): 539–50.

Van Maanen, J. (1988a) Some Notes on the Importance of Writing in Organizational Studies. Working paper, Sloan School of Management, Massachusetts Institute of Technology, Cambridge, MA.

Van Maanen, J. (1988b) *Tales of the Field: On writing ethnography.* Chicago, IL: The University of Chicago Press.

Van Maanen, J. (1995) An end to innocence: The ethnography of ethnography. In *Representation in Ethnography,* edited by J. Van Maanen. Thousand Oaks, CA: Sage Publications, pp. 1–35.

Whyte, W.F. (1961) *Men at Work.* Homewood, IL: Dorsey-Irwin.

Wigren, C. (2003) *The Spirit of Gnosjö: The grand narrative and beyond.* Doctoral thesis, JIBS Dissertation Series, no. 017, Jönköping.

Wolcott, H.F. (1995) Making a study 'more ethnographic'. In *Representation in Ethnography,* edited by J. Van Maanen. Thousand Oaks, CA: Sage Publications, pp. 79–111.

Yin, R.K. (1994) *Case Study Research: Design and methods.* Thousand Oaks, CA: Sage.

16 A critical realist approach to quality in observation studies
Anne Bøllingtoft

Entrepreneurship research and observation studies

Observation can broadly be defined as 'the act of noting a phenomenon, often with instruments, and recording it for scientific or other purposes' (Adler and Adler 1994). Thus observation studies are a matter of going 'where the action is', and simply watching and listening. Generally speaking, we engage in observation whenever we observe or participate in social behaviour and try to understand it – whether in a doctor's waiting room, in the supermarket, the office or elsewhere. The researcher's task is, however, somewhat more complicated than merely an individual trying to decide on a course of action through observation (Adler and Adler 1994; Crano and Brewer 1973). Hence *scientific* observation differs from 'everyday' observation in its emphasis on the *systematic* and *purposive* nature of the observational operations. Thus scientific observation involves systematic recording, description, analysis and interpretation of the observed individual's behaviour (Saunders et al. 2000).

In general, very few articles based on observational research are published, even in qualitative journals. According to Adler and Adler (1994), editors of scholarly journals have found it difficult to accept the legitimacy of solely (qualitative) observational research, and will probably continue to do so. The main problem is that the technique suffers from subjectivity and excessive reliance on observer articulation (Adler and Adler 1994). Moreover, it is no exaggeration to say that entrepreneurship research has no tradition of publishing studies using any type of observation. The studies published have been – and still are – dominated by positivistic inquiry (surveys) (Bouckenooghe et al. 2004; Chandler and Lyon 2001; McDonald et al. 2004).

Chandler and Lyon (2001) reviewed the methodologies employed in entrepreneurship research in nine peer-reviewed journals between 1989 and 2000.[1] In total there were 416 articles. Of these, only four studies (2 per cent) used observation.[2]

Similar results were found in a study by McDonald et al. (2004). They examined the methods and methodologies of research published in top entrepreneurship journals, covering the period 1985–2004.[3] In all, they assessed more than 2200 articles from the five journals. Twelve per cent of the articles were found to have no empirical content, and 19 per cent of the methods employed were secondary research techniques relying on published or other publicly available data, for example financial databases. Of the remaining articles, only about 2 per cent used observation as primary data collection method.[4] Hence observation is still an unexploited way of collecting data within entrepreneurship research, while the use of observation has the potential for adding new contributions and aspects to the field.

In the methodological literature, unstructured observation is in general treated as only one research strategy among many data-gathering techniques. Many textbooks, or sections in textbooks, describe how to *do* observation studies (for example Jorgensen 1989; Spradley 1980), but most books on observation ignore, or only implicitly deal with, paradigmatic questions. There are two important points here:

1. The paradigm concerned affects (i) the questions the researcher asks, (ii) the methods the researcher chooses, and (iii) how the researcher analyses the data (Guba and Lincoln 1994).
2. The evaluation of a study depends on what is considered good and valid research, which is not always the same within different paradigms (Smith 1990).

Thus the paradigmatic position is important, because it tells something about the worldview that guides the researcher, what the researcher perceives and what others should perceive and judge as 'quality', or, put another way, which evaluation criteria will be used in order to ensure rigorous and meaningful results.

This chapter deals with *qualitative* observation from a critical realist perspective. It will focus on how quality criteria can be incorporated into the process of an observation study, and thus reduce or eliminate some of the main problems of this technique as pointed out. This chapter will not discuss paradigmatic issues and questions in detail, as this is dealt with in Chapter 2. This chapter will only provide a short introduction to critical realism in order to clarify the role of observation within this paradigm. It will draw on my own experience with observation when relevant. This should provide the reader with a better understanding of how to overcome some of the difficulties related to quality issues when using observation.

The chapter is organized as follows: the first section examines the role of observation within critical realism. This is followed by an account of what observation entails. Next, the chapter deals with the question of how to judge qualitative research in general from a critical realist approach. A set of quality criteria is presented, and the chapter discusses the extent to which these criteria can be applied when using qualitative observation and how they can be incorporated into the process of an observation study. In conclusion, the chapter reflects on the limitations of the suggested criteria for judging the quality of observation studies in entrepreneurship.

The role of observation in critical realism
Within critical realism, the world is perceived as consisting of three ontological domains: (i) the real, (ii) the actual and (iii) the empirical (Bhaskar 1975; Danermark et al. 2002). The real domain can be seen as an 'invisible' layer, consisting of underlying mechanisms that produce observable events. When mechanisms produce a factual event, it takes place in the actual domain, while the last domain, the empirical domain, consists of what is experienced.

The distinction between these three domains is central. It lays the grounds for the assumption within critical realism that there is a reality that exists independently of our awareness of it. This reality, termed 'the intransitive object of science' (Bhaskar 1975; Danermark et al. 2002; Guba 1990; Guba and Lincoln 1994), is to be distinguished from what constitutes 'knowledge of reality', namely theories and notions of reality (the reader is referred to Chapter 2 for a more exhaustive explication). This 'created knowledge' of science is termed 'transitive objects' (Danermark et al. 2002) and these are dependent on theoretical conceptions. Empirical observation is part of this transitive object of science, as observation contains an interpretive element.

Within critical realism the researcher's attention is directed towards identification of the underlying mechanisms or structures that produce and/or are capable of explaining the events or the phenomena under study – the focus is not just the events/phenomena. The mode of inference used for this identification is called 'retroduction', which is a thought operation involving a reconstruction of the basic conditions for anything to be what it is (Danermark et al. 2002).

Within a critical realist framework, both qualitative and quantitative methodologies can be used to analyse the underlying mechanisms that drive actions and events (Danermark et al. 2002). However, using observation in order to identify mechanisms or structures does not require that the questions of interest be stated in advance. Consequently, the use of observation opens up the possibility of uncovering aspects not thought of or unknown to be relevant *ex ante*. Thus the researcher is given the opportunity to approach the field with the purpose of getting an in-depth understanding of the phenomena, and later use this knowledge in the process of identifying mechanisms or structures.

As critical realism is dealing with 'open systems', the mechanisms studied operate in complex and dynamic interaction with other mechanisms. Consequently, mechanisms are only *contingently* related to observable empirical events, and therefore the researcher must be able to specify the contexts in which these mechanisms operate (Danermark et al. 2002). Also, in order to examine and obtain an understanding of the context, observation can be a valuable approach as the researcher is given the possibility of observing the natural context from a multitude of perspectives. Box 16.1 gives the background to my PhD project.

BOX 16.1   INTRODUCTION TO OBSERVATION STUDY

The empirical context of my PhD project was a phenomenon with many of the same characteristics as business incubators,[5] as it was a network of new and young entrepreneurial companies, all located in the same building.

The entrepreneurs were offered access to shared office services such as Internet and printers, meeting rooms, and so on. In short, the business incubator was based on:

- The prospect of economies of scale
- Flexibility
- Cooperation between the companies
- Social and professional gathering

The fundamental idea underlying the phenomenon was networking between the entrepreneurs. The business incubator seemed to be based on trust, shared beliefs and norms, and a positive attitude towards cooperation as opposed to competition. In this respect, the phenomenon differed from most other traditional incubators. Furthermore, it did not provide any 'specialist' advice service, such as assistance in developing business and marketing plans, obtaining capital and building management teams. Furthermore, there was no professional manager, and the building was rented by the companies jointly.

I chose to carry out an (introductory) observation study because the phenomenon was the first of its kind in Denmark of this size. Furthermore, the business incubator seemed to be very successful as regards the survival of the companies. Thus I wanted to understand what was going on *inside* the incubator and *between* the entrepreneurial companies.

> I did not look for any specific aspects or themes in the beginning, just an understanding of the phenomenon and the mechanisms underlying it. What was it all about? It was very important for me to get a more in-depth understanding of, for example, the day-to-day interactions between the entrepreneurial firms. How did the companies create relations? Which relations did they create? Why did they create the relations? How did they perceive and define networks? Thus an observation study seemed to be an appropriate choice of method.

Using observation

The aim of most social science research is to acquire an understanding of a basic phenomenon. However, research is often undertaken in isolation from the natural context, thus giving the researcher an incomplete picture of the 'real world' (Crano and Brewer 1973). Observation, on the other hand, enables the researcher to collect data about a phenomenon in its broad *natural* context, at different times and from a multitude of perspectives (Babbie 1986; Glaser 1996).

Observation is a useful method in which it is important to determine human behaviour and attitudes (Miles and Huberman 1994; Spradley 1980). Observation can, for example, give important information about (informal) relations between informants, which can be difficult to obtain through interviews. Moreover, observation may also help uncover implicit problems, which cannot easily be discovered through interviews.

Because observation can assume various forms, it can be used for several purposes (Robson 2002). It is commonly used in the exploratory phase of a study, often in an unstructured form, in order to try to establish what is going on in a given situation. Further, observation is often used as a supportive or supplementary method of collecting data that may complement or put in perspective data obtained by other means. According to Adler and Adler (1994), observation is the most likely method to be used in conjunction with other methods. Consequently, it is not unusual for observation to be used in a multi-method case study or in other types of flexible design (Jankowski and Wester 1991).

Types of observation

The literature distinguishes between at least two 'extreme' types of observation: *participant observation* and *structured observation*. They can be found at each end of a continuum in between which there may be other types (Robson 2002; Saunders et al. 2000).[6] The two extremes will be elaborated below.

Participant observation

At one end of the continuum is participant observation, which is qualitative, often unstructured and focused on discovering the meanings that people attach to their actions (Saunders et al. 2000). The word 'participant' refers to the observer's participation (either openly or covertly) in the daily life of the people under study.[7] It has its origins in the work of anthropologists (Bogdewic 1999; Jorgensen 1989; Spradley 1980), and is in particular associated with the Chicago school of sociology (Robson 2002).

According to Saunders et al. (2000), one of the best-known examples of participant observation is that of Whyte (1955), who lived among a poor American-Italian community in order to understand the 'street corner society'. While participant observation is much less used in management and business research, Saunders et al. (2000) mention Roy (1952) as a well-known example of a researcher who worked as an employee in a machine shop for ten months in order to understand how and why his 'fellow workers' operated the piecework bonus system.

Structured observation

At the other end of the continuum we find structured observation, which is quantitative, and, in contrast to participant observation, concerned with the frequency of actions or with quantifying behaviour (Saunders et al. 2000). This type of observation is systematic, and has a high level of predetermined structure, where coding schemes contain predetermined categories for recording what is observed (Robson 2002). It has been used in a variety of disciplines, and is almost exclusively linked to fixed designs, both experimental and non-experimental.

One of the best-known examples of structured observation in managerial research is Mintzberg's study of senior managers (Martinko and Gardner 1985; Saunders et al. 2000). This study led Mintzberg (1970, 1971) to cast doubt on the long-held theory that managerial work was a rational process of planning, controlling and directing. In his study of what five chief executives actually did during one of each of the executives' working weeks, Mintzberg combined unstructured and structured observation. First, he used unstructured observation, where he developed the categories of activity that formed the basis for his coding schedules. Thus Mintzberg 'grounded' his structured observation on data collected by use of participant observation.

Participant observation versus structured observation

The short description of participant and structured observation above highlights one very important difference in the approach to observation: the degree of pre-structure in the observation exercise. This can further be dichotomized as informal and formal observation respectively (Robson 2002).

The informal approach is less structured, and allows the observer considerable freedom in dealing with the information gathered and how it is recorded, since there are no predetermined categories. The more formal approach imposes a high degree of structure and direction on what is to be observed. The observer focuses only on the prespecified aspects; everything else is considered irrelevant with regard to the study. Consequently, while structured observation is characterized by a high degree of reliability and validity, this is achieved at the loss of complexity and completeness in comparison with the more informal approach (Robson 2002).

The less structured approach often used in participant observation does not mean that this type of approach cannot be systematic. However, this is more in terms of the logical inference system applied than the actual degree of prestructure of observational categories.

Judging qualitative research from a critical realist approach

The adoption of the critical realist approach has an impact upon the criteria used to ensure rigorous and meaningful results. Critical realism has traditionally relied on a mix of the criteria that have been developed for positivism and/or constructivism research (Healy and Perry 2000), and even though it has become an important perspective, it has been conspicuous by its absence in evaluation methodology (Healy and Perry 2000; Pawson and Tilley 1997).

Healy and Perry (2000), however, have identified six criteria that can be used explicitly to judge research within this paradigm. They are shown in Table 16.1, where they are linked to the basic beliefs of critical realism. The table also contains the practical implications for qualitative researchers, that is to say some possible techniques that the researcher can use, according to Healy and Perry (2000).

The criteria developed by Healy and Perry are rather 'general' criteria, in the sense that they deal with case study research (Healy and Perry 2000).[8] The criteria are not 'designed' for observation studies, but can still be applied – in a somewhat modified form – within such a study. The criteria will shortly be commented upon below, where they also will be linked to observation studies as regards the possible techniques.

Ontological appropriateness

The first criterion that Healy and Perry (2000) focus on is that of 'ontological appropriateness'. Ontology is, as previously described in Chapter 15, concerned with the character of the phenomena to be investigated. Is it an abstract 'thing' or idea born of people's minds or does it exist independently

Table 16.1   Basic beliefs of critical realism and quality criteria

Level	Basic beliefs	Criteria	Some possible techniques
Ontology	Reality is 'real' – but only imperfectly apprehensible	Ontological appropriateness	Selection of research problem, for example, it is a 'how' and 'why' problem
		Contingent validity	In-depth questions, emphasis on 'why issues', description of the context of the cases
Epistemology	Modified objectivist: findings are probably true	Multiple perceptions of participants and of peer researchers	Multiple interviews, supporting evidence, triangulation. Published reports for peer review
Methodology	Triangulation and interpretation of research issues by both qualitative and quantitative approaches	Methodological trustworthiness (the research can be audited by third person)	Case study database, use in the report of relevant quotations, and descriptions of procedures such as case selection and interview procedures
		Analytic generalization	Identify research issues before data collection, to formulate an interview protocol that will provide data for confirming or disconfirming theory
		Construct validity	Use of prior theory, case study database, triangulation

Source: Adapted from Healy and Perry (2000: 122).

of any one person? The main issue here is that often researchers only tacitly acknowledge their ontological position. This may lead to a discrepancy between the tacit ontology and the tangible methods used, and ultimately for the assessment of quality.

In this chapter 'ontological appropriateness' will not be elaborated further as it is difficult to discuss this criterion without going beyond the focus of this chapter (Healy and Perry 2000 also merely suggest a selection of a 'how' and 'why' research problem).

Contingent validity

'Contingent validity' corresponds to the criterion of internal validity as it is used for example by Yin (1994). Where internal validity is about being sure of the pertinence and internal coherence of the results produced by the study (Drucker-Godard et al. 2001), 'contingent validity' is validity about (generative) mechanisms and the contexts that make them contingent.[9]

As critical realist research deals with open systems, the world is not seen as a laboratory where the conditions for the effective triggering of causal mechanisms can be created (Danermark et al. 2002; Sayer 1992; Tsang and Kwan 1999). Social phenomena are by nature fragile, so causal impacts are not fixed but contingent upon their environment; hence focus on the context is necessary. The use of observation facilitates the study of the natural context, thus providing the researcher with a broader and fuller understanding.

In order to uncover mechanisms, focus should be on the reasons *why* things happen – they should not only be described but explained. In this connection, it is vital to uncover different participants' perceptions (Danermark et al. 2002; Healy and Perry 2000). The suggested technique of in-depth questions put to different participants can cause problems when using observation studies, but it depends on the researcher's observer role, as some roles do 'allow' the researcher to ask questions of the participants under study. The different observer roles as well as the advantages and disadvantages of the roles will be elaborated upon later.

Multiple perceptions of participants and of peer researchers

Positivism assumes that reality is 'out there' to be discovered objectively and is value-free, while constructivism assumes a subjective relationship between the researcher and the respondent, thus being value-laden (Guba and Lincoln 1994; Healy and Perry 2000). Between these two positions critical realism can be found. Healy and Perry (2000) characterize critical realism researchers as being 'value-aware' (see also Danermark et al. 2002). There is a real world to discover – but it is only imperfectly and probabilistically apprehensible (Danermark et al. 2002).

Differently put, a participant's perception is not reality, but rather 'a window to reality' through which a picture of reality can be triangulated with other perceptions (Healy and Perry 2000). According to Healy and Perry (ibid.), these multiple perceptions involve triangulation of several data sources, and of several peer researchers' interpretations of those triangulations. The use of triangulation within observation studies is not problematic. There are many different kinds of triangulation, and they will be elaborated upon later. Here it should just be noted that nothing prevents the researcher from triangulating observation notes with, for example, other archival documents or access to mailing lists. The suggested use of multiple interviews will depend on the researcher's observer role.

Methodological trustworthiness

'Methodological trustworthiness' is central, and refers to the extent to which the research can be audited by a third person, this person very often being another researcher. Possible techniques suggested by Healy and Perry (ibid.) is the development of a case study database and the use of quotations in the written report. When using observation, a database consisting of the researcher's observations can be built. Central in this process is that the researcher registers what is observed. Whether this 'database' contains quotations depends on the researcher's observer role.

Descriptions of the procedures used in the observation study should also be available in the written report, and generally these descriptions should include the necessary details so that a third person is able to follow the different steps throughout the research project. Differently put, the researcher should have the ability and honesty to describe the entire research process employed.

The criterion of 'methodological trustworthiness' is somewhat similar to that of reliability. However, as also explicitly stated by Healy and Perry (ibid.), the criterion of 'methodological trustworthiness' should be considered as broader than the criterion of reliability. Furthermore, evaluating the reliability of research consists in establishing and verifying that the various processes involved will be repeatable, with the same results being obtained by different researchers and/or at different periods. Within critical realism, approaches to replication are viewed as an attempt to confirm the structures and mechanisms identified in the original study under similar contingent conditions. However, since studies are rarely conducted under conditions of closure, replication does not produce conclusive verification of the mechanisms' existence. Similarly, a failure to replicate previous findings does not conclusively falsify the theory (Bhaskar 1979; Robson 2002; Tsang and Kwan 1999).[10]

Analytical generalization

Because critical realism relies on retroduction, the approach to generalization is in the form of analytical generalization (Danermark et al. 2002). The main point made by Healy and Perry (2000) with this criterion is that this form of generalization is different from that of statistical generalization. The use of analytical generalization has to do with the analysis of data and the establishment of the domain to which the study's findings can be generalized, thus corresponding to the well-known criterion of external validity. The criterion will not be elaborated further in this chapter, though it should be noted that the use of observation does not exclude analytical generalization.

Construct validity

The final, and also very central, criterion mentioned by Healy and Perry (ibid.) is similar to the construct validity of positivistic research and refers to how well information about the constructs in the theory being built is measured in the research. Construct validity is not usual in the social sciences, where research often draws on one or several abstract concepts that are not always directly observable (Drucker-Godard et al. 2001). This quality criterion is primarily related to the analysis of data, and will hence not be elaborated further in this chapter.

Quality issues related to the process of observation

This section focuses on how the quality criteria suggested by Healy and Perry (contingent validity, multiple perceptions of participants and methodological trustworthiness) can be incorporated into the process of an observation study. On the basis of the previous section, four issues stand out as being particularly central: (i) awareness of the researcher's observer role, and thus the possibilities and limitations following this role; (ii) descriptions of the procedures used within the observation study; (iii) registration of the researcher's observations; and (iv) the use of triangulation. These four issues will be elaborated upon in the following subsections.

Observer roles

Depending on the problem concerned and the degree of access to the field, the researcher has to decide which role to take as observer. This aspect is vital, as the role of the observer says something about which data are collected (for example if only observation has been used, or if the observations have been supplemented with, for example, unstructured interviews) and the way in which the data are collected (Miles and Huberman 1994). Also, the observer role of the researcher reflects the relations to the informants.

Overt versus covert participant observation   Overall, observation can be divided into two major categories: (i) *covert* and (ii) *overt* (Stafford and Stafford 1993), also sometimes called *complete insider* and *complete outsider* respectively (Jorgensen 1989).

When the researcher becomes an insider, the research is considered covert. The true identity of the researcher remains concealed, and the people being studied believe that the individual is a new member of their group. The major advantage of this approach is that the data will not be 'contaminated' by respondent reaction. However, certain ethical considerations must be taken into account when using this method. As expressed by Stafford and Stafford (1993: 67),

Deception in the use of covert techniques may take two forms: (1) the subjects being studied are not informed of the research; and (2) because they are unaware of the research, subjects are not asked for the traditionally required 'informed consent'. For these reasons, some researchers maintain that covert strategies violate the rights of human subjects, particularly the right to informed consent.

The other major category is overt observation. Here, the researcher openly requests permission to observe a situation, and makes his or her identity, objectives and intentions known. In general, this research is considered ethically acceptable, but also obtrusive, leading to two kinds of problems (Stafford and Stafford 1993): (i) the researcher may be refused access, or (ii) subjects may react to the researcher's presence.

However, between these two extreme roles, the researcher can be an outsider or an insider to a greater or lesser degree. Raymond Gold (1958) has discussed four different positions on a continuum of roles that observers may play in this regard: a complete participant, a participant as observer, an observer as participant or a complete observer.[11] The two points of view mentioned above can be integrated, as shown in Table 16.2.

The complete participant In the role of complete participant, people are only allowed to see the researcher as a participant, never as a researcher (Babbie 1986; Gold 1958; Stafford and Stafford 1993). According to Gold (1958), there can be two potential problems affiliated with this particular role, however: (i) the researcher may become so self-conscious about revealing his/her own identity that it is difficult to perform convincingly in the assumed role, or (ii) the researcher may 'go native'.[12]

However, the researcher thinks that informants will be more natural and honest if they do not know that s/he is doing a research project (Babbie 1986). If people know they are being studied, they might modify their behaviour in a variety of ways: (i) they might expel the researcher, (ii) they might modify their speech and behaviour so as to appear more respectable than would otherwise be the case, or (iii) the social process itself might be radically changed.

To play the role of participant, the researcher *must participate* (ibid.), and this participation may affect the social process under study in important ways. For example, if the researcher is asked what the group should do next, then no matter what s/he says, it will affect the process in some way. Ultimately, *anything* that the participant observer does or does not do will have some effect on what is being observed; it is simply inevitable (ibid.).

Participant as observer In this case, the researcher is able to assume an investigative role while at the same time maintaining membership of the group. The researcher participates fully in all group activities, and informants

Table 16.2   Continuum of observer roles

	Complete insider		Complete outsider	
	Complete participant	Participant as observer	Observer as participant	Complete observer
Role	Interacts with field as naturally as possible, and becomes a member of the group	Participates fully with the group under study, but researcher makes it clear that he is also undertaking research	Identifies himself as a researcher and attempts to interact with the group. Does not participate in group activities and relies mostly on informants	Observing from a distance. Is isolated from phenomena, allowed no direct contact or interplay
Visibility	Covert	Overt	Overt	Overt
Advantage(s)	Informants more honest and natural	Able to assume a stranger's role and ask questions from a position of ignorance. Ability to establish an insider's identity – from a researcher's point of view	Able to assume a stranger's role and ask questions from a position of ignorance	Most closely approximates the traditional ideal of the 'objective' observer
Disadvantage(s)	Risk of going native. The researcher might affect the area of study	Risk of going native. Informants may shift attention to the research project itself rather than carrying on with their natural behaviour. Friendship between researcher and informant(s)	Risk of going native (albeit to a lesser extent than the two former roles). Informants may shift attention to the research project itself rather than carrying on with their natural behaviour. Possibility of misunderstanding the informant	Possibility of ethnocentrism. Lack of richness and detail. Potential for misunderstanding and inaccuracy

are completely aware of being under observation (Stafford and Stafford 1993). The risk here, however, is that they may shift their attention to the research project itself rather than carrying on with their natural behaviour. Thus the processes studied may not be typical (Babbie 1986).

Sometimes the researcher observes formally, as in scheduled interviews, and other times the researcher observes informally – when attending parties, for example (Gold 1958). During the early stages of his/her stay, informants may be somewhat uneasy about the researcher in both formal and informal situations, but their uneasiness is likely to disappear when they learn to trust him/her and s/he them.

As pointed out by Gold (1958), a potential problem here is that, if the researcher and the informant begin to interact in more or less the same way as ordinary friends, they tend to jeopardize their field roles in at least two important ways: (i) the informant may become too identified with the field worker to continue functioning as merely an informant, and (ii) the field worker may over-identify with the informant and start to lose his research perspective by 'going native'.

Observer as participant The researcher identifies him-/herself as a researcher and interacts with the participants in the social process, but makes no pretence of actually being a participant (Babbie 1986). An example could be a newspaper reporter covering a social movement, where he would follow some of the people from the movement and also interview some of them.

According to Gold (1958), the observer-as-participant role is often used in studies involving one-visit interviews. The observer-as-participant role describes researchers primarily observing their subjects for extremely brief periods during structured interviews (Adler and Adler 1994). The observer's identity remains strongly research-oriented and does not cross into the friendship domain.

There is less risk of 'going native' compared with the two former roles. However, because the observer-as-participant's contact with an informant is so brief, and perhaps also superficial, he is more likely to misunderstand the informant, and vice versa – informants misunderstand the researcher.

The complete observer The role as complete observer most closely approx- imates the traditional ideal of the 'objective' observer (Adler and Adler 1994). The complete observer observes a social process without becoming a part of it in any way (Babbie 1986), and, quite possibly, the subjects might not realize they are being studied because of the researcher's unobtrusive- ness. Thus the researcher watches or observes from a distance, and is iso- lated from the phenomena and allowed no direct contact or interplay.

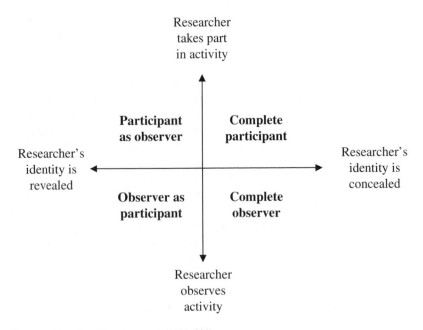

Source: Based on Saunders et al. (2000: 223).

Figure 16.1   The four observer roles

The disadvantage of this approach is the potential lack of richness and detail (Babbie 1986; Hirschman 1986), and because the complete observer remains entirely outside the observed interaction, he runs the greatest risk of misunderstanding the observed (Babbie 1986; Gold 1958). For the same reason, in this role he is least likely to 'go native', though there is a greater possibility of ethnocentrism.[13]

Concluding remarks on the observer role
The researcher is advised to be aware of his own role as a researcher as well as the advantages and disadvantages of this role. The role reflects the relation to the informants (Spradley 1980), and the character of field relations heavily influences the researcher's ability to collect information (Jorgensen 1989). Thus the observer role of the researcher concerns the quality criteria of contingent validity, multiple perceptions of participants as well as methodological trustworthiness.

It should be emphasized, however, that it is not always easy to define one's role in the field. The role of the researcher can either be defined by the researcher him-/herself or ascribed by the informants. Furthermore, it is very likely to be extremely fluid, changing when observing different informants or situations. Box 16.2 describes my observer role in conducting my PhD project.

BOX 16.2   OBSERVER ROLE

My observer role can be described as a mix of participant as observer, and observer as participant:

- The entrepreneurs were informed about the project, and thus knew that I was a researcher. From the start, therefore, complete participation was not possible in my case, since I clearly had the role as a researcher trying to understand what the studied business incubator was all about.
- In some situations, I participated fully in the firms under study, while at other times I only observed.

It was very important for me to get to know the entrepreneurs – and also that they got to know me. This would hopefully facilitate small-talking with the entrepreneurs and my intention was that they should avoid feeling that they were being interviewed every time they talked to me. The role described above made this possible, and the role also made possible that I could ask questions/do informal interviews.

I sometimes felt pressured by the entrepreneurs to become more involved in the business incubator. As they expressed it: 'the best way to get to know people is to participate in the events and help arrange them'. But I saw problems in this – I did not want to get too close to them, because I was afraid to become too involved – to go native. So I tried to keep a distance, and often only participated in the events as observer. Of course, I was not silent all the time, as this would have seemed strange, but I was very careful not to give my opinion, suggestions and advice.

It is hard to say whether or not the entrepreneurs were affected by my presence. However, it seemed to me that they were so busy working, that they did not have time to be affected. Most of the time, they did not even notice me – a tendency that became clearer after a couple of months. In part, this also had to do with the way in which the companies in the business incubator were organized – most of the companies had open landscape offices. This made it possible for me to sit at a desk working at my computer, while at the same time observing all the entrepreneurial companies around me.

My observer role varied with the situation. When they had 'Friday afternoon bar', I took part in the 'social small-talk', whereas when the entrepreneurs had a formal meeting or arrangement, I only observed. My participation in the 'Friday afternoon bar' turned out to be a 'good investment'. Here, I got to know many of the entrepreneurs in a social context, and I was no longer an outsider sitting in a corner taking notes, but a more natural part of their environment. This also resulted in many of the entrepreneurs coming to tell me if something new was happening, for example if new entrepreneurs were moving in or if a company had won a huge contract. More sensitive information also came to my knowledge this way.

Observation procedures used

As also mentioned by Healy and Perry (2000), descriptions of the procedures used should be available in order to ensure methodological trustworthiness. The procedures used within an observation study can vary a great deal, and therefore the following has a more general character.

As mentioned in the introduction, observation is commonly used in the exploratory phase of a study, often in an unstructured form, in order to identify what is going on in a given situation. Consequently, the nature of the researcher's observations inevitably shifts in range and character from the early to the later stages of an observational project (Adler and Adler 1994). Spradley (1980) and Jorgensen (1989) characterize initial observations as primarily 'descriptive' in nature. They are often unfocused and general in scope, and are usually based on broad questions. This reflects the fact that, in the beginning, it can be difficult to know what is important. Aspects that seem to be important at the first meeting with the field can later prove to be irrelevant. Conversely, aspects that initially do not seem important may later turn out to be very central or lead to new problems.

These first descriptive observations provide a base from which the researcher can branch out in a myriad of directions. Once the observer becomes more familiar with the settings, the social groups and the processes in operation, he/she can begin to distinguish the most interesting features. At this point, the researcher is likely to shift to more 'focused' observations. This stage of observation often generates clearer research questions and concepts, which then require selected observations (Adler and Adler 1994). The process can be illustrated as in Figure 16.2.

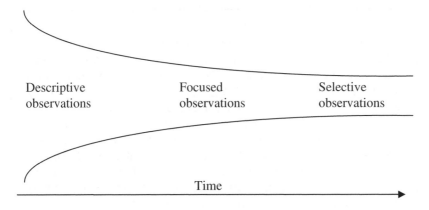

Source: Based on Spradley (1980: 34).

Figure 16.2   Development of the observation process

A description of this development is vital in order to make clear how the research project develops, which choices are made during the research project and why the researcher ends up by focusing on the chosen research questions.

Here it should be noted that, within observation studies, data collection and analysis activities may take place interchangeably in the research process (Robson 2002; Sayer 1992). Often analysis takes place in the middle of data collection and is used to help shape its development. This makes it difficult to discuss the details of the process of observation without including some overall details about the analysis. Box 16.3 describes the process and procedures I used in my PhD project.

BOX 16.3   DEVELOPMENT OF THE OBSERVATION PROCESS AND DESCRIPTIONS OF PROCEDURES USED

In the beginning, I systematically recorded field notes in relation to what I saw, heard, and how I experienced the atmosphere. This was done without thinking specifically of any research questions. I basically made notes of everything – especially the actions/ situations that confused or surprised me.

After having observed the entrepreneurial companies for a couple of weeks, I began – through my initial analysis of my

---

observations – to get an understanding of the business incubator and what was going on between the companies. My data collection and analysis was, without any doubt, part of the same process. When I observed something interesting, I often added my own interpretation of it (written in italics). Previous observations and interpretations had some influence on my focus, as you naturally follow up on the most interesting aspects observed.[14]

For reasons too extensive to elaborate upon here, I made the choice to focus my observations towards companies especially 'visible' and active in a social way, and active with respect to cooperation with other companies. In a way, this choice can be compared to a 'case selection', and naturally it should be argued why the cases are selected as they are. However, a first step towards this explicit argumentation is to be aware of it during the observation process.

A frustrating aspect about observation is that it is not possible to decide in the morning: 'today I will focus more on (subject) x and y' or 'today I will focus more on the mechanisms underlying cooperation'. Because you cannot be certain that any of the owners of the companies will even talk to each other that day. Expressed in other words, I could not 'control' what to observe or look at the next day. From this point of view, observing is very different from scheduled interviews, where you can bring up a specific subject of interest.

Further to assign form and precision to the data, I asked questions about some situations/events. This may seem to go against the notion of direct observation, and be more akin to interviewing. The distinction is indeed blurred. However, as also noted by Robson (2002), in participant observation the researcher is much less likely to have 'set-piece' interviews and much more likely to have opportunistic 'on the wing' discussions or informal interviews with individuals. Thus, the way I asked questions in order to assign form and precision to my data can be described as 'on the wing' discussions and short informal interviews.

Registration of the researcher's observations

Also related to the quality criterion of methodological trustworthiness is the registration of the observations. When doing an observation study, it is possible to construct a database containing information about, for example, when each kind of observation has taken place, the main results from the observations, quotations from 'on the wing' discussions or informal interviews. Ultimately, this registration can help the researcher to provide the necessary information in the written report, making it possible for a third person to audit the research.

In general, there are several ways to record observations, for example video recording, tapes and taking notes. The observer chooses the 'tool' that fits the situation. However, no matter how the researcher chooses to record the observations, s/he should be aware that it is not possible to observe everything. The abilities of the researcher, as well as convenience, opportunity, resources and interests, all influence what to observe. Nor can everything observed be recorded. However, Babbie (1986: 250) provides a few basic rules that may be helpful in the process:

- Do not trust memory any more than necessary – it is untrustworthy. It is a 'must' to take notes during observation, or as soon afterward as possible
- It is a good idea to take notes in 'stages'. First stage is just keywords on what is observed. Second stage is a rewriting of the notes in more detail. Do it as soon as possible after the events observed
- How much to record? In general, in observation studies it is impossible to be sure of what is important and what is unimportant until there has been a chance to review and analyze the great volume of information. So it is a good idea to record as much as possible – even though it does not seem important at the time

Adler and Adler (1994) also suggest that all observation records should contain explicit reference to participants, interactions, routines, rituals, interpretations and so on. Robson (2002) as well as Saunders et al. (2000) find that it is of vital importance to develop some kind of system to distinguish different types of material. They suggest that, in general, the following should be included:

- It is common practice to start with descriptive observation. The basic aim here is to describe the setting, the people and the events that have taken place
- Interpretative ideas and notes offering an analysis of the situation
- Personal impressions, feelings and subjective reactions. This also includes notes on how the researcher's personal values have intervened, or changed, during the research process
- Finally, notes about roles played by key participants and how these may have changed, organizational structures, communication patterns, and so on, are also relevant

According to Babbie (1986), it is of key importance to distinguish between empirical observations and the researcher's interpretations of them. Thus the researcher should separate what is 'known' to have happened and what s/he 'thinks' has happened. My method of recording observations is described in Box 16.4.

BOX 16.4   THE RECORDING OF OBSERVATIONS

I chose not to use video or tapes for the following reasons: tape was not a possibility at all, partly because I was moving around and partly because there would be so much noise on the tape due to the open office landscapes. Moreover, a tape would not catch behaviour. If I used a video camera, they would definitely notice me, and I also think it would bother quite a lot of the entrepreneurs.

Most of the time I was just sitting at a desk, minding my own business, working and taking notes. If I observed something interesting, I changed document on my computer and wrote it down immediately. If I had observed events where it was not possible to complete the notes, I wrote them as soon as I got back to the office, or sometimes in full view of those who I was observing. A restroom is also a good place to write notes.

I was very careful about separating empirical observations and my interpretation of what was going on. However, I found this difficult in the beginning, and even after six months of training I still found it difficult in some situations. My own thoughts and interpretations were written in italics to distinguish them from the descriptive observations.

A more than six-month observation study generates enormous amounts of notes! It is my experience that it is extremely important to be careful with regard to note-taking. Furthermore, the notes must be taken in such a way that they can also be understood one year later.

Triangulation

Triangulation plays a major role when dealing with observation studies from the perspective of critical realism. Empirical observation within critical realism is part of the transitive object of science (that is, our created knowledge of science), as the observation contains an interpretive element (Danermark et al. 2002).[15] Thus, empirical observation can never be the same as an actual reality, which is independent of the cognitive subject/individual (Danermark et al. 2002). However, it is possible to get closer to the actual reality by triangulating different perceptions (Healy and Perry 2000).

'Stripped to its basics, triangulation is supposed to support a finding by showing that independent measures of it agree with it or, at least, do not contradict it' (Miles and Huberman 1994). Triangulation is not a tool or a strategy of validation, but an alternative to validation (Denzin and Lincoln 1994). The combination of, for example, multiple methods and observers in a single study is best understood, then, as a strategy that in general adds rigour, breadth and depth to any investigation.

There are many different kinds of triangulation and the list below should therefore not be seen as exhaustive. For a variety of types, see for example Adler and Adler (1994); Denzin (1978); Hammersley and Atkinson (1997); Jorgensen (1989); Miles and Huberman (1994); Stafford and Stafford (1993) and Sykes (1990). In the following, the point of departure is taken from Denzin (1978):

- **Data triangulation**
  Data triangulation has three subtypes: (i) time, (ii) space, and (iii) person
- **Investigator triangulation (observer A, B and C)**
  This form of triangulation is aimed at reducing researcher bias by using more than one observer of the same object (Adler and Adler 1994; Hammersley and Atkinson 1997). However, this is often not possible for different reasons, and therefore alternatives to investigator triangulation may be used:
  (i) Focus on conclusions drawn: did s/he really mean that? What other interpretations could have been put on this?
  (ii) Informant verification is another option. Write up the conclusions, and let the informants verify the content
- **Theory triangulation**
  This kind of triangulation refers to the use of a variety of theoretical perspectives within a study. Multiple theoretical perspectives are a tool which provides alternative interpretations of the same data (see also Miles and Huberman 1994)
- **Methodological triangulation**
  Methodological triangulation can entail within-method triangulation and between-method triangulation
  - **Within-method triangulation (e.g. observation, interviews)**
    Data produced by different data collection techniques are compared. It may thus be possible to assess the validity by examining other data relating to the same study, for example data from observation, interviews, access to mailing list or other archival documents (see also Hammersley and Atkinson 1997)
  - **Between-method triangulation (qualitative, quantitative)**
    In the critical realism approach, different kinds of data can be used. Often, this kind of triangulation refers to the process of comparing the results and conclusions of a current research study

with those of a similar, previous study (see also Miles and Huberman 1994)

Doing an observation study does not exclude the researcher from using triangulation. The form of triangulation used, however, depends on the specific design of the study. Here it should be noted, though, that Adler and Adler (1994) specifically advise that the observations be conducted systematically and repeatedly under varying conditions. If observations carried out in this way show the same findings, they are more credible than those gathered in a more *ad hoc* way. Thus the two keywords here are *time* and *place* – in order to ensure the widest range of observational consistency. My use of triangulation in my PhD project is described in Box 16.5.

BOX 16.5   THE USE OF TRIANGULATION

The entrepreneurs were observed closely over a period of more than six months, one or two days a week. I observed different places within the business incubator, thus observing different entrepreneurs, on different days of the week and at different times of the day.

The entrepreneurial companies I observed belonged to different industries, the companies differed in size, and some of them had been in the business incubator for a long period of time, others for only a couple of months. Some of the firms were 'born' in the incubator, while others were 'born' outside. Thus, I tried to observe a broad range of entrepreneurs, and to observe systematically and repeatedly, but under varying conditions.

In the beginning, I relied on observation only. However, because of my observer role, I small-talked quite a lot with the entrepreneurs and had many 'on the wing' discussions. As I acquired a better understanding of the phenomenon and what was going on, I also carried out some informal interviews (within-method triangulation).

For practical reasons, it was not possible to involve other observers. Thus, I had to rely solely on my own observations. I tried to be extremely careful by asking myself questions about my conclusions. I also focused on getting my conclusions 'verified' during small-talk with the entrepreneurs and during the informal interviews.

The business incubator had a webpage, which I also studied. In addition, I was given access to the internal website, which only contained information concerning the entrepreneurs. I also studied any printed material or folders I could find.

Since I was also on their mailing list, it meant that (a) I was not dependent solely on observation and my physical presence to know what was going on, and (b) I could collect more 'physical evidence' on some of the 'networking activities' between the firms.

Concluding remarks

The use of observation within entrepreneurship research can add depth of understanding regarding the questions *how* and *why*. Observing entrepreneurs provides a different angle to these questions, and, furthermore, it can be of great value to actually observe what the entrepreneurs *do* instead of *asking* them (via interviews) what they do.

Moreover, a total lack of predetermined categories means that the observer is free to change any problems and questions which crop up during the study. This flexibility makes it possible to discover aspects that might otherwise be overlooked. Thus, compared with more structured methods, observation has the flexibility to yield insight into new realities or new ways of looking at old realities (Adler and Adler 1994; Jorgensen 1989; Miles and Huberman 1994; Spradley 1980).

As also argued by Adler and Adler (1994), from a journal editor's point of view, the value of observation studies lies in their capacity to provide insights through rich detail (Adler and Adler 1994). Looking at observation from the more 'dark side', some of the chief criticisms levelled against observational research are that the technique can suffer from subjectivity (the observer is forced to rely more on their own perceptions), and excessive reliance on observer articulation (there is always the possibility that the findings are the result of chance) (Adler and Adler 1994; Hammersley and Atkinson 1997).

There are several ways to deal with these criticisms levelled against observational research. But what is important is that the observer is aware of these aspects before undertaking the observation study and during the observation study.

Even though this chapter does not include the analysis of data, a few remarks related to Healy and Perry's (2000) quality criteria of 'analytic generalization' should be made. The approach to generalization in the form of analytic generalization stems from the reliance on retroduction. Retroduction is an un-formalized mode of inference, where there are no formalized descriptions of the various procedures, ways of reasoning and arguing (Danermark et al. 2002). This means that the working processes can be very varied within different studies. On the positive side, this makes room for creativity in the working process. But it also makes it difficult to evaluate the working process. The main point made here is that 'analytic generalization', suggested by Healy and Perry (2000) as quality criteria, is not adequate in itself. The use of analytic generalization does not say anything about which strategies are used in order to arrive at the conclusions. Critical realism's reliance on retroduction necessitates that the researcher is being very explicit in regard to what is done during the whole working process – this also includes the process of analysis. Differently put, the 'road' to the conclusions must be made clear.

The evaluation criteria identified by Healy and Perry capture many important and relevant aspects. By making references from their suggested evaluation criteria to other well-known evaluation criteria, Healy and Perry are creating a link to a well-known frame that most researchers can relate to. However, by focusing on established criteria used to evaluate research within other paradigms, the overall frame is somehow already set. A potential drawback with this 'strategy' is that the reseach is not evaluated on its own paradigmatic terms. Evaluation of a research study should not be reduced to only a 'checklist', where reflection and critical thinking are put aside by the researcher.

Notes

1. *Entrepreneurship Theory and Practice*; *Journal of Business Venturing*; *Strategic Management Journal*; *Academy of Management Journal*; *Academy of Management Review*; *Organizational Science*; *Management Science*; *Journal of Management and Administrative Science*.
2. The 'top score' was surveys with 66 per cent, whereas only 25 per cent used interview methodologies, 3 per cent used phone interviews, 4 per cent used experiments, and 3 per cent combined survey and interview methodologies (Chandler and Lyon 2001). Regarding the type of observation used, Chandler and Lyon (2001) mention it as participant observation. However, no further specific details are provided.
3. The examined journals were *Entrepreneurship and Regional Development*; *Entrepreneurship Theory and Practice*; *International Small Business Journal*; *Journal of Business Venturing* and *Journal of Small Business Management*.
4. The 'top score' was surveys with about 64 per cent. About 16 per cent used case studies, about 12 per cent used interviews, and the rest were divided between other qualitative methods, document analysis, other quantitative methods, focus groups and diary studies (McDonald et al. 2004). As in the study by Chandler and Lyon (2001), no details are provided as regards the type of observation applied.
5. 'Business incubator' is an umbrella term for any organization that provides access to affordable office space and shared administrative services (Allen and McCluskey 1990; Fry 1987).
6. Robson argues that the focus on these two approaches has tended to eclipse a third type, which can be called unobtrusive observation (Robson 2002). In the literature, this is also referred to as naturalistic observation. As also argued by Adler (Adler and Adler 1994), it has remained a stepchild to its more widely recognized offshoot: participant observation. Its defining characteristic is that it is non-participatory in the interests of being non-reactive. It can be structured, but is more often unstructured and informal (Robson 2002).
7. A definition of participant observation is offered by Becker and Geer: 'by participation observation we mean that method in which the observer participates in the daily life of the people under study, either openly in the role of researcher or covertly in some disguised

role, observing things that happen, listening to what is said, and questioning people, over some length of time' (Becker and Geer 1957, cited in Jankowski and Wester 1991: 61).

8. The term 'case research' is generally used very loosely (Easton 2001; Stake 1994). If research is described as a case study, this does not imply the use of a standard research method (Saunders et al. 2000; Yin 1994), and it does not call for a particular approach to the analysis of the data which it produces (Robson 2002).

9. As with internal validity, there is no particular method of ensuring the 'favourable' level of contingent validity of a research project.

10. As expressed by Tsang and Kwan (1999: 769), 'One explanation of this failure is that the structures and mechanisms as postulated in the theory are inaccurate: in this case we have had a true falsification. However, another possible explanation is that, in the replicated study, there is a different set of contingencies that either modifies the postulated mechanisms or invokes previously inactive countervailing mechanisms. This results in a different set of events being observed.' However, even though replication does not result in conclusive verification or falsification of theories, replicated studies do help to support or discredit theories (Tsang and Kwan 1999).

11. According to Adler, new conceptions of qualitative research have evolved since then, and it is argued that three membership roles appear to dominate: (i) the complete member researcher, (ii) the active member researcher, and (iii) the peripheral member researcher (Adler and Adler 1994). However, Gold's four roles are found to be more appropriate in this context.

12. To 'go native' basically means that the researcher stops wondering about what is observed, and accepts the informant's views as the researcher's own.

13. Ethnocentrism occurs whenever a field worker cannot or will not interact meaningfully with an informant. He then seemingly or actually rejects the informant's views without ever getting to the point of understanding them.

14. In practical terms I developed a coding system for my observation notes, and started by developing rough categories. This coding system was quite simple in the beginning, but as the months passed by and my understanding of the phenomenon under study grew, the coding system became more nuanced. More general patterns were split up into sub-patterns, and along the way, I also changed some of my initial categories. It was a very iterative process, where the observations analysed helped to focus the next observations.

15. The meaning of two observations of one and the same phenomenon can therefore differ, depending on the pre-understanding and conceptual starting point (Danermark et al. 2002).

Recommended further readings

Adler, P.A. and Adler, P. (1994) Observational techniques. In N.K. Denzin and Y.S. Lincoln (eds), *Handbook of Qualitative Research*. Thousand Oaks, London, New Delhi: Sage Publications, pp. 377–92. This chapter provides a good introduction to observation. It examines some of the essential features of observation, and discusses methodological issues, strengths, and weaknesses in its practice. The authors also consider several theoretical traditions underlying observation.

Healy, M. and Perry, C. (2000) Comprehensive criteria to judge validity and reliability of qualitative research within the realism paradigm. *Qualitative Market Research: An International Journal*, 3(3): 118–26. The article by Healy and Perry aims to address a gap in the literature on quality criteria in qualitative research within the realism paradigm. Building on a comparison with criteria in other paradigms, particularly positivism and constructivism, they develop six criteria for judging realism research, drawing on the three elements of a paradigm: ontology, epistemology and methodology.

References

Adler, P.A. and Adler, P. (1994) Observational techniques. In N.K. Denzin and Y.S. Lincoln (eds), *Handbook of Qualitative Research*. Thousand Oaks, London, New Delhi: Sage Publications, pp. 377–92.

Allen, D.N. and McCluskey, R. (1990) Structure, policy, services and performance in the business incubator industry. *Entrepreneurship: Theory and Practice*, **15**(2): 61–77.

Babbie, E. (1986) *The Practice of Social Research*, 4th edn. Belmont, CA: Wadsworth Publishing Co.

Becker, H.S. and Geer, B. (1957) Participant observation and interviewing: a comparison. *Human Organization*, **16**(3): 28–32.

Bhaskar, R. (1975) *A Realist Theory of Science.* Leeds: Leeds Books.

Bhaskar, R. (1979) *The Possibility of Naturalism.* Brighton: Harvester.

Bogdewic, S.P. (1999) Participant observation. In B.F. Crabtree and W.L. Miller (eds), *Doing Qualitative Research*, 2nd edn. Thousand Oaks, London, New Delhi: Sage Publications, pp. 47–69.

Bouckenooghe, D., Bulelens, M., De Clercq, D. and Willem, A. (2004) *A Review of Research Methodology in Entrepreneurship: Current Practices and Trends (1999–2003).* Paper presented at the RENT XVIII, Copenhagen, Denmark.

Chandler, G.N. and Lyon, D.W. (2001) Issues of research design and construct measurement in entrepreneurship research: The past decade. *Entrepreneurship Theory and Practice*, **25**(4): 101–14.

Crano, W.D. and Brewer, M.B. (1973) *Principles of Research in Social Psychology.* New York: McGraw-Hill.

Danermark, B., Ekström, M., Jakobsen, L. and Karlsson, J.C. (2002) *Explaining Society. Critical realism in the social sciences.* London and New York: Routledge.

Denzin, N.K. (1978) *The Research Act in Sociology*, 2nd edn. New York: McGraw-Hill.

Denzin, N.K. and Lincoln, Y.S. (1994) *Handbook of Qualitative Research.* Thousand Oaks, CA: Sage Publications.

Drucker-Godard, C., Ehlinger, S. and Grenier, C. (2001) Validity and reliability. In R.A. Thiétart et al. (ed.), *Doing Management Research.* London, Thousand Oaks, New Delhi: Sage Publications, pp. 198–219.

Easton, G. (2001) Case research as a method for industrial networks. A realist apologia. In S. Ackroyd and S. Fleetwood (eds), *Realist Perspectives on Management and Organization.* London: Routledge, pp. 205–19.

Fry, F.L. (1987) The role of incubators in small business planning. *American Journal of Small Business*, **12**(1): 51–62.

Glaser, J.M. (1996) The challenge of campaign watching: Seven lessons of participant-observation research. *Political Science and Politics*, **29**(3): 533–7.

Gold, R.L. (1958) Roles in sociological field observations. *Social Forces*, **36**(3): 217–23.

Guba, E.G. (1990) *The Paradigm Dialog.* Newbury Park, London, New Delhi: Sage Publications.

Guba, E.G. and Lincoln, Y.S. (1994) Competing paradigms in qualitative research. In N.K. Denzin and Y.S. Lincoln (eds), *Handbook of Qualitative Research.* Thousand Oaks, London, New Delhi: Sage Publications, pp. 105–17.

Hammersley, M. and Atkinson, P. (1997) *Ethnography, Principles in Practice.* London: Routledge.

Healy, M. and Perry, C. (2000) Comprehensive criteria to judge validity and reliability of qualitative research within the realism paradigm. *Qualitative Market Research: An International Journal*, **3**(3): 118–26.

Hirschman, E.C. (1986) Humanistic inquiry in marketing research: Philosophy, method, and criteria. *Journal of Marketing Research*, **XXIII**(August): 237–49.

Jankowski, N.W. and Wester, F. (1991) The qualitative tradition in social science inquiry: contributions to mass communication research. In K.B. Jensen and N.W. Jankowski (eds), *A Handbook of Qualitative Methodologies for Mass Communication Research.* London, New York: Routledge, pp. 44–74.

Jorgensen, D.L. (1989) *Participant Observation. A Methodology for Human Studies* (Vol. 15). Newbury Park, London, New Delhi: Sage Publications.

Martinko, M.J. and Gardner, W.L. (1985) Beyond structured observation: Methodological issues and new directions. *Academy of Management Review*, **10**(4): 676–95.

McDonald, S., Gan, B.C. and Anderson, A. (2004) *Studying Entrepreneurship: A review of methods employed in entrepreneurship research 1985–2004.* Paper presented at the RENT XVIII, Copenhagen, Denmark.

Miles, M.B. (1979) Qualitative data as an attractive nuisance: The problem of analysis. *Administrative Science Quarterly*, **24**(4): 590–601.

Miles, M.B. and Huberman, M.A. (1994) *Qualitative Data Analysis*, 2nd edn. Thousand Oaks, London, New Delhi: Sage Publications.

Mintzberg, H. (1970) Structured observation as a method to study managerial work. *The Journal of Management Studies*, **7**(February): 87–104.

Mintzberg, H. (1971) Managerial work: Analysis from observation. *Management Science*, **18**(2): B97–B110.

Pawson, R. and Tilley, N. (1997) *Realistic Evaluation.* London, Thousand Oaks, New Delhi: Sage Publications.

Robson, C. (2002) *Real World Research. A resource for social scientists and practitioner-researchers*, 2nd edn. Malden, MA: Blackwell Publishing.

Roy, D. (1952) Quota restriction and goldbricking in a machine shop. *American Journal of Sociology*, **57**: 427–42.

Saunders, M.N.K., Lewis, P. and Thornhill, A. (2000) *Research Methods for Business Students*, 2nd edn. Harlow, UK: Prentice-Hall.

Sayer, A. (1992) *Method in Social Science. A realist approach*, 2nd edn. London and New York: Routledge.

Smith, J.K. (1990) Goodness criteria. Alternative research paradigms and the problem of criteria. In E.G. Guba (ed.), *The Paradigm Dialog.* Newbury Park, London, New Delhi: Sage Publications, pp. 167–87.

Spradley, J.P. (1980) *Participant Observation.* Fort Worth, TX: Harcourt Brace College Publishers.

Stafford, M.R. and Stafford, T.F. (1993) Participant observation and the pursuit of truth: Methodological and ethical considerations. *Journal of the Market Research Society*, **35**(1): 63–76.

Stake, R.E. (1994) Case studies. In N.K. Denzin and Y.S. Lincoln (eds), *Handbook of Qualitative Research.* Thousand Oaks, London, New Delhi: Sage Publications, pp. 236–47.

Sykes, W. (1990) Validity and reliability in qualitative market research: a review of the literature. *Journal of the Market Research Society*, **32**(3): 289–328.

Tsang, E.W. and Kwan, K.-M. (1999) Replication and theory development in organizatinal science: A critical realist perspective. *Academy of Management Review*, **24**(4): 759–80.

Whyte, W. (1955) *Street Corner Society*, 2nd edn. Chicago, IL: University of Chicago Press.

Yin, R.K. (1994) *Case Study Research, Design and Methods*, 2nd edn, Vol. 5. Thousand Oaks, London, New Delhi: Sage Publications.

17 Daring to be different: a dialogue on the problems of getting qualitative research published
Robert Smith and Alistair R. Anderson

Introduction

I consider this brief section necessary because it introduces the problem to be discussed, namely how to market qualitative research that is visibly and qualitatively different from the 'conventions' of logico-deductive empiricalism. As such, it lies at the heart of the spirit of this handbook – namely, researching at the frontiers of entrepreneurship using qualitative methodologies. The aim is to clarify the focus of the chapter, that is, to articulate the problems faced by me, as a junior researcher, in achieving publication in academic outlets of work steeped in the qualitative methodologies of social constructivism and semiotics[1].

In keeping with the title of this chapter, it should be stressed that its style and format are different from what one would normally expect to encounter. This is no scholarly mimesis, relying on the familiar crutches of literary review, followed by the setting of research questions, methodology, analysis and conclusions. It is not the aim of the chapter to be different, nor to justify its difference. Notwithstanding this, writing outside the box is even scarier than thinking outside the box, because thoughts and spoken words can be ephemeral, but the written word is not. This is perhaps apt, as achieving publication is a continuing creative process of ontogenesis.

We hope other doctoral students and experienced scholars find this chapter useful because it poses a number of challenges to mainstream research practices and protocols. It should also be helpful because it documents and examines the learning processes that I underwent during my doctoral programme. Hence the chapter should be read in the spirit of inquiry in which it was written. What is most striking is that both anonymous reviewers, my supervisor (and mentor) Professor Alistair R. Anderson and both editors patently entered into this spirit, while acknowledging that they had refrained from applying their normal reviewing methods in critiquing earlier drafts. This enabled a genuine dialogue to develop. For this I thank them. In addition, on reading the first draft one of the editors commented that Alistair and I had articulated many valid points which they had thought but had never dared to write.

In this chapter, I present my voice as 'the voice of inquiry' seeking answers to several questions. The opening question is: 'Why do we see so little semiotic research in entrepreneurship journals?' This is important because perhaps the answer lies in that semiotics shares and indeed exemplifies some of the problems of a qualitative approach. I am interested in values, morality and other socio-subjective elements of the entrepreneurial process that are difficult to research empirically. This dialogic commentary seeks answers to the question why, if qualitative methodologies are extensively used in the social sciences such as anthropology and sociology, are they not used more frequently in the field of entrepreneurship research? Notwithstanding this uptake elsewhere, qualitative research currently exists on the margins of entrepreneurship research. This led Rae (2001) to criticize entrepreneurship researchers for failing to make fuller use of qualitative methodologies in researching at the frontiers of entrepreneurship. Why is this so? As will be demonstrated, there are sound academic reasons. The second question to be answered is two-fold, namely, 'Is it worth trying to publish such research, and what are the benefits?'

In the next section my supervisor and mentor introduces the problems as he perceives them, namely (1) that qualitative methods are held in some suspicion in certain academic circles; and that (2) the problematic nature of entrepreneurship and ways of explaining it. In the following two sections, in response to Alistair, I justify the use of a more impressionistic approach and explain why I chose to write this chapter as an impressionistic tale of the field in the manner of Van Maanen (1988). Thereafter I provide a critique of the academic cultures of modesty and perfection. This is followed by sections on being qualitatively different, discussing the craft of learning to write qualitatively; and on daring to write differently, which explains why qualitative writing is different from other forms of academic writing. Thereafter, I continue the discussion on the generic problems of getting published *per se*. Later sections concentrate on strategies for making the most of one's differences; and a 'how to' section setting out further traditional and alternative strategies for getting published. The penultimate section deals with developing the vital skill of learning to be self-critical. The final section sets out the argument for the necessity of compiling a research/publication strategy. The chapter ends with some concluding thoughts by Alistair R. Anderson.

Introducing the problem (as narrated by Alistair R. Anderson)
I find that there is a dual problem. First, qualitative work is held in some suspicion by certain circles. It lacks the apparent scientific basis of positivism. It moves outside the well-established realm of hypotheses testing. Because positivism has provided all the advances in hard science since the

Enlightenment, qualitative approaches may be seen as drifting back to the metaphysics of supposition. Journal editors want to be confident that what they publish will withstand academic scrutiny, so there may be an understandable reluctance to risk publishing anything that might be construed as too subjective, too interpretative and hence lacking in verifiable objectivity. Of course, those of us who recognize that human beings are subjective creatures also know that humanity does not respond according to any universal laws. As qualitative researchers, we see our task as trying to understand what is going on, and to provide some explanation of what and why this happens. Consequently we need to have editors and reviewers who share our epistemological and ontological view of the world and the processes that happen within it. But we also need to be constantly aware of the issue and address critical issues.

Consider, for example, how many qualitative papers purport to use grounded theory. Yet few actually do because, in practice, it is difficult to operationalize usefully. However, it is a quasi-scientific methodology and appears to objectify the analysis of the research process. What is worse is that many researchers believe that grounded theory is based on the social constructivist paradigm whereas it is in reality based on the critical realist paradigm! Compare grounded theory with ethnographic work and narrative, where we are convinced by the seeming accuracy of naturalism; where we recognize the processes described; in this way we come to *believe* the story. Consequentially, we are open to be persuaded by the analysis, but this analysis may well be developed from flights of imagination and intuition (as can the entrepreneurial act). Again compare this with the statistical analysis of positivism. Rarely is this questioned, but do we ever know who really completes the questionnaires? Do we really know how accurate these ticks are? Yet these data 'facts' appear so much more rigorous than the 'feelings' we try to describe in social constructionism.

The second problem lies in the nature of entrepreneurship and ways of explaining it. These aspects cross-cut each other and, I think, lie at the root of our work. Entrepreneurship is a practice; it is *doing*. Only academics, and perhaps politicians, try to shift it from an action form into any sort of objectification. So when we talk about entrepreneurship we attempt to freeze it, capture aspects of it by looking only at one side of an unfolding process. This may be the wrong way to go about it, but what else can we do? However, entrepreneurship is creative. It is about creating futures, from a whole range of possible futures. It needs imagination to form ideas and even more imagination to turn these into new realities. Thus entrepreneurship is an economic art form. In turning to how to tell (and attempt to understand) entrepreneurship, perhaps we might try to emulate the conventions of the art world. Painters try to capture reality in two dimensions on canvas; we try to capture social constructions of entrepreneurship in the single dimension of the written word. Just as a good picture should invoke emotions about its content, surely our efforts in print should also excite the imagination. The words should reach out to tell the story and incite the imagination to soar to complete the picture. If we are right, and not on a flight of fancy ourselves, what we should be doing in our written down work is to engage the reader. We should do this by capturing attention, by telling the story. But that is only the beginning – we need to engage attention and imagination, forcing the reader to think about our words. I don't think it matters too much whether they agree or disagree with our analysis. Even if they disagree, they have engaged and developed their own ideas to refute ours. The pool of our collective understanding is richer for this. It is to the matter of engaging that Robert now turns.

Justifying a different more impressionistic approach (RS)
The narrative tone of this chapter is intentionally anecdotal, conversational and mentorial. This is very relevant, bearing in mind the advice of Wolcott (1990: 69), who succinctly noted that we tend to remember 'material presented through anecdotes and personal asides'. This chapter is also written in a dialogical format, which deviates from traditional academic style. There are precedents for this – see for example, Atherton and Elsmore (2004) and Hosking and Hjorth (2004). This chapter did not begin its existence with the intention of being different, but genuinely evolved as a dialogue between the different viewpoints between Alistair and me. However, I took refuge in the assertion of Gartner (2001) that entrepreneurship, as a phenomenon, is inherently about 'being different'. We are also grateful to one of the anonymous reviewers who suggested that we concentrate on the dialogic aspect of the chapter, even at the risk of making it deviate even further from the norm. However, it is necessary at this stage to explain why it is an impressionistic tale of the field.

An impressionist's tale of the field
I consider this chapter to be an impressionist tale of the field because it describes the ontological process and the development of a qualitative research style that 'dared to be different' and as such required to adopt a writing style consistent with the difference of the material. As academics, in a research community we are all to a greater or lesser degree in the same field – the field of publication. It is apt that John Van Maanen (1988) named one of his categories of tales from the field 'impressionistic tales' in recognition of the creative and poetic dimensions of ethnographic writing. Van Maanen drew his inspiration from art historians, which is fitting because the practice of entrepreneurship can be viewed as an art form; for example,

Anderson and Jack (1997) argue so. According to Van Maanen (1988: 102), such tales present 'the doing of the fieldwork, rather than the doer or the done'. It is the doing of the research that most of us find stimulating. All too often the writing up is a chore. There is no getting away from the fact that qualitative research is definitely characterized by 'doing', as appreciated by Silverman (2000). Writing in his characteristic and hypnotic style, Van Maanen stresses that impressionist writings try to keep both subject and object in constant view with the epistemological aim of 'braiding' the 'knower' to the 'known'. The notion of narrator and story becoming as one is appealing but difficult to achieve outside the framework of face-to-face communication. This does not excuse one from trying to fuse daring, or different research, with scholarly writing. It is a dilemma which must be faced.

Furthermore, Van Maanen (1988: 101–3) artfully describes impressionistic tales as startling, striking stories in which words, metaphors, phrases and imagery are crafted to reconstruct past events into a vibrant, dramatic form in which the author reflectively participates in the rendition of a rolling narrative. For Van Maanen such stories draw an audience into an unfamiliar story world and allow them to practically see, hear and feel the action. Another refreshingly marvellous and appealing factor of such tales is that they do not masquerade as anything but stories (Van Maanen 1988: 108). Exaggeration, embellishment and creativity are thus permitted to avoid tedium as long as they drive the story forward. Indeed, Van Maanen (ibid.: 117) argues that well-told tales must be elaborated and embellished. According to him (ibid.: 110), such tales work better when orated and can appear stilted in print. Also, they permit us to say things that we would otherwise not have been permitted to broach in conventional academic writing. Instead, they are judged in story terms on interest/attraction, on coherence, and on fidelity/truth value. Impressionist tales are often informal or irreverent, and very pragmatic because one is permitted to skip in and out of the impressionist style into academic and reflective modes of address. It is clearly a useful tool in the qualitative researcher's epistemological tool kit, but would you dare try this out – or any other unusual qualitative methodology, for that matter? Perhaps not, unless, like me, you have an understanding supervisor and liberally minded sympathetic editors. This is a pity because, in many respects, a certain genre of entrepreneurial narrative and qualitative research methodology is best told as impressionistic tales. When narrated, or orated, properly with passion they are powerful, inspirational stories, which certainly leave an impression upon the audience. What follows is an attempt to write differently by me, a young[2] researcher in the field of entrepreneurship engaged on a grail-like quest to achieve the heady elixir of publication and of course to make a modest contribution to existing knowledge in the field. Moreover, in attempting to conduct research that is different and to articulate oneself differently, I found that I had to overcome the academic cultures of modesty and perfectionism. In reading the following critique I would like readers to consider whether I am justified in thinking along these lines.

A critique of the academic culture of modesty and perfection

Initially, when learning the craft of academic writing, I came to the conclusion that there appears to exist in the academic research community an endemic culture of modesty and a desire for perfection. In my impatience to become published, I found this both galling and frustrating, particularly since management textbooks contain the sagacious advice that perfectionism is anti-entrepreneurial. However, as I later came to realize, there are valid structural and career-oriented reasons why this is so. Whereas 'daring to be different' may be a valued entrepreneurial trait, it is perhaps not a trait appreciated by some journal editors or reviewers. Indeed, academic careers and reputations are built upon the basis of achieving repeated publication in respected journals, in other words, by adhering to conformity and accepted disciplinary peer conventions. This dictates that academic papers conform to a general length, format and layout. As such they are a peculiar 'social construction', which may conspire to limit the creativity of authors, as it seriously restricts the amount of research variables and type of material that we can include in our research agenda. Yet the best academic arguments are often those that are complex but couched in simplicity. Alistair's supervisor, the late Mike Scott, put this very sensibly when reproaching him for some verbosity: 'Any fool can make the simple complex, but it takes a clever man or woman to render the complex simpler.'

In addition, time constraints associated with other personal and academic activities and the part-time nature of my studies limited the amount of time available to me for actual research. Also, the need to research tidy, achievable projects as well as meet conference deadlines and preferred styles limited my creativity as a researcher. Combine this with the humanistic instinct to conform and of not to appear different in any way, and one can begin to understand the scale of the problem. I found that all these factors initially conspired against me to produce innovative research with an entrepreneurial bent. I railed against papers that in my opinion were technically efficient, yet uninspiring albeit that they echoed the prevailing mood of the field. Thus I perhaps consciously (or subconsciously) set out to write differently. I wanted to publish in top-flight journals but was put off by what I considered to be the lengthy 'gestation' period from first draft to publication. I know from personal experience this can be well in excess of 12 months. It is hardly surprising that the attrition rate is considerable.

The academic axiom of 'publish or perish' springs to mind! Yet qualitative research by its very nature often exceeds the constraints of academic journals.

The problem is exacerbated when one's research interests are clearly delineated as being 'qualitative' and no other alternative 'quantitative' methodologies are suitable, as was the case with me. Should I be apologetic, or should I embrace the opportunity as a challenge (in true entrepreneurial style)? For me, the former course of action was never an option, but the latter was. Unfortunately, as is the theme of this book, qualitative research in entrepreneurship is often rejected by mainstream journals for a variety of reasons. This problem is compounded if one is interested in subjective criteria such as values, morality and legitimacy that lie at the centre of entrepreneurial action, as I am. As academics we are trained to cleanse our work of all notions of subjectivity. Adopting a 'moralist stance' can be viewed as being suspect. It is often easier to metaphorically 'sit on the fence' because although we are happy exhorting students to 'think outside the box', we are less able to do so ourselves when it involves writing up outside the box. After all, it can be dangerous to one's career, particularly to a young researcher beginning a career in academia. It is a dilemma that is often not fully confronted head on. I unknowingly accepted the challenge upon entering into a verbal agreement to submit a chapter to this compilation. At the time of taking up the challenge, I now acknowledge that I was impatient to become published and was literally brimming over with exciting ideas which I found difficult to articulate (and still do).

Another problem that I, like many academics, have to overcome when discussing my research with others is to avoid the pitfalls of being considered too self-referential. It does not come easily to cite one's own work (echoes of Narcissus). Nevertheless, disseminating one's work often requires one to blatantly blow one's own trumpet, although decency and self-deprecation prevent one from ever being comfortable with doing so. Also, there is an innate fear of writing 'how-to articles' such as this one because of the fear of setting oneself up for a fall. This fear of *hubris* is not confined to the entrepreneur. Consequentially, during the doctoral process and the writing up of this chapter (June 2003 to September 2004) I have come to appreciate the virtues of modesty and perfectionism. There are advantages and disadvantages of daring to be different and Table 17.1 sets out the pros and cons. The most important aspect of the learning process is that I had fun on the way.

On being qualitatively different!
While learning to write qualitatively, I came to the conclusion that practising qualitative methodologies mirrors the entrepreneurial process, as they

Table 17.1   Advantages and disadvantages of daring to be different

Advantages

- It allows you freedom to create, to be playful, and to be expressive. I liken it to an artist learning a craft. You try various combinations of qualitative methodologies and then sit back and judge if it has worked. Often it does not. You must learn to experiment, because qualitative methodologies (unlike quantitative) are not linear equations to be followed rigorously. They do not guarantee you a result.
- It imbues your work with a sense of fun. The entrepreneurial process is embedded in the spirit of fun and should be researched in the same vein.
- Research becomes more interesting because you become attached to it – often over-attached. It allows you to form an illusion that you are in control of your academic destiny because you are freed of the obligations to conform. But with this privilege comes the pitfalls and perils discussed below.

Disadvantages

- You place yourself in the invidious position of the artist whereby you become your own self-critic, which can be counterproductive and countercreative. You do not want to let go of your work. Yet work that is not 'put to work' is not work; it is a private indulgence. Whether you like it or not, as an artist you must test the market and there is no alternative but to target journals. The patronage of an intellectual readership requires to be cultivated.
- The line between imaginative, creative work and idiosyncratic dogma is a very thin one indeed. But I feel that madness and sanity are negotiable subjective human frameworks. You take a risk when you act or write differently.
- There is a danger that, in being different, you become insular. Even different work requires to be marketed to establish a dialogue with others.
- It requires you to be self-confident because 'going against the grain' runs contrary to human nature. Yet I do not see myself in that light; I can only hope that others agree with me and that my work resonates with them, and if it does I feel vindicated. There is a real danger of being type-cast as an eccentric or other assigned roles. Thus I may be viewed by others as an impressionist, a deconstructionist, a rebel, a maverick when those are not the qualities I seek to emphasize. We should be free to alternate between methodologies. Having been type-cast as anti-establishment, there is often no turning back. Being different is thus a personal choice. To use an old trading idiom, 'You have to set out your stall.' If people like what they see, they may become customers.
- There is a danger that you start to believe your own ideological rhetoric. It is vital to become involved in the more conventional research projects of others to keep yourself focused and down to earth.

imbue social research with an air of excitement and spirit of risk-taking, in which rhetoric and narrative devices replace quantitative logic to a certain extent. But this comes at a price because there is nothing worse than a story that fails to captivate an audience. Also, in both practices, one must invest so much of one's time and energy in the process, with no concrete guarantee of return. It may seem strange to begin with a conclusion, but not to me. Story-time permits it too. Bear in mind that Wolcott (1990: 55) argues that 'qualitative research helps others understand themselves by seeing things through our perspective'. The perspective in qualitative methodology must therefore be carried in a narrative framework. Irrespective of how exciting a piece of research was to carry out, writing up is an integral part of the qualitative research process. Indeed, the iterative process between data and analysis may even be what provides the qualitative edge to research.

The allegory of art does not end with Van Maanen, for Lomask (1987) has likened academic writing to a 'craft' that needs to be learned in a similar vein to the 'biographer's craft'. Indeed, the writing should emerge from the research and be tinged with the atmosphere in which the field research was conducted. It should possess what Becker (1986: 56) refers to as a 'physical embodiment'. Good qualitative writing should have a presence, but like the art of entrepreneuring it is best learned by doing. This encompasses learning by experience and from failures. I had to school myself to learn how to let go of my work. I still have a feeling of trepidation when sending work to a publisher or editor, for bold undertakings do not come without an element of risk or danger. Qualitative writing is no longer such a pioneering field and, indeed, qualitative methodologies have become well established. For example, they no longer require to be written in an apologetic, justificatory style, replete with extensive and explanatory methodology sections. However, extensive and explanatory methodology sections document the stringency of qualitative research and offer proof that we do not do haphazard work, as positivists are prone to believe.

On daring to write differently and getting published!
Qualitative writing is different and we should not be embarrassed to acknowledge its difference. Wolcott (1990: 34–5) writes that one of the major problems of conducting qualitative research is that 'it generates an immense amount of data, quotes, vignettes, observations and insights that must be "canned" (got rid of) not written. Perhaps articulating themes, nuances and essences is all one can hope for.' Wolcott also advocates keeping writing simple, and encourages writers to write in the past tense as it kills off actions as they occur, framing one's writing in a timeless style. Perhaps this is why entrepreneurial narrative is often written in the present

tense, where the action colours the dialogue. According to Wolcott, qualitative methodologies wed us to prose. He develops this theme by stressing that in qualitative research, writing makes or breaks the study and that poor writing can dull the dialogue. He advises us to write solid pieces that stand the test of time, as opposed to capturing the mood of the moment. For Wolcott, good writing enhances what is being written about. Thus articulating qualitative research may entail making use of the pictorial elements of visual representation; hence semiotics should be a constant companion to the qualitative researcher because we should make more use of pictures and images in explaining our work.

I am interested in such complex issues as entrepreneurial narrative, entrepreneurial drama, entrepreneurial identity and identifying alternative constructions of the entrepreneur, and consequentially embrace social constructionism and semiotics. I am also fascinated with the notion of criminal entrepreneurship. This has to a certain extent forced my hand, as in the push/pull theories of entrepreneurship. I had to 'dare to be different' as both my research interests and workload conspired against me achieving publication. I was constantly aware that I was researching at the margins of entrepreneurship research using qualitative methodologies. I was also acutely aware that disciplinary purists may even consider that what I research and write is not entrepreneurship research *per se*. Anyway, writing differently is probably the easy part. It is getting published that is the difficulty. However, Wolcott (1990: 87) was right to counsel that the qualitative research act is not completed until our work is completed and accessible to others – however this may be achieved. The following sections discuss my progress as a *rite de passage*, documenting the false starts, enlightening the problems and the solutions.

Getting published (or, more significantly, not getting published) is a major dilemma facing experienced and novice researchers alike. During my doctoral process, this was a factor that increasingly occupied my thoughts. I felt a significant (self-imposed) pressure to publish. This is not a process unique to me because, as de Sola Pool (1983) stresses, young academics are encouraged to publish as much as possible in their first five to six years. Thus, whether we like it or not, publishing is the lifeblood of academic careers, and failure to achieve in this respect can blight and destroy promising careers in academia. It is interesting that the decision of where or whether to publish centres around the thorny issues of tenure and promotion (Sweeney 1998). Tenure and promotion revolve around publishing 'scholarly work' in top-flight peer-reviewed journals. Indeed, scholarly publications count significantly toward salary and job security (Varian 1997). Quality and quantity both count. Academics who fail to publish are definitely marginalized in their professional networks. We are frequently told this by our tutors and at doctoral consortiums. I consider myself fortunate because not all supervisors permit their research students the degree of freedom that I have been given to write, to make mistakes and learn from them. Freedom to express, but also freedom to fail! I enjoy writing and reading. I like writing short stories, writing in the style of Dickens, in the style of Tolkien, or tragedies. Good writing requires practice. I write best to music playing in the background. Yet none of this is apparent in a completed article.

Writing up can be a time-consuming, stressful activity, which pervades the research process. This pressure can have a detrimental effect upon the creativity of the researcher and can in turn affect the quality of the writing. The personal and institutional pressure to conduct and write up research can be intense. Writing ability and the integrity of research are important but ultimately I will be measured by the bottom line – the number and quality of my publications. It is the academic's equivalent of the gunslinger's notches on the barrel of his gun, or the fighter pilot's killing tally, and as such is a particularly masculine ritual. Likewise, quantity is often associated and erroneously conflated with prowess and ability. I argue that this can lead to research being designed and carried out expressly for the purpose of writing a reputation-enhancing journal article or to attend a specific conference. More important but less easily researched topics are often ignored and sidelined. It is a narrative or dialogue which impinges upon the personal conversations of many academics but is silent in academic journals.

It is surprising, but there may be sound structural reasons why getting qualitative research published is difficult, given the incisive suggestion of Wolcott (1990), who notes that a major problem of qualitative methodologies is that they are difficult to conclude. Indeed, he advocates against trying to do so. This structural defect actually makes it difficult to write up such research for quality journals, because the journal article by its very nature drives one towards providing conclusions and implications. In qualitative studies, it is sometimes the actual research that is interesting *per se*, not the conclusion. It is also a common mistake to conclude a qualitative study with a flourish. Yet good writing style demands a flourish. Similarly, Wolcott (1990) advocates that one should avoid summarizing. An alternative strategy is to invoke reflection and posit one's judgements. Such reflectivity pervades qualitative writing, because such accounts often read like an unfinished tale, and indeed they are. They are part of a continuing learning process in which the author engages in trying to achieve *Verstehen*: a full understanding and appreciation of the phenomenon. In writing apparently different papers I find myself engaging in a continuing dialogue with myself. When I read the consecutive papers sequentially, a rather different picture emerges. I find that I have (as perhaps other qualitative researchers do) left unanswered questions and themes in a preceding paper and sub-consciously answer them in the next. It does not always make tidy reading, but in tidying up qualitative work, one can lose some of its power, vitality and charm. So how does one make the most of one's differences? Does one tone them down or accentuate them? It is a personal choice.

Making the most of one's differences

I first became aware that I may, perhaps, be qualitatively different when I conducted action-based research into the entrepreneurial narrative and pre-sented an award-winning paper at the 2002 Babson–Kaufman Research Conference. The paper was entitled 'Inspirational tales: Propagating the entrepreneurial narrative amongst children' (Smith 2002) and was based upon action research in the form of a children's story book entitled *Ernie the Entrepreneur.*[3] The paper achieved publication but the seminal narrative from which it sprang did not. It would be wrong of me to say that I was prouder of my innovative children's story than I was of the prestigious award, but one can get very attached to one's first piece of creative writing. Yet in vain I searched for a publisher. After two rejections from publishers of children's books, I gave up. Imagine my shock and surprise when the next paper I wrote jointly with Eleanor Hamilton (Hamilton and Smith 2003) from Lancaster University entitled 'The entrepreneuse' also won a best-paper award. The feeling of euphoria was immense. It would be easy to be conceited. I had to suffer the mock 'golden boy' taunts of my peers. But everybody knows the fate of those who submit to *hubris* and believe in invin-cibility. The myths of Iciris and Midas are there to remind us, lest we forget.

I continued with my frenetic pace of researching and writing. I find that writing papers drove my doctoral research forward. I became interested in semiotic aspects of entrepreneurial identity and researched visual images of entrepreneurs and images associated with entrepreneurship. I gathered semiotic data from books, magazines, newspapers and the television. This led to gathering sufficient data to write two conference papers. I presented the first paper, entitled 'Entrepreneurial identity and bad boy iconology' (Smith 2003) at a research seminar at Strathclyde University in April 2003. At that seminar, I was commended/applauded by my peer group for pre-senting research that was uniquely different. A professor whom I had never met before advised me never to attempt to conform myself to academic convention and to continue researching in the maverick vein I had obvi-ously adopted. Heady stuff, indeed.

Alistair and I jointly presented the second paper, entitled 'Conforming non-conformists: semiotic manifestations of an entrepreneurial identity' (Smith and Anderson 2003) at the Babson–Kaufman Research Conference,

2003, which examined selected images associated with entrepreneurial identity. It too was well received by a small audience. However, the problem with such research is that it was our perception that editors of journals and publishers are often unwilling to print photographs and images because of technical and financial constraints. This may deter research into such issues. It was clear to us that an alternative venue for achieving dissemination of the research had to be formulated that would allow us to write conventional journal articles while enabling readers to access the images at will. This led us to give serious consideration to the important issues of getting unusual qualitative research published, or if not published, at least alternatively disseminated in one's academic community. Alistair and I obviously had to consider establishing alternative avenues of dissemination. But how? It is to this question that I now turn.

Establishing alternative avenues of dissemination

In this section, I tender some observations, albeit in a tentative manner, for I find telling others 'how to' is a difficult task to accomplish with grace. I will focus on some issues that I consider important in getting qualitative research published. I also address the disseminating of research by traditional methods and discuss alternative forms of writing up the findings, for example layers and voices, genres and stances, narratives and stories. In doing so, I obviously had to consider making the most of traditional methods of dissemination because only a fool would expend their efforts in shaping an alternative strategy if the existing one sufficed.

Making the most of traditional methods of dissemination

I started by considering the traditional methods of dissemination available to me. These included conference papers, targeting top-flight journals, targeting lesser-ranked journals with a smaller turnaround time; targeting journals outside one's academic field; targeting calls for book chapters; targeting publishers to publish interesting research in book format; and finally self-publishing (both on the Internet and in the amateur press). As can be seen, the relevant word in this section is targeting. It is worth considering the merits and pitfalls of these methods in turn, because it is all too easy to take them for granted. Table 17.2 sets out traditional methods of disseminating research.

In order of merit Alistair and I chose to target the book chapters market, conference papers and lesser-known journals. I do not advocate turning one's back on the quality journals because conference papers are sometimes only reviewed as abstracts whereas the respected journals imbue one's writing with a sense of gravitas. Like good investors, Alistair and I also sent off papers to top-flight journals. Their respectability of output is appealing

Table 17.2   Traditional methods of disseminating research

Conference papers	Play a major part in driving entrepreneurship research forward, being fun to write and present, but can vary considerably in the quality of the research. These were a major part of my eventual strategy because they often evolve into journal articles and book chapters. I like them because they are usually published in a folder presented to participants and thus act as a concrete sign of achievement. Although it is a basic method of disseminating research, it allowed me freedom to develop my writing and presentation skills while learning to work to a deadline. I liked it because I achieved a sense of closure and was able to quickly build up elements of my CV – a point often forgotten. According to Wolcott (1990: 89), they contribute towards academic credibility and visibility.
Top-flight journals	It is an understandable tendency to target one's work towards quality journals, but as I have found, this can prove to be a soul-destroying, frustrating learning curve. It is a high-risk/high-gain strategy. Competition is fierce and time scales can be frustrating. One submits one's work in the hope that it resonates with the anonymous reviewers. I liken it metaphorically to sending one's child into the wilderness in the hope that it will end in a fairy-tale format. I am perhaps being unkind but it is also like the childhood activity of sending messages in a bottle out to sea. One launches them full of hope and quickly forgets about them. I am a social being and thrive on positive feedback. I do not want it in sixth months' time, nor in a year's time. I am like a child: I want everything now. I know that this is being unrealistic, but am I alone? By the time I receive feedback I have moved on. It is possible to achieve publication, providing the research topic and methodology are progressive and the resulting paper is well written (especially if it mirrors the aims of the journal), but acceptance can be slow. One of the frustrations is that one writes creatively and then agonizes ponderously and torturously over one's creation, line by line. In polishing, one can be destroying that which made special – its spontaneity. Scholarly writing has its place but is a skill in its own right. Varian (1997) also cites the cost of publishing journals, resulting in editors encouraging short articles to capture the attention span of the readers. This entails stripping them of unnecessary prose, the very mechanism that brings qualitative work to life. Varian argues that all publications are not equal and that competition to publish in top-ranked journals is often intense, with the process often taking 12 months to two years. Laband and Piette (1994) argue that citation counts are

Table 17.2   (continued)

	often used as a measure of the impact of articles and journals, making publishing in top-flight journals a necessity.
Lesser-ranked journals	I found that targeting lesser-rated journals is a more realistic strategy, especially if one is using a lesser-known qualitative methodology such as social constructivism and semiotics. Such journals can take more risks and welcome well-written research that dares to be different.
Alternative journals	Targeting alternative journals is an excellent strategy because it increases the size of one's target audience and has the added benefit of making one work hard to ensure that one is communicating one's knowledge at a suitable level. Research occurring at the margins of entrepreneurship may contain material that makes it of mainstream interest to other disciplines. In my case I have targeted criminology journals because I can tailor my work towards them. It also keeps my other writing fresh.
On-line journals	Sweeney (1998) asks, 'Should you publish in electronic journals?', arguing that the rapid growth of information and communication technology since the early 1990s has greatly influenced the accessibility of information on a global level, playing a critical role in restructuring the mechanisms by which specialized academic knowledge is validated, distributed and made available to consumers. Sweeney (1998) and Dixon (1997) argue that the pressure to publish can be marginally alleviated by easy and straightforward electronic submission and refereeing of papers. Such electronic journals have rapid turnaround times and offer speed of dissemination. Yet electronic journals have yet to be fully accepted as legitimate publication outlets (Kling and Covi 1995). Varian argues that best-paper prizes are an attractive method to overcome young authors' reluctance to publish in electronic journals.
Book chapters	Alistair and I have made a deliberate choice to target the book market. It has the benefit of being a relatively frequent opportunity. I like the spirit of excitement which they engender and also the spirit of competitiveness. These combine to imbue our writing with a tone of excitement. I like the fact they are scheduled for publication and this enables me to work to set guidelines, time scales and have the benefit of editorial advice and direction. I like the security of gaining an acceptance which guarantees me a publication two years hence. The eclecticism engendered by creative writing and artful editing ensures that they are exciting projects to be involved in. I have found them invaluable in gaining writing experience and building a network of writers with whom I am happy writing with.

Table 17.2   (continued)

The book market	I find the book market to be a bit more risky a strategy. Perhaps this view will change when I have established a reputation or can collaborate with an author who has. I consider it to be a very viable, but time-consuming strategy, which permits one the luxury of avoiding the pitfalls of writing for journals. One can be more expressive and take more liberties with structure and content. I considered this but it is a strategy for the future.

to me and is in direct relation to the prestige of the publication. It was the book chapter market which paid off for me/us, with seven acceptances in a two-year period. Notwithstanding this, I still pondered why work submitted to top-flight journals did not pay dividends. I thought that perhaps my work was just too different for the reviewers. I have also had to come to the realization that perhaps the time has not come for my writing to be accepted by a serious journal. As a research community, we are good at writing, but not very good at talking, or writing about writing. I now turn to developing alternative methods of dissemination.

Developing alternative methods of dissemination
Again, I tender some observations, and discuss some alternative methods of dissemination available to me. The most obvious of these was self-publishing. This method is often frowned upon in academic circles by old-school academics as being academically lax and unprofessional. Indeed, it is a strategy fraught with danger. It can leave you open to derision from other respected academics who have had to earn their reputations the hard way. There are two methods, conventional printing and by desktop, or by self-publishing on the Internet. With the advent of PCs, word processing, scanners etc., desktop publishing has lost much of its earlier amateur stigma. Self-publishing of any sort can be viewed as being undesirable, eccentric and associated with the vanity press, leaving one open to the charge of being self-conceited, self-aggrandizing and a self-publicist. For this reason, vanity-style publishing is rare in academic circles; many academics have the ability and social cachet to develop their own outlets/publishing contacts. Yet I find it strangely appealing. Am I alone? It has all the drama of being a labour of love. Perhaps in the future I will be brave enough to try it – but not yet.

I find it disappointing that this attitude exists because self-publishing is a channel used by local historians and amateur ethnographers alike. In my humble opinion, it is an under-used and perfectly viable method of disseminating research that cannot be truncated to fit journal articles. A

40–50-page booklet or pamphlet, particularly if it contains photographs and other images, can be produced and disseminated reasonably cheaply. It may take the form of teaching material before being reworked into an academic article. It can be very effective if your academic audience is relatively small or if your non-academic audience exceeds the former. Such amateur publications can even be sold at local outlets (to defray costs) and distributed to local libraries. It can allow you to tone down academic style to that which is necessary only to complement the research. It lets research speak for itself and permits the author to control content and style.[4] In the short term I rejected this strategy, although I may dabble in it in the future.

I seriously considered self-publishing on the Internet, in my view an under-used academic tool. It has the added advantage of allowing one to post several connected studies into a complementary anthology of studies. A growing number of researchers use the strategy of creating their own webpages where they report on ongoing research and working papers before seeking publication in journals. The disadvantages are that it is time-consuming and may damage their longer-term desirability as publications in different format. I have been impressed by some very good websites, for example the one on semiotics by Daniel Chandler of the University of Wales. However, I recognize their drawbacks. For a start they can be relatively expensive to post and maintain. They do not target – they maintain a presence awaiting to be accessed by anyone. Their strengths are that you as an author can control and amend content as arguments develop and crystallize. You can post pictures and drawings, providing you address copyright issues. You can count the number of hits, thereby assessing your following/readership. An added advantage is that you can post ongoing work for others to read as it develops. Also, there is no frustrating delay from writing to publication. It is certainly a strategy (albeit a risky one) that can pay dividends because one can reach a wider audience. Yet, I too rejected this as a strategy because I feared that I would be damaging my chances of achieving future publication of the material in a quality journal. Notwithstanding this, the work of Daniel Chandler (1994) eventually achieved publication in book form in 2001. Another factor in the decision to reject this strategy is that I do not have sufficient time and in addition I am a technophobe.

The most frequent generic criticism of all these self-publishing methods is that such work is not peer-reviewed. For it to become an academically viable strategy it would be necessary to have the work edited by another party and peer-reviewed by other leading academics in the field as well as subjected to some sort of 'blind reviewing'. I find the possibility of publishing my email address and encouraging respondents to comment upon the material to be strangely appealing and could foresee establishing a meaningful dialogue as a distinct advantage. To return to the issue of conference papers, if I cannot develop them into journal articles and book chapters, I will give serious consideration to posting them on the Internet or at the very least disseminated via alternative forms of writing up.

Alternative forms of writing up

I also considered some alternative forms of writing up qualitative research, including organizing a symposium or seminar; writing a magazine column; and the most radical decision of all – not to write up. I will discuss these in turn; see Table 17.3.

To return to the introduction and in particular the assertion of Van Maanen (1988) that one can become as one with one's stories, in seminars and in symposia this can and does happen. It is my favourite dissemination methodology. It is a natural venue in which I can tentatively express my findings in a semi-structured manner. I can experiment with the

Table 17.3   Alternative methods of disseminating research

Symposiums and seminars	I like presenting my work at symposia and seminars. I like the structure of a maximum of a 15-minute presentation time. It enables me to articulate my work succinctly and allows me to empty it of academic references. It crystallizes my arguments and renders my work more understandable to non-academic or marginally interested audiences. In academic contexts it allows me to dispense with formality and discuss the important issues underlying my research. These are time-consuming to organize and manage but are well worthwhile. I appreciate the ability they provide me to practise presentational styles and techniques and to perform.
Magazine columns	I gave consideration to publishing my work as an editor of a magazine or professional journal. I like this idea because again it would enable me to spread the message of the research, again emptied of academic parlance and style. To date I have not found a serious venue prepared to take me on. I therefore self-rejected this avenue.
Non-publishing	I find the assertion of Wolcott (1990: 88–9) that one should give serious consideration to not publishing strangely appealing as a viable strategy, especially for studies of limited appeal. Not all work must be published, but all work must be written up. Disseminating your work may entail merely making copies of it available on request. At the very least one should consider sending drafts to members of one's peer group to see if the work resonates with them.

different layers of meaning, with different genres and even in different voices, genres and styles. I obtain the benefit of almost instantaneous feedback. I am forced to learn how to perform academically and lean towards the dramatic and expressive, and to learn the art of injecting oratory passion into my stories within stories. If I 'pull it off', the effect can be electrifying. Chance and risk go hand in hand. Of course it can bomb too! However, I find that the minute I utter those magic words 'I will now tell you a story', or I produce a book and begin to read, or even invite the audience to form a circle around me, something primeval and strangely magical happens! As a storyteller I become as one, braided with my story. It beats the buzz of achieving a publication by a long stretch, but it is alas ephemeral. However, its most important facet is that it brings my research to life in a memorable way. It helps me forget for a moment the nagging doubts of self-criticality.

On the need to be self-critical

After much reflection and in collectively reviewing my lack of progress in achieving a finished article which I considered worthy of sending to the publisher of a top-flight journal, Alistair and I came to the conclusions that my writing contained specific generic faults. The papers discussed invariably suffered from the same generic problems. For instance:

1. Being qualitative, novel and often prone to being subjective;
2. Their use of semiotics – which requires explanation and justification;
3. Adopting a social constructivist stance;
4. Being wedded to prose and stylistic writing – hence their inherent excitement;
5. Perhaps even being idiosyncratic (in that writings contain much of my foibles);
6. They were 'busy' and perhaps attempted too much.

The last point is interesting as the writings definitely mirror the characters of their authors. I would also have been wise to heed the advice of Wolcott (1990) to beware of tangential interests as I spread myself too thinly on many occasions. Frustratingly, as papers they were exciting to write, discuss and present. I found the collective effect worked well – a synthesis of seductive words and pictorial images. In all, in the interest of academic research, I have disseminated about 20 copies of each, complete with images. However, when one separates the words from their illustrative images they simply lack the dimension of the completed article. In my opinion, qualitative writing works best, like the qualitative methods embedded within them when the correct balance is struck and they work at a taken-for-granted level. When this authorial harmony with writing is achieved there is no need to explain the methods for the techniques, if adequately mastered, do it all for you. The finished result is a pleasure to read. I would by far have preferred to publish one of my/our papers by way of illustration than to write about them. Writing about creating them is a vexing, self-doubting destructive process. But if I am truly self-critical, the inability to achieve publication may lie closer to home than is comfortable for me to accept. Perhaps my work to date has been developmental in nature or even poor. I am grateful for the comments of an anonymous reviewer, who suggested that it was unfair to assert that papers that might dare to be different are unlikely to receive a fair hearing from mainstream, high-end journals, because of other factors such as the possibility that it is poor work. This forced me to acknowledge that I had in fact been self-policing my work and that the divide was as much of my own making as that of editors and publishers. Whilst perceptual influences are critical in such valuation and perhaps there are high degrees of subjectivity, defensiveness and the desire to protect my work played a significant part in where I decided to publish.

Another problem with qualitative writing is that it benefits from the maturity that comes with allowing it time to embed it within itself, time for it to mature, time to consider whether it still pleased me, time to play, time to tinker with it, amend it, time to procrastinate, to rewrite it and so forth. This causes another set of problems in that it is so easy to run out of time and it goes stale. As a result of critical self-analysis it was apparent that what I lacked was a competent research publication strategy.

Compiling a research publication strategy (as narrated by Robert Smith)
I have found to my cost that to avoid all the pitfalls of literary stagnation, it is essential to compile a research publication strategy. What I had failed to do was to make time to plan creatively, to build in time after a conference to rewrite when the material and responses were fresh and to send my work away for a more critical peer review process. It is a process that is best documented, particularly if one, like me, is absentminded or, worse still, driven by intellectual curiosity towards new work. This is the curse of being a qualitative researcher. If this vital process is not in place, then it is easy to allow promising work to 'drift' while also running the risk of it becoming tired and dated. I did not always make my work 'work' for me. It must be released to the outside world. The actual research and the writing are the most exciting aspects. However, creative minds have an inherent flaw of generating ideas, which, if left unbridled, or not effectively managed, means that as an avid researcher I had moved onto other projects before finalizing the previous one. It is a trap into which I, and many, fall. Granted un-disseminated research may eventually consolidate into quality

publications later in one's academic career, but trusting to luck, serendipity or providence are not serious publication strategies. I now have a growing number of conference papers waiting to be rewritten as journal articles when I finish my Ph.D. I cannot turn the clock back, but wish I had considered this sooner.

Developing an integrated research publication strategy is similar to any portfolio project. It is an investment in time and in one's future. One may metaphorically strike 'pay dirt' by high-risk strategies, but spreading the risks is always a more viable strategy. Targeting a variety of venues avoids the pitfalls of academic stagnation. With this in mind, I made the decision to target book chapters, lesser-known journals and, if all else failed, to self-publish. An integrated research publication strategy is an essential mentoring tool in matching the expertise and experience of the supervisor with the enthusiasm and high work rate of the doctoral student. This is specifically true of academia in Britain, where very few Ph.D. dissertations are ever published in their original format. If you are lucky, you may be able to publish an edited version as a book. Different academic disciplines have better track records than others. For instance, sociological and anthropological works are more readily marketable than entrepreneurship, where the track record is poorer.

There are a few exceptions to this rule in the entrepreneurship field, for example Dibben (2000) and Rae (2001). In Sweden a higher percentage of Ph.D. dissertations are made public by recourse to publishing them. A prime example is Hjorth (2001). Also, compendiums of research are encouraged, for example *Images of Entrepreneurship and Small Businesses*, by Johannisson and Landström (2001) (eds) brings together the work of 12 entrepreneurship doctoral students. This is a strategy worth encouraging. It permits the development of 'schools' or 'stables' of promising researchers. Seeing your work in print as a book can be immensely satisfying and has the added benefit of permitting qualitative studies to be disseminated in full. Having a presence is essential if you desire to be cited by others, but bear in mind the advice of Wolcott (1990: 84–5) that qualitative research is disseminated in a closed system, with writers of such research also being its buyers; this makes the market commercially non-viable. This more than any other factor makes it essential to consider alternative forms of writing up and of marketing your qualitative research elsewhere.

One of the most surprising aspects about the disappointing uptake of qualitative methodologies in the entrepreneurship research field is that there is a definite spirit and celebration of difference. For example, the Swedish ESBRI seminars, with their grounded themes, positively encourage diversity, difference and the dramatic. These are propagated via their seminal *Movements in Entrepreneurship* book series.

At one point Alistair and I also seriously considered submitting my/our work to journals by compromising and either making them entirely text-dependent or describing one or two of the pictorial facets contained in the original to capture some of the aura of the original. Fortunately we resisted this most obvious of solutions as it was our vision that readers of academic journals could click on a pre-coded web address to view individual images in a similar manner to a web address.[5] This led to further discussion and we initially decided to set up a gallery of images annexed to the Robert Gordon University website. This led to a time-consuming round of discussions and permissions to be sought. In the end the technical requirements (as well as pressure of work) dulled our enthusiasm. Being innovative is easier to talk about than to accomplish. More time elapsed. In the interim period, I had committed Alistair and myself to submitting the abstract for this book chapter, based solely upon our honest intentions to progress the project.

An alternative thought we had while attending yet another conference was to download the images onto a CD disc to accompany each copy of the journal/book chapters. This is standard practice outside entrepreneurship circles. Ideas were kicked about like a proverbial football. The acceptance of this chapter forced our hand. It did not help that both Alistair and I are 'dyed-in-the wool' technophobes. We prefer the feel of paper and the permanence of the printed word in a completed book. Thus webpages, CD ROMS and Internet 'Google' image searches do not come naturally to us. Even mastering the IT of PowerPoint systems taxed us considerably. We were to find that technical problems beset us. Like all good impressionistic tales, it is beneficial to include an element of the confessional in it too. It is easier to write about being innovative than to actually do it. In the interim period, I did achieve sufficient publications to quell my impatience. Also, I changed, in that I became less impatient and dare I say perhaps more conventional. Alistair and I are still exploring new avenues of making our work more accessible to our peers. I would prefer to try to publish my work in a respected journal before setting up a stand-alone website. If that fails I will try to publish my qualitative research as a monograph or even book. What caused this drastic turnaround? Maturity perhaps? Or perhaps I have just changed? I admit to being influenced by the perseverance of Bill Gartner, who in Gartner (2004: 245–54) tells his story of how his much-cited article 'Who is the entrepreneur is the wrong question' (Gartner 1988) very nearly did not achieve publication. Gartner stresses that it took him a four-year period, numerous rejections from an equally numerous number of different journals, actual confrontations with reviewers and editors plus a plethora of rewrites before he eventually achieved publication. It is a wonderful story, but then Bill Gartner dared to be different.

Conclusion

Some concluding thoughts (as narrated by Robert Smith)

I trust that the contents of this chapter have demonstrated in some small way 'why we see so little semiotic research in entrepreneurship journals'. In seeking to answer the two-part question of whether it is 'worth trying to publish such research' and 'what are the benefits', it is necessary to adopt a personal stance and declare that I personally have come to believe that it is worth it; hence my determination to find a suitable method of writing up such research to permit my work to be published in a top-flight journal. The benefits are self-evident but are often only achieved as part of a longer-term strategy.

To relate the contents of this chapter to the serious issues, and laudable aims, that this handbook seeks to address, it is now necessary to 'braid' together what we have learned. First, the writing style chosen for this chapter is obviously a symbolic form to literally and figuratively denote difference. I do not suggest for a moment that we have to develop a bohemian style, grow our hair long, read poetry, take up painting and obscure hobbies. None the less, these suggestions, although posited in jest, will improve your writing. However, writing must retain passion and be allowed to express difference. It is how entrepreneurs brand themselves, and we should learn from our subjects. Nor is it enough to mimic sociological and anthropological methods of using qualitative research, despite the assertion of Casson (2000) that anthropology possesses an affinity with the romantic. We, that is you and I, must develop our own styles and conventions of difference with which we are happy as a discipline. Only then will the uptake of qualitative methods increase, as confidence levels improve. The only advice I can give is to follow your heart, articulate your ideas, write from the heart with passion, be creative but realistic. Pursue a career but remain true to yourself, for integrity comes from within, be daring but pragmatic, and even consider developing your own methodology. Only then will 'daring to be different' become a valued disciplinary trait. Also, develop a dissemination strategy and work hard at it.

Nevertheless, we cannot do it all on our own. As a discipline we need to organize and form writing schools, we need to set aside time to mentor, to tutor, to share and read our works with each other. If a daring publisher trailed an issue of *Qualitative Writings on Entreprenaria*,[6] it would be surprising how many would answer the call for papers. This daring handbook on qualitative research is a welcome beginning. Until then, conduct research that stretches your imagination, that pushes the boundaries, for entrepreneurship perhaps has no boundaries, pursue any avenue of dissemination available to you, go to seminars, tell your stories and publish on the Internet. Make your impression, as I hope to make mine. As I have found, researching at the frontiers of entrepreneurship using qualitative methodologies positions me firmly on the edge of the discipline; it also entails writing on the edge. It can be exhilarating at times. But I am always aware that I can also fall over the edge. Being different is a precarious privilege, as is being an entrepreneur. In a chapter such as this, there can often be no conclusion.

A reflective reply grounded in experience (as narrated by Alistair R. Anderson)

Well, this chapter certainly fulfils the promise of its title and I like the theme a lot. It engendered a spirit of genuine discussion and caused me to reflect upon my own experiences. The idea for the chapter was presented to me almost as a *fait accompli* when Robert enthusiastically responded to the call for papers. I had reservations, because how different can one be in academia? Different work like this has to overcome the fear of setting oneself up. We discussed many ideas for the chapter, but many times it appeared as though it would not materialize. Robert wrote the first draft and presented it to me almost as it appears now. My first response on reading it was to reply to each section in the manner of a dialogue, but I dismissed this as pretentious; after all, who am I to present an 'expert' discourse on somebody else's work? Whilst the chapter was different, I realized that it nevertheless required to be reviewed as a potential publication so I started by responding in its reflective spirit. Here are some of my thoughts.

It is helpful because what Robert has done is to 'tell us a story' about his views and experiences concerning research and publishing. This allows us to relate to this, in our own terms. This is surely a classic element in recounting narrative and a worthy objective. Such stories do need to be assertive, but to have real and lasting value they need to combine this with some careful reflection. Being different is a wonderful quality, but it also requires to be tempered by experience. In writing up experiences of difference, one has to make the distinctions between what one finds and objective realities. The two can become blurred. It is difficult to get into a conversation with a reader, because of the nature of writing. It is, after all, a one-sided rendition and there is a danger that in building up an atmosphere one slides into discoursing and dogma. Thus one needs to try to maintain an open-ended conversational style; this is no mean feat and perhaps helps explain why we stick to convention. In such a chapter, maintaining a friendly exchange is essential because it presents experiences and views in a user-friendly way, as well as inviting a reflective response. This is doubly difficult because, as researchers, when we find out things we tend to present our findings as if they were facts, when they may be better narrated as readings of experiences. Narrating research in terms of these research experiences requires a different writing style and perspective. Reflective writing avoids some of the necessity of stating facts. Moreover, writing about qualitative research is difficult because it covers such a potentially enormous field. Given that our experience relates to researching narrative and social constructivist fields, what Robert narrates is especially true of such work. But might it be argued to be less true of more general qualitative work?

However, having said all that about reflection, there is little value in merely perpetuating a 'stream of consciousness' approach. While this might be interesting, it does not make for a good book chapter. Reflective writing and impressionistic tales of the field have to braid our experiences as researchers with our reflections as individuals – turning them into a well-grounded narrative. We also need to avoid a diatribe against the establishment. What one must seek to do is what Robert has tried to do – to open minds, not close them. Was it a story worth telling? Did it engage you? You need to decide.

Notes

1.   Professor Alistair R. Anderson is a well-published veteran of the field, having written numerous journal articles and presented a considerable number of conference papers. In comparison, doctoral student Robert Smith has written and presented a few conference papers, but has only a few journal articles to his credit.
2.   Although young in terms of scholarship, the author is not young in years. Note how impressionistic tales allow one to exaggerate and embellish, or, if one is unkind, to deceive.
3.   The paper itself won the 'The Raymond Family Business Institute' best-paper award and was published in the book – *Frontiers of Entrepreneurship Research* (2002). However, the desire to publish the story itself remains. Initially it was proposed that it would be posted on the Internet. This led to further time-consuming discussions and the eventual abandonment of the project. After all, a children's storybook is a book – not a flashy webpage. Authorial pride brooks no compromise.
4.   This novel methodology is currently being developed by the author for a historically oriented socioeconomic study into subsistence entrepreneurship in a Scottish fishing community for presentation at a future rural entrepreneurship conference. This method of dissemination was chosen since the research incorporates photographic images. It is being written up as an ethnographic social commentary (with an anthropological bias) that will, it is hoped, appeal to a wider audience.
5.   Initially it had been our intention in this chapter to track attempts to achieve publication of the three articles mentioned above and the compromises that we had to make to accommodate conformity. However, it soon became apparent that this was not feasible given the lengthy waiting time in getting published in some quality scholarly journals.
6.   Pertaining to all things entrepreneurial.

References

Anderson, A.R. and Jack, S.L. (1997) Teaching the entrepreneurial art. In Evans, D.S. (ed.), *International Dimensions of Teaching Entrepreneurship: A collection of invited working papers under the direction of the Ecole superieure de commerce et de management.*

Atherton, A. and Elsmore, P. (2004) *A Dialogue (And Dialectic) Between Users: What sense can we make of software 'support' and protocols for qualitative data analysis in the research process?* Paper presented at the First International Co-Sponsored Conference Research Methods Division, Academy of Management (USA), Crossing Frontiers in Quantitative and Qualitative Research Methods, Lyon, France, 18–20 March.

Becker, H.S. (1986) *Writing For Social Scientists: How to start and finish your thesis, book or article*, Chicago, IL: University of Chicago Press.

Casson, M.C. (2000) *Enterprise and Leadership: Studies on Firms, Markets and Networks*, Cheltenham UK and Northampton, MA, USA: Edward Elgar.

Chandler, D. (1994) http://www.aber.ac.uk/media/Documents/S4B/semiotic.html.

Chandler, D. (2001) *Semiotics: The basics*. London: Routledge.

de Sola Pool, I. (1983) Tracking the flow of information. *Science*, **221**(4611): 609–13.

Dibben, M. (2000) *Exploring Interpersonal Trust In the Entrepreneurial Venture*, Basingstoke: Palgrave Macmillan.

Dixon, A. (1997) Electronic publishing and the academic community: A publisher's perspective. In Ian Butterworth (ed.), *The impact of electronic publishing on the academic community* (Session 1: The present situation and the likely future). International Workshop organized by the Academia Europaea and the Wenner-Gren Foundation, Wenner-Gren Center, Stockholm, Sweden, 16–20 April. Available: http://tiepac.portlandpress.co.uk/books/online/tiepac/session1/ch2.htm.

Gartner, W. (1988) Who is the entrepreneur is the wrong question. *American Journal of Small Business*, **12**(1): 11–32.

Gartner, W. (2001) Is there an elephant in entrepreneurship? Blind assumptions in theory development, *Entrepreneurship Theory and Practice*, **25**(4): 27–39.

Gartner, W. (2004) Saying what entrepreneurship is (not). In Hjorth, D. and Steyaert, C. (eds), *Narrative and Discursive Approaches in Entrepreneurship*. Cheltenham, UK and Northampton, MA, USA: Edward Elgar, pp. 245–54.

Hamilton, E. and Smith, R. (2003) *The Entrepreneuse: A Silent Entrepreneurial Narrative*, Paper presented at the SBED Conference, Surrey, April.

Hjorth, D. (2001) *Rewriting Entrepreneurship: Enterprise discourse and entrepreneurship in the case of re-organising ES*, Växjö, Sweden: Växjo University Press.

Hosking, D. and Hjorth, D. (2004) Relational constructionism and entrepreneurship: some key notes, in Hjorth, D. and Steyaert, C. (eds), *Narrative and Discursive Approaches in Entrepreneurship*. Cheltenham, UK and Northampton, MA, USA: Edward Elgar.

Johannisson, B. and Landström, H. (eds) (2001) *Images of Entrepreneurship and Small Business*, Sire: Växjo, Sweden: Växjö University Press.

Kling, R. and Covi, L. (1995) Electronic journals and legitimate media in the systems of scholarly communication. *The Information Society*, **11**(4): 261–71. [Online]. Available: http://www.ics.uci.edu/~kling/klingej2.html.

Laband, D.N. and Piette, M. (1994) The relative impact of economics journals: 1970–1990, *Journal of Economic Literature*, **32**(2): 640–66.

Lomask, M. (1987) *The Biographer's Craft*. New York: Harper & Row.

Rae, D. (2001) *The Entrepreneurial Spirit: Learning to unlock value*. London: Silverlink Publishing.

Silverman, D. (2000) *Doing Qualitative Research*. London: Sage Publications.

Smith, R. (2002) *Inspirational Tales: Propagating the Entrepreneurial Narrative Amongst Children*. Paper presented at the Babson–Kauffman Entrepreneurship Research Conference, Boulder, CO, June, 2003.

Smith, R. and Anderson, A.R. (2003) *Conforming Non Conformists: A semiotic analysis of entrepreneurial identity*. Paper presented at the Babson–Kauffman Entrepreneurship Research Conference, Boston, June 2003.

Smith, R. (2003) *Entrepreneurial Identity and Bad Boy Iconology*. Paper presented at an Entrepreneurship Research Seminar at Strathclyde University, April.

Sweeney, A.E. (1998) Tenure and Promotion – Should you publish in Electronic Journals?, *The Journal of Electronic Publishing*, September, Volume 4, Issue 1. ISSN 1080-2711 http://www.press.umich.edu/jep/04-01/varian.html.

Van Mannen, J. (1988) *Tales of the Field: On Writing Ethnography*, Chicago, IL: University of Chicago Press.

Varian, H.R. (1997) *The future of electronic journals: Some speculations about the evolution of academic electronic publishing*. Paper presented at the Scholarly Communication and Technology Conference, Emory University, Atlanta, GA, April 1997. [Online]. Available: http://arl.cni.org/scomm/scat/varian.html.

Wolcott, H.F. (1990) *Writing up Qualitative Research*. Newbury Park and London: Sage Publications.

18 Avoiding a strike-out in the first innings
Candida Brush

The rules of the game (see Box 18.1)

BOX 18.1 HOW TO PLAY

Baseball is known as 'America's national pastime', and has been played for more than 150 years now, thanks to a West Point Cadet by the name of Abner Doubleday who is credited with having invented the game in 1839.

The game is played on a baseball field or diamond. There is the home plate, where each batter stands when it is their turn at bat, the first base, second base, and third base. There are two teams consisting of nine players each. The player's positions are the pitcher, the catcher, the first baseman, the second baseman, the third baseman, the shortstop, the left fielder, the center fielder, and the right fielder, when that team is playing on the field. When one team is on the field, the other team takes turns among its members, at batting the ball (the authors). The object of the game is to score runs or keep the other team from scoring runs. Runs are scored by the batter hitting the ball any place inside the foul lines and then running to first, second, and third bases, consecutively, and then returning to home base.

This whole thing may sound easy, but there is a trick to this. For while the batter is running, the opposing team is chasing after the ball. When it is caught, it is immediately thrown to the baseman (reviewers) standing where the runner is heading. If the baseman catches the ball before the runner touches or tags the base, then an 'out' is called against the runner and his team. Each team, while at bat, gets a total of three outs before they lose their batting privilege.

A ball hit far enough for the batter to reach first base safely without being tagged out is called a single (getting past desk reject). If the ball is hit and two bases are reached, it is called a double (getting a 1st revision). And when a ball is hit far enough for all three bases to be reached, it is called a triple, or triple play

---

(getting a 2nd revision). When a ball is hit out of the playing field, which is every batter's dream, it is called a home run (getting thru in the first go with no revision) and all three bases are run, then the batter returns to the home plate. The batter's team then scores a point.

Another key figure in the game of baseball is the umpire (editors). The umpire is positioned behind the batter and 'calls' or judges every ball that is pitched to the batter. They also rule on the plays. That is, the umpire decides whether a runner has safely reached a base without being tagged out. This is called being 'safe'. If the runner fails to reach the base before begin tagged, the umpire calls the player 'out'. A strike is called every time the batter swings at the pitched ball and nicks it or misses it. A ball hit outside of the foul lines is called a foul ball.

Finally, a normal game consists of nine innings, or nine rounds of play in which each team has a turn at bat. In the case of a tied score at the end of nine innings, additional innings are played until one team wins.

Scoring a home run: how to publish your entrepreneurial work

Getting your work published is analogous to playing the American game of baseball. In baseball, when you step up to the plate, you want to do your best to avoid a strike-out by hitting the ball as far as possible and scoring a run. In writing, submitting your work is a bit like stepping up to the plate. You work hard to prepare your manuscript to avoid being rejected upon submission. In baseball, you want to get to first base (revise and resubmit) so you have a chance of scoring (getting accepted for publication).

The entrepreneurship area is generally defined by creation activities, innovation and processes followed by nascent entrepreneurs associated with opportunity recognition and evaluation (Aldrich 1999; Shane and Venkataraman 2000). For this reason, qualitative methods such as case studies, in-depth interviews, direct observations and analyses of new venture documents are particularly appropriate (Gartner and Birley 2002). However, getting qualitative work published presents a challenge, as explained in the preceding chapter. Indeed, Hindle (2004: 577) finds that 'There has been an explosion in the use of qualitative methods in almost every domain of the social sciences *except entrepreneurship* [emphasis added]'.

Drawing on the baseball analogy, this chapter considers the steps that need to be taken in order to avoid rejection as you step up to the plate. With a particular focus on qualitative research, this chapter draws from various well-known scholars to identify steps you can take to avoid costly mistakes, better target and position your work, increase chances of satisfying reviewers and editors.

Costly mistakes
In baseball, costly mistakes are referred to as errors. An error occurs when an outfielder drops a ball that should be caught, or when a third baseman throws the ball to the first baseman but it sails well over his head into the viewing stands. For the batter, a costly mistake is swinging wildly at a pitch that is way over your head, or way below your knees. In writing, we like to avoid errors and striking out.

No matter how experienced at writing and scholarship you are, receiving a letter that says something like the following causes your heart to sink.

> After seriously considering the comments of the reviewers and the issues raised, we sincerely regret that we cannot offer you an opportunity to publish in the *Journal of Outstanding Theoretical Innovations and Wonderments.* The core ideas have limited scholarly value, the logic is flawed, findings are unimportant and the literature review is inaccurate.

While everyone reacts differently, most people never get used to words of rejection. There is a tendency to feel badly when you receive a rejection letter, causing you to question your ideas and capabilities. Usually after a few days, you can overcome these feelings and start to consider how to reposition the manuscript, re-analyze the data, rewrite the article and revise it for submission elsewhere. But it is always better to avoid costly mistakes at the outset and increase the odds of an invitation to revise and resubmit your work, or better yet, to have it published with minimal revision. The latter, of course, is more like hitting a home run in your first at bat.

So what are the major errors that guarantee being called out at your first bat? Regardless of editors and reviewers, pet peeves that push them over the top to rejection rather than revision, there are six basic issues that if not attended to, will guarantee rejection either by the editor (desk reject) or by the reviewers. These include:

1. Inappropriate target (submitting your paper to a journal which does not accept qualitative research)
2. Unclear or inappropriate theoretical foundation (the articulation of a clear theoretical basis is insufficient)
3. Poor positioning within the literature (not making clear what 'gap' your paper fills)

4. Inappropriate methodology
5. Flawed analysis and measures
6. Unclear contribution to the field.

Each of these issues can be mitigated. You can considerably reduce your risk of getting called out on your first bat by following the major league checklist proposed below.

Major league checklist
What do I know about the journal?
Every journal has a statement describing the specifications and focus of articles published. The specifications vary from quantitative to qualitative, practitioner to academic, or general management to particular disciplinary focus. Submissions that do not 'fit' the target journal risk being rejected by the editors without having the manuscript reviewed. For example, if an article grounded in practitioner literature with normative prescriptions for managers is sent to a scholarly outlet requiring strong theory such as *Entrepreneurship Theory and Practice*, it will likely be returned without review. Similarly, some journals are unequivocally pro-quantitative work such as *Journal of Small Business Economics*, which is described as having become a premier academic journal since it was founded to focus on entrepreneurship and small business. In the journal's mission statement you can read the following:

> High quality research is published employing theoretical or *quantitative* analyses, along with contributions focusing on institutions and public policies, within both a national and international context. (Emphasis added)

Or the following extract from mission statement and guidelines for authors in the *Journal of Small Business Management*:

> Both shorter and longer manuscripts should use *statistical techniques*. (Emphasis added)

Clearly, it would be a mistake to target these journals if your work is purely qualitative in nature. There are outlets that are much less restrictive and take an interdisciplinary approach.

Therefore, when you step up to the plate to hit the ball, you need to have a target in mind. What direction would you like to hit the ball? If center field is well covered, you probably would not want to aim there. Or, if the third baseman has won the prestigious 'golden glove award for outstanding fielding', you may want to avoid hitting to this player as well. In entrepreneurship this would be analogous to writing a piece that criticizes a theory proposed by the receiver of an award for excellence in research, and that person being on the review board, hence being likely to review your work. Instead, you want to aim for the part of the field where it is unlikely to be caught. This presupposes that you have taken time to learn about the other players, knowing what their strengths and capabilities are.

The same applies in targeting your article. At the outset, you should carefully identify your target journal. Before you consider sending your article for review, do your homework on the journal. In the entrepreneurship arena, there are more than 36 journals with about 20 commercially produced (Katz 2003) (see Appendix A for listing). Each of these journals has a slightly different focus; for example, *Entrepreneurship and Regional Development* and *Small Business and Enterprise Development* prefer manuscripts that are policy-oriented. You want to increase your chances of getting the article reviewed by insuring that the reviewers will know something about the topic. Start by reading the mission statement of the journal. This generally provides a guideline as to what is the editorial philosophy and objective of the journal. What topics do they cover? Then, to fully understand the kinds of articles published, read several articles out of the most recent three years of issues. Consider who is the editor and who is on the review board – what are their areas of interest and expertise? What have they published? After this assessment, think about how your paper fits the journal – is it appropriate for the audience? Will the reviewers have the expertise to review the paper? Does it fit the mission of the journal?

If the answer to these questions is yes, then go a step further and consider the review process and criteria as outlined in the authors' guidelines. You might also want to talk with the editor about the specifics with regard to length of time for reviews, percentage of papers offered revision, and rate of acceptance overall. In other words, do your homework.

How does my paper fit within the literature?
In baseball, there is always a 'batting order'. Each player has different strengths and capabilities depending on whether you come to bat first, second or eighth. Where the player is situated in the batting rotation makes a difference to the 'gap' you are filling on the team. If a paper is not clearly positioned in a stream of literature, there is a risk that the reviewers will send it back for retooling. For instance, a paper that compares two entrepreneurs' approaches to opportunity exploration but offers no evidence that relevant literature was reviewed or considered risks an early rejection. A reviewer comment leading to rejection by the editor might state:

> Both reviewers acknowledge the potential importance of the topic and message of your paper; however, you need to justify this paper by more showing what

this paper contributes to the field, as well as what is distinctive and novel about this effort.

Hence it is important to 'locate' your work in a stream of literature. Each new research project should fill a 'gap' in the literature or our knowledge. In part, this has to do with the explicit purpose of the paper (or research question), but it also means connecting the paper to other work. As we are a community of entrepreneurship scholars, collectively we hope that knowledge will be cumulative. It is therefore of the utmost import that you show the reviewers where your paper 'fits' into literature by indicating if it is testing current theory, extending theory, replicating a study, or extending existing work in another context.

Is the theoretical basis for the paper articulated?

All articles need to be anchored in some literature. For each research effort, a theory or perspective provides the foundation for the exploration. If the theory is unclear or inappropriate to the research question or the data, there is a great risk that your article will be returned swiftly. For example, a case study offering a mere description of an entrepreneur and her founding of the organization that is not connected to any theory would be considered conceptually weak. On the other hand, an empirical piece that mines the data without reference to theory or a conceptual framework within which to explore relationships would be similarly lacking. Most review criteria for academic journals include an item such as 'conceptual development' or 'conceptual adequacy' that asks reviewers to examine the theoretical foundation of a submission. If theory or conceptual logic is half-baked, chances are it will be rejected.

Each hitter is schooled and trained in a different way, according to different approaches of hitting. This means that some hitters are taught to hit balls on the outside of the plate, others relish hitting those that are fast and high, and some prefer slow breaking balls.[2] Similarly, scholars in entrepreneurship are probably either trained and have expertise in quantitative or qualitative research, although some are well versed in both, for example there is a tradition among European scholars to emphasize qualitative methods (cf. Parker and Gartner 2004). Whatever foundation for training, the author and reviewer both need to understand this.

Therefore, every good paper articulates a clear theoretical basis or anchor. This is the explicit foundation or perspective upon which the research rests. If it is blurred, reviewers will use their own lens and perhaps misinterpret the meaning and/or results. David Whetten (1989: 492), quoting Dubin (1978), says:

A theoretical perspective should explain WHAT (factors constructs, concepts) logically should be considered part of the explanation, HOW these are related, WHY these are related and WHO, WHEN and WHERE these might apply (contextual limits).

Whether the paper is designed to test or develop theory, it needs to offer clear definitions, articulate the assumptions and explain who, where and when the theory applies. This means more than just describing characteristics, the what and how (Whetten 1989).

Are my definitions clear?

To be a successful hitter, you need to know what your capabilities are, how you define yourself as a player. Because every pitcher has a different arsenal of pitches, you need to be clear about what you can and can't do. If you can hit fast balls, this suggests you have a quick eye and fast acceleration through the ball. On the other hand, if you can hit a knuckleball,[3] chances are that you have an adaptable swing and quick reaction time as the movement on the ball is greater than most pitches. Either is an advantage in entrepreneurship research. With regard to the former, you may be a fast mover within one specific area of entrepreneurship where you dig in your heels and get in the fast track. In the latter, you may be an innovator or fast adapter of new research ideas.

The same is true for your paper. Since reviewers often come from areas outside of your expertise, it is very important to be sure you have carefully defined every major construct, and use these definitions consistently. For instance, the term 'entrepreneurship' might be defined as opportunity identification and exploitation (Shane and Venkataraman 2000); new venture creation (Gartner 1985), new combinations of activities (Schumpeter 1934) or a variety of other ways. Another example is the definition of an entrepreneurial team – a number of researchers equates the entrepreneurial founding team with the top management team, but the founding team may well be made up from other persons than the top management team. Hence it is a contestable point and your paper should state which definition you are using so reviewers know about the basis from which to assess the paper, for example 'two or more individuals who jointly establish a business in which they have an equity interest' (Kamm et al. 1990: 7).

Your paper should also pay attention to operational definitions. For example, if you are discussing entrepreneurs, it may not be appropriate to use owner, founder, self-employed, inventor, manager or small business manager interchangeably. Even the term 'performance' has been operationalized more than 50 different ways (Brush and VanderWerf 1992).

Is my literature review relevant, analytical and complete?

In baseball, to hit the ball soundly, you need a foundation. This foundation is generally gained through years of training, experience and study. While most players have some natural talent, this is enhanced by studying other elite players, how they watch the ball and how they swing. At the same time, good hitters study statistics about different pitchers, the types of pitches they can throw (slider or sinker), the velocity and the location of the ball. Studying the background and knowing the foundation of pitches is essential to hitting the ball.

Like baseball, your paper needs to be based on existing knowledge in the shape of a literature review of some sort. A literature review demonstrates that you have read and analyzed the received literature in a way that informs your investigation and interpretation of results. For example, an ethnographic case study considering relationships between entrepreneurship, structuration and embeddedness carefully reviews current theory and empirical work related to these three concepts (Jack and Anderson 2002). However, a literature review needs to be analytical rather than descriptive. If the review simply restates everyone else's work, it will be lacking. The review should be relevant specifically to theory and studies regarding your research question. Another aspect of the literature review is the timeliness. A review that includes nothing more recent than 1995 or older than 1995 will be considered dated, and reviewers will almost always catch this. A good review should synthesize, evaluate and show, rather than tell or describe.

Is my methodology appropriate for the research questions addressed in the paper?

Methodology encompasses the research design and approach to answering the research question/s. A paper that relies on a convenience sample, with little attention to response bias, reliability of responses or rigor in sample design is likely to be rejected. For any empirical paper, whether qualitative or quantitative, whether using primary or secondary data, if the methodology is poorly explained or inconsistent with the data, this will probably be considered a major flaw. However, a drawback in qualitative methodology is that the methodological explication is often lengthy. Hence you need to consider how to trim this to size while still getting the message through.

One way to convince reviewers of the thoroughness of your approach is also to refer to well-reputed scholars with a qualitative twist, for example Mahesh Bhave (1994) in his well-known qualitative study of the venture creation process presents his methodology as follows:

> Simon (1969) writes, 'One should not let one's discipline determine the choice of method; rather one should fit the method to the problem.' Further,

'entrepreneurship is one of the youngest paradigms in management science' (Bygrave 1989a, p. 7), there is no general agreement on defining concepts and variables characterizing it, and the processes of birth of firms are not well understood (Low and MacMillan 1988). Given this situation, an exploratory field study involving interviews, 'mapping systems' according to Simon (1969), was undertaken to obtain an overview of venture creation processes. (Bhave 1994: 226)

Thus technique and routines are a crucial part of hitting the ball. Some players hold the bat high, others hold it low. Some open their stance wide and others keep it narrow. Tapping the bat on the plate, fastening and unfastening gloves, touching the helmet – all of these are part of the methodology that hitters follow before the hit the baseball.

Further, in writing a manuscript, your methodology has to do with the data collected and the purpose for which the data were collected. A paper should explain the research methodology and show that choices concerning the sample, variables and measures are driven by the theory and an interesting question. In other words, the theory and the data should be related. Your paper should clearly state the method by which data were collected, explain the sampling frame, and carefully describe the respondent group, in addition to specifics of your measures. Answer the question; how and why does this theory fit the research question and method chosen to investigate it? Be careful and detailed in explaining your choices, especially when you use qualitative data. Because the criteria for judging qualitative data may be poorly understood or even disputed, it is better to be more detailed (Patton 2001) (see also Chapters 16 and 17 in this volume for an in-depth discussion). At the same time, don't assume that every reviewer knows the ins and outs of 'grounded theory' or 'ethnographic research'. It's better to provide a detailed explanation of what these involve by being specific about your approach (Pratt 2005).[4]

Even if you write a conceptual paper, there needs to be a methodology. If you are developing or proposing theory, are you using illustrative cases? A literature review? Hegelian debate? Historical analysis? Whatever your method, it needs to be articulated and argued.

Have I used the appropriate test(s) for the data, and
addressed issues of quality?

Baseball is a game of statistics. Statistics are kept for hitting, pitching, earned runs, strike-outs and a multitude of other details. Each time you step up to the plate, you are testing and adding to a statistic.

In the case of qualitative research the concern is more with meaning than measurement (Daft 1983). While qualitative researchers often have the richness of data, going beyond the descriptive and delving into questions of 'why' the phenomenon is more appropriate (Gartner and Birley 2002).

For this reason, the complexity and nuances of the methodological choices should be thoroughly discussed and described. Several authors have articulated methodology for designing case study research (Yin 1984; Patton 2001), analyzing case data (Miles and Huberman 1984) grounded theory and building theory from cases (Glaser and Strauss 1967; Eisenhardt 1989). Indeed, Hindle (2004: 599) refers to Miles and Huberman as the ultimate sourcebook for techniques of qualitative analysis. Using tables, graphs or figures or techniques such as critical incidence or repertory grid creates an illusion of quantification and promotes understanding.

You should also explain how the quality of the contribution should be judged. Have you considered the correct criteria, for example dependability (Lincoln and Guba 1985) versus external validity (Yin 1984)? Is the design strategy for collecting data articulated and is the sampling approach clearly described (Patton 2001; Chapter 10 in this volume)? Have you considered issues of content validity, or the degree to which items measure what they are supposed to measure (Denzin 1978; Kerlinger 1964)? Have you triangulated across sources such as interviews, documents, and newspaper articles (Jick 1979)? Even in qualitative papers attention to issues such as inter-rater reliability in coding of data is essential (Boyatzis 1998). Ultimately, it is always a good idea to have a strong methods person pre-review your paper.

Careful attention to these issues will substantially increase your chances of getting past first base.

What is the contribution of my work?

In baseball, to stay on the team you have to make a contribution. Because a baseball season is a series of games, you have many chances to add value, but it must be clear. Those players not adding value are sent back to the minor leagues.

So, whatever the topic of your paper, the most important thing is its contribution. Consider the value of the below – which would guarantee rejection:

> The main advantage of this study is that it uses a large data set and has a strong response rate. No differences in business demographics are found unless industry and size are considered.

Not only is the advantage trivial, but the differences suggest unexplored areas that might shed light on the data. Other conclusions such as: 'age matters in performance of new ventures' or 'the entrepreneur's human capital is of crucial importance in crafting strategy' are examples of contributions that add little or nothing to our knowledge. A paper concluding with obvious or trivial results will surely be called out at the plate. With qualitative work there is another concern: generalizability (Pratt 2005). The generalizability issue concerns the fact that qualitative research is based on small groups of people or contexts that provide rich details. Qualitative research is likely to be rejected by reviewers with a strong quantitative persuasion. Consider the following genuine extract from a rejection:

> I find it hard to accept that this paper can truly point to any solid conclusion of any impact with *so very small a study* [24 case studies] – the discussion of the literature was of some value, but the actual study itself is so very small that I find it difficult to accept its value as a possible *representative study of the 'universe'*. I would urge the author to expand the study to a size where the results would really have impact and meaning – and to use the research to provide the entrepreneurial community with conclusions and recommendations that can truly have an impact, based on a study that is *large enough* where we would say Wow! (Emphasis and explanation added)

The author has simply not been sufficiently persuasive in showing how the context of the study may be similar to other contexts and has failed to link insights from the study to existing theory, in order to mitigate this concern (Pratt 2005).

This is one of the key considerations in the evaluation of a paper. Building new knowledge is the motive for doing research in the first place. A good paper will provide new insights, crystallize our thinking about some issue, offer new constructs or conceptualizations, present creative prescriptions for management action, explain or predict industry or executive behavior, or add to an ongoing debate by confirming or refuting existing beliefs (Cavusgil 1994).

If you consider these major areas in your paper, you have done more than half the work by avoiding the fatal flaws. But there is no guarantee of getting past first base unless you address the minor league issues as well. The following are things that really 'bug' reviewers. Reviewers are the 'gatekeepers' to getting your paper published, and they can be 'ruthless' in their review (Cavusgil 1994). It's better to anticipate their potential objections and address these at the outset.

Minor league mistakes that will keep you at first base
Tension and balance
Hitting the baseball is an art. To get that home run means everything must work together – your swing, your judgement, the angle and acceleration of the bat, and of course, your movement towards the ball. But you can't rely only on one aspect – just swinging hard doesn't necessarily result in a hit. It's the combination of balance of multiple actions at the same time, not the overwhelming power of a single motion.

Research is similar. It is a craft, inherently uncertain and unpredictable, even though we try to plan our work so it comes out as predicted. But, quality work is measured by the intensity of surprise (Daft 1984). This means that your paper should have an element of tension or balance. If you present only one side of the argument, or half the story, chances are that you haven't considered all aspects of the theory, data or results.

Points of the argument, hypotheses and data need to be 'discussed' thoughtfully in a way that considers supporting points and limitations. If you only present literature supporting your logic, and don't recognize competing theories or results, reviewers will almost surely doubt the credibility and contribution of your results. You should also avoid 'cherry-picking' theory or studies simply to support a particular view. Reviewers will catch this and conclude you have not synthesized and thought about the logic of your paper.

Assertions

It is a dangerous thing to brag about your ability to hit the baseball if you can't back it up. The same holds true with your manuscript. Doctoral training encourages persuasive and positive writing styles. However, being persuasive and positive is not the same thing as being arrogant. While passion for ideas and beliefs can be appropriate, assertions without foundation almost certainly will be recognized for what they are – unsupported statements. For instance, a statement with no references or discussion like the following would be questioned:

> Organizations control basic sets of resources that confer competitive advantage in and of themselves. But, resource sets change as a venture grows either incrementally or in a punctuated fashion.

It is better if you support your statements with clear logic; for example:

> Many resource based theorists assume that an organization already controls a basic set of resources (e.g. Wernerfelt 1984) and that these resources confer competitive advantage in and of themselves (e.g. Barney 1991; Hall 1992). However, there is growing recognition that resource bundles develop and change as a new venture grows (Galunic and Rodan 1998; Brush, Greene and Hart 2001) . . . For most new ventures, an optimal set of resources is not developed instantly, but rather evolves and changes over a period of weeks, months and years. This development process relies on certain combinations and re-combinations of organizational resources, and the prudent sequencing of these resources over time (Amit and Schoemaker 1993; Ropo and Hunt 1995). (Lichtenstein and Brush 2001: 40–41)

Packaging and readability

In baseball, if you show up with a sloppy uniform, your coach will think that you are not ready to play, and do not care about the game.

The same is true of your manuscript. Every journal has a style guide that should be reviewed and followed. Ignoring the details of specific journal style requirements can put off reviewers, giving them the impression you did not take the time to consider putting your article in the format appropriate for the journal. This includes referencing, use of charts and tables, length, abstract and summary requirements. In addition, the appearance of your manuscript (margins, typeface, headings) can bias the reader. Attention to word and paragraph redundancy, spelling and grammatical mistakes is essential. There is no substitute for careful editing. You want your manuscript to create an immediately favorable impression in the mind of the reviewer, rather than drawing attention to mistakes at the outset.

Tips for getting into scoring position (third base)
Getting into scoring position requires practice. Before any baseball game, there is a warm-up session where hitters take batting practice, the coaches offer suggestions on technique and everyone warms up for the game.

Before submitting your manuscript, it is likewise a good idea to have your paper pre-reviewed or given what is often referred to as a 'friendly review'. Identify a colleague who can read and comment on your paper within a timely fashion. You might offer to reciprocate by reviewing his/her paper in exchange. Professor Howard Aldrich says in his instructions to doctoral students: 'You should perceive writing as a "social process". We don't sit in a cabin in the woods and write furiously without input from others.'[5] Our writing benefits from constructive and thoughtful review, and is shaped by these to make it a better product. Of course, this should not be carried to an extreme – a few pre-reviews before submission by those willing and knowledgeable about your area are appropriate. After receiving the friendly advice, you should revise the paper accordingly, with appropriate thanks to the reviewer.

Another suggestion is to review or analyze your own paper. What is the point of every paragraph? Is the argument clear in each section? Does it flow logically (is the structure clear and reasonable?) Is each exhibit necessary? Is it self-explanatory?

Spend time on your cover letter. A covering letter should provide a succinct three-sentence summary of your paper (question, method and findings). It should communicate the most salient contribution of your manuscript.

Finally, anticipate the reviewer comments. Close your eyes: who is reading your paper? What will he/she ask about? What are potential objections and questions? Does your paper answer these? For example:

> This is the first study to examine the impact of effective networking in a social setting such as golf games. Using a qualitative methodology involving network

mapping of contacts measured over three separate periods, this study shows that entrepreneurs are more likely to engage new golf partners than managers, who are more likely to have the same partners week after week.

Scoring the run

If you have hit the ball and gotten to first or second base, chances are that you may score a run. But, to do this, you have to pay attention to the coaches, who will guide you across the plate.

This is similar to responding to reviewers. If you received revise and resubmit advice, you can be very happy to have the opportunity to work with the reviewers. While you probably won't agree with all the comments of the reviewers, and you may even complain about what you need to fix, modify or delete, remember they can improve your chances of scoring a run.

Reviewers are a bit like coaches, often telling you things you don't want to hear, but, in the long run, providing guidance and advice that will help you get your manuscript published. As a strategy, after reading the reviewer comments, yell and write a scathing reply but leave it on your desk. Two days later, rip up your letter and re-read the comments from the reviewers and the editor alongside your paper. Evaluate each comment and ask yourself the following:

- What is the issue?
- Is this a major issue requiring a comprehensive rewrite or is it an editorial problem?
- What do I need to read to fix this issue?
- What do I need to do to fix this issue?
- Who can provide guidance?

After reviewing each point, think about how you might address these issues and how you will revise the paper. In your response to reviewers, be specific and careful in addressing each point. Maintain a positive and polite tone explaining how you address each issue. Be timely in your replies to the editor.

If you have successfully avoided all the major and minor league mistakes, chances are you will score a run. You will get that letter in the mail that says:

> Congratulations! We are pleased to inform you that your manuscript, 'The Impact of Entrepreneurial Networking in Social Settings', will be published in the March issue of the *Journal of Outstanding Theoretical Innovations and Wonderments*.

Notes

1. These fatal flaws are courtesy of Cavusgil (1994).
2. Fast balls are pitches that come off the ends of the tip of a pitcher's second and third fingers and have high velocity (e.g. 85–97 miles per hour). A breaking ball is a pitch that

comes off the inside tip of the pitcher's third finger and starts outside of the strike zone (the area over the plate between the hitter's shoulders and knees) and moves across over the strike zone at the last second.

3.   A knuckleball is a pitch that appears to 'dance' in the air. It is thrown with little rotation, with one or more fingers curled so as to grip with the knuckles, fingertips, or sides of the fingers. Funny things happen with a slowly rotating ball. A large pocket of swirling air develops behind it, and how the rotation is will change this pocket, larger, smaller, back and forth, and this pocket pulls against the ball, sometimes in one direction for a moment, then another. It can be gripped anywhere, any way, with success.

4.   For examples of carefully described context, methods, analysis, reliability and validity issues, see Jack and Anderson (2002); Rosa (1998); Lichtenstein and Brush (2001).

5.   Presentation by Prof. Howard Aldrich at the 2001 Doctoral Consortium, Entrepreneurship Division of the Academy of Management, Washington, DC.

Recommended further resources

Katz, J. (2003) Core Publications in Entrepreneurship and Related Fields: A Guide to Getting Published. Version 4.1.1, http://eweb.slu.edu/booklist.htm

References

Aldrich, H. (1999) *Organizations Evolving*. Thousand Oaks, CA: Sage Publications.

Bhave, M. (1994) A process model of entrepreneurial venture creation. *Journal of Business Venturing*, **9**(3): 223–42.

Boyatzis, R. (1998) *Transforming Qualitative Information: Thematic analysis and code development*. San Francisco, CA: Sage Publications.

Brush, C.G. and VanderWerf, P. (1992) A comparison of methods and sources for obtaining estimates of new venture performance. *Journal of Business Venturing*, **7**(2): 157–70.

Cavusgil, S.T. (1994) From the Editor in Chief. *Journal of International Business*, **2**(1): 1–5.

Daft, R.L. (1984) Learning the craft of organizational research. *Academy of Management Review*, **8**(4): 539–46.

Denzin, N.K. (1978) *The Research Act: A theoretical introduction to sociological methods*, 2nd edn. New York: McGraw-Hill.

Dubin, R. (1978) *Theory Development*. New York: Free Press.

Eisenhardt, K. (1989) Building theories from case study research. *Academy of Mangement Review*, **14**(4): 532–50.

Gartner, W.B. (1985) A conceptual framework for describing the phenomenon of new venture creation. *Academy of Management Review*, **10**(4): 696–706.

Gartner, W.B. and Birley, S. (2002) Introduction to the special issue on qualitative methods in entrepreneurship research. *Journal of Business Venturing*, **17**(5): 387–95.

Glaser, B. and Strauss, A. (1967) *The Discovery of Grounded Theory: Strategies of qualitative research.* London: Weidenfeld and Nicolson.

Hindle, K. (2004) Choosing qualitative methods for entrepreneurial cognition research: A canonical development approach. *Entrepreneurship Theory and Practice*, **28**(6): 575–607.

Jack, S.L. and Anderson, A.R. (2002) The effects of embeddedness on the entrepreneurial process. *Journal of Business Venturing*, **17**(5): 467–88.

Jick, T. (1979) Mixing qualitative and quantitative methods: Triangulation in action. *Administrative Sciences Quarterly*, **24**(4): 602–11.

Kamm, J., Shuman, J., Seeger, J. and Nurick, A. (1990) Entrepreneurial teams in new venture creation: A research agenda. *Entrepreneurship Theory and Practice*, **14**(4): 7–14.

Katz, J. (2003) Core Publications in Entrepreneurship and Related Fields: A Guide to Getting Published. Version 4.1.1, http://eweb.slu.edu/booklist.htm

Kerlinger, F.N. (1964) *Foundations of Behavioral Research*, 2nd edn. New York: Holt, Rinehart and Winston.

Lichtenstein, B. and Brush, C.G. (2001) How do 'resource bundles' develop and change in new ventures? A dynamic model and longitudinal exploration. *Entrepreneurship Theory and Practice*, **25**(3): 37–58.

Lincoln, Y.S. and Guba, E. (1985) *Naturalistic Inquiry*. Beverly Hills, CA: Sage Publications.

Miles, M. and Huberman, A.M. (1984) *Qualitative Data Analysis*. Beverly Hills, CA: Sage Publications.

Parker, S.C. and Gartner, W.B. (2004) Introduction to the special issue on entrepreneurship and new venture creation. *Entrepreneurship Theory and Practice*, **28**(5): 413–19.

Patton, M.Q. (2001) *Qualitative Research and Evaluation Methods*. Thousand Oaks, CA: Sage Publications.

Pratt, M. (2005) Some thoughts on publishing qualitative research. http://www.aom.pace.edu.rmd/pratt_files/pratt.htm

Rosa, P. (1999) Entrepreneurial processes of business cluster formation and growth by habitual entrepreneurs. *Entrepreneurship Theory and Practice*, **22**(4): 43–62.

Schumpeter, J. (1934) *The Theory of Economic Development*. New York: Harper & Row.

Shane, S. and Venkataraman, S. (2000) The promise of entrepreneurship as a field of research. *Academy of Management Review*, **25**(1): 217–26.

Whetten, D.A. (1989) What constitutes a theoretical contribution? *Academy of Management Review*, **14**(4): 490–95.

Yin, R. (1984) *Case Study Research*. Beverly Hills, CA: Sage Publications.

Zeller, R.A. and Carmines, E.G. (1980) *Measurement in the Social Sciences: The link between theory and data*. London: Cambridge University Press.

Appendix
This entire appendix is from Katz (2003).

Annual research review
Katz, J.A. (ed.) *Advances in the Study of Entrepreneurship Firm Emergence and Growth*. Greenwich, CT: JAI Press.
Liebcap, G. (ed.) *Advances in the Study of Entrepreneurship, Innovation and Economic Growth*. Greenwich, CT: JAI Press.
McGee, J. and Thomas, H. *The Technology, Innovation, Entrepreneurship and Competitive Strategy Series*. New York: Elsevier Science.

Annual proceedings
Babson Entrepreneurship Research Conference, *Frontiers of Entrepreneurship Research*. Babson College: Babson Park, MA.
International Council For Small Business World Conference Proceedings and the US Association for Small Business and Entrepreneurship Proceedings are organized by year by the Small Business Advancement Electronic Resource.
Research at the Marketing/Entrepreneurship Interface, sponsored by the AMA-MEIG. If this link does not work, contact Gerald Hills.

The generally recognized 'Big 5' of entrepreneurship research

1. *Journal of Business Venturing* (Publisher: Elsevier) (ABI) (SSCI).
2. *The Journal of Small Business Management* (Publisher: West Virginia University and ICSB) (ABI) (SSCI).
3. *Small Business Economics* (ABI) (SSCI) (Publisher: Kluwer).
4. *Entrepreneurship and Regional Development* (Publisher: Taylor and Francis).
5. *Entrepreneurship: Theory and Practice* (Publisher: Baylor University) (ABI).

Postscript: Unresolved challenges?
John Parm Ulhøi and Helle Neergaard

'Entrepreneurship is about creating the future' states one of the contributors in this handbook (Smith in Chapter 17). While we concur with this observation, we also find that qualitative research in entrepreneurship is about understanding the premises underlying the activities that create this future. We hope that the entrepreneurial spirit, the craft, and the professional dedication exhibited by the contributors will increase the understanding and smooth the path for different high-quality 'soft' approaches to entrepreneurship research to become more used and accepted as valid and legitimate options to consider in entrepreneurship research.

As the preceding chapters show, the contributors to this handbook are all passionate about their craft and convinced of the applicability and value their research brings to the field of entrepreneurship. It is an essential feature of qualitative methodology that immersion in empirical reality sparks new challenges all the time, challenges to which researchers often respond by executing creativity and innovation. Several of the chapters constitute examples of such methodological imagination, creativity, variety and richness. We only regret that it was not possible to provide an even greater coverage of the methods and techniques that we know exist. However, we entertain the hope that this book may pave the way for other volumes that will fill any gap we may leave. We know of some such initiatives.

There is little doubt that empirical reality rubs off on researchers in the field: in the process of conducting research scholars become immersed in their context and often they become smitten with the enthusiasm of their research subjects or informants. This may be one of the reasons why the field apparently attracts newcomers in increasing numbers from many other fields. If we look at the background of most of the scholars who are today prominent in the field, few of these were actually graduates of entrepreneurship. This has given entrepreneurship its distinct multi- and trans-disciplinary characteristic. It has also generated a field that has the methodological variation and scope needed to capture the dynamics and complexity of the empirical reality, a field that is also rich with insight from other research areas. However, this also means that there is no superior methodology *per se* for researching entrepreneurship – the methodological choice remains always to be decided in the light and context of the questions to be answered.

It is crucial that we look at the field to establish how we may learn the most from it – and in turn consider what we can give back.

Within the social sciences in general and business research in particular researchers often need to have a clear sense of the real-life settings of the domain they are studying. Some degree of first- or second-hand experience is necessary to understand the practical, technical, social and psychological dimensions of entrepreneurship. The full scope and dynamics of entrepreneurship may possibly only be fully understood if the researcher has been actively involved in entrepreneurial activities. Indeed, many of the most acknowledged scholars in the field have been or are themselves entrepreneurs. Entrepreneurship research cannot be approached at arm's length. Indeed, most entrepreneurs would agree that it is necessary to have been in an entrepreneur's shoes to know what it takes.

Entrepreneurship researchers should therefore be willing, at least occasionally, to get their hands dirty. It is in and through a close interaction with the field that we become familiar with and gain new insight into entrepreneurial phenomena. This closeness to the 'matter' is essential if we are to advance our understanding of entrepreneurship, entrepreneurs and entrepreneurial processes. Qualitative methods invite the researcher to observe, talk to and interact with real-life entrepreneurs. They help capture the 'intangibles', the tacit and not immediately observable knowledge, those events and occurrences that are taken for granted by those who are immersed in the act.

A key remaining challenge of qualitative research in the field of entrepreneurship, one that we probably share with qualitative research in many other fields – is the danger of becoming entrapped by our own passion in a position as self-righteous missionaries. We need to acknowledge the relevance of exploring new combinations of methods in our field studies, including both quantitative and qualitative, a choice which should not be rigidly dictated by paradigmatic preference but rather by the nature of the problem or phenomenon at hand. Moreover, the focus needs not be so directed on inventing new ways of investigating the field that it overlooks the value of refining existing methods. As important as it may be to develop new methods, it is equally important to develop a broader awareness and familiarity with existing methods and combinations thereof. We are convinced that such endeavours will not render research results incommensurable, but rather that they may facilitate a multi-faceted and more holistic understanding of entrepreneurial phenomena. Finally, most methods in general and qualitative methods in particular constitute a craftmanship that cannot be learned and mastered exclusively by reading books and papers about such methods. Indeed, they can only be adequately mastered after a good deal of practical first-hand experience.

There is still some way to go before the majority of journal editors and reviewers become as familiar with the most frequently used qualitative methods as they are with quantitative methods. A critical challenge for journal editors in this respect is to ensure that they have reviewers on their boards who have sufficient experience with qualitative methods and to be very careful in selecting the reviewers to whom they assign a prospective qualitative article. Moreover, it is vital for qualitative researchers to be more visible at editorial advisory boards of mainstream journals as this will signal to potential contributors that the journal is not excluding qualitative research as inferior to quantitatively based research. However, difficulties encountered in the publication process are no excuse for not attempting to publish qualitative research. When using qualitative methods in entrepreneurship research we should not overlook our own shortcomings. Rather we should focus on how to further enhance the methodological robustness and documentation of our research to achieve higher publication rates (in mainstream journals). Experience shows that one way in which junior researchers can increase their hit rate is by allying with more seasoned qualitative researchers who are familiar with and have worked out strategies for overcoming the obstacles. Sharing experiences constitutes an important road towards broader dissemination.

Ultimately, even if the road to publication is both long and winding, we should take comfort from the overall rationale, which is both directly and indirectly apparent throughout this volume: that qualitative methods should not be perceived merely as an equal or superior alternative to quantitative methods, but rather as an obvious choice dictated by the nature of the research puzzle. In expanding our collective methodological repertoire and tolerance, there is hope that we may eventually produce a richer understanding of nature of the dynamic and complex phenomenon that is usually referred to as 'entrepreneurship'.

Index